AN EXPERIENTIAL APPROACH TO ORGANIZATION DEVELOPMENT

Fifth Edition

AN EXPERIENTIAL APPROACH TO ORGANIZATION DEVELOPMENT

Don Harvey
California State University–Berkeley

Donald R. Brown
Antelope Valley College

PRENTICE HALL, Upper Saddle River, New Jersey 07458

Library of Congress Cataloging-in-Publication Data

HARVEY, DONALD F.
 An experiential approach to organization development / DONALD F.
HARVEY, DONALD R. BROWN.—5th ed.
 p. cm.
 Includes bibliographical references and index.
 ISBN 0-13-517988-2
 1. Organizational change. I. Brown, Donald R., [date].
II. Title
HD58.8.H37 1996
658.4'063—dc20 95-40567

Acquisitions editor: *Natalie Anderson*
Associate editor: *Lisamarie Brassini*
Project management: *Edie Riker*
Marketing manager: *Jo-Ann DeLuca*
Cover design: *Wendy Alling Judy*
Buyer: *Vincent Scelta*

 © 1996, 1992, 1988, 1982, 1976 by Prentice-Hall, Inc.
A Simon & Schuster Company
Upper Saddle River, New Jersey 07458

Printed in the United States of America

10 9 8 7 6 5 4 3 2 1

ISBN 0-13-517988-2

Prentice-Hall International (UK) Limited, *London*
Prentice-Hall of Australia Pty. Limited, *Sydney*
Prentice-Hall Canada Inc., *Toronto*
Prentice-Hall Hispanoamericana, S.A., *Mexico*
Prentice-Hall of India Private Limited, *New Delhi*
Prentice-Hall of Japan, Inc., *Tokyo*
Simon & Schuster Asia Pte. Ltd., *Singapore*
Editora Prentice-Hall do Brasil, Ltda., *Rio de Janeiro*

Contents in Brief

Contents

9 APR

SURE

SURE

5 The OD Consultant: Diagnostic Process 122

PART III DEVELOPING HIGH PERFORMANCE

6 Overcoming Resistance to Change 152

7 Process Consulting Skills 177

8 OD Intervention Strategies 204

14 High Performing Systems: Systemwide Interventions 384

15 Organization Transformation: Strategy Interventions 405

PART VI FOCUSING ON THE FUTURE

PREFACE

The first edition of this text appeared over a decade ago, and what changes have taken place! We live in a world that has been turned upside down. Fortune 500 companies are pouring money, technology, and management expertise into regions that were once off-limits, acquiring new enterprises, forming joint ventures, or creating new global businesses from the ground up. Many major companies are going through significant changes including downsizing, reengineering, using self-managed work teams, flattening organizations, and doing routine jobs with automation and computers. The added stress on people makes it increasingly difficult to create and maintain a culture that motivates and satisfies human potential.

The fifth edition has undergone major changes, much like the world we live in. In the past, managers aimed for success in a relatively stable and predictable world. However, in the hyperturbulent environment of the twenty-first century, managers will be confronting an accelerating rate of change. They are facing constant innovation in computer and information technology and a chaotic world of changing markets and consumer lifestyles. Today's organization must be able to transform and renew to meet these changing forces.

This is a book about Organization Development: the management discipline aimed at improving organizational effectiveness by means of increasing use of Human Resources. It is also about managing in a changing world. We have tried to make this the most "user friendly" text available.

This text offers a practical and realistic approach to the study of Organization Development. Through the application of a new paradigm—the OD Process Model—each of the OD stages is described from the standpoint of its relationship to an overall program of change. The book is written primarily for students who are learning about Organization Development for the first time. The text relates the student to the real world through the use of numerous illustrations and company examples showing how Organization Development is being applied in today's organizations.

Organization Development is an emerging behavioral science discipline that provides a set of methodologies for systematically bringing about high-performing organizations. The goals of Organization Development are to make an organization more effective and to enhance the opportunity for the individual to develop his or her potential. It is our view that these Organization Development goals can best be accomplished by using the experiential approach to learning.

This text differs from most Organization Development (OD) texts in providing both conceptual and experiential approaches to the study of OD. A revolution is under way in how individuals use education to improve their performance. Our approach is focusing on the development of interpersonal skills. Students are provided with a conceptual framework necessary for understanding the relevant issues in OD. In addition, individuals will be actively participating in individual and team exercises that require the application of chapter content to specific organizational situations. This approach is aimed at developing those critical interpersonal skills needed to manage in a changing world.

This text is the first to directly relate student learning experiences in OD with these skills judged by experts to be essential for potential OD consultants. As noted in Chapter 1, recent studies have been critical of today's business graduates for deficiencies in a number of areas, including communication skills, problem solving, decision-making ability, and leadership potential. This approach provides coverage of OD topics while also developing student skills in a "learn by doing" context.

OBJECTIVES

The basic objective is to provide the student and practicing manager with an integrated and comprehensive view of the field of OD. We hope to present, in a clear and organized manner, the newest approaches, concepts, and techniques of this emerging discipline. We have attempted to include most of the current state-of-the-art OD techniques and whatever empirical findings exist on the results. The stages of the OD Process Model are presented so as to provide a step-by-step description of the various techniques and problems involved in OD efforts.

Our second objective is to present OD from an experiential learning approach; that is, the student not only reads the concepts, but also practices and experiments by doing and using these techniques in a simulated organizational situation.

There is much evidence to support the success of this approach. Our own experience and student evaluations support this: students report an enhanced level of learning, greater course satisfaction, and rate the overall course learning higher than in more traditional courses.

The OD concepts, techniques, and skills that make up this book were selected because of their usefulness to practitioners. To achieve this goal, we have had to integrate materials from a diverse set of approaches. Our strategy has been to try to integrate these various approaches to provide a comprehensive view of the field of OD.

OD is an organized body of knowledge, with its own concepts, techniques, and necessary skills, which are discussed in this book. The practice of OD concerns people in organizations; thus there is an emphasis on developing improved interpersonal skills.

Every successful OD program is the result of a concerted group effort, and each failure is a failure for all organization members. Therefore, people as agents of change, not forces or structures, determine whether the OD practitioner will manage change effectively. Because the OD practitioners' effectiveness results not only from the concepts learned, but also from their managerial style and the way they influence others, our emphasis in this book is on the experiential approach to learning.

As students progress in the book, the simulations will allow them to continually utilize growing knowledge and experience, thereby building a foundation of management experience to carry forward into their managerial career. By analyzing successes and failure, students begin to develop the ability to learn from experience and to develop insights into organizational functioning that would normally take years to acquire.

NEW METHODOLOGIES

This OD text is designed to present the complex and fascinating world of managing people in an easy-to-grasp, "user-friendly" way. In addition to its comprehensive, innovative coverage, the text provides an OD practitioner or managerial approach to the field. It provides a rich depth of practical examples and applications, showing the major problems that managers face in their efforts to change organizations to meet a changing environment.

Each chapter presents an OD skills application, a major example describing an actual company situation, practical examples, a case, and a behavioral problem-solving simulation. Finally, this OD text makes learning this field easy and enjoyable. Its writing style and level are well suited to the beginning OD student.

The text sets forth incidents that reveal the drama of today's human resource manager, such as how Apple Computer's culture focuses not just on products, but on the hopes and dreams of its members; Walt Disney's legendary emphasis on making the customer happy; and Johnson & Johnson's attempt to change to an entrepreneurial culture.

The manager of the future will probably be acting as a people manager and will be involved in initiating, designing, or implementing organization change programs. The material in the text will provide the manager with new methodologies and techniques for implementing OD programs, as well as an opportunity for personal growth and development. The book is designed so that each one may assess his or her own behavior and begin setting some personal development goals. Also, opportunities are created for feedback on how effective one's behavioral style is, which encourages greater effectiveness.

The text is designed so that the instructor may incorporate new methodologies into the learning situation, including simulations and cases. All of the experiential skill exercises in this text were designed to focus on critical personal skills in the OD field.

Video cases and Accumen personal computer software, commercially available, can be integrated into the text. Lotus 1-2-3® templates are provided to the instructor, which can be used with selected simulations.

The text is organized to present an overview of OD concepts and theories and provides behavioral skill simulations for each major stage of an OD program. This book may be used as an independent study guide for those wanting to learn more about organization change or as a comprehensive set of materials on how to initiate OD programs for the practicing OD consultant or operating manager.

NEW FEATURES

This OD text gives the student a comprehensive, innovative, and practical introduction to the field. Its style and extensive use of applications and exercises make the book straightforward, easy to read, and enjoyable.

The text contains 16 chapters to fit a one-semester course, and has been thoroughly edited to improve readability. Illustrations and figures add to the book's visual appeal. All tables, facts, figures, references, and dozens of current examples are provided within the text materials. Chapter objectives and a list of key terms are supplied for each chapter to enhance learning.

An Experiential Approach to Organization Development offers substantial new coverage on several important topics: organization transformation, organization renewal, changing the corporate culture, self-managed work teams, organization compensation, managing diversity, total quality management, and empowerment.

The text has many significant features. We have included several features to promote the readability and understanding of important organization development concepts.

1. The OD Process Model presents a visual, graphic display of the major stages relating all organization development topics. We believe that the model will serve as an excellent teaching device.
2. The approach is dynamic, rather than static. Time is considered as a significant variable in changing organizations.
3. Case studies involving OD examples are provided at the end of each chapter to provide for discussion of the major topics.
4. OD examples are included in each chapter. These examples allow the student to become involved in situations that are occurring in the business world.
5. A comprehensive exercise called OD Skills Simulation is provided for each chapter. These exercises provide for an extensive class learning situation.

This book was designed to provide a variety of learning methods. The skill exercises are fun and involving, cases often make the concepts more understandable, and text readings provide a set of concepts to be applied and challenged. The book can be used as the primary text or as a supplemental text for courses at the junior, senior, or graduate level. We have successfully used the material with undergraduate students, as well as with graduate students from many fields, including communications, public administration, engineering, administration, and health care. The material has also been used for management training and executive development programs in a variety of fields with bankers, engineers, nurses, teachers, public administrators, military officers, production managers, and marketing managers; and at a variety of levels from first-line supervision to top management teams.

NEW TOPICS

First, corporate culture, goal setting, total quality management, empowerment, and self-managed work teams are the subjects of chapters. These chapters represent the most recent theory, research, and applications available in the literature.

Second, each case emphasizes a particular OD issue or managerial technique. They cover a variety of different types and sizes of organizations and include problems of all levels of management.

Third, the "OD In Practice" segments have been enthusiastically received by students and instructors. They report actual applications of the concepts and theories presented in the chapter and appear at the exact point in the text where the concept or theory is being discussed. Each of the chapters in this edition contains an "OD In Practice" application. Through the identification of actual organizational applications of text materials, the gap between the classroom and the real world can hopefully be narrowed.

Fourth, we have added an international emphasis by including "Our Changing World" sections in application of OD concepts in a global context to each chapter.

We have also included a number of self-report questionnaires for the reader to complete. These questionnaires get the reader involved and let him or her take a close look at personal style, attitudes, and behavior patterns. We provide norms and averages so the reader can make comparisons.

Finally, the supplements for the text are thorough and should be secured from the publisher. Both the student and instructor were considered in preparing these supplements, which add to the student's understanding and the instructor's ability to teach an exciting course. The *Instructor's Manual*, which includes a suggested lecture outline, a test bank, suggestions for facilitating classroom simulations, and additional simulations, provides an excellent source of in-class and out-of-class assignments. A set of transparency masters is also available upon adoption.

LEARNING AIDS

Many learning aids are provided within this book to help students learn about OD. The main ones are:

- *Chapter Objectives*. Each chapter presents objectives that prepare the student for the chapter material and point out learning goals.
- *Figures, Photographs, and Illustrations*. Throughout each chapter, key concepts and applications are illustrated with strong, visual materials.
- *OD Applications/Highlights*. Current examples of OD practices and important information are highlighted in boxed exhibits throughout the text.
- *OD International Applications/Highlights*. To focus upon global changes.
- *Summaries*. Each chapter ends with a summary that wraps up the main points and concepts.
- *Review Questions*. Each chapter has a set of review questions covering the main chapter points.
- *Key Terms*. Key Terms are highlighted within each chapter, and a list of key terms is provided at the end of each chapter.
- *OD Skills Simulations (Exercises)*. These self-learning, experiential exercises include both individual and team learning. The exercises take theories and principles covered in the text and bring them to life in team activities. This hands-on, team interaction serves to generate feedback, lively discussions, the testing of personal ideas, and the sharing of information.
- *Case Studies*. Cases for the class discussion or written assignment are provided at the end of each chapter. The cases challenge students to apply OD principles to real companies in real situations.
- *Index*. A subject index helps students quickly find information and examples in the book.

Many other important changes have been incorporated into this edition.

1. The nature of open systems and contingencies has more thorough coverage.
2. Cases have been added at the end of chapters on topics directly related to the text material.
3. Approximately 75 percent of the simulations are new or extensively revised.
4. Review questions have been added at the end of each chapter.
5. The footnote references have been updated and expanded.
6. There is an opportunity to incorporate video cases and Accumen and Lightyear software into the learning situation. Both the cases and software are readily available commercially.

The book is organized into six major parts. Part I, Anticipating Change, has been revised in a substantial way, primarily by the more complete explanation of organization transformation and the systems approach in Chapter 2 and organizational renewal and corporate cultures in Chapter 3. Part II, Consulting for High Performance, focuses on the skills, techniques, and roles of the OD practitioner and includes expanded material on consultant styles. Part III, Developing High Performance, has been revised and updated to reflect the state-of-the-art in the field of OD. Part IV, Motivating for High Performance, covers self-managed teams and team development. Part V, Changing for Success, presents TQM and other system change programs. Finally, Part VI, Focusing on the Future, examines future trends and challenges of the field.

We are grateful to the many people who contributed to this fifth edition. Steve Dye and Dawn Zimmer provided extensive help in reviewing and editing the manuscript. Special thanks go to Professor John Hulpke, CSUB, for "Our Changing World"; to Dean V.K. Unni of CSUB for his support; to Donna Meyer, Antelope Valley Hospital Medical Center; and to Julie White for her fine support. Many students and managers have been involved in the development of the simulations and cases.

Our sincere appreciation is also extended to Natalie Anderson and Lisamarie Brassini of Prentice Hall for their support and assistance; and to Edie Riker for her valuable help as production editor.

The authors would like to extend a public and personal note of thanks to family and friends. From Don Harvey of the authors' team: My sons Scott and Dave (who are playing soccer and basketball at Trafalger Junior High) have contributed in more ways than I can enumerate—not just in allowing the time for writing but in a form of involvement that can never be fully appreciated or repaid. And from Don Brown: My family and friends contributed the encouragement and support necessary to pursue the project.

MEMO TO: The Readers

FROM: The Authors

SUBJECT: Use of This "User Friendly" Text

Perhaps we can reflect on some of the things we tried to develop in this book to make your task easier. Since our major goal is to present knowledge (and yours, we hope, to acquire it), we thought it would be helpful to preview some of the learning tools so that you can use them as you progress.

First, there is a set of **behavioral objectives** at the beginning of each chapter. These are general guides to the major points in each chapter, and they are tied into the **Review Questions** provided at the end of each chapter.

In addition, throughout the text we have identified **key terms** and concepts for you to remember. There are OD terms and concepts which you should be able to use as you complete each chapter. For motivation: exams are often designed around these key concepts, so when a concept is introduced and defined, it will appear in **bold type** in the text. Also, at the end of each chapter, key concepts will be listed with space for you to note the pages on which they are defined. In review, you can scan the text, define each concept for yourself, and—if you are unsure—move back into the text to clarify the meaning. Also, you can review the questions at the end of each chapter and then go back into the text for those you may have missed.

We hope these aids will be helpful to you. We have done our part, the rest is up to you.

Don Harvey
Donald R. Brown

AN EXPERIENTIAL APPROACH TO ORGANIZATION DEVELOPMENT

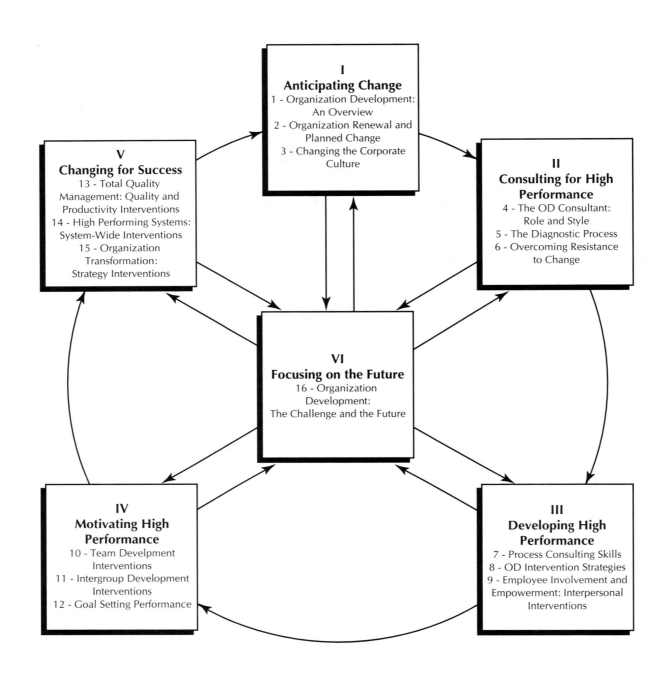

The OD Model

Part I: Anticipating Change

Team meetings play a crucial role in the management of IBM. *Photo courtesy of International Business Machines.*

Organization Development: An Overview

1

OBJECTIVES

Upon completing this chapter, you will be able to:

1. Define the concept of organization development and recognize the need for change and renewal.
2. Describe organization culture and understand its impact on the behavior of individuals in an organization.
3. Understand the expectations of the psychological contract formed on joining an organization.

PREMEETING PREPARATION

1. Read the Background Information.
2. Read and prepare analysis for Case 1: T.G.I.F.

BACKGROUND INFORMATION

Change is avalanching down upon our heads and most people are utterly unprepared to cope with it. Tomorrow's world will be different from today's, calling for new organizational approaches. Organizations will need to be adapting to these changing market conditions and at the same time coping with the need for a renewing rather than reactive workforce. Every day managers are confronting massive and accelerating change. As one writer comments, "Call it whatever you like—reengineering, restructuring, transformation, flattening, downsizing, rightsizing, a quest for global competitiveness—it's real, it's radical and it's arriving every day at a company near you."[1]

Boeing Co., long a leader in the airplane production field, is experiencing severe problems including declining orders for new planes, increasing competition and the need to downsize by some 40,000 employees. According to Dean Thornton, president of Boeing Commercial Aircraft group, the company is dedicated to avoiding the fate of other major companies—getting to the top and then resting on their laurels. As a result, Boeing is radically reinventing itself, finding ways to change, to do things faster, better and cheaper.

Global competition and economic downturns have exposed a glaring weakness in American organizations: the fact that many organizations have become overstaffed, cumbersome, slow and inefficient.[2] To increase productivity, enhance competitiveness and contain costs, organizations are changing the way they are organized and managed.

The successful twenty-first century manager must deal with a chaotic world of new competitors and constant innovation. Tom Peters, (author) suggests that "the time for 10 percent staff cuts and 20 percent quality improvement is past . . . the rate of change demanded . . . and the boldness of goals suggested will be unfailingly new—and frightening."[3]

In the future, the only winning companies will be those that respond quickly to change. Preparing managers to cope with today's accelerating role of change is the central concern of this book. The modern manager must not only be flexible and adaptive in a changing environment but must also be able to diagnose problems and implement change programs.

Organizations are never completely static. They are in continuous interaction with external forces (see Figure 1.1). Changing consumer lifestyles and technological breakthroughs all act on the organization to cause it to change. The degree of change may vary from one organization to another, but all face the need for adaptation to external forces. Many of these changes are forced upon the organization, whereas others are generated internally. Because change is occurring so rapidly, there is a need for new ways to manage.

FIGURE 1.1 The Organizational Environment

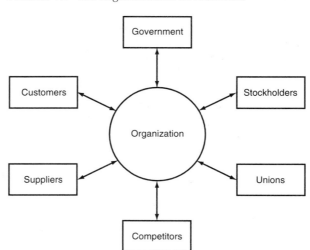

One new approach being used in many organizations is termed **Total Quality Management (TQM)**. This approach involves ensuring that an organization operates with a commitment to quality and continuous improvement in meeting its customer's needs. Organization's are changing and will continue to do so in order to survive in this complex environment. **Organization Development (OD)** is a discipline applying behavioral science to help organizations adapt to these changes. Organization development is aimed not only at improving the organization's effectiveness, but also at enhancing the development of organization members.

This book introduces the practicing manager and student to the field of organization development. The purpose is twofold: (1) to create an awareness of the changing environmental forces confronting the modern manager and (2) to provide the techniques and skills needed for dealing with change in organizations. As author and consultant, Tom Peters has advised today's students, "Remember that: (1) education is the ticket to success and (2) it doesn't stop with the last certificate you pick up. Education is the 'big game' in the globally interdependent economy."[4]

Organizations are using OD techniques to increase their effectiveness and adaptiveness to changing conditions. In this chapter, you will learn about this exciting field: What OD is, why it has emerged, and some basic concepts about the organization change process. You will be introduced to the experiential approach to learning and will be given an overview of the field of study.

What Is Organization Development?

What makes one organization a winner, while another fails to make use of the same opportunities? The key to survival and success lies not in the rational, quantitative approaches, but rather in a commitment to irrational, difficult-to-measure things like people, quality, customer service, and most importantly, developing the flexibility to meet changing conditions. Richard E. Dutton, for example, examined the "high tech-high touch" phenomenon at Citicorp and found that the crucial component in adapting to technological change was the human factor.[5] The true key to successful change is employee involvement and commitment.

Organization development is an emerging discipline aimed at improving the effectiveness of the organization and its members by means of a systematic change program. Chester Barnard and Chris Argyris, among other management theorists, have noted that the truly effective organization is one in which both the organization and the individual can grow and develop. Such an environment may be termed a "healthy" organization. This is what organization development is all about: making organizations healthier and more effective. These concepts apply to all types of organizations including schools, churches, military, government, and industrial concerns. John Sculley (former CEO of Apple Computer), in his book, *Odyssey*, discusses the notion of the **third-wave** company by comparing Pepsi, one of the best second-wave companies of the industrial age, and Apple, one of the best third-wave companies in the age of information. Third-wave companies are the emerging form, not only for high-tech companies, but for all organizations. Their strength lies in *change*—in the ability to transform their products and organization in response to changes in the economy.[6]

Change is a way of life in today's organization. But organizations are also faced with maintaining a stable identity and operations in order to accomplish their primary goals. Consequently, organizations involved in managing change have found that the way in which change is handled is critical. There is a need for a systematic approach, discriminating among those features that are healthy and effective and those that are not. Erratic, short-term, unplanned, or haphazard changes may well introduce problems that did not exist before or allow side effects of the change that may be worse than the original problem. Managers should also be aware that stability or equilibrium can contribute to a healthy state. Change

inevitably involves the disruption of that steady state. Change just for the sake of change is not necessarily effective; in fact, it may be dysfunctional.[7]

A Definition of Organization Development

Organization development (OD) is defined as a long-range effort to improve an organization's ability to cope with change and its problem-solving and renewal processes through effective management of organization culture.

OD involves moving towards a third-wave organization and an attempt to achieve corporate excellence by integrating the desires of individuals for growth and development with organizational goals. According to Richard Beckhard, "organization development is an effort: (1) planned, (2) organization wide, (3) managed from the top, (4) to increase organization effectiveness and health, through (5) planned interventions in the organization's processes using behavioral science knowledge."[8]

Organization development efforts, then, are planned, systematic approaches to change. They involve changes to the total organization or to relatively large segments of it. The purpose of OD efforts is to increase the effectiveness of the system and, also, to develop the potential of all individual members. Finally, a series of planned behavioral science intervention activities are carried out in collaboration with organization members to help find improved ways of working together toward individual and organizational goals.

Another way of understanding OD is to explain what it is not:

- *OD is not a micro approach to change.* Management development, for example, is aimed at changing individual behavior, whereas OD is focused on the macro goal of developing an organization-wide improvement in managerial style.
- *OD is more than any single technique.* Whereas OD consultants use many differing techniques, such as total quality management, or job enrichment, no single technique represents the OD discipline.
- *OD does not include random or ad hoc changes.* OD is based on a systematic appraisal and diagnosis of problems, leading to specific types of change efforts.
- *OD is aimed at more than raising morale or attitudes.* OD is aimed at overall organization health and effectiveness. This may include participant satisfaction as one aspect of the change effort, but includes other effectiveness parameters as well.

The Characteristics of Organization Development

To enlarge upon the definition of OD, let us examine some of the basic characteristics of OD programs (see Table 1.1 on page 5.)

- **Planned change**. OD is a planned strategy to bring about organizational change. The change effort aims at specific objectives and is based on a diagnosis of problem areas.
- **Collaborative**. OD typically involves a collaborative approach to change which includes the involvement and participation of those organization members most affected by the changes.
- **Performance**. OD programs include an emphasis on ways to improve and enhance performance and quality (TQM).
- **Humanistic**. OD relies on a set of humanistic values about people and organizations that aims at gaining more effective organizations by opening up new opportunities for increased use of human potential.
- **Systems**. OD represents a systems approach concerned with the interrelationship of various divisions, departments, groups, and individuals as interdependent subsystems of the total organization.
- **Scientific**. OD is based upon scientific approaches to increase organization effectiveness.

In more general terms, organizational development is based on the notion that an organization to be effective (accomplish its goal), must be more than merely efficient. It must also adapt to change.

Table 1.1 Major Characteristics of the Field of OD

Characteristics	Focal Area
1. Planned Change	Change is planned by managers to achieve goals.
2. Collaborative approach	Involves collaborative approach and involvement
3. Performance orientation	Emphasis on ways to improve and enhance performance.
4. Humantistic orientation	Emphasis upon increased opportunity and use of human potential.
5. Systems approach	Relationship among elements and excellence.
6. Scientific method	Scientific approaches supplement practical experience.

An OD practitioner (either manager or consultant) is a person in an organization responsible for changing existing patterns to obtain more effective organizational performance. Organization development practitioners have come to realize that conventional training techniques are no longer sufficient for effecting the type of behavioral changes needed to create adaptive organizations. New techniques have been developed to provide participants with the competence and motivation to alter ineffective patterns of behavior. One interesting question is, can OD be used to change nations as well as organizations? (See Our Changing World on page 6.)

There are many OD techniques, and any individual practitioner may rely on one or a combination of approaches. Regardless of the method selected, the objectives are to work from an overall organization perspective, thus increasing the ability of the "whole" to respond to a changing environment.

Organizations have objectives such as making profits, surviving, and growing; but individual members also have desires to achieve, unsatisfied needs to fulfill, and career goals to accomplish within the organization. OD, then, is a process for change which can benefit both the organization and the individual. In today's business environment, managers must continuously monitor change and adapt their systems to survive by staying competitive in a turbulent arena.

Why Organization Development?

Why has such a fast-growing field emerged? Organizations are designed to accomplish some purpose or function and to continue doing so for as long as possible. Because of this, organizations are not necessarily intended to change.

But change can affect all types of organizations from giants such as IBM and Boeing to the smallest business. No one can escape change. This is why managers must be skilled in organization change and renewal techniques. As Richard Beckhard (a leading OD practitioner and MIT professor) notes, "Corporations are so hard up for answers these days that I'd say there's a $3 billion or $4 billion market for transformational (OD) consulting out there."[9]

One study examining why organizations initiate large-scale change programs found the most cited reasons for beginning a change program were: (1) *the level of competition:* 68 percent of respondents indicated that the organizations were experiencing a high or very high level of competition; (2) *survival:* some 15 percent indicated that the organization would cease to exist within the next few years without some type of change program; and (3) *improved performance*: 82 percent indicated that without a program, the organization would gradually suffer a decline in performance. This study also identified the primary goals of change programs as shown in Table 1.2 on page 7.[10] Other goals cited included changing the corporate culture, becoming more adaptive, and increasing competitiveness. At IBM, for example, changing conditions are forcing the firm to become more effective in order to remain competitive. (See OD in Practice on page 7.) In the coming decades, changes in the external environment will be occurring so rapidly that organizations will need OD techniques just to keep pace with the accelerating rate of innovation.

OUR CHANGING WORLD:
OD IN THE PRC? IN EASTERN EUROPE?[11]

OD Changing Nations

As stated in the text, OD is not a micro approach to change. OD focuses on the macro goal of developing an organization-wide improvement in managerial style.

While OD focuses on organizations rather than on entire societies, it is interesting to consider the following: Can the principles of OD be implemented across an entire nation? In thousands of organizations simultaneously?

In the 1990s, country after country in Eastern Europe is wrestling with this precise issue. Decisions made at the macro level, for example to cut governmental subsidies to individual plants, are causing massive headaches to "newly freed" managers. These organization managers, with the new freedom to seek profits, now also face a new risk-failure. "At the start, we were told how much to produce, given so much yarn, sent all this stuff to Russia, and nobody expected us to make a profit," says Mrs. Gyorgy Olah, manager in Hungary's Texcoop Textile Factory. But now with state subsidies cut off, machines are idle and unsold sweaters are piled up in boxes in the hallways. "I'm afraid we don't have much to be proud of," says Mrs. Olah.

Can We Use OD?

Can the principles of OD help? Certainly, every lesson in this book could help in Eastern Europe. Should we expect an easy transition away from the tightly state controlled economies in Eastern Europe? Lessons from China give some hints.

Back in the late 1970s, newly empowered Chinese leader Deng Xiao Ping set out to modernize his one-billion population nation. China had achieved much through socialism, for all practical purposes wiping out famine and insuring universal free elementary education. But China still remained very poor overall. Guaranteed jobs and food, Chairman Deng figured, had lowered the overall national incentive to work. Motivation was dulled when everyone, hard worker and laggard alike, ate out of the "One Big Rice Bowl."

The solution, according to Deng, was to "Break the Iron Rice Bowl." Individuals who failed to work would begin to feel hunger. Those who excelled would be rewarded. As Chairman Deng proclaimed, "To be rich is glorious" and "Some must become rich before others."

Did it work? Yes and no. Some decided if wealth was in, any methods, including corruption, should be used to become rich. Other leaders at the organization level faced worker apathy or resistance. Worker productivity bonuses, designed to reward those with initiative, were often distributed to each worker in exactly equal proportions—laggard and superworker receiving identical "bonuses."

But where it did work (typically in organizations small enough to have a cohesive team feeling), the new freedom worked famously. As one co-op manager put it, "I think China has found a wonderful way to realize its goal of modernization," describing her Jinghua Food Company. Manager Liu Zhihua was named a "model rural entrepreneur" at China's first National Conference of Rural Entrepreneurs. Her company, founded by a group of farmers, has developed into an enterprise running several factories, with more than 350 workers. How did the Jinghua Food Company change from a group of farmers to a successful business? Many of the ideas of this book mirror changes in that organization.

So what is the lesson for countries aiming to move from centrally planned economies towards more open markets? Success comes step by step, one organization at a time. OD is not a micro approach, but change at the national level must be matched by change and renewal at the level of the organization. If not, look for trouble. In the case of China, the tensions between those who wanted stability and those who wanted change erupted into violence and huge steps backward on the national level. Yet, even after the Tiananmen Square massacre of June 4, 1989, individual firms in China have forged ahead.

What Next?

What next for China, the Soviet Union, and Eastern Europe? Without a doubt, the principles of organizational development and change outlined in this book will have direct application. But the lessons of China should be remembered: massive change and renewal does not come automatically.

And what next for the countries of North America? Today, the countries of North America are attempting to open markets and allow free trade. The North American Free Trade agreement (NAFTA) will open up free trade from Mexico to Canada with 370 million people and a gross domestic product of $6.8 trillion—the largest free-trade zone in the world today. As mentioned earlier, national change must be matched at the organizational level. Competition and the struggle for corporate survival will be fierce. Successful organizations will be those who diligently employ organizational development strategies. Managers and entrepreneurs alike must be careful not to forget the lessons learned at Tiananmen Square.

Questions

1. Identify the uses of OD approaches to changing nations.
2. How does the application of OD differ between closed markets and open markets?

Table 1.2 Major Goals of Large-Scale Change Programs

Goals	Percent of Organization
To increase productivity	20%
To increase responsiveness to clients	19
To improve competitive positioning (increase productivity/decrease costs)	19
To increase employee involvement and participation	19
To increase employee morale	18
To develop new managerial skills and strategies	14

OD IN PRACTICE:
BIG CHANGES AT BIG BLUE[12]

IBM, once America's premier growth company, is now talking mostly about cutbacks. To come to grips with a changing market place and nine years of lackluster performance, IBM announced plans to cut an additional 35,000 jobs and carve $1.75 billion from annual costs.

Many industry analysts feel IBM has been slow to react to changes in the computer industry. While rushing to get its first personal computer out quickly, IBM ceded control of the operating system to Microsoft Corp. and the microprocessor standard to Intel Corp. IBM blindly lost architectural control of its own personal computer market and was consequently unable to reap the financial rewards of upgrade rights.

Chief Executive Officer Louis V. Gerstner Jr. has begun implementing measures to hack old IBM bureaucracy, improve product distribution and develop a greater sense of customer needs. Gerstner was appointed to his position shortly after IBM posted its first-ever operating loss under former head John F. Akers. He has set up task forces to explore growth opportunities and promised that IBM will execute its strategies better.

Just Like IBM

The 52-year-old Mr. Gerstner has played this tune before. He graduated from Dartmouth and earned an M.B.A. at Harvard in 1965. He joined McKinsey & Co., at age 31 becoming its youngest senior partner ever. In 1978 he left to run American Express's travel-services business. A decade later he became CEO of RJR.

There, he forged himself as a leader who could cut through red tape and overhaul corporate culture. RJR headquarters was bloated and ineffective, just like at IBM. Line managers were suspicious and resentful of the reining-in he was imposing, just like at IBM. They relied too much on overhead foils. Just like IBM.

Tougher Competition— Waving a Samurai Sword

Over the past few years, as other makers of IBM-compatible mainframes have gained credibility and cut prices, IBM's response has been to get tough. When that didn't work, they got even tougher.

One survey found that nearly a third of IBM customers are getting discounts on their mainframes. One large customer says he found he could get a better price just by taking a large Japanese Samurai sword off the wall, waving it over his head, and yelling the name of a Japanese computer company.

Amdahl, one of IBM's biggest competitors, uses what it terms the "million dollar coffee mug"; they tell customers to just leave an Amdahl coffee mug on their desk when an IBM salesman comes calling and they will get $1 million knocked off the IBM price.

But for all the changes and despite price discounts, IBM is losing market share.

The Big Blue Corporate Culture

One of Lou Gerstner's central challenges will be to make the monolithic IBM of old, more cohesive. Gerstner commented he had "never seen a company that is so introspective, caught up in its own underwear, so preoccupied with internal processes . . . People in this company tell me it's easier doing business with people outside the company than inside." He already created an executive panel of operating chiefs to find ways of working better together. He also changed the incentive pay for panel members to focus upon companywide results instead of unit numbers. He plans to manage by principle rather than procedure. Gerstner also has a plan to change IBM's training and management development programs to reflect his new ideas. He adds, "There is no formal way to change attitudes. It takes communication and reinforcement. A corporate culture has to be built around expectations of performance, not rules of behavior." Hence, no more formal dress codes.

Mr. Gerstner is learning that it is easier to talk about change than it is to dismantle seven decades of culture. An internal IBM survey of 1,200 top managers shows that 40% still don't accept "the need for change." At the annual meeting of shareholders in Toronto last month, Mr. Gerstner put it bluntly: "When it comes to a results-oriented corporate culture, we're not there yet, not by a long shot."

Turning New Technologies Into Appealing New Products

Gerstner believes IBM must begin spreading its technology across the different product lines. IBM has already secured production of a highly advanced microprocessor called PowerPC that was developed in a joint effort with Motorola Corp. and Apple Corp. IBM will start incorporating the PowerPC chips into nearly every one of their computer architecture systems. They are working feverishly to better understand the scope of needs among customers and to provide a desired product for the new and changing needs. The rapidly expanding personal computer market appears to be their next frontier.

In one move, IBM acquired Lotus Development, a leading software company, and now has a chance of regaining some of its prior glory, even while downsizing its work force.

In summary, Lou Gerstner has no simple task in trying to shape the competitive posture of IBM after years of neglect. Many analysts feel that the proposed changes alone will not bring IBM back atop the industry. So far, the employees appear to accept Gerstner's concepts of change. Their ability to manage success will also be a key determinant of future growth potential.

Questions

1. Do you agree with Lou Gerstner that IBM needs to change?
2. Would an OD program be appropriate here?
3. What changes would you recommend?

While many organizations have been able to keep pace with changes in information technology, few firms have been able to adapt to changing social and cultural conditions. In a dynamic environment, change is unavoidable. The pace of change has become so rapid today that it is difficult to adjust or compensate for one change before another is necessary. The technological, social, and economic environment is rapidly changing, and an organization will be able to survive only if it can effectively respond to these changing demands. As we move into the twenty-first century, increases in productivity of 500 percent, not 10 percent, will be required for corporations to compete effectively.[13]

Given this increasingly complex environment, it becomes even more critical for management to identify and respond to forces of social and technical change. In attempting to manage today's organizations, many executives find that insufficient consideration of the changing environment in the past is creating problems for them. For example, 3M Corporation has developed an outstanding reputation for innovation. 3M is big but acts small. 3M's 15 percent rule allows its people to spend up to 15 percent of the work week on anything as long as it is product related. The most famous example to come out of this is the Post-it note which now creates $300 million in sales.[14]

Another company, Oregon Steel Mills, was suffering from past losses when Thomas Boklund took over. Boklund overcame rising costs, aging equipment, falling productivity, and a workforce with little or no experience. He introduced changes, such as self managed teams, to increase productivity by over 300 percent and actually averaged sales and earnings growth above 40 percent over the next four years. Boklund spearheaded the turnaround with a management-led buyout giving the employees 95 percent of the company. But loyal employees are not the only reason Oregon Steel has enjoyed such a dramatic turnaround. The company has changed with the times.[15]

One firm which has failed to change with the times is Bain & Company. This group of management consultants was extremely successful through the 1980s. A series of setbacks, two rounds of layoffs, and the defections of several key executives left serious doubts as to the future of the company. Several defectors were younger managers, unhappy with their limited roles in the firm and seeking a greater share of the profits.[16] In this case, Bain & Company lost valuable talent because top management failed to perceive the need to allow individuals to fulfill personal objectives as well as to attain company goals. The loss of key managers can greatly affect the performance of an organization and alter its ability to attract and develop new leadership.

The Emergence of OD

Organization development is one of the primary means of creating more adaptive organizations. Warren Bennis, a leading OD pioneer, has suggested three factors underlying the emergence of OD.

1. *The need for new organizational forms.* Organizations tend to adopt a form that is more appropriate to a particular time, and the current rate of change requires more adaptive forms.
2. *The focus on cultural change.* Because each organization forms a culture—a system of beliefs and values—the only real way to change is to alter this organizational culture.
3. *The increase in social awareness.* Because of the changing social climate, tomorrow's employee will no longer accept autocratic styles of management; therefore, greater social awareness is required in the organization.[17]

The Organization of the Twenty-First Century

The management theorists suggest that to be a successful firm in the next century will require changes as shown in Figure 1.2. They suggest that predictability is a thing of the past and that today's and tomorrow's winning organization is becoming increasingly clear—based upon quality, innovation, and flexibility.[18] Yogi Berra, echoing this sentiment, reportedly once said, "The future ain't what it used to be."

These successful firms will share common traits including:

- *Faster*—more responsive to innovation and change.
- *Quality Conscious*—a total commitment to quality.
- *Employee Involvement*—adding value through human resources.
- *Customer Oriented*—creating niche markets.
- *Smaller*—more autonomous units.

FIGURE 1.2 The Changing Organization of the Twenty-First Century

Today's managers exist in shifting organizational structures and can be the central force in initiating change and establishing the means for adaption. Most organizations strive to be creative, efficient, and highly competitive, maintaining a leading edge in their respective fields rather than following trends set by others. Effective managers are vital to the continuing self-renewal and ultimate survival of the organization. The consultant (manager) must recognize when changes are occurring in the external environment and possess the necessary competence to bring about change when it is needed. The manager must also be aware of the internal system and recognize that the major element in planned change is the organizational culture: the feelings, norms, and behaviors of its members.

The Evolution of Organization Development

It is not within the scope of this book to provide a detailed history of OD, but a brief explanation of the evolution of this field may give you a better understanding of its application today. Organization development has evolved over the past 40 years from the application of behavioral science knowledge and techniques to solving organizational problems. What has become OD started in the late 1940s at MIT and is deeply rooted in the pioneering work of applied social scientists such as Kurt Lewin, and also strongly influenced by the work of psychologists such as Carl Rogers and Abraham Maslow. The term **organization development** is widely attributed to Robert Blake and Jane Mouton (the originators of the Managerial Grid) and Herbert Shepard (a leading OD pioneer); however, Richard Beckhard (an OD consultant) claims this distinction as well. Regardless of who first coined the term, it emerged about 1957 and is generally conceded to have evolved from two basic sources: the application of laboratory methods by National Training Laboratories (NTL) and the survey research methods originated by the Survey Research Center. Both methods were pioneered by Kurt Lewin in about 1945.

NTL—Laboratory-Training Methods

In the late 1940s and early 1950s laboratory-training methods were developed and applied by a group of behavioral scientists at Bethel, Maine. Douglas McGregor (Theory X and Theory Y), working with Richard Beckhard, began applying laboratory-training methods to industry, at General Mills in 1956 and at Union Carbide in 1957. At Union Carbide, McGregor and John Paul Jones (an internal consultant) formed the first internal OD consulting group.

About this same time, Herbert Shepard and Robert Blake were initiating a series of applied behavioral science interventions at Esso, using mainly laboratory-training techniques (see Chapter 9) to improve work team processes. These early training sessions provided the basis for what Blake and Mouton later developed as an instrumented training system they called the Managerial Grid (see Chapter 14). The success of these programs led to a dissemination of such efforts to other corporations.

Survey Research and Feedback

About the same time, a group at the Survey Research Center at the University of Michigan began to apply to organizations the action research model of Kurt Lewin. Rensis Likert and Floyd Mann administered an organization-wide survey to Detroit Edison Co., involving the systematic feedback of data to participating departments (see Chapter 14). They used what is termed an "interlocking series of conferences," feeding data back to the top management group and then down to work teams throughout the organization. Since that time, many organizations have used the survey feedback approach. General Motors, for example, has reported success in applying Likert's survey feedback approach to organizational improvement.

In summary, the major sources of current OD practice were the pioneering work at NTL (laboratory-training techniques) and the Survey Research Center (survey feedback methods). This brief look at the past is important because OD is a new and still developing field, and you as a future OD practitioner may build upon these earlier foundations in pioneering other new approaches.

The Extent of OD Applications

From these early beginnings OD has experienced a rapid growth. A growing number of organizations worldwide are applying OD techniques and many, including most major corporations, have formed internal OD consulting groups.

The OD Network, an organization of OD practitioners, has been in existence for only a little over two decades and has grown to a membership of more than 2,000 members. The National Training Laboratories, American Psychological Association, American Society for Training and Development, and Academy of Management all have professional divisions relating to organization development. The first doctoral program for training OD specialists, called the Organizational Behavior Group, was started by Shepard in 1960 at what is now the Department of Organization and Administration at Case Western Reserve University. Shepard applied these OD techniques, in an educational setting, to the development of OD practitioners. The Organizational Behavior Group has since graduated over 100 specialists, who are involved in teaching and consulting throughout the world. Other universities with graduate programs bearing on OD include Brigham Young, Harvard, MIT, Southern Methodist, UCLA, University of Washington, Gonzaga, Pepperdine, and Yale, with many others beginning to include OD in the curriculum.

Organization development is an exciting and rapidly growing field. OD efforts have grown into a multitude of differing approaches and are now applied in a number of organizations around the world by an expanding number of OD practitioners.

OD and TQM

Because change is occurring so rapidly, there is a need for new ways to manage focusing on product quality and individual involvement. Total Quality Management is an approach to managing work focusing on the evaluation of work processes; the development of a quality energized culture; and the empowerment of employees, for the purpose of continuous improvement of products and services.

Since TQM is a powerful new management technique requiring increased employee participation, the first step is a dramatic change in corporate culture. Any successful change in corporate culture will depend upon the active consultation and involvement of the management team.

The Organization Culture

One element of an organization system which a manager needs to understand is the **organization culture**. The term culture refers to a specific civilization, society, or group that are its distinguishing characteristics. As B. F. Skinner has commented: "A culture is not the behavior of the people 'living in it'; it is the 'it' in which they live—contingencies of social reinforcement which generate and sustain their behavior."[19] The *organization culture* refer to a system of shared meanings, including the language, dress, patterns of behavior, value system, feelings, attitudes, interactions, and group norms of the members. You may examine the patterns of behavior on your campus or in your company. How do people dress or wear their hair? What jargon or unique terms are used? (See B. C. comic strip.) These are the elements that make up a culture: the accepted patterns of behavior.[20] One example is the culture at Federal Express, carefully crafted by Frederick Smith, the chairman, to reflect a combat situation. Flights are called "missions" and competitors are "enemies." Fred Smith,

SOURCE: *B.C.* by permission of Johnny Hart and Creators Syndicate, Inc.

a Vietnam veteran, gives a Bravo Zulu award (Navy jargon meaning "job well done"), and his managers are sometimes called "Ho Chi Minh's Guerrillas."[21] This provides a set of values and behavioral norms for the organization.

Norms are the organized and shared ideas regarding what members should do and feel, how this behavior should be regulated, and what sanctions should be applied when behavior does not coincide with social expectations. The values and behaviors of each organization are also unique as shown by Oliver Stone's movie, *Wall Street*, which examines the cultural norms of investment banking firms or the book, *Maverick*, a description of a unique industry culture. Some patterns of behavior may be functional and may facilitate the accomplishment of organization goals. Other patterns of behavior or cultural norms may actually inhibit or restrict the accomplishment of organization goals.

It is helpful to look at the types of norms that exist in an organization to gain a better understanding of the culture of that organization. Norms generally are enforced only for behaviors that are viewed as most important by most group members.[22] Norms essential to accomplishing the organization's objectives are called **pivotal norms**. Norms that support and contribute to the pivotal norms but are not essential to the organization's objectives are called **peripheral norms**. For example, norms requiring a student to conform to a certain dress code are peripheral. Pivotal and peripheral norms constantly confront an individual in an organization, and he or she must decide whether or not to conform. The pressure to conform to these norms varies, allowing individuals some degree of freedom in responding to these organizational pressures depending on how they perceive the rewards or punishments. The organization also has latitude in the degree of conformity it requires of its members.

The Socialization Process

Even though an organization does an effective job of recruiting, new employees must still adjust to the organizational culture. Because they are not aware of the culture, new employees are likely to disagree with or question the customs and values that exist. **Socialization** may be defined as the process that adapts employees to the organization's culture.[23] (See Figure 1.3.)

FIGURE 1.3 The Socialization Process

New Employee Expectations

To function effectively, a manager or a member must be aware of the norms within the organization. He or she must recognize how sharply norms are defined and how strongly they are enforced. The individual's initial entry into any new situation often results in some degree of anxiety or stress. The less an individual can relate the new situation to previous situations, the greater the feelings of anxiety and discomfort. The more the individual can meet expectations, the less are the feelings of anxiety and discomfort.

One example of this is at Bain & Co., a Boston consulting firm. Like many other companies, the cultural atmosphere at Bain & Co. reflects many of the values of its founder, Bill Bain. For example, desks are kept clear. Any paper left on desks overnight is shredded. Partners have offices but other employees work in open areas designed to increase team morale. The company tries to hire only the "best and brightest" young MBAs, and expects them to dress in the company uniform, the so-called "power suit": dark suit, handmade shirt, and red tie (or its female equivalent).[24]

Encounter Organizational Culture

The organizational culture provides a way of meeting and getting along with organization members. Three important aspects of socialization when joining an organization are:

1. deciding who is a member and who is not;
2. developing an informal understanding of behavioral norms; and
3. separating friends from enemies.

To work together effectively, individuals need to understand things like power, status, rewards, and sanctions for specific types of behaviors. For instance, what behavior gets one a good grade, and so on.

While the individual is experiencing a new situation, the organization may be attempting to influence the person. If a new member comes to an organization expecting to find a certain set of norms, he or she is looking for those expectations to be affirmed. If these expectations reflect the actual norms of that organization, the integration process for both the new member and the organization is relatively painless.

Adjustment to Norms

The new member often finds that the norms are unclear, confusing, and restrictive. As a result, he or she may react in several different ways when entering an organization (see Figure 1.4). At one extreme the new member may choose to conform to all the norms of the organization, resulting in uniformity of behavior and complete acceptance of organization values. In an organization this conformity may result in stagnation, nonresponsiveness, and a loss of creativeness. At the other extreme the new member may choose to rebel, to reject all values, or to leave the organization altogether.[25]

FIGURE 1.4 Basic Responses to Socialization

Another less obvious alternative is for the new member to accept the pivotal norms and seriously question the peripheral norms, which Schein has termed **creative individualism**. This would be the ideal behavior for a healthy and effective organization, but it is often difficult for a newcomer to correctly determine which norms are peripheral and which are pivotal. What may be a pivotal norm in one department may be peripheral or not a norm at all in another department of the same organization. Since norms are changing and dynamic, it requires an awareness on the part of the organization member to discern the differences between pivotal and peripheral norms.

Results

Only the more healthy organizations allow their members to challenge the norms. The aim of OD is to develop an organization climate that is appropriate to its mission and its members. In a sense, OD involves changing the culture of organizations and work groups so that a more effective means of interacting, relating, and problem solving will result. OD is involved in developing an organization to the point that it feels comfortable in allowing its members to openly examine the norms, both pivotal and peripheral, with the ultimate goal of building a more effective organization. The reaction of the individual to these norms results in the formation of an unwritten agreement with the organization.

At 3M, for example, employees believe that it is their responsibliity to innovate and be creative. They use these behaviors in developing new and improved products and processes. They believe that team discussion, challenging ideas and taking risks are appropriate behaviors for achieving these goals. However, in many auto plants, employees believe that following procedures, reaching quantitative outcome targets, and following orders consistent with work rules are behavioral goals. Each person tends to do the following:

1. separate more important from less important goals;
2. develop ways to measure their accomplishments; and
3. create explanations for why goals may not always be met.

Psychological Contract

Psychological contract may be defined as an unwritten agreement between individuals and the organization of which they are members.[26] It describes certain expectations that the organization has of the individual and the individual's expectations of the organization. Because the two parties are growing and changing, the contract must be open-ended, so that old issues and new issues may be renegotiated.

An organization has certain expectations of its members. If it is a business organization, certain expectations of member behavior will probably be spelled out very clearly. It undoubtedly expects its members to be on the job during certain hours of the day. It is probably concerned with quality and quantity of work, loyalty, appearance, and various other things unique to the organization. For the organization to be satisfied, the individual will need to comply to some degree with the expectations. In other words, the organization has certain requirements, and the individual must do certain things to meet those requirements if there is to be a lasting and healthy relationship. In many instances, these unfulfilled expectations result in high turnover, absenteeism, sabotage, and worker alienation.[27]

Similarly, the individual has certain expectations of the organization. An individual may expect to gain work experience, security, and advancement. The individual probably expects to have an opportunity to meet people, make friends, and form social relationships; and undoubtedly expects remuneration from the organization. For the individual to be satisfied and stay, the organization will have to meet the individual's expectations.

When either the organization's or individual's expectations are not being satisfied adequately by the other party, friction, and difficulties may develop. If these problems cannot

be solved, they may culminate in the individual leaving the organization by either his or her or the organization's choice. All too often, the problem is solved by not solving it: it takes too much effort to reach a real solution, so both parties must continue with a tenuous and unharmonious relationship.

In some psychological contracts between the organization and the individual, key expectations may not even be addressed. One or both of these parties may assume that the other party agrees to some unstated expectations. The phrase "it is intuitively obvious to the most casual observer" may be the underlying assumption of one or both parties. Such unstated or assumed expectations can lead to an organization manned by individuals who feel cheated or managers who feel disappointed in their subordinates. To avoid such misunderstandings, it is suggested that both parties—the members and the representatives of the organization—form a psychological contract that is continually being renegotiated.

The Experiential Approach to Learning

To learn OD techniques, a manager or student needs both the knowledge of content material and the experience of putting theory into practice. Consequently, to create a learning environment for the field of organization development at either the undergraduate or graduate level, the emphasis should be on experience.[28] In this book you will be experiencing OD techniques by means of behavioral simulations at the same time that you are learning OD theories.

You will perhaps discover a different approach to the study of organizational change. Many courses in OD approach change in a structured and traditional manner. By means of lectures and readings, useful concepts and theories are presented to the student, whose role is largely passive. This book utilizes an innovative and significantly different approach to teaching OD: the *experiential approach*. It is based on learning OD techniques by experiencing simulated organizational situations. You will experience situations in which you are developing a relationship with a client or diagnosing a problem rather than simply reading about them.

The Basic Concepts of Experiential Learning

Experiential learning is based upon three basic concepts:

1. You learn best when you are involved in the learning experience.
2. Concepts have to be experienced or discovered by you, the learner, if they are to change your behavior.
3. Your commitment to learning will be greatest when you are responsible for setting your own learning objectives.

In the experiential approach, the major responsibility for learning is placed upon you, the learner. You will determine your own learning objectives and influence how the class goes about achieving these objectives. You set your own goals, decide which theories you want to learn, practice the skills or techniques you want to improve, and develop the behavioral style you want to develop.

Experiential learning also involves an active, rather than a passive role. Often you may sit in a class, listen, take notes, or perhaps daydream while the instructor "does his or her thing" for an hour. In this class, you will be actively deciding what to do and how to do it. You will be doing, communicating, and participating in learning. You will find that you cannot learn in isolation. As in a job situation, you are dependent upon others and they upon you for ideas, reactions, experiences, and feedback about behavior. The same will be true in this class. Experiential learning is also the method most corporations use to teach OD concepts to their employees. So, you will be experiencing the same kinds of activities that occur in most "real world" OD programs.

FIGURE 1.5 Schematic Diagram of Experiential Learning Cycle

What is different about the experiential learning process? First, you will generate from your own experience in this class a set of concepts that will guide your behavior. These concepts will be continually modified over time and in various managerial situations to improve your effectiveness. The experiential learning process can be presented as a four-stage cycle (see Figure 1.5):

1. *Gaining conceptual knowledge and theories*—you will be reading about OD concepts and theories and doing preclass preparation.
2. *Activity in a behavioral simulation*—you will be problem solving, making decisions, and communicating, actively practicing the concepts and theories.
3. *Analysis of activity*—you will be analyzing, critiquing, and discussing the way you solved problems, and comparing the results of different approaches.
4. *Connecting the theory and activity with prior on-the-job or life situations*—you will be connecting your learning to past experiences, reflecting upon the results, and generalizing into the future. The end result should be improved skill and performance in applying these learnings to life and job situations.

"Student-centered" learning places the learning responsibility upon you. There will be an opportunity in the class for a high level of participation and for a challenging learning experience. Small-group learning environments will be formed wherein you may share learning with others, thus encountering feedback. Each of the learning units presents a conceptual background and a framework for a behavioral simulation. The focal point for each chapter is the action-oriented behavioral simulation.

As part of the experiential learning model in OD, feelings, and emotions represent important data for learning. Open and authentic relationships in which you share your feelings with others and provide honest feedback are a necessary part of the learning situation. Each chapter is organized to help you learn concepts and skills, and each provides cases, simulations, and diagnostic instruments to help you learn more about OD. Although experiential learning can be stimulating and often fun, it is important to remember that you learn from the combination of theory and experience.[29]

An Overview of the Field of Study

In this book we present the field of organization development—both theory and practice. The material has been selected to provide you with most of what is known at this time about the field of OD: the current state of the art. This includes issues, critiques, and controversy as well, for the field of OD is itself evolving and being questioned. This is the fifth edition of this book and it is a very different book than when it was first written.

The book is intended to assist the participant, the manager, and the practitioner in understanding the strategies and techniques of OD and moves from the more basic elements

to the more complex. The OD model is shown in Figure 1.6 which also identifies the chapter in which each topic area is discussed. The arrows and feedback loops show the notion of interrelationship among the various sections.

Part I: Anticipating change. This introduces the concepts and techniques of organization development and organization renewal. This includes what OD is, why it has emerged and the nature of changing the corporate culture.

Part II: Consulting for high performance. This presents the basic roles and styles, the diagnostic process and overcoming resistance to change.

Part III: Developing high performance. This covers OD consulting skills, basic OD strategies, and employee involvement approaches.

Part IV: Motivating high performance. Here we present team, intergroup, and goal setting OD strategies.

Part V: Changing for success. This presents high performance teams, systems, and organizations.

Part VI: Focusing on the future. Here we examine the results of the OD process and discuss future challenges and problems.

FIGURE 1.6 The OD Model

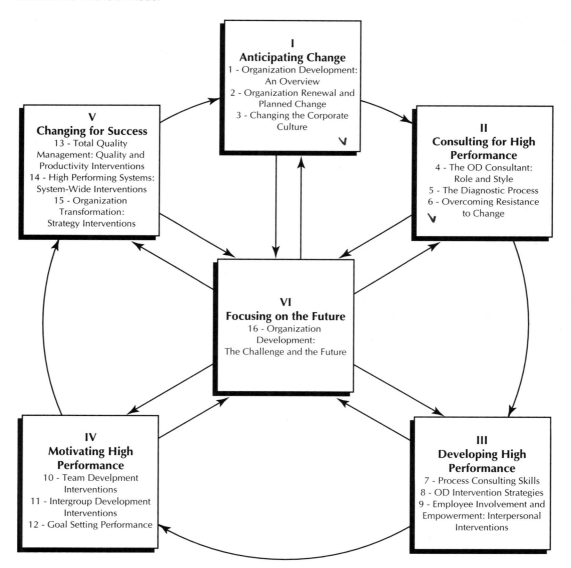

We hope you find this approach interesting, and that it answers some significant questions about OD, and raises additional questions regarding this dynamic field. Basically, there is an opportunity for you to improve your consultant skills, gain an overall grasp of OD, and learn to make better predictions about the implications and consequences of any future change activities that you may undertake.

REVIEW QUESTIONS

1. How would you define "organization development?"

2. How does OD differ from a single change technique such as management training?

3. Identify and demonstrate the uses of the psychological contract.

4. Contrast the difference between pivotal and peripheral norms.

5. Compare and contrast planned versus unplanned change.

6. Explain three basic responses an individual has to socialization.

7. Read a book or view a video/movie and identify organization culture and norms. (For example, *Wall Street* or *The Firm*.)

KEY WORDS AND CONCEPTS

Define and be able to use the following:

Creative Individualism
Experiential Learning
Norms
Organization Culture
Organization Development (OD)
Organization Renewal

Peripheral Norms
Pivotal Norms
Psychological Contract
Socialization
Third Wave
Total Quality Management (TQM)

OD SKILLS SIMULATION 1.1
AUDITIONING FOR THE "SATURDAY NIGHT LIVE" GUEST HOST SPOT

Total time suggested: 1 hour

A. PURPOSE

The goal of this exercise is to begin building trust within the group by sharing information about yourself with others and exploring group members values and norms. You will gain experience interviewing another person which is a key skill for a potential OD consultant.

B. PROCEDURES

Step 1. Members form into dyads (pairs).

Step 2. Each dyad member (A) interview their partner (B) to find out who she/he is. The purpose is for you to gain enough information to introduce the other person to the group with an emphasis on behavior. The partners then reverse roles, with B interviewing A. A set of questions are provided as a departure point for your discussion on the Interview Format.

Time suggested for Steps 1 and 2: 20 minutes.

Step 3. The total group is re-formed. Each person (A) then introduces her/his partner. Introduce your partner to the class with a focus on positive accomplishments, yet add some humor and demonstrate your own "guest host" style. The class may ask questions to find more relevant information about (B). This proceeds around the class until each partner has been introduced.

At the end of the introductions, how many potential guest hosts did you discover?

Step 4. Meeting with the entire class, discuss the following questions:

1. Based on the introductions, can you foresee the formation of any norms?
2. In the introduction process, did you learn more about the person being introduced or the person doing the introduction?
3. What seems to be the type and level of participation of the members?

Time suggested for Steps 3 and 4: 40 minutes.

(Interview Format follows on next page)

INTERVIEW FORMAT

Name of Person Interviewed _____

1. Tell me a little bit about yourself.

 a. _____

 b. _____

 c. _____

2. How would you describe the strengths you bring to the group?

 a. _____

 b. _____

 c. _____

3. What do you consider your past accomplishments or highlights?

 a. _____

 b. _____

 c. _____

4. What are your hobbies, interests, and astrological sign?

5. What is your favorite:

Color	Music	Car	Food	TV Star	Other
_____	_____	_____	_____	_____	_____

6. What are your goals for this class?

 a. _____

 b. _____

 c. _____

7. What resources can you contribute?

8. Anything else we've not covered?

OD SKILLS SIMULATION 1.2
THE PSYCHOLOGICAL CONTRACT[30]

Total time suggested: 1 hour

A. PURPOSE

The goal of this exercise is to make explicit and share some of the major expectations and obligations between students and instructor.[31] It provides an opportunity for the instructor to find out what the class expects and for the students to learn what the instructor expects.

B. PROCEDURES

PART A. INSTRUCTOR'S INTERVIEW OF STUDENTS

Step 1. The class forms into groups of four to five persons.

Step 2. Each group elects one person as representative.

Step 3. Each group prepares its representative for the interview, and should be sure that they understand the group's position. (See the Suggested Question Guide for Instructor's Interview of Students.)

Time suggested for Steps 1 to 3: 15 Minutes

Step 4. The representatives, one from each group, meet with the instructor. The instuctor interviews them about their expectations while the rest of the class observes.

Time suggested for Step 4: 20 minutes

SUGGESTED QUESTION GUIDE FOR
INSTRUCTOR'S INTERVIEW OF STUDENTS

1. What are your objectives for this course?
 a. To learn theories?
 b. To reach some desired level of knowledge?
 c. To learn new skills?
 d. To gain new behaviors?
 e. To get a good grade?
 f. To get required credit hours?

2. How can the instructor best help you to achieve your goals?
 a. By giving lectures?
 b. By assigning and discussing readings?
 c. By giving exams?
 d. By leading seminar discussions?
 e. By relating personal experiences?
 f. By letting you work on your own?
 g. By being a stern task master?
 h. By being warm and supportive?

3. How can other class members help you achieve your goals?
 a. By sharing prior experiences?

 b. By participating in group discussions?

 c. By coming to classs prepared?

 d. By sharing educational background?

 e. By doing nothing?

 f. By being enthusiastic and supportive?

 g. By being critical?

 h. By being flattering?

 i. By giving honest appraisals?

 4. How should class members be evaluated?

 a. By quizzes, exams, and tests?

 b. By instructor?

 c. By peers?

 d. By quantity or quality of work?

 5. How should the class be motivated and how would you in reality act toward this motivation?

 a. By self-motivation?

 b. By peer pressure?

 c. By instructor pressure?

 d. By class interest?

 e. By grade pressure?

 6. What is the best thing that could happen in this class?

PART B: WHAT DO I WANT FROM THIS COURSE?

A. PURPOSE

 1. To focus on key goals for this course.

 2. To share expectations of what you want from this course.

 3. To form a psychological contract for the class.

B. PROCEDURES

 Step 1. Individually complete Column I of the Psychological Contract Worksheet.

 Step 2. In small groups, exchange views, achieve consensus in completing Column II of the Worksheet, and develop group responses to the questions.

 Step 3. Each group discusses any questions it would like its representative to ask the instructors. He/she should be sure to understand the group's questions and concerns. (See the Suggested Question Guide for Students' Interview of Instructor, p. 23.)

 Time suggested for Steps 1 to 3: 15 minutes.

 Step 4. The representatives, one from each group, interview the instructor to clarify the instructor's expectations of the class.

 Time suggested for Step 4: 20 minutes.

 It might be helpful to incorporate into Step 4 the following: The representatives and the instructor should write on the blackboard a consessus of course objectives. This will not only reaffirm and support objectives listed in the syllabus (by allowing the class to come up with the objectives), but will let the students and instructor delete or add other objectives which they feel may be important to the learning process.

DISCUSSION QUESTIONS

1. In what ways did course objectives differ from student to student?
2. What kind of class culture is desired?

THE PSYCHOLOGICAL CONTRACT WORKSHEET

Issues	Column I Individual Responses	Column II Group Responses
1. What were my expectations from this course when I enrolled in it?	_____	_____
2. What do you expect to get out of this course?	_____	_____
3. What will be the most enjoyable part of the course?	_____	_____
4. What skills do you feel will be the most critical to becoming an effective manager?	_____	_____
5. What skills and topics must you work on?	_____	_____

SUGGESTED QUESTION GUIDE FOR STUDENTS' INTERVIEW OF INSTRUCTOR

You may ask the instructor any questions you feel are relevant to effective learning. Some areas you may want to discuss are:

1. How do people learn?
2. What are expectations about attendance?
3. What is the philosophy of evaluation? How are students evaluated?
4. What is the instructor's role in the class?
5. What stereotypes about students are held?
6. Is there anything else that you feel is important?

PART C. IDENTIFYING AND ESTABLISHING NORMS

Step 1. Meeting in class session, discuss the following:

1. Identify the pivotal and peripheral norms that are being established.
2. Which of these norms are functional or dysfunctional to the class?
3. Which of these norms would you like to change?
4. Do you have any additional behaviors you would like to see become norms?
5. How much trust is being developed among students, and between students and instructor?

Step 2. For the norms you would like to change, make some specific plans for the changes.

Time suggested for Steps 1 and 2: 15 minutes.

CASE ANALYSIS GUIDELINES

WHY USE CASES?

Case studies allow a learning-by-doing approach. The material in the case provides the data for analysis and decision making. Cases require you to diagnose and make decisions about the situation and to defend those decisions to your peers.

OBJECTIVES OF THE CASE METHOD

1. Helping you to acquire the skills of putting textbook knowledge about management into practice.
2. Getting you out of the habit of being a receiver of facts, concepts, and techniques, and into the habit of diagnosing problems, analyzing and evaluating alternatives, and formulating workable plans of action.
3. Training you to work out answers and solutions for yourself, as opposed to relying upon the authoritative crutch of the professor or a textbook.
4. Providing you with exposure to a range of firms and managerial situations (which might take a lifetime to experience personally), thus offering you a basis for comparison when you begin your own management career.

HOW TO PREPARE A CASE

1. Begin your analysis by reading the case once for familiarity.
2. On the second reading, attempt to gain full command of the facts, organizational goals, objectives, strategies, policies, symptoms of problems, problems, basic causes of problems, unresolved issues, and roles of key individuals.
3. Who are the key players in this situation—their roles, styles?
4. Arrive at a solid evaluation of the organization, based on the information in the case. Developing an ability to evaluate organizations and size up their situations is the key to case analysis.
5. Decide what you think the organization needs to do to improve its performance and to set forth a workable plan of action.

•

CASE 1: T.G.I.F.[32]

It's 4:30 on a Friday afternoon and the weekly beer bust is in full swing at Quantum Software's[33] Seattle headquarters. The sun shines on the volleyball court and beyond, the patio sparkles over a dazzling view of Lake Washington. Every week most of the employees drop in to unwind and relax at the beer bust for an hour as a reward for extra effort.

Quantum Software was founded three years ago by Stan Albright and Erin Barber based upon an idea they came up with in college for forming a business aimed at developing and selling computer software specifically oriented to the needs of independent oil businesses. Few of these firms grow large enough to do their own data processing systems. Quantum has grown to over 200 employees and $15 million in sales over the past three years. One Friday afternoon, Bill Carter, the corporate attorney, had dropped in to attend a business meeting. After the meeting, he was invited to mix in with employees at the weekly beer bust.

"What a great place to work!" several people told Bill. The spirit of Quantum continually amazed Bill. Stan and Erin knew how to keep things hopping and yet hold morale at an enthusiastic level. To counter the frantic work pace of 16-hour days and six-day weeks, Quantum had a beer bust every Friday afternoon. Everyone was invited, from Stan and Erin to the part-time janitor who worked nights.

[handwritten margin note: ALL INCLUDED GOODS BAD]

No ties, no suit coats, first names only: this was a great way to encourage the team concept. Lately though, Bill Carter had been having second thoughts about serving alcohol at a company sponsored party. He made up his mind to speak to CEO Stan Albright about it and started over toward the pool where Stan and Erin were holding a lively discussion with three employees. Just then, John Hooker, a new programmer in software development, lost his balance and fell on the snack table sending finger sandwiches flying in all directions and getting a round of applause. "All right, John!" several people called out. More determined than ever, Bill approached Stan and Erin and said, "Don't you think this party thing is getting a little out of hand? It used to be a lot of fun, but now maybe we're growing too fast. We're getting more people like John there, who just seem to overdo it."

[handwritten margin note: STARTING TO GET OUT OF HAND]

"Take it easy, Bill," said Stan. "The atmosphere around here would get stale real fast if we couldn't blow off a little steam now and then."

"Come on, Bill," Erin added, "lighten up. We need this time to relax and for everyone to socialize over a beer without the pressure of work."

[handwritten margin note: WORK HARD PLAY HARD]

"You should know, Bill, how much these parties mean to our success. I really feel that one of the keys to our continued growth has been the family feeling among our employees. On Fridays at our TGIF get-togethers, we all get to know one another as equals. That gives me the right to kick butts when I have to because they know I like them and want them to succeed. That's the real value of these parties."

[handwritten margin note: FAMILY KEY TO GROWTH]

"Okay, Stan, so you tell me," asked Bill, "what's the value in having someone like John who has had too many beers driving home and possibly causing a serious accident? Do you realize that Quantum could be held liable in such an instance?"

[handwritten margin note: LIABILITY]

"Bill," responded Erin, "you know I'm the one who first thought up the idea of having a Friday bash and I still think it's a great idea. I agree with Stan that this company is a success thanks to our employees and the *esprit-de-corps* that we've developed. If we drop the TGIFs as a time to unwind, what can we replace it with? I can see the point you're trying to raise. I agree that something bad could come out of this, but if we can't take a few risks we may as well close the doors. These parties are great for recruitment and they define our corporate culture. I feel it would be a big mistake to drop the parties."

[handwritten margin note: ESPRIT]

"I think you two are missing the point," answered Bill. "Of course, I realize how important it is to keep our team spirit. What I'm trying to say is, isn't there a way to keep that spirit and put some limit to our liability exposure at the same time?"

QUESTIONS

1. Does Quantum have a problem or not?
2. How would you respond to Bill?
3. Examine the pros and cons of the various actions.
4. What do you think Quantum should do?

CASE ANALYSIS FORM

Name: _____

I. Problems

 A. Macro

 1. ___MASSIVE CHANGES CULTURE CHANGING_____

 2. _____

 B. Micro

 1. ___LIAB SCRV ALC_____

 2. _____

II. Causes

 1. ___WEEKLY BEER BUST – CULTURE (PIVOTTAL OR PGRIPH)___

 2. _____

 3. _____

III. Systems affected

 1. Structural _____

 2. Psychosocial ___PSYCH CONTRACT_____

 3. Technical _____

 4. Managerial_____

 5. Goals _____

IV. Alternatives

 1. ___DO NOTHING_____

 2. ___DON'T SERVE ALCOHOL_____

 3. ___USE NO HOST BAR_____

 4. ___DESIG DRWGR OR CO. BUS_____

 5. _____

V. Recommendations

 1. _____

 2. _____

 3. _____

SUMMARY

This chapter has focused on several major issues. One is that organizations operate in a dynamic and changing environment and consequently must be adaptive. You have been introduced to the emerging field of organization development (OD) and the ways it is used to improve organizational effectiveness.

• **Change.** One of the manager's most difficult tasks is initiating organization change and renewal. You, as a manager, must be sensitive to changes in markets, products, and competition and be aware of the need for an adaptive and flexible organization. The first step in the change process is an awareness that a problem exists.

You have had an opportunity to experience the need for organization change in this class meeting. Students frequently complain about the lack of effectiveness and learning in the classroom. In OD we call this the awareness of a problem. The university environment is changing, and today's student is not the same as the student who attended the university 10 or 20 years ago. Today's students' backgrounds, their motivation, and their expectations are different, but they face basically the same learning environment that students experienced 20 years ago.

• **Socialization.** Entering a class for the first time is very similar to the first day on the job. You may decide to rebel and reject the classroom norms, you may conform by accepting classroom norms, or you may respond with creative individualism.

• **Experiential.** In this class your role will be active. You will be an active participant, and your degree of learning and that of your fellow class members depends to a large degree upon your involvement and contributions. In this session you have become aware of the potential within other individuals and within yourself, and of the factors of organization culture and norms. We create and maintain the culture and norms, and we can change them. Frequently, organizations must change these attitudes, values, beliefs, and behaviors if they are to become more effective.

• **Ownership.** In the classroom students often feel that a course is boring, dull, and unsatisfying. Instructors often feel similarly: that students are lazy, apathetic, and immature. It is often easier to sit back passively and complain rather than attempt to change the situation. Students become accustomed to placing full responsibility for learning upon the instructor. When they are confronted with an opportunity to express expectations and to participate in setting learning goals, students may become confused, suspicious, or frustrated. Yet both students and instructor share objectives and responsibility for the learning environment.

• **Psychological Contract.** In this class you have examined the organization culture and the norms. In the simulation you have experienced the formation of a psychological contract. As a result of the contract formation process, many underlying expectations have been brought out into the open and explained, and the interdependence and shared responsibility of student and instructor have been demonstrated.

• **OD.** Organization development is the discipline that applies behavioral science techniques to management problems. Since the essential task of management is to deal with change, it is the purpose of this book to better prepare managers for this task. We have found that this can best be accomplished by students and using the experiential approach—an approach that differs significantly from the traditional lecture-exam approach. We think you will enjoy it.

NOTES

1. Thomas A. Stewart, "Welcome to the Revolution," *Fortune*, December 13, 1993, p. 66.
2. Laura Rubach, "Downsizing: How Quality is Affected as Companies Shrink," *Quality Progress*, Vol. 28, No. 4, April, 1995, p. 23.
3. Thomas J. Peters, "Thriving on Chaos," (New York: Alfred A. Knopf, 1992), p. 66. Also see Rosabeth Moss Kanter, "Championing Change," *Harvard Business Review,* Jan-Feb, 1991, pp. 119–30.
4. Thomas J. Peters, "Thriving on Chaos," *Working Woman*, September, 1993, p. 43.
5. Richard E. Dutton, "High Technology with the Human Touch," paper presented at Academy of Management, Washington, D.C., 1989. Also see Jeannie Coyle, "Aligning Human Resources Processes with Total Quality," *Employment Relations Today*, Autumn 1991, p. 273.
6. John Sculley, *Odyssey* (New York: Harper & Row, 1987), p. 92.
7. Marie McKendall, "The Tyranny of Change: Organizational Development Revisited," *Journal of Business Ethics*, February, 1993, p. 97
8. Richard Beckhard, *Organizational Development: Strategies and Models* (Reading, Mass.: Addison-Wesley Publishing Co., Inc., 1969), p. 9. Also see Jyotsna Sanzgiri and Jonathan Z. Gottlieb, "Philosophic and Pragmatic Influences on the Practice of Organization Development, 1950–2000," *Organizational Dynamics*, Autumn 1992, pp. 57-69.
9. *The Wall Street Journal*, July 24, 1987, p. A1. David Kirkpatrick, "IBM Moves to Fix Its Micro Soft Problem," *Fortune*, July 10, 1995, p. 102–105.
10. Teresa J. Colvin and Ralph H. Kilmann, "A Profile of Large Scale Change Programs," Proceedings, Southern Management Assn., 1989, p. 202.
11. John F. Hulpke, California State University, Bakersfield, Bakersfield, CA 1994.
12. David Kirkpatrick, "Gerstner's New Vision for IBM," *Fortune*, November 15,1993, p. 120; Laurie Hays "Blue Period," *The Wall Street Journal*, May 13, 1994, p. A1.

13. T. Mantz, "Guiding I/T Inspired Transformation," Nolan, Norton & Co. Symposium, September 19–20, 1988, San Francisco.

14. Russell Mitchell, "Masters of Innovation," *Business Week*, April 10, 1989, pp. 58–63.

15. R. Lee Sullivan, "Metals," *Forbes*, January 4, 1993, p. 170.

16. Keith H. Hammonds, "Can Bain Consultants Get Bain & Co. Out of this Jam?," *Business Week*, February 11, 1991, pp. 52–3.

17. Warren Bennis, *Organization Development: Its Nature, Origins, and Prospects* (Reading, Mass.: Addison-Welsley Publishing Co., Inc., 1969).

18. Peters, *Thriving on Chaos,* p. 29.

19. B. F. Skinner, *Contingencies of Reinforcement* (Englewood Cliffs, N.J.: Prentice Hall, Inc., 1969), p. 13.

20. See H. S. Becker, "Culture: A Sociological View," *Yale Review*, Summer 1982, pp. 513–27; and E. H. Schein, *Organizational Culture and Leadership* (San Francisco: Jossey-Bass, 1985), p. 168.

21. Peter Waldman, "Federal Express Faces Test of Pilot's Loyalty Since Purchasing Tiger," *The Wall Street Journal*, October 23, 1989, p. A1.

22. Edgar H. Schein, "Coming to a New Awareness of Organizational Culture," *Sloan Management Review*, Winter 1984, pp. 3–16; Daniel C. Feldman, "The Development of Group Norms," *Academy of Management Review,* vol. 9, no. 1 (1984), pp. 47–53.

23. See, for example, J. E. Hebden, "Adopting an Organization's Culture," *Organizational Dynamics* , Summer 1986, pp. 54–72; and G. R. Jones, "Socialization Tactics," *Academy of Management Journal*, June 1986, pp. 262–79.

24. Nancy J. Perry, "A Consulting Firm Too Hot Too Handle," *Fortune*, April 27, 1987, p. 91.

25. Edgar H. Schein, "Organization Socialization and the Profession of Management," *Industrial Management Review*, vol. 9 (1968), p. 8.

26. H. G. Baker, "The Unwritten Contract, *Personnel Journal*, July 1985, pp. 37–41; see also Edgar H. Schein, *Organizational Psychology*, (Englewood Cliffs, N.J.: Prentice Hall, Inc., 1970), pp. 76–79.

27. Robert W. Goddard, "The Psychological Contract," *Management World*, vol. 13, no. 7 (August 1984), p. 12.

28. Michael C. Ehrhardt, "Managerial Education: A Guide to Curriculum and Content," *Survey of Business*, Summer 1992, pp. 13–17.

29. Ibid. Also see John A. Byrne, "Harvard B-School: An American Institution in Need of Reform," *Business Week,* July 19, 1993, pp. 58–65.

30. This exercise is adapted from David A. Kolb, Irwin M. Rubine, and James M. McIntyre, *Organizational Psychology: An Experiential Approach*, 2nd ed. (Englewood Cliffs, N.J.: Prentice Hall, 1974), pp. 9–17.

31. For some interesting ideas and approaches, see William P. Ferris, Russell Funelli, and Peter Hess, "Innovative Evaluation Techniques," paper presented at OBTS Conference, 1982.

32. Don Harvey, John Hulpke, and Joe Hudson, California State University, Bakersfield, Bakersfield, CA 1994.

33. Any resemblence in name to an actual corporation is coincidental.

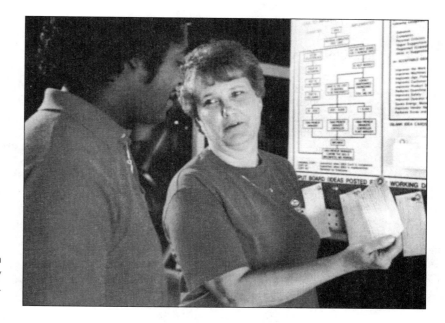

People discussing Dana's "Excellence in Manufacturing" program at the Oklahoma City facility of the Aftermarket Production Division. *Photo courtesy of Dana Corporation.*

Organization Renewal and Planned Change

2

OBJECTIVES

Upon completing this chapter, you will be able to:

1. Recognize the factors contributing to an accelerating rate of change.
2. Identify the ways an organization uses renewing processes to adapt to change.
3. Determine the individual and group methods of coping with change.
4. Understand and apply the systems approach to OD.
5. Describe the five stages of the OD process model.

PREMEETING PREPARATION

1. Read the Background Information (Section III).
2. Read the instructions for OD Skills Simulation 2.1. Complete OD Consultant Profile I (Part A), and the Performance Interview Form (Part B). Become familiar with material in Step 2, Part B.
3. Read and prepare analysis for Case 2: The NoGo Railroad.

BACKGROUND INFORMATION

Change is the name of the game in management today. Market, product, and competitive conditions are rapidly changing. Under these pressures, organizations are changing. They are downsizing, reengineering, flattening structures, going global, and initiating more sophisticated technologies. However, in many organizational changes, such as downsizing, there are often unintended effects or consequences on the productivity of individual work units. A recent survey of 900 downsizing U.S. firms found that 79 percent of senior managers surveyed, indicated that morale, trust and productivity had decreased after downsizing.[1] As the environment changes, organizations must adapt if they are to be successful. For example, through changing times 3M has managed to keep its creative spirit alive. Almost everyone now uses Post-It notes, yet they were an accidental discovery of 3M scientist Art Fry, who became the product champion for Post-It's and started what has now become a $300 million business. The outcome is a big company that still manages to develop new products faster than its competition. About one-third of 3M's $10.6 billion in revenues comes from new products developed within the past five years. The reason: commitment to innovation and lack of corporate rules leaves room for plenty of experimentation—and failure.[2]

Organization renewal requires that top managers make adaptive changes to their strategic models following significant changes to the environment. One study suggests that the strategic models of top managers play a crucial role in directing organizational responses to keep pace with changing industry conditions.[3] In today's business environment, more than at any time in history, the only constant is change. As Robert Waterman (author/consultant) has noted, "Somehow there are organizations that effectively manage change, continuously adapting their bureaucracies, strategies, systems, products, and cultures to survive the shocks and prosper from the forces that decimate their competition They are *masters of renewal*."[4] The fact is that managers are going to have to become masters of change and renewal to be effective in the future.

The changes facing management in the twenty-first century are likely to be even more dynamic and challenging. Therefore, the focus of OD is on changing organizational systems, stressing the situational nature of problems and their system-wide impact. In solving a given problem managers must analyze the organization, its departmental subsystem interrelationships, and the possible effects on the internal environment as well. This approach is termed the **systems approach**, and provides a way of observing, analyzing, and solving problems in organizations. The systems approach, then, is concerned with the relationships among departments and the interdependencies between these elements and the external environment.

An example of changing conditions that face organizations can be seen in the sudden decline in the sewing machine market, compared to the projected increase in the demand for laptop computers. The Singer Company has had to reorganize, sell off unprofitable units, and change its marketing strategy because the number of people buying sewing machines has declined drastically. The market for notebook computers, on the other hand, virtually nonexistent a few years ago, today constitutes a several-billion dollar market.

Because of the rapid pace of technology, firms are confronted with early technological obsolescence of products. In the past, companies could grow during the long life span of a proprietary invention, but today they find their innovations are often quickly overtaken by competitors with technological improvements. Tom Peters summarizes this new challenge well: "Excellent firms don't believe in excellence—only in constant improvement and constant change."[5]

These problems are the result of an increasing rate of change and are made more difficult because of the impact of future shock on management. Managers today face risk situations unlike those of the past, and in an era of accelerating change, management's degree of excellence results from its ability to cope with these changes. Organizations either become more adaptive, flexible, and anticipative, or they become rigid and stagnant, reacting to change after the fact often when it is too late. Seldom can management decisions be based

solely on the extrapolation of historical experience. Many decisions are unique, innovative, and risky, involving new products and new areas of opportunity. Putting a new product or a new process into production is a major business decision.

Because an organization exists in a changing environment, it must have the capacity to adapt. At Sun Microsystems (a fast growing computer maker), for example, company executives have outlined a bold strategy to lead a revolution in the computer industry by offering industry-wide standards for hardware and software. In response to criticism, Sun CEO Scott McNealy, responds, "I guess that's what happens when you're trying to change the whole industry."[6] Because high-tech firms are moving faster on the experience curve, the consequences of being slow to respond to change are most severe in that business.

In this chapter, we examine the way managers react to this accelerating rate of change. The pressure of future shock results in new perspectives for management strategies and decisions. Managers must do more than just react: they must be able to anticipate the changing patterns of people, markets, products, and technology. Three areas will be covered:

1. Organization renewal—adapting to change.
2. The systems approach—a dynamic model of change.
3. Organization transformation and development.

Organization Renewal—Adapting to Change

A major challenge facing organizations today is to manage effectively. When an organization fails to change, the cost of that failure may mean its very survival. Since the environment is composed of systems outside the immediate influence of the organization, the organization must attempt to adapt itself to these forces by introducing internal changes that will allow the organization to be more effective. To be successful, organizations must develop a management style and culture that will adequately handle the challenges and opportunities which they face. A management style that was adequate under one set of conditions may become progressively less effective under changing circumstances. The OD practitioner, then, is ultimately interested in changing human behavior and organization processes to create a more adaptive and flexible organization.

Organization renewal is important. If a company is to survive in an increasingly competitive marketplace, the organization must continuously adapt to its environment: without renewal, management cannot maintain excellence.[7] **Organization renewal** may be defined as an on-going process of building innovation and adaptation into the organization.

Robert Waterman suggests eight key factors from the leaders who generate excellence and how they find ways to renew their organizations. Table 2.1 on page 32 lists and discusses his eight prescriptions for corporate renewal.[8]

The renewal dilemma, as Waterman notes, is that stability is necessary on one hand, but is also the major obstruction to change. For most organizations, it seems that the more effective they have been in the past, the more likely they are to resist change. As noted in the next section, entropy is a principle of physics that suggests that everything that is organized will break down or run down unless it is maintained. Organization renewal, then, is an approach to preventing corporate **entropy**.

Why is change so difficult? Possibly because the culture of the organization becomes a part of the people who perform the work. In changing these old patterns, people must alter not only their behavior but also their values and view of themselves. The organization structure, procedures, and relationships continue to reinforce prior patterns of behavior and to resist the new ones. As a result, organization change sometimes results in upheaval and dissatisfaction, and possibly even in resignations, dismissals, or transfers. Consequently, an organization must develop an adaptive orientation and management style which is geared to its environment. Managers in different organizations deal with situations that may be dramatically different. Some organizations exist in relatively stable environments, whereas others operate in highly dynamic settings. Each requires a different orientation to the environment.

Table 2.1 Lessons in Corporate Renewal

1. *Informed Opportunism*
 Renewing organizations set directions, not detailed strategy. These companies treat information as their main strategic advantage and flexibility as their main strategic weapon.

2. *Direction and Empowerment*
 The renewing companies treat everyone as a source of creative input. They give up some control over subordinates to gain what counts: results.

3. *Friendly Facts*
 The renewing companies treat facts as friends, and financial controls as liberating. They love facts and information that removes decision making from mere opinion.

4. *A Different Mirror*
 The leaders of renewing organizations seem to get their determination from their singular ability to anticipate crisis. This stems from their willingness to listen to all sources—to look into a different mirror.

5. *Teamwork and Trust*
 Renewers constantly use such words as teamwork and trust. They are relentless at fighting office politics.

6. *Stability in Motion*
 The renewing companies know how to keep things moving. Renewing companies undergo constant change against a base of underlying stability.

7. *Attitudes and Attention*
 In renewing companies visible management attention gets things done. Action may start with words, but must be backed by behaviors.

8. *Causes and Commitment*
 Renewing organizations seem to run on causes. Commitment results from management's ability to turn grand causes into small actions so that everyone can contribute.

Orientation to Change

Every organization must have enough stability to continue to function satisfactorily and still prevent itself from becoming too static or stagnant to adapt to changing conditions. Both stability and adaptation are essential to continued survival and growth.

An organization that operates in a mature field with a stable product and relatively few competitors needs a different adaptive orientation than a firm operating in a high-growth market, among numerous competitors, and with a high degree of innovation. The former operates in an environment that is relatively stable, whereas the latter faces a more dynamic and turbulent set of conditions. A stable environment is characterized by unchanging basic products and services, a static level of competition, a low level of technological innovation, a formalized and centralized structure, and a steady, slow rate of growth. Such an environment remains relatively stable over long periods.

A **hyperturbulent environment**, on the other hand, is characterized by rapidly changing product lines, an increasing and changing set of competitors, rapid and continual technological innovation, and rapid market growth. For today's organization, the idea of change is clear. A static organization can no longer survive. Yesterday's accomplishments amount to little in an environment of rapidly advancing markets, products, and life styles. To survive, organizations must devise methods of continuous self-renewal. Organizations must recognize when it is necessary to change, and they must develop the ability to implement change when needed. To meet these conditions, many companies have created specialized OD units whose primary purpose is implementing organizational changes. These units are developing new programs to help the organization improve its level of adaptation to its envi-

ronment and to maintain a stable identity, so that change is not overwhelming. To achieve successful change, both of these goals must be satisfied.

A Model of Adaptive Orientation

The topic of transformational change as opposed to gradual change has been receiving much attention. David Miller argues that some organizations resist change until a critical state of incongruence is reached, at which point a "quantum" change occurs.[9] Joan Ash and Ellen West examined 12 non-profit organizations to investigate the transformational change process.[10] Teresa Colvin and Ralph Kilmann also investigated large-scale change in some 300 organizations.[11]

From theses studies, a simplified model of adaptative orientation has been developed, as shown in Figure 2.1. One dimension represents the degree of change in the organization's environment, and the second represents the degree of adaptiveness or flexibility present in

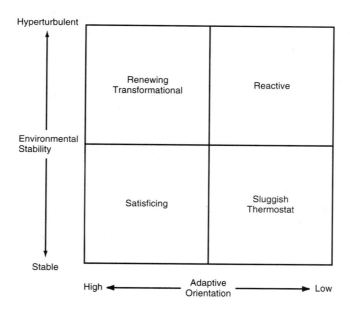

FIGURE 2.1 A Model of Adaptive Orientation in Organizations

the internal orientation of the organization. Organizations can vary greatly on these dimensions, and the various combinations of these orientations can lead to differing adaptive styles. Certain types of possible orientations are described next.

Sluggish-Thermostat Management (Stable Environment, Low Adaptation)

Sluggish-thermostat management is a term originated by David Miller to describe organizations that resist change until cost trade-offs favor it.[12] This term is a good analogy because many organizations have their thermostats set so low they become insensitive to change.

Sluggish management refers to a style of management based on low risk, with formalized procedures and a high degree of structure and control. Typically, organizations that utilize sluggish management have very stable goals and a highly centralized structure. They also tend to have more managerial levels, a higher ratio of superiors to subordinates and an

emphasis upon formal control systems. There may be a tendency to value tradition, to keep on doing things as they have always been done, to value seniority more than performance, and an aversion to accepting new ideas. Although this is a low-risk style of managing, it may lead to serious problems in the long run. Referring to Ford Motor Company's sluggish management and inability to meet new customer demands, CEO Donald Petersen (since retired) said, "We learned that there's no market for lousy cars: we tested it."[13]

One study of change programs reported that only three percent of respondents indicated that they could continue to succeed without some form of change program. Such organizations may succumb to forces of entropy. Ian Mitroff argues that slowness to adapt stems not from failure, but from success.[14] In the auto industry, for example, for 60 years, the rules for competing remained the same, and the assumptions about customers, markets, and suppliers remained valid.

Satisficing Management (Stable Environment, High Adaptation)

Satisficing management, a play off the word satisfactory, is a management that is adequate and average. It is a style of managing that emphasizes a more centralized decision-making structure with problems being referred to the top. Because of the stable environment there tends to be more levels of management, with coordination done by formal committees. Planning and decision making are usually concentrated at the top, with high clarity of procedures and roles. Change is accomplished at a rate that is "good enough" to keep up with the industry, but certainly well behind the state of the art. Such organizations often tend to accept strategies that are "good enough," because of the low level of pressure for change from the environment. Eighty-two percent of the respondents in the Colvin/Kilmann study reported that without change, they would gradually suffer a decline in performance.[15]

Reactive Management (Hyperturbulent Environment, Low Adaptation)

Organizations with a low level of adaptation, but existing in a rapidly changing environment, tend to deal with problems on a short-run, crisis basis. **Reactive management** refers to a style of reacting to a stimulus after conditions in the environment have changed. It is a short-term, crisis type of adaptation, often involving replacement of key people, hasty reorganization, and drastic cutting of people and product lines. A major food corporation, for example, was feeling the pressures of changing business conditions, losing momentum, experiencing product failures, and reporting decreased earnings. The new chief executive instituted some massive changes, including a major management reorganization, a company-wide efficiency drive, cutting salaried personnel by 10 percent, and taking a very hard look at all marketing programs. The reactive approach to change implies waiting until serious problems emerge which can no longer be ignored and then taking drastic corrective measures. Colvin and Kilmann reported that 68 percent of the firms studied were experiencing a high or very high level of competition, thus forcing some form of response.[16]

One example of Reactive Management is IBM. IBM has set cost reductions of $5 billion a year with already-announced moves to cut 45,000 jobs, shut outdated plants and sell off real estate over the next three years. Now, CFO Jerome York must whittle almost $2 billion more by focusing on the small stuff, ferreting out inefficiencies and fundamentally challenging business practices locked in over decades of die-hard habits. "There's a lot of waste in this company." The new chief financial officer says, "We're going to find it and root it out."

York, the former auto executive, must take on all of this while being regarded as a techno-neophyte and a stranger by dozens of lifelong IBMers whom he must enlist in his effort. Mr York's preoccupation with costs and his lack of high-tech basics clearly rankle some current and recently departed IBMers. Others contend, however, that only an outsider can usher in the new era of cutbacks and coldhearted reality that Big Blue requires.[17]

Renewing/Transformational Management
(Hyperturbulent Environment, High Adaptation)

Organizations which exist in a hyperturbulent environment must not only respond to change, but must proactively take advantage of new opportunity and innovation. These organizations tend to fit the renewal/transformational orientation and, like 3M, tend to be champions of innovation and are faster at developing new ideas, more responsive to competitive changes (a more sensitive thermostat), and more participative in getting commitment and involvement of organization members in the renewal process. Organizations with a high level of adaptation existing in a rapidly changing environment tend to utilize the renewing management style.

Renewing/transformational management refers to introducing change to deal with future conditions before these conditions actually occur. Examples of renewing management include the innovations of corporations such as General Electric, 3M, and Merck which have actively initiated programs of innovation before conditions became critical. A renewing management orientation has both the ability and need to respond to a hyperturbulent environment. It seems that most modern organizations are increasingly finding the need for this adaptive orientation.

Change can provide new opportunity for growth or an increase in the state of organizational entropy—an ability to change. The renewing or transformational manager is constantly fighting entropy and proactively building for the future. Today organizations need to develop a renewal/transformational orientation if they are to maintain a competitive edge and even to survive as shown in Figure 2.1.

The Systems Approach:
A Dynamic Model of Change

The systems approach to managing change views the organization as a unified system composed of interrelated units. This gives managers a way of looking at the organization as a whole and as a part of a larger external environment. In an organization using a downsizing approach, managers may use a systems approach to determine how to cut costs. One approach, the "horizontal corporation," refers to breaking the company into its key processes, and creating teams from different departments to run them. It's about managing across, rather than up and down.

This suggests that managers can no longer function within the traditional organization chart, but must integrate their department with the goals and strategy of the whole organization. To accomplish this, managers must communicate with other departments as well as with employees and customers. By using a systems perspective, a manager can maintain a balance between the needs of various units of the enterprise as well as total system goals and objectives.

Downsizing, alone, does little to change the fundamental way that work gets done in a corporation. To do that takes a different organizational model: the "horizontal corporation." Already, some of corporate America's biggest names, from American Telephone & Telegraph and DuPont to General Electric and Motorola, are moving toward the idea. In the quest for greater efficiency and productivity, they're beginning to flatten the hierarchical organization charts that have defined corporate life. Some of these changes have been under way for several years such as "total quality management," reengineering, or process redesign. But the trend is toward flatter more adaptive organizations.[18]

At this point, we will discuss three systems perspectives to managing change: the systems approach, sociotechnical/contingency approaches, and future shock.

What Is a System?

A **system** is a set of interrelated parts unified by design to achieve some purpose or goal. Organizations are systems. Each organization can be viewed as a number of interrelated, interdependent parts, each of which contributes to total organizational functioning and to the achievement of its goal. The systems approach is one of the most important concepts in OD because it deals with change and interrelationships in complex organizations. The notion of system interdependency is critical because a change in one part of an organization system has consequences in other parts of the organization.

The term *system* is used in many different contexts: for example, defense system, weapons system, solar system, and stereo system. A system has been defined as an "organized unitary whole composed of two or more interdependent parts, components or subsystems and delineated by identifiable boundaries from its environment."

A system has several basic qualities:

- A system must be designed to accomplish an objective.
- The elements of a system must have an established arrangement.
- Interrelationships must exist among the individual elements of a system.
- The basic ingredients of a process (the flows of information, energy, and materials) are more vital than the basic elements of a system.
- Organization objectives are ore important than the objectives of its elements, and thus there is a deemphasis of the parochial objectives of the elements of a system.

The focus of the systems approach is the recognition of the effect of managerial functions and the interrelationship between subelements of the organization. Rather than view the organization as a static set of relationships, the organization is viewed as a set of flows of information, personnel, and material. Time and change become critical aspects. The flow of inputs and outputs is a basic starting point in the description of the system (see Figure 2.2). There are three basic elements that make up such a system:

1. *Inputs* are the resources that are applied to the processing function.
2. *Processes* are the activities and functions that are performed to produce goods and services.
3. *Outputs* are the products and services produced by the organization.

FIGURE 2.2 The Organization as an Open System.

A business firm takes such inputs as materials, people, and energy, and converts them into the products or services desired by consumers. The organization receives inputs from its environment, acts on those inputs by transforming them, and returns these transformed

elements to the environment as products. The inputs to a hospital include money, equipment, trained staff, information, patients, and physicians; the outputs include new research, well patients, improved medicine, trained doctors and nurses, and other medical benefits.

The Organization as an Open System

There are two basic types of systems: open and closed. A **closed system** is one that is self-contained and isolated from its environment. In the strictest sense, closed systems exist only in theory, for all real systems interact with their environment. Our emphasis is on treating organizations as open systems.

By far the most important type of system is the open system. An *open system* influences and is influenced by the environment through the process of interdependency, which results in a *dynamic (changing) equilibrium.* A business organization provides an excellent example of the process of reciprocity and, therefore, of an open system. The **open system** is in continual interaction with its environment and therefore achieves a steady state of **dynamic equilibrium**. The system could not continue to survive without the continuous influence of transformational outflow. As the open system interacts with its environment, it continually receives information termed **feedback,** from its environment, which helps it adjust. The departments also interact with one another, because they have interacting tasks to perform. Therefore the overall efficiency of the system depends upon the level and degree of interaction with other elements.

The Characteristics of Open Systems

Although there are various types of systems, there are certain characteristics that tend to occur in all open systems. The various organizational functions are not isolated elements. They are components interacting with each other and with the outside environment. The decisions of any one manager may well have repercussions upon other parts of the organization. The systems model is based on a number of characteristics, including the following:

- *Subsystems.* A system is composed of interrelated parts called subsystems. Any subsystem is dependent on the other elements and change in any one means that some adjustment will occur in the others.
- *Synergy.* The system is a whole, not merely the sum of its parts, and its performance should be viewed as an integrated system. Synergy means that the whole is greater than the sum of its parts, so that functional departments which cooperate can become more productive.
- *Input/output model.* All systems transform inputs into outputs. The system is viewed as a transformation process in dynamic interaction with its environment.
- *Goal seeking—open system.* Open systems exchange information, energy, or material with their environment. Interaction between elements results in some final state or goal.
- *Entropy.* Every transformation process involves the degradation or use of energy and resources. The tendency toward entropy is a movement toward disorder and eventually termination of functioning. To keep a system operating there must be an infusion of energy and resources.
- *Steady state.* The notion that systems are goal seeking implies that they are adaptive and self-regulating. The open system seeks a state of dynamic equilibrium.
- *Feedback.* The feedback of information regarding performance is used to adjust and control performance. Feedback is informational input which indicates that the system is deviating from goals and needs to readjust.

One of the current trends in OD is a shift toward using a more integrated, systems approach to organization improvement.[19] The systems approach, then, allows managers to anticipate both immediate and far-reaching consequences of organizational changes. One example of a situation where a systems analysis approach is useful is at Union Carbide Industries, Ltd. (See Our Changing World.)

OUR CHANGING WORLD:
UNION CARBIDE AND BHOPAL[20]

Attempts to change only people, or only technology, or only structure are heading for trouble, according to the text. The Union Carbide Corporation's plant in India provides an illustration of these problems, even though all three were changed to some extent. The trouble is, the changes weren't coordinated, didn't fit together well, and in the long run, helped set the stage for the world's most horrendous industrial disaster.

An Industrial Disaster

A little after midnight on the night of December 2, 1984, a cloud of poisonous gas escaped from the Union Carbide Plant near Bhopal, India. By morning some 2,500 people had died and thousands of others were blinded or suffered other serious injuries. Some accounts place the final death toll at "more than 3,700."

More than $35 billion in lawsuits were filed against Union Carbide and stockholders filed another $1 billion in suits alleging management malfeasance. As a result, the company's stock price fell and its image as an investment has suffered. What had gone wrong? While the exact cause may never be completely unravelled, several elements contributed.

Management. The Union Carbide India, Ltd. plant was a subsidiary of the Union Carbide Corporation which held a bare majority interest (50.9) and had only one American executive on the Board of Directors. Although the U.S. headquarters set major policies, the Indian plant operated almost autonomously.

Another factor that may have contributed to the accident was that the India plant had been losing money and had initiated cost-saving measures including layoffs of operational workers and a reduction of maintenance budgets. The plant, previously managed and run by managers with high-quality goals, was now being managed by executives with orders to watch costs closely. Every rupee had to be accounted for. No waste was to be tolerated. Accordingly, staffing levels were cut by attrition. As people left, their positions were often unfilled.

Technology. Although newer, more modern production equipment might have allowed the plant to operate with less staff, in fact no new technology was added. The equipment on hand was getting older and, at the very time more maintenance might be required, less was being provided.

Structure. The organization structure changed also. In the decade proceeding the tragedy, the Bhopal plant had changed reporting procedures several times. In 1970, the plant was under the safety and managerial guidance of Union Carbide, USA. By the time of the accident, the Bhopal plant reported to Union Carbide India, Ltd., to a management that had higher priorities than one small marginal plant producing pesticides in a very competitive market.

A Systems Approach

If people, technology, and structure had been considered simultaneously using a systems approach to change, could the Bhopal disaster have been avoided? No one knows, but if an OD consultant had visited Bhopal in 1984, one would surely have been able to predict trouble. An unhealthy organization can, quite literally, be a killer.

Questions

1. Using a systems approach, identify the various problems at Union Carbide.
2. Describe the differences between the cultural environments in the U.S. and India, and how OD principles might apply.

The Organization as a Sociotechnical System

Organization development and renewal may be referred to as a systems approach to change. An organization is viewed as an open **sociotechnical system** of coordinated human and technical activities. The various organizational functions and processes are not considered as isolated elements but as parts reacting to and influencing other system elements. This approach uses the following:

1. Organize around process—not tasks.
2. Flatten the hierarchy.
3. Use teams to manage everything.
4. Let customers drive performance.
5. Reward team performance.

As a result, changes in any one process of the organization can have effects throughout the organization, because all processes are related. Therefore, by its very nature, OD seeks to consider the interrelationships among all basic elements of the system when changes are planned. The organization can be viewed as an open system in interaction with its environment and consisting of five primary components (see Figure 2.3).

The structural subsystem. This includes the formal design, policies, procedures, and so on. It is usually set forth by the organization chart and includes division of work and patterns of authority.

The technical subsystem. This includes the primary functions, activities, and operations, including the techniques, equipment, and so on, used to produce the output of the system.

The psychosocial subsystem (culture). This includes the network of social relationships and behavioral patterns of members, such as norms, roles, and communications.

FIGURE 2.3 The Sociotechnical System.

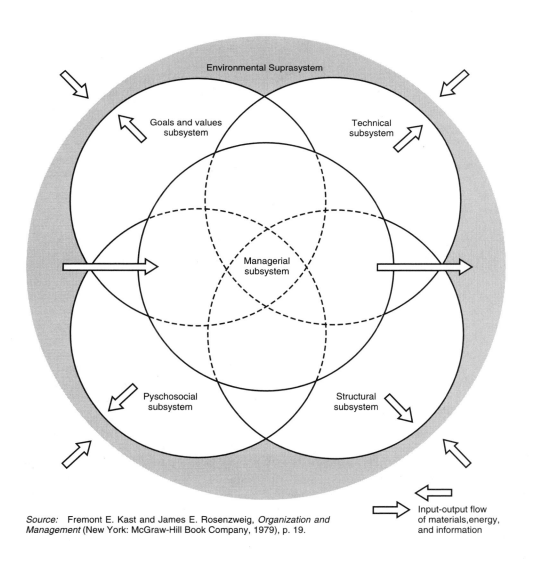

Source: Fremont E. Kast and James E. Rosenzweig, *Organization and Management* (New York: McGraw-Hill Book Company, 1979), p. 19.

The goals and values subsystem. This includes the basic mission and vision of the organization. Such goals might include profits, growth, or survival and are often taken from the larger environment.

The managerial subsystem. This subsystem spans the entire organization by directing, organizing, and coordinating all activities toward the basic mission. The managerial function is important in integrating the activities of the other subsystems.

One of the earliest applications of the sociotechnical systems concept was in British coal mining. The traditional "short wall" method utilized small, cohesive work groups working as autonomous teams. Technological advances by engineering efficiency experts determined that the short wall method was inefficient, and introduced an improved technical system termed the "long wall" method. Unfortunately, the long wall method resulted in lower performance and higher absenteeism. Production decreased because they had failed to consider the impact of the changes on the psychosocial system. Researchers found, as a result of reintroducing a team approach and providing team pay incentives, that productivity and morale improved substantially. The sociotechnical systems OD approach is considered one of the most sophisticated techniques involving large-scale effort and considerable skill on the part of the OD consultant.[21]

High-Performance Systems

A more recent development is to apply the sociotechnical systems approach in designing a high-performance organization. David P. Hanna argues that high-performance organizations do not occur by chance or by policy or decree: they are designed—"and all organizations are perfectly designed to get the results they get!"[22]

Hanna's high-performance model focuses on five key variables (similar to Figure 2.3) that need to be considered if managers wish to improve performance.[23] These key variables include:

1. the business situation (forces in the environment);
2. the business strategy (the goals and values);
3. the design elements (technology, structure, and so on);
4. the culture; and
5. the business results (the outputs produced).

These models can be used to identify the real drivers of organizational success used in organization development and renewal programs to improve system performance.

The Contingency Approach

Systems theory provides a conceptual overview of organizational functioning, but the manager needs to know how the subsystems of a particular organization are uniquely related in that specific environment and how best to deal with its particular problems. Contingency theory recognizes that such differences do exist and that what constitutes effective management in one system may not in another setting. Contingency views tend to emphasize the characteristics of a specific organization, and suggest that to organize and manage a change program, one must consider the set of conditions in that particular setting.[24]

The **contingency approach** suggests that there is no one best way of managing in all situations. Given certain combinations of contingencies (such as a stable external environment and a low adaptive orientation to change), one can specify general approaches to change that are likely to be more effective than others. In other words, the contingency approach identifies various types of "if-then" relationships and suggests general directions for change, depending on the situation. The contingency approach is also based on certain conceptual

skills, such as diagnosing and understanding the various types of situations that are likely to confront the OD practitioner.

The contingency view suggests that managers in differing departmental units face situations that may be very different on a number of dimensions. There may be varying degrees of structure, differing motivation levels, and a diverse potential for conflict. The OD practitioner, then, must recognize that there is "no one best way" for all organizations, although some practitioners would take issue with this statement.[25] The contingency approach to OD suggest that the effectiveness of various consulting styles, intervention techniques, or strategies will vary according to the circumstances. The contingency variables that need to be considered and the relative emphasis will depend on the type of problem being considered.

Future Shock and Change

Alvin Toffler, in *Future Shock,* suggests that most people are utterly unprepared to cope with the accelerated rate of change. "**Future shock** is a time phenomenon, a product of a greatly accelerated rate of change in society. It arises from the superimposition of a new culture on an old one."[26] Future shock, too much change in too short a time, affects managers and organizations as well.

When change occurs too rapidly, the capacity of management to react is strained, creating the danger of future shock. As a result, managers must become more adaptable and flexible than ever before. As an example, fast-changing technology has spurred growth and change in the semiconductor industry, including a bewildering array of manufacturing processes and new techniques to build more and more electronic circuitry onto a quarter-inch-square silicon chip. Yet industry leaders expect to see more changes in the next decade than have been seen in the past 10 years.

The U.S. Department of Labor report on "Workforce 2000" and a journal of the American Academy of Arts and Sciences suggest evidence of widespread changes including:

- Work increasingly relies on knowledge rather than physical effort. At least half of all employees are information workers.
- Up to 90 percent of all American jobs will be influenced, some even replaced, by expert and artificial intelligence computer systems.
- More than 90 percent of all new workers will be minorities and women.
- More than 25 percent of all families in the United States now have dual incomes and a large percentage are full-time, two-income professional career families.
- About 80 percent of jobs in the near future will require education past high school. Jobs are demanding much higher skill levels.
- A movement away from a production-oriented economy toward an economy relying on services is occurring. Unfortunately, productivity gains in the service sector have been more difficult to attain than in manufacturing.
- The need for more environmentally sound products will open up new industries and opportunities. At the same time, some products and manufacturing processes will be forced from the market. Products like Freon, foam cups, and high-sulphur coal may no longer be used.
- There will be an increased emphasis on long-term strategic planning.
- Traditional methods of managing that rely on an autocratic style will become obsolete.

For corporate planners and top managers, the environment has never seemed as turbulent as it does today. The very uncertainties, from the cloudy economic outlook to the energy crisis, make accurate planning for the future much more difficult. In such a rapidly changing environment, some plans are out of date within three to six months.

The world is constantly changing in economics, social values, and technology, and these changes seem to have accelerated in recent years. These technological changes have shortened the life cycle of many products and services, and when product life cycles are shortened, organizations must become more adaptive by shortening their lead times to get into production.

There is an increasing need for new organizational forms and systems. Further, individuals within organizations are affected by change. No longer satisfied to be passive members, individuals increasingly assert their right to change the organization for their own reasons.

America's present environment is in a state of turbulent change, suggests John Naisbitt in his books *Megatrends* and *Megatrends 2000,* because we are moving into a new era.[27] The shift in the United States from an industrially based economy to a technologically based economy is creating a state of turbulent change, both for workers and corporations. John Naisbitt predicts widespread changes throughout society as shown in Table 2.2.

These changing trends will have a significant impact on organizations, as managers are developing new organizational models and finding novel ways of motivating employees.[28] As a result, managers will need to scan the environment to be aware of issues which will have a major impact on their industry or organization. As Naisbitt notes, "By identifying the forces pushing the future, rather than those that have contained the past, you possess the power to engage with your reality."[29]

Technological advancements are occurring so rapidly that most scientists' education is technically obsolete within 10 years after graduation from college. There is so much information that a professional operating in a narrow field may find it impossible to keep current on information pertinent to his or her specialty. The term **information overload**, once reserved for computer storage ability, aptly applies to managers trying to act responsibly in a changing environment.

During the past decade, society has been placing new demands on business firms for social responsibility, environmental, and pollution controls. Other social changes also impinge upon the organization. In the past, jobs were thought of as tasks to be done, not something to be questioned or evaluated. In the United States, more workers earn their pay in knowledge-based jobs than in skilled and nonskilled jobs. For many years, managers will be searching for newer, more relevant, and more effective ways of managing this increasingly intelligent and sophisticated work force.

The organization must adapt to these changing conditions. Each day brings a new set of conditions, and internal realignment is often required. Product and market strategies need to be more flexible and must depend upon raw material logistics and the ability of a company to recognize the need for change. Consequently, management will need to place an increased emphasis on human resource development. An unprecedented opportunity exists for the OD practitioner to apply specialized skills to seeking solutions for these problems of industry. In view of these factors, whether an organization can remain effective is largely dependent upon whether it is sufficiently adaptive to changing conditions as shown at Next, Inc. (See OD in Practice.)

Table 2.2 The Millennial Megatrends: Gateways to the Twenty-First Century

As we enter this new decade, our candidates for the most important, the overarching trends influencing our lives are:

1. The Booming Global Economy.
2. A Renaissance in the Arts
3. The Emergence of Free-Market Socialism.
4. Global Lifestyles and Cultural Nationalism.
5. The Privatization of the Welfare State.
6. The Rise of the Pacific Rim.
7. The Decade of Women in Leadership.
8. The Age of Biology.
9. The Religious Revival of the New Millennium.
10. The Triumph of the Individual.

Source: Adapted from John Naisbitt and Patrician Aburdene. *Megatrends 2000* (New York: William Morrow and Company, Inc, 1990).

OD IN PRACTICE:
COMPUTER VISIONARY OR MANAGEMENT MYOPIA[30]

Steve Jobs, computer visionary, or terrible manager? In 1984, Steve, then 29, was the chairman of Apple Computer, and he and John Sculley launched the Macintosh PC, with the famous Big Brother television commercial. Forced to resign from Apple, the company he founded, Steve Jobs started a new company, Next, Inc. Jobs felt that the Next computer, a starkly elegant black cube with a powerful array of new features could impact the industry even more than the Macintosh.

After he unveiled his latest computer, sources suggested that sales were slower than expected, running at 500 to 600 per month or roughly $4 million. But Jobs tried a new marketing strategy—going for what he called "the whole enchilada,"—establishing a third major general purpose computer aimed mainly at the business market.

Charismatic Leadership

In the past, many have felt that Steve Job's charismatic leadership and idiosyncrasies have caused some internal problems. At Apple, he was seen as a leader whose brilliance and idealistic vision of "providing computers as a tool to change the world," drew other talented people to him. Yet, by the same token, his management style tended toward throwing tantrums and to berating and humiliating employees who disagreed with his ideas. Also, his habit of making decisions and then suddenly changing his mind has been given as part of the reason he was forced out of Apple.

The Next Startup

Steve Jobs shocked Apple by leaving to start his own company and taking along five of the Macintosh team's brightest talents, including software whiz Bud Tribble. Jobs held company-wide retreats of the kind he used at Apple. At the retreats, Jobs told his small, select crew that the Next computer could not cost more than $3,000 and that the machine must be ready by the spring of 1987. The machine was finally introduced in 1989 for a price of $9,995.

Steve Job's perfectionism extended to every detail. He insisted on a perfect finish inside the machine's magnesium shell, even though it would never be seen by the consumer, and once flew to Chicago to persuade a die caster to retool.

The Steve Job's Reality Distortion Field

Where did Steve Jobs go wrong? He is an impassioned leader whose personality and reputation lend him charisma, but he often tends to get impassioned about the wrong things. As noted Jobs the perfectionist, hired a West German designer to come up with the machine's sleek black casing, and reportedly paid $100,000 for the Next logo. But, while preoccupied with the appearance of the computer and corporate headquarters, he overlooked the design features of the computer. One former employee calls it, "the Steven Job's reality distortion field."

What's Next?

All of this eccentricity adds to the allure of Steve Jobs. His unusual behavior, considered merely odd at most companies, became part of the Jobs legend at Next. Steve and his small band set out to develop a revolutionary new product, and his single-minded pursuit of these goals is the source of much of his charisma. Dressed in his usual black turtle neck and faded blue jeans, Steve uses a whirling-dervish approach to management, dashing from meeting to meeting, making decisions, giving advice, delegating orders without breaking stride, as he puts in his customary 75-hour work week. Steve's strong opinion about doing things his way also hurts his relations with employees. Some associates claim Steve has changed very little from his days as the fiery leader of Apple, where he frequently berated subordinates over minor details and lost faith in loyalists who failed to meet his demanding expectations.

Steve Job's later announced plans to scrap its slow selling workstations and focus solely on software. Saying he could not allow the struggling firm to remain "a second tier hardware company," Jobs unveiled a radical restructuring that included the dismissal of 280 of 536 employees. At stake is nothing less than the survival of the company.

Once again, Steve Jobs has brought changes into the computer industry. The next question is: can he build his startup into a successful corporation or is he just a visionary leader? So far the answer is no!

Questions

1. Is this an example of organization renewal or transformation? Why?
2. Do entrepreneurs like Steve Jobs have to leave large organizations to achieve innovation, or can they successfully transform larger companies?
3. What adaptive orientation was used?

Organization Transformation and Development

There are many ways to respond to the pressures for change. Some responses may be ineffective or even ultimately destructive. There are many examples of companies that have been driven out of business due to competitive forces or to unwise financial maneuvers. In this section, we will examine two major approaches to change and present a model of the planned change process.

Organization transformation (OT) and Organization development (OD) are both approaches to managing change in organizations. **Organization transformation** (OT) may be defined as the action of changing organization form, shape, or appearance, or changing organization energy from one form to another. The term OT has been used by some theorists to focus on unplanned changes from within the system in response to crises and life-cycle considerations, and are often of a second-order nature—in other words, they transform the very framework and assumptions of an organization.[31] OD, on the other hand, focuses more on planned changes introduced by outside consultants often of a first-order nature.

The authors would suggest that the difference between OT and OD appears to be in the magnitude and time of the change: between revolution and evolution. OT appears to refer to significant changes introduced in short, almost immediate time frame to deal with survival or crisis-type problems. OD involves large-scale change over a longer time frame on a more gradual basis. Organizations must interact with their external environment to survive. Those factors that interfere with the organization's ability to produce or market its products, or to attract the human, technical, and financial resources it needs, become a force for change.

OD—The Planned Change Process

OD or *planned organizational change* is a deliberate attempt to modify the functioning of the total organization or one of its major parts in order to bring about improved effectiveness.[32] The persons attempting to bring about this change will be referred to as **consultants** and the organization being changed will be referred to as the **client system**. Planned change efforts can focus on individual, group, or organization behavior.

Individual Effectiveness

An organization is made up of individual members and each member has unique values, beliefs, and motivations. The leadership style of top management and the norms, values, and beliefs of the organization's members combine to form the organization culture. Organization effectiveness can be increased by creating a culture that achieves organizational goals and at the same time satisfies members' needs. Empowering the individual employee by letting workers make decisions can often improve quality, productivity, and employee commitment. Recent use of empowerment in companies like Delta Air, Federal Express, and WalMart suggests that empowering employees pays off. Managers who can find the key to unlock the human potential of their employees will be able to tap an immense source of productive energy.[33]

Change efforts that focus on individual effectiveness range from empowerment training programs to high-powered executive development programs. These include empowerment activities that are designed to improve the skills, abilities, or motivational levels of organization members. The goals are improved technical skills or improved interpersonal competence. Such change efforts may also be directed toward improved leadership, decision making, or problem solving among organization members. The assumption underlying such efforts is that by developing better managers and employees, a more effective organization will result. As Tom Peters suggests, "Involve everyone in everything—truly involved people can do anything."[34]

Team Effectiveness

Change efforts may also focus on the fundamental unit of an organization, the team or work group, as a means for improving the effectiveness of the organization. Today, we are in the midst of revolutionary changes in how people are managed in industrial organizations. Organizations, including Ford, Boeing, and others, are moving toward what are termed "high involvement" or "self-managed" work teams (see Chapter 13).[35] The premise of this emerging approach is that organizations must elicit the commitment of their employees, if they are to achieve a sustainable competitive advantage in a turbulent marketplace. There is an emphasis on improving problem-solving processes while working through conflicts and issues surrounding ways the group can improve its effectiveness and productivity.

These activities are designed to improve the operations of work teams and may focus on **task activities**, what the team does, or they may deal with **team process**, how the team works and the quality of relationships among team members. The assumption is that work teams are the primary unit of the organization and that more effective teams will lead to improved organizations. More effective teams may increase work motivation, improve performance, and decrease turnover and absenteeism.

Process Observation

One technique that is often used in examining groups is called **process observation**. As we observe and analyze work groups as systems, two separate dimensions may be identified:

1. *content*—the task of the group; and
2. *process*—the way the group functions.

Group process includes such factors as leadership, decision making, communication, and conflict. The content is *what* is being discussed; the process is *how* the group operates.

By observing the behavior of group members, one can determine the way in which a group is functioning. The observer describes group functioning in a systematic manner, such as who talks to whom, the frequency of certain behaviors, and so on. The observations are then summarized and presented to the group. The purpose is to clarify and improve team functioning. It is helpful for the OD consultant to develop skills in process observation and to learn to be a **participant-observer**, that is, to actively participate and at the same time be aware of group process. Such skills are particularly useful in developing an effective consulting team.

Organization Effectiveness

Another focus for OD planned change efforts is the organization system. The total organization may be examined by use of climate surveys: planned change programs are then designed to deal with the specific problem areas identified in the survey. As one management theorist notes, "You don't put two turkeys together and make an eagle." These activities aim at improving effectiveness by structural, technical, or managerial subsystem changes. The objective of such system-wide operations is to increase the effectiveness, the efficiency, and the morale of total organization functioning. Tom Peters, for example, argues, "Excellent firms don't believe in excellence—only in constant improvement and constant change."[36]

Each of these planned change efforts aims at improving the overall goal attainment of the system, but each has a specific target or focus for the change program. Organization development occurs when the change effort is focused on the total system. OD may involve individual, group, and intergroup approaches, but it becomes OD only when the total system is the target for change. In an OD program, a set of goals or purposes is identified, and a course of action is undertaken involving the commitment of organization members toward organization improvement.

Teresa Colvin and Ralph Kilmann found evidence that there is a relationship between the level of employee participation in the change and the success of the change program.[37] Frank Friedlander and L. Dave Brown (OD practitioners/professors) have also noted that attempts to change only people, only technology, or only structure are likely to meet resis-

tance or failure.[38] In the next section, we examine the sequence of stages involved in implementing a program of planned change.

A Model for Organization Change

OD is a continuing process of long-term organizational improvement consisting of a series of stages, as shown in Figure 2.4. At 3M, one of the most imaginative and innovative major U.S. companies, managers have been willing to take big risks for a large corporation to develop an entrepreneurial culture. OD techniques have also been applied at Xerox to get organization units to operate more efficiently.[39] In an OD program the emphasis is placed on individual, group, and organization relationships.

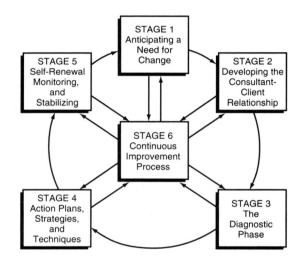

FIGURE 2.4 New Paradigm: Organization Development Stages.

The primary difference between OD and other behavioral science techniques is an emphasis upon viewing the organization as a total system of interacting and interrelated elements. Organization development is the application of a **systems approach** to the functional, structural, technical, and personal relationships in organizations. OD programs are based upon a systematic analysis of problems and a top management actively committed to the change effort. The purpose of such a program is to increase organization effectiveness by the application of OD values and techniques. Many organization development programs use the **action research model**. Action research involves collecting information about the organization, feeding this information back to the client system, and developing and implementing action programs to improve system performance. The manager also needs to be aware of the processes that should be considered when attempting to create change. In this section a five-stage model of the total organization change process is presented. Each stage is dependent on the prior one and successful change is more probable when each of these stages is considered in a logical sequence. (See B.C. Cartoon, p. 47.)

Stage One: Anticipating Change

Before a program of change can be implemented, the organization must anticipate the need for change. The first step is the manager's perception that the organization is somehow in a state of disequilibrium or needs improvement. This state of disequilibrium may result

Source: B.C. by permission of Johnny Hart and Creators Syndicate, Inc.

from growth or decline or from competitive, technological, legal, or social changes in the external environment. There must be a felt need, since only felt needs convince individuals to adopt new ways. Managers must be sensitive to changes in the competitive environment—"To what's going on out there."

At General Electric a reorganization was implemented to enhance GE's competitiveness in a global area. The stimulus for this change was an awareness by organization members that "GE was too slow to make decisions, too slow to respond to changing conditions, and too slow to make thrusts into profitable new markets." At the root of GE's problems was a cultural resistance to change. As the economic and competitive circumstances facing the industry altered, GE had failed to adapt to them. To counter these problems, GE embarked on a change program to give managers more operating authority and responsibility for profits.[40]

Stage Two: Developing the Consultant-Client Relationship

After an organization recognizes a need for change and a consultant contacts the system, a relationship begins to develop between the consultant and the client system. The development of this relationship is an important determinant of the probable success or failure of an OD program. As with many interpersonal relationships, the exchange of expectations and obligations (the formation of a psychological contract) depends to a high degree upon a good first impression or match between consultant and client system. The consultant may be a manager or other member of the organization, referred to as an **internal consultant**, or an outside resource, referred to as an **external consultant**. The consultant attempts to establish a pattern of open communication, a relationship of trust, and an atmosphere of shared responsibility. Issues dealing with responsibility, rewards, and objectives must be clarified, defined, or worked through at this point.

The consultant must decide at what point to enter the system and what his or her role should be. For instance, the consultant may intervene with the sanction and approval of top management and either with or without the sanction and support of members in the lower levels of the organization. At one company, for example, OD started at the vice-presidential level and by using internal OD consultants was gradually expanded to include line managers and workers. At another company an outside consultant from a university was invited in by the organization's industrial relations group to initiate the OD program.

For example, one major corporation was afflicted with autocratic management and intergroup rivalries. However, a new top manager took charge and began totally overhauling the corporate personality. A management consulting group was contacted and the com-

pany embarked on a change program aimed at role negotiation and improving intergroup cooperation.

Stage Three: The Diagnostic Phase

After the consultant has intervened and developed a working relationship with the client, the consultant and the client begin to gather data about the system. The collection of data is an important activity providing the organization and the consultant with a better understanding of client system problems: the diagnosis.

One rule or *modus operandi* for the OD consultant is to question the client's diagnosis of the problem, because the client may well be biased in its perspective. After acquiring information relevant to the situation perceived to be in disequilibrium, the consultant and client together analyze the data to identify problem areas and causal relationships. A weak, inaccurate, or faulty diagnosis can lead to a costly and ineffective change program. The diagnostic phase, then, is used to determine the exact problem that needs solution, to identify the causal forces in the situation, and to provide a basis for selecting effective change strategies and techniques.

Although organizations usually generate a large amount of "hard" or operational data, still the data may present an incomplete picture of organizational performance. The consultant and client, then, may agree to increase the range or depth of the available data by interview or questionnaire as a basis for further action programs. One organization, for instance, was having a problem of high employee turnover. In such a case the consultant investigated the high turnover rate by means of interview or questionnaire to determine why this problem existed, and from these data an OD program was designed to correct the problems. This firm's employees felt that it had become a bureaucratic organization clogged with red tape, causing high turnover. OD programs have since reduced employee turnover to 19 percent, compared with 34 percent for the industry.

At a major food company, a new executive vice president needed to move quickly to improve the division's performance. With the help of an outside consultant, data were gathered by conducting intensive interviews with top management, as well as with outsiders, to determine key problem areas. Then, without identifying the source of comments, the management team worked on the information in a 10-hour session until solutions to the major problems were hammered out and action plans developed.

Stage Four: Action Plans, Strategies, and Techniques

The diagnostic phase leads to a series of interventions, activities, or programs aimed at resolving problems and increasing organization effectiveness. These programs apply OD techniques such as TQM, Managerial Grid programs, management by objectives programs, team building, or intergroup development to the causes specified in the diagnostic phase.

In many organizations there had to be more emphasis on changing the ongoing organization on a day-to-day basis, so they began to focus on the work team itself rather than on individual hang-ups. Team building, intergroup building, organization mirrors—all of these have proved more relevant to the job situation as the team evolved its own brand of management training.[41]

Stage Five: Self-Renewal, Monitoring, and Stabilizing the Action Programs

Once an action program is implemented, the next step is to monitor the results and stabilize the desired changes. This stage concerns the assessment of the effectiveness of change strategies in attaining stated objectives. Each stage of an OD program needs to be monitored to gain feedback on member reaction to the change efforts. The system members need to know the results of change efforts in order to determine whether they ought to modify, continue, or discontinue the activities. Once a problem has been corrected and a change program implemented and monitored, means must be devised to make sure that the new behavior is

stabilized and internalized. If this is not done, the tendency is for the system to regress to previous ineffective modes or states. The client system needs to develop the capability to maintain innovation without outside support.

The problem of stabilizing change and the possibility of managers reverting to previous, ingrained modes of behavior is a very real problem in many corporations. At Xerox, for example, change was needed because manufacturing costs had become way too high, overhead was too large, and the organization was too complicated and slow to react. They also lacked a real understanding about what customers really needed. Xerox used competitive benchmarking and employee involvement to ingrain the quality process into the organization.[42] At another company, on the other hand, top management felt that OD was successful because turnover was reduced to 19 percent and innovation was encouraged at all levels.

This model shows how varying OD methods and approaches are used to continuously improve performance so the vision can be achieved. It is important to remember that no model or paradigm is perfect, but still provides useful approaches to change.

As an OD program stabilizes, the need for the consultant should decrease. If the client moves toward independence and evidences a self-renewal capacity, the gradual termination of the consultant-client system relationship is easily accomplished. If the client system has become overly dependent upon the consultant, termination of the relationship can be a difficult and awkward issue. At one company for example, the program has produced tangible benefits. Of 264 managers involved in the program, 93 percent reported that the program led to improved teamwork.

One important issue in the implementation of an OD program is whether or not the OD consultant is able to deal effectively with power and the use of power. Hierarchical organizations, whether they be industrial, governmental, or academic, rely on power. The individuals in positions of influence generally constitute the power structure and frequently are power-motivated people. Managers complete for promotions, and departments and divisions conflict over budget allocations.

Political infighting is a reality (and often a dysfunctional factor) in most organizations and the issue is whether OD consultants deal with these power issues in bringing about a change. In one study of high-speed decision making Kathleen Eisenhardt and L. J. Bourgeois, III, found that politics do influence decisions and that political conflicts within top management teams are associated with poor firm performance.[43]

The OD consultant acts as a facilitator to promote team problem solving and collaboration, and values such as trust, openness, and consensus. Given the nature of an OD program, it is our view that OD is not a political/power type of intervention. But, given the political nature of organization decision making, the OD consultant must be aware of politics and use a problem-solving approach which is compatible with power-oriented situations.

REVIEW QUESTIONS

1. What is the implication of organization renewal and organization transformation to today's organizations?

2. Identify the basic stages of an OD program.

 1. _____

 2. _____

 3. _____

4. _____

5. _____

3. Contrast the differences between a stable and a hyperturbulent environment.

4. Compare and contrast the four types of management orientations used in relating to the environment.

KEY WORDS AND CONCEPTS

Action Research
Client Systems
Closed System
Content
Contingency Approach
Dynamic Equilibrium
Entropy
External Consultant
Feedback
Future Shock
Hyperturbulent Environment
Internal Consultant
Information Overload
OD Stages Model
Open System
Organization Renewal

Organization Transformation (OT)
Participant-Observer
Planned Change
Process
Process Observation
Reactive Management
Renewing/Transformational
 Management
Satisficing Management
Sluggish Management
Sociotechnical System
Synergy
System
System's Approach
Task Activities
Team Process

OD SKILLS SIMULATION 2.1
OD CONSULTANT BEHAVIOR PROFILE I

Total time suggested: 1 hour.

A. PURPOSE

In most organizations there is a lot of untapped human potential. In an excellent, renewing organization, this potential can be released, resulting in personal growth for the individual. Personal development and organization renewal involve changes in attitudes and behavior which are related to your self concept, role, goals, and values.

The behavior profile which you will generate in this simulation is intended to illustrate some growth dimensions for interpersonal competence and career planning. By recognizing your strengths and accomplishments, you may be encouraged to improve your self image and interpersonal skills. Hopefully, a honest self appraisal may aid you in becoming a more effective individual and team member. During this course you will be afforded additional opportunities to obtain information about yourself on how you behave in organizational situations. This feedback may provide the impetus for you to change, but the ultimate responsibility for that change is with you. Retain this survey, as it will be used again near the end of this course in Chapter 16.

B. PROCEDURES

Part A: Profile Survey

Step 1. Before class, complete the profile on a Lotus 1-2-3® computer template furnished by your instructor or on the following survey. How you respond reflects how you view yourself, which in turn reveals something of your behavioral style. Based on the following scale, select the number to indicate the degree to which you feel each description is characteristic of you. Record your choice in the blank to the right. If you are taking the survey on the template, save the template before quitting as you will need the completed survey again in OD Skills 16.1.

PROFILE SURVEY

```
::          :          :          :          :          :          :          ::
      1          2          3          4          5          6          7
  Not at All                     Somewhat                        Very
Characteristic                 Characteristic                Characteristic
```

1. Having the ability to communicate in a clear, concise, and persuasive manner _____

2. Being spontaneous—saying and doing things that seem natural on the spur of the moment _____

3. Doing things "by the book"—noticing appropriate rules and procedures and following them _____

4. Being creative—having a lot of unusual, original ideas, thinking of new approaches to problems others do not often come up with _____

5. Being competitive—wanting to win and be the best _____

6. Being able to listen to and understand others _____

7. Being aware of other people's moods and feelings _____

8. Being careful in your work—taking pains to make sure everything is "just right" _____

9. Being resourceful in coming up with possible ways of dealing with problems _____

10. Being a leader—having other people look to you for direction; taking over when things are confused _____

11. Having the ability to accept feedback without reacting defensively, becoming hostile, or withdrawing _____

12. Having the ability to deal with conflict and anger _____

13. Having written work neat and organized; making plans before starting on a difficult task; organizing details of work _____

14. Thinking clearly and logically; attempting to deal with ambiguity, complexity, and confusion in a situation by thoughtful, logical analysis _____

15. Having self-confidence when faced with a challenging situation _____

16. Having the ability to level with others, to give feedback to others _____

17. Doing new and different things; meeting new people; experimenting and trying out new ideas or activities _____

18. Having a high level of aspiration, setting difficult goals _____

19. Analyzing a situation carefully before acting; working out a course of action in detail before embarking on it _____

20. Being effective at initiating projects and innovative ideas _____

21. Seeking ideas from others; drawing others into discussion _____

22. Having a tendency to seek close personal relationships, participating in social activities with friends; giving affection and receiving it from others _____

23. Being dependable—staying on the job; doing what is expected _____

24. Having the ability to work as a catalyst, to stimulate and encourage others to develop their own resources for solving their own problems _____

25. Taking responsibility; relying on your own abilities and judgment rather than those of others _____

26. Selling your own ideas effectively _____

27. Being the dominant person; having a strong need for control or recognition _____

28. Getting deeply involved in your work; being extremely committed to ideas or work you are doing _____

29. Having the ability to evaluate possible solutions critically _____

30. Having the ability to work in unstructured situations, with little or no support and to continue to work effectively even if faced with lack of cooperation, resistance, or hostility _____

Step 2. Complete Table 2.3. Profile Form, by coloring in the bar graph for Chapter 2 in the appropriate line (or bring in computer printout) relative to the behavior profile you have just completed. Note that the 30 descriptions have been reordered to fit into five categories. The profile provides information about your behavioral style and allows you to see where you stand in each category. It also lets you directly compare your score on different scales by looking at the difference in the bar graph. The profile may indicate items on which your score is less desirable than you would like. You may also find categories in which you have generally low ratings. These may suggest areas for improvement during this course and for assessing the kinds of changes you may wish to make in order to become a more effective consultant or manager.

Table 2.3 Profile Form

		Score	Not at All Characteristic		Somewhat Characteristic		Very Characteristic		
			1	2	3	4	5	6	7
A. Communicating Skills									
1. Communicates	Ch. 2								
	Ch. 16								
6. Listens	Ch. 2								
	Ch. 16								
11. Receives Feedback	Ch. 2								
	Ch. 16								
16. Gives Feedback	Ch. 2								
	Ch. 16								
21. Seeks Ideas	Ch. 2								
	Ch. 16								
26. Sells Ideas	Ch. 2								
	Ch. 16								
Mean Score A	Ch. 2								
	Ch. 16								
B. Interpersonal Skills									
2. Is Spontaneous	Ch. 2								
	Ch. 16								
7. Is Aware	Ch. 2								
	Ch. 16								
12. Deals with Conflict	Ch. 2								
	Ch. 16								
17. Experiments	Ch. 2								
	Ch. 16								
22. Seeks Close Relationships	Ch. 2								
	Ch. 16								
27. Is Dominant	Ch. 2								
	Ch. 16								
Mean Score B	Ch. 2								
	Ch. 16								
C. Aspiration-Achievement Levels									
3. Conforms	Ch. 2								
	Ch. 16								
8. Is Careful	Ch. 2								
	Ch. 16								
13. Is Organized	Ch. 2								
	Ch. 16								
18. Aspires	Ch. 2								
	Ch. 16								
23. Is Dependable	Ch. 2								
	Ch. 16								
28. Is Committed to Ideas or work	Ch. 2								
	Ch. 16								
Mean Score C	Ch. 2								
	Ch. 16								

Continued

Table 2.3 *Continued*

		Score	Not at All Characteristic		Somewhat Characteristic		Very Characteristic	
D. *Problem-Solving Skills*								
4. Is Creative	Ch. 2							
	Ch. 16							
9. Is Resourceful	Ch. 2							
	Ch. 16							
14. Is Logical	Ch. 2							
	Ch. 16							
19. Analyzes	Ch. 2							
	Ch. 16							
24. Is Catalyst	Ch. 2							
	Ch. 16							
29. Evaluates	Ch. 2							
	Ch. 16							
Mean Score D	Ch. 2							
	Ch. 16							
E. *Leadership Skills*								
5. Is Competitive	Ch. 2							
	Ch. 16							
10. Is a Leader	Ch. 2							
	Ch. 16							
15. Is Confident	Ch. 2							
	Ch. 16							
20. Initiates	Ch. 2							
	Ch. 16							
25. Takes Responsibility	Ch. 2							
	Ch. 16							
30. Can Work in Unstructured Situations	Ch. 2							
	Ch. 16							
Mean Score E	Ch. 2							
	Ch. 16							
Overall Profile Mean (A + B + C + D + E) ÷ 5	Ch. 2							
	Ch. 16							

Part B Goal Setting—Personal Objectives for Course

Step 1. After completing Table 2.3, Profile Form, outside of class list some of the *specific* objectives and expectations you have for this class on the Performance Interview Form. These objectives should describe what you will be able to do and the time required. Refer to the Profile Form you have just completed and select some behaviors you would like to emphasize for change.

Sample: to develop more self-confidence in doing class presentations by doing three short presentations in class.

PERFORMANCE INTERVIEW FORM

I. Aspiration—Achievement Levels

	100%–95%	94%–90%	89%–80%	79%–70%	69%–60%	59%–50%	49%–0%
1. Attendance							
2. Preparation							
3. Be careful in work—ready to contribute to team							

II. Communicating Skills

	100%–95%	94%–90%	89%–80%	79%–70%	69%–60%	59%–50%	49%–0%
1. Communicates ideas clearly in class							
2. Listens and shows interest in fellow team members							
3. Provides feedback to fellow team members							

Continued

PERFORMANCE INTERVIEW FORM, CONTINUED

III. Interpersonal Skills

	100%–95%	94%–90%	89%–80%	79%–70%	69%–60%	59%–50%	49%–0%
1. Shows interest in meeting							
2. Initiates team/class discussions							
3. Gets along with team members							

IV. Problem-Solving Skills

	100%–95%	94%–90%	89%–80%	79%–70%	69%–60%	59%–50%	49%–0%
1. Encourages others to develop problem-solving							
2. Prepares problem solutions for cases/simulations							
3. Prepares and evaluates team solutions							

V. Leadership Skills

	100%–95%	94%–90%	89%–80%	79%–70%	69%–60%	59%–50%	49%–0%
1. Provides team leadership, leading discussions							
2. Initiates team projects							
3. Takes responsibility							

Try referring to the preceding objectives often and at least before coming to class for the remainder of the course. Do not hesitate to experiment with the new behaviors you would like to cultivate. You will be referring to these objectives again later in the book.

Step 2. The profile can be used as a feedback tool. You will be able to learn more about yourself by assessing the kinds of changes you may need to make in order to become more effective. Form into trios, with one person acting as the client, a second as the consultant, and the third as observer (see the Profile Form and Process Observer Forms, p. 58). Refer to the end of this simulation for "Instructions for Developing Consultant/Client Roles and Skills." The consultant will help you to develop a fuller understanding of how your styles play a part in your overall effectiveness and how you may build on your strengths during this course. The consultant will review the client's Profile Form and Performance Interview Form for the following:

1. How accurate are the profile assessments relative to observations in class?
2. Are they a complete and challenging set of goals?
3. Are they realistic and feasible?
4. Are they specific and measurable?
5. Are they things the client can do and demonstrate by the end of the course?

The observer will observe the consulting relationship using the Process Observer Forms and try to provide feedback on the consulting style. At the end of each interview, the observer gives observations providing feedback to the consultant using the Process Observer Form. Then rotate roles so that each person is in each of the three roles. Continue the simulation by switching roles until all have played each of the roles.

Time suggested for Step 2: 15-20 minutes per person (in each of the rotating roles).

Step 3. Meeting with the entire class, discuss:

1. How can we improve performance?
2. What consultant role seemed to work best?
3. Whether we view change as positive or negative.
4. The role of the consultant. Was it helpful? How?
5. How effective was our team?

Time suggested for Step 3: 15 minutes.

(Process Observer Forms follow on page 58)

PROCESS OBSERVER FORM

Your role during this part of the simulation is important because your goal is to give individuals feedback on their strategies of change. Following are listed ten criteria of helping relationships. Rate the consultant by circling the appropriate number.

NOTES:
Words,
behaviors

1. Level of involvement:
 Cautious Low 1 : 2 : 3 : 4 : 5 : 6 : 7 : 8 : 9 : 10 High Interested _____

2. Level of communication:
 Doesn't listen Low 1 : 2 : 3 : 4 : 5 : 6 : 7 : 8 : 9 : 10 High Listens _____

3. Level of openness, trust:
 Shy, uncertain Low 1 : 2 : 3 : 4 : 5 : 6 : 7 : 8 : 9 : 10 High Warm, friendly _____

4. Level of collaboration:
 Authoritative Low 1 : 2 : 3 : 4 : 5 : 6 : 7 : 8 : 9 : 10 High Seeks agreement _____

5. Level of influence:
 Gives in Low 1 : 2 : 3 : 4 : 5 : 6 : 7 : 8 : 9 : 10 High Convincing

6. Level of supportiveness:
 Disagrees Low 1 : 2 : 3 : 4 : 5 : 6 : 7 : 8 : 9 : 10 High Supports _____

7. Level of direction:
 Easygoing,
 agreeable Low 1 : 2 : 3 : 4 : 5 : 6 : 7 : 8 : 9 : 10 High Gives directions _____

8. Level of competence
 Unsure Low 1 : 2 : 3 : 4 : 5 : 6 : 7 : 8 : 9 : 10 High Competent _____

9. Reflects Feelings-Summaries:
 Never Low 1 : 2 : 3 : 4 : 5 : 6 : 7 : 8 : 9 : 10 High Often _____

10. Overall style:
 Ineffective Low 1 : 2 : 3 : 4 : 5 : 6 : 7 : 8 : 9 : 10 High Effective _____

PROCESS OBSERVER: COMMUNICATION FLOW

Observer _____

Use arrows to indicate direction, frequency of communication between consultant and client.

Behaviors

Client

1. _____
2. _____
3. _____
4. _____

Consultant

1. _____
2. _____
3. _____
4. _____

INSTRUCTIONS FOR DEVELOPING
CONSULTANT-CLIENT ROLES AND SKILLS

In this course there has been an opportunity to develop the interaction and communication atmosphere conducive to experiential learning. In experiential learning the interrelationship among students is as important as that between instructor and students. Some characteristics of the OD consultant role are:

1. Two-way communication and influence. Use open-ended questions.
2. Openness of expression of views, feelings, and emotions. Being able to tell it like it is!
3. Supportiveness. When you are in agreement with your clients, give them your support. Learn to express differences without offending. Often two people in confrontation are 90 percent in agreement on the issues, but they focus only on their differences.
4. Awareness that conflict can be creative when differences are expressed appropriately.
5. Recognition of individual differences.
6. Confrontation of client.
 a. The courage to express your own convictions.
 b. Can you give and take feedback?
 c. Are you worried about being shot down?
 d. Are you willing to attempt risk-taking behavior?
 e. Are you overusing your share of the air time?
7. Reflections of the feelings of the client. You might say, "You seem to feel very strongly about this."
8. Disclosure of something about yourself. You might say, "This is a problem for me, also."
9. Use of silence or nonresponse; just let the client talk.
10. Use of nonverbal signals such as eye contact or nod of head indicate that you hear what is said.

CASE 2: THE NoGo RAILROAD[44]

INTRODUCTION

Allen Yates, the Northwestern Division Manager of the NoGo Railroad, promoted the Chief Dispatcher, Dave Keller, to Communication Manager in the division. Dave Keller was a recent graduate of State University, but his management experience was limited to only five years as Chief Dispatcher. Yates announced that Dave demonstrated that he had the guts to do what was needed and the ability to act intelligently, rationally, and quickly in a crisis. Dave was advised that his selection was based on his being single, being willing to accept a temporary position, and agreeing to extensive traveling, as well as on his effective, independent, decision-making capabilities.

BACKGROUND

Dave's original hiring as Dispatcher was based on his prior military experience. After six years of outstanding service, he was promoted to Chief Dispatcher due in part to his youth and his excellent physical condition, attributes needed to stand the stress of the position. The previous Chief Dispatcher had had a heart attack on the job and was unable to return

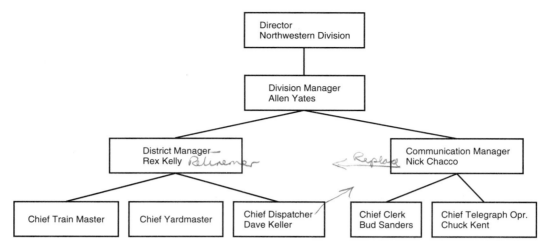

EXHIBIT 2.1 Organizational Chart: NoGo Railroad

to work. Dave's yearly performance evaluations as Chief Dispatcher were consistently rated satisfactory by Rex Kelly, the District Manager. (See Exhibit 2.1 for Organization Chart).

Rex was scheduled for retirement and Nick Chacco, the Communication Manager, would assume Rex's responsibilities. Dave accepted the vacated Communication Manager position, but was uneasy about his ability to perform the tasks ahead. He felt extremely uncomfortable about his people skills, educational background, and experience. Having expressed this to Allen, Dave was quickly dismissed by the Division Manager, who told him not to worry about it.

COMMUNICATIONS DEPARTMENT

Officially, his territory encompassed the states of Washington, Idaho, and Montana. His responsibility included the personnel who performed radio, teletype, telephone, and computer operations. These communication operations were performed by two groups of unionized employees: the telegraph operators and the clerks.

Unofficially, Allen had made arrangements for Dave to meet and travel with several experienced individuals. His purpose was to tour remote areas, observe different job functions, eliminate obsolete practices and modernize wherever possible.

Dave discovered that the clerks were predominantly women. In addition, these clerks had an agreement in the contract which stated they could not work directly with radio communications and train crews. Their daily functions varied from teletype and computer operations to general clerical duties. Their contract stated that they could not be sent more than 30 miles away from their home on assignments. In rural districts, this led to having a large force of clerks that could not cover for vacations and emergencies. Hence, Dave found an overabundance of clerks without enough work to keep them all busy.

The telegraph operators, predominantly men, no longer had to know Morse Code, but were highly trained in radio, teletype, and computer operations. However, such skills as knot tying were still essential. Proper knot tying was important in handing paperwork extended on a pole to the conductor and engineer passing by in a speeding train. The taller the employee, the easier and safer this practice.

Placing small "torpedoes" on the rails of the tracks to signal the crew in an oncoming train was another function of the telegraph operators. This loud explosion would alert the crew in the engine car of danger or of any new information to be picked up ahead. These and many other archaic traditions and procedures were still practiced in the mountainous areas where communication by radio was still impossible or difficult between train dispatchers, train crews, and telegraph operators.

UNION CONTRACTS

40 hr guarantee The telegraph operators had an agreement in their contract guaranteeing them 40 hours of weekly pay even if no work was available. This concession was granted years ago because of the large amount of time that they spent on call or away from home and family. Each telegraph operator managed to receive this benefit four to six weeks per year during the slow winter season. Their pay was also higher than that of the clerks.

higher pay than clerks
op to op
clerk to clerk
op does any clerk idle

The telegraph operators could be sent anywhere, replacing only telegraph operators. Clerks could only replace other clerks. It was not uncommon during major derailments for telegraph operators to be hundreds of miles from their home, on overtime, living on expenses paid by the railroad, yet working next to clerks who had nothing to do.

layoff fears Dave was aware of the rumors that were running rampant in the company and that employee fears of layoffs were justified. In addition, attempts to combine job descriptions and job functions in different departments were also in debate.

featherbedding Dave knew that the removal of the fireman position from the engine car of the train was meeting with an organized covert slowdown of work. The fireman position was left over from the days when the shoveling of coal was required to heat the boiler on the steam locomotive. The train crew in the engine consisted of the engineer, fireman, and brakeman. The fireman's only new function, since the advent of the internal combustion engine, was to take over the controls of the engine should the engineer need assistance. Since the decline of the steam engine locomotive, several unsuccessful attempts to remove the fireman position by incorporating duties with those of the brakeman had occurred.

inflexible
in work assignments

Employees that believed they had enough seniority to remain after a layoff saw this as increasing their work without increasing their pay. When seasoned employees were asked to do a different task or function previously done by another job title, they would openly refuse. Backed by the union, they stated that it was not in their job description or in their contract.

ORGANIZATION PROBLEMS

reduce expenses
improve morale

After extensive research, Dave realized he had two immediate problems facing him: reducing crushing employee expenses necessary in day-to-day operations and improving the attitude of employees to accept necessary changes to insure the railroad's survival.

relatives
↓
High resistance
to change

He believed that the morale problem was created by a recruitment process which traditionally favored the hiring of relatives. This was a common practice throughout the Western United States. Dave had observed employees working beside spouses, brothers, cousins, and children. This nepotism saturated many different levels of the organization. Due to this high degree of nepotism within the railroads, featherbedding proliferated. (Featherbedding is the practice of limiting work our output in order to provide more jobs and prevent unemployment.) Resistance to change was high, especially when cooperation could result in loss of employment for one or more family members.

Dave believed that if he could eliminate the featherbedding, reduction in expenses would follow. This would assist in avoiding a major layoff of clerks and telegraph operators. Both groups would have to accept some changes and take on additional or different duties. But this action would reduce the yearly income of many individuals who had grown to count on their guarantees, expense accounts, and overtime pay.

2 years to new
union contract

A new union contract was still two years away, and experience had shown extreme rigidity by the union for concessions in these areas. Gathering enough information and evidence to substantiate changes in job descriptions with union representatives would be impossible without help from upper management.

The thing he was uncertain about was whether or not organized resistance by seasoned employees under his jurisdiction would occur. Twice during his eleven years with the railroad he had witnessed such subversive group resistance. Its effects were extremely devastating to the company and the responsible managers. The present slowdown by the train crews over the fireman issue attests to the power, strength, and attitude of the employees.

slowdowns
resistance

CONCLUSION

[handwritten margin notes: vulnerable / why him / old job filled / not in / writing / set up? / trust / paid own / MBA / candidate]

Dave was aware of his own career vulnerability if such an organized effort took place against him. He knew he was only temporary and wondered why someone with more experience hadn't been given these difficult tasks. Why was his being single an important criteria?

Originally, Dave believed that temporary meant that he would champion a specific task, then be reinstated as Chief Dispatcher, but that position was immediately filled by Rex's son-in-law, Chuck Kent, Chief Telegraph Operator.

He tried unsuccessfully to get written backing from Allen Yates to support his unofficial directives. Allen's only advice was to do what is best for the railroad, not to fill Chuck's position and that Bud would be retiring very soon.

After much soul searching, he was unsure if he was being set up as a helmsman on a sinking ship or if he was being unnecessarily paranoid. If he implemented the needed changes, he would lose employee support and fail to meet official expectations, possibly causing his dismissal if Allen didn't back him. If he didn't make the required changes, Allen would dismiss him creating the same results. Dave felt forced to give Allen the changes he wanted, but didn't trust him for support afterwards.

Things were changing fast and Dave wanted a fresh perspective. He felt the need for outside consultation before taking any action, however using company funds was out of the question. So for a small fee, out of his own pocket, he consulted and confided in a small group of outstanding MBA candidates at the local college. You are one of those outstanding students. What problems, recommendations, advice, and actions would your group identify? (Use Case Analysis Form.)

CASE ANALYSIS FORM

Name: _____

I. Problems

 A. Macro

 1. _____

 2. _____

 B. Micro

 1. _____

 2. _____

II. Causes

 1. _____

 2. _____

 3. _____

III. Systems affected

 1. Structural _____

 2. Psychosocial _____

 3. Technical _____

 4. Managerial_____

 5. Goals _____

IV. Alternatives

 1. _____

 2. _____

 3. _____

 4. _____

 5. _____

V. Recommendations

 1. _____

 2. _____

 3. _____

SUMMARY

- **Change** is all around us, and for managers the idea of future shock—too much change in too short a time—can be a very real problem. Managers and organizations face rapid changes in three areas: technological advancements, environmental changes, and social changes. The organization must renew and adapt to these changing situations as each day presents a new set of conditions.

- **Systems.** Each organization must maintain a dynamic equilibrium between stability and innovation. A systems model may be used to identify the sources of impetus for change. The environmental suprasystem has an impact on organizations through technological, economic, and cultural forces. Organizational change also comes from forces within the organizational subsystems.

- **Adaptive.** Organizations may adapt to changes with four different orientations. A sluggish management orientation has little ability to adapt to changes, but there is no great need because of a stable environment. A reactive management orientation has the need to respond to a rapidly changing environment but does not have the ability. A satisficing management orientation has the ability to respond to a chang-

ing environment but finds itself in a relatively stable environment. A renewing management orientation has both the ability and the need to respond to a rapidly changing environment.

- **Organization Renewal.** It seems that most modern organizations are increasingly finding the need for organization renewal. Renewing management predicts future conditions and makes planned changes before the conditions actually occur. For an organization to have the capacity to adapt to change and become more effective, management must initiate and create a climate that encourages creativity and innovation.

- **OD Model.** *Organization development* involves the long-term, system-wide application of behavioral science techniques to increase organization effectiveness. OD works on the idea that organization change involves improving the way people work together on teams and the way team activities are integrated with organizational goals.

OD is a continuing process of organization improvement usually involving a sequence of steps, or stages. The five stages presented here are typical of most OD programs,

but they are not always exactly followed, since a change program is an unpredictable and turbulent thing. The stages may not occur in the sequence described or some of the stages may occur simultaneously, but they can be regarded as an ideal or a typical model rather than as the actual representation of every OD program. The objective of OD is a payoff in increased adaptability and productivity.

• **OD Skills.** In the simulation you may have begun to sense the responsibility of being an OD consultant. What kinds of systems or individuals would you choose to help or not help? What financial criteria would you use? Would you consult with a client system even though it could not pay you? These are among the factors that a consultant must consider, and you must also be aware of your own value system: What do you believe in and stand for?

Change is the name of the game in management today, requiring rapid solving of complex problems within time constraints. In the simulation you had an opportunity to deal with these factors.

NOTES

1. Rubuch, Laura, "Downsizing: How Quality is Affected as Companies Shrink," *Quality Progress*, vol. 28, no. 4, April 1995, p. 24.
2. Dumaine, Brian, "The Bureaucracy Busters," *Fortune*, June 17, 1991, pp. 36–50 and Russel Mitchell, "Masters of Innovation," *Business Week*, April 10, 1989, p. 58.
3. Barr, Pamela, Stimpart J., and Huff, Anne S., "Cognitive Change, Strategic Action and Organizational Renewal," *Strategic Management Journal*, Summer, 1992, pp. 15–36.
4. Waterman, Jr., Robert H., *The Renewal Factor* (New York: Bantam Books, 1987).
5. Peters, Thomas J., *Thriving on Chaos* (New York, Alfred A. Knopf, 1987), p. 3.
6. "New Trends in the Computer Industry," *The Management Journal*, March 18, 1988, p. 1.
7. See Kathleen M. Eisenhardt, "Making Fast Strategic Decisions in High-Velocity Environments," *Academy of Management Journal*, vol. 32, no. 3, (1989), pp. 543–76.
8. Waterman, *The Renewal Factor*, pp. 6–12.
9. See David Miller, "Evolution and Revolution: A Quantum View of Structural Change in Organizations," *Journal of Management Studies*, (April 1982), pp. 131–51.
10. Ash, Joan, and Ellen West, "High Performance Systems and Transformational Change," paper presented at Academy of Management meeting, August, 1989, Washington, D.C.
11. Colvin, Teresa J., and Ralph H. Kilmann, "A Profile of Large Scale Change Programs," Proceedings, Southern Management Assn., 1989, p. 202.
12. Miller, David, *Evolution*, pp. 133–35.
13. Simon, Ruth, "What I Learned in the Eighties," *Forbes*, January 8, 1990, p. 100.
14. Mitroff, Ian I., *Break-Away Thinking* (New York: John Wiley & Sons, 1988), p. 21.
15. Colvin, *A Profile of Large Scale Change Programs*, p. 202.
16. *Ibid.*
17. Hays, Laurie, "IBM's Finance Chief Cuts Costs," *The Wall Street Journal*, January 26, 1994, p. 1.
18. "The Horizontal Corporation," *Business Week*, December 20, 1993, p. 76.
19. See Peter R. Hybert, "Managing the Interactions of People with Your Product," *Quality Progress*, vol . 27, no. 7, July 1994, p. 67.
20. Hulpke, John F., California State Univesity, Bakersfield, Bakersfield, CA 1991.
21. Sashkin, Marshal, and others, "OD Approaches," *Training and Development Journal* , vol. 39, no. 2 (February 1985), p. 46.
22. Hanna, David P., *Designing Organizations for High Performance*, (Reading, Mass: Addison-Wesley, 1988), p.38.
23. *Ibid*, p.42.
24. See Henry L. Tosi, Jr., and John W. Slocum, Jr., "Contingency Theory: Some Suggested Directions," *Journal of Management*, vol. 10, no. 1 (1984), pp. 9–26.
25. See Robert R. Blake and Jane S. Mouton, "OD Technology for the Future," *Training and Development Journal*, (November 1979), p. 55. Blake contends that there is "one best way."
26. From *Future Shock*, by Alvin Toffler, Copyright ©1970 by Alvin Toffler. Reprinted by permission of Random House, Inc. Originally appeared in *Playboy* in slightly different form. Also by permission of the Bodley Head, London. See also *The Third Wave*, 1982.
27. Naisbitt, John, and Patricia Aburdene, *Megatrends 2000* (New York: William Morrow and Company, Inc., 1990). See also John Naisbitt and Patricia Aburdene, *Re-Inventing the Corporation* (New York: Warner Books, 1985).
28. Serwer, Andrew E., "Lessons from America's Fastest Growing Companies," *Fortune*, August 8, 1984, p. 42.
29. Naisbitt, *Megatrends 2000*.
30. Deutschman, Alan, "Next KOs Workstation Line," *Computer World*, (February 15, 1993), p. 2; "Steve Jobs' Next Big Gamble," *Fortune*, (February 8, 1993), p. 99; and Patton, Julie, "The Steven Jobs Reality Distortion Field," *Forbes*, (April 22, 1991), p. 24.
31. Latham, John R., "Visioning: The Concept, Trilogy and Process", *Quality Progress*, vol 28, no. 4, April 1995, p. 65.
32. Chin, Robert, and Kenneth D. Benne, "General Strategies for Effecting Changes in Human Systems," in *The Planning of Change*.
33. Stewart, Thomas A., "Rate Your Readiness for Change," *Fortune*, February 7, 1994, p. 106.
34. Peters, *Thriving on Chaos*, p. 286.
35. Panchak, Patricia L., "How To Implement a Quality Management Initiative," *Modern Office Technology*, February 1992, p. 27–31.
36. Peters, *Thriving on Chaos*, p. 4.
37. Colvin and Kilmann, *A Profile*, p. 202.
38. Friedlander, Frank, and L. Dave Brown, "Organization Development," in *Annual Review of Psychology*, vol. 25, (1974), p. 336.
39. Cuadron, Shari, "How Xerox Won the Baldrige," *Personnel Journal*, April 1991, pp. 98–102.
40. Dumaine, Brian, "The Bureaucracy Busters," *Fortune*, June 17, 1991, pp. 36–50, and "Team Work Through Conflict," *Business Week*, March 20, 1974, p. 45.
41. Mann, Robert W., "A Building Blocks Approach to Strategic Change," *Training and Development Journal*, August 1990, pp. 23–25.
42. Kearns, David, "Xerox: Satisfying Customer Needs With a New Culture," *Management Review*, February 1989, pp. 61–63.
43. Eisenhardt, Kathleen M., and L. J. Bourgeois III, "Politics of Strategic Decision Making in High Velocity Environments," *Academy of Management Journal* , vol. 31, no. 4., (December 1988), p. 38.
44. This case was written by Mark Mangiaracina and Don Harvey, "The NoGo Railroad," Eastern Washington University, used by permission, 1991.

Involvement of employees helps mold the culture of Texas Instruments. *Photo reprinted by Permission of Texas Instruments Incorporated.*

Organization Renewal: Changing the Corporate Culture

3

OBJECTIVES

Upon completing this chapter, you will be able to:

1. Recognize the importance of corporate culture to organizational success.
2. Identify the key factors used in assessing the corporate culture.
3. Describe the cultural and organizational factors which lead to effective organizations.

PREMEETING PREPARATION

1. Read the Background Information.
2. Prior to class, form into groups of five and select roles. Read instructions for OD Skills Simulation 3.1. Complete Step 1, prepare Individual Decision Worksheet (Or Lotus/Excel spreadsheet).
3. Read and analyze Case 3: The Dim Lighting Co.

BACKGROUND INFORMATION

Change, massive change, is impacting on all facets of society, creating new dimensions and great uncertainty. The issue facing us today is how to manage such change. Organization development provides a renewal process enabling managers to adapt their style and goals to meet the changing demands of the environment. These changes—improving quality, increasing innovation, adopting a customer orientation—are so fundamental that it usually means changing the organization's culture.[1]

Change is inevitable. Executives are adapting to changing market conditions and at the same time facing the need for creating a "renewing" rather than a "reactive" managerial system. They are searching for ways to manage an increasingly complex technology and a more sophisticated work force. To accomplish these diverse goals, managers need more than piece-meal, ad hoc change programs dealing only with current crises. They need long-term efforts to prepare for future organization requirements.[2]

In such a chaotic world, the only excellent managers will be those who are constantly adapting to change—those not only able to deal proactively with shifting forces, but those able to take advantage of the opportunities that arise.

An effective organizational climate and a realistic vision of the future are both essential to future success. At Citicorp for example, "We're in the business of managing change. That requires a combination of vision and execution," says CEO John S. Reed.[3] As R. H. Kilmann has noted:

> The organization itself has an invisible quality—a certain style, a character, a way of doing things—that may be more powerful than the dictates of any one person or any formal system. To understand the soul of the organization requires that we travel below the charts, rule books, machines, and buildings into the underground world of corporate culture.[4]

The lessons of management seem to point out that companies with outstanding financial performance often have powerful corporate cultures, suggesting that "culture" is the key to an organization's success. Cultural change does not just happen in an organization, rather, it is usually the result of a complex change strategy implemented by the company's management.

Given an environment of rapid change, a static organization culture can no longer be effective. Managers must be able to recognize when changes are needed and must possess the necessary skills and competence to implement these changes. The organization must try to adapt itself to a dynamic environment by introducing internal changes that will allow the organization to become more effective.

One method for bringing about such a proactive management culture is organization development. Organization development has been described earlier as a long-range effort to introduce planned change throughout an organization. In this chapter, we will examine: (1) the concept of corporate culture; (2) the impact of key cultural factors; and (3) the goals and values of an OD program.

The Corporate Culture

Every organization has a culture. For example, at IBM, service to the customer is a dominant value that forms a basis for action from top management down through all levels of the company.

Pepsi Cola, also, has its own culture. "Pepsi's values reflect the desire to overtake Coca Cola. Managers engage in fierce competition against each other to acquire market share, to squeeze more profits out of their business, and to work harder. Employees who do not succeed are terminated. They must win to get ahead. A career can be made or broken on one-tenth of a point of market share. Everyone knows the corporate culture and thrives on the creative tension thus generated. The internal structure is lean and adaptable. The company picnic is characterized by intensively competitive team sports. Managers change jobs frequently and are motivated to excel. The culture is characterized by a go-go atmosphere and success at all costs."[5] (See Our Changing World)

OUR CHANGING WORLD
PEPSI, COKE, AND GO-GO-CULTURES[6]

The Cola Wars

The news clips were impressive. While the Berlin Wall was being torn down, there, hustling through those gaps in the wall, were Coca-Cola trucks, loaded with Coke for thirsty East Berliners. Coke gave away thousands of free Cokes as the wall came down, demonstrating that Cola Wars are not confined to any one country.

Coke approaches the twenty-first century with a pretty significant amount of cash on hand, including the $1.1 billion it got from selling Coke's 49 percent interest in Columbia Pictures to Sony. Coca-Cola's president, Robert Goizueta, plans to spend some of the cash on new international bottling joint ventures, according to Fortune. Why go overseas? Goizueta responds: "Why did Willie Sutton rob banks? That's where the money is."

The Pepsi Challenge

In years to come, look for aggressive moves from Pepsi on the international front, too. As a Forbes article puts it, "Pepsi wants to go international in the worst way." But they have not really arrived yet, in spite of Pizza Hut franchises in Russia, Kentucky Fried Chicken outlets in Beijing and elsewhere, and Pepsi just about everywhere. The truth is that Pepsi isn't yet turning those overseas ventures into the kinds of profits that Coke earns. Coke earns 66 percent of its soft drink revenues, and 80 percent of its soft drink profits, outside the United States. Pepsi, by contrast, earns 50 percent of its soft drink revenues and only 15 percent of its soft drink profits from foreign operations. But the Pepsi Challenge is going global. As PepsiCo chairman, D. Wayne Calloway, put it, "We are still basically an American company with offshore interests. As the '90s progress, that's going to change. We'll be a truly global consumer products company."

India: A Case in Point

A case in point is India. Coca-Cola was forced out of India in a political move where one faction attempted to embarrass another faction that had given Coca-Cola access to India. Coke was ordered to give the locals the secret Coke formula as a condition of staying in business. To no one's surprise, Coke shut down its operation and left.

Meanwhile, PepsiCo had its eyes on the Indian market. Indians don't drink much cola now, but Pepsi figured aggressive marketing might pay off. After all, in neighboring Pakistan, soft drink consumption is 13 bottles per person per year, compared to only three bottles per person per year in India. Egypt, by comparison, boosted consumption to 80 bottles per capita per year after a Cola War broke out there.

Go-Go at Any Cost

The details of the Pepsi deal allowing it to go into India are complex, but at least Pepsi is there. Were risks involved? You bet. But they are just part of the Pepsi Go-Go win-at-any-cost culture. Under the new Pepsi culture, there was no option. Given even a slim chance at such a large potential market, there was simply no choice: Pepsi had to go ahead and give it a try.

Questions

1. Identify differences between the Pepsi and Coca-Cola cultures.

2. What explains the different consumption in differing countries?

What Is Corporate Culture?

A corporate culture is a system of shared values and beliefs which interact with an organization's people, structure, and systems to produce behavioral norms (the way things are done around here) (see Figure 3.1 on page 68.) Corporate culture is defined as "an interdependent set of beliefs, values, ways of behaving, and tools for living that are so common in a community that they tend to perpetuate themselves, sometimes over long periods of time. This continuity is the product of a variety of social forces that are frequently subtle, bordering on invisible, through which people to learn a group's norms and values, are rewarded when they accept them, and are ostracized when they do not."[7]

What makes up a culture? There are several factors including:

Managerial. Bruce Crockett's (CEO, COMSAT) desk has no drawers, indeed none of the furniture in his office has any, and that is a deliberate attempt to change the corporate cul-

Feedback

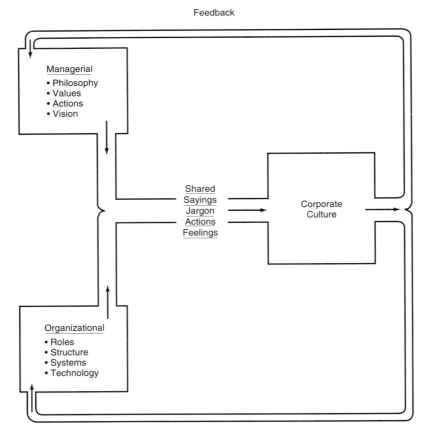

FIGURE 3.1 Culture Formation.

ture. Without places to stash paper, Bruce feels he's more efficient, memos are read once, and decisions are made quickly. "On a good day," says Crockett, "my desk will be totally empty. That means I have done something with everything." In an increasingly competitive world, Bruce Crockett feels his values and actions will influence how the organization reacts.

Organizational. At one time, COMSAT was not particularly customer oriented. But employees have recognized the reality if they did not create a competitive, customer oriented culture, the world was likely to leave the company behind. Organizational roles, structure, and technology must reinforce changes.

Corporate Culture. Changing the corporate culture involves a "lot of hardheadedness, vigilance, and constant fighting to keep change open," says Bruce Crockett. "Some people can change, you encourage all of them to change, but if they can't, then they have to be changed out."[8]

We shall use the term **corporate culture** to refer to all types of organizations: thus a university or a city government has a corporate culture, even though they are not corporations. An organization may also have subcultures with differing or even conflicting corporate cultures for example—Pillsbury Corporation's Minneapolis headquarters was a formal, gray-flannel suit culture, termed "Minneapolis Ice," while the Burger King subsidiary in Miami was very informal, dressed in pastels, no ties, and so on, and was known as "Miami Vice."

Management style and corporate culture are central factors in the success of a company. One of the most critical factors in organizational strategy is management style and culture. This sets the tone for the whole organization and influences the communication,

decision making, and leadership patterns of the entire system. There is no basic culture that works best for all organizations. The management style and the set of norms, values, and beliefs of the organization's members combine to form the corporate culture. According to Terrence Deal and Allan Kennedy, "A shared history between members builds a distinct corporate identity or character."[9]

A corporate culture must achieve goals as well as satisfy the needs of members in order for the organization to be effective. Culture influences how managers and employees approach problems, serve customers, react to competitors and carry out activities.

Sam Walton, founder of Wal-Mart, created a culture for his firm that reflected his own personal values. Although he was worth some $8 billion, Walton lived in a modest ranch home in Bentonville, Arkansas. He drove a Ford pickup truck, and ate breakfast almost daily at the local Ramada Inn. He went out on Friday nights to Fred's Hickory Inn for ribs and cheesecake. He worked out of a small office with plywood paneling. He visited every store and led the company cheer.[10] Wal-Mart continues to reflect Sam's values: frugality, simplicity, and humility.

A strong, widely internalized corporate culture is frequently cited as a reason for the success of such companies as 3M and Hewlett-Packard. In these organizations, the rewards, ceremonies, and other symbolic forms of communications maintain a culture that guides the actions of its members.[11] Similarly, in a study of 24 organizations, Henry Migliore has identified a set of 20 cultural factors which may be used to measure the organizational culture, termed the Corporate Culture Index.[12] These factors include the following characteristics:

- *Member Identity*: employees identify with the organization as a whole on their type of job or field of professional expertise.
- *Team Emphasis*: the degree to which work activities are organized around teams rather than individuals.
- *People Focus*: the degree to which management empowers the employees within the organization.
- *Autonomy:* the degree to which departments within the organization are encouraged to operate in a coordinated or interdependent manner.
- *Control*: the degree to which rules, regulations, and direct supervision are used to control employee behavior.
- *Risk Tolerance:* the degree to which employees are encouraged to be aggressive, innovative, and risk-seeking.

The Corporate Culture and Success

A corporate culture gives the whole organization a sense of how to behave, what to do, and where to place priorities in getting the job done. Culture helps members fill in the blanks between formal directives and how the work actually gets done. Because of this, culture is of critical importance in the implementation of strategy.

A great majority of outstanding companies trace their culture back to an influential founder who personified a value system and relentlessly hammered in a few basic values which became the cultural core of the company.[13] However, with today's rapidly changing environment, many corporate cultures fail to adapt to change and therefore fail as economic entities.

For some organizations, especially those in the service sector, the company's culture is what helps set it apart from its competition. One organization where this is the case, is the powerful, prestigious, and highly successful consulting firm of McKinsey & Co. It is that culture, unique to McKinsey which sets the firm apart from virtually any other business organization and which often mystifies even those who engage the services of "The Firm," as its members have long called it.[14]

Another example of clashing corporate cultures occurred when GM acquired Electronic Data Systems (EDS). Former GM CEO, Roger Smith, allowed EDS to keep their corporate culture, GM management then transferred 10,000 employees from GM to EDS. The GM employees had a difficult time dealing with EDS' corporate culture which was rad-

ically different from GM's culture. In fact, there was a near revolt. The GM employees couldn't deal with the strict rules and regulations of EDS; for example, no tassels on shoes, no alcoholic drinks at lunch, and so on. Over 600 of the transferred employees quit.

One example of cultural change occurred at Cadillac Motors division of GM. They focused on employee involvement, quality, and customer satisfaction. This required a change in a culture that was individual and union rule oriented, to one that valued teamwork and employee involvement as a source of competitive advantage. The employees were empowered to take responsibility for making things happen.[15] Indeed, many of the once-great corporations such as IBM, Sears, and General Motors, previously thought of as model organizations, incapable of losing their dominating position in the marketplace; almost met ruin because of their cultures' reluctance to change.

Cultures often clash following corporate mergers, downsizings, or other restructurings. Mitchell Marks notes:

> Mergers and internal restructurings bring together work forces with diverse characteristics and firms and business units with diverse cultures. In the case of international mergers, diverse national cultures also are combined. Successful integration following a major reorganization—be it a domestic merger, an international merger, or an internal restructuring—requires that employee and cultural diversity be carefully managed as products, services, policies, and structures are integrated.[16]

Following a merger, differences in corporate beliefs concerning gender, race, geography, religion, and nationalism can manifest a non-productive "we" versus "they" situation if all parties involved are not made aware of, and sensitive to, the cultural differences.

Creating a Winning Culture

What makes for excellence in the management of an organization? Today's key words are flexibility and innovation. Organizations are being forced to make dramatic changes just to remain competitive. These changes such as improving product quality, increasing speed of responsiveness, and expanding customer orientation are so basic and fundamental that managers must alter the corporate culture. However, cultural change implies a change in the basic values, in the hearts and minds of the individual employee. The "reengineering," or the radical redesign of how businesses are organized and operate, requires starting from scratch, with a clean sheet of paper. Complete redesign of a business' core processes virtually requires significant changes in the organization's culture.[17]

Peters and Waterman, in their first book, *In Search of Excellence* studied the practices of 43 companies that are often used as examples of well-managed organizations, including 3M, McDonalds, and Hewlett-Packard. The book's basic message was that U.S. organizations can regain their competitive edge by paying more attention to the culture and to people—customers and employees—and by developing those core skills and values that employees know how to do best.

In Search of Excellence was a response to management's emphasis on traditional structures and values and on "number crunching" as an answer to all problems. Perhaps the most important message is that the excellent companies of today will not necessarily be the well-run companies of tomorrow. An excellent company must develop a core culture which leads to innovation and adaptation to the changing environment. At 3M, McDonald's, and Hewlett-Packard, for example, the culture and values that drive the behavior of employees are harmonious with the market-driven strategies of the companies. In their later books both Tom Peters and Bob Waterman suggest that the only excellent firms are those that are rapidly changing.

The Impact of Key Factors

In order to create a winning culture, managers need to adapt their managerial style, values, and goals to fit the changing demands of the environment.

As we move into the twenty-first century, the question is not "Will corporate cultures continue to exist?" but rather, "What type of corporate culture will be most effective in

enabling our company to survive and excel? To understand the performance of an organization, one must first investigate the corporate culture."[18] The focus of OD is to improve an organization's self-renewal process so managers can quickly initiate changes to the corporate culture to meet new problems which are emerging. Tomorrow's leaders will be those who are most flexible and innovative.

There are several key factors which organizations need to be aware of to improve the level of effectiveness:

- *Create a Vision for the Future.* A shared vision provides direction, focus, and commitment. Harold Leavett has termed this action "pathfinding," and it involves the dreamer, the innovator, the creator, and the entrepreneur.[19] Some very successful organizations began with a vision. Steve Jobs at Apple Computer, for example, dreamed of a computer for everyone, "one person, one computer" as a way toward a better world. Fred Smith at Federal Express bet his personal fortune on overnight delivery, on the need for faster information processing in a high-speed world. These visions are compelling and involve all members in striving toward goals: vision provides meaning.

- *Develop a Model for Change.* Total organization change often starts in one unit or sub-culture of the organization. When Steve Jobs started to develop the Macintosh at Apple, he started with a handpicked team of young dedicated designers, whom he termed the "pirates," working under the black skull and crossbones flag. Similarly, at a large utility, one department manager instituted an MBO program even though most corporate managers said it would never work. This change led to increased performance of this department, and ultimately the whole organization was motivated to use this system. Though it may be coincidental, this manager is now the president of his company.

- *Reward Changes.* One of the basic underlying concepts of motivation is that people tend to behave in ways that provide rewards or reinforcement for them. If the system still rewards the old culture, then it won't make sense for people to change. This, of course, includes pay and promotion, but other incentives as well. For example, in Japan, Sharp Corporation rewards top performers by putting them on an elite "gold badge" project team. At Apple, awards and recognition were used to gain employee involvement and people were willing to work incredible hours to bring out products. They wore T-shirts that celebrated their dedication like: "Working ninety-hours a week and loving it."[20]

Corporate cultures are the very essence of organizations. Whether effective or ineffective, organizational cultures exist—usually reflecting the personality of the top executive. Corporate cultures often affect the success or failure of the organization and are determined in various ways by all employees. There is considerable debate over whether changing these deeply held values is possible. In the next sections, we examine cultural resistance to change and some power tools suggested to use in change programs.

Cultural Resistance to Change

Changing a corporate culture is not easy. Culture emerges out of the shared behaviors of organization members and working relationships which have developed over time. Consequently, it takes time for a cultural transformation to take effect. Many firms, confronted with international competition and technological change, have no choice but to slim down. Though accelerated by recession, this trend is likely to continue even after economic growth returns. Whether it is called "reengineering," "downsizing," or "delayering," the goals are the same: to eliminate levels of middle managers in order to delegate responsibility to those actually making products or dealing with the customers. Ideally, companies should emerge from these reorganizations more flexible, entrepreneurial, and effective. But, unless they find new ways to motivate the remaining employees, most managers are unlikely to achieve the gains that are supposed to justify such drastic changes.[21]

A culture can also prevent a company from remaining competitive or adapting to a changing environment. UPS has radically changed its corporate culture. After losing business to such aggressive competitors as Federal Express Corp. and Roadway Package System, UPS Chief Executive Kent C. "Oz" Nelson has been overhauling the way the world's largest package carrier does business. Gone is the we-know-what's-best-for-you attitude that was UPS's hallmark for decades. In its place, UPS stresses customer satisfaction. Flexible pickup

and delivery items and customized shipment plans are available to corporate clients. UPS also offers discount prices to volume shippers.[22]

UPS is one example of the importance of culture in managing a company's strategy. As a result, changing the culture to successfully implement a strategy is critical. "OD in Practice" illustrates this difficulty at Procter & Gamble.

OD IN PRACTICE:
NO MORE MR. NICE GUY—REINVENTING THE CORPORATE CULTURE[23]

Procter & Gamble, once considered very slow and cumbersome, is pushing authority down, speeding up decisions, and becoming more responsive to its customers. P & G is reinventing its corporate culture and undergoing a radical restructuring under chairman, Edwin Artzt. In the process, P & G is reinventing the packaged goods industry for the year 2000 and beyond. But can a large and bureaucratic organization make these radical changes without totally destroying the culture that made it great?

Traditional Values

P & G has been known as a corporation with traditional, old-fashioned values. The organization man in the gray flannel suit feels right at home and hierarchy and tradition reign—drinking at lunch, wearing light colored socks, or red suspenders is discouraged. Middle managers rarely make key decisions and the decision process often travels through several management layers. But as John G. Smale, former CEO commented, "You can't be old fashioned and be successful in the markets in which we compete."

A New Vision

In an effort to imprint Ed Artzt's view of what the P & G culture should be like, new hires spend three to four days at P & G college within their first year. There are additional courses for first time supervisors and for higher level managers. In total, some 4,000 employees per year attend courses on the art of competition. Like most of Mr. Artzt's new ideas, the college, which he calls combat training, is designed to focus on winning in the marketplace. In the first two years of restructuring, Procter & Gamble has reorganized its marketing, sales, manufacturing, and distribution.

Driving the reorganization is the long-term vision to become the market leader in each of P & G's 349 product categories. As part of the reorganization, CEO Edwin Artzt is changing the vaunted brand management system. Only one of every three new hires ever makes it through the four-year process to become a brand manager, a position responsible for every part of their brand's marketing, advertising, and development. But Procter & Gamble's brand managers were so focused on one single product that they often lost sight of the total market. This led to the creation of the category manager position who has total profit and loss responsibility for an entire product line. The category manager has the authority to make quick decisions, which is an attempt to create small stand-alone businesses within the corporation.

No more Mr. Nice Guy at P & G

Is Ed Artzt's like-it-or-leave-it management style doing more harm than good? By now P & G knows their CEO doesn't play by the same rules as his predecessors. Gone is the low profile, gray suited leadership of P & G. Ed Artzt wants results. He aims to build a tougher, faster, more global P & G, and to do this, he is promoting individual accountability and turning back the clock from the "team approach" of recent years. He has overhauled P & G's corporate training program in favor of a squash the competition version. He sees lightning quick reflexes as essential at a time when P & G's rivals are globalizing, streamlining, and investing in innovation. Vows Mr. Artzt, "We are going to make a quantum leap in the quality and speed of our execution."

Edwin Artzt, CEO and leader of the change, who spends 60 to 70 percent of his time on the road says, "I give everybody the opportunity for input, and—consensus or no consensus—off we go." He has earned the nickname, "the prince of darkness," because he comes in, makes changes, and moves to the next problem. Artzt's goal is for a new management structure, a fresh global approach, an enduring corporate culture, and a commitment to the long term.

Most of Artzt's strategies for dealing with these competitive pressures make sense even to his critics. But many inside the company think he is pushing his agenda too hard. Some top employees have left in the past year, and many who remain "feel their behavior is being changed, but their heart isn't being changed." They do not feel enrolled in the vision. Critics also argue that Artzt is abandoning many of the progressive changes of an era, which brought a more questioning multi-functional, people oriented approach to the business. Unfortunately, many of these critics have either been silenced or have left the company. Although he insists he is a proponent of teams, Artzt wants them to have explicit missions and clearer goals for individual team members.

Questions

1. Do you agree that P & G needs to make changes? Why?
2. Do you see any problems in trying to change the old line culture? Why?
3. Do you see any OD or organization renewal approaches being used?

The need for devising and executing better strategies is becoming readily apparent. Recession, deregulation, technological upheavals, social factors, foreign competition, and markets that seem to emerge and vanish as quickly as they come have increased the pressure on companies to be flexible and adaptable. One of the biggest stumbling blocks on the path to adaptation is often an inappropriate culture.[24] Dennis Nowlin, manager of executive development at 3M, expressed this idea when he said, "Obviously, when the vision of the future is created, you have to let go of the present and the past. We have a very strong culture and letting go was a significant challenge in itself."[25]

POWER TOOLS FOR CHANGE

Management changes to improve strategy are more likely to succeed if the factors that shape the culture can be identified and managed. In a comparison of high-innovation companies with low-innovation ones, Rosabeth Moss Kanter describes how *change masters and corporate entrepreneurs* are allowed to flourish in high-innovation companies.[26] Three organization **power tools** are required in the adaptive organization: information, support, and resources.

Information. The first tool is to provide people with information or an ability to gather information. People feel free to go outside of their own department to gather information and open communication patterns across departments. General Electric and Wang Laboratories have rules prohibiting closed meetings. Other organizations like Hewlett-Packard and Digital Equipment have information exchange meetings that cut across employee levels. "MBWA" (Management by Wandering Around) is an expression at Hewlett-Packard is increasingly becoming a practice for managers at all levels. Making information available at all levels increases employee motivation and permits faster decision making.

One new trend is termed, **open book management**, used by companies such as Allstate, MCI, and Harris Semiconductor. Open book organizations teach employees to understand accounting and financial statements and to use that knowledge in their work and planning. The basic element involves getting key information to employees so that job decisions can be made by work teams.[27]

Support. The second tool is to provide the corporate entrepreneur with the support and necessary "go ahead" from higher management as well as the cooperation of peers and subordinates. If the project will cut across organization lines, support and collaboration from other departments is needed. For example, interdepartment meetings and training sessions that normally bring people together can provide the opportunity to build support for projects. Organizations can remove the fear to fail and provide a climate that supports people in taking risks. At 3M, management encourages risk-taking and supports research—knowing that some projects will fail. They feel that an intolerant management kills initiative.

Resources. The third tool is providing the resources, including funds, staff, equipment, and materials to carry out the project. One normal process of funding innovation is through budgetary channels, but traditionally this process is too time consuming to respond to the project in a timely manner. Some organizations support projects from bootlegged funds budgeted for other projects. Lockheed Aircraft is particularly known for its "skunk works" projects, and 3M normally requires a certain percent of a funded project be devoted to bootlegged projects. "Venture capital" and "innovation banks" also provide support for innovative projects. W. L. Gore and Associates, another example of a highly adaptive company, does not have employees; it has instead associates, and the company encourages people to develop their ideas into projects.

In one study, Don Harvey and Richard Wald investigated an OD program aimed at changing the culture of an old-line manufacturing company. They found that while high-tech firms operate in a more dynamic environment and require frequent changes, an equally important problem involves implementing change in the old-line, traditional companies.[28] They reported that such changes are difficult and take time. Change does not take place quickly in a strongly established culture. Some of the key factors in changing an ingrained culture are shown in Table 3.1.

Any changes to the organization culture must focus on what people value and what they do. If the OD consultant can get members to behave in new ways, then cultural change is possible.

Table 3.1 Key Factors in Cultural Change

- **Understand the old culture**. Managers can't change their course until they know where they are.
- **Encourage change in employees**. Reinforce people in changing the old culture and those with new ideas.
- **Follow outstanding units**. Recognize outstanding units in the organization, and use them as a model for change.
- **Don't impose cultural change**. Let employees be involved in finding their own new approaches to change and an improved culture will emerge.
- **Lead with a vision**. The vision provides a guiding principle for change, but must be bought into by employees.
- **Large-scale change takes time**. It may take three to five years for significant, organization-wide cultural change to take effect.
- **Live the new culture**. Top management values , behaviors, and actions speak louder than words.

The Goals and Values of OD

Now that a macro approach to organizational change has been described, let us examine some of the micro issues involved in change: the underlying goals, assumptions, and values basic to most OD programs. The ultimate purpose of increasing an organization's ability to adapt to a changing environment is to make it more effective. What makes an organization effective or ineffective? Etzioni has suggested that effectiveness is the degree of goal achievement or, as he further elaborates, the amount of resources an organization needs to use in order to produce units of output.[29]

In general, OD programs are aimed at three basic organizational dimensions which affect performance. **Managerial Effectiveness** refers to the accomplishment of specific organizational goals and objectives, or "doing the right thing." If organizations are using their resources to attain long-term goals, the managers are being effective. The closer an organization comes to achieving its strategic goals, the more effective the organization. **Managerial Efficiency** refers to the ratio of output (results) to input (resources), or "doing the things right." The higher this proportion, the more efficient the manager. When managers are able to minimize the cost of resources used to attain performance, they are managing efficiently. An organization may thus be efficient, but not effective, or vice versa. The third factor may be termed **motivational climate,** consisting of the set of employee attitudes and morale which influence the level of performance.

Three other criteria as indicators of organizational effectiveness or health are:

- *Adaptability*—the ability to solve problems and to react with flexibility to changing environmental demands.
- *A sense of identity and vision*—knowledge and insight on the part of the organization of what its goals are, and what it is to do.
- *Capacity to test reality*—the ability to search out and accurately and correctly interpret the real properties of the environment, particularly those that have relevance for the functioning of the organization.[30]

Some OD consultants have suggested that effectiveness comes from conditions that permit the integration of organization goals with individual goals. In a similar vein, others indicate that organizational excellence is derived from the integration of concern for production with concern for people. **Organizational effectiveness** is the end result of an OD program. It is a multiple rather than a singular goal, involving all of these factors.

Organizations that are reacting to change become increasingly slow to adapt as the rate of change increases. Renewing management results in a source of organizational flexibility, thus allowing increased adaptation to changing conditions and a more effective organization. OD seeks to improve the anticipative nature of the culture and to improve the way the organization's mission is accomplished. Because of the impact of corporate culture, the OD practitioner must also examine the relationship between the values of OD and those of the client system, as noted in the following.

OD Professional Values and Ethics

Almost every organizational decision involves an ethical question, such as how people should treat others, conflicts of interest, and so on. In attempting to change organizations, **OD consultants** must consider the ethical consequences of various actions and develop a set of ethical standards to guide them when competing interests collide.

There is also the question of professional values. OD is an emerging profession, and its practitioners tend to describe themselves as professionals. Even though the OD discipline may be classified as having some degree of professionalization, the individuals working in the field may vary greatly in their **professionalism**. By professionalism we refer to the internalization of a value system that is a part of the concept of the profession.

The professionalism of an individual depends on the degree to which certain values pertinent to the profession have been internalized. Although there is some disagreement, four areas appear to be important.

1. *Expertise*. The professional requires some *expertise*. This includes specialized knowledge and skills that can be obtained only through training (usually academic).
2. *Autonomy*. The professional claims *autonomy*. Professionals reserve the right to decide how their function is to be performed and to be free from restrictions.
3. *Commitment*. Professionals feel a *commitment* to the discipline. They are more likely to identify with members of their profession in other organizations than with their own organization.
4. Code of ethics. Finally, there is a *responsibility to society* for the maintenance of professional standards of work. They adhere to professional self-discipline and a code of ethics.[31]

In any program of organizational change, the OD practitioner must take into account the individual members whose lives and livelihood could be impacted by the change being introduced. Lou Holtz, (football coach, University of Notre Dame) has suggested three principles which are useful to OD professionals as well:

- Do what is right.
- Do your best.
- Treat others the way you want to be treated.

OD Implementation Issues

One important factor to recognize is that the success of the OD program is, to a large extent, dependent upon the fit between OD values and those of the organization. One of the key issues to be resolved between the OD practitioner and the client concerns the relative value orientations of each party. These include beliefs about people, the methods used to reach change goals, and the purpose of the change program.

There is a value system underlying OD approaches. These values emphasize increasing individual growth and effectiveness by creating an organizational climate that develops

human potential together with achieving organizational goals. The value systems underlying OD have been derived from a number of basic ideas and approaches, including those of Chris Argyris, Warren Bennis, Abraham Maslow, Douglas McGregor, Frederick Perls, and Carl Rogers. Wendell L. French and Cecil H. Bell, Jr. have commented:

> Organization development activities rest on a number of assumptions about people as individuals, in groups, and in total systems, about the transactional nature of organization improvement, and about values. These assumptions tend to be humanistic, developmental, and optimistic. Assumptions and values held by change agents need to be made explicit, both for enhancing working relationships with clients, and for continuous testing through practice and research.[32]

To achieve the OD goals, the consultant has to consider certain ethical or value implications of his or her role in initiating a change program. There are a range of these ethical issues associated with an OD program; including:

The degree of value congruence. The OD consultant's values may not be compatible with the organization culture of the client system. The OD consultant brings a certain set of values to the client organization, which has its own basic values and mission. The question, then, is the degree to which the consultant's personal values are congruent with those of the client. For example, should an OD change agent help an organization doing biochemical warfare research to become more effective if his or her personal value system is opposed to the organization's methods or mission?

Many OD consultants feel that this is an initial issue to be considered prior to accepting any consulting relationship. If the client's goals are unacceptable, he or she should not try to make a system more effective. To do so, these consultants feel, would be unethical.

Others have argued that such companies are legal and follow the directions chosen by elected governmental representatives, and therefore organization development is valid in these situations. OD has been applied in defense organizations and in the military, and some practitioners believe that OD should have a value-free orientation. Just as a doctor treats both friend and foe, the OD consultant works to help organizations of all types and the individuals within these organizations to develop into a more healthy orientation.

A related issue concerns which client systems the consultant chooses to help or not to help. Some OD consultants offer their professional assistance to all potential clients regardless of financial remuneration; others limit themselves to client systems that can afford their professional fees. (See B.C. comic strip.)

The Politics of Change. Since organizations are political systems, another ethical consideration for the OD consultant is the question of choice in deciding to implement a change program. The decision to initiate an OD program is usually made by the top management

Source: B.C. By permission of Johnny Hart and Creators Syndicate, Inc.

group, yet it is likely to affect all members and parts of the organization. At one major company, for example, the top executives and the OD consultant decided on the OD program, which involved all members. Lower-level members may or may not have had a real choice regarding their participation in the program. If organization members do not have a choice, the consultant may tend to become an instrument for imposing change upon the rest of the organization.

One example that illustrates this issue is reported by William J. Crockett, concerning his experience in introducing change into the U.S. Department of State.

> One of the first things that happened to me was a summons from Robert Kennedy, the Attorney General, to come to his office. There was no greeting, no small talk, and no chance for response by me except, "yes, sir," to his cryptic monologue. He said: "*First of all get your loyalties straight.* No matter whom you think you work for, the President appointed you, and he is your boss. He will expect your absolute loyalty. *Second, get your job straight.* The State Department must be made to be loyal and responsive to the President. It must become more positive and proactive. It must be made to assume a leadership position in the Foreign Affairs Community. Your job is to make this happen. And thirdly, do you know how to make this happen . . . ?"
>
> While I was trying to think up an answer, he held up his hand to silence my response and added, "*You will make it happen* by giving orders and firing people who don't produce."[33]

Organization politics are a factor in any change program, because change has the potential to disrupt the current balance of power among members and units. The OD consultant cannot afford to ignore the reality of power and politics in implementing change.

The Ethics of Control. A third issue involves which of the goals of an OD program is likely to be given precedence. As noted earlier, change programs generally are aimed at improved effectiveness, efficiency, and participant satisfaction. The question then arises: Which, or to what degree is emphasis to be placed on each goal? Are organizational or individual goals to take precedence? Although this sounds relatively simple in theory, in practice the executives who are paying for the OD program are frequently under pressure to improve efficiency and profitability, even though they also seek increased participant satisfaction and morale. The question is: How can the OD consultant help improve the productive efficiency of the organization and at the same time improve the quality of job existence for its members?

So one challenge for the OD consultant is to try to develop a balanced intervention—one where member rights and well-being are considered, as well as improvements in productivity. Underlying the challenges and dilemmas of OD are a set of values about the nature of human beings and their positions in an organizational context as shown in Table 3.2. In this environment of change, OD practitioners face both exciting challenges and serious dilemmas over how to fully meet the changing values and processes of change.

Table 3.2 OD Values

- *Respect for people.* Individuals are allowed to function as human beings, perceived as being responsible, authentic, and caring. People should be treated with dignity and respect, not just as resources.
- *Trust and support.* Develop an effective and healthy organization characterized by trust, authenticity, openness, and a supportive climate.
- *Power equalization.* Provide opportunities for people to influence their work environment. Effective organizations are those with less reliance on hierarchical authority and control.
- *Confrontation.* Provide an environment of open communication where problems aren't swept under the rug. Issues and strategies should be openly confronted and decided.
- *Participation.* Provide opportunities for each individual to develop their full potential. The more that people who will be affected by a change are involved in the decisions leading to that change, the more they will be committed to implementing those changes.

There has been a growing concern about the philosophical issues surrounding the field of OD. These ethical issues arise from basic inconsistencies between the values of OD practitioners and those held by client organizations. The technology and value system of OD is itself undergoing change and revitalization; hence the feelings expressed by one OD practitioner, Jerry B. Harvey, who feels that OD consultants are becoming trapped in the rituals of their own discipline.[34]

In summary, the objectives of OD are to create organizational cultures that are more effective, more potent, more innovative, and better equipped to accomplish both organization and member goals.

REVIEW QUESTIONS

1. Describe or compare the corporate cultures of organizations you have worked in. What makes one more effective than another?

2. Compare and contrast management efficiency and effectiveness.

3. Identify the key factors in cultural change.

KEY WORDS AND CONCEPTS

Define and be able to use the following:

Corporate Culture
Excellence
Managerial Effectiveness
Managerial Efficiency
Motivational Climate
OD Consultant

OD Ethics
OD Professional Values
Open Book Management
Organizational Effectiveness
Professionalism
Three Power Tools
Winning Culture

OD SKILLS SIMULATION 3.1
DOWNSIZING: A CONSENSUS-SEEKING ACTIVITY

Total time suggested 1 hour.

A. PURPOSE

The purpose of this simulation is to examine the interdependence among team members and to provide insights into the concept of culture. To study culture, we may examine the culture of a group which share certain cultural traits. The goals include:

1. To compare decisions made by individuals with those made by the group.
2. To practice effective consensus-seeking techniques.
3. To gain insights into the concept of cultural values.

B. PROCEDURES

Step 1. Prior to class, form into groups of five members, each group constituting an executive committee. Assign each member of your group as one of the committee members. (Extras act as observers.) Use Individual Decision Work Sheet, or if your instructor prefers, use this format for a Lotus or Excel spreadsheet and bring it to class. Observers may use Observer Form located at the end of this simulation to gather data on group process.

1. Executive Vice President, Marketing
2. Executive Vice President, Finance
3. Executive Vice President, Manufacturing
4. Executive Vice President, Human Resource Management
5. Executive Vice President, Research and Development
6. Observer (extras)

Before class, individually read the employee profiles that follow and in the Individual Decision Worksheet rank-order the 10 employees on the work sheet from "1" for least likely to "10" for most likely to be expendable. Participants are to enter their ranking in column (1) on the Executive Committee Decision Work Sheet (See p. 82).

Step 2. Executive Committee Meeting

Through group discussion, exploration, and examination, try to reach a *consensus decision* reflecting the integrated thinking and consensus of all members. Remember, a consensus decision involves reaching mutual agreement by discussion until all agree on the final decision.

Follow these instructions for reaching consensus:

1. Try to reach the best possible decision, but at the same time defending the importance of your department.
2. Avoid changing your mind simply to reach agreement and to avoid conflict, but support solutions with which you are able to agree.
3. Avoid "conflict-reducing" techniques, such as majority vote, averaging, or trading in reaching your decision.
4. View differences of opinion as a help rather than a hindrance in decision making. *better decision*

At this point, meet together as the Executive Committee and enter your results in column (2) on the Executive Committee Decision Work Sheet. (See page 82)

Time suggested for Step 2: 35 minutes.

Step 3. Each team lists its results on the blackboard, and the instructor posts the actual performance ranking. Enter the performance ranking in column (3).

Time suggested for Step 3: 5 minutes.

Step 4. Using the answers given by the instructor, score your individual and team answers by subtracting the Personal Ranking (column 1) and Committee Ranking (column 2) each from the Actual Performance Ranking (column 3). Then record the absolute difference as the Individual Score (column 4) and Team Score (column 5), respectively. By totaling the points, an individual and a team score can be calculated. Column (4) provides an indication of the individual participant's "correctness," and column (5) provides an equivalent measure of each group's performance.

Individuals and teams can be compared based on these scores. However, individuals have varying degrees of knowledge and the final score may not reflect how decisions were made during the team discussion.

Time suggested for Step 4: 5 minutes.

Step 5a. Team members individually complete the Value Survey and Conflict Survey Forms. (See page 83)

Step 5b. As a team, discuss and come to team rating on the Value and Conflict Survey Forms. Observer feeds back information on team process using the Observer Form as a guide. (See page 84)

Time suggested for Step 5: 10 minutes.

Step 6. The instructor leads a discussion of the activity, letting each team explain its scores on the Value Survey and Conflict Survey forms. Consider the following points and compare results for each team:

1. The consensus process within each group: things that went well and difficulties, whether the rules were followed, and the dynamics behind the posted scores.
2. The extent to which efficiency, effectiveness, and member satisfaction was emphasized in the meeting.
3. The culture that will likely develop at Delta as a result of the decisions made in the meeting.
4. How could an OD program help Delta and your management team?

Time suggested for Step 6: 5 minutes.

DOWNSIZING: DELTA CORPORATION

Delta, started in 1988, is a small, family-owned firm in the microcomputer business. The company grew rapidly because of its microcomputer boards, disk drives, optical disks, tape backup drives, and innovative approaches to solving computer hardware problems. Both managers and workers have put in long hours, often sacrificing their personal time to get the company off the ground.

Unfortunately, a significant downturn in the economy has caused a reduction in sales, and it is increasingly apparent that some adjustments will have to be made if the company is to survive.

Your committee will have to make a series of recommendations for a downsizing (lay-off) of employees, all of whom are married, of the same age (28), and all with no previous experience before joining Delta.

The president has asked you to examine the personal information of the 10 employees in the company who are most expendable. They are all good employees but because of reduced sales and earnings and declining economy, Delta needs to be prepared for a ten percent reduction in work force (RIF). Therefore, you are meeting to rank-order from "1" for least likely, to "10" for most likely to be "riffed." There are at least 11 employees in each of the five departments. The employees other than those on the list given to you have been with the company at least eight years, and it is not feasible to RIF them at this time.

Among the criteria you may want to consider are:

1. Education
2. Performance
3. Seniority
4. Technical ability
5. Attitude
6. Leadership
7. Effectiveness
8. Efficiency
9. Job function
10. Social ability

EMPLOYEE PROFILES

Finance

Gwen—seniority three and one-half years; four-year college education; has performed about average on annual appraisal (75 percent); average technical abilities and leadership potential; a steady, grinding worker; works long hours, has been working on employee benefit plan for two years; is a nonsmoker and nondrinker; has frequently complained about working with cigarette smokers.

Hal— seniority five and one-half years; four-year college education; has been rated average and above in annual appraisals (80 percent); high technical abilities; average leadership; always in on Saturday mornings; frequently works through lunch hour; has been working on committee to computerize payroll for past 18 months; is well liked and gets along with fellow workers; is a very neat and stylish dresser.

Research and Development

Carole—Ph.D. in engineering; seniority two and one-half years; has been above-average research engineer in performance appraisal (90 percent); high technical and leadership abilities; works unusual hours (sometimes works late at night, then doesn't come in until noon the next day); developed patent on a new solid-state circuit device last year; seldom attends social events, and is said to be friendly but often disagrees and conflicts with fellow workers.

Dave—M.S. in engineering; seniority three and one-half years; has been average to above average on performance appraisal (75 percent); average technical abilities; average leadership; works steady 8 AM to 5 PM, is working on several R&D projects but none yet completed; always ready for a coffee break or joke-telling session; is well liked by coworkers; and never complains about bad assignments.

Marketing

Tony—M.B.A. degree; seniority two years; has been rated as performing better than 90 percent on performance appraisal; high technical abilities; above average leadership; works erratic hours (often comes into office at 9:30 and frequently plays golf on Wednesday afternoons); sold the highest number of product units in his product line; seldom socializes with fellow workers; and is often criticized because his desk is messy and disorganized, piled with correspondence and unanswered memos.

Ken—four-year college degree; seniority 18 months; has been rated an above-average to outstanding performer (80 percent); high technical abilities; average leadership has been criticized for not making all his sales calls, but has a good sales record and developed advertising campaign for new product line, although a good bowler refuses to bowl on company team; and has been rumored to drink quite heavily on occasion.

Human Resource Management

Eduardo—four-year college degree; seniority 18 months; has been rated above average as performer (80 percent); average technical abilities; high leadership; is frequently away from desk and often misses meetings; has designed and implemented a new management development program; is well liked although frequently has differences of opinion with line managers; and often takes long coffee breaks and lunch hours.

Frank—two-year college degree; seniority four years; has been rated average to above average as performer (70 percent); low technical abilities; above average leadership; works long hours; regularly attends all meetings; has been redesigning performance appraisal systems for past two years; is involved in many company activities; belongs to Toast Masters, Inc.; and is known as a friendly, easy going guy.

Manufacturing

Irv—four-year college degree; seniority 15 months; rated an outstanding performer (90 percent); high technical abilities; moderate leadership; has been criticized for not attending committee meetings; designed and implemented the computerized production control process; does not socialize with fellow employees; and is known as a sloppy dresser (often wearing white or red socks with a suit).

Jackie—high school; seniority six years; rated an average performer (75 percent); average technical abilities; low leadership; always attends meetings; works steady 8 AM to 5 PM hours and Saturday mornings; has chaired committee to improve plant safety for past two years; participates in all social events; plays on company bowling and softball teams; and is known for a very neat, organized office.

EXECUTIVE COMMITTEE DECISION WORKSHEET

Employee	(1) Personal Ranking	(2) Committee Ranking	(3) Actual Performance Ranking	(4) Individual Score	(5) Team Score
Gwen			10 1 394		
Hal			3 8 546		
Carole			1 10 582		
Dave			6 5 506		
Tony			2 9 555		
Ken			5 6 508		
Eduardo			9 2 476		
Frank			8 3 478		
Irv			7 4 496		
Jack			4 7 522		
			Total Scores		

INDIVIDUAL DECISION WORK SHEET

Employee	Department	Education	Performance	Seniority	Technical Ability	Attitude	Leadership	Effectiveness	Efficiency	Job Function	Social Ability	Total
Gwen	Finance											
Hal	Finance											
Carole	Res. & Dev.											
Dave	Res. & Dev.											
Tony	Marketing											
Ken	Marketing											
Eduardo	Personnel											
Frank	Personnel											
Irv	Manufacturing											
Jackie	Manufacturing											

VALUES SURVEY FORM

Below are several value orientations. Based on the following scale, individually rate the values at Delta based on your team's decision. Record your choice in the left column (Step 5a) and record the team rating in the right column (Step 5b).

```
::      :      :      :      :      :      :      ::
  1      2      3      4      5      6      7
Not at All           Somewhat             Very
Characteristic       Characteristic       Characteristic
```

RATING THE COMPANY

Values	Individual Rating	Team Rating
1. High Productivity	_____	_____
2. Effective Relationships	_____	_____
3. High Quality	_____	_____
4. High Achievement	_____	_____
5. Seniority	_____	_____
6. Time Consciousness	_____	_____
7. Dress/Neatness	_____	_____
8. Amount of Education	_____	_____
9. Positive Attitudes	_____	_____
10. High Professionalism	_____	_____

CONFLICT SURVEY FORM

Rate your team, individually, on how differences were resolved during your team's meeting. Record your choice in the left column (Step 5a) and your team rating in the right column (Step 5b).

```
::      :      :      :      :      :      :      ::
  1      2      3      4      5      6      7
Not at All           Somewhat             Very
Characteristic       Characteristic       Characteristic
```

RATING THE TEAM!

Factor	Individual Rating	Team Rating
1. Not Afraid of Conflict	_____	_____
2. Express Differences	_____	_____
3. Ignore Disagreements	_____	_____
4. Open Discussion	_____	_____
5. Analysis of Differences	_____	_____
6. Debate of Issues	_____	_____
7. Trust	_____	_____
8. Confrontation	_____	_____
9. Encourage Openess	_____	_____
10. Flexibility	_____	_____

OBSERVER FORM

Name: _____

Position: _____

Behaviors

1. _____
2. _____
3. _____

Name: _____

Position: _____

Behaviors

1. _____
2. _____
3. _____

Name: _____

Position: _____

Behaviors

1. _____
2. _____
3. _____

Name: _____

Position: _____

Behaviors

1. _____
2. _____
3. _____

Name: _____

Position: _____

Behaviors

1. _____
2. _____
3. _____

Name: _____

Position: _____

Behaviors

1. _____
2. _____
3. _____

NOTE: Draw direction arrows for communication flow. Identify behaviors shown by participants.

CASE 3: THE DIM LIGHTING CO.

The Dim Lighting Company is a subsidiary of a major producer of electrical products. Each subsidiary division operates as a profit center and reports to regional, group, and product vice presidents in corporate headquarters. The Dim Lighting subsidiary produces electrical lamps, employing about 2,000 workers. The general manager is Jim West, an M.B.A. from Wharton, who has been running this subsidiary successfully for the past five years. However, last year the division failed to realize its operating targets, as profit margins dropped by 15 percent. In developing next year's budget and profit plan, Jim West feels that he is under pressure to have a good year because two bad years in a row might hurt his long-term potential for advancement. (See Exhibit 1.)

EXHIBIT 1 The Organizational Environment

DOCTOR SPINKS, DIRECTOR OF R&D

Leon Spinks, director of R&D, was hired by West three years ago, after resigning from a major competitor. Dr. Spinks has received a number of awards from various scientific societies and his group of scientists and engineers respect his technical competence and have a high level of morale.

Although he is recognized as a talented scientist, other managers feel that Spinks is often autocratic, strong-minded, and impatient. Dr. Spinks left his former company because management lacked creativity and innovation in R&D.

THE PROPOSAL

Dr. Spinks has submitted a budget request for a major research project: the micro-miniaturization of lighting sources, to greatly reduce energy requirements. He sees this as the Lamp of the Future. The proposed budget would require $250,000 per year for two years, plus another $300,000 to begin production. Jim West immediately contacted corporate headquarters, and although his idea was highly praised, they were reluctant to expand any share in the proposed project. Dr. Spinks feels the project has a 70 percent chance of success, and will develop a net cash flow of $1 million by the third year.

THE BUDGET MEETING

West called a meeting of his management group on Wednesday morning to discuss the proposed budget. Dr. Spinks presented a very rational and high-powered sale pitch for his project. He suggested that the energy crunch had long-term implications and that if they failed to move into new technologies, they would be competitively obsolete.

Carl Preston, accountant, presented a financial analysis of the proposed project, noting the high risk, the uncertain results, and the length of time before it would contribute to operating profits. "These scientists are prima donnas, who can afford to wait for long-term results. Unfortunately, if we don't do something about the bottom line right now, we may not be here to enjoy it," he noted.

Bill Boswell, production manager, agreed with Preston: "We need new machinery for our production line also, and that has a very direct payback."

Pete Newell, marketing, agreed with Dr. Spinks: "I don't feel we can put our heads in the sand. If we don't keep up competitively, how will our salespeople be able to keep selling obsolete lighting products? Besides, I'm not sure that all of Carl's figures are completely accurate in measuring the actual return on this low-energy project." A stormy debate followed, with heated arguments both for and against the project put forth, until West called the meeting to a halt.

Later in his office, thinking it over, he considered the situation. Going ahead with the micro-miniaturization project was a big gamble with high uncertainty. But if he decided against it, it was quite possible that Dr. Spinks would resign, which would shatter the R&D department he had worked so hard to assemble.

Case Ananlysis Form follows on page 87

SUMMARY

• **Change**. Change is an inevitable consequence of operating in a dynamic environment. For OD consultants and managers it is important to recognize that organization changes can be initiated by organization members (renewing) or as a reaction to external forces (reactive). This chapter focuses on the idea that a key aspect of implementing change is the need to institutionalize the change into organizational value systems. Consequently, one important element in implementing a change program is the corporate culture.

• **Culture**. Whether change is anticipative or reactive, it is likely to be most successful when the organization proceeds with a planned approach which takes into account the nature of the culture. In recent years, corporate culture has been recognized as a pervasive force influencing organization effectiveness. Culture has been defined as the shared values and behaviors of organizational members and represents a key factor in implementing planned change in organizations.

• **Teamwork**. You have had an opportunity in the OD Skills Simulation to experience and observe a situation of organization change. You probably found that initiating planned change is not always as easy as it looks. You may

have discovered that the functioning of a group is difficult to analyze, and gaining acceptance of change strategies presents difficulties. In reflecting upon the simulation, you may feel that the quality of your group's decision was not what it could have been. In addition to helping group members work better and more harmoniously with each other, OD programs assist employees in making more effective decisions for both the organization and its members. This simulation demonstrates many of the interpersonal and organizational factors that inhibit change. If the essential task of management is to deal with change, a manager must be able to initiate change and to implement the stages of an OD program.

• **Goals**. Planned change efforts concentrate on problems of efficiency, effectiveness, and participant satisfaction. The focus of planned change efforts toward organization improvement includes individual behavior, group and intergroup relations, and overall organization problems.

• **OD.** OD is not a panacea, but many organizations have improved effectiveness by the application of these techniques. In the following chapters, each stage of an OD program is examined and explained in greater depth.

CASE ANALYSIS FORM

Name: _____

I. Problems

 A. Macro

 1. _____

 2. _____

 B. Micro

 1. _____

 2. _____

II. Causes

 1. _____

 2. _____

 3. _____

III. Systems affected

 1. Structural _____

 2. Psychosocial _____

 3. Technical _____

 4. Managerial _____

 5. Goals _____

IV. Alternatives

 1. _____

 2. _____

 3. _____

 4. _____

 5. _____

V. Recommendations

 1. _____

 2. _____

 3. _____

NOTES

1. Wilhelm, Warren, "Changing Corporate Culture—or Corporate Behavior? How to Change Your Company," *Academy of Management Executive*, vol. 6, no. 4, (1992), pp. 72–77.

2. Latham, John R., "Visioning the Concept, Trilogy and the Process," *Quarterly Progress*, vol. 28, no. 9, April 1995, p. 65.

3. See Karen Bemowski, "Codes, Cultural, Archetypes and the Collective Cultural Unconscious", *Quarterly Progress*, vol. 28, no. 1, January 1995, p. 33.

4. Kilmann, R. H., "Corporate Culture," *Psychology Today*, April 1985, p. 63.

5. Shrivastra, P., "Integrating Strategy Formulation with Organizational Culture," *Journal of Business Strategy*, (Winter 1984), pp. 103–4.

6. John Hulpke, CSUB, 1994, sources: "The Cola Superpowers' Outrageous New Arsenals," *Business Week*, March 20, 1989, p. 162; Chakrabarty, Subrata N., "How Pepsi Broke Into India," *Forbes*, November 27, 1989, pp. 43–44; Sellers, Patricia, "Financial Soundness," *Fortune*, January 29, 1990, pp. 46–47.

7. See Karen Bemowski, "Codes, Cultural, Archetypes and the Collective Cultural Unconscious," *Quarterly Progress*, vol. 28, no. 1, January 1995, p. 34 and Wilhelm, Warren, "Changing Corporate Culture—or Corporate Behavior? How to Change Your Company," *Academy of Management Executive*, 1992, vol. 6, no. 4, p. 72.

8. MacLanahan, John S., "Bruce Crockett Communicates Change at Comsat," *Industry Week*, June 15, 1992, p. 57.

9. Deal, Terrence E., and Allan A. Kennedy, "Culture: A New Look Through Old Lenses," *The Journal of Applied Behavioral Science*, vol. 19, no. 4, (1983), p. 108.

10. Walton, Sam and John Huey, *Sam Walton—Made in America, My Story*, (New York: Doubleday, 1992), pp. 156–158.

11. See Brian Dumaine, "Creating a New Company Culture," Fortune, January 15, 1990, 127–31.

12. Migliore, Henry, R. T. Martin, Tim Baer, and Jeffrey L. Horvath, "Corporate Culture Index," Proceedings, Southern Management Association, 1989, p. 217.

13. See Richard D. Teach, R. G. Schwartz, and Fred A. Tarpley Jr., "Small Firm Cultures," Proceedings, Southern Management Association, 1989, p. 211.

14. Huey, John, "How McKinsey Does It," *Fortune,* November 1, 1993, p. 56.

15. Roberts, Roy S., "A Winning Approach," *Executive Management*, May, 1992, p. 16.

16. Marks, Mitchell, L., "Managing the Diversity that Follows Mergers and Restructurings," *Employee Relations Today*, Winter 1991/1992, pp. 453–458.

17. Byrne, John A., "The Horizontal Corporation," *Business Week*, December 20, 1993, p. 77.

18. Higginson, Thomas J., and Robert P. Waxier, "Corporate Cultures for the 1990s: What Is Needed?" *Corporate Environment,* January/February 1993, pp. 11–13.

19. Leavitt, Harold, *Corporate Pathfinders*, (Homewood, IL: Dow Jones-Irwin, 1986), pp. 10–11.

20. See Rubach, Laura, "Downsizing: How Quality is Affected as Companies Shrink," *Quality Progress*, vol. 28, no. 4, April 1995, p. 24.

21. "The death of corporate loyalty," *The Economist*, April 3, 1993, p. 53.

22. "After a U-Turn, UPS Really Delivers," *Business Week,* May 31, 1993, pp. 92–93.

23. Sources: Brian Dumaine, "P & G Rewrites the Marketing Rules," *Fortune*, November 6, 1989, pp. 35–48. Alecia Swasy, "Slow and Steady," *The Wall Street Journal*, September 21, 1989, p. 1.

24. Uttal, Bro, "The Corporate Culture Vultures," *Fortune,* vol. 108, no. 8 (October 17, 1983), p. 66.

25. Lawrence, Stephanie, "Voices of HR Experience," *Personnel Journal*, April 1989, p. 72.

26. Kanter, Rosabeth Moss, "SMR Forum: Innovation—The Only Hope for Times Ahead," *Sloan Management Review*, vol. 25, no. 4 (Summer 1984), pp. 51–55.

27. Rubis, Leon, "Playing By the Books," *HR Magazine*, vol. 40, no. 5, May 1995, p. 38.

28. Harvey, Donald F., and Richard A. Wald, "Changing an Organizational Culture . . . ," Proceedings, Southern Management Association, 1989, p. 214.

29. Etzioni, A., *Modern Organizations*, (Englewood Cliffs, N.J.: Prentice Hall, Inc, 1964), p. 8.

30. Bennis, Warren, *Organization Development, Its Nature, Origins, and Prospects,* (Reading, Mass.: Addison-Wesley, Publishing Co., Inc., 1969), pp. 26–32.

31. Strauss, George, "Professionalism and Occupational Associations," *Industrial Relations,* vol. 2 (May 1963), p. 8.

32. French, Wendell L., and Cecil H. Bell, Jr., *Organization Development: Behavioral Science Interventions for Organization Improvement,* 4th ed. (Englewood Cliffs, N.J.: Prentice Hall, Inc., 1990), p. 18.

33. Crockett, William, "Introducing Change to a Government Agency," in *Failures in Organization Development and Change*, ed. Phillip Mirvis and David Berg (New York: John Wiley & Sons, Inc., 1978), p. 113.

34. Harvey, Jerry B., "Eight Myths OD Consultants Believe In . . . and Die By," *OD Practitioner*, February 1974, p. 3.

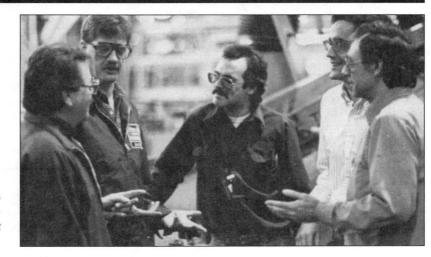

Total Quality Management project teams help solve problems through consensus at Owens-Corning. *Photo courtesy of Owens-Corning Fiberglas Corporation*

The OD Consultant: Role and Style

4

OBJECTIVES

Upon completing this chapter, you will be able to:

1. Define the role of an OD consultant.
2. Identify your strengths and areas of improvement as a potential consultant.
3. Experience and practice your own style of intervention and influence in a group.

PREMEETING PREPARATION

1. Read the Background Information.
2. Complete Steps 1 through 4 of OD Skills Simulation 4.1.
3. Read and prepare Case 4: The Grayson Chemical Company.

BACKGROUND INFORMATION

The globalization of markets, the downsizing of the workforce, the flattening of hierarchy, the reengineering of work processes, and the spread of information technology are all part of a revolution in the way we do business. These changes are happening at the same time and fast. Because these changes interact, business and society are in the midst of revolution comparable to the industrial revolution. In a turbulent and changing environment, managers are concerned not only with managing organizations as they exist at the present time, but also with changes to meet future conditions. Change programs do not happen accidentally. Instead, they are initiated with a specific purpose and require some form of leadership to function properly. The **OD consultant** must deal proactively with these changing competitive forces. In an effective organization, the OD consultant tries to build a consensus among top management to initiate changes quickly in order to take advantage of shifting circumstances.[1] For example, in the new, horizontal corporation self managed teams are becoming the building blocks of the changing organization. Performance objectives are then linked to customer satisfaction rather than profit. And employees are rewarded not just for individual performance, but for team performance.[2]

One study reported that a typical large-scale change effort is initiated in response to, or in anticipation of, external environmental changes.[3] These change programs often represent a major alteration of organizational processes. For example, organizations are reengineering, restructuring, and downsizing to meet changing times. Organizations consist of groups of people working together. Changes alter the way the people work together, how they relate with others, and even how they see themselves. The OD consultant facilitates such changes by training, educating, and collaboratively designing new ways of functioning.

There are two types of change that may take place in an organization. The first type, termed *random* or *haphazard change*, is forced on the organization by the external environment. This type of change is not prepared for; it simply occurs and is dealt with as it happens, a practice usually called *firefighting*. This type of change includes downsizing where sizeable numbers of employees are laid off. When a large organization, such as IBM, implements a downsizing program, such changes can be extremely difficult, because it involves a major cultural transformation.[4]

The second type of change results from deliberate attempts to modify organizational operations by persons seeking to promote improvement. One example of this type of program is Total Quality Management (TQM), with a focus on continuous improvement. To sustain the long term success of OD programs requires commitment and leadership as organizational relationships are changed. These changes do not automatically occur simply because someone in the organization decided an OD program would be helpful. The implementation of these steps depends largely on the consultant's abilities. Prior to the entry of the OD consultant, there must be an awareness of the need for change: usually some problem or disequilibrium causing the client system to seek help. To implement a program of planned change, the management must first identify a gap between the current situation and some desired condition. OD change programs are then aimed at improving effectiveness, efficiency, and participant well-being. Too often, management will have introduced short-run, expedient change programs aimed solely at cost savings. Such programs often have unintended dysfunctional effects on participant satisfaction and the long-term goals of the organization. The OD consultant helps the organization identify differences between where it is and where it would like to be, and then proceeds to design and implement appropriate OD interventions. For example, one important element in developing a TQM culture is the development of a shared vision. The OD consultant involves all members of an organization in developing a vision and improving the corporate culture.[5]

Every OD program must begin with a good working relationship between the OD consultant and the individual or department being helped. If this relationship is weak or superficial, the program is unlikely to succeed. The success of almost any OD project depends to

a large degree on the nature of this relationship, which must be developed in the initial stages of the change program.

This chapter focuses on the skills of the consultant and the initial intervention into the ongoing client system. We'll examine the major OD consultant roles and styles, the intervention process, and the major factors in creating a climate for change.

External and Internal Consultant Roles

In every large-scale change program, some person or group is usually designated to initiate the change: the OD consultant. The OD consultant, then, is the person leading or guiding the process of change in an organization. The OD consultant may already be a member of the organization or may be a consultant brought in from outside.

In the past few years a growing number of major organizations (including IBM, General Electric, General Motors, Honeywell, TRW, Union Carbide, and the U.S. Army and Navy) have created internal OD consulting groups. (In fact, the U. S. Army OD program seems to be turning out a large number of internal OD consultants for private industry.) Consequently, the OD consultant is either an external consultant (an outside consultant called in by the client) or an internal consultant (an organization member acting as consultant). There are advantages and disadvantages to both roles.

The External Consultant

The external consultant is someone not previously associated with the client system. Coming from the outside, the external consultant sees things from a different viewpoint and from a position of objectivity. Because the external consultant is invited into the organization, he or she has increased leverage (the degree of influence and status within the client system) and greater freedom of operation than an internal consultant. There is research evidence to suggest that top managers view outside consultants as having a more positive role in large-scale change programs than internal consultants.[6]

Furthermore, because external consultants are not a part of the organization, they are less in awe of the power that various members may wield. They do not depend upon the client system for raises, approval, or promotion, as an internal consultant must. Since they usually have a very broad career base and other clients to fall back on, they usually have a more independent attitude regarding risk taking and confrontations with the client system. At McKinsey & Co., a leading consulting firm, consultants are direct, outspoken and challenge the clients opinions. Once The Firm (as McKinsey is called) is hired, an 'engagement team' of four to six people is assembled, with an experienced consultant to coordinate the effort.[7]

The disadvantages of external consultants result from these same factors. Generally, they are unfamiliar with the organization system and may be less than totally knowledgeable of its technology, such as aerospace or chemistry. They are unfamiliar with the culture, communication networks, and the formal or informal power system. In some situations, consultants may have difficulty gathering pertinent information simply because they are outsiders. (See Our Changing World on page 92.)

The Internal Consultant

The internal consultant is already a member of the organization; either a top executive; a manager of personnel, human resources, or industrial relations departments; or simply an organization member who initiates change. Recently, many large organizations have established offices with the specific responsibility of helping the organization implement change programs. These internal consultants often operate out of the human resources area and may report directly to the president of the organization.

OUR CHANGING WORLD
MATSHUSITA GOES GLOBAL[8]

It's a few minutes before the morning shift at a Matshusita Electric Industrial Co. semiconductor plant. Workers are shuffling toward locker rooms to don "bunny suits" and other sanitized apparel. So strict are the cleanliness guidelines that salespeople, secretaries, janitors, cafeteria workers, and even the top brass must change into geeky white shoes around the place. Shortly, the rousing company anthem rises throughout the complex. Outside, the imposing silhouette of one of the world's most majestic mountains provides the perfect backdrop to this typical Japanese factory scene.

But this isn't Japan. The mountain is Rainier, the town Puyallup, Washington, and the factory is the home of Matshusita Semiconductor Corp. of America, one of the Japanese company's more than 150 overseas industrial outposts.

But all this success abroad creates a quandary for Matshusita. Many overseas plants are beginning to compete with the company's factories back in Japan. Already the company is importing a lot of the TVs, air conditioners, VCRs, and electronic components it sells in Japan. While that may be great for Japanese customers and for the country's trade surplus, it puts a lot of pressure on Matshusita's managers and engineers to devise other, more advanced products to keep its 254,000 Japanese employees gainfully busy. (Matshusita employs 99,000 outside Japan.)

President Yoichi Morishita, 60, acknowledges the dilemma but contends that it's part of becoming a truly global enterprise. Says he: "Our success manufacturing abroad helps us in more ways than it hurts us, because that is where the fastest-growing markets are and because it gives us even more incentive to develop new products and technologies back here in Japan."

Matshusita's Lessons for Going Global

- Be a good corporate citizen in every country, respecting cultures, customs, and languages.

- Give overseas operations your best manufacturing technology.
- Keep expatriate headcount down and groom local managers to take over.
- Let plants set their own rules, fine-tuning manufacturing processes to match skills of workers.
- Develop local R&D to tailor products to markets.
- Encourage competition among overseas outposts and with plants back home.

Despite Matshusita's obvious success overseas, the company is falling short of one of its loftier goals - bringing the best of its foreign managers into the corporation's highest ranks. Its most senior foreign executive is a woman from Singapore who is executive vice president of Matshusita's regional headquarters there. Back in Osaka, gaijin are a rare sight. Says President Morishita: "We recognize that to become a truly global company we have to have diversity in top management. That might be realized in the twenty-first century."

Since taking over early last year, Morishita has instilled a new sense of urgency at Matshusita and has reorganized the entire corporation to speed up product development. He also has reassigned hundreds of managers and engineers to explore business opportunities in multimedia, software, and digital telecommunications. But it is too early to tell what kinds of products might result. Matshusita is doing a lot of things right overseas, and for the moment at least, any success abroad buys the company a little more time to get its house in order back home. Over the long term Matsushita needs innovative ideas for new products. Its overseas subsidiaries can help make it more creative.

Question:

1. Can you think of other examples of change problems in multinational firms?

Internal consultants have certain advantages inherent in their relationship with the organization. They are familiar with the organization's culture and norms and probably accept and behave in accordance with the norms. This can save considerable time in becoming familiar with the system and becoming accepted. The internal consultant knows the power structure, who are strategic people, and how to apply leverage. He or she is already known to the employees, and has a personal interest in seeing the organization succeed. Unfortunately, acquiring effective internal consulting skills is not as easy as it sounds. The proof is in the problems encountered by new, not quite ready, internal consultants or staff members who take on projects before they are fully comfortable with their consulting roles in the organization, and before they understand and have developed the skills that are critical to effective consulting.

The position of internal consultant also has disadvantages, one of the most significant of which may be the lack of specialized skills needed for organization development. Another disadvantage relates to lack of objectivity. There is evidence to suggest that internal change

agents may be more likely to accept the organizational system as a given and accommodate their change tactics to the needs of management. Being a familiar person has advantages, but it can also work against the internal consultant. Other employees may not understand the consultant's new role and will certainly be influenced by his or her previous work and relationships, particularly if the work and relationships have in any way been questionable. Finally, the internal consultant may lack the necessary power and authority, as it is too often the case that internal consultants are in some remote staff position and report to a mid-level manager.[9]

In an interview, Admiral Elmo R. Zumwalt, Jr., past chief of naval operations (who was responsible for setting up the U.S. military's first OD program), commented as follows on implementing change from within:

> I think every young generation's approach to the world is to generalize idealistically—dissatisfied with what they see—hoping for a better world. The process of maturing improves the society as they work to achieve their ideals. They also learn that the only way in which they can arrive at positions of influence sufficient to improve society is to make certain compromises. It seems to me that the essence of growth is to learn how to do that without giving up one's fundamental beliefs and aspirations. When people achieve positions of importance, the real test, for naval officers or petty officers or anybody, is whether they recall those youthful aspirations and measure themselves against those early ideals, modified by maturity, but hopefully not too much . . . [10]

The OD consultant must break through the barriers of bureaucracy and organizational politics to develop innovation, creativity, teamwork, and trust within the organization.

The External-Internal Consulting Team

The implementation of a large-scale change program is almost impossible without the involvement of all levels and elements of the organization. One approach to creating a climate of change uses a team formed of an external consultant working directly with an internal consultant to initiate and facilitate change programs. This is probably the most effective approach. John Lewis, for example, found that the more successful OD consultants worked upon the development of their internal counterparts.[11] Each partner brings to the consulting team complementary resources, that is, advantages and strengths that offset the disadvantages and weaknesses of the other. The external consultant brings expertise, objectivity, and new insights to organization problems. The internal consultant, on the other hand, brings detailed knowledge of organization issues and norms, a long-time acquaintance with members, and an awareness of system strengths and weaknesses.[12]

The collaborative relationship between internal and external consultants provides an integration of abilities, skills, and resources. The relationship serves as a model for the rest of the organization—a model that members can observe and see in operation, one that embodies such qualities as trust, respect, honesty, confrontation, and collaboration. The team approach allows a dividing of change program workload and a sharing of the diagnosis, plans, and strategies. The external-internal consulting team is also less likely to accept watered-down or compromise change programs because each team member tends to provide support to the other. As an example, during the U.S. Navy's Command Development (OD) Program, the internal change agents recommended that training seminars be conducted away from the navy environment (i.e., at a resort) and that participants dress in civilian clothing to lessen authority issues. Higher authority, however, ordered the seminars to be held on naval bases and in uniform—ground rules that the internal consultants reluctantly accepted. In this situation an external consultant with greater leverage might have provided enough support and influence to have gained approval of the desired program.

Another reason for using an external-internal consulting team is to achieve greater continuity over the entire OD program. Because external consultants are involved in other outside activities, they generally are available to the organization only a few days a month, with two- or three-week intervals between visits. The internal consultant, on the other hand,

provides a continuing point of contact for organization members at any time problems or questions arise. Since many OD programs are long-term efforts, often lasting three to five years, the external-internal consulting team also provides continuing support for maintaining the momentum of the OD program. Most programs will hit low spots or stumbling blocks, and the external-internal combination may provide the stimulation and motivation needed to keep the change program moving during periods of resistance. The team effort is probably most effective, as it combines the advantages of both the external and internal consultants while minimizing the disadvantages.

Types Of Consultants

The OD consultant is the person who initiates, stimulates, or facilitates a change program, and may be an executive, a member of the organization, or an outside consultant. Change begins with the intervention of the consultant in the system to be changed. **Intervention** refers to the entrance into the client system and includes a variety of roles and activities.

One recent study suggests that OD consultants are involved in and are using different skills and intervention activities than in the past. In the past, much of OD was focused on team development, but today there is greater emphasis on organization transformation and change.[13] A number of consulting styles or approaches can be identified. Each style varies according to its underlying character—shaped by the kinds of skills and techniques consultants use, the values they bring to their clients, and the manner in which they carry out their assignments. Other research has also examined the degree of emphasis the consultant places upon two interrelated goals or dimensions of the change process. One method of classification involves the consultant's orientation to the two interrelated dimensions:

1. The degree of emphasis upon effectiveness or goal accomplishment.
2. The degree of emphasis upon relationships, morale, and participant satisfaction.

Based upon these two dimensions, five different types of consultant styles or roles may be identified (see Figure 4.1).

FIGURE 4.1 Consultant Styles

The Stabilizer Style. The goal of the stabilizer style consultant is neither effectiveness nor participant satisfaction. Rather, the consultant is trying to keep from rocking the boat, and to maintain a low profile. The underlying motivation is often survival, or merely following the directives of top management. Such a role is usually found in large organizations where development programs may be part of the staff function and are not highly regarded by top management. This style is usually regarded as forced upon the individual by organization pressures, so that the individual has learned to conform and suppress internal motivations.

The Cheerleader Style. The cheerleader style places emphasis on the satisfaction of organization members and is chiefly concerned with employee motivation and morale. The cheerleader consultant seeks warm working relationships and in general is more comfortable in nonconfrontative situations. Effectiveness per se is not emphasized, the assumption being that if member satisfaction is high, effectiveness will also be high. Unfortunately, there is a great deal of evidence that contradicts these assumptions. The cheerleader style strongly pushes for improved morale and open conflict or locking horns is avoided by attempts to smooth over differences and maintain harmony.

The Analyzer Style. The analyzer style places greatest emphasis on efficiency with little emphasis given to member satisfaction. The analyzer feels most comfortable with a rational assessment of problems and assumes that the facts will lead to a solution. This type of consultant may be quite confrontative, usually relying on authority to resolve conflict and on rational problem-solving processes.

The analyzer consultant has a background of specialized expertise, knowledge, and experience applicable to the solution of specific problems. The client needs to have a problem solved, a service performed, or a study made; the analyzer consultant takes responsibility for providing these functions. This type of consultation is based on the belief that the client does not need to know or cannot learn the skills to solve its problems. The success of the consultant is largely dependent on the client's having properly diagnosed its problem and having called in the right kind of consultant.

The Persuader Style. The persuader style focuses on both dimensions, effectiveness and morale, yet optimizes neither. Such a style provides a relatively low-risk strategy, yet avoids direct confrontation with other forces. This approach may be used when the consultant's power or leverage is low relative to other participants. This style is motivated primarily by a desire to satisfy, that is, to achieve something that is "good enough." A great deal of effort is applied in attempting to satisfy the differing forces, thus gaining a majority block of support for prepared changes. The resulting change program often may be watered down or weakened to the point where organization improvement is unlikely.

The Pathfinder Style. The pathfinder style seeks both a high degree of effectiveness and a high degree of member satisfaction, believing that greater effectiveness is possible when all members are involved and problem solving is done through teamwork. There is an awareness that confrontation and conflict are often a means to a more effective organization and to more satisfied individual members. The pathfinder approach uses collaborative problem solving and challenges the underlying patterns of member behavior.

Harold J. Leavitt uses this term to refer to developing a sense of value and vision.[14] In this sense, the pathfinder consultant is helping the organization to focus on its most critical issues and questions.

In a survey of about 1,000 OD practitioners, it was found that the OD skills rated as most important were listening, integrity, and organizational diagnosis.[15] The pathfinder consultant uses these skills to give the client new insights into its activities and to help the client system determine how it wishes to change and how it might go about implementing such changes. The consultant rarely informs or instructs the client system, but instead tries to discover client system problems and to challenge the underlying patterns of behavior of organ-

ization members. The pathfinder consultant focuses on six types of processes essential for effective organization performance: (1) communication, (2) member roles and functions in groups, (3) group problem solving and decision making, (4) group norms and growth, (5) leadership and authority, and (6) intergroup cooperation and competition.[16]

One familiar approach which might provide a useful example is to look at the style used by Lieutenant Columbo—the irreverent detective played by actor Peter Falk in the colorful television series. While Columbo is not a consultant, per se, he uses a similar approach in eliciting information to solve problems. What can we learn from Columbo about consulting? Well first, he always develops a relationship with his client (in this case, the brilliant master criminal who thinks he or she has committed the perfect crime) and continues to use this communication channel to get vital information about the problem. Here he uses a stabilizer or "don't rock the boat" style.

Second, Columbo is very supportive and non-threatening to the client, with his bumbling, rumpled approach. He often asks questions like, "Gee, I don't understand this, can you explain this to me?" and so forth. Frequently, the "bad guy" actually likes the bumbling detective, as Columbo assures him that he is not a suspect. In a sense, he is using the cheerleader style to build a supportive relationship.

Third, he takes the client where he is, that is he expresses approval and acceptance. He is agreeable, supportive, and persuasive. He raises issues and questions, but avoids direct conflict—the persuader style.

Finally, his success is usually due to persistent research and asking in his famous last second, on the way out queries such as "Oh, pardon me but could I bother you with one more question" In this sense, he is using the analyzer and the pathfinder styles to elicit client information to find a problem solution.

We have identified five different consultant styles in this section. At the end of the chapter, you will have an opportunity to find out where your own style fits in this classification system. Most organization problems are complex situations, however, and may not neatly fit with any one particular change approach but will depend upon the particular consultant, the nature of the problem, and the type of organization climate that exists.

In summary, these five consulting styles are not mutually exclusive. All consultant styles can be effective and are interrelated. A consultant may use different styles at various times to meet changing client system needs and deal with diverse situations. Frequently, some combination of the types may be applied.

The Readiness of the Organization for OD

Upon first contacting the client system, the OD consultant begins evaluating its receptiveness for any OD program. It is a mistake to assume that because most organizations can benefit greatly from an OD program, they all must, and should, have one. The ironic element is that the very organizations most in need of such a program are precisely the ones least receptive. Their inflexibility and insensitivity to the need for change seem almost proverbial: "There are none so blind as those that will not see." Rather than impose organization development upon them, the consultant needs to wait until key personnel decide whether change is really needed. The motivation for any change program is then built in, not artificially contrived. To aid the consultant in gauging the preparedness of an organization for an OD program, there are four questions which the consultant needs to obtain definite, precise, and positive answers before venturing further:

1. Are the learning goals of OD *appropriate*?
2. Is the cultural state of the client system *ready* for organization development?
3. Are the *key* people involved?
4. Are *members* of the client system adequately *prepared and oriented* to organization development?[17]

Once these questions have been satisfactorily answered, then, and only then, should the consultant proceed. There is an old saying, which often holds true in OD consulting. "If it ain't broke, don't fix it." But Tom Peters proposes that in today's management this should be modified to "If it ain't broke, you just haven't looked hard enough. Fix it anyway."[18] OD change programs often deal with developing higher involvement, increased performance and a more free-wheeling, faster responding organization.

The Intervention Process

The OD process involves a collaborative relationship between a consultant and a client system. OD consultants may possess differing consulting styles, philosophies, and approaches but, in general, they perform a certain set of functions with regard to the client system. These functions include (1) helping the client determine its current level or state (data gathering), (2) assisting in a collaborative analysis of problem areas and planning strategies of change (diagnosis), and (3) intervening and facilitating change from the current level to some ideal or desired level. One example of the consulting process in action is at Bain & Co. (See OD in Practice.)

OD IN PRACTICE
BAIN & CO.: A NEW CONSULTING ROLE[19]

Bain & Co., a management consulting firm founded by Bill Bain, may be at the most critical juncture in its twenty year history. Bill Bain is turning control and management of his company over to a group of younger executives. Through the 1980's Bain was among the very best in the consulting industry. Now, however, Bain itself seems to need a consultant after a series of setbacks has tarnished its once sterling image.

William W. "Bill" Bain, Jr. who created a new type of management consultant role—the quasi-insider—one who is privy to his clients' secrets and works directly with the CEO to implement consulting recommendations, is letting go of his firm. Bain & Co. has seen spectacular growth since its founding in 1973: revenues have grown at 50 percent annually to $150 million and staff size has more than tripled with a worldwide staff of more than 1,000 consultants.

But, now Bain may need its own consulting wisdom, as the firm's workforce is down by 30 percent, thinned by two rounds of layoffs and by the defection of key executives. Revenues fell by 10 percent, the first decline in Bain's history.

The Bain Consultant

Bain is known for the shrewd, suave people it employs. With starting salaries in excess of $60,000, they were able to attract and recruit the top MBAs from Harvard and Stanford. The Bain consultant dresses in the company uniform—the dark "power suit", monogrammed, handmade shirts, and red tie (or its female equivalent). They tend to be attractive, articulate, meticulously groomed, well-mannered, and exceedingly charming. Bain employees are notoriously secretive about their organization and its work for clients and dedicate themselves to improving their customer's competitive position. Business is a war that their clients must win.

New Types of Consultants

Bill Bain is known as the creator of "relationship consulting." The consultants build their business on the close relationship they develop with clients. Bain focuses on the total system, on the profitability of the entire organization. Such knowledge demands lots of data-gathering and a great deal of time for analysis. Bain consultants also insist on working directly with the chief executive, who they feel is the key to the firm's success. The goal of the Bain consultant is to produce a value for its client that is worth 10 times the cost of its consulting fees.

What happened to these earlier successes? Some say Bain fell victim to the same mistake it warns its clients against, relying too heavily on a few profitable client accounts and on a small team of senior executives who generated the majority of revenues.

Problems

Bain has some problems. Clients such as Chrysler, Baxter, Dun & Bradstreet, and Canadian Pacific, each of whom had been spending $20 million or more a year for Bain's services, ended their relationships.

A new managing director has led a financial restructuring that is intended to get the firm back on track. It is hoped that a redistribution of ownership will give incentives to a wider group of executives to rebuild the business. But Bain executives privately confess to being nervous. They must undo the damage that has already been done to the firm's mystique in the marketplace.

Questions

1. Would you agree with the relationship consulting approach?

The Intervention

When the external or the internal consultant contacts the client system, he or she has already begun to intervene. *Intervention* refers to a coming between or among members or groups of an organization for the purpose of effecting change. More specifically, intervention refers to an array of planned activities participated in by both the consultant and the client, including shared observations of the processes occurring between members of a group or of an organization for the purpose of improving the effectiveness of the processes. The intent of the intervention is to alter the status quo. Richard Beckhard suggests that a planned intervention is "moving into an existing organization and helping it, in effect, 'stop the music,' examine its present ways of work, norms, and values, and look at alternative ways of working, relating, or rewarding."[20]

In a very broad sense, stages 2 through 5 of the OD process (explained in Chapter 2 and in the succeeding chapters of this book) describe the intervention process. During the course of an OD program there will be many interventions: interventions for gathering data, team-building activities, and so forth, but here we are concerned with the consultant's initial contact with the client system. The initial contact with the client system by the consultant is an intervention if for no other reason than it is a message to the organization members that the climate of the organization is under scrutiny and that new and more effective ways of doing things are being sought. Just this promise of a better future can effect change and therefore constitute an intervention.

The external consultant generally intervenes through either a top manager or a personnel director. As an example, when TRW decided to initiate change, an external consultant was brought in by the industrial relations section. It is easier to bring about change when the intervention is made at higher levels of the client system, since greater power to influence others is concentrated there. At McKinsey & Co., for example, they insist on working directly with the top management team as noted earlier. Although change programs have been initiated at lower levels, many OD practitioners feel that if real and lasting change is to take place, it must begin at the top. Michael Beer and Edgar Huse, however, contend that change can, and does begin at lower levels of an organization, but the lack of top support does increase the risk involved.[21]

The consultant must face many different types of situations when intervening in an organization. These may be categorized in terms of client system support. In the most favorable type of situation, all levels of the organization recognize the need for and support change programs. In another type of situation, top management recognizes the need for change and provides support, but lower levels are nonsupportive or resistant. One example might be the new CEO at Volkswagen, Ferdinand Piech, who is trying to reverse the growth strategy by cutting the workforce by 12,500, a strategy not popular with the rank and file. When he toured headquarters, he asked a section leader how many people worked there. Eighty-nine came the answer, "That's one nine too many," said Piech. The section leader breathed a sigh of relief, but then he realized Piech meant he would be left with a staff of 8, not 80.[22] Still another type of situation occurs when lower levels of the organization are supportive while top management is resistant to change.

Who Is the Client?

"Who is the client?" at first may appear to be an unimportant question, or one with an obvious answer. But in reality, this is one of the most critical questions facing the consultant. This is because dealing with the wrong, or misidentified client may lead to ineffective, or even disastrous consequences. The decision of who the client is becomes more complex as the consultant intervenes into more segments of the organization. At some point, the consultant needs to determine who the client actually is. Is it the total organization? Is it certain divisions, departments, or groups? Or is it the individual who contracted for the

consultant's services? This is a question that sometimes appears easy to answer at the beginning of an OD program but becomes increasingly unclear as the program develops. The client initially will be the person with whom the consultant first makes contact. But it may soon become apparent that the organization is more realistically the client. The consultant's concern may thus extend to include work groups or subsystems of the organization and even the individual members of the system. One OD consulting team, for example, reported on OD intervention with the Cincinnati Department of Health. They were originally contacted by the commissioner of health as their initial client; however, during the course of the intervention they eventually determined that the "real" client was the city council.[23] As it can be seen, the question of identifying the client is more complicated than it might appear.

The OD Consulting Role in the Intervention

The OD consultant (as noted earlier) can be categorized into five general styles: stabilizer, persuader, analyzer, cheerleader, and pathfinder. The OD consultant tends to work in the pathfinder style. This style is similar to that of the process consultant, which has been documented by Schein in his book *Process Consultation* and is discussed in Chapter 7 of this book. OD process consulting operates on the belief that the team is the basic building block of an organization. One of the newer innovations is the self managed work team, which gives workers more automomy and control over their immediate behavior. The workers are organized into teams on the basis of task functions. They make decisions on many key issues including work schedules and assignments and how to deal with quality problems.[24] Therefore, team behavior is analyzed in terms of communications, member roles and functions in groups, group problem solving and decision making, group norms and growth, and leadership and authority.[25]

OD consultants are primarily concerned with how these five processes occur in an organization. Their role involves sharing observations of these five processes and thus helping the client improve the effectiveness of the organization. Simultaneously and equally important, the client is learning to observe and improve its own process skills and problem-solving abilities for use in the future as well as in the present. Since the client is learning to make process interventions similar to those made by the consultant, the client is also learning how to solve its own problems without having to rely on the consultant.

One basic assumption underlying the OD consultant role is that the client needs to learn to identify problems, to participate in the diagnosis, and to be actively involved in problem solution. The consultant recognizes that either the client has useful skills and resources but does not know how to use them effectively, or the client does not have the requisite skills but has the capacity to develop the needed skills and resources. As a result, the client solves its own problems with the consultant "helping to sharpen the diagnosis and in providing alternative remedies which may not have occurred to the client."[26] The OD consultant operates on the notion that by assisting instead of taking control, the client's problems will be solved in a more lasting manner. Furthermore, the client will have increased its skills so that it will be able to solve future problems. The process consultant teaches the client how to diagnose and solve its own problems but does not advise or suggest solutions. Initially, the client may fumble around a bit and take longer than it would with expert assistance but in the long run the client will grow and mature.

Although most writers on OD support the idea of OD process consultation, they also recognize that because clients have various needs and maturity levels, it may be necessary at times to provide expert and technical advice. The need for working in a style other than the pathfinder style may be more apparent at the beginning of the consulting relationship. But as a rule of thumb, the OD consultant should not encourage and perpetuate a dependent relationship. As the maturity of the client increases, the consultant tends to operate more in the process consultation or pathfinder style.

OD Consultant Skills and Activities

The role of the OD consultant is changing and becoming more complex. Ellen Fagenson and W. Warner Burke found that the most practiced OD skill or activity was team development, while the least employed was the integration of technology. (See Table 4.1.)[27]

The results of this study reinforce what other theorists have also suggested. The OD practitioners of today are no longer just process facilitators, but are expected to know something about strategy, structure, reward systems, corporate culture, leadership, human resource development, and the nature of the business of the client organization. As a result, the role of the OD consultant today is more challenging and more in the mainstream of the client organization than in the past.

Table 4.1 OD Consulting Skills and Activities

Skill	Average Use
1. Team development	2.97
2. Corporate change	2.91
3. Strategy development	2.60
4. Management development	2.45
5 Employee (career) development	2.04
6. Technology integration	1.97

NOTE: Ratings on 5-point scale with 5.0 to a great extent, being high.

Susan Gebelein has suggested six key consulting skill areas, which are critical to the success of the internal consultant as shown in Figure 4.2. The relative emphasis on each type of skill will vary depending upon the situation, but, all are vital in achieving OD program goals. The skills which focus on the people oriented nature of consulting include:

- *Leadership.* Consultants must know how to initiate action and be able to motivate others.
- *Project Management.* This includes planning, organizing, clarifying goals and setting priorities.
- *Communication.* The need to communicate and listen effectively so that all key players are kept informed.
- *Problem Solving.* This includes technical expertise, knowledge of business operations, and diagnostic and decision making skills.

FIGURE 4.2 The Consulting Wheel

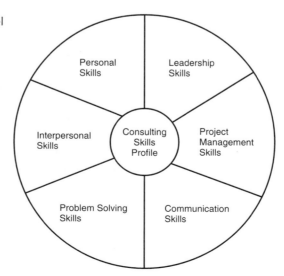

- *Interpersonal.* This includes facilitating, building relationships and process consulting skills.
- *Personal.* This includes a focus on helping, on results and on ethical and trust worthy behavior.[28]

The OD consultant's role is to help employees create their own solutions, systems and concepts. When the consultant is using these skills to accomplish these goals, the employees will work hard to make them succeed, because they are the owners of the change programs.

The Initial Intervention, Perception, and Assessment

One way of examining the consultant-client relationship is to view it as a system of interacting elements as shown in Figure 4.3. One important element is the *consultant*: the internal or external OD consultant or manager who initiates the change program aimed at improving the effectiveness of the client system. A second element, within the client system, may be termed the **client sponsor** or contact. This is the person or group within the client organization who has requested the consultant's help, and who interfaces with the consultant. The third element consists of the organizational unit or units that are to be changed, and the set of behaviors and values that have been traditionally practiced. This element may be termed the **client target system**: the actual target of the OD intervention.

For example, the authors were contacted about consulting with a medium-sized manufacturing company to develop an OD program for one major division of the company. The client contact people, or sponsors, were the vice president of industrial relations and the division manager (also a vice president). The target system was to be the division, with the goal of developing a more participative management style and increasing productivity. The members of the division, however, had little voice in determining the proposed change program. It was found in preliminary discussions that some were strongly in favor of such changes, whereas others were strongly opposed or even hostile to the proposed changes. Consequently, this combination of elements needs to be considered prior to beginning any change program.

Forming the Consultant-Client Relationship

In developing the consultant-client relationship, the first stage involves an interaction between the parties which includes initial perceptions and assessments by each of the other. Such assessments involve the consultant's determination of whether or not to enter into a

FIGURE 4.3 A System's View of the Change Relationship

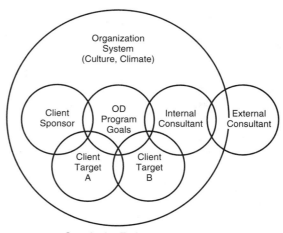

consulting relationship. This decision is based upon the consultant's assessment of the degree of congruence between his or her values and those of the client system. These include the attitudes of the client system toward OD and change, the ability of OD techniques to deal with the problems, and the potential of the consultant's efforts to help solve the client's problems.

The consultant's first intervention will probably be tentative. As Warren Bennis comments: "I enter a relationship on the basis that neither the client nor I know what the underlying problems are and that I need to explore and get a 'feel' for the situation before committing myself fully to the client system and before it fully entrusts itself to me."[29] This initial intervention might therefore be termed a reconnaissance on both sides. The OD practitioner is trying to evaluate the organization's readiness and commitment for change while the client system is assessing the consultant's capabilities.

Lynda McDermott and Warner Burke have suggested that power networks are important because they will influence the OD strategy that is chosen. The OD consultant has to be aware of where the power is in the organization, because that represents the major lever for change.[30] In these exploratory interactions, first impressions are rather important in setting the climate for any future relationships. (See B.C. comic strip.) Research by Polansky and Kounin shows that very early in the relationship, the client system makes judgments on the capabilities of the consultant.[31]

Perception can be defined as the process individuals use to give meaning to their environment by interpreting and organizing sensory impressions; however, what one perceives can be substantially different from reality. *Perception* is a basic factor in understanding behavior in the consultant-client relationship because once an impression is made, regardless of its correlation with reality, that impression is difficult to change. Clients form early impressions that become very quickly entrenched. Several studies indicate that impressions are formed very early, possibly in the *first four or five minutes* of the meeting. This is because people behave on the basis of what is *perceived* versus what really *is*. A basic model of the way such perceptions are formed is shown in Figure 4.4. There are many factors involved including one's past experiences, the degree of stress in the situation, the amount of group pressure that exists, and the type of role system involved. There are several basic factors affecting the formation of perceptions that can be identified.

Selective perception refers to the selectivity of information that is perceived. People tend to ignore information that they do not want to hear, that might be distracting or conflict with other ideas or values. However, people tend to accept information that is satisfying, pleasurable, and in agreement with their ideas and values.

Also, a similar stimulus may be interpreted differently by different individuals. Each one's **interpretation** depends upon his or her unique background and experience. Consequently, individuals tend to interpret situations in ways that reflect more favorably upon themselves.

Another process involved in perception is termed **closure.** This refers to the tendency of the individual to fill in any missing information, to complete the perception, and to give

Source: B.C. By permission of Johnny Hart and Creators Syndicates, Inc.

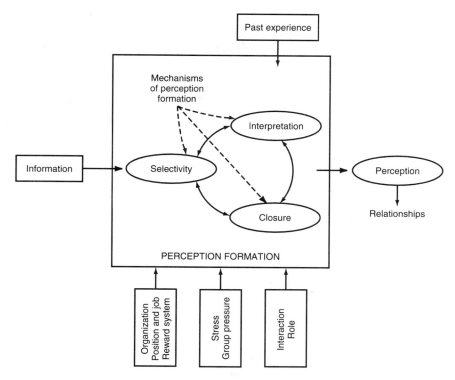

FIGURE 4.4 Perception Formation and Its Effect on Relationships

Source: Adapted from Joseph A. Litterer, *The Analysis of Organizations* (New York: John Wiley & Sons, Inc., 1965), p. 64.

it meaning and wholeness. In this way, a person may perceive more in a given situation than is already there, adding information to make the picture seem complete.

During this initial intervention each party may be selling itself to the other and trying to second-guess the other party's expectations. "Often the client system seems to be seeking assurance that the potential consultant is different enough from the client system to be a real expert and yet enough like it to be thoroughly understandable and approachable. But for the consultant, the process of selling one's self has certain dangers and could possibly lead to future problems. The consultant should ideally be free of the pressure of needing the consulting work, so that one can remain neutral to judge whether the client system needs the services and whether the consultant could be helpful.

These elements are often termed **dilemma interactions**. Such dilemma interactions result from questions by the consultant regarding the client's definition of the problem, the awareness of the need for change, the reduction of possible client overexpectations, the client's misuse of power, and value differences between client and consultant. The issue of dependency is a real problem in many consultant-client relationships. At the beginning of any OD consulting relationship, there is bound to be some amount of dependence on the consultant by the client.

As the relationship continues, the client is likely to become more independent of the consultant and to want to reject either the help or the helper or both. This is a critical point in the relationship and the effective OD consultant must be able to let this independence flourish while maintaining the relationship. Operationally, this may mean changing roles in the problem solving and letting the client assume a greater role in the change process. In the mature relationship, a condition of interdependence exists. In this situation the client is able to make optimum use of the resources of the consultant, knowing when to use exper-

tise, when to take the initiative, and how to accept suggestions or ideas for consideration. The consultant feels free to give ideas and suggestions knowing that the client will use these as appropriate. One essential condition of the sound consulting relationship is a mutual confidence between the consultant and the client.

Often there is a probable gap existing between the consultant's and the client's understanding about OD and change. The consultant needs to assess the degree of this gap, since a relationship is possible only if the consultant can be flexible enough to understand where the client is and help the client to learn about the OD change process. In this sense, the OD consultant's clarity about one's own purpose in the organization is crucial, as shown in Figure 4.5. The consultant brings a certain knowledge, skills, values, and so forth to the consulting situation. In turn, the client system has its own, often differing values, and a set of expectations for the consultant.

The consulting task, the changes that are to be implemented, the scope, difficulty, and complexity, affect the relationship, as well. Finally, the target organization, its readiness for change, level of resistance, and culture, all influence the consulting style and change approaches which may be successful in a given situation. The OD consultant needs to involve organization members at all levels and convince them to "buy in" to the change program— in effect, to get members involved in solving the problems.

Developing a Trust Relationship

One essential aspect of the OD program is the development of openness and trust between consultant and client. This is important because trust is necessary for cooperation and communication. When the trust level is low, people will tend to be dishonest, evasive, and not authentic with one another, and communication is often inaccurate, distorted, or incomplete. In developing a trust relationship, there are several basic responses which the consultant may use in the communication process, including:

- *Questions*—"How do you see the organization?"
- *Applied expertise* (advising)—"One possible intervention is team building."
- *Reflection*—"It sounds like you would like to see a participative form of leadership."
- *Interpretation*—"From your description, intergroup conflict could be the problem."
- *Self-disclosure* —"I've felt discouraged myself when my ideas were rejected."
- *Silence*—say nothing, let the client sort out his or her thoughts.

FIGURE 4.5 Consulting Style Model

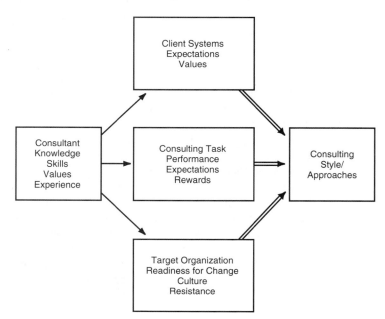

How these basic responses are used is important in developing the consultant-client relationship. In general, the more balanced the consultant's use of these responses and the more open the range of responses, the higher the level of trust. For example, a consultant might rely almost exclusively on questions. This may tend to create a one-way flow of information but does not do any sharing or disclosing of one's own ideas or feelings. Another consultant may rely heavily on advisement responses, which may tend to develop a dependent relationship. Therefore, it is important for the consultant to be aware of the response range and to use a broad variety of responses in building toward an open, trusting relationship.

When the consultant first contacts the client system, the following types of questions may be reflected upon:

- What is the attitude of the client system toward OD? Is there a real underlying desire for change? Or is the attitude superficial?
- What is the "gut-level meaning" of the client's problem? How realistic is the client's appraisal of its own problems?
- What are the possibilities that an OD program will alleviate the problem? Can OD solve the problem or are other change programs more appropriate?
- What is the consultant's potential impact on the system? Based on feedback from the client, how probable is it that the consultant can bring about significant change?

Once these questions have been answered, the consultant may then decide whether to continue the change efforts or to discontinue and terminate the relationship. Most OD practitioners recommend an open discussion with the client on these issues at an early stage.

Creating a Climate For Change

Most OD consultants would agree that an open give-and-take relationship between the consultant and the client is desirable. To some extent this depends on the ability of the consultant to form relationships of openness and trust. Good relationships do not fit into a formula or equation, but OD practitioners have noted a number of recognizable characteristics of which the potential consultant may be aware. Bennis states that "the change agent should act **congruently (authentically)**, in accordance with the values he is attempting to superimpose upon the client system's value system." Or, to use an old expression, the consultant should "practice what he preaches." The consultant must think and act in ways that will create and enhance a positive climate for participation and learning.

Value System Conflicts

The basic value system of the OD practitioner may not be compatible with the organization culture. As a result, there may be conflicts between the value system of the consultant and that of the client system. Michael Maccoby summarizes his findings on the type of manager who holds the leadership in large American companies. Maccoby isolated four basic types:

- *The Craftsman*: holds traditional values and is concerned with the process of making something. This person sees others in terms of whether they will help or hinder him or her in doing a craftsmanlike job.
- *The Jungle Fighter*: lusts for power and experiences life and work as a jungle. Others are seen as either accomplices or enemies.
- *The Company Man*: identity is based on being part of the organization. This person tends to sustain an atmosphere of cooperation, but lacks the daring to be innovative or competitive.
- *The Gamesman*: sees life in terms of options and possibilities as if playing a game. This person likes to take calculated risks and is fascinated by new technologies and methods. The main goal is to be known as a winner, the deepest fear to be labeled a loser.

The OD consultant, in a general sense, will usually find clients fitting into some of Maccoby's characteristic patterns and so must understand some of the needs, drives, and ambitions of the client system environment. The modern manager, in Maccoby's view, is molded by the requirements of the organization, presenting an emotional and spiritual underdevelopment. Consequently, Maccoby asks: "Where will we find future leaders who possess moral strength to know right from wrong and the courage to act on those convictions?"[32]

To assess the degree of difference and the likelihood of working these differences through is part of the OD practitioner's initial intervention. The consultant may desire to create a relationship of openness, authenticity, and trust. The client system managers, however, may tend not to be open, may have learned not to behave authentically, and may even feel threatened by any exploration of feelings or confrontation by the consultant. If the discrepancy between values is too great, the consultant may have reservations about the probability of a successful program. The consultant also examines the degree of conflict and collaboration between organization units and needs to be aware of this to avoid being party to any existing conflicts. "One of the most frequent forms of resistance to change," comments Lippitt, "is the perception by certain subgroups that the consultant is more closely related to other subgroups and is 'on their side' in any conflict of interests."[33]

Consultant-Client Relationship Modes

Eric H. Neilsen has identified several basic dimensions in the consultant-client relationship which can be used as indicators of the climate for change.[34] In order to collaboratively change the organization's culture: (1) members need to share their assumptions, perceptions, and feelings; and (2) members need to accept personal responsibility for their own behavior. Based upon these two dimensions, Neilsen has identified four possible modes in the consultant-client relationship (see Figure 4.6).

The Apathetic Mode. Members keep their true ideas about self-fulfillment and organization effectiveness to themselves. They assume that sharing this information will not make any difference, so why bother. In general, they follow established routines and avoid accepting responsibility for their actions. They simply do as they are told by others. They tend to relate to the consultant in the same manner by assuming that higher authority has sanctioned the change, but viewing it with skepticism.

The Gamesmanship Mode. Members keep their true feelings about self-fulfillment and organizational effectiveness to themselves, under the assumption that sharing information may threaten personally desired outcomes. Members make their own decisions about how to behave, thus taking responsibility for their behavior. This may include conforming outwardly to any decision-making procedure, while manipulating strategic factors to gain per-

FIGURE 4.6 Four Consultant-Client Relationship Modes

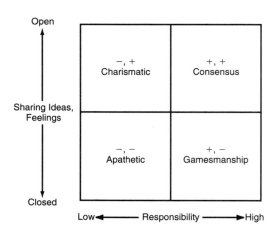

sonal goals. Members may favor change if they can see ways in which it can serve their personal interests.

The Charismatic Mode. In this mode, there is open sharing of ideas and feelings between a limited number of members and the rest, based on perceptions of leadership. The followers are looking for cues from their leaders, so that responsibility is low for most members. Members view the change process as desirable, if the leaders approve. However, they rely on the leaders to interpret the results.

The Consensus Mode. Members continuously share perceptions and feelings openly, both on self-fulfillment and organizational effectiveness. Personal viewpoints are seen as relevant to organization functioning and are expressed. Decisions are made through the sharing of viewpoints and differences are resolved. This process involves both sharing of data and maintaining one's responsibility for actions. Members see the OD process as consistent with their way of operating and find the results interesting and useful.

The consultant, by his or her own attitudes and behavior, makes it possible for the client to create a climate where feelings can be freely and honestly expressed regarding the client system. The consultant also has the ability to listen effectively and to express ideas clearly and concisely. The consultant is honest with the client, as facades have no place in the relationship. By operating on the basis of power equalization, the consultant ensures that the power differential between consultant and client is not too great, or else it will become difficult to develop a collaborative relationship. This is particularly true with internal consultants, who may be in a subordinate position in the organization power structure. The consultant also makes certain that all key parties in the client system are involved to some degree in the OD program. The consultant must determine to what degree the involvement of different individuals or groups is appropriate. But the outcome of ignoring key people is increased resistance and probable ineffectiveness in the change program.

These are not all the dimensions that are involved in a complex consultant-client relationship, but they are intended to provide the beginning practitioner with an awareness of some of the important dimensions that should be examined and considered. The consultant must keep in mind that this relationship is analogous to one's impact on the total system. The practitioner's behavior will actually be a model for the organization members. When a person is attempting to create a climate of openness and collaboration between organization members and departments, one strives to develop relationships based on similar qualities. A good relationship increases the probability of a successful OD program. A tenuous or superficial relationship increases the probability that the OD program will be ineffective or unsuccessful.

The Formalization of Operating Ground Rules

Generally, the first contact between the consultant and the client is informal, exploratory, and tentative. As many consultants (e.g., Beckhard, Bennis, and Schein) point out, successful relationships require some definition of roles and procedures. The formalization of obligations in the form of a contract is usually advisable for an external consultant. Although it is not necessary for the internal consultant to have a contract, key **operating ground rules** should be formalized in some manner. The contract with the external consultant will probably be incorporated in several letters transpiring between the consultant and the client. The formalization or contract normally specifies such items as:

1. *The point of contact*. Which person in the client system will the consultant be contacting and who will be contacting the consultant?
2. *The role of the consultant*. Is he or she to be an expert, a process helper, or some other role?
3. *The fees*. The amount the consultant charges for services varies, depending on the financial status of the client system and the amount of time devoted to consulting. Fees are usually based

upon hourly or daily rates, on a project basis, or a retainer. (McKinsey & Co., for example, reportedly charges a base fee of $200,000 per month plus all expenses incurred.)

4. *The schedule.* For example, "the objectives can be accomplished over an anticipated two-year program devoting five days of consulting time per month." The schedule might also include a tentative list of activities and meetings.

5. *The anticipated results.* The outcome should be stated as specifically as possible; however, some consultants warn against providing any guarantee of value to the organization, as this tends to put the responsibility for change with the consultant instead of with the client. The consultant may promise to develop a valid diagnosis of organization problems, and might suggest in a very general way areas of change that would develop. For example, for its fee from Federated Department Stores, McKinsey agreed to evaluate:
 - The relative economic performance of the company's stores.
 - The relative economic performance of product categories.
 - Consumers perceptions of the stores.
 - The strengths and weaknesses of major competitors.[35]

6. *The operating ground rules.* Such ground rules could include but are not limited to the following:
 - The point of contact, which will usually include the top manager.
 - The requirements of the organization members, such as being prepared for meetings.
 - The confidentiality of consulting information.
 - The process role, rather than having an expert coming in to define problems and implement solutions.

Although these are not all the factors involved in a consulting agreement, they have been presented as guidelines for the beginning practitioner.

Red Flags In The Consultant-Client Relationship

As previously noted, the initial meeting is a critical stage in the OD process. Consultants must decide whether or not to obligate themselves to a change project at this time. An unpromising beginning may lead to a frustrating change effort and to an OD program that is predestined to end as an unrewarding experience. Some of the critical warning signals for the consultant to consider are as follows:

The Level of Commitment to Change. At times the client system is not really committed to a change program. Members may verbally express commitment to the proposed OD program, but their behaviors are not congruent with their words. They may be going through the motions only to please top management.

The Degree of Leverage or Power to Influence Change. Sometimes a lower-level manager invites the consultant into the organization. This member is committed to change, but lacks any real capability to influence the system. Here the consultant must realistically assess the probability of gaining enough leverage to effectively bring about change in such a situation. If a member of the human resources department invites the consultant into the organization, the consultant may first wish to ascertain the degree of top management's receptiveness and support for any proposed change before entering into an OD program.

The Client's Manipulative Use of the Consultant. In certain situations there may be a conflict or an internal power struggle, and the client may wish to involve the consultant as a weapon against other factions or individuals within the organization system. The person in the client system requesting external assistance may want others in the organization to change their ideas or may want to use the consultant to enforce a position which is already committed. The resulting conflict would probably result in a destructive rather than constructive type of change effort, with the consultant caught in the middle. In other situations the client may intend only to use the consultant to gather information about others in the organization that would otherwise be unobtainable.

REVIEW QUESTIONS

1. Compare and contrast the five basic consultant, styles.

2. What are the pros and cons of external and internal consultants? Why is the team approach a viable alternative?

3. What is the importance of an organization being ready for an OD program?

4. Compare and contrast values and goals of client versus consultant.

5. Identify the basic problems in the consultant-client relationship.

KEY WORDS AND CONCEPTS

Define and be able to use the following:

Analyzer Style Consultant
Apathetic Mode
Change Agent
Charismatic Mode
Cheerleader Style Consultant
Client Sponsor
Client Target System
Company Man
Congruent (Authentic)
Consensus Mode
Craftsman
Dilemma Interactions
Entry
External Consultant
External-Internal Consulting Team

Gamesman
Historical Resistance to Change
Internal Consultant
Intervention
Jungle Fighter
Leverage
OD Consultant (Practitioner)
Operating Ground Rules
Pathfinder Style Consultant
Perception
Persuader Style Consultant
Relationship Consulting
Selective Perception
Stabilizer Style Consultant
Trust Relationship

OD SKILLS SIMULATION 4.1
CONSULTANT STYLE MATRIX

Total time suggested: 35 minutes.

A. PURPOSE

The role of the OD consultant is both difficult and challenging The consultant style matrix has been designed to give you information about your characteristic approaches to a consulting relationship. This information may serve to reinforce existing strengths, or it may indicate areas of needed improvement. In either case, the data from the survey should prove helpful in learning more about your style.

At various times there are many people trying to bring about change. They probably do not operate under the guise of a "consultant" but are more commonly referred to as man-

agers, teachers, social workers, ministers, and parents and so on. You may now be, in some aspects of your life, a consultant, and at some time in the future you will most certainly be a consultant. That is, you now are or will be trying to initiate and implement change in an individual or organization. This survey will help you gain some insights into ways you implement change.

B. CHANGE

Step 1. You will find in this survey ten situations that call for your response. Each of the ten situations presents five alternative ways of responding. Because you will be asked to rank these five responses to the situation, it is important that you read through all the responses before answering. Once you have read through all five responses, select the response that is most similar to the way you think you would actually behave or think in such a situation. Place the letter corresponding to that response (a, b, c, d, or e) somewhere on the "Most Similar" end of the 10-point scale appropriate to the intensity of your feeling. Next, select the response that is least similar to the way you would actually act or think. Again place the letter corresponding to that response somewhere on the "Least Similar" end of the scale. Complete the answers by placing the remaining three responses that reflect your actions or thoughts for those responses within range of previously selected most-least points. You may use the Lotus 1-2-3® spreadsheet template provided by your instructor to take the survey, tabulate, and print out the results.

As an example, the answer to a situation could be:

Most Similar	10	9	c 8	b 7	6	5	e 4	d 3	2	a 1	Least Similar

THE CONSULTANT STYLE MATRIX

In answering these questions, think of how you would actually handle or act in the situation or how you think about change and the nature of change.

1. As a consultant relating to a client, I will
 a. Support the client to work out their goals aiming at high morale.
 b. Generally set ground rules and then leave it up to the client.
 c. Identify with the client the goals of the change program and then jointly work through the alternatives.
 d. Try to develop a friendly relationship, while suggesting change goals.
 e. Provide expertise and use logic to convince the client.

Most Similar	10	9	8	7	6	5	4	3	2	1	Least Similar

2. As a consultant, change in a client can best be initiated when
 a. I avoid involving too many people.
 b. The logic for the change is pointed out and results emphasized.
 c. The client first has a good opinion of me and then I urge changes.

 d. I help the client to gain self-confidence and satisfaction.

 e. The client makes a choice for change on the basis of mutual needs and goals.

Most Similar | 10 | 9 | 8 | 7 | 6 | 5 | 4 | 3 | 2 | 1 | Least Similar

3. If I am talking with a client, I usually
 a. Try to be supportive by letting the client do most of the talking.
 b. Try to let the client talk and then slowly sell the client on my methods of change.
 c. Try to be sure the client understands the logic of the decision.
 d. Share about equally in the conversation and attempt to reach a shared conclusion.
 e. Say very little and only present my opinion when asked.

Most Similar | 10 | 9 | 8 | 7 | 6 | 5 | 4 | 3 | 2 | 1 | Least Similar

4. To achieve change in the client, I feel
 a. The client has to be convinced that the plan for change has benefits as well as employee satisfaction.
 b. The client and the consultant can mutually agree on alternatives.
 c. The change and its implementation is left up to the client.
 d. The client decides what change is needed with support given by consultant.
 e. The change is logically presented by the consultant.

Most Similar | 10 | 9 | 8 | 7 | 6 | 5 | 4 | 3 | 2 | 1 | Least Similar

5. When a consulting proposal is suggested and a client reacts negatively to it, I am likely to
 a. Accept the client's position and search for mutual agreement.
 b. Suggest the best course of action.
 c. Go along with the client's ideas.
 d. Point out the requirements of the situation but avoid becoming involved in fruitless argument.
 e. Search for a compromise position that satisfies both points of view.

Most Similar | 10 | 9 | 8 | 7 | 6 | 5 | 4 | 3 | 2 | 1 | Least Similar

6. The client will probably be more accepting of the change if
 a. The consultant emphasizes the rewards to the client and downplays any problems.
 b. The change will result in increased personal satisfaction and morale.
 c. The client is responsible for taking a course of action deemed appropriate.
 d. It is made clear how changes will effect the bottom line.
 e. The client is an active participant along with the consultant in planning for the change.

Most Similar | 10 | 9 | 8 | 7 | 6 | 5 | 4 | 3 | 2 | 1 | Least Similar

7. As a consultant, a decision to change is most effective when the consultant
 a. Tells the client logically what is expected and how to best accomplish the change.
 b. Gains the approval and friendship of the client to get acceptable changes.
 c. Actively participates with the client in setting the change goals.
 d. Leaves the client to make its own decision whether or not to change.
 e. Allows the client to take responsibility for the changes while giving personal support.

8. In evaluating a change as a consultant, I usually use
 a. The degree to which the client complies with the change as well as the amount of pushing from me needed to gain conformance.
 b. The client's performance as measured by goals jointly set by both the client and myself.
 c. The client's evaluation of his or her performance.
 d. An adequate degree of satisfaction to ensure the client's compliance in meeting change requirements.
 e. A high level of morale in the client as well as a friendly relationship between the client and myself.

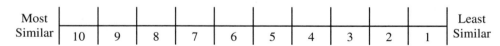

9. In evaluating the client's performance, the consultant should
 a. Look at evaluation as a mutual responsibility.
 b. Use a standard evaluation form to ensure objectivity and equal treatment among persons.
 c. Present one's ideas, then allow questions, but casually push for specific improvement.
 d. Compare performance with quantitative productivity standards.
 e. Encourage the client to make own evaluation with my moral support.

10. As a consultant, if there seems to be a personality conflict, I usually
 a. Try to ignore the conflict, avoid taking sides.
 b. Confront, use logic to gain acceptance of my position.
 c. Try to relieve tension, smooth over differences.
 d. Try to explore differences, resolve conflict, and reach mutual goals.
 e. Try to find areas of commonality, maintain morale, and seek compromise.

Step 2. Scoring instructions for Table 4.2: In Step 1 you wrote your answers (a, b, c, d, and e) above a number. Now transfer from each of the 10 situations your number values for each letter to Table 4.2. For each situation look at the questionnaire to determine what number value you assigned to that letter and then place that number in the columns. These

computations will be made by the template if you are using the computer spreadsheet. The sum of each of the five columns is your score for each of the change styles. There is further explanation of the five change styles in Step 4.

Table 4.2

Situation	Analytical Style	Cheerleader Style	Stabilizer Style	Persuader Style	Pathfinder Style
1.	e = _____	a = _____	b = _____	d = _____	c = _____
2.	b = _____	d = _____	a = _____	c = _____	e = _____
3.	c = _____	a = _____	e = _____	b = _____	d = _____
4.	e = _____	d = _____	c = _____	a = _____	b = _____
5.	b = _____	c = _____	d = _____	e = _____	a = _____
6.	d = _____	b = _____	c = _____	a = _____	e = _____
7.	a = _____	e = _____	d = _____	b = _____	c = _____
8.	a = _____	e = _____	c = _____	d = _____	b = _____
9.	d = _____	e = _____	b = _____	c = _____	a = _____
10.	b = _____	c = _____	a = _____	e = _____	d = _____
Total Points	_____	_____	_____	_____	_____

Step 3. Scoring instructions for Table 4.3:

1. Transfer the numerical sums from the score sheet in Table 4.2 to Table 4.3, column 2 by rearranging them from highest to lowest score.
2. In column 1 write the appropriate Word Description of Approach to Change beside the score.
3. Take the difference of the scores (column 2) for your first and second choices and record the difference on the first line of column 3. Then take the difference for your second and third choices and record the difference on the second line of column 3. Continue taking the differences between the third and fourth choices, and the fourth and fifth choices. The difference between scores indicates the likelihood that a person will shift styles: a low score (1–10) suggests switching, a high score (over 20) suggests resistance to shifting.

Table 4.3

Your Choice	Word Description of Approach to Change (Col. 1)	Score (high to low) (Col. 2)	Difference between Scores (Col. 3)
1st Primary	_____	_____	_____
2nd Backup	_____	_____	_____
3rd Backup	_____	_____	_____
4th Backup	_____	_____	_____
5th Backup	_____	_____	_____

Time suggested for Steps 2 and 3: 15 minutes.

Step 4. Styles of implementing change: You have just completed and scored your consultant survey. Following is a brief explanation of the five styles.

The pathfinder style. The person using this style constantly strives for achievement of the change goals by other people in the change program and at the same time has maximum concern that the people involved in implementing the change are personally committed to the change and to the vision of the future.

The persuader style. This type of consulting style has medium concern for achievement of the change goals and medium concern that the people implementing the change are committed to the change goals. As a result, the consultant using this style is not consistent in behavior, and often shifts the emphasis from concern for change goals to concern for the people involved in the change program. The consultant believes too rapid a change will be disruptive and, therefore, attempts to implement change in small steps which allow people to become gradually accustomed to the changes and to avoid conflict.

The cheerleader style. The consultant using this style has minimum concern that the stated change goals are accomplished, but does have maximum concern that the people involved in the change program are personally committed to and happy with the change. There may be as many change programs as there are people, because the cheerleader style consultant encourages members of a system to design and implement their own programs of change. The emphasis is on moral and friendly relationships.

The analyzer style. The person using this style has maximum concern for efficient accomplishment of the change goals and little concern that the people involved in implementing the change are personally committed to these goals. The analyzer style sees people as a means to accomplish the change and believes that people must be closely guided and directed because they lack the desire or capacity to change. A person using this style tends to use an expert-based style and sets demanding performance standards as a method of implementing change.

The stabilizer style. This style of consultant has very minimum concern for goal accomplishment and minimum concern for the people involved. The consultant does not care to get involved and is only biding time until new orders come down. Change is viewed as a disruption of a well-ordered and secure environment.

You may now plot your average style scores on the graph in Table 4.4 Consulting Styles. Complete the bar chart by shading in the score for each style (or the Lotus template will automatically plot it). This provides a profile of your scores.

A person does not operate using one style to the exclusion of others. The purpose of the scoring in Step 3 was to give you an indication of the importance you place on each of the five styles. The difference between your primary and backup styles indicates the strength of your preference and how quickly you will fall back on another style. Little difference between scores could indicate a tendency to vacillate between styles or vague thoughts about how to handle change. A large difference could indicate a strong reliance on the predominant change style.

This survey should be used as a point of departure for further reflection and observation concerning the way you attempt to change and influence other people. To obtain a better understanding of your change style, try to become aware in your associations with friends, peers, and working associates of how you handle change. It may also be helpful to observe other people when they try to change or influence your behavior and to become aware of how you react to their change methods.

Step 5. In class session, discuss the five consulting styles. Does your score for your primary and backup change style seem congruent with the way you think you operate in change situations? Share your scores with class members with whom you have been working and get their feedback. Does this feedback correlate with your scores on the matrix?

Time suggested for Steps 4 and 5: 20 minutes.

Table 4.4 Consulting Style

	0	10	20	30	40	50	60	70	80	90	100
Pathfinder											
Persuader											
Cheerleader											
Analyzer											
Stabilizer											

OD SKILLS SIMULATION 4.2
CONFLICT STYLES

Total time suggested: 1 hour.

A. PURPOSE

This simulation is designed to allow you the opportunity to influence and change other individuals as well as to be influenced and changed by others. Although the story may seem minor, it describes a situation about which most of us have some rather strong feelings and ideas. Through diverse usage we have found it to be a means to quickly get involvement and commitment to certain issues which you will select. This personal involvement is necessary so that in a later part of the simulation that requires you to change others' ideas and others to change your ideas, there will be a real and prior commitment to those ideas. The goals include: (1) to identify ways of dealing with organizational or group conflict, (2) to discuss when and why different methods of resolving conflict are appropriate to different situations, and (3) to provide an experience in group decision making.

B. PROCEDURES

Step 1. Form groups of five members each. Any extra persons may join as the sixth member of a group, but no group should have more than six or fewer than four members.

Step 2. The following is a short story you are to read. Answer the question that directly follows the story *individually*. Spaces are provided on Line A for your answer.

THE YOUNG WOMAN

In a house is a young woman married to a man who works very hard. She feels neglected. When her husband goes off on still another trip, the young wife meets an attractive man who invites her to his house. She spends the night and at dawn she leaves, knowing her husband is coming home. Alas! The bridge is blocked by a madman who kills everyone who

comes near him. The young wife follows the river and meets the ferryman, but he demands one hundred francs to take her to the other side. The young wife has no money. She runs back to her lover and asks for one hundred francs; he refuses to help. The woman remembers that a platonic friend lives nearby. She runs to him and explains her plight. The friend refuses to help; she has disillusioned him by her conduct. Her only choice is to go by the bridge in spite of the danger, and the madman kills her. That is the story.[35]

In what order do you hold the principals (woman, husband, lover, madman, ferryman, and friend) responsible for the tragedy?

Line A	1.	2.	3.	4.	5.	6.
Line B	1.	2.	3.	4.	5.	6.
Line C	1.	2.	3.	4.	5.	6.

Step 3. In your groups you are to arrive at a group consensus for the answer to the question. Most members will not have the same answer, but it is important that your group make its decision in 15 minutes. Place the group's answer on Line B.

Time suggested for Steps 1-3: 20 minutes.

Step 4. Form a class group again and focus your discussion on the following questions:

1. Was there much disagreement within your group?
2. If there was, to what could it be attributed?
3. How did your group reach its decision (consensus, voting, etc.)?
4. To what extent do you feel that other members of your group support the group's decision?

Time suggested for Step 4: 5 minutes.

Step 5. Go back to the story and on Line C answer the question again, but on an *individual basis.* Your answers may be the same as when you first responded to the story or you may alter your original position based on the team discussion.

Step 6. Meet back in your groups to observe how individuals responded on Line C. Observe to see if Line C answers are the same as those on Line B and Line A, or perhaps different from any previous answers.

Time suggested for Steps 5 and 6: 5 minutes.

Step 7. Complete Table 4.5 Team Member Styles, by recording what you observed to be the primary and backup consulting styles (pathfinder, persuader, cheerleader, analyzer, or stabilizer) of members in your group. Add any observations or comments about why that style seems to fit.

Time suggested for Step 7: 10 minutes.

Step 8. In Table 4.6 Individual Style Feedback, transfer the information from what the other team members recorded about you in their Table 4.5. From Table 4.6 try to draw some conclusion about your style of consulting. Discuss your conclusions with the other team members.

1. How did your survey style compare with the information received from your team?
2. Was there general agreement from your team on your consultant style? If there were differences, to what could they be attributed?

Time suggested for Step 8: 10 minutes.

Step 9. Meeting with the entire class, discuss the following questions:

1. How congruent were your scores from Simulation 4.1 with the feedback from your group members?
2. If there was any difference, to what could it be attributed?
3. What consulting styles do you feel are most effective in an OD program? Why?

Time suggested for Step 9: 5 minutes.

Table 4.5 Team Member Styles

Group Member's Name	Primary Style	Backup Style	Comments/ Observations

Table 4.6 Individual Style Feedback

	Information Received From	Primary Style	Backup Style	Comments/Observations
1				
2				
3				
4				
5				
6				
Consensus				

CASE 4
THE GRAYSON CHEMICAL COMPANY

THE COMPANY

The Grayson Chemical Co. manufactured industrial chemicals for sale to other industrial companies. The company was about 40 years old and had been run by a stable management under only two presidents. Within the past few years, however, declining earnings and sales had brought pressure from the board of directors, investment bankers, and stockholder groups to name a new president. The company had grown increasingly stagnant—although at

Grayson they refer to it as conservative—and had steadily lost market standing and profitability. Finally, the Board decided to go outside the company to find a new CEO and was able to recruit a dynamic manager from another major corporation, Tom Baker. Baker is 47, an M.B.A. and had helped build his prior company into a leadership position. However, when another executive was chosen for the top job, Baker decided to accept the position with Grayson.

Baker was clear about what he needed to do. He knew that he needed to develop a top management team that could provide the leadership to turn the company around. Unfortunately, the situation at Grayson was not very favorable.

Decisions were made by the book, or taken to the next higher level. Things were done because "they have always been done this way," and incompetent managers were often promoted to high-level jobs.

THE MEETING

In a meeting with three members of the Board, Robert Temple (chairman), James Allen, and Hartley Ashford each had a different bit if advice to offer.

Robert Temple said: "Look, Tom, you can't just get rid of the old organization if you want to maintain any semblance of morale. Your existing people are all fairly competent technically, but it's up to you to develop performance goals and motivate them to achieve these standards. Make it clear that achievement will be rewarded and that those who can't hack it will have to go."

James Allen, puffing on his pipe, noted: "Let's face it, Tom, you need to bring in a new top management team. Probably only six or so, but people who know what top performance means, people who are using innovative methods of managing and, above all, people you trust. That means people whom you've worked with closely, from ABC or other companies, but people you know. You can't retread the old people and you don't have time to develop young MBAs, so you need to bring in your own team even though it might upset some of the old timers."

Hartley Ashford smiled and said: "Sure, you're going to have to bring in a new team from the outside, but rather than bring in people you've worked with before, bring in only managers with proven track records. People who have proven their ability to lead, motivate and perform, from different industries. This way you will get a synergistic effect from a number of successful organizations. And the old people will see that favoritism is not the way to get ahead. So get a top performance team, and if you lose a few old timers, so much the better."

CASE ANALYSIS FORM

Name: _____

I. Problems

 A. Macro

 1. _____

 2. _____

 B. Micro

 1. _____

 2. _____

II. Causes

 1. _____

 2. _____

 3. _____

III. Systems affected

 1. Structural _____

 2. Psychosocial _____

 3. Technical _____

 4. Managerial_____

 5. Goals _____

IV. Alternatives

 1. _____

 2. _____

 3. _____

 4. _____

 5. _____

V. Recommendations

 1. _____

 2. _____

 3. _____

SUMMARY

- **OD Goals.** The organization is a system. The OD consultant intervenes in the system and its plans, structures, leadership, and controls for various purposes. But the overriding change goal is to develop and maintain the dynamic fit between members and tasks which is necessary to yield organization effectiveness and human satisfaction.

- **Consulting Roles.** You have examined the various types of consultants, also roles and possible approaches. The problems of entry into the client system were also explored. The consultant must decide at exactly what point, how, and with whom to intervene. The receptivity of the system to change must not be overlooked or taken for granted but ought to be carefully probed and realistically determined prior to further intervention.

- **Consulting Skills.** You have had the opportunity to gain insights into your own consulting style, to assess your own strengths and areas of improvement as a potential OD consultant, and to examine briefly the impact of a given style upon others. One important aspect of being a consultant is to *know yourself.* Only by being aware of your own motives, reactions, and needs can you successfully hope to influence others.

- **OD Consultant Styles.** The Consultant Style Matrix provided an opportunity for you to gain some insights into how you approach change situations. It is important to rec-

ognize that your answers to the survey may reflect more the way you wish to behave—an ideal—than the way you actually do behave. Your first objective is to get a clear reading on your actual consultant style by getting feedback from your fellow participants. Their reports on how your actions affect them will enable you to move to a more effective style. You have begun this integration process here, but it should be a continuing process of feedback, reappraisal, and experimentation throughout this course and beyond.

- **Feedback.** The last simulation was intended to provide a situation where you could gain feedback on your consultant style. During the intervention in a decision situation, you have encountered the problems of developing a change strategy and observed the consequences of different styles and approaches. You have also been receiving feedback from other members of your team, which should enable you to become more proficient in handling change situations.

- **Innovation.** Today we need organizations with flexibility and responsiveness, ever faster innovations and higher involvement among employees. The OD consultant is the person who initiates, stimulates, or facilitates a change program. In this section, you have experienced a situation where you have gained insights into your own consulting style and its degree of influence in a group.

NOTES

1. Thomas A. Stewart, "Welcome to the Revolution," *Fortune*, December 13, 1993, p. 66.
2. John A. Byrne, "The Horizontal Corporation," *Business Week*, December 20, 1993, p. 77.
3. Teresa Colvin and Ralph Kilmann, "A Profile of Large Scale Change Programs," *Proceedings*, Southern Management Association, 1989, p. 202.
4. "Decade of Downsizing Eases Stigma of Layoffs," *The Wall Street Journal*, February 8, 1994, p. 1.
5. Shari Caudren, "Change Keeps TQM Programs Thriving," *Personnel Journal*, October 1993, p. 104.
6. Teresa Colvin.
7. "How McKinsey Does It," *Fortune*, November 1, 1993, p. 60.
8. John Hulpke, California State University, Bakersfield. See also "Matshusita Goes Global," *Fortune*, July 11, 1994, p. 160.
9. Philip Hunsaker, "Strategies for Organizational Change: The Role of the Inside Change Agent," *Personnel*, September/October 1982, pp. 10–28.
10. Excerpt from the "Playboy Interview with Admiral Elmo Zumwalt." Originally appeared in *Playboy* Magazine; copyright® 1974 by *Playboy.*
11. John Lewis III, "Growth of Internal Change Agents in Organization Development," doctoral dissertation, Case Western Reserve University, 1970.
12. Hunsaker, "Strategies for Change," pp. 18–28.
13. Susan Gebelein, "Profile of an Internal Consultant: Roles and Skills," *Training & Development Journal*, March 1989, p. 52.
14. See Harold J. Leavitt, *Corporate Pathfinders*, (Homewood, IL: Dow Jones-Irwin, 1986), p. 10.
15. Lynda C. McDermott, "The Many Faces of the OD Professional," *Training and Development Journal*, Vol. 38, No. 2, February 1984, pp. 14–19.
16. Edgar Schein, *Process Consultation: Its Role in Organization Development*, (Reading, Mass.: Addison-Wesley Publishing Co., Inc., 1988), p. 13.
17. Warren Bennis, *Organization Development: Its Nature, Origins, and Prospects*, (Reading, MA: Addison-Wesley Publishing Co., Inc., 1969), p. 48.
18. Thomas J. Peters, *Thriving on Chaos*, (New York: Alfred A. Knopf, 1987), p. 3.
19. Keith H. Hammonds, "Can Bain Consultants Get Bain Out of this Jam?," *Business Week*, February 11, 1991, p. 52–53.
20. See Richard Beckhard, *Organization Development: Strategies and Models*, (Reading, MA: Addison-Wesley Publishing Co., Inc., 1969), p. 13.
21. Michael Beer and Edgar Huse, "A Systems Approach to Organization Development," *Journal of Applied Behavioral Science*, Vol. 1, No. 8, 1979, pp. 79–101.
22. John Templeman, "A Hard U-Turn at VW," *Business Week*, March 15, 1993, p. 47.
23. L. Goodstein and R. Boyer, "Crisis Intervention in a Municipal Agency: A Conceptual Case History," *Journal of Applied Behavioral Science*, (May–June 1972), pp. 318–40.

24. Charles C. Manz, David Keating & Anne Donnellon, "Preparing for an Organizational Change to Employee Self Management," *Organizational Dynamics*, Vol. 19, Autumn, 1990, p. 15.

25. Edgar Schein, *Process Consultation, Volume I: Its Role in Organization Development*, (Reading, MA: Addison-Wesley Publishing Co., Inc., 1988), p. 11.

26. *Ibid.*

27. See Fagensona and Burke, *The Current Activities*, p. 251.

28. Susan Gebelein, "Profile of an Internal Consultant: Roles and Skills," *Training & Development Journal*, March 1989, p. 52.

29. Bennis, *Organization Development*, p. 43.

30. Patricia Hurley, "What in the Name of OD Do We Do?" *Training and Development Journal*, Vol. 37, No. 4, April 1983, p. 44.

31. N. Polansky and J. Kounin, "Client's Reactions to Initial Interviews: A Field Study," *Human Relations*, No. 9 (1956), pp. 237–65.

32. Michael Maccoby, *The Gamesman: The New Corporate Leaders*, (New York: Simon & Schuster, Inc., 1976).

33. Ronald Lippitt, "Dimensions of the Consultant's Job," in *The Planning of Change*, ed W. Bennis, K. Benne, and R Chin (New York: Holt, Rinehart & Winston, 1961), p. 160.

34. Eric H. Neilsen, "Reading Clients' Values from Their Reactions to an Intervention/Feedback Process," *Academy of Management Proceedings*, 1978, p. 318.

35. John Huey, "How McKinsey Does It," *Fortune*, November 1, 1993, p. 66.

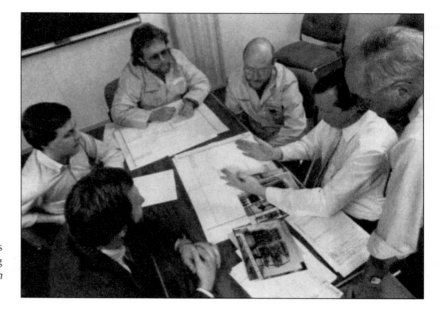

Design Excellence Team members discuss Peacekeeper engineering refinements during a tabletop review. *Photo courtesy of Martin Marietta Corporation.*

The OD Consultant: The Diagnostic Process

5

OBJECTIVES

Upon completing this chapter, you will be able to:

1. Identify system parameters and recognize symptoms, problems, and causes of organization ineffectiveness.
2. Recognize the various techniques for gathering information from client systems.
3. Describe the major diagnostic models and techniques used in OD programs.
4. Apply a systematic diagnosis to organizational situations.

PREMEETING PREPARATION

1. Read the Background Information.
2. Prepare for OD Skills Simulation 5.1. Complete Step 1. Form groups of 5 and select roles.
3. Read and analyze Case 5: The Old Family Bank.

BACKGROUND INFORMATION

The successful organization in the twenty-first century will need flexibility and the ability for rapid transformation. The organization moves along a well-worn path and often problems are concealed or hidden by other factors.

An important element in developing a high performance organization is the identification of areas for improvement or problems. During a time of downsizing and restructuring, many American companies are finding that they must learn to manage more effectively. Organizational problem solving means that all members of an organization participate in developing a vision and improving the corporate culture. In any change program, you must know where you are before you can chart a course for where you want to be. Therefore, before implementing TQM, or another program, it is important to assess the organization in terms of its current quality or performance level and to define the level of performance or quality you wish to achieve.[1] Organization diagnosis provides information which allows a faster reacting organization to emerge, one which can deal proactively with changing forces. Organization diagnosis is often mentioned as the most critical element in the OD process. In a recent survey of OD practitioners, it was reported that a diagnostic phase of some type occurred in 85 percent of the projects.[2]

Organization diagnosis is aimed at providing a rigorous analysis of data on the structure, administration, interaction, procedures, interfaces, and other essential elements of the client system. The diagnosis, then, provides a basis for structural, behavioral, or technical interventions to improve organizational performance. Diagnosing a problem requires a systematic approach throughout the process. If organization change is to be effective, it must be based on a specific diagnosis of the problem.

One rule, or **modus operandi (M/O),** for the organization development consultant is to question the client's diagnosis of the problem. The client may have some preconceived ideas as to what the problem is, but these ideas should be accepted only after having been verified by research. The client is part of the system that has a problem, and this may prevent the client from taking an objective view of the situation. Also, the client will probably be operating from one part of a larger system, and it may be difficult if not impossible to see the total system. It would be appropriate for the consultant to listen to the client's definition and ideas of the problem, but the consultant should openly seek permission to verify these ideas with properly conducted research. Diagnosis is a process that helps organizations improve their capacity to assess and change inefficient patterns of behavior as a basis for developing greater effectiveness and ensuring continuous improvement.

An OD program must be based on a sound analysis of relevant data about the problem situation. To make a sound diagnosis, it is important to have valid information about the situation and to arrange available data into a meaningful pattern. The simple fact of sharing performance information can become a powerful force for change.

In this chapter, the diagnostic stage of an OD program is examined. This includes a general definition of diagnosis, the major diagnostic models, the data collection process, and red flag situations.

What Is Diagnosis?

Today's intense global competition and deregulation have created much higher uncertainty for firms in virtually every industry. Increased competition requires constant response to initiatives by other firms. It calls for continuous improvement of quality and products while decreasing costs. Michael Beer has suggested, diagnosis as a method of analyzing organizational problems and learning new patterns of behavior. It can be a process that helps organizations by doing the following:

1. Enhancing their capacity to assess and change the culture of the organization.
2. Providing an opportunity for organizational members to acquire new insights into the dysfunctional aspects of their culture and patterns of behavior as a basis for developing a more effective organization.
3. Ensuring that the organization remains engaged in a process of continuous improvement.[3]

Because diagnosis provides these opportunities, it becomes an indispensable step in the process of organizational revitalization. Organization development is a data-based activity. One of the characteristics of OD is the reliance on valid information about current problems and possible opportunities for improvement. A study of over 1,000 practitioners, found that organizational diagnosis was one of the major consulting skills.[4] The diagnosis provides a starting point (a set of current conditions) and the change objective (an ideal or desired set of conditions). The *diagnosis* usually examines two broad areas. First, a diagnosis is made of the various subelements that make up the organization. These include the divisions, department, products, and the relationships between these interacting elements. This may also include a comparison of managerial levels among the top, middle, and lower levels of the organization.

The second area of diagnosis is based on the organizational processes. These include communication networks, team problem solving, decision making, leadership and authority styles, goal setting and planning methods, and the management of conflict and competition.

In organizational diagnosis, the consultant is looking for causality—that is, the implication that changes in one factor (such as compensation) will cause change in another factor (productivity): a cause-effect relationship. Often the client is aware of the evidence of the problem, such as declining sales, high turnover, or loss of market share—the symptoms of a problem. In the diagnostic phase, the consultant tries to identify what factors are causing the problems, and therefore what needs to be changed to fix it.

The critical issues in diagnosis include:

- *Simplicity*. Keep data as simple as possible and use simplicity in presentation, or KISS—Keep It Simple, Stupid.
- *Visibility*. Use visible measures of what's happening.
- *Involvement*. Emphasize participation and involvement of organization members in the diagnosis.
- *Primary Factors*. Use undistorted collection of primary operating variables in diagnosis.
- *Measure What's Important*. Pursue the straightforward assessment of variables that are critical to success.
- *A Sense of Urgency*. During diagnosis, gain an overall sense of urgency for change.[5]

At McKinsey & Co., the diagnostic process is "hypothesis-driven". The consulting team develops hypotheses such as, "People who sell big orders make more money for the company." The consulting team then gathers data to test these hypotheses before recommending solutions. The team may interview many managers at many companies, and collect factual data to prove or disprove and may discover, in fact, that large sales orders may be the least profitable. The secret of diagnosis, then, is in the rigor of fact-finding, things are proved with facts, not opinions.[6]

Diagnosis is a systematic approach to understanding and describing the present state of the organization. The purpose of the diagnostic phase is to specify the nature of the exact problem requiring solution, to identify the underlying causal forces, and to provide a basis for selecting effective change strategies and techniques. The outcome of a weak, inaccurate, or faulty diagnosis will be a costly and ineffective OD program. Organization diagnosis, then, involves the systematic analysis of data regarding the organization processes and culture with the intention of discovering problems and areas for improvement.

The Process

Diagnosis is a cyclical process which involves data gathering, interpretation, and identification of problem areas and potential action programs, as shown in Figure 5.1. The first step

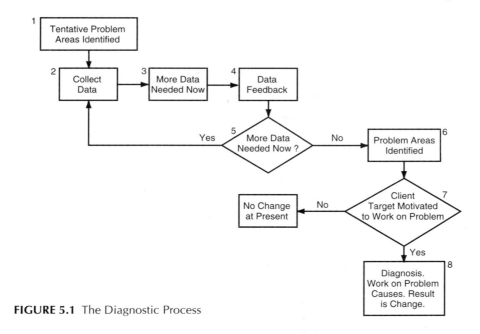

FIGURE 5.1 The Diagnostic Process

is the preliminary identification of possible problem areas. Often these preliminary attempts tend to bring out symptoms as well as possible problem areas.

The second step involves gathering data based on the preliminary problem that was identified in the previous step. These data are then categorized, analyzed, and presented to the client in a feedback session (steps 3 and 4). If it is determined that enough data is available (step 5), then the client and consultant jointly diagnose and identify likely problem areas (step 6). At this point, the level of motivation of the client to work on the problems is determined (step 7). Based upon the diagnosis, the target systems are identified and the change strategy is designed (step 8). Finally (step 9), the results are monitored to determine the level of degree of change that has been attained versus the desired change goals.

The Performance Gap

One method in the diagnostic process is to determine the **performance gap**—the difference between what the organization could do by virtue of its opportunity in its environment and what it actually does in taking advantage of the opportunity. This leads to an approach that may be termed *gap analysis*. In this method, data are collected on the actual state of the organization on a varying set of dimensions and also on the ideal or desired state, that is, "where the organization should be." As shown in Figure 5.2, the gaps or discrepancy between the actual state and the ideal forms a basis for diagnosis and the design of interventions. The gap may be characterized by ineffective performance among internal units or emerge because of other competitive changes or new innovations. Performance gap may also occur when the organization fails to adapt to changes in its external environment.

Competent organizational diagnosis not only provides information about the nature of the system, but it is also helpful in designing and introducing action alternatives for correcting possible problems. The diagnosis affirms the need for change and the benefits of possible changes in the client system. Many times, important problems are hidden or obscure while more conspicuous and obvious problems may be relatively unimportant. In such situations, dealing with the obvious may not be a very effective way to manage change, and points out the importance of the diagnostic stage.

As noted earlier, some 85 percent of OD practitioners reported using some form of diagnostic process. One example of data collection and diagnosis occurred at Eastman Kodak

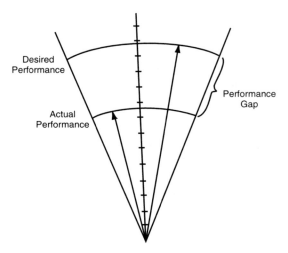

FIGURE 5.2 The Performance Gap

and is described in OD in Practice. Kodak management is examining its performance to identify "performance gaps"—gaps between actual and desired performance.

The performance gap may continue for some time before it is recognized, as at Kodak. In fact, it may never be recognized. One consultant, for example, says of IBM, "IBM still clings to outmoded technology out of fear of alienating its existing customers who have invested heavily in the older systems. Somewhere between one and four years from now the company is going to enter another period of crisis." This performance gap will be a technological gap, and will take more than financial or organizational changes.

OD IN PRACTICE
DIAGNOSIS FOR KODAK: THE MULTIMEDIA REVOLUTION[7]

Eastman Kodak, after cutting tens of thousands of jobs, is betting heavily that new CEO George M. C. Fisher can transform Kodak from a cost cutting, slow changing company into a leader on the cutting edge of the multimedia revolution. In choosing a builder instead of a bloodletter for its new CEO, Kodak is clearly reversing its former strategy. Fisher, the soft spoken wizard who put Motorola atop the evolving electronic world, envisions turning Kodak into a leader in the electronic age.

Data Collection and Analysis

Kodak polled a widening corps of its managers and called in outside consultants. McKinsey & Co. even conducted "trap teams," where managers were invited to test out scenarios that might cause problems. Finally, Kodak's core photo businesses were reshuffled into 17 entrepreneurial units. Such a measured approach to change has been the very essence of Kodak, a company that has raised careful deliberation—some would say procrastination—to a high art. In the last decade, Kodak dragged its feet while competitors ran away with new markets such as instant photography, 35mm cameras, video recorders, and copying machines.

Kodak faces several dilemmas: they must hold down prices or risk losing market share to foreign competitors, but at the same time, investors want improved returns now. Competition is especially fierce in the color print film business, Kodak's mainstay. Yet back in 1970, Kodak came up with the video recorder technology, but decided not to pursue it. Now it seems the long-term future of photography is in electronics, not film. Today, growth is slowing in Kodak's photographic products, the mainstays of the company for 105 years. The betting is that Mr. Fisher will accelerate development of more powerful and cheaper versions of electronic-imaging equipment.

Diagnosis and Change

George Fisher laid out his vision for Kodak as a treasured brand name in a fast moving multimedia revolution in which images and information merge, and won over the Board of Directors. The directors began to believe his vision of combining Kodak's image technology with wireless technology. For Fisher, the job of making Kodak more effective will require changing a 100-year-old culture that guaranteed employment, but fostered

complacency and resistance to change. In the past, Kodak was known to favor caution over risk taking, which was possible when Kodak controlled the market. But now young managers are being given authority over new product development.

What's so tough about the job of remaking Kodak? First, it is a chemical company that must transform itself, at least in part, into an electronics company. The chemical business, silver halide photography, is mature and slow growing. The electronics business involves translating images into the digital language of computing so they can be manipulated on computer screens and transported electronically; it is still a small, fast-growing industry full of startups. The two businesses are like an elephant and mouse.

New Products and Markets

One of Kodak's greatest challenges will be managing its many new ventures, something it has muffed in the past. Fisher's task is to make a big company act like a small one. Still, Kodak's diversifications are minimal so far. Fisher believes the company needs to build market share by combining Kodak's image technology with wireless technology.

Indeed, the company has been moving away from consumer electronics, such as its 8mm video camera market, to focus its attention on nonconsumer applications of electronics. Kodak has failed to introduce new consumer electronic products "in an industry where you obsolete your own products every month," notes a trade newsletter. So far, the impact of such new technologies on the bottom line has been negligible. But in the future, electronics could make up fully half of Kodak's business.

Since the late 1980's, Kodak's share in consumer film has eroded from 80% to as low as 60%, according to some estimates. Customers, once fiercely loyal to the little yellow box, now often turn to Fuji or private-label film to save money. Mr. Fisher's challenge is to get the costs out of the business to better compete for today's more frugal customer. Mr. Fisher said his marketing strategy is simply to "give customers what they want, when they want it, at a value that allows you to make some money."

But will George Fisher's diagnosis and vision bring about the desired changes, and will Kodak's managers after years in the old culture, be able to break out of the former ineffective patterns? But the new strategy isn't without risk. Kodak has to combine still images with information pipelines and processing content for the digital highways of tomorrow could be the long term bet Mr. Fisher makes for Kodak. The new CEO needs to pick his own management team, and needs to motivate current Kodak employees to be more productive. The big question is, "Can Fisher transform a sluggish giant into a technology leader?"

Questions

1. What data or information would be necessary to develop a change program?
2. What kind of performance gaps might you identify at Kodak?
3. Why is it so important to use diagnosis prior to implementing a change program?

The awareness of a performance gap may unfreeze functions within the organization that are most in need of change. When this occurs, conditions are present for altering the structure and function of the organization by introducing OD interventions.

One OD practitioner suggests a self-assessment version of gap analysis using questionnaires to gather information in four key areas:

1. The organization's strengths.
2. What can be done to take advantage of those strengths.
3. The organization's weaknesses.
4. What can be done to alleviate those weaknesses.[8]

These diagnostic approaches point to a common problem—organizations that are data-rich but information poor: lots of data, but little or no information. The process of identifying the organization's strengths and weaknesses often leads to recognition of performance gaps and to change programs.

Diagnostic Models

Diagnosis is based on some understanding of how an organization functions. OD practitioners use diagnostic models to assess an organization.[9] In an investigation of 245 OD practitioners, Burke, Clark, and Koopman found that 70 percent used a model to help diagnose the organization.[10] One method of diagnosis (presented earlier in Chapter 2) is the system model. Diagnostic models play a critical role in an organization development program. The trend now is to ask employees to rate the organization's progress on issues like corporate change, empowerment, and so on. Each of the various diagnostic models may be used to analyze the structure, culture, and behavior of the organization. Several diagnostic models will be examined in this section.

The Analytical Model

The **analytical model**, sometimes referred to as the *differentiation-integration model*, stresses the importance of a sound analytical diagnosis as the basis for planned change in organizations.[11] The model was developed to study and understand interdepartmental issues by conducting a careful diagnosis of the organization's problem areas. Most organizations are composed of departments or divisions; that is, the organization is composed of differentiated function or units that must be integrated into a unified effort if the organization is to be effective. The various tasks that the units work on can be examined in respect to four characteristics of the organization's environment: (1) the degree of departmental structure; (2) the time orientation of members; (3) the interpersonal orientation of members toward others, and (4) organization members' orientation toward goals (see Table 5.1).

One example of how this model can be used is shown in Table 5.1, which presents the survey results of four departments of a typical company. The data shows the finance and research departments are fairly wide apart in how the members view time, orientation toward others, and goals. Despite these differences, the two departments must work together. By using the analytical model, it may be possible for the two departments to understand why they have differences and to develop ways to work better together. The data on these four characteristics provides a basis for structural or cultural changes in the department. When the groups in an organization tend to be highly differentiated, cooperation between them becomes difficult and it may be necessary for the organization to design methods for achieving integration.

The Emergent-Group Behavior Model

The **emergent-group behavior model** is based primarily on the work of George Homans and provides a conceptual scheme for analyzing behavior in work groups, particularly the

Table 5.1 The Orientation of Functional Departments

Organization Units	Degree of Departmental Structure	Members' Orientation toward Time	Members' Orientation toward Others	Members' Goal Orientation
Finance	High	Short	Controlling	Investment
Research	Low	Long	Permissive	Science
Marketing	Medium	Short	Permissive	Market
Production	High	Short	Directive	Product

interdependence of groups.[12] According to this diagnostic model, a complex pattern of behavior consisting of activities, interactions, sentiments, and norms develops from the set of behaviors and relationships required to perform the work of the group. In addition, there are a complex set of behaviors that emerge in addition to those required, such as social activity. The behavior may or may not assist the group in the performance of their duties. The emergent-group behavior model helps in understanding how teams operate. This model is used to gather observations and information on these four characteristics and uses these data to diagnose problems among or within teams.

Management Consulting Model

In a study of over 900 consulting cases, Terry Armstrong and Walter Wheatley have developed a diagnostic model for use in management consulting which analyzes six basic factors as shown in Figure 5.3. These include:

- *Basic Planning*—do they have a mission, vision, and goals?
- *General Business Practices*—do they have appropriate management systems?
- *Finance* —are they operating with timely and accurate financial data and plans?
- *Advertising and Promotion*—are they aware of the link between advertising and sales?
- *Market Research*—are they aware of competitors' strategies, policies, etc., and customer's needs?
- *Personnel*— do they have appropriate systems for recruiting, training, and retaining human resources?

They suggest that it is possible to ask a few basic questions in each area to gain an indication of where the client's problems may be located.[13] See Our Changing World (p. 130) for an example of diagnosis at Asahi Brewery.

FIGURE 5.3 Managerial Consulting Diagnostic Model

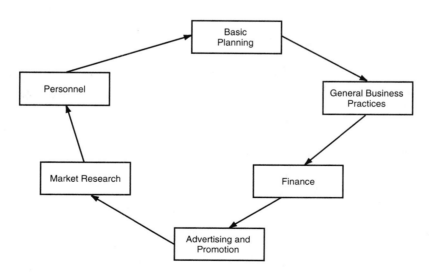

Source: Adapted from Armstrong and Wheatley, p. 8.

OUR CHANGING WORLD
WHEN TROUBLE BREWED AT ASAHI[14]

The purpose of the diagnostic phase is to specify the nature of the exact problem requiring solution, to identify the underlying causal forces, and to provide a basis for selecting effective strategies for change. One method is to check for a performance gap—the difference between what an organization could do and what it is doing. Unfortunately, the performance gap may go unrecognized for quite a while. A look at Japan's Asahi Brewery provides a case in point.

Sometimes things seem to be going smoothly when in fact trouble is brewing. Consider the Asahi story.

Growth in Sales

Originally incorporated in 1886 as Osaka Brewery, this firm grew into the number one brewery in Japan by two kinds of growth. Internal expansion accounted for some growth, and in 1906 the growing firm merged with both Nippon Brewery and Sapporo Brewery. The newly merged company grew steadily so that by 1949, the firm controlled 70 percent of the Japanese beer market. However, a post-World War II antimonopoly law forced a breakup of the firm into two parts. Asahi came out of the breakup with a respectable business, and a healthy 36.1 percent of the Japanese market. From 1949 on, the new Asahi Brewery, Limited exhibited the following growth in sales:

Year	Sales in Billion Yen
1949	2
1955	27
1960	50
1965	89
1970	109
1975	145
1980	185
1985	236

Market Share Data

The figures look impressive, showing an obviously healthy growing organization, right? Wrong! Unfortunately for Asahi, the growth in sales completely obscured some other pertinent facts. Things were not really going all that well. The truth is that Japan's beer market was undergoing an explosive rate of growth, and a lethargic Asahi was accidentally gaining some of the increasing beer sales. At the very same time, Asahi was losing ground to competitors, as the market share figures for the same years show:

Year	Sales in Bilion Yen	Asahi Market Share
1949	2	36.1%
1955	27	31.8%
1960	50	28.2%
1965	89	24.2%
1970	109	17.2%
1975	145	13.5%
1980	185	11.0%
1985	236	9.6%

There were many reasons for the decline, but the point here is that without some kind of diagnostic process, a serious performance gap can exist and the organization may not even realize it. For Asahi, things declined for 35 years. The declining market share also contributed to a stagnating corporate culture, which in turn accelerated the decline in market share.

A New President

How did the diagnosis process start at Asahi? Part of the answer is that a new president looked at the situation and didn't like what he saw. In 1982, Tsutomu Murai, who had previously led a successful turnaround at Mazda Motors, took charge at Asahi. Murai discovered that although market share had eroded steadily, there was no feeling of crisis within management. The growing beer market had lulled the organization and its members into complacency.

What happened next is another story, but it is worth noting that as an important step, Murai worked to evoke a feeling of crisis throughout Asahi. But even before this, Murai had to look at the data and go through the process of diagnosing the situation. The Asahi sales figures illustrate how important it is not just to "look at the data." Murai knew (as the text points out) that you have to look at the RIGHT data in this case, starting with market share figures. The awareness of a performance gap at Asahi provided the impetus for a successful organizational change program.

Question

1. How can an organization go so long without recognizing a performance gap?

The Sociotechnical Systems Model

The **sociotechnical systems model**, developed from the work of Eric Trist and others at the Tavistock Institute, is used to analyze the organization as a sociotechnical system interacting with its external environment.[15] According to Trist and his colleagues, there exists in the organization a social system consisting of the network of interpersonal relationships and a technological system consisting of the task, activities, and tools used to accomplish the basic purpose of the organization. These two systems—the social system and the technological system—are interrelated and interdependent. The diagnosis then determines how these systems interrelate and particularly the type of feedback or lack of feedback between the various subsystems.

Cause Maps and Social Network Analysis Model

Reed E. Nelson and K. Michael Mathews have suggested the use of cause maps and social network analysis in diagnosis.[16] **Cause maps** are mathematical representations of perceived causal relationships among variables. First, a list of the most important factors is generated (such as quantity, speed, frequency, quality, morale, and so forth.) through group discussion. Then participants are asked to identify what causal relationships exist among the variables. The results can then be incorporated into a matrix of relationships.

The **social network analysis model** is based upon mathematical representation of relations between individuals or groups (i.e., marketing department). By analyzing the causal makeup of the organization and information about specific interdepartmental relationships, knowledge is gained of important interdependencies.

The Force-Field Analysis Model

The **force-field analysis model**, originated by Kurt Lewin, is a general-purpose diagnostic technique.[17] Lewin views organization behavior not as a static pattern but as a dynamic balance of forces working in opposite directions. In any organization situation there are forces that push for change as well as forces that hinder change. Those forces acting on the organization to keep it stable are called **restraining forces** and put pressure on the organization not to change. Opposite forces, called **driving forces**, put pressure on the organization to change. If the forces for change and the forces against change are equal, the result is organization equilibrium and the organization remains stable, as shown in Figure 5.4. Lewin termed this state *quasi-stationary equilibrium*. This technique assumes that at any given moment an organization is in a state of **equilibrium**; that is, it is balanced.

Change takes place when there is an imbalance between the two forces and continues until the opposing forces are brought back into equilibrium. The imbalance can be planned, and specifically brought about by increasing the strength of any one of the forces, by adding a new force, by decreasing the strength of any one of the forces, or by a combination of these methods. One example of how force-field analysis can be used might prove

FIGURE 5.4

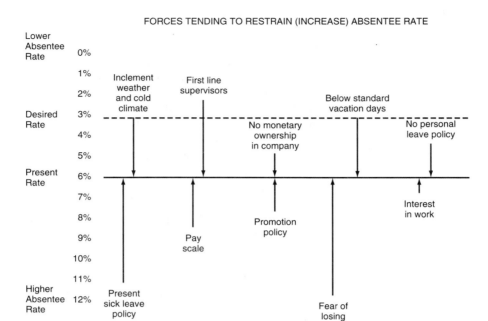

FIGURE 5.5 Example of the Use of Force-Field Analysis

helpful. The general manager of a hospital employing 300 workers and her immediate subordinates identified the six percent daily absentee rate as an area of concern. They determined that a three percent absentee rate would be much more acceptable. In other words, they found a "performance gap." After going over the survey results with the OD consultant, it was decided to use force-field analysis to gain an improved diagnosis of this problem. In a brainstorming session, the work team listed all of the forces tending to restrain and increase absenteeism (see Figure 5.5).

The managers made the length of the arrows proportionate to the strength of the force. The managers could then use several strategies to reduce the performance gap. They could decrease the strength of the restraining forces, increase the strength of the driving forces, or a combination of both. Generally, if those forces that put pressure on people (such as fear of losing their job) are increased, the tension within the system will also increase, bringing about possible stronger resistance and unpredictability in behavior, so it is often better to increase forces that do not put pressure on people (for instance, promotion policy that is more closely tied to an employee's absentee rate), to reduce restraining forces, or to add new driving forces.

The Data Collection Process

Information quality is a critical factor in any successful organization. Developing an innovative culture, like 3M, and finding new ways to meet customer needs are strongly influenced by the way information is gathered and processed. Organization development is a data-based change activity. The data collected are used by the members who provide the data and often lead to insights into ways of improving effectiveness. The data collection process itself involves an investigation, a body of data, and some form of processing information. For our purposes the word **data**, which is derived from the Latin verb *do, dare*,

meaning "to give," is more appropriately applied to unstructured, unformed facts. It is an aggregation of all signs, signals, clues, facts, statistics, opinions, assumptions, and speculations including accurate and inaccurate, and relevant and irrelevant items. The word **information** is derived from the Latin verb *informo, informare*, meaning "to give form to," and is used here to mean data that have form and structure.

The Definition of Objectives

The first and most obvious step in data collection is defining the objectives of change program. A clear understanding of these broad goals is necessary to determine what information is relevant. Unless the purpose of data collection is clearly defined, it becomes difficult to select methods and standards. The OD practioner must first gain enough information to allow a preliminary diagnosis and then decide what further information is required to verify the problem conditions. Usually, some preliminary data gathering is needed simply to clarify the problem conditions before further large-scale data collection is undertaken.

This is usually accomplished by a session of interviews with key members of the organization, investigating possible problem areas and what an ideal organization may be like. This provides a basis for the organization and the OD practitioner to understand the way things are, versus the way members would like them to be.

Most practitioners emphasize the importance of collecting data as a significant step in the OD process. First, data gathering provides the basis for the organization to begin looking at its own processes, to focus upon *how* they are doing things and the way this affects performance. Second, data collection often begins a process of self-examination or assessment by members and work teams in the organization, leading to improved problem-solving capabilities.

The Selection of Factors

The second step in data collection is to identify the central variables involved in the situation (such as turnover, suboptimization, and so on). The consultant and the client decide which factors are important and what additional information is necessary to systematically diagnose the client system's problems. The traditional approach was to select factors along narrow issues such as pay and immediate supervisors. More recently, the trend is to gauge the organization's progress and status more broadly. Broader issues include selecting factors that determine the culture and values of the organization. There is normally a considerable amount of "hard" data generated by the organization, including production reports, budgets, turnover ratios, and so forth, which may be useful as indicators of potential problems. The consultant may find, however, that it is necessary to increase the range of depth of data beyond what is readily available. (See B.C. comic strip.) The practitioner may wish

Source: B.C. by permission of Johnny Hart and Crators Syndicate, Inc.

to gain additional insights into other dimensions of the organization system, particularly those dealing with the quality of the transactions or relationship between individuals or groups. This additional data gathering may examine the following dimensions:

- What is the degree of dependence between operating teams, departments, or units?
- What is the quantity and quality of the exchange of information and communication between units?
- What is the degree to which the vision, mission and the goals of the organization are shared and understood by members?
- What are the norms, the attitudes, and the motivations of organization members?
- What are the effects of the distribution of power and status within the system?

In this step, then, the consultant and client determine which factors are important and which factors can and should be investigated.

The Selection of Data-Gathering Method

The third step in data collection is selecting a method of gathering data. There are many different types of data and also many different methods of tapping these data sources. There is no one best way to gather data—the selection of a method depends on the nature of the problem. The data should be acquired in a systematic manner, thus allowing quantitative or qualitative comparison between elements of the system. The task in this step is to identify certain characteristics that may be measured to help in the achievement of the OD program objectives and then to select an appropriate method to gather the required data. Some major data-collecting methods follow.

Secondary sources of data. When the OD practitioner begins the data-gathering process, it may be assumed that data are not presently available. But there are often large amounts of organization data already generated which can be used in identifying problem areas. These data may be termed secondary data or measures. Examples of secondary sources include accounting data, productivity data, quality data, and performance indicators such as employee thefts, turnover, and absentee rates. One organization used accounting data as a technique for organizational diagnosis, and found that it substantially increased their insight into planning assumptions and goals.[18]

There are certainly some limitations associated with the use of secondary data. Although the secondary data may be available, it may not be in a usable format. For example, lateness and absentee figures may not provide information by department. An additional problem involves the interpretation of the data: What are the causes underlying a given absentee rate or number of grievance reports?

Employee Surveys. Employee surveys, or **questionaires** are used to provide an important source of information, on past, present and future improvement efforts. Surveys have two important functions:

1. Surveys serve as information/improvement tools. They can help identify opportunities for improvement and help evaluate the impact of changes being implemented.
2. Surveys are an effective communication tool. They facilitate dialogue on potential improvements between managers and employees.

Questionnaires are used to gather a large number of quantitative responses. The questionnaire is particularly useful for studies of attitudes, values, and beliefs of respondents. Questionnaire data tend to be impersonal and anonymous and are often lacking in feeling and richness, but this method easily lends itself to quantitative analysis.

There are many problems involved in designing and administering an effective questionnaire. There are often problems of validity: Does the questionnaire measure what it is

intended to measure? There are also possible problems of the accuracy of information obtained: Did the person answer it realistically or just to make a good impression? For example, one researcher found in a follow-up study that 29 percent of questionnaire respondents admitted answering falsely to some questions.[19] To deal with these problems, there are statistical techniques available that attempt to measure the reliability of the survey responses. There are also problems of nonresponse. Those who choose to respond may be those who have strong feelings, either positive or negative, about the content of the survey but may represent only a small percentage of the total sample.

The use of the questionnaire method depends upon the depth of information desired and the purpose of the information. In some organizations survey follows survey, but without any effective change. This often leads to apathy and indifference in answering any subsequent surveys. Therefore, it is usually beneficial to inform the respondents beforehand about the purpose of the survey, how the information will be used, and how feedback of the results will be made available to them. The OD consultant also has an obligation to the client to: (1) insure confidentiality of all data; and (2) insure that feedback of data will be made to all who participate.

Surveys seem to achieve better information in terms of quantity and validity if the questionnaire shows that the researchers are familiar with key issues in the organization.[20] Such event-based questionnaires, making clear that researchers are acquainted with important aspects of the organization, are more likely to reveal information about the organization than vague, theory-based questionnaires.

Other types of instruments. Another technique for collecting data on work groups is called the *sociometric approach*. This method, developed by Jacob Moreno, is a means of obtaining quantitative data about the network of interrelationships within groups, usually on certain given dimensions.[21] Basically, Moreno's sociometric analysis provides a means of analyzing data about the choices or preferences within a group. The sociometric instrument asks specific questions, such as "Whom do you prefer to work with?" "Whom do you communicate with?" "Who helps you the most with technical problems?" Such data enable the investigator to diagram the structure and patterns of group interaction. The results are usually presented in what is called a **sociogram** (see Figure 5.6). The highly chosen individu-

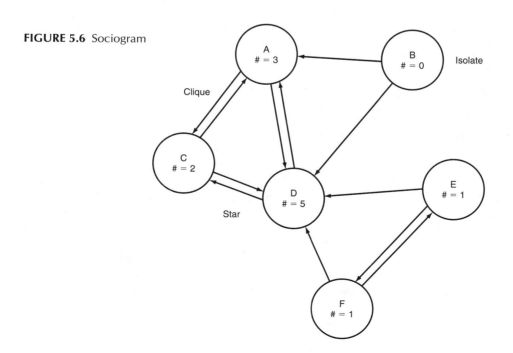

FIGURE 5.6 Sociogram

als are called **stars;** those with few or no choices are called **isolates.** Certain individuals will choose one another this is known as **mutual choice.** When an individual chooses another but is not chosen in return, this designates a **one-way choice.** When three or more persons within a larger group select one another (mutual choices), this is termed a **clique.** The existence of these subgroups may indicate lack of group cohesion and coordination.

In the sociogram each member of the group is represented by a circle, with choices designated by arrows indicating the direction of choice. The number of choices may be written in the circle under the name or code letter of the person. Sociometric techniques are useful because they provide insights into the informal structure, give some indications of group cohesiveness, and aid in pointing out possible operating problems.

Other data-collecting methods include the use of indirect questions or ambiguous stimuli to gain information. An example of this would be the thematic apperception test (TAT) used to measure the intensity of achievement, power, and affiliation motivation profiles of organization members.[22] Others have also reported the use of collages and drawings made by organization members as a means of inferring organization climate.[23]

Direct observation. Another important source of data for the OD practitioner is direct observation of member behaviors and interactions. The consultant observes how people go about task performance and how they act or react in response to specific situations. The norms and attitudes expressed by members also present an important source of data. The observer looks for inconsistent or discordant behaviors: situations in which the observed actions are different from what has been previously described or expected.

The OD consultant may use a diagram (such as a sociogram) to chart the communication process in team meetings, for example, to identify communications flows and patterns. Many consultants recommend that the observer be as inconspicuous as possible, should not use a stop watch (or other equipment), and should not take notes while observing. If the observer needs to make notes, one should leave the area. Often the observer may use indirect observation; that is, while seemingly observing one section, the observer may actually be observing another section across the room.

It is frequently valuable to visit work sites, field locations, or assembly-line operations to compare observed with reported behavior. This is obviously of greater value if the observer has a reasonably clear idea of what to look for. Observation varies from highly systematic, structured observations to nonsystematic, random observations. The more systematic the planning, recording, and observing, the greater the likelihood that observation will yield reliable and useful data. Too often, the observer's own biases influence what they see.

Interviews. One study of 245 OD practitioners, reinforced the fact that interviewing is the most widely used data-gathering technique in OD programs.[24] The interview has the advantage of being more direct, personal, and flexible than a survey and is particularly well-suited for studies of interaction and behavior. There are two advantages that set interviewing apart from other techniques. First, *it's flexible* and can be used for many different types of situations. For example, interviews can be used to determine motives, values, and attitudes. Second, *it's the only technique that provides two-way communication.* This permits the interviewer to learn more about the problems, challenges, and limitations of the organization. Interviewing usually begins with the initial intervention and is best administered in a systematic manner by a trained interviewer. Data-gathering interviews usually last at least one hour and the purpose is to get the interviewee to talk freely about things that are important to him or her and to share these perceptions in an honest and straightforward manner. It has been the authors' experience that people really want to talk about things that are important to them. If the OD consultant can ask appropriate questions, then interviewing can yield important results.

The advantage of the interview method is that it provides data that are virtually unobtainable through other methods. Subjective data, such as norms, attitudes, and values, which

are largely inaccessible through observation, may be readily inferred from effective interviews. The disadvantages to the interview are the amount of time involved, the training and skill required of the interviewer, the biases and resistances of the respondent, and the difficulty of ensuring comparability of data across respondents.

The interview itself may take on several different formats. The interview can be directed or nondirected. In the **directed interview**, certain kinds of data are desired. Therefore, specific questions are asked. Usually, the questions are formulated in advance to ensure uniformity of responses. The questions themselves may be open-ended or closed. **Open-ended questions** allow the respondent to be free and unconstrained in the answers, such as "How would you describe the work atmosphere of this organization?" The responses may be very enlightening, but may also be difficult to record and quantify. **Closed questions**, which can be answered by either a yes, no, or some other similarly abbreviated response, are easily recorded and are readily quantifiable.

In the **nondirected interview** the interview direction is chosen by the respondent and is given little guidance or direction by the interviewer. If questions are used in the nondirected interview, open-ended questions will be more appropriate than closed questions. A nondirected interview could begin with the interviewer saying, "Tell me about your job here." Possibly followed by, "You seem to be excited about your work." The data can be very detailed and significant, but because the interview is unstructured, the analysis of the data can be difficult.

The Implementation of the Program

First, one decides from whom in the organization data will be obtained and from how many. The use of interviews may limit the number of possible respondents, whereas the use of a questionnaire may expand the number. Data should be collected from several levels and departments in the organization, but different questions may be needed for varying levels or departments. The results of a survey of OD practitioners concerning the types of methods used to gather data is reported by Burke, Clark, and Koopman.[25] The one-to-one interview is the most common type of data gathering method, used by 87 percent of those responding. Other methods include observation used by 60 percent, group interviews used by 52 percent, questionnaires used by 45 percent, and existing documents used by 37 percent. The survey also shows that consultants normally rely on a variety of data gathering methods.

After an appropriate technique has been selected, the actual data collection program must be accomplished. This includes the operational aspects of designing, printing, distributing, and collecting the data collection instrument. It has been found that having an outside data collection agent is more effective than using internal personnel. The use of an outside data collection agent is recommended, as respondents apparently feel more secure and trusting that candid answers will not be used against them.

Once again, confidentiality of data is a critical issue. It is also recommended that a small pilot study or beta test be accomplished on the data collection instrument, including a practice analysis, before commencing with a large-scale data collection to insure that all possible problems are corrected prior to the data collection program.

The Analysis of Data

The techniques for analyzing data vary from relatively straightforward, simple methods, to highly sophisticated statistical techniques. Several important questions must be considered prior to the selection of a data-collecting method: How are the data to be analyzed? Are they to be analyzed statistically, and if so, what type of analysis is to be used? Will the data be processed by hand or by computer? How are they to be coded? These questions must be taken into account prior to data collection so that the data may be used to draw inferences and conclusions. This is particularly true when large-scale surveys or interviews are undertaken and the quantity of data makes processing a difficult task. The analysis may include

comparisons between different divisions within the organization. Comparisons can also be made between management levels. To make comparisons, however, it is necessary to properly code the surveys or interviews.

Despite the advanced statistical methods available, OD practitioners in one survey reported giving the data only the simplest analysis. Specifically, in over 80 percent of the projects the data was either "eyeballed" or subjected only to simple statistics. Only 10 percent of the consultants used advanced statistics to analyze the data.[26]

Evaluating the Effectiveness of Data Collection

In a systematic data collection program, some criteria for how well the data meet the objectives in quantity and quality need to be established. Obviously, a large enough sample needs to be included to enable generalization of results. The accuracy of the data, that is, the degree to which the data deviate from the truth, is also an important factor.

A number of criteria may be used to compare various data collection techniques. The OD practitioner needs to consider the trade-off between the quantity and the accuracy of information versus the cost and the amount of time involved in collecting information. The consultant must determine what is the best available information that can be generated within given cost and time constraints. The following criteria present some guidelines.

The validity of the data. Probably the most important question to ask is: Are we measuring and collecting information on the dimensions that we intend to measure? Frequently, OD programs are dealing with difficult, subjective parameters such as attitudes and values.

The time to collect data. How long will it take to gather the information using any given technique? How much time is available? Our experience suggests that data collection usually takes longer than planned.

The cost of data collection. How much does the information cost? It may cost several thousand dollars to design and administer a survey. A large-scale interviewing program also costs a great deal of time and money. The consultant and the client must determine how much money can be spent on a given OD program in the information-gathering stage. They should also consider the problem of diminishing returns: What is the minimum number of interviews needed to be a reliable measure?

The organization culture and norms. The OD practitioner should consider which techniques are best suited to a given organization culture and will yield the most valid information given these constraints. For example: Are people likely to be open and candid, or hidden and resistant? Does the climate call for open confrontation and questions or a more indirect form of data gathering?

The Hawthorne Effect In Data Collecting. One of the most difficult factors to eliminate is the effect of the observer upon the subject, which is called the **Hawthorne effect**. The very act of investigating and observing may influence the behavior of those being investigated.

As Larry Greiner has pointed out, one characteristic of successful change programs is the fact that some attempt to gather data about organization problems has been made prior to the change effort.[27] An effective data collection process enables the change effort to focus on specific problems rather than rely upon a generalized program. The data collection stage also presents managers and organization members with some hard data which may be compared with intuitive, subjective problem awareness.

Red Flags in the Diagnosis

The change strategy and OD intervention techniques follow from the diagnosis. An inappropriate intervention can be very costly. Such programs can disrupt operations, generate resistance or even hostility among employees, and create additional problems. These improper change strategies can simply fail to produce needed changes, or create unnecessary changes at the expense of the client system. Such ineffective change programs are usually the result of an inaccurate diagnosis.

The OD practitioner needs to recognize some of the special problems that the diagnostic phase presents. Because diagnosis is one of the most important stages in the OD process, the practitioner should be aware of the following warning signals.

Confidentiality

One critical problem area in diagnosis is the issue of confidentiality. As noted earlier in the discussion of consultant ethics, the relationship is based upon privileged communication between client and consultant. This often represents information which may be potentially damaging. The consultant is entrusted with private information about the client. Larry Pate and Larry Greiner report on an interesting illustration:

Two consultants carried on a casual conversation in the elevator about sensitive material revealed to them by the CEO, only to learn later that they had been overheard by an attorney who was a close personal friend of the CEO.[28]

There are many similar examples that suggest that the consultant cannot be too careful about the handling of confidential information. This goes back to the level of trust that the consultant must be able to develop with organization members.

The Over Diagnosis

At times, the diagnosis may continue to the extent that it avoids any corrective programs. The diagnosis itself may become a ritual of continual analysis. An executive at Control Data Corporation, for example, commenting on the company's tendency to over diagnose a problem, said "Everything has to be studied to death."[29] The diagnosis may continue to a point where so many problems are identified that the client becomes overwhelmed by the complexity of the situation. While diagnosis is an important step, it can also be a delaying factor and prevent change programs from even getting started. In most situations, there are several problems that need correction. But if managers are faced with too many alternatives, the most important ones may be obscured or overlooked.

The Crisis Diagnosis

The OD practitioner is often in danger of falling into the trap of attending only to the immediate, short-term crises which the client sees as immediate and important. Energy is often wasted on fighting symptoms or dealing with small crises as a way of avoiding the long-run change programs necessary to develop a more effective organization. Because of time pressures, a consultant may go through an organization in a few days and quickly diagnose the problems. Often, this results in dealing only with the conspicuous problems, while more important but less visible problems may be missed.

The Threatening and Overwhelming Diagnosis

As the OD practitioner interacts with the client system and begins to perceive possible problem areas, he or she may begin to confront the client on these problems. There is a danger, however, that the consultant may come across so blunt or so strong that the relationship with the client is weakened. It may be rather difficult for the client to face and accept informa-

tion concerning problem areas. The client can also be inundated with so much information that there is difficulty dealing with the information in any meaningful way. If the diagnosis becomes too threatening or overwhelming, the client may resist or reject the entire change program.

The Consultant's Favorite Diagnosis

There can be a tendency for the consultant to fall victim to his or her own biases and selective perceptions. This may result in imposing a special or favorite diagnosis regardless of the nature of the problem. As an example, certain OD practitioners may always view a problem as caused by organization structure regardless of the actual organization problems. Other consultants may see every problem as arising from interpersonal behavior. The consultant has to be aware that there may be a tendency to impose a favorite diagnosis on the problem. "One danger . . . is that the academician, fortified with his technique, is likely to warp the problem so that he can find a solution. He may omit variables that don't fit in and get an elegant solution to something that is not a problem."[30]

As Lippitt, Watson, and Westley have pointed out:

> The diagnostic orientation of the change agent is in many ways a self-fulfilling prediction. If he looks for difficulties in communication, for instance, he will find them; and if his help is directed toward improving communication patterns, success will demonstrate to the client system that a solution of communication problems necessarily result in a more satisfactory state of affairs The orientation of the change agent is a primary factor in determining the "facts" which the client system will discover to be true about its own situations.[31]

The Diagnosis of Symptoms

As noted earlier, there is often a tendency to focus on the symptoms rather than on the underlying problems. The OD practitioner may be unduly influenced by certain data such as high turnover rates, and identify turnover as the problem. However, this may be merely a symptom of other problems, such as poor supervision, inadequate performance appraisal, or lack of compensation. In short, the diagnostic phase is an important and critical step in the OD process.

REVIEW QUESTIONS

1. Describe the use of performance gap analysis.

2. Compare and contrast the interview and survey methods of data collection. (Find examples from *Business Week, The Wall street Journal, Fortune,* etc.)

3. List some possible types of organization data that you might find in your own organization (or one with which you are familiar with) that might be used in planning an OD program.

4. Describe the difference between symptoms and causes.

5. Identify and give examples of the force-field analysis model.

KEY WORDS AND CONCEPTS

Define and be able to use the following:

Analytical Model
Cause Maps Model
Causality
Closed Questions
Confidentiality
Data
Diagnosis
Directed Interview
Driving Forces
Emergent-Group Behavior Model
Equilibrium
Force-Field Analysis Model

Hawthorne Effect
Information
Modus Operandi (M/O)
Nondirected Interview
Open-Ended Questions
Performance Gap
Questionnaires
Restraining Forces
Social Network Analysis Model
Sociogram
Sociotechnical Systems Model
Symptoms

OD SKILLS SIMULATION 5.1
THE ACQUISITION DECISION

Total time suggested: 1 hour

A. PURPOSE

The purpose of this simulation is to experience and observe how information affects team decision making. Specifically, it is to experience interdependence and to observe:

1. How task information is shared among team members.
2. How various problem-solving strategies influence results.
3. How collaboration and competition affect group problem solving.

B. PROCEDURES

The two parameters of group effectiveness include (1) the determination of an optimum solution to the problem and (2) the completion in the shortest amount of time.

Step 1. Prior to class form groups of five members. Each individual is to select and prepare one role from the following:

1. Vice President, Finance
2. Vice President, Marketing
3. Vice President, Human Resources
4. Vice President, Production
5. Vice President, Research and Development
 Observer-OD Consultant (extras)

Any extra persons may serve as observers. If there are fewer than six members, a member may select more than one general manager role, but each team should have at least one observer.

Read the Acquisitions Briefing Sheet on p. 143 and your Role Description before the class meeting. Complete the Acquisition Alternative Summary Sheet (Table 5.2). Fill in the Individual Decision Form, or develop a Lotus or Excel spreadsheet. Record your decision on the Executive Committee Decision Work Sheet on p. 145. Record individual decisions in Column 1 of the Work Sheet. The observer should see the Observer Forms located on pp. 146, 147 after the role description and the questions in *Step 3*.

INDIVIDUAL DECISION WORK SHEET

Role: V. President_____ **Name:**_____

	Previous Annual Sales	Current Annual Est. Sales	% Sales Growth	Previous Annual Earnings	Current Annual Est. Earnings	Price	P&E Ratio	R&D	Expected Annual Savings	Payback	Antitrust Reaction	Availability	Wall Street Reaction	Total Reaction
A														
B														
C														
D														
E														
F														
G														
H														

Read *Only* Your Own Role

Step 2. Executive Committee Meeting. Your team is to select the correct acquisition candidate. Use your Individual Decision Forms and record your Team Decision or Executive Committee Decision on Column 2 of the Worksheet. Decisions are to be reached independently of the other groups. The Observer-OD Consultant will not take an active part during this phase of the simulation.

Time Suggested for Step 2:30 minutes.

Step 3 In your teams the Observer-OD Consultant will provide feedback and guide the discussion using the Observer Forms and the following questions. All team members are encouraged to provide feedback using the Team Critique Form on p. 147.

1. What behaviors seemed to help your group to successfully complete its task?
2. What factors inhibited problem solving?
3. How much time was spent on deciding how to solve the problem?
4. How was information shared among the group? What does the sociogram for the team look like?
5. How did issues of authority or power affect the group?

Time suggested for Step 3: 15 minutes.

Step 4. Each team lists its committee decision on the board. Discuss the questions in Step 3 with the entire class.

Time suggested for Step 4: 15 minutes.

ACQUISITION BRIEFING SHEET

A. Instructions to the group
 1. You are a committee made up of the key managers of SOS.
 2. This is the meeting to make a decision about the acquisition.
 3. Basically, the data you bring with you are in your head.
 4. Your job is to select an acquisition from among the possible candidates.
 5. You may use a calculator or a personal computer with an electronic spread sheet.

B. 1. Assume that there is an optimum solution.
 2. Assume that all data are correct.
 3. You have 45 minutes to work the exercise.
 4. There must be substantial consensus when the problem has been solved.
 5. You must work the problem as a team.

GENERAL COMPANY INFORMATION

Your committee is made up of the managers of SOS Corporation, a young and growing medium-sized software company. Your mission is to locate and identify the best acquisition candidate for your firm. Your company is quick to exit businesses that don't offer high-growth, high-performance opportunities.

You have already examined the data on eight companies. Your first order of business is to gain a consensus on the best selection from among the candidates listed on the Acquisition Alternative Summary Sheet.

ROLE DESCRIPTIONS (READ ONLY YOUR ROLE)

Vice President, Finance. Your mission is to locate and identify the best financial acquisition candidate for your firm. Your company is quick to exit businesses that don't offer high-growth, high-growth performance opportunities.

You have already examined the data on eight companies. You think that the sales growth rate must be greater than 10 percent over the previous year in order to fit this criteria and the P/E ratio should be 11 or less. Should you decide to consider payback (price paid divided by expected annual savings) in the acquisition decision, anything seven years or more is a low payback. You feel Wall Street reaction will be important, as well as future earnings.

Vice President, Human Resources. Your mission is to locate and identify the best acquisition candidate for your firm. Your company is quick to exit businesses that don't offer high-growth, high-performance opportunities.

You have already examined the data on eight companies. You think that the reaction of the investment community on Wall Street must be better than fair if you are to maintain performance. Also, the company should have at least a moderate chance of being available. If you decide to consider the earnings growth rate, use the previous year's earnings as the base year. You want to avoid any large scale downsizing, in order to achieve savings of over 30 million.

Vice President, Research and Development. Your mission is to locate and identify the best acquisition candidate for your firm. Your company is quick to exit businesses that don't offer high-growth, high-performance opportunities.

You have already examined the data on eight companies. You think that Research and Development should be at least six percent of sales in order to maintain technological capabilities and annual sales must be at least $225 million. Also, if you decide to consider the rate of sales growth, use the previous year's sales as the base year. The company has decided

to use a modified P/E ration of using the ratio of price paid for the company to its current earnings. You feel availability is important to avoid prolonged negotiations.

Vice President, Marketing. Your mission is to locate and identify the best acquisition candidate for your firm. Your company is quick to exit businesses that don't offer high-growth, high-performance opportunities.

You have already examined the data on eight companies. You think that the price should be less than $300 million to fit the performance goal; and earnings growth rate should be greater than five percent over the previous year. Should you decide to consider an appropriate payback, anything less than five years is a high payback. The annual savings of the acquisition is an average projected for the next eight years. You are not concerned about antitrust reactions.

Vice President, Production. Your mission is to locate and identify the best acquisition candidate for your firm. Your company is quick to exit businesses that don't offer high-growth, high-performance opportunities.

You have already examined the data on eight companies. You think that the payback should be moderate or high to gain economies of scale. You would like a favorable price-earnings (P/E) ratio but the lower the ratio the better. Antitrust reaction should be moderate or less. You want a high level of expected annual savings.

OD Consultant Guidelines. Your job is to collect information during the Executive Committee Meeting. Use the three Observer-OD Consultant Forms (pp. 145-147). Also, refer to the questions in *Step 3*. You should not take part in the decision that is made during the SOS Committee Meeting (*Step 2*). In *Step 3* you will provide feedback from the Observer-OD Consultant Forms.

Table 5.2 Acquisition Alternative Summary Sheet

Company	Previous Annual Sales (millions)	Current Annual Estimated Sales (millions)	Previous Annual Earnings (millions)	Current Annual Estimated Earnings (millions)	Price (millions)	Research and Development (millions)	Expected Annual Savings (millions)	Antitrust Reaction	Availability	Wall Street Reaction
A	330	400	20	24	240	24	38	Moderate	Most likely	Good
B	185	200	9	10	120	10	35	Minimum	Moderate	Fair
C	325	350	27	30	315	21	65	High	Most likely	Poor
D	210	250	10	13	172	20	35	Low	Definite	Good
E	135	150	7	8	75	6	10	Extreme	Moderate	Fair
F	350	380	20	22	228	23	50	Absent	Low	Poor
G	460	500	16	18	157	40	23	Moderate	Moderate	Fair
H	185	220	10	14	185	14	30	Minimum	Moderate	Fantastic

EXECUTIVE COMMITTEE DECISION WORK SHEET

Company	(1) Personal Ranking	(2) Committee Ranking
A		
B		
C		
D		
E		
F		
G		
H		

OBSERVER FORM A

Name: _____

Position: _____

1. _____
2. _____
3. _____

Name: _____

Position: _____

1. _____
2. _____
3. _____

Name: _____

Position: _____

1. _____
2. _____
3. _____

Name: _____

Position: _____

1. _____
2. _____
3. _____

Name: _____

Position: _____

1. _____
2. _____
3. _____

NOTE: Draw direction arrows for communication flow. Identify behaviors shown.

OBSERVER FORM B

Description of Behavior	Names of Individuals Observed
Encourager—friendly and responsive to others; offers praise; accepts others' points of view.	
Harmonizer—mediates differences; relives tension in conflict situations; gets people to explore their differences.	
Compromiser—when own idea is involved in a conflict, offers compromise and admits error. Tries to maintain group cohesion.	
Expresses group feelings—senses the feeling or mood of the group, others, and self and shares this with the group.	
Gatekeeper—keeps communications open; suggests procedures for sharing information with others.	
Initiator—proposes tasks or goals; suggests ways to solve problems.	
Information or opinion giver—offers facts; states own belief or opinion.	
Clarifier—interprets ideas or suggestions; clears up confusion; gives examples.	
Summarizer—pulls together related suggestions; offers conclusion for the group to accept or reject	
Others:	

TEAM CRITIQUE FORM

Instructions: The observer is to complete this form for each member, with the member being critiqued listening to the process. Place one check mark in the appropriate block under each of the five headings. Each member rates the others and reaches a consensus.

	Finance	Marketing	Human Resource	Production	R & D
1. In planning, this person					
a. Showed little interest in the activities or objectives	❑	❑	❑	❑	❑
b. Gave most of his/her attention to the social aspects of the situation, with eager acceptance of any idea	❑	❑	❑	❑	❑
c. Went along with suggestions that seemed acceptable to the majority	❑	❑	❑	❑	❑
d. Did all the planning of how and what to do	❑	❑	❑	❑	❑
e. Made many inputs on plans and procedures, with challenge and review of all suggestions	❑	❑	❑	❑	❑
2. In making decision, this person					
a. Did not receive or respond to inputs	❑	❑	❑	❑	❑
b. Showed quick, eager agreement with happy approving looks	❑	❑	❑	❑	❑
c. Sought to achieve compromise	❑	❑	❑	❑	❑
d. Pushed hard toward a particular point	❑	❑	❑	❑	❑
e. Made decisions after a thorough review of all alternatives, understood and agreed upon by all	❑	❑	❑	❑	❑
3. In communicating, this person					
a. Voiced ideas and comments with little interest or concern	❑	❑	❑	❑	❑
b. Listened politely with joking and friendly conversation	❑	❑	❑	❑	❑
c. Expressed different viewpoints and opinions, but conformed to the majority viewpoint	❑	❑	❑	❑	❑
d. Engaged in discussion of a win-lose type, with much effort to out-argue others and very little active listening	❑	❑	❑	❑	❑
e. Expressed differing viewpoints, listened to others' ideas and suggestions, asked for clarification, and gave and received feedback	❑	❑	❑	❑	❑
4. In conflict, this person					
a. Avoided discussion of differences in opinion	❑	❑	❑	❑	❑
b. Tried to soothe ruffled feelings, change the subject, or soft-pedal differences	❑	❑	❑	❑	❑
c. Made for the middle ground, compromise or areas of mutual agreement in order to settle the differences	❑	❑	❑	❑	❑
d. Suppressed differences by overpowering argument or detraction from others' positions in a competitive atmosphere	❑	❑	❑	❑	❑
e. Confronted differences by examining closely their underlying causes and seeking to complete understanding	❑	❑	❑	❑	❑
5. In the group meeting, this person					
a. Paid very little, if any, attention to team process or procedures	❑	❑	❑	❑	❑
b. Made only complimentary remarks of group actions	❑	❑	❑	❑	❑
c. Suggested minor improvements to keep things moving at a reasonable pace	❑	❑	❑	❑	❑
d. Presented fault-finding criticism and negative remarks on team behavior	❑	❑	❑	❑	❑
e. Paid attention to team action and procedures, and made suggestions for team process	❑	❑	❑	❑	❑

CASE 5:
THE OLD FAMILY BANK

The Old Family Bank is a large bank in a southeastern city. As a part of a comprehensive internal management study, H. Day, the data processing vice president, examined the turnover, absenteeism, and productivity figures of all work groups in the organization. The results Day obtained contained no real surprises except in the case of the check-sorting and data-processing departments.

THE STUDY

The study revealed that in general the departments displaying high turnover and absenteeism rates had low production figures, and those with low turnover and absenteeism were highly productive. When analysis began on the check-sorting and data-processing figures, Day discovered that both departments were tied for the lead for the lowest turnover and absenteeism figures. What was surprising was that the check-sorting department ranked first as the most productive unit, whereas the electronic data-processing department ranked last.

That inconsistency was further complicated by the fact that the working conditions for check-sorting employees is extremely undesirable. They work in a large open room that is hot in the summer and cold in the winter. They work alone and operate high-speed check-sorting machines requiring a high degree of accuracy and concentration. There is little chance for interaction because they all take rotating coffee breaks.

The computer room is air-conditioned, with a stable temperature the year round; it has perfect lighting and is extremely quiet and comfortable. It was known that both groups are highly cohesive and that the workers function well with others in their department. This observation was reinforced by the study's finding of the low levels of turnover and absenteeism.

THE INTERVIEW DATA

In an effort to understand this phenomenon, vice president Day decided to interview the members of both departments. Day hoped to gain some insight into the dynamics of each group's behavior. It was discovered that the check-sorting department displayed a great deal of loyalty to the company. Most of the group are unskilled or semiskilled workers, although they have no organized union, and each person felt that the company had made special efforts to keep their wages and benefits in line with unionized operations. They knew that their work required team effort and were committed to high performance.

A quite different situation existed in the data-processing department. Although the workers liked their fellow employees, there was a uniform feeling among this highly skilled group that management placed more emphasis on production than on staff units. It was their contention that pay increases had been better for operating departments and that the gap between the wage earners and salaried employees did not reflect the skill differences. Because of that, a large percentage of the group displayed little loyalty toward the company, even though they were very close among themselves.

CASE ANALYSIS FORM

Name: _____

I. Problems

 A. Macro

 1. _____

 2. _____

 B. Micro

 1. _____

 2. _____

II. Causes

 1. _____

 2. _____

 3. _____

III. Systems affected

 1. Structural _____

 2. Psychosocial _____

 3. Technical _____

 4. Managerial _____

 5. Goals _____

IV. Alternatives

 1. _____

 2. _____

 3. _____

 4. _____

 5. _____

V. Recommendations

 1. _____

 2. _____

 3. _____

SUMMARY

• **Diagnosis.** Organizational diagnosis is one of the most critical and difficult elements in the OD process. The OD practitioner has to recognize the importance of this process because the diagnosis leads to problem-solving action. A weak or inaccurate diagnosis leads to an ineffective change program. A sound diagnosis enables the consultant and the client to specify the nature of the problem by identifying underlying forces and multiple causality.

• **Data Collection.** In an OD program, intervention and data gathering occur throughout the program. The decisions about what information to collect and how it should be collected are difficult and important. No data-gathering methods is of itself either right of wrong; rather, each method has its own limitations as well as its strong points. The process of collecting information is an important step in an OD program because it provides a foundation for the diagnosis of problems and the selection of change strategies and techniques. What must be determined is whether a particular method is most appropriate for the specific objectives and climate of each unique situation.

• **Problem Solving.** In diagnosing organization problems, the consultant and the client try to specify the problems, determine the underlying causes, and identify the opportunities for change. The OD consultant tries to sort out factual from nonfactual information and searches for multiple sources of the problem condition. The outcome is an explicit and specific diagnosis upon which to base change efforts.

• **OD Consultant.** The consultant needs maximum participation from members of the client system in the diagnostic process and needs to consider the impact of the diagnosis upon his or her relationship with the client. The OD consultant may confront the client with unpleasant facts, so the more objective the data and the more the analysis includes both strengths and weaknesses, the better the resultant OD program will be. During the diagnostic phase the OD consultant should also be alert for danger signals or red-flag conditions.

• **Diagnostic Models.** Several diagnostic models have been described, including the analytical model, the emergent-group model, the sociotechnical systems model, and the force-field model. The models may be used by the consultant to facilitate the analysis of client system problems. You have had the opportunity to practice using various methods for diagnosing problems.

• **Diagnostic Process.** In the simulation you had a chance to experience using information and diagnosing organization problems. You may have found that diagnosis is not a simple process, since it includes both the client's needs and system problems. The diagnostic process involves identifying the problems and assessing the readiness for change in the client system. It requires an understanding of the client's felt needs by attempting to see the problem from the client's viewpoint. Similarly, the OD consultant must apply a system's approach by specifying the interrelationships of various elements of the client system. This requires organizing the available data or evidence into some meaningful patterns.

• **OD.** In the chapter, the important factors and models in the diagnostic process have been described, and you have had an opportunity to practice and apply these concepts. This stage provides the foundation for subsequent OD interventions.

NOTES

1. Laura Rubach, "Downsizing," *Quality Progress*, April 1995, p. 24.
2. W. Warner Burke, Lawrence P. Clark, and Cheryl Koopman, "Improve Your OD Project's Chances for Success," *Training and Development Journal*, vol. 38, no. 9 (September 1984), p. 65.
3. Michael Beer, Bert Spector, "Organizational Diagnosis," *Journal of Counseling & Development*, vol. 71, Jul/Aug, 1993, pp. 643–650.
4. Linda C. McDermott, "The Many Faces of the OD Professional," *Training & Development Journal*, Feb. 1984, pp. 14–19.
5. John H. Johnson, "Another Look at Employee Surveys," *Training & Development*, July 1993, p. 15–18.
6. John Huey, "How McKinsey Does It," *Fortune*, Nov. 1, 1993, p. 56.
7. *Sources*: Peter Nulte, "Kodak Grabs for Growth Again," *Fortune*, May 16, 1994, pp. 76–78; "Kodak Pictures Eastern Europe as Profit Center," *The Wall Street Journal*, May 10, 1990, p. A-7; Bill Saporito, "Companies That Compete Best," *Fortune*, May 22, 1989, p. 37; Clare Ansberry and Carol Hymowitz, "Last Chance," *The Wall Street Journal*, September 19, 1989, p. A-1.
8. Sally Ver Schere, "Assessing the Strengths and Challenges of Your Group," *Fund Raising Management*, December 1984, pp. 60–61.
9. D. Nadler, "Role of Models in Organizational Assessment," in *Organizational Assessment*, eds. E. Lawler III, D. Nadler, and C. Camman (New York: John Wiley & Sons, Inc., 1980), pp. 119–31.
10. Burke, Clark, and Koopman, "Improve Your OD Project's Chances," p. 65.
11. Paul Lawrence and Jay Lorsch, *Developing Organizations: Diagnosis and Action* (Reading, Mass.: Addison-Wesley Publishing Co., Inc., 1969), pp. 11–14.
12. George Homans, *The Human Group* (New York: Harcourt Brace Jovanovich, Inc. 1950).
13. Terry R. Armstrong and Walter J. Wheatley, "Identifying Client Needs: A Diagnostic Model for Consultants," paper presented at Academy of Management Meeting, 1989.
14. John F. Hulpke, California State University, Bakersfield, Bakersfield, Calif., 1994.
15. F. Emergy, *Characteristics of Sociotechnical Systems* (London: Tavistock Institute, 1959).
16. Reed E. Nelson and K. Michael Mathews, "The Use of Cause Maps and Social Network Analysis in Organizational Diagnosis," paper presented at Academy of Management Meeting, 1989.

17. Kurt Lewin, "Frontiers in Group Dynamics, Concepts, Methods and Reality in Social Science," *Human Relations*, (June 1974), pp. 5–42.

18. Lem Rubin, "Playing by the Books," *H. R. Magazine*, May 1995, p. 39.

19. L. Dean, "Interaction Reported and Observed: The Case of One Local Union," *Human Organization*, Fall 1958, pp. 36–44.

20. See Edward J. Conlon, "Survey Feedback as a Large-Scale Change Device: An Empirical Examination," *Group and Organization Studies*, September 1984, pp. 399–416; and also Clayton P. Alderfer and L. Dave Brown, "Designing an 'Empathetic Questionnaire' for Organizational Research," *Journal of Applied Psychology*, vol. 56, no. 6 (1972), pp. 456–60.

21. Jacob Moreno, *Who Shall Survive?* 2nd ed. (New York: Beacon House, Inc., 1953).

22. David C. McClelland, *The Achieving Society* (Princeton, N. J.: D. Van Nostrand Company, 1961).

23. Jack Fordyce and Raymond Weil, *Managing with People* (Reading, Mass.: Addison-Wesley Publishing Co., Inc., 1971), pp. 146–52.

24. Michael A. Hitt and Robert L. Mathis, "Survey Results Shed Light Upon Important Developmental Tools," *Personal Administrator*, vol. 28, no. 2 (February 1983), pp. 89–97.

25. Burke, Clark, and Koopman, "Improve Your OD Project's Chances," p. 65.

26. Ibid.

27. Larry Greiner, "Patterns of Organization Change," *Harvard Business Review*, May–June 1967, pp. 119–30.

28. Larry E. Pate and Larry E. Greiner, "Invited Commentary: Resolving Dilemmas in Power and OD with the Four Aces Technique," *Consultation*, vol. 8, no. 1 (Spring 1989), p. 58.

29. Russell Mitchell, "Fine Job, Larry—But Don't Get Too Settled," *Business Week*, October 16, 1989, p. 34.

30. Tom Alexander, "Computers Can't Solve Everything," *Fortune*, October 1969, p. 128.

31. Ronald Lippitt, Jeanne Watson, and Bruce Westley, *The Dynamics of Planned Change* (New York: Harcourt Brace Jovanovich, Inc., 1958), p. 65.

Planned change at Texas Instruments helps insure success of programs. *Photo reprinted by permission of Texas Instruments Incorporated.*

Overcoming Resistance to Change

6

OBJECTIVES

Upon completing this chapter, you will be able to:

1. Identify the forces within individuals and organizations causing resistance to change programs.
2. Recognize strategies that can increase motivation to change.
3. Experience reaction to a change situation.
4. Diagnose the resistant forces in organization change.

PREMEETING PREPARATION

1. Read the Background Information.
2. Prepare for OD Skills Simulation 6.1. Read the company background and complete Step 1.
3. Read and analyze Case 6: The Keyboard Company.

BACKGROUND INFORMATION

Faced with continuing economic pressures and increasing competition, organizations are being forced to radically change and reinvent their processes. Reengineering, rightsizing, and downsizing are frequent responses to these pressures. Organizational downsizing is one of the frequent change programs undertaken during the past decade to increase productivity. But many surveys have found there are often unintended consequences of these changes. The Society for Human Resource Management (SHRM) for example, reported that more than half of 1,468 downsizing firms indicated that productivity had deteriorated as a result of downsizing. Next to the death of a relative or a friend, there are few things as stressful as losing one's job. Corporate downsizing, then, threatens the self esteem of both laid off employees and the survivors.[1]

Organizations today face a major challenge in managing change effectively. When an organization fails to change in necessary ways, the costs of failure are often high. In a dynamic environment, organizations must have the capacity to adapt quickly in order to survive. At GM's 36 assembly plants, morale among workers is said to be at an all time low because of skimpy bonuses and worries about job security. General Motors has had difficulty adapting to change despite a string of reorganizations over the decades. An auto industry consultant, James Womack, says, "It seems to me they still have a pretty good case of organization cirrhosis. They're so much more complex than anyone else in this business."[2]

The most serious challenges to improvement programs have common focus: people. OD consultants in developing and implementing programs to keep today's organizations competitive in a tough, constantly changing environment, must deal with resistance to change. At GM's Opel plant, for example, they reorganized the 35,000 workforce into teams of 5 to 15 members. The team approach has proven to be successful, but not without overcoming cultural and communication barriers. In most cases, the speed and complexity of change may severely test the capabilities of both managers and members. Unless members prepare themselves emotionally for change, the sheer speed with which change occurs can be overwhelming.

Solving organizational problems usually involves the introduction of change. If the required changes are small or isolated, they can usually be accomplished without major problems. However, when the changes are on a larger scale and involve many individuals and subunits, there are often significant problems. As organizational problems emerge, managers attempt to take corrective actions. Often, these corrective actions impact upon patterns of work or values, and resistance is encountered. Although many potential problems may emerge while initiating organizational change programs, the problem most likely to be encountered is associated with human resistance to changing patterns of work and behavior.

As noted in the GM example, employees often strongly resist changes. On a personal level, change represents altering set patterns of behavior, defined relationships with others, work procedures, and job skills. On an organizational level, change represents altering policies, procedures, sunk costs, organization structures, manufacturing processes, and work flows. Both people and organizations have vested interests in the status quo. Prior to the implementation of any OD strategy or technique, the OD consultant must deal with potential resistance to change.

This chapter examines an important issue to any OD program: the motivation of the client system. What is it that makes an individual, a group, or an organization believe that a change would be beneficial? What forces interfere with and restrict the implementation of a change program? What phases of resistance does a typical change program encounter? Finally, what can a manager or OD consultant do to increase the probability of acceptance of a change program?[3]

It would obviously be helpful to answer these questions very specifically; however, specific answers can only be given when speaking of a single client system. The answers will be formulated with the purpose of developing a criterion of forces tending to increase and decrease the acceptance of a change program. Those forces pushing for and enhancing a change program will be called *driving forces* and those resisting and interfering with a change program will be called *restraining forces* (see force-field analysis in Chapter 5).

Once the organization or its key members have made the decision to implement a change program and the OD practitioner has been brought in to work with the organization, it is the task of these parties to energize the forces favoring the change program. So that you can more fully appreciate this process, this chapter deals with the phases of resistance of change programs, driving and restraining forces, and the actions increasing the probability of change.

THE LIFE CYCLE OF RESISTANCE TO CHANGE

Organization programs such as downsizing, reengineering and TQM programs involve innovation and change which will probably encounter some degree of resistance. This resistance will be evident in individuals and groups in such forms as controversy, hostility, and conflict, either overtly or covertly. The change itself tends to move through a life cycle.[4]

Phase 1. In the first phase, there are only a few people who see the need for change and take reform seriously. They represent a fringe element of the organization and may be openly criticized, ridiculed, and persecuted by whatever methods the organization has at its disposal and thinks appropriate to handle the dissidents and force them to conform to established organization norms. Resistance appears massive. At this point the change program may die or it may continue to grow. One of IBM's business partners has said that trying to get action from IBM is like swimming through "giant pools of peanut butter."[5]

As an example, during the 1970s and 1980s the environmental movement seemed to grow. The first Earth Day was held in 1970. Widespread interest in environmental concerns subsided during the 1980s and much of the 1990s. Some political officials neglected environmental concerns and environmentalists were often portrayed as extremists and radicals. The forces for change were small but persisted through court actions, pressure on elected officials, and group actions.

Phase 2. As the movement for change begins to grow, the forces for the change and against the change become identifiable. The change is discussed, and it is more thoroughly understood by more of the organization's members. The threat associated with the change can be lessened because of increased understanding. In time, the novelty and strangeness of the change tends to disappear.

Environmental supporters and opponents became more identifiable during the 1980s. James Watt, a Secretary of Interior, was perhaps the most vocal and visible opponent of environmental concerns and served as a "lightening rod" for pro-environmental forces such as the Sierra Club and Wilderness Society. But with time environmental groups through education increasingly delivered their message. The public had more information and scientific data to understand the nature of the problem.

Phase 3. In this phase there is a direct conflict and a showdown between the forces pro and con. This phase will probably mean life or death to the change effort, as those enthusiastic about the change frequently underestimate the strength of those resistant to the change. Those in an organization who see a change as good and needed find it difficult to believe the extent to which the opposition will go to put a stop to the change.

The Clean-Air Act passed by Congress in 1990 represented the culmination of years of confrontation between pro- and anti-environmental forces. The bill was passed several months after national and worldwide Earth Day events. Corporations that previously were pointed to as contributors of environmental problems took out large newspaper and television advertisements to explain how they were reducing pollution and cleaning up the environment. The "greening" of corporations became very popular.

Phase 4. If, after the decisive battles, the supporters of the change are in power, the remaining resistance is seen as stubborn and a nuisance. There is still a possibility that the resisters to the change will mobilize enough support to shift the balance of power. Wisdom is necessary in dealing with the overt opposition and with that element which, although not openly opposed, is not yet thoroughly convinced about the benefit of the change.

One example is the confrontation between Green Peace (an environmentalist group) and Shell Oil. The Greenpeace group had been campaigning for weeks to block Royal Dutch/Shell group from disposing of the towering Bent Spar oil-storage rig by sinking it deep in the Atlantic Ocean. As a small helicopter sought to land Greenpeace protestors on the rig's deck, Shell blasted high powered water cannons to fend off the aircraft. This was all captured on film and shown around the world. This shows how high profile cases like this and the Exxon Valdez can ignite world-wide public interest. Four days after the incident, Shell executives made a humiliating about face, they agreed to comply with Greenpeace requests and dispose of the Brent Spar on land.[6]

Phase 5. In the last phase the resisters to the change are as few and as alienated as were the advocates in the first phase. Although these phases may give the impression that a battle is being waged between those trying to bring about change and those resisting the change (and sometimes this is the situation), the actual conflict is usually more subtle and may only surface in small verbal disagreements, questions, reluctance, and so forth.

Regardless of the degree of resistance to the organization change program, the change will to some extent evolve through the five phases previously described. In some change programs, however, some of the phases may be brief, omitted, or repeated. The last phase may not even be solidified and the change process will move again into the first phase. General Electric's CEO, John F. Welch has written:

> People always ask, "Is the change over? Can we stop now?" You've got to tell them, "No, it's just begun." They must come to understand that it is never ending. Leaders must create an atmosphere where people understand that change is a continuing process, not an event.[7]

MANAGING CHANGE FORCES

Changing an organization involves modifying existing organizational systems, structure, and culture to some different standard or level of performance. The purpose of change is to increase organizational effectiveness or even to ensure survival. Most managers agree that if an organization is to continue to be excellent, it must continually respond to significant environmental developments.

According to a study by John P. Kotter and Leonard A. Schlesinger, "Most companies or divisions of major corporations find that they must undertake moderate organizational changes at least once a year and major changes every four or five."[8] This is borne out by organizations which introduced quality circles (an early OD intervention) in the early 1980s and left them alone. The circles tended to lose their effectiveness after a couple of years. Other organizations using the circles continued to introduce changes and followed with self-managed work teams or total quality management (see Chapter 13). Managing change is therefore not only a challenge for managers, it is necessary for survival.

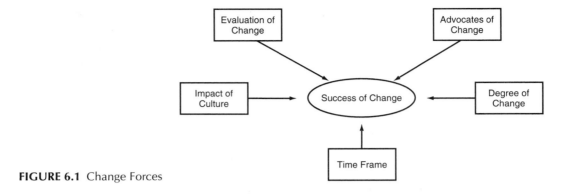

FIGURE 6.1 Change Forces

Often other managers consider change to be so critical to the success of the organization that they continuously search for ways to make positive organizational changes. The major forces in the change process include advocates of change, degree of change, time frame, impact on culture, and evaluation of change. (See Figure 6.1.)

Advocates of change. Perhaps the most important factor is determining who will spearhead the change program. This may be an executive, a manager, an internal consultant, or an outside consultant brought in for a specific change project.

Degree of change. A second factor is the degree of change to be made. Is it a relatively minor change such as a change in sales order forms? Or is it a major change in strategy such as a new product line? The greater the degree of change, the more difficult it is to implement successfully.

Time frame. A third factor is the length of time chosen to implement the change program: whether a gradual change implemented over several months or years, or an abrupt change implemented immediately. In general, the more gradual the change and the longer the time frame, the greater the chance of success. Some organizations, however, have become so ineffective that any chance they have for survival depends on radical change introduced swiftly.

Impact of culture. The change program's impact on existing systems and culture is important because the greater the impact on existing cultural norms, the greater the amount of resistance likely to emerge, and thus the greater the difficulty in implementing the change program. As an example, the breakup of AT&T caused a lot of problems with many of the senior employees who sometimes clashed with the newer workers. The senior employees were brought up in an environment where competition meant getting in a rate increase request on time. When what is now Bell Atlantic Corporation was a division within the AT&T system, there was a manual covering virtually every contingency. The manual, in three ring binders, took up about 24 feet in shelf space and the section on "How to Properly Take an Order" was more than 1,200 pages long. A system like this attracts and breeds a certain kind of person. After years in such a system, change becomes difficult. One manager who had first been with AT&T and then with Bell Atlantic Corporation after the breakup said, "This certainly isn't the cruise ship I signed up for 30 years ago."[9]

Evaluation of change. Finally, some system of evaluating the change must be considered. Standards or levels of performance are developed to measure the degree of change and its impact on organization effectiveness.

A CHANGE MODEL

Two major considerations in making changes in an organization are the degree of change and the impact on the culture. Evidence suggests that change is difficult to accomplish and resistance can be expected whenever a change involves a significant impact on the traditional behavior, power, culture, and structure within an organization. The degree of change and the impact on the existing culture is shown in The Change Model in Figure 6.2. The areas in the divisions of the figure show the relative resistance encountered to four possible change situations.

1. *Minor change, minor impact on culture.* Where the change to be introduced is relatively minor and the impact on the existing culture small, there will predictably occur the lowest level of resistance and the highest probability of a successful change.
2. *Minor change, major impact on culture.* Where the change is minor, but has a large impact on the culture, some resistance can be expected, depending on the size of the threat, and the speed of the change.
3. *Major change, minor impact on culture.* Here the change is major, but the impact on existing culture is minor, so while some resistance is likely, good management can probably overcome resistance.
4. *Major change, major impact on culture.* When the degree of change is large and the impact on the existing culture is high, the greatest resistance can be predicted. In this situation, the probability of success is low.

In managing change, experience suggests that both the level of resistance and the time it takes to implement change tend to be underestimated. An alternative plan, assuming the organization has the time, is to break the change into smaller components that will be introduced over a longer time. Each component will encounter low resistance by representing a small degree of change and small impact on the culture.

FIGURE 6.2 The Change Model

The larger the area, the greater the resistance

THE DRIVING FORCES TOWARD ACCEPTANCE OF A CHANGE PROGRAM

Driving forces are anything that increases the inclination of the client system to implement the proposed change program. These forces vary in intensity, depending on the specifics of the individual client system and its immediate situation. Some of the forces help to create the need for and to initiate the change program; other forces develop later, as the change program progresses.

Dissatisfaction with the Present Situation

Initially, the client may feel some dissatisfaction or even pain with the present situation. The client many not know why it is dissatisfied, but it does have a desire for relief. This could be likened to a person who is sick: he does not know why or what to do to be cured, but he does want to be relieved of the pain. He may try some home remedies or seek the help of a doctor.

Organizations sometimes find themselves in a similar situation: that is, they come to realize that they are unhealthy or ineffective and seek the help of a consultant. The more intense the dissatisfaction with the present situation, the greater will be the motivation to change. Members of an organization may become dissatisfied with their personal position and push for change on the belief that things cannot get much worse.

In other situations the client system may be more aware of the need to change. Members of the client system may perceive a difference between the present situation and the situation as they would like it to be. They may not be really dissatisfied with the situation as it is, but perhaps after observing other organizations, they recognize a need for some improvements. The organization may have operating records that are compatible with standards for their type of organization, but they may not be satisfied with being average. They may believe that they have an untapped potential, but are not sure how to release their talents in a way that will further the development of their organization.

For other organizations, the need to change may be more obvious. The client system may not be meeting its industry's standards on such matters as rate-of-return on invested capital or employee turnover. Internal goals, such as group production quotas, may not have been achieved. Or there may be attempts of a stockholder revolt or an unfriendly takeover. As a consequence, internal pressures are brought to bear to change the present situation. There is an obvious felt need that "we had better do something, anything, and fast." The CEO of AlliedSignal, Lawrence Bossidy, has called this the "burning platform" condition. When Bossidy took over AlliedSignal, the company had poor margins, too much debt, and negative cash flow. He writes of change:

> . . . the people of AlliedSignal obviously were on a burning platform. . . . To inaugurate large-scale change, you may have to create the burning platform. You have to give people a reason to do something differently. . . . Scaring people isn't the answer. You try to appeal to them. The more they understand why you want change, the easier it is to commit to it.[10]

External Pressures Toward Change

An organization does not exist in a vacuum. It is part of a larger external environment that imposes certain forces upon the organization. Sometimes various external pressures will cause the client system to change some of its present methods of operation. These pressures can vary widely from voluntary actions to involuntary legal requirements. In industry the corporation may need to adopt new technologies to remain competitive, or an organization may be required by law to make a change necessitated by environmental or civil rights legislation. International competition and lowering of trade barriers—**the global market**—is probably doing more to force changes on organizations than any other external force. (See Our Changing World.)

OUR CHANGING WORLD:
WHY EUROPE RESISTS CHANGE[11]

"Change or Die." This is the choice many U.S. companies are facing. One company after another is going the way of the dinosaur. Companies such as IBM that were once considered invulnerable are losing market share, seeing declining share price, laying off large numbers of employees, and experiencing falling profits. Many companies are taking the advice of a Walt Disney Co. studio president who says, "If you're not part of the steamroller, you're part of the road."

Tom Peters says, "It is more urgent today than ever that we try to understand the dynamics of renewal. . . . Excellent firms don't believe in excellence—only in constant improvement and constant change."

Change in Europe

Is resistance to change an American phenomenon? Apparently not. "I get the same . . . questions in Europe that I get in Chicago," says Peters. "Apparently business people everywhere have more common points than differences today."

Robert Waterman writes in *The Renewal Factor* that the Europeans might have an even harder time in adapting, transforming, and revitalizing than Americans. "European companies tend to surround themselves with altogether too much tradition," Waterman says. "There is too much emphasis on title and position; too much communication through hierarchy." Europe today, with long familiar trade barriers crumbling, must adopt attitudes of change and renewal. Will management respond, overcoming inherent resistance to change? The odds don't look too good. Waterman says "My feeling is that it takes a crisis to make things change."

Eurosclerosis

Economists at Oxford Economic Forecasting, Ltd., use the term "Eurosclerosis" to describe current European problems. They contend that the solution to Europe's problems is not as simple as excessive factory wages (which often exceed pay scales in both the U.S. and Japan) or high interest rates. These economists contend that European workers are inflexible, as exemplified by the lack of worker mobility. U.S. and Japanese workers are more likely to move to areas where jobs are available, but Europeans are more likely to stay put, even within their own national boundaries. The cause of the problem may be culture and the high cost of buying and selling a house.

Change or Die

Germany, the largest economy in Europe, seems to be particularly reticent to change. Interest groups in Germany, such as labor unions, are formed into nationwide organizations. This means that fundamental changes in the way Germans work require wide agreement. Alarms for change must be sounded again and again until Germans are scared into change. Says one labor economist, "You need lots of consensus. You have to make people aware that they're facing serious change."

Change is coming to Europe, but it is also coming to the rest of the world as well. But do crises have to occur before people and companies are willing to change?

Questions

1. Do you agree that tradition causes Europeans to have a more difficult time than Americans in adapting to change? Support your position.
2. If older traditions can mean a country has more problems adapting to change than a younger country, how might this apply to companies, such as IBM and Compaq, which have significant age differences?

Momentum Toward Change

When a change program has gotten under way, certain forces tend to push the program along. An OD program is built around client involvement. The client system plays a major part in directing the change, and it will probably become committed to the program. There will be forces within the client that want to see the project carried through to completion; the client will want to see "the fruits of its labor." Also, as change programs and consultants usually do not come cheap and some money has probably been spent on the program, the client may want to continue in order to get its money's worth.

Once a change program is under way in one part of an organization, it may set off a chain reaction requiring or permitting changes in other parts of the organization. This is often the case with self-managed work teams, which are usually set up on a trial basis within a department. Other workers, hearing of the teams, often ask for self-managed teams in their units so they can participate. This notion of change is compatible with the OD fundamen-

tal that effective change is organization-wide, or if the change is in a subpart of an organization, the subpart is reasonably well isolated.

Motivation by the Consultant

The consultant should not be overlooked as a motivating force. Words of assurance and encouragement from the consultant can have a strong motivating effect on the client system. The consultant has been involved in many planned change programs, but for the client it could easily be the first major planned change program. The client system may become discouraged at the seemingly slow pace at which the change is moving. Or after having been involved in the diagnosis of problems, it may be overwhelmed by the variety and magnitude of the problems. Although the consultant should be selective in relating "war stories," the sharing of similar situations and past successes in other organizations can be helpful.

The consultant's own behavior can often serve as a motivating force, especially if the consultant is held in high esteem by the client system. Members of the client system may be closed, untrusting, and dishonest in their relations with each other, whereas the consultant believes that effective organizations are built on openness, trust, honesty, and collaboration among the system's members. If the consultant personally behaves in this manner and is held in high regard, the client system may change its behavior.

THE RESTRAINING FORCES BLOCKING IMPLEMENTATION OF CHANGE PROGRAMS

Another critical factor to be considered prior to the implementation of any OD strategy or technique is the probability of forces restraining change. The consultant may assume that because the goals of the program are worthwhile, members will actively support the changes, but this is not always true. Since change always alters the status quo, the consultant should anticipate some resistance among members and plan for this eventuality in the change strategy. The experience of OD practitioners indicates that one of the significant hindrances to OD is not the inadequacy of change techniques, but rather the failure of management and consultants to gain acceptance of proposed changes.

The success of organization development programs may depend to a great extent on the ability of the consultant doing the planning. OD practitioners can benefit from the knowledge gained by sociologists, social psychologists, and cultural anthropologists who have studied the process of change. Resistance to organization development programs is a complex rather than a simple problem; it is the cumulative effect of many factors that make up the acceptance or rejection of change.

Uncertainty Regarding Change

Organization members may have a psychological resistance to change because they seek to avoid uncertainty. Past ways of doing things are well-known and predictable, and the unwillingness to give up familiar tasks or relationships may cause resistance.

Fear of the unknown. A large part of resistance to change stems from a fear of the uncertain or unknown. People become anxious when they exchange the old and familiar for something new and uncertain. A lack of information or understanding often leaves a vacuum which is filled by rumor, speculation, and insecurity.

Disruption of routine. Proposed changes that disturb habitual routines or patterns are likely to encounter resistance because a person's behavior is governed largely by habit and routine. When a person first successfully copes with a situation, he or she will usually continue to operate in a similar manner. The familiar is preferred, and this is especially true when the established behavior has resulted in past successes.

There is little incentive to change when the old way of behaving has been tried and is successful. Once these habits and attitudes have been firmly established, a person responds to his or her environment and to new ideas through this framework. Even situations that are in conflict with these old attitudes are sometimes altered and perceived in a way that is congruent with those attitudes. The old adage "We hear what we want to hear" has some degree of truth. People may conveniently forget some learning if it is in conflict with their present behavior. This notion of selective perception means that people will successfully resist and negate the possible influence of new information upon their earlier attitudes and behavior.

Loss of Existing Benefits

When the change causes employees to feel pressured, they may interpret change as a loss of individual security. There may be an emotional loss associated with the change, a loss of the prior "comfort zone."

Any proposed change is more readily accepted if it promises to benefit those affected by it; however, the motivation of top management to change may not be shared at the operating level. In some cases resistance may be due to a lack of interest or practical appreciation of the reason for the change. In a similar vein, the expectations of a group toward a proposed change will influence its reception. A group that favors a change and expects to benefit will change more readily than one that starts with a negative attitude. People affected by a change tend to resist unless they see the need for it.

Lynda McDermott, an OD consultant, comments "My experience of organization change is that typically the focus is on 'what's in it for the organization,' but to counter resistance to change there has to be a focus, for some periods of time, on 'what's in it for the individual.' "[12]

Threat to Position Power

Any change that causes a manager or group to "lose face" will be resisted. Changes that threaten to lower the status or prestige of the individual or group will probably meet resistance. For example, a department manager who sees a change as reducing his or her sphere of authority is not likely to be in favor of such a change. A former CEO of General Motors referred to the tens of thousands of managers made complacent by the golden days of GM as the "frozen middle." Where a proposed change appears to be detrimental to the vested interest of any group, the groups will resist the change. Thus, even though a change to a modular organization structure may benefit the organization as a whole, functional departments may view the change as a threat to their best interest and therefore resist.[13]

Threat to security. Change sometimes results in a potential disadvantage to an individual employee or group, and people tend to resist changes that threaten the security of their environment. There may be concern for such vested interests as the loss of job, reduced promotional potential, change in career opportunities, reduction in wages or benefits, or an increase in job demands. There are many incidents where work groups have withheld a secretly invented tool or improved work method from management for fear the job will be retimed and people laid off or transferred. These fears induce a loss of security and result in resistance to change.

Redistribution of power. A major factor in resistance to innovation is that reorganization invariably implies a redistribution of power and influence. Individuals or groups who perceive that a change will lessen their degree of influence will strongly resist such changes. Those who have the most to lose will be most likely to disapprove or resist proposed changes.

Disturb existing social networks. Generally, technical changes are more readily accepted when they do not disturb existing social networks. Friendships, social cliques, or informal teams may be threatened by changes. There is research evidence to indicate that the stronger the group ties, the greater the resistance to change.

Conformity to Norms and Culture

Norms are the organized and shared ideas of what members of an organization should do and feel. The members themselves define what the norms are, as well as enforce individual behavior to conform to the norms. The enforcement is imposed by the individual and by the group through peer pressure upon the individual. Because norms generally have strong support from the group, they cannot easily be changed. This is especially true of an individual attempting to alter a norm, for this person faces exclusion by the group. When a person is external to the group (say, an external consultant or a manager), the change process may be even more difficult because of lack of familiarity with the group.

The organization culture includes the language, dress, patterns of behavior, value system, feelings, attitudes, interactions, and group norms of the members. Larger organizations will have subcultures formed around smaller work or social groups. According to the system view of organization behavior, it is difficult to change the ways of behaving in one part of the organization without influencing and being influenced by (perhaps through resistance) the other parts. Unless the consultant begins by considering the possible resistance from the organization as a whole, the ultimate acceptance of the change program is in serious question.

CONSULTANT STRATEGIES TO LESSEN RESISTANCE

If resistance to change can be minimized, the chances of a successful OD program are enhanced. Initially, two things in reducing resistance should be recognized by both the manager and the OD practitioner: (1) resistance to change can be predicted; and (2) resistance cannot be repressed effectively in the long run. Change of some type is inevitable. The task of the manager or the consultant is to make conflict resulting from the resistance creative for organizational good. That is, as the repression of conflict is unwise and even futile, the objective is to turn the energies generated in the resistance of the change to good advantage. A manager or consultant can, however, minimize the threat that underlies resistance. Certain actions may be implemented to make resistance creative for the organization and to reduce resistance. See OD in Practice for an example of how Du Pont has initiated a change program.

OD IN PRACTICE
DU PONT MAKES A SEA CHANGE[14]

E. I. du Pont de Nemours and Company, one of the country's largest corporations, is a diversified chemical manufacturer. They produce, among other products, Freon for refrigerators and coal from West Virginia.

Over 80 chemical plants are located throughout the United States and additional plants are located worldwide. Du Pont consumes about half of one percent of all electricity generated in the United States. By any standards Du Pont is big. Yet within *Fortune* magazine's chemical product group, they rank number-one as the most respected chemical company.

Operating Problems at Industrial Polymers Division

One division, the Industrial Polymers Division (IPD), gives an indication of how Du Pont is able to remain successful when other large corporations are faltering. When it was created,

this division pulled together products that accounted for annual sales of $1 billion. The products placed in this division had been labeled "mature" or "outdated" by many employees. The problems from the beginning included low morale, high costs, low productivity, and an old product line. The division's top and middle management understood the need to improve the division's operations, but this objective was not understood by those lower in the division.

A Sea Change

The IPD head was Joe Miller, who decided after much research that only a major change or "*sea change*" would turn the division around in the long run. In the first few months after the division's creation, Miller held a series of meetings with the help of internal consultants where IDP's mission statement was

formulated. The document was less than a page long. There were several things going for adoption of the document. People were aware of the commonplace performance of the products now located within the division, and they had a desire to turn things around. There was a widely held belief that survival of the division and its personnel hung in the balance. There had already been personnel cutbacks through early retirement plans.

Developing a Vision

Additional meetings were attended by about 300 employees including managers of all levels and professionals to further develop the mission statement. From the information gathered at the meetings, a five-point vision statement was written. At a later meeting attended by 350 technicians, representatives from manufacturing, secretaries, supervisors, and professionals, the vision statement was presented and discussions were held. Out of this meeting came ideas to implement team efforts, self-management, and partnerships with suppliers and customers.

Within three years, sales of IDP were up 55 percent and operating income up about 200 percent. Du Pont recognizes, however, it is too soon to tell if the changes sought for will bring long run changes to IDP's culture.

Questions

1. What did IDP do to build acceptance within the lower ranks of the change program?
2. What were the driving forces to change?

Resistance to the change are signals to the consultant that something is not working in the implementation of the program. These signals include delays and inefficiencies, failure to produce anticipated results, or even efforts to sabotage the change program. There are several methods for dealing with resistance to change.

Education and Communication

The uncertainty and fear of the unknown associated with change can be minimized by an effective communication program. (See B.C. comic strip.) The lack of reliable information leads to rumors and uncertainty. Information concerning the *what* and *why* involved in the change program should be provided to all organization members. In a survey commissioned by *Fortune* magazine of 1,500 senior executives from 20 countries, 89 percent believed the need to communicate frequently with employees will be one of a CEO's top characteristics compared to 59 percent saying it currently was a top characteristic.[15]

Many companies, including Dana Corporation and General Motors, have shown employees commercial television programs on the ability of U.S. companies to compete internationally in an attempt to increase awareness of the need for a change. When employees are told of falling sales, sharply rising costs, declining profits, decreasing quality, customer complaints, high absenteeism, and other statistics that compare unfavorably with the competition or where the company would like to be, organization members are much more likely to support changes.

Source: B.C. by permission of Johnny Hart and Creators Syndicate, Inc.

Organizations such as General Mills and Aetna Life & Casualty are spending a significant amount of time training production-line employees to read accounting and production documents, and then making sure they have all relevant cost and production information. A major benefit is that employees are able to analyze and understand the problems for themselves. The importance for change is appreciated directly by employees—line workers to top executives. The longer members speculate in the absence of reliable facts, the more likely it is that resistance will emerge. Most managers underestimate the amount of communication needed, so it is better to use "overkill" than to understate the situation.

The advantages and rewards of the **communication of proposed changes** should be emphasized for opposition to change disappears as the fears it generates are explained away. Once the reasons underlying a change program are made clear and how individuals will benefit, employees involved can more readily understand and accept the impact of the change.

Create a Vision

In the *Fortune* magazine survey of senior executives, 98 percent of the respondents said conveying a strong sense of vision would be an important characteristics for a CEO in the year 2000, compared to 75 percent who describe themselves or their current CEO as having this characteristic now.[16] A study of effective leaders at all levels of an organization, not just CEOs, found that one of the most powerful impacts they can have is through communicating their vision of the organization.[17]

Some of the more competitive organizations have a well-articulated vision that all members understand. For example, Motorola's CEO, Robert Galvin, began a Total Quality Management program (TQM) and made Six-Sigma quality a goal to attain in five years. Six Sigma is a quality term meaning being perfect 99.9999998 percent of the time—near perfect manufacturing. Motorola spent $25 million in the first year on education programs to explain the complicated concepts to all employees. Six Sigma posters hung throughout every building and memos came out nearly weekly from Galvin on quality. It was a mammoth job to get 105,000 Motorola employees to adopt Six Sigma, but it was a vision CEO Robert Galvin held, and he successfully communicated it to all Motorola's employees.[18]

Participation of Members in the Change Program

One basic technique for increasing the acceptance of change is to be certain that the individuals involved are allowed to share in the decision process rather than being forced. The **participation** of the individual in matters of concern increases the probability of having an acceptable program. An individual who has participated in the formation of a program has an interest and ownership in the program which is likely to lead to increased motivation and understanding.

A change program "prepared on high and cast as pearls before swine" will most certainly be destined to failure. Captain Queeg, in the following excerpt from *The Caine Mutiny*, very enthusiastically follows the policy of dictated change, which later contributed to the crew's mutiny:

> "Now, there are four ways of doing a thing aboard ship—the right way, the wrong way, the Navy way, and my way. I want things on this ship done my way. Don't worry about the other ways. Do things my way, and we'll get along—okay. Now are there any questions?" He looked around. There were no questions. He nodded with smiling satisfaction.[19]

If there is a union in the workplace, it needs to be involved and supportive of the change program. Some OD interventions, such as quality of worklife and self-managed work teams (discussed in Chapter 13), directly involve the union. When potential resisters are drawn into the planning and implementation process, resistance to the change may be reduced or eliminated.

Facilitation and Support

Reinforcing the change process and providing support for those involved is another way OD practitioners can deal with resistance. If the situation allows, the OD consultant can arrange promotions, monetary rewards, or public recognition for those participating in the change program. In one OD program in which the authors were involved, a well-publicized promotion was arranged for a manager who had endorsed and participated in the OD program despite considerable risk of criticism by his peers and immediate superiors when he volunteered for the program. The result was a dramatic acceptance of the OD program by other managers.

Negotiation and Agreement

Another technique is negotiation with potential resisters. Some examples include union agreements, increasing an employee's pension benefits in exchange for early retirement, transferring employees to other divisions instead of laying them off, and negotiating agreements with the heads of departments that would be affected by the change.

Leadership

The leadership of key managers in the organization is critical. "Today's chief executives can't have an emotional commitment to the past. They can't be afraid to shake things up."[20] Other managers who are affected by the change need to be involved and supportive. Many companies provide management development seminars to open up managers to the acceptance of changes. Other than the formal leadership in the organization, the informal leaders' support is also important. Bringing in informal leaders early in the planning stages can build "grass-roots" support for the change.

Reward Systems

Flexible reward systems that take account of individual differences in employees can help in the acceptance of changes. Profit-sharing, bonuses, skill and knowledge-based pay, gain-sharing, and stock ownership plans have recently become more common in large and small businesses.[21] **Profit-sharing** uses the performance of the business to calculate pay. **Knowledge-based pay** or skill-based pay uses the knowledge or skills a worker has to determine pay. **Gain-sharing** recognizes the value of a specific group based on measurable characteristics in the basis for calculating pay.

The trend in more flexible reward systems will likely continue during the 1990s. As of 1990, estimates show that there are at least 10,000 employee-owned businesses employing more than 10 million people. With 76,000 employees, UAL Corp., parent of United Airlines, is the largest U.S. company that is majority-owned by employees.[22] Ford Motor Company has a profit-sharing plan in place that recently rewarded hourly employees with $2,800 for the year. General Motors at its Saturn plant pays workers and executives 80 percent of the base pay of other plants; but employees can make up the difference and more if they meet productivity, quality, and sales targets.[23]

One study found that employee ownership "can have a positive effect on a work group's norms, cohesiveness, and cooperative behaviors; on an employee's work-related attitudes, motivation, and behavior; and on an organization's performance and profitability. Ownership *per se* does not, however, automatically and directly produce these social-psychological and behavioral effects." The researchers concluded that, "An employee-ownership system designed and operated with strong equity, information, and influence components will help produce psychologically experienced ownership and build employees' commitment to and integration into the organization."[24]

Explicit and Implicit Coercion

Managers may force people to go along with a change by explicit or implicit threats involving loss of jobs, or loss of promotion, or raises, and so forth. At one company that was introducing quality improvement teams, managers who were ordered by their president over their objections to participate sat with their backs to the conference table.[25] In some situations, managers may also dismiss or transfer employees who refuse to change. Such methods, though not uncommon, pose risks and make it more difficult to gain support for future change programs. Organizations that have introduced teamwork have found a few employees can't make the transition of working cooperatively with others in teams. They have provided opportunities for these workers to transfer to work situations where they are not working interdependently with others.

Climate Conducive to Communications

Creating a climate where everyone involved in the change program feels free and not threatened to communicate with others can minimize resistance in the long run. If attitudes of respect, understanding, and communication prevail, this will help to break a cycle of reciprocal threat and aggressiveness on the part of the resisters and the advocates of the change program. The consultant insures that parties do not sit in judgment of each other, but instead focuses attention on the basic issues and the relevant facts.

Power Strategies

OD programs historically have been reluctant to deal with the use of power in organizations. To some extent, **power strategies** are antithetical to OD values. But most organizations operate within some type of system that sanctions and uses power, and the organization's members are motivated to some extent by the perceived power of the organization. It may be necessary for an OD program to use the power structure in an organization to convince its members of the worthiness of the program.

In an OD program being implemented in one of the branches of the U.S. military, it was necessary to resort to a power strategy, although it was fairly low key and nonthreatening. After more than a year of trying to find a unit to participate in an OD program, a volunteer unit was finally obtained. Once the program was in progress, it was decided to arrange a visit by that branch's Chief of Operations (who reported to the President) to communicate his personal appreciation for the unit's participation in the OD program. The visit served a dual purpose: it built a high degree of enthusiasm within the client for the remaining phases of the OD program, and it convinced other units sitting on the sidelines that the OD program was to be taken seriously.

This power strategy was employed after many months of attempts to obtain a client and as the result of heated debates by the team of OD practitioners. This was certainly not the only reason for the successful spread of the OD program throughout that military branch, but it did give added impetus when the future of the program was at a crucial stage. This will be the case when dealing with an organization that traditionally relies upon power.

Overcoming resistance to change will involve using more than one of these approaches. The OD practitioner must decide which techniques to use and how to put them into effective action.

REVIEW QUESTIONS

1. Trace the life cycle of change in an organization or government.

2. What are major forces in the change process?

3. What strategies might be used in gaining acceptance for an OD program?

KEY WORDS AND CONCEPTS

Define and be able to use the following concepts:

Communication of Proposed Changes
Driving Forces
Gain-Sharing
Global Market
Knowledge-Based Pay

Participation
Power Strategies
Profit-Sharing
Restraining Forces

**OD SKILLS SIMULATION 6.1
DOWNSIZING IN THE ENIGMA COMPANY**

Total time suggested: 1 hour

A. PURPOSE

This chapter discusses how people react to possible changes. In this simulation you will have an opportunity to be involved in a small-group decision on change and begin to see how different individuals may perceive a situation in differing ways. The purposes include:

1. To examine how you and others attempt to exert influence in an attempt to change another's position.
2. To understand the relationship between motivation and the acceptance or rejection of change.
3. To consider how change situations are influenced by multiple criteria, and subjective versus objective considerations.

B. PROCEDURES

Step 1. Before coming to class, read the Company Situation on p. 168. Use the data in Table 6.1 on page 169 to fill in the Individual Decision Form on p. 169 (or develop your own Lotus® or Excell® worksheet). Each participant should then make an individual ranking of the employees from 1 (the first to be laid off) to 8 (the last to be laid off). Transfer your answers to Column 1 of the Enigma Rating Form on page 169.

Step 2. Form groups of five members each with one person (plus any additional class members) serving as an observer. Each group is to reach a consensus on the ranking. Remember, a consensus decision involves reaching mutual agreement by discussion until all agree on the final decision. Follow these instructions for reaching consensus:

1. Try to reach the best possible decision.
2. Avoid changing your mind simply to reach agreement and to avoid conflict, but support solutions with which you are able to agree.
3. Avoid "conflict-reducing" techniques, such as majority vote, averaging, or trading in reaching your decision.
4. View differences of opinion as a help rather than a hindrance in decision making.

Record your team decision on the Enigma Rating Form, Column 2. The observer can use the Observer Form at the end of the simulation.

Time suggested for Step 2: 30 minutes.

Step 3. List each group's ranking on the blackboard and compare and discuss differences in ranking. The observer will provide feedback using the Observer Form as a guide. Also consider the following questions with the observer leading the discussion:

1. How did members differ in the criteria used to lay people off?
2. Was there any resistance among team members to changing their positions?
3. What were the strategies used to influence and change team members' positions?
4. How were the differences resolved? To what extent was the group decision really based on consensus?

Time suggested for Step 3: 20 minutes.

Step 4. Record the answers given by your instructor in Column 3. Score your individual and team answers. Where the actual and correct answers match, put + 10 in Columns 4 and 5 on the Enigma Rating Form. If the actual and correct answers do not match, put 0 in Columns 4 and 5. By totaling the points, an individual and team score can be calculated. Column 4 provides an indication of the individual participant's "correctness," and Column 5 provides an equivalent measure of each team's performance.

Compare the individual and team scores. Individuals come to teams with varying degrees of preparation, and the final score may not reflect how decisions were made by the team. As a class, compare the scores of the teams.

Time suggested for Step 4: 10 minutes.

COMPANY SITUATION:
ENIGMA ENGINEERING COMPANY

The Enigma Engineering Company is a medium-sized manufacturing company located in the suburbs of Chicago, Illinois. The company is nonunionized and has attempted during the past two years to incorporate an objective performance-review system that has been designed purposefully to provide feedback to employees. The system is designed to be objective, time-oriented, and representative.

The loss of a contract bid to a competitor has forced the Enigma management to consider laying off one, two, or three of the poorest performers next week in the circuit board unit. This unit produces circuit boards that are sold to electronic firms. The layoff may only be temporary, but management wants to be sure that they have been fair in presenting an objectively based decision to the employees.

The people in the unit to be cut back are:

1. Albert Banks: white; age 42; married; three children; two years of high school; 14 years with the company.
2. Bob Brown: black; age 37; widower; two children; high school graduate; eight years with the company.
3. Christine Newton: black; age 24; single; high school graduate; two years with the company.
4. Dave Fram: white; age 50; single; finished junior college while working; 15 years with the company.
5. Carla Peters: Native American; age 36; married; four children; high school graduate; three years with the company.
6. Ray Salgado: Hispanic; age 40; married; one child; high school graduate; four years with the company.
7. Valarie Green: white; age 39; divorced; two children; 2 years of college; 7 years with the company.
8. Richard Chu: Asian; age 42; married; no children; one year of college; nine years with the company.

The company has evaluated these unit employees on a number of factors listed in Table 6.1. The ratings shown have been averaged over the past 18 months of performance evaluation.

Table 6.1 Enigma Performance Review Data; Factors Evaluated by Supervisor

Employee	Average Weekly Output[a]	(%) Rejects[b]	(%) Absences[c]	Cooperative Attitude[d]	Loyalty[d]	Potential for Promotion[d]
Albert Banks	39.6	4.9	6.3	Good	Good	Fair
Bob Brown	43.4	5.3	7.9	Poor	Fair	Fair
Christine Newton	35.2	0.9	0.4	Excellent	Good	Good
Dave Fram	40.4	4.7	13.2	Excellent	Excellent	Fair
Carla Peters	40.2	9.6	9.3	Poor	Fair	Poor
Ray Salgado	39.6	3.4	6.1	Good	Fair	Poor
Valarie Green	36.2	4.8	5.0	Good	Good	Fair
Richard Chu	45.2	7.0	3.6	Fair	Fair	Good

[a]Higher score = more output.
[b]Lower score = fewer rejects.
[c]Lower score = fewer absences.
[d]Possible ratings: poor, fair, good, excellent.

THE ENIGMA COMPANY INDIVIDUAL DECISION FORM

	Education	Working Output	Seniority	Rejects	Absences	Attitude	Loyalty	Promotion Potential	AVERAGE
A. Banks									
B. Brown									
C. Newton									
D. Fram									
C. Peters									
R. Salgado									
V. Green									
R. Chu									

Education:
* No H.S. Diploma = 2
*High School Diploma = 4
*1 Year College = 6
*2+ Years College = 8

Seniority:
*2 years = 1
*3 Years = 2
*4 years = 3
*7 Years = 4
*8 Years = 5
*9 Years = 6
*14 Years = 7
*15 Years = 8

Attitude, Loyalty, & Potential for Promo:
*Poor = 2
*Fair = 4
*Good = 6
*Excellent = 8

ENIGMA RATING FORM

Employee	Individual Rating Col. 1	Team Rating Col. 2	Correct Rating Col. 3	Individual Score Col. 4	Team Score Col. 5
1. A. Banks					
2. B. Brown					
3. C. Newton					
4. D. Fram					
5. C. Peters					
6. R. Salgado					
7. V. Green					
8. R. Chu					
Total Scores					

OBSERVER FORM

Low	:	:	:	:	:	:	High
	1	2	3	4	5	6	7

Based on the following scale, rate the team on how it performed on the following scale.
Record your choice in the blank.

Factor	Individual Rating	Team Rating
1. Cooperative teamwork	_____	_____
2. Member satisfaction	_____	_____
3. Team motivation	_____	_____
4. Information sharing	_____	_____
5. Consensual decision making	_____	_____
6. Conflict directly faced and resolved	_____	_____
7. Participative leadership	_____	_____
8. Clearly defined goals	_____	_____
9. Trust	_____	_____
10. Encouraged openness	_____	_____

OD SKILLS SIMULATION 6.2
DRIVING AND RESTRAINING FORCES

Total time suggested: 50 minutes.

A. PURPOSE

This simulation draws on the change situation posed in Simulation 6.1. This simulation should help you further understand the diagnosis process and overcoming resistance to change.

B. PROCEDURES

Step 1. Form into the same groups as Simulation 6.1 and identify your team's operating problems encountered in solving the task in Simulation 6.1. Then make two lists on the Force Field Analysis Form on page 171: one on driving forces (behaviors and actions that helped in solving the problem) and the other on the restraining forces (behaviors and actions that hindered in solving the problem). Put a star next to those forces in which you will probably play a part.

Make additional charts depending on the number of problems identified.

Time suggested for Step 1: 25 minutes.

Step 2. Meeting as a class, report on the significant problems and the driving and restraining forces. Determine to what extent are the problems similar and different between groups.

Time suggested for Step 2: 25 minutes.

FORCE FIELD ANALYSIS FORM

Problem: _____

Driving Forces	Restraining Forces
_____	_____
_____	_____
_____	_____

Problem: _____

Driving Forces	Restraining Forces
_____	_____
_____	_____
_____	_____

Problem: _____

Driving Forces	Restraining Forces
_____	_____
_____	_____
_____	_____

Problem: _____

Driving Forces	Restraining Forces
_____	_____
_____	_____
_____	_____

CASE 6:
THE KEYBOARD COMPANY

The Keyboard Company is a medium-sized manufacturing firm supplying computer keyboards to many national computer manufacturers. The company has experienced rapid growth since its beginning by president John Zoltan and is now moving into advanced electronics from the electromechanical assembly of the past. John Zoltan had recently attended a university executive seminar, and was so impressed that he brought in the professor as a consultant. At one of their meetings, it was decided that to achieve the "organizational excellence" that Zoltan desired for his company, he should start an internal OD consulting group. The president ran an ad in *The Wall Street Journal*, and he and the consultant selected four young M.B.A.'s. These four, and one young internal prospect from human resources, were formed into what was called the *OD group*. (See Exhibit 1.)

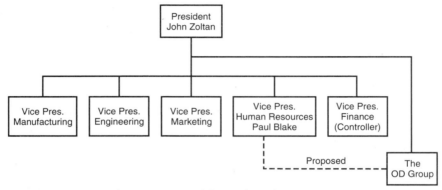

EXHIBIT 6.1 Partial Organization of the Keyboard Company.

THE OD GROUP

The OD group was housed in an old conference room and began with a high level of enthusiasm and energy. The members of the group ranged in age from 23 to 34. The members were Pete Loomis, 25, M.B.A., a behavioral specialist, who had done training in industry; Kay Hughes, 27, M.B.A., who had been a sales representative prior to graduate school; Bill Heller, 26, M.B.A., specializing in group dynamics with no industry experience; Don Morgan, 34, M.B.A., with OD experience in the military; and George Kessler, 23, three years of experience in the human resources department.

The group spent their first month getting to know the various members of the organization, and held weekly conferences with John Zoltan, who was very interested and active in the planning stages of the OD program.

At that point the group (the "hot-shots" as they were known in the plant) started a company-wide training program focusing on managerial style. The program involved three-day training sessions at an off-site location, a resort motel with good meals and so on. This was called the "country club" by disparaging employees.

The group itself was a highly cohesive work team. Because of their open office, they spent long hours tossing ideas around and providing support and enthusiasm for each other's ideas. They were all involved in the design of the program (as was Zoltan) and worked hard to make it a success. Often the group would sit around until nine or ten o'clock or even midnight, critiquing the sessions and planning new approaches for change.

Within the group there was a diversity of dress and so on, but with individuality and openness being a norm. Pete, George, and Bill usually dressed informally in Levi's and sport

shirts, while Don and Kay dressed in more of an executive style wearing sport jackets and the like. This difference in dress also reflected a division of thought within the group. Pete, George, and Bill wanted to be more confrontational and aggressive in approach. They wanted innovative changes and wanted to overhaul the production operations. . . . The others felt that they needed to be accepted first and favored more gradual changes. They felt that the group needed to start "where the system was" if they were to be effective. About this time, Zoltan left for a visit to Asia to inspect new marketing opportunities.

THE ACTIVITIES

As the training continued through all levels of the organization, they were also collecting organization-survey data to be used in planning the next phase of the OD program. Here the controversy began to emerge. Some wanted to hold feedback sessions and to confront the members with the data, then begin a job-design program leading to quality-control circles. The second group, including Don and Kay, suggested a slower and more gradual approach. They thought that given their low level of acceptance in the organization, they should start with something less threatening, such as data gathering and feedback.

A second rift occurred when they began to see less and less of Zoltan as the training progressed. However, Kay could call the president's office and get an appointment anytime, which she often did. Don Morgan also held a weekly briefing session with Zoltan when he was in town.

The other members, particularly Pete, made a lot of jokes about this fact, but there was often an edge of seriousness under the humor. For example, Pete and Bill had been trying for two weeks to see Zoltan to explain their ideas, but he was unavailable. Yet his secretary called for Kay Hughes to join him for coffee. When this was discussed by the group, Don and Kay simply stated that they were trying to maintain and develop the group's relationship with the client. Peter replied, "I thought the whole organization was our client."

Unfortunately, the evaluation of the training program was mixed. Some managers and departments were full of praise for the program, whereas others were highly negative, calling it "a waste of time and money."

In a meeting with John Zoltan, the controller expressed the idea that, in view of the disappointing results, it would be a good idea to move the OD group to the human resources section for budgeting purposes. The group was currently charging over $200,000 per year into overhead, and this was highly unpopular among the line managers since overhead costs were allocated. Zoltan said he would give the matter some thought and discuss this possibility with the Executive Committee.

THE MEETING

Shortly after this (approximately one year after the group had been formed), the members of the group were invited into the Executive Committee meeting, where the performance of the OD program was discussed and evaluated. John Zoltan and others expressed high praise for the work of the group. However, the Executive Committee suggested some ideas for improving the group in the future.

Since Zoltan suggested a need for more coordination and integration of training activities and for improved budgetary control, the committee recommended that the group be placed within the human resources department for budgeting purposes, reporting to Paul Blake. The committee assured the group that this would not affect the way the group operated. Second, the committee suggested that one person be designated central contact person. Don Morgan was the one person that they all felt would be acceptable to a majority of the company managers, and they recommended him, but left the decision up to the group.

As the group walked back to the office, several angry suggestions were made along the line that Zoltan "could take this job and shove it!" Both Kay and Pete said they were considering resigning from the company.

CASE ANALYSIS FORM

Name: _____

I. Problems

 A. Macro

 1. _____

 2. _____

 B. Micro

 1. _____

 2. _____

II. Causes

 1. _____

 2. _____

 3. _____

III. Systems affected

 1. Structural _____

 2. Psychosocial _____

 3. Technical _____

 4. Managerial_____

 5. Goals _____

IV. Alternatives

 1. _____

 2. _____

 3. _____

 4. _____

 5. _____

V. Recommendations

 1. _____

 2. _____

 3. _____

SUMMARY

- **Change**. In the hyperturbulent environment of the 1990s, change is the norm. The bottom line *is* today's organization must focus on what has to be changed: a radically new environment demands radically new forms of organization and ways of managing. In this chapter, we have examined some of the forces motivating individuals toward change, some factors that restrain the likelihood of change, and some change strategies that are likely to enhance acceptance. The process of change is complex because of the interaction of social, technical, and psychological factors. People often become satisfied with the status quo and react with insecurity or anxiety when change occurs.

- **OD Strategy**. An important factor to be considered prior to the implementation of any OD strategy is the motivation of the client system toward change. Some resistance to proposed changes may arise from perceived (real or unreal) threats to personal security.

- **Resistance**. Resistance to change is usually a reaction to methods used in implementing a change rather than any inherent human characteristic. People tend to resist changes that do not make sense to them or that are forced upon them against their will. Certain factors, such as loss of security or status, lead to resistance to change. There are ways to reduce this resistance, including good *communication* and *participation* in the change process.

- **Identify forces**. You have had an opportunity to role play and observe a situation of change, to identify forces of resistance, and to apply change strategies to a situation. You may have found in the simulation or from other personal experiences, that it is difficult to motivate a person. The motivation must come from within and as psychologist, Abraham Maslow, has noted, a satisfied need is *not* a motivator. There must be a perceived need for change within the client system before change can take place.

- **Acceptance**. You may have found that acceptance of change can be improved when certain conditions are present that minimize the potential threat or discomfort of a proposed change. These conditions include careful planning and thorough communication of the change to the target individual, group, or system. You may also have found that when you or others are allowed to participate in making it a self-designed change program, the degree of acceptance also increases. If you, as a consultant, can create a climate where people feel free to change, rather than being coerced, the probability of acceptance will also be higher.

NOTES

1. Laura Rubach, "Downsizing: How Quality is affected as companies shrink," *Quality Progress,* vol. 28, no. 4, April 1995, pp. 24–25.
 For additional information on how companies are managing change, see Noel. M. Tichy and Stratford Sherman, *Control Your Destiny or Someone Else Will: How Jack Welch Is Turning General Electric into the World's Most Competitive Corporation*, (New York: Doubleday and Co., Inc., 1993); and Rosabeth Moss Kanter, *When Giants Learn to Dance: Mastering the Challenge of Strategy, Management, and Careers in the 1990s*, (New York: Simon and Schuster, 1989).
2. See Gabriella Stern, "GM Puts Saturn in Small-Car Group, Shakes Up North American Operations," *The Wall Street Journal*, October 5, 1994, p. A-5. Alex Taylor III. "GM: Some Gain, Much Pain," *Fortune,* May 29, 1995 p. 78.
3. For additional information, see "Managing Change," *Business Week*, special issue "Reinventing America, 1992," pp. 59–74; Yoram Zeira and Joyce Avedisian, "Organizational Planned Change: Assessing the Chances for Success," *Organizational Dynamics*, Winter 1989, pp. 31–45
4. Goodwin Watson, "Resistance to Change," in *Concepts for Social Change*. Cooperative Project for Educational Development Series, vol. 1 (Washington, D.C.: National Training Laboratories, 1966).
5. Carol J. Loomis, "Dinosaurs?," *Fortune*, May 3, 1993, pp. 36–42.
6. *The Wall Street Journal*, July 7, 1995, p. A1.
7. John F. Welch, "A Master Class in Radical Change," *Fortune*, December 13, 1993, pp. 82–90.
8. John P. Kotter and Leonard A. Schlesinger, "Choosing Strategies for Change," *Harvard Business Review*, vol. 57, no. 2 (March–April 1979), p. 106.
9. Julie Lopez, "For the Baby Bells, New Business Ventures Beget a Culture Clash," *The Wall Street Journal*, March 15, 1989, p. A1.
10. Welch, "A Master Class in Radical Change."
11. John F. Hulpke, California State University, Bakersfield, 1994, sources: Richard Turner, "Hollywood Is Seeing the Future, and It Is Interactive Show Biz," *The Wall Street Journal*, May 19, 1993, p. A1; Daniel Benjamin, "Germany Is Troubled By How Little Work Its Workers Are Doing," *The Wall Street Journal*, May 6, 1993, p. A1; Gene Koretz, "Europe's Work Force Isn't Moving With The Money," *Business Week*, June 21, 1993, p. 24; Tom Peters, *Thriving on Chaos; Handbook for a Management Revolution*, (New York: Alfred A. Knopf, 1987); and Robert H. Waterman Jr., *The Renewal Factor: How the Best Get and Keep the Competitive Edge*, (New York: Bantam Books, 1987).
12. Linda McDermott, "What in the Name of OD Do We Do?" *Training and Development Journal*, vol. 37, no. 4, April 1983, p. 45.
13. Shawn Tully, "Modular Corporation," *Fortune*, February 8, 1993, pp. 106–15.
14. Tircia Welsh, "Best and Worst Corporate Reputations," *Fortune*, February 7, 1994, pp. 58–95; Barbara Rosewicz and Richard Koenig, "How Clean-Air Bill Will Force Du Pont into Costly Moves," *The Wall Street Journal*, May 25, 1990, p. A1; Brian Dumain, "Creating a New Company Culture," *Fortune*, January 15, 1990; and Bernard A. Rausch, "Du Pont Transforms a Division's Culture," *Management Review*, March 1989, pp. 37–42.
15. Lester B. Korn, "How the Next CEO Will Be Different," *Fortune*, May 22, 1989, pp. 157–61.
16. Korn, "How the Next CEO Will Be Different."
17. W. Bennis and B. Nanus, *Leaders*, (New York: Harper & Row, 1985).

18. Kenneth R. Thompson, "A Conversation with Robert W. Galvin," *Organizational Dynamics*, Spring 1992, pp. 56–69; and Mark S. Gill, "Stalking Six Sigma," *Business Month*, January 1990, pp. 42–46.

19. *The Caine Mutiny: A Novel of World War II* (Garden City, N.Y.: Doubleday & Co., Inc., 1951), p. 131. Copyright © 1951 by Herman Wouk.

20. Noel M. Tichy, University of Michigan management professor quoted in "Requiem For Yesterday's CEO," John A. Byrne, *Business Week*, February 15, 1993, pp. 32.

21. For a more detailed discussion of reward systems, see Robert L. Rose, "Employee Ownership Is Catching On in Airline Industry," *The Wall Street Journal*, July 23, 1993, p. B-3; and Kanter, *When Giants Learn to Dance*, pp. 229–66; and Henry Tosi and Lisa Tosi, "What Managers Need to Know About Knowledge-Based Pay," *Organizational Dynamics*, Winter 1986, pp. 52–64.

22. Michael J. McCarthy and Carl Quintanilla, "Holders of UAL Approve Bold Buyout That Gives Workers Majority Control," *The Wall Street Journal*, July 13, 1994, p. A-3.

23. Neal Templin, "GM Unit Posts Operating Profit For First Time," *The Wall Street Journal*, June 14, 1993, p. A5; and James B. Treece, "Here Comes GM's Saturn," *Business Week*, April 9, 1990, pp. 56–62.

24. Jon L. Pierce and Candace A. Furo, "Employee Ownership: Implications for Management," *Organizational Dynamics*, Winter 1990, p. 42.

25. Thomas M. Rohan, "A New Culture," *Industry Week*, April 17, 1989, pp. 43–56.

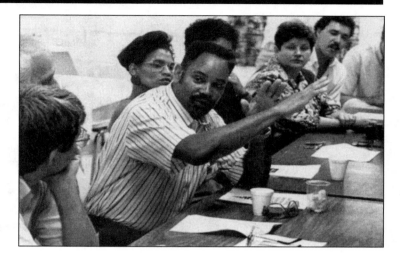

The Aiken plant of Owens-Corning have formed product style teams with customers to address quality issues. *Photo courtesy of Owens-Corning Fiberglas Corporation.*

Process Consulting Skills

7

OBJECTIVES

Upon completing this chapter, you will be able to:

1. Understand the key OD consulting skills, including process consultation skills, and determine how they may be applied.
2. Practice using OD consulting skills.
3. Identify and gain insights into your own OD consulting style.

PREMEETING PREPARATION

1. Read the Background Information.
2. Read the company information and role description in OD Skills Simulation 7.1. Complete Step 1, form teams of six, and assign roles.
3. Read and complete Step 1 of OD Skills Simulation 7.2.
4. Read and prepare for Step 1 OD Skills of Simulation 7.3.
5. Read and analyze Case 7: The OD Letters.

BACKGROUND INFORMATION

OD consultants focus on long-term benefits for the organization rather than on short-term, cosmetic success. The consultant's role is primarily to help employees create their own solutions, systems, and concepts, not to decree problem solutions.[1] The challenge of changing organizations and developing corporate excellence increasingly focuses on the OD consultant/manager team. This is because OD change efforts can result in performance gains or losses for the entire organization. The OD consultant is the person responsible for developing change programs and thus brings a variety of skills to the client system. For the most part these skills will have broad impact on future organization success. These skills include an understanding of management and business principles, problem-solving and analytical skills, and interpersonal and communication skills. The OD consultant will at various times be teacher, counselor, cheerleader, coach, and advisor. This chapter will describe one of the basic OD consultant skills: process consultation.

The role of managers—especially middle managers—is changing to more of a process consultant. One management consultant, Michael Hammer, says, "Middle management as we currently know it will simply disappear." He believes that three-quarters of middle managers will vanish and return to the work they did before they were promoted into management. The remainder, "will fill a role that will change almost beyond recognition."[2] More simply, there will be two types of new-style managers: The first will oversee, beginning to end, a reengineered process, such as order fulfillment or product development. They will need skills in performance management and work redesign. The second manager type Hammer calls employee coaches. He says, "Employee coaches will support and nurture employees—much as senior managers do in corporate America today."[3] This chapter will describe one of the basic OD consultant skills: process consultation.

Process consultation is one of the most-used OD consulting skills. Its purpose is to help the client system become more aware of its processes, particularly those that relate to group behavior and interpersonal communications. When a work team becomes more keenly aware of how it operates, it will be better able to analyze and solve its own problems. The process consultant helps the work group learn to solve its own problems.

The skills discussed in this chapter should not be viewed as a cook-book approach for the OD consultant. As the OD consultant gains experience using these and other skills, the consultant will become more comfortable using them. Then the skills can be applied during various stages of the OD process.

Process Consultation

Process consultation is an OD consulting skill for helping work groups become more effective. In one survey of OD consultants, it was found that 80 percent of the consultants used process-consulting skills, more than any other OD skill mentioned.[4] Edgar Schein has perhaps best described process consultation in his book, *Process Consultation: Its Role in Organization Development*. Schein defines process consultation as a "set of activities on the part of the consultant that help the client to perceive, understand, and act upon the process events that occur in the client's environment in order to improve the situation as defined by the client."[5] Process consultation aims at helping the work group to become more aware of its own processes and to use its own problem-solving ability and resources. "Process consultation is not a technique; it is a philosophy of *how to be helpful*."[6] Process consultation is based upon a very thorough diagnosis of the problems made jointly by the consultant and the client.

One of the major characteristics of process consultation is that the clients learn to identify problems and then initiate their own solutions. The process consultant observes individuals and teams in action and helps the client organization learn to diagnose and solve its own problems. The underlying assumption is that the solutions will be more accepted by members.

Group Process

The foundation of process consultation is the study of how groups and individuals within those groups behave.[7] While *content* is *what* a group does (its task), *process* is *how* the group goes about accomplishing its task. Process consultation is only concerned with the content or the actual product of the group to the extent that the content is a function of the process.

Because process consultation often leads to the use of other OD approaches, the consultation process should start at the highest level of the client organization. This way the impact will be as far reaching as possible. The process consultant tries to help the organization solve its own problems by making it aware of organization process. The process consultant deals with five areas crucial to effective organization performance: communication, member roles and functions in groups, group problem solving and decision making, group norms and growth, and leadership and authority.[8]

Communications

The process consultant uses several techniques for analyzing the communications processes within a group.

- *Observe*. One method is to observe the frequency and length of time each member talks during a group discussion. These observations can be easily recorded on paper and referred to later when analyzing group behavior. It is also useful to keep a record of who talks to whom or to use a sociogram.
- *Identify*. Sometimes it is also helpful to identify the "most influential listeners" in a group. Noticing eye contact between members can give insights to the communication processes. Often one person, who may speak little, is the one being focused on by others as they speak.
- *Interruptions*. Another valuable observation concerns interruptions: Who interrupts whom? Is there a pattern to the interruptions? What are the apparent effects of the interruptions? Is there a pattern of who talks after whom? (See Our Changing World.)

OUR CHANGING WORLD
DO JAPANESE COMMUNICATE MORE BY SPEAKING LESS?[9]

Consultants often try to change attitudes and challenge biases. Multicultural management has become much in demand since so many companies are becoming global organizations. Companies quickly realized that international management was much more complicated than it appeared initially. Anglo-Saxon business practices are often poorly suited for much of the world outside the United States and Great Britain.

Multicultural Management

Many training programs emphasize teamwork and focus on building global business- and interpersonal-skills. One trainer says multicultural management is "a question of attitude, an openness to human variety, not a question of knowledge."

The Japanese vs. American Cowboys

Participants often address communication issues at such sessions. At one training program run by University of Michigan's Professor Noel Tichy, the challenge was to draw the Japanese out of their shells and get them to speak more often and openly. The Americans who participated had the opposite problem.

Professor Tichy chided them saying, "You're a bunch of cowboys. You're not listening."

The participants continued to explore their communication differences and discovered many of their differences were culturally based. Though they found no single answer, the participants gained several insights into themselves and others.

Typically, up-and-coming American executives pride themselves on aggressiveness and openness. They assume that more communication is naturally better. On the other hand, the Japanese seem to realize that they can learn a great deal by listening. In the Japanese culture, the most successful executive is more likely the one who listens best, rather than the one who talks most. Professor Tichy concludes that in the end the executives learned how to work "across cultures and across languages."

Questions

1. Do you agree with the ideas about listening?
2. To what other factors can you attribute the difference between the behavior of American and Japanese business people?

Member Roles and Functions

The process consultant must also be aware of the different **roles** which individual members play in the group. Group members have several issues to resolve at the same time they are working on their group's task.[10] Members will be working on acting out the roles in which they feel most comfortable. Many of these roles will probably not be explicitly stated but will evolve and include such roles as who is the technical expert, who is aggressive, who initiates the conversation, and who is the joke teller or tension reliever. The group will also resolve control, power, and influence issues.

Members of existing groups take on roles which can be categorized as group task functions, group building and maintenance functions, or individual functions (see Table 7.1). *Group task functions* include member behaviors that directly help the group solve its task. These behaviors include *initiating and suggesting* what is the goal of the group and how the group can proceed to accomplish its goal. Other behaviors include *seeking opinions and information* from other members and giving opinions and information. *Asking questions* of clarification and elaborating on information helps the group to work on its goal. *Summarizing* occurs when a member pulls together and reviews briefly what the group has said or done thus far. A related function is a member *testing for group consensus* by asking such questions as "What I seem to be hearing the group say is. . . . Is this correct?" or "Are we ready to make our decision?"

Group building and maintenance functions include behaviors that help the group grow and improve its members' interpersonal relationships. *Harmonizing* and *compromising* behavior help to reduce conflict and tension between members. *Encouraging* behavior helps people to better develop their ideas and helps the quieter members to make more contributions. *Gatekeeping*, another maintenance function, gives everyone a chance to be heard. A person with *following* behavior passively accepts the ideas of others and serves as an audience for the group.

Individual functions are behaviors that satisfy individual needs and are inconsequential to the group's task and maintenance. The behaviors are frequently dysfunctional to the group. *Dominating* behavior attempts through displaying flattery, behaving authoritatively, and interrupting others to assert superiority. The *playboy* displays a lack of involvement through horseplay, cynicism, and other inappropriate behavior. *Blocking* behavior carries disagreement and stubbornness beyond reason. *Recognition-seeking* behavior calls attention through such acts as bragging, to avoid being placed in an inferior position. *Pleading* for special interest is behavior that disguises the person's own beliefs or biases by projecting them through others such as "the union guy down on the floor says . . ." or "the average consumer believes. . . ."

Problem Solving and Decision Making

An effective group must be able to identify problems, examine possible actions, and make decisions. The process consultant helps members understand how the group makes deci-

Table 7.1 Group Member Behaviors

Group Task Functions	Group Building and Maintenance Functions	Individual Functions
Initiating and suggesting	Harmonizing	Dominating
Seeking opinions	Compromising	Acting the playboy
Asking questions	Encouraging	Blocking
Elaborating	Gatekeeping	Seeking recognition
Summarizing	Following	Pleading for special interest
Testing for consensus		

sions and the consequences of each method of decision making. Problem solving begins with gathering the necessary information and identifying problem areas. Alternatives are then generated, along with forecasts of possible results. An alternative is chosen, and a detailed plan of action is formulated. The decision is implemented and finally an evaluation of the decision is made.

Group consensus is an effective method for making group decisions. A decision made by group consensus is one that all members can support. This is the ideal technique, though it is the most difficult to obtain. This type of group decision making is especially effective when the group members must carry out the decision, and their acceptance and cooperation is required. The process consultant then helps the group understand how it makes decisions and the possible consequences of decision processes.

Group Norms and Growth

Norms have been defined as the organized and shared ideas regarding what group members should do and feel, how this behavior should be regulated, and what sanctions should be applied when behavior does not coincide within social expectations. The process consultant helps the group understand its own norms and whether these are helpful or dysfunctional. As the group continues to meet, they should move forward from the acquaintance stage to an effectively functioning team. The members will become more supportive, use member talents and resources, and understand how the group operates and improves upon their decision-making process.

Leadership and Authority

The process consultant can help the group understand the impact of leadership styles. Groups may have a formal and an informal leader. It is common for the leadership function to be shared by group members; for example, the member who performs functions of gatekeeping, summarizing, or one of the other task or maintenance functions, is behaving in the role of a leader.

The Types of Process Interventions

Process interventions are varied but the interventions never involve the consultant in the task of the group. The concern is *how* the group is going about accomplishing its task. The interventions should be as brief and crisp as possible and focus on only one level of behavior at a time. They should provide maximum impact with minimum interruption.

The types of process interventions that may be used include clarifying, summarizing, synthesizing, generalizing, probing, questioning, listening, reflecting feelings, providing support, coaching, counseling, modeling, setting the agenda, feeding back observations, and providing structural suggestions.[11]

Clarifying and Summarizing

Clarifying refers to resolving misunderstandings or incorrect perceptions in what members are saying. For example, "Mary, I seem to be hearing you say. . . . Is this correct?" Providing a summary of the major points and accomplishments of a discussion may be helpful. This sometimes helps the group to understand where it is and also provides a link to the next topic on the agenda.

Synthesizing and Generalizing

Synthesizing occurs when several points and ideas are put together into a common theme. Generalizing refers to taking the ideas or feelings of one person and attaching them to the

entire group. For example, when one person expresses reservations about dealing with a particular issue, a process observation is, "Am I correct in assuming the rest of you share Irwin's position?"

Probing and Questioning

When the group needs additional information or needs to explore additional ideas, it may be important to seek additional information and ask questions. As an example, "Larisa, you mentioned. . . . I'm not sure everyone understands your point. Could you explain it in more detail?" Probing and questioning may be especially useful at the beginning of a discussion if members are reaching hasty conclusions.

Listening

One of the most important skills of the OD consultant is listening. Listening in this context is not only passively hearing what another is saying, but it is also a very involved activity. It is important for the process consultant to communicate nonverbally through eye contact, nods of the head, and posture that the speaker is being listened to. Listening refers to hearing the entire message including any feelings. The feelings of the speaker are rarely expressed in words but are often communicated nonverbally: tone of voice, facial expressions, hand and arm movements, body posture, eye movements, and so forth.

Reflecting Feelings

Most messages have two parts: one is the content and the other is the feeling of the speaker, often expressed nonverbally. (See B.C. comic strip.) The listener needs to practice *empathy*, that is, the listener tries to see the world from the speaker's point of view. Reflecting feelings refer to communicating back to the speaker the feeling part of the message that has been heard. Several examples are, "By the looks of most of your faces, you seem confused by what Carlos has said. Is this correct?"; and after seeing a member slowly push her chair back from the table and fold her arms tightly, "Yoshiko, am I correct in assuming you have a problem with what Murphy has just reported?" The purpose of reflecting feelings is to check out perceptions and to get members more involved in the discussion.

It is important for the OD consultant to test constantly for an understanding of what the client is saying. Empathizing with the client and then reflecting back what the speaker seems to be saying from both a content and feeling point of view builds positive relations with the client and is at the foundation of problem solving and change.

Source: B.C. by permission of Johnny Hart and Creators Syndicate, Inc.

Providing Support, Coaching, and Counseling

Providing support includes encouraging group members to talk and express their ideas. It also includes complimenting the group for a particularly productive meeting. The question sometimes arises by individuals or the group about what behavior or action can be changed to improve group functioning. Coaching and counseling may occur in a private meeting with individuals, particularly the formal manager or supervisor of the group. Suggestions of appropriate behavior and ways of dealing with group issues are appropriate, but the process consultant should first be sure that the client understands the feedback and is interested in trying to solve the problem. It is important for the OD consultant to remember that the objective of process consultation is to help the client to be an active participant in identifying and solving his or her own problems. General Motors and U.S. President Bill Clinton have both hired consultants to help them work on improving group processes. (See OD in Practice.)

OD IN PRACTICE
THANK YOU FOR SHARING THAT MR. PRESIDENT[12]

Several presidents have tried process consultation: one president was General Motors President Roger Smith, who has since retired, and another was U.S. President Bill Clinton.

General Motors Attempts Improved Communications

General Motors hired a full-time facilitator, or process consultant, to work with CEO Roger Smith and 17 other top executives. The consultant, Mark Sarkady of Forum (a Boston consulting firm), frequently says, "Thank you for sharing that" in GM's team-building sessions. Many of these are held off-site, away from company property, which removes the participants from the old GM culture and puts them in a more neutral setting.

Sarkady has set up sessions that bring together lower-level managers and top executives. The idea is to promote honest, frank, and frequent communications. He is normally present. In one such GM session, Roger Smith asked a subordinate a hostile question. Sarkady intervened and asked, "How would you feel, Roger, if somebody asked you a question like that?" Smith then apologized and rephrased the question.

In the sessions the executives get to know each other better. They talk informally about strategy and even share plans, something that in the past rarely occurred. One team-building session had pairs of executives stretch a rubber band between them, each trusting the other not to let go and snap the band at the partner. Ideas like trust and openness were often discussed. The tone of the sessions threw people off guard, but part of the goal was to shift their thinking to a new way of managing.

What's Good for GM Is Good for the United States

More recently President Clinton held a cabinet meeting at Camp David. Two facilitators were brought in by presidential invitation. They asked cabinet members to bring their resumes and be prepared to talk about the "passions" of their lives. In addition, at the first session participants were asked to talk about significant personal events not mentioned in their resumes.

The facilitators expect to meet regularly with the cabinet every six months. Some cabinet people thought that the sessions were worth while. One cabinet member intends to take his senior managers on a similar retreat.

Some OD consultants think that OD can work in government, but they also think that it is difficult to achieve because of conflicting personal agendas. Other OD consultants thought Mr. Clinton's approach was too "touchy-feely." They expressed the idea that facilitators today focus more on trying to get people to understand how they can use their own characteristics to contribute to the group.

Mr. Clinton, never-the-less, seems comfortable with his approach. For several years he has been attending Renaissance Weekends at Hilton Head, South Carolina, where participants engage in scheduled joggings on the beach that include a facilitator.

Questions

1. How would you describe Mark Sarkady's consulting style?
2. Were process-consulting skills used and, if so, what types?
3. What do you think of President Clinton's approach?

Modeling

As the process consultant will be with the group for only a limited time, it is important for group members to learn how to make process interventions. These types of interventions can be very helpful to the group for accomplishing its task on a regular basis, not just sessions when a consultant is present. One of the better methods to learn how to give process observations is through observing someone else giving process observations. Members should be encouraged to take over the role of providing process interventions. Ideally, and with time, the consultant's role in providing process interventions will become less frequent until group members are providing their own process interventions.

Setting the Agenda

Agenda-setting interventions include setting aside time when process issues will be specifically discussed apart from content issues. Agenda-setting interventions do not include determining the task items to be discussed. The process consultant may encourage the group to allocate time in its regular meetings to discuss the processes of the meeting or may suggest that the group hold a separate meeting just to deal with process issues. These issues may include how well members communicated with each other, how satisfied members were with the meeting, and how involved members were in the meeting.

Feeding Back Observations

Feedback to groups can occur during their meetings or to individuals after meetings. The process consultant often has a strong temptation to share some interesting observations regardless of the client's ability to receive this feedback. Before any feedback is given to either individuals or groups, it is crucial that there is a readiness to receive feedback. The feedback may be more useful if it is limited in scope and quantity, and given over a period of time. This will better enable the clients to gradually integrate the feedback into their behavior.[13]

Structural Suggestions

The process consultant also makes structural suggestions about group membership, communication patterns, allocation of work, assignment of responsibility, and lines of authority. The consultant often makes suggestions on how work should be organized, who should be on what committees, and who should be working on specific projects. The process consultant helps the manager or work group determine the results of their actions or suggest alternatives. It is critical for the process consultant to avoid stepping in and taking over. Otherwise the client will not learn to solve its own problems and may develop a dependency relationship with the consultant.

The Results of Process-Consultation

Process consultation skills used by managers, in dealing with their subordinates and peers can be helpful. Edgar Schein, who has taught middle-level executives at the Sloan School of Management at Massachusetts Institute of Technology, says that students frequently reported that they often had to use process consultant skills with their subordinates and superiors. Process consultation, they said, is a method useful in relating with people where organization members can learn to solve their own problems.[14] Robin Burns, the Chief Executive Officer of Estee Lauder USA, uses process consultation skills by carefully soliciting the ideas of people she works with. One of her former managers, Minnetonka founder Robert Taylor, says "She leads without being a dictator. She's the best I've met in terms of building relationships with the people she works with."[15]

Richard Walton in his book, *Managing Conflict, Interpersonal Dialogue and Third Party Roles*, maintains that, while process skills were the domain of OD specialists in the 1970s and 1980s, they are now a part of normal management activity.[16] Such major corporations as IBM and General Motors brought process skills to the managerial level in the 1980s when they regularly sent managers to workshops that were designed to help participants become more effective in analyzing group process. These managers in the 1990s use process skills as a part of their daily management activities. This will be more common as companies rely on the team approach in managing their companies.

While OD consultants report improved organization health and functioning as an outcome of process consultation interventions, there is little empirical evidence to document such changes. The assumption is that a group that is aware of and acting upon its problems is likely to be more effective than a group that is not. Also, process consultation is usually a technique that is practiced as part of an OD program, and it is often difficult to evaluate process consultation separately from the total OD program.

One evaluation of process consultation studies supports the problems of measuring results.[17] The survey examines published studies in three categories: (1) reports in which process intervention is the causal variable, but performance is measured inadequately or not at all; (2) reports in which performance is measured, but process consultation is not isolated as the independent variable (the case in many instances); and (3) research in which process consultation is isolated as the causal variable and performance is adequately measured. The findings suggest that process consultation does have positive effects on participants (according to self-reports): increases in personal involvement, higher mutual influence, group effectiveness, and similar variables. However, there is little if any research that clearly demonstrates that task effectiveness was increased. Most of the field studies either did not directly measure performance or the effect of process intervention was intermixed with other variables.

Nonetheless, process consultation is relied upon by OD consultants in their interactions with clients. Furthermore, the technique is becoming a method more frequently relied upon by managers and supervisors in working with subordinates. It is highly compatible with and is typically used by consultants to introduce OD interventions such as employee empowerment, laboratory training, team building, intergroup development, self-managed work teams, and total quality management (to be discussed in future chapters).

REVIEW QUESTIONS

1. Explain how process consultation can be used in an OD program.

2. What is the difference between group task functions and group maintenance functions?

KEY WORDS AND CONCEPTS

Define and be able to use the following:

Agenda-Setting Interventions
Empathy
Group Consensus
Group Process
Group Content
Individual Functions

Maintenance Functions
Member Roles
Modeling
Process Consultation Skills
Process Interventions
Task Functions

OD SKILLS SIMULATION 7.1
APEX OIL SPILL

Total time suggested: 1 hour.

A. PURPOSE

To identify the forces acting upon individuals as they interact with others and to practice using process consultation interventions. The goals include:

1. To examine behaviors that facilitate and inhibit group functioning.
2. To identify functions and roles of group members.
3. To explore group processes.

B. PROCEDURES

Step 1. Form into groups of six members each before the class meeting and make role assignments. Additional people may act as observers. The six roles are:

1. Assistant to the Governor
2. State Economic Development Director
3. State Environment Director
4. Petroleum Producers Representative
5. Environmental Defense Representative
6. OD Consultant
 Observer (optional)

Read the APEX Oil Spill Background Information that follows on page 187 and your role description before the class meeting. Do not read the role description of other members. The observer should use the Observer Forms on pages 191, 192.

Step 2. The committee (including the OD consultant and the observer) meets to decide its recommendation. The OD consultant will assist the committee in arriving at a decision, but the observer will not take part in the committee decision. Record your individual and team position on the Apex Decision Form on page 190.
Time suggested for Step 2: 40 minutes.

Step 3. After the committee reaches its decision, discuss the process. If there is an observer, the observer can also share information recorded on the Observer Forms Parts A and B on pages 191, 192. All team members are encouraged to provide feedback. Answer the following questions:

1. How was a decision reached? (By consensus, vote, etc.)

2. What type of process skills did the consultant use? Try to be specific and give examples?

3. Did the consultant make the client feel at ease? How?

4. What did the consultant do or say that was helpful?

5. What consultant verbal and nonverbal communications seemed to help the meeting?

Time suggested for Step 3: 10 minutes.

Step 4. As a class discuss the questions in Step 3.
Time suggested for Step 4: 10 minutes.

APEX OIL SPILL BACKGROUND INFORMATION

Several months ago an APEX Oil Corporation underwater oil pipeline split open and allowed four million barrels of heavy crude to spill into coastal waters. The pipeline carries oil from off-shore pumping platforms where the oil is pumped through another pipeline to a refinery 75 miles inland. The spill was the largest to hit your state and the damage to the wildlife and coastal towns has been significant.

APEX has said through its representatives that the equipment monitoring the pipeline had been periodically registering false alarms indicating a pipeline leak for the past three months. When technicians saw that the gauges showed a problem, they assumed that it was another false alarm and did not take any action. It was not until 10 hours later, when local fishermen reported an oil slick, that the pipeline was shut down. The oil, however, continued to drain out of the pipe for another six hours.

A 100-mile stretch of state beaches and state coastal wildlife preserves were moderately to heavily fouled with the oil slick. Cleanup is proceeding by crews hired by APEX and a large number of volunteers organized by environmental groups. A large number of fish were killed, plus lobster and crab have been virtually wiped out. Seals, porpoises, otters, and many species of birds suffered large losses. Attempts to remove the oil from these animals has been proceeding, but most efforts have been largely unsuccessful because of the ingestion of oil by the animals.

The oil spill also affected the human population in economic terms. The economies of four coastal towns in the area depend on a combination of commercial and recreational fishing and tourism. The fishing industry became nonexistent overnight when the State Environment Director acted immediately to bar commercial and recreational fishing in an area that affects one-third of the state coastal fishing waters. The restriction will probably be effective for at least two years, and the time it will take for fish production to be close to normal will probably be six years. Tourism, including out-of-state tourism, is down 90 percent. It will probably be two years before the beaches will be in a condition that tourists will return in normal numbers.

On the brighter side, a few businesses such as motels and restaurants, were not hit as hard because of an influx of scientists, government officials, and cleanup crews. Some of the displaced commercial fishermen were hired by APEX to clean up the beaches, and half of the fish processing plants have been turned into rescue facilities for some of the affected wildlife.

APEX has publicly taken responsibility for the oil spill and a representative from the company has said it will pay for the cleanup of the beaches and the animal rescue centers sponsored by the company. In a news conference, APEX rejected any responsibility for incidental costs such as reduced income to the commercial fishermen, the fish-processing plants, and local town businesses.

APEX has also said it is not subject to laws relating to killing endangered or threatened species as the intent of the law did not pertain to this type of accidental killing. According to APEX, the cleanup operation is running expeditiously and should be completed in three months.

On the other hand, state officials, scientists, and environmentalists assert that APEX's cleanup operation is proceeding at a slow pace because of the company's bureaucracy, inexperience in handling operations of this type, and a company expectation that public concern will diminish with time.

The economy of the state as a whole has also been affected. The state receives 15 percent of its revenue from off-shore oil production and the platforms involved in the spill account for 30 percent of the state's off-shore oil production. The State Environment Director (all state directors are elected positions and can operate independently of the Governor) obtained a court injunction to shut down all off-shore oil production until a complete investigation could be conducted to determine the safe operating condition of all platforms and equipment operating in state waters.

The investigation by state engineers will take at least nine months and meanwhile the state will lose its tax revenue from the production of the oil. The court action has been highly popular with the state's citizens though the Governor and the Economic Development Director have expressed some reservations with the court injunction.

There have been news reports for the past five years that the equipment from several companies with off-shore facilities was old and preventive maintenance had been lax. There was speculation that contributions to the election funds of members of the state legislature and a previous governor was partly responsible for the lack of enforcement of safety regulations. Recent opinion surveys show that the environment is the most important concern of the voters.

The Governor has called this committee together to make a recommendation to her. Though the suggestions may take action in court to enforce, the Governor has publicly stated that she wants all options to be explored. In addition to the recommendation, the Governor would also like the following issues addressed (see APEX Oil Spill Decision Form, p. 190):

1. Should the state try to shut down future off-shore oil drilling operations?
2. Should the state try to shut down all off-shore oil production pending an investigation of all platforms and pipelines by state authorities? Or shut down just platforms and pipelines involved in this oil spill?
3. Should the state try to shut down oil production in the area affected until the environment can be stabilized (about 18 months)?
4. Should the state go into court and try to force APEX to pay for all direct and indirect costs plus pay fines for pollution and killing wildlife?

ROLE DESCRIPTIONS (READ ONLY YOUR ROLE)

Assistant to the Governor. You have been instructed by the governor to make sure her interests are represented. The Governor is concerned about the state's economy—especially as she hopes to be reelected in two years. That means trying to keep tax revenue from oil as high as possible in order to avoid a tax increase. The Governor has repeatedly told the voters there would be no new taxes while she is governor. You believe the future of the state economically is dependent on increasing oil production. You must, at least, make appear-

ances that the environment is important because of voter concern. You have received a secret preliminary draft from the Federal Environmental Protection Agency that recommends federal legislation be passed banning new off-shore oil drilling in environmentally sensitive waters under federal control. It is important, therefore, to get the committee to recommend continued production and drilling in state waters before the federal report is released. The governor also owes some favors to the petroleum industry because of their legal campaign contributions to the governor.

State Economic Development Director. Your job is to assure that the economic development of the state progresses on track in order to meet its 10-year plan. Reduced tax revenues from oil, commercial fishing, and out-of-state tourism will reduce tax revenues as much as 20 percent for the next two years. An immediate problem is what to do with the economies of the four coastal towns after the cleanup crews and environmentalists leave. You believe indirect costs such as unemployed fishermen, fish-processing plants not operating, and loss of business to other town businesses such as motels, restaurants, and tourist shops should be pursued against APEX. The effect of future oil spills to the fishing and tourist industry concerns you. A recent study you had conducted by a reliable economic "think tank" found that oil tax revenue is offset by the economic costs if a major oil spill occurs every 40 years. Despite these concerns, you realize that without tax revenue from oil production and the jobs it brings in will mean either a tax increase, reduced expenditures, or some combination of the two. Because of these conflicting concerns, you favor some sort of compromise. However, if you learn of new and persuasive information during the meeting, you will be willing to support either the pro-oil or pro-environment forces.

State Environment Director. Your job is to protect the environment of the state. You would like to halt all off-shore oil production in state and federal waters off your state until a thorough investigation is made of each oil field. Only then will the oil field be brought on line. For the future, a very rigid state monitoring system of existing oil platforms and pipelines should be implemented. Future drilling in state waters should be permanently barred. You suspect the cost to the fishing and tourist industries offset any gains the state may make through oil tax revenues. Recent studies by scientists from your office show a major oil spill can be expected every 35 years. You believe the oil industry in your state has a long history of acting irresponsibly and trying to buy themselves (through campaign contributions) out of regulations being enforced against them. In addition to the imposition of heavy fines for pollution and killing wildlife, all direct and indirect costs should be pursued against APEX.

Petroleum Industry Representative. You represent all the oil companies doing business in the state. It is imperative that you get the committee to allow your companies to have unencumbered access to drilling and oil production in the state. Off-shore drilling represents a minimum risk to the environment but one that is acceptable given the economic gains and the necessity of oil. Studies conducted by scientists and business experts from your organization show that a medium-size spill can be expected every 25 years and that a major spill would occur only once every 75 years. You are aware of other studies from environmental groups contradicting these figures, but you seriously question the credentials of the scientists conducting the studies. You do not want any drilling and production restrictions for fear they will spread to other states. As a last resort, it may be necessary to let APEX be the "sacrificial lamb" to preserve oil development for the other companies. However, you must be discreet about abandoning APEX so as not to alienate them from your organization. You will need to stress the importance of oil production in terms of jobs and tax revenue to the state for both the short and long run. Legal contributions have been made by your organization to the governor's reelection campaign. You expect the Governor's representative will be helpful in the meeting.

Environmental Defense Representative. You were chosen by environmental organizations to represent them at the meeting. You have been directed to take a very strong position about protecting the environment for both the short and long term. You want APEX to pay for all cleanup and to pay heavy fines for pollution and killing endangered and threatened wildlife. You also want APEX officers charged with criminal neglect. Some of the cleanup crews and animal rescue centers have been funded by the environmental organizations and you want to make sure they are reimbursed by APEX. You want to halt all off-shore oil production and drilling now and in the future in state and federal waters. Studies made by your highly reputable scientists show off-shore drilling is environmentally unsafe and that a major oil spill can be expected every 20 years. There have been recent rumors from your Washington sources that a letter was sent to the Governor informing her that the Federal Environmental Protection Agency will soon be recommending legislation be passed by Congress banning all off-shore oil drilling and production in both state and federal waters. You want to make sure APEX pays for their negligence in order to set a strong example for other companies. The lack of enforcement of existing regulations by state agencies concerns you and you expect campaign contributions to elected officials are part of the problem. There is a saying among environmentalists that "the state elected office-holders are the best that money can buy."

OD Consultant. Review the section in this chapter titled "The Types of Process Interventions." Use these process consultation skills to help the committee reach a decision. Be careful not to take over and run the committee. You should not take a position or support one group of people. Your job is to help them so they can make their own decision.

Observer. Do not take part in the committee meeting. Your role as an observer is to provide information later in Steps 3 and 4. Use the Observer Form Parts A and B to record your observations.

APEX OIL SPILL DECISION FORM

	My Decision	Team Decision
1. Shut down future off-shore drilling?	_____	_____
2. Shut down off-shore production pending investigation of all platforms?	_____	_____
Or shut down platforms involved in this spill?	_____	_____
3. Shut down production in affected area for about 18 months?	_____	_____
4. State goes to court to force APEX to pay?	_____	_____

OBSERVER FORM PART A

Instructions: Put the names of the individuals in your group in the spaces at the top of the chart. Read and become familiar with the behavior discriptions. Put a check in the appropriate block *each* time you observe the behavior.

Description of Behavior	Names of Individuals Observed					
Initiating						
Suggesting						
Seeking opinions						
Asking questions						
Elaborating						
Summarizing						
Testing for consensus						
Harmonizing						
Compromising						
Encouraging						
Gatekeeping						
Following						
Dominating						
Acting the playboy						
Blocking						
Seeking recognition						
Pleading for special interest						
Others:						

OBSERVER FORM PART B

Use the communication flow diagram to plot frequency and direction of communication. Draw direction arrows for communication flow. Identify behaviors shown in meeting.

Name: _____

Position: _____

 1. _____
 2. _____
 3. _____

Name: _____

Position: _____

 1. _____
 2. _____
 3. _____

Name: _____

Position: _____

 1. _____
 2. _____
 3. _____

Name: _____

Position: _____

 1. _____
 2. _____
 3. _____

Name: _____

Position: _____

 1. _____
 2. _____
 3. _____

Name: _____

Position: _____

 1. _____
 2. _____
 3. _____

OD SKILLS SIMULATION 7.2
TRUST BUILDING

Total time suggested: 30 minutes.

A. PURPOSE

The purpose of this simulation is to provide a comparison between your perception of trust behavior and how it is perceived by others.

B. PROCEDURES

Step 1. Based on your group work in Simulation 7.1, complete and score the Group Behavior Questionnaire.

Time suggested for Step 1: 5 minutes.

Complete Figure 7.1, the Trust Diagram, on page 195, by drawing horizontal and vertical lines at the appropriate numbers representing your score.

GROUP BEHAVIOR QUESTIONNAIRE

The following are a series of questions[18] about your behavior in your group. Answer each question as honestly as you can. There are no right or wrong answers. It is important for you to describe your behavior as accurately as possible. Place a number in the blank to the right representing your choice based on the following scale.

[Never 1 : 2 : 3 : 4 : 5 : 6 : 7 Always]

1. I offer facts, give my opinions and ideas, provide suggestions and relevant information to help the group discussion. _____

2. I express my willingness to cooperate with other group members and my expectations that they will also be cooperative. _____

3. I am open and candid in my dealings with the entire group. _____

4. I give support to group members who are on the spot and struggling to express themselves intellectually or emotionally. _____

5. I keep my thoughts, ideas, feelings, and reactions to myself during group discussions. _____

6. I evaluate the contributions of other group members in terms of whether their contributions are useful to me and whether they are right or wrong. _____

7. I take risks in expressing new ideas and current feelings during a group discussion. _____

8. I communicate to other group members that I am aware of, and appreciate, their abilities, talents, capabilities, skills, and resources. _____

9. I offer help and assistance to anyone in the group in order to bring up the performance of everyone. _____

10. I accept and support the openness of other group members, supporting them for taking risks, and encouraging individuality in group members. _____

11. I share any materials, books, sources of information, or other resources I have with the other group members in order to promote the success of all members and the group as a whole. _____

12. I often paraphrase or summarize what other members have said before I respond or comment. _____

13. I level with other group members. _____

14. I warmly encourage all members to participate, giving them recognition for their contributions, demonstrating acceptance and openness to their ideas, and generally being friendly and responsive to them. _____

SCORING OF GROUP BEHAVIOR QUESTIONNAIRE

To score this questionnaire, add the scores in the following way, reversing the scoring on the questions that are starred. Find the average response by dividing the total scores by 7.

Openness and Sharing	**Acceptance and Support**
1. _____	2. _____
3. _____	4. _____
*5. _____	*6. _____
7. _____	8. _____
9. _____	10. _____
11. _____	12. _____
13. _____	14. _____
Total _____	Total _____
Average _____	Average _____

*Reverse the scoring on these questions. In other words, a value of 2 would be recorded as 6.

FIGURE 7.1 Trust Diagram

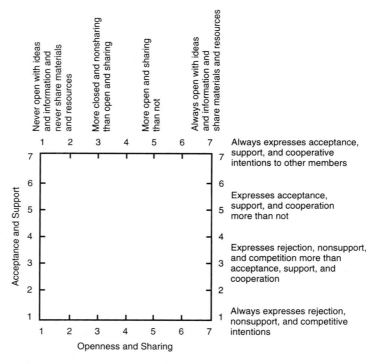

Source: David Johnson and Frank Johnson. *Joining Together: Group Therapy and Group Skills.* © 1975, p. 244. Adapted by permission of Prentice Hall, Inc., Englewood Cliffs, New Jersey.

Step 2. After completing Simulation 7.1 each member of the group rates every other group member on two dimensions from 1 (low) to 7 (high).

Member	Openness and Sharing		Acceptance and Support	
	Low	High	Low	High
1 _____	1 2 3 4 5 6 7		1 2 3 4 5 6 7	
2 _____	1 2 3 4 5 6 7		1 2 3 4 5 6 7	
3 _____	1 2 3 4 5 6 7		1 2 3 4 5 6 7	
4 _____	1 2 3 4 5 6 7		1 2 3 4 5 6 7	
5 _____	1 2 3 4 5 6 7		1 2 3 4 5 6 7	
6 _____	1 2 3 4 5 6 7		1 2 3 4 5 6 7	

Step 3. Give each member his or her scores.

Time suggested for Steps 2 and 3: 10 minutes.

Step 4. Compute and enter the averages of the two sets of scores received from group members by drawing dotted horizontal and vertical lines at the appropriate numbers in Figure 7.1. Each member has the results of the Group Behavior Questionnaire and the results of the feedback received from his or her fellow group members. Meeting with your group, each group member answers the following questions:

1. How similar are the results from others and your answers about yourself?
2. Is there a close match? If not, what factors do you think contribute to the other group members' seeing your behavior differently from the way you do?
3. How could this modify your behavior?

Time suggested for Step 4: 15 minutes.

OD SKILLS SIMULATION 7.3
PROCESS CONSULTATION

Total time suggested: 50 minutes.

A. PURPOSE

This simulation will provide you with additional practice in OD practitioner skills and will give you an opportunity to practice using process consultation and active listening. You will have an opportunity to meet with a client who has a problem, and your responsibility is to help him or her clarify the problem by formulating a diagnosis. In the role play you will also experience being consulted with as a client. And you will be able, as an observer, to observe the consultant-client process.

B. PROCEDURES

Step 1. Form into triads. There are three roles, and all members will be able to play each role. The three roles are client, consultant, and observer. Before beginning the role play, all members should read each of the following guidelines:

Client: Take a class problem or a work problem that involves you and explain this to your consultant.

Consultant: Your role is to help the client by practicing process consultation. See the Observer Form to familiarize yourself with appropriate and inappropriate helping skills.

Observer: Your job is to observe as carefully as possible both the client and the consultant. Use the Observer Form to record your observations.

Step 2. Take about 10 minutes for each role play. At the end of *each* role play, the observer will share his or her observations. Also during this time, the consultant and the client should critique each other's style. The following questions will help serve as a starting point for the critique:

1. As the client, how did you feel about responses of the consultant? Were they helpful or dysfunctional? Try to be specific.
2. As the consultant, how did you feel about the way the client behaved? Did any of his or her behaviors bother you? If so, did you share this with him or her? Try to be specific.
3. How did you feel about playing the part of the consultant or the client? Were you able to really "get into" your roles? Why?
4. Can you think of doing anything differently that might help in the next role play?
5. Any other comments or thoughts?

Continue the simulation by switching roles until all have played each of the roles.
Time suggested for Step 2: 40 minutes.

Step 3. In class session, critique the role plays. You may want to look at the questions in Step 2.
Time suggested for Step 3: 10 minutes.

OBSERVER FORM

As an observer, score the consultant on the following items. Items 1 through 6 are appropriate behaviors for process consultation, while items 7 through 10 are inappropriate behaviors.

REMARKS

1. Practiced empathy:

Low 1 : 2 : 3 : 4 : 5 : 6: 7 High _____

2. Made eye contact:

Low 1 : 2 : 3 : 4 : 5 : 6: 7 High _____

3. Practiced nonverbal communications:

Low 1 : 2 : 3 : 4 : 5 : 6: 7 High _____

4. Reflected back content of message:

Low 1 : 2 : 3 : 4 : 5 : 6: 7 High _____

5. Reflected back feeling of message:

Low 1 : 2 : 3 : 4 : 5 : 6: 7 High _____

6. Demonstrated approval and acceptance:

Low 1 : 2 : 3 : 4 : 5 : 6: 7 High _____

7. Sent solutions:

Low 1 : 2 : 3 : 4 : 5 : 6: 7 High _____

8. Blamed or acted in judgment:

Low 1 : 2 : 3 : 4 : 5 : 6: 7 High _____

9. Expressed sarcasm or humor:

Low 1 : 2 : 3 : 4 : 5 : 6: 7 High _____

10. Participated in a large degree of "small talk":

Low 1 : 2 : 3 : 4 : 5 : 6: 7 High _____

CASE 7:
THE OD LETTERS

February 11

Dear Larry,

I enjoyed seeing you last summer at the Academy of Management convention. I've been trying to reach you by phone, but no luck. Your secretary said you were on a job out of state. I have several clients and my workload is getting pretty hectic. Are you interested in working together again? I've been contacted by Memorial Hospital here in town to come by and discuss some management training, possibly OD. It seems like you worked with them several years ago. Is this correct or have I got my hospitals mixed up?

Hope to hear from you soon and maybe we can work something out at Memorial.

Ryan

February 19

Dear Ryan,

Sorry to have missed your calls but I was in Oklahoma City doing some work with the State Department. And now that I'm back, your secretary said you were out of the area on a consulting job.

I thought I would drop you this note instead of waiting for you to get back in town. Your note triggered some old memories. Excuse my rambling in what I will share with you about Memorial Hospital. Please keep this confidential.

Yes, you were right about me working with Memorial. I looked in my records and it was nine years ago. I have been indirectly keeping in touch with how things are going there through some of my old contacts.

Their Chief Administrator, John Everet, has been under severe pressure from three of their five board members. They are a public hospital you know. I can't say he doesn't deserve at least some of the blame for their current problems, though I suspect the board members have their own political agendas.

I was contacted nine years ago by Irwin from their training department to go on their annual retreat with the middle and top administrators. Irwin is OK and if he has a fault, it's his taking his work too seriously given the current culture at Memorial. I was to initially do some management development training on a very superficial level. John Everet had only been at the hospital for several months. Irwin and I decided it would be prudent to go easy at first until John got the lay of the land. Irwin, not John, was my contact person as Irwin was responsible for all of the management and technical training.

Anyway, the three-day retreat was "weird" but, reflecting back on things, not at all unusual. The retreat started when we were all loaded up in a bus. None of the participants were told where they were going so it was to be a big surprise. We traveled about three hours to a dude ranch in the local mountains. I was supposed to provide the training for one afternoon and the following morning. Irwin helped out. We did a few ice breaker exercises, followed by some kind of nonthreatening team exercise. This was followed by reports from the teams on what they thought were effective supervision skills. It was really low-key stuff. I arranged the teams to be composed of managers from both middle and top levels.

You know, I can remember what happened as if it was yesterday. John remained real aloof. I had previously arranged for him, like everyone else to be in a team. He joked around with several other men for about 30 minutes before joining his team. Meanwhile, his team went to work without him. He finally joined them but did not say much. After a few minutes he got up and went over to another team and talked with them about the tennis game they had the previous day. I did not confront him at the time, which, reflecting on things,

may have been a mistake on my part. But I rationalized that because he was new, he wanted to get to know his people on a social basis. Besides, don't us OD types say we should take our clients "where they're at?"

Well, that was the afternoon session. Not exactly a roaring success, but a number of the participants were really getting in to the exercises. The morning session the next day went about the same. John played the part of the social butterfly. His behavior was a bit obvious to others. Reflecting back on things, I think he was intimidated. This was his first job as a Chief Administrator. We had a team-building exercise followed by a discussion on how departments in general could work better together—nothing specific. I remember one fellow got real annoyed at some of the other teams for joking around. He said something to the effect that this was why it took so long to get anything done at the hospital. Several others agreed but then John said what we were doing in the teams was just a fun game and did not mean anything. The morning session ended OK, for the most part, though John and several others left early.

Nothing more happened with me and the hospital. Irwin called me to say his budget had been cut, and they were not able to do any more training for a while. I read between the lines and politely wished him well. Several years ago, I heard from a friend, Shannon, who I have worked with on other jobs. She said she had been recruited to conduct training at Memorial's annual retreat. They flew over a thousand miles to a retreat at Cape Cod. Big bucks on this trip. It was for five days, and she was to provide training for four half-day sessions. Halfway through the first session, John recruited three of his top administrators and they went for a canoe ride. Shannon said you could hear them out on the lake while the rest of them were working. At each of the other three sessions, participation dropped off dramatically until she ended up with about 15 percent in the last session. She said she had never seen anything like it.

Their training sessions occur every May so it looks like it is your turn. No consultant seems to get past the annual retreat. I would like to work with you again, but I think it would be in everyone's best interest that I pass on this one. The pay is good and maybe you will get a good vacation out of it. On the other hand, don't take your lack of success personally. You may have a different experience as the board might have mixed up the pot, so-to-speak. Stay in touch and give me a call.

Sincerely,
Larry

QUESTIONS

1. If you were in Ryan's position, how would you proceed with Memorial Hospital?
2. How could process-consulting skills help?

CASE ANALYSIS FORM

Name: _____

I. Problems

 A. Macro

 1. _____

 2. _____

 B. Micro

 1. _____

 2. _____

II. Causes

 1. _____

 2. _____

 3. _____

III. Systems affected

 1. Structural _____

 2. Psychosocial _____

 3. Technical _____

 4. Managerial _____

 5. Goals _____

IV. Alternatives

 1. _____

 2. _____

 3. _____

 4. _____

 5. _____

V. Recommendations

 1. _____

 2. _____

 3. _____

SUMMARY

• **Most used.** This chapter has presented an overview of process consultation. As one of the most used OD consulting skills, process consultation is often utilized to develop more effective teams. It is used to assist groups in diagnosing and solving their own team problems and to increase the functioning of work groups by helping team members work together.

• **Own solutions.** One of the major characteristics of process consultation is that the clients learn to identify problems and then initiate their own solutions. The process consultant observes individuals and teams in action and helps the client organization learn to diagnose and solve its own problems.

• **Performance.** The foundation of process consultation is the study of how groups and individuals within those groups behave. The process consultant deals with five areas crucial to effective organization performance: communication, member roles and functions in groups, group problem solving and decision making, group norms and growth, and leadership and authority.

• **Types.** The types of process interventions that may be used include clarifying, summarizing, synthesizing, generalizing, probing, questioning, listening, reflecting feelings, providing support, coaching, counseling, modeling, setting the agenda, feeding back observations, and providing structural suggestions. The interventions should be as brief and crisp as possible. The concern is *how* the group is going about accomplishing its task.

• **Interventions.** The consultant and the client must examine several factors in deciding upon an intervention. They must determine not only the depth of the intervention desired but also the relative advantages and disadvantages of various possible interventions in selecting one that best fits their target system. You had a chance in the simulations to experience and practice process consultation skills. You may have gained some insights into your own relational style and recognized how such techniques might be used in an OD program. Often process consultation can be used as a means to enhance team functioning and performance.

Throughout the remainder of this text, you will be participating in simulations where the application of process skills will be appropriate. Enact the practice of these skills to the point that their use becomes natural and comfortable.

NOTES

1. See Hugh Williamson, "What it Takes to be a Quality Consultant," *Quality Progress*, vol. 28, no. 4, April, 1995, p. 31.

2. See William Bridges, "The End of the Job," *Fortune*, September 19, 1994, p. 74.

3. Ibid.

4. W. Warner Burke, Lawrence P. Clark, and Cheryl Koopman, "Improve Your OD Project's Chances for Success," *Training and Development Journal*, September 1984, p. 67.

5. Edgar Schein, *Process Consultation, Volume I: Its Role in Organization Development* (Reading, Mass.: Addison-Wesley Publishing Co., Inc., 1988), p. 11.

6. Fred Luthans, "Conversation with Edgar H. Schein," *Organizational Dynamics*, Spring 1989, p. 66.

7. For additional information on process consultation see: Michael Donovan and Leta Letize, "*Lessons from the Wizard,*" *Journal for Quality and Participation*, vol. 16, no. 4 (July/August, 1993), pp. 44–47; John Keltner, "Catalyst for Group Problem Solving," *Management Communication Quarterly*, vol. 3, no. 1 (August 1989), pp. 8–32; Benjamin J. Broome, David B. Keever, "Next Generation Group Facilitation," *Management Communication Quarterly*, vol. 3, no. 1 (August 1989), pp. 107–27; Luthans, "Conversation with Edgar H. Schein," pp. 60–76.

8. Schein, *Process Consultation, Volume I*, p. 15.

9. John F. Hulpke, California State University–Bakersfield, 1994, sources: Gautam Naik, "Beyond the Borders," *The Wall Street Journal* September 10, 1993, p. R10; and Bob Hagerty, "Trainers Help Expatriate Employees Build Bridges to Different Cultures," *The Wall Street Journal*, June 14, 1993, p. B1.

10. Kenneth D. Benne and Paul Sheats, "Functional Roles of Group Members," *The Journal of Social Issues*, vol. 4, no. 2 (Spring 1948), pp. 42–47.

11. For additional information see Schein, *Process Consultation, Volume I*; Paul H. Ephross, and Thomas V. Vassil, *Groups That Work: Structure and Process*, (New York: Columbia University Press, 1988), pp. 140–65; David Coghlan, "In Defence of Process Consultation," *Leadership and Organization Development*, vol. 2, no. 2 (1988), pp. 27–31; Carl R. Rogers and F. J. Roethlisberger, "Barriers and Gateways to Communication," *Harvard Business Review*, July–August 1952, pp. 28–34.

12. Sandra Younger, "Who Was That Masked Facilitator?," *Training and Development Journal*, vol. 47, no. 6 (June 1993), p. 9; James M. Perry, "Using 'Team Builders' May Become Common in Clinton Administration," *The Wall Street Journal*, March 5, 1993, p. A7A; Jacob M. Schlesinger and Paul Ingrassia, "GM Woos Employees By Listening to Them, Talking of Its 'Team'," *The Wall Street Journal*, January 12, 1989, p. A1; and M. M. Petty, James Cashman, Anson Seers, Robert Stevenson, Charles Barker, and Grady Cook, "Better Communication at General Motors," *Personnel Journal*, September 1989, pp. 40–49.

13. Leroy Wells, Jr., "Feedback, The Group Unconscious, and the Unstated Effects of Experimental Methods," *Journal of Applied Behavioral Science*, vol. 28, no. 1 (March 1992), pp. 46–53; and Poppy L. McLeod, Jeffrey K. Liker, and Sharon A. Lobel, "Process Feedback in Task Groups: An Application of Goal Setting," *Journal of Applied Behavioral Science*, vol. 28, no. 1 (March 1992), pp. 15–41.

14. Luthans, "Conversation with Edgar H. Schein," p. 68.

15. Kathleen Deveny, "In a More Than Cosmetic Move, Burns Walks Softly to Lauder," *The Wall Street Journal*, January 12, 1990, p. 31. For other examples of effective corporate communications, see Fay Rice, "Champions of Communication," *Fortune*, June 3, 1991, pp. 111–20.

16. See Hugh Williamson, "What it Takes to be a Quality Consultant." *Quality Progress* vol. 28 no. 4 April, 1995, p. 34.

17. R. Kaplan, "The Conspicuous Absence of Evidence that Process Consultation Enhances Task Performance," *Journal of Applied Behavioral Science*, vol. 15 (1979), pp. 346–60.

18. David Johnson and Frank Johnson, *Joining Together: Group Theory and Group Skills*, © 1975, p. 244. Adapted by permission of Prentice Hall, Inc., Englewood Cliffs, N.J.

Much of the success of Ford Motor Company comes from an emphasis on human resource management programs. (Courtesy of Ford Motor Company)

OD Intervention Strategies

8

OBJECTIVES

Upon completing this chapter, you will be able to:

1. Identify and understand the range of major OD intervention techniques and how they may be applied.
2. Identify the way various interpersonal, team, and intergroup techniques fit into an OD program.
3. Understand the change strategies.

PREMEETING PREPARATION

1. Read the Background Information.
2. Read the instructions for OD Skill Simulation 8.1 (Section VI). Complete Step 1. Form teams of six and assign roles the preceding class meeting.
3. Read and analyze Case 8: The Farm Bank.

FIGURE 8.1 The OD Process

BACKGROUND INFORMATION

Organizational change, or OD, programs such as reengineering and downsizing are attempts to increase organizational efficiency. These corporate revolutions are aimed at increasing productivity through invigorated employees who can work in self managed teams and who are able to develop creativity, performance and innovation beyond traditional levels.[1] Managing organizational change is an important and complex action. In attempting to increase organizational and individual effectiveness, the OD consultant must understand the nature of changes needed and the possible effects of various alternative change strategies.[2]

The starting point for setting a change program in motion is the definition of a total change strategy. The consultant's role and relationship with the client and the organizational climate will influence the selection of specific OD strategies aimed at improving organization effectiveness. A graphic illustration of the OD process is shown in Figure 8.1.

The diagnostic phase leads to the interventions, activities, and programs aimed at resolving problems and increasing organization effectiveness. At this point, the OD consultant designs specific OD strategies to improve an organization's structure and processes. After diagnosing the problem areas associated with current performance, the opportunities for improvement are identified and a strategy to apply techniques and technologies for change are selected. **Strategy** involves the planning and direction of OD projects or programs; **intervention techniques** are the specific means by which change goals can be attained.

Before OD techniques can be implemented, the consultant and the client develop a set of strategies to guide future actions. OD is based primarily upon a collaborative change strategy: the client is actively involved in defining problems and selecting the means for improvement. Within this basic approach to change, an OD change strategy is developed to meet the needs of a specific client system. This chapter describes several major OD strategies for setting up a program of change.

Basic Approaches

Three basic approaches to organization change are structural, technical, and behavioral.[3] **Organization structure** is important since it provides the framework that relates elements of the organization to one another. A poor structure may inhibit efficiency. Restructuring corporations to make them more competitive has been a major goal of corporations during much of the 1990s.

Downsizing, often associated with restructuring efforts, has become a term synonymous with layoffs. But restructuring has not been a panacea to companies attempting to improve their operations. An analysis of manufacturing productivity at 140,000 factories that employed a total of about 12.7 million people was conducted for the Center of Economic Study at the Census Bureau. The 10-year study found that while 55 percent of productivity gains occurred at factories where the work force shrunk, the other 45 percent of gains occurred at plants with growing employment. At these growing plants, total output more than doubled over the period.[4]

Another survey conducted by the American Management Association found similar results. Of the 547 companies that downsized during the six years of the study, only 43.5 percent improved their operating profits. With such a poor record for downsizing, other companies such as 3M reassign excess workers to other divisions. Vice-President of Human Resources Richard A. Lidstad says, "Our employees are corporate assets, not assets of a given business. It's like production machinery. In a downturn, you don't just throw it out."[5]

Eastman Kodak Company is an example of a company that has tried restructuring—five times within a decade—but is still experiencing problems. New CEO George Fisher does not intend to lay off any more than the 10,000 employees (out of 110,000 total employees) that had already been marked before he came to Kodak. Though more layoffs might send the stock up in the short run, Fisher has judged that additional cuts could damage Kodak's long-run capabilities.[6]

Technical processes also need to be given careful analysis and often changes are required to bring them up to the state of the art in machinery, methods, automation, and job design. (See CROCK comic strip.) IBM's large investment in robotic-controlled production lines to build their personal computers has enabled IBM to bring new models on line quickly and at prices competitive with imported personal computers.

Another approach, the **behavioral,** places emphasis on the use of human resources. In the past, managers placed emphasis upon fully analyzing an organizations' technical and mechanical capacities, but managers often neglected a vast untapped resource: its human assets. Furthermore, people generally have higher morale, and are motivated toward organization goals when their personal resources and talents are being fully used. By increasing the level of morale, motivation, and commitment of members, organization performance can also be improved.

Ford and General Motors illustrate the implementation of different change strategies. At one time, Ford was coming close to declaring bankruptcy. Lacking capital and facing a need to improve, Ford made structural and behavioral changes on the production line. Capital rich GM, on the other hand, invested in expensive technological innovations such as new assembly lines and robotics. Ford's strategy paid off and its profits surpassed those of GM for the first time. The technological innovations at GM had a high cost but low yield, while Ford carried out comparably low-cost behavioral and structural change strategies that had a high yield. Carl Thor, President of the American Productivity and Quality Center says that

Source: CROCK by Rechin, Parker and Wilder © Field Enterprises, Inc. by permission of North American Syndicate, Inc.

managers will have to restructure the workplace and eliminate layers of bureaucracy to enable employees to adapt more readily to new technologies.[7]

For OD strategies to be successful, the consultant must consider the interdependencies that exist among the various subelements of the organization. A change in one subsystem will have some impact upon other elements of the system. Richard J. Selfridge and Stanley L. Sokolik have suggested a comprehensive approach that considers technical and structural variables as well as behavioral variables of the system.[8] They propose a diagnosis based on the analogy of an "iceberg." There are surface or overt organization elements which are easily observed, such as organization structure and policy; and there are subsurface or covert elements, such as patterns of communication, trust, and openness which are often obscured or hidden (see Figure 8.2). Often the diagnosis examines only the more visible and overt aspects of the organization and ignores the many powerful but hidden problem areas. It is essential in any change program to consider all possible problem areas, both overt and covert, if the strategy is to be successful.

Once a diagnosis of client-system problems has been made, a strategy for accomplishing the change goal needs to be determined. An OD strategy may be defined as the plan

FIGURE 8.2 The "Organization Iceberg" Approach to OD

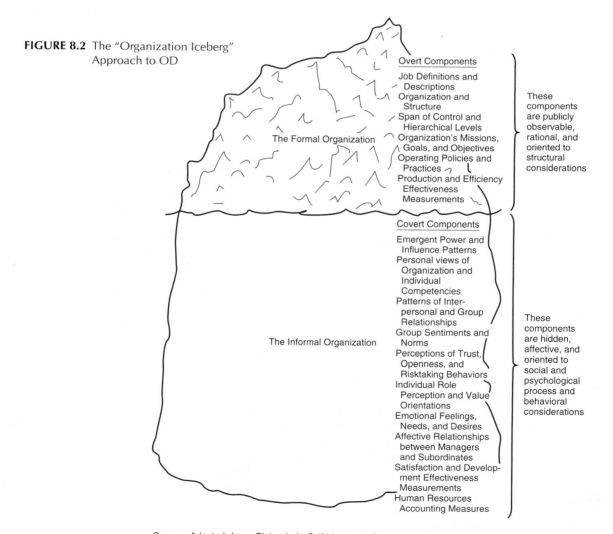

Overt Components

The Formal Organization

Job Definitions and Descriptions
Organization and Structure
Span of Control and Hierarchical Levels
Organization's Missions, Goals, and Objectives
Operating Policies and Practices
Production and Efficiency Effectiveness Measurements

These components are publicly observable, rational, and oriented to structural considerations

Covert Components

The Informal Organization

Emergent Power and Influence Patterns
Personal views of Organization and Individual Competencies
Patterns of Interpersonal and Group Relationships
Group Sentiments and Norms
Perceptions of Trust, Openness, and Risktaking Behaviors
Individual Role Perception and Value Orientations
Emotional Feelings, Needs, and Desires
Affective Relationships between Managers and Subordinates
Satisfaction and Development Effectiveness Measurements
Human Resources Accounting Measures

These components are hidden, affective, and oriented to social and psychological process and behavioral considerations

Source: Adapted from Richard J. Selfridge and Stanley L. Sokolik, "A Comprehensive View of Organizational Development," p. 47, *Business Topics*, Winter 1975. Reprinted by permission of the publisher, Division of Research, Graduate School of Business Administration, Michigan State University.

for relating and integrating the different organization improvement activities engaged in over a period of time to accomplish objectives. **Developing a strategy** is the planning of activities that is intended to resolve difficulties and build on strengths in order to improve the effectiveness and efficiency of the organization. (See Our Changing World.)

Although OD traditionally has been associated with behavioral strategies, this chapter attempts to provide a balanced description of the change process by including *structural* and *technological* strategies. It is our belief that OD techniques are an effective means for carrying out many change strategies including technical and structural. Any major change effort, regardless of emphasis, must deal with the total organization system, which includes structure, technology, and people. Each of these approaches appears in most OD strategies, but they receive different emphasis.

OUR CHANGING WORLD
RESTRUCTURING JAPAN[9]

It seems that throughout most of the 1980s Japanese companies could do no wrong. Companies from the rest of the world were beating a path to Japan to see how they were building the better mouse trap. Terms like zero defects, quality circles, teamwork, bottom-up decision-making, keiretsu (loosely defined as close cooperation within a group of manufacturers and suppliers), just-in-time inventory, lifetime employment, and robotics were discussed in board rooms, on factory floors, and in union meetings around the world. But something happened to Japan, Inc., on the way to the 21st century. For the first time in years, many top executives and policy makers in Japan fear that their competitiveness is threatened.

Japan's New Credo

Changes are happening on many fronts in Japan. Their new credo may become, "Average can be good enough." For example, Honda Motor Co. is asking, "If the market accepts lower standards, is it really a good idea to keep standards at our level?"

An Ashtray to Fit Any Size Cigarette

Nissan Motor Co. has announced the first major factory closing in Japanese auto-industry history. It is also cutting back on the number of models and options it offers. It offered more than 300 varieties of ashtrays. One car model had 87 different variations of steering wheels. Nissan set a goal of cutting back the possible model variations, which exceed 2,200, by 35 percent. With the price of an average Japanese car exceeding that of a Detroit car by $2,300 and little difference in quality, Nissan and the other Japanese auto companies are scrambling to get costs under control.

A Layoff by Any Other Name Is Still a Layoff

Lifetime employment is another practice that is coming under scrutiny. With more than a million surplus workers on company payrolls, a Vice-Minister at Japan's Ministry for International Trade and Industry has called Japanese companies lazy. Japanese companies usually take a circuitous method to laying off workers. The method generally takes the form of a cut in pay, fewer overtime hours, and not-so-subtle hints from bosses like, "Oh, are you still here?"

Team Pay Checks Are on the Way Out

As for teamwork and bottom-up decision-making, they too are being rethought. Says one Japanese executive, "When things aren't moving fast, the old consensus style was fine. Now, it's not enough." Some companies are altering their compensation system to move away from one that is almost automatic and based largely on group results. Instead, performance-related compensation is being employed. The idea is to emphasize personal accountability, not group results.

Is There Time?

Most experts say it is too early to count Japan out. Much of its industry is going through the restructuring and shakeouts that U.S. companies have already begun. In the final analysis, it's not a question of if Japan will change, but a matter of how soon and how much.

Questions

1. Do you think the changes that Japanese companies are making will help them become more competitive in the world marketplace?

2. With companies from other countries adapting Japanese management practices, what do you predict will be their reaction to these newer Japanese changes?

After the OD consultant and the client select a strategy, they decide upon specific OD techniques to achieve the desired changes. These OD intervention techniques, such as goal setting, confrontation meetings, survey feedback, total quality management, and team building (discussed in detail in later chapters) are then implemented systematically to revitalize the organization.

The flow in developing an OD program is from the diagnosis of problems and opportunities for change (where we are now) to the setting of objectives (where we want to be). The program then moves to deciding upon change strategies and finally selecting specific intervention techniques (how we get from here to there).

The task of the OD practitioner is: (1) to help the client system generate valid information, (2) to provide free choice for the client among decision alternatives, and (3) to provide client ownership of the chosen alternatives or action plans. Structural, technical, and behavioral change strategies are not OD change strategies per se. The determining feature of an OD strategy is the process used to arrive at and carry out the strategy. As Edgar Schein, a leading OD practitioner, said in an interview, "I believe OD is a philosophy of *how* you do things, not a technology of *what* you do."[10] The OD consultant helps the client to develop their own problem solutions. The primary task is helping the clients learn to diagnose and solve their own problems.

The Integration of Change Strategies

Organization development has evolved during the past decade from a narrow viewpoint favoring one specific intervention strategy to a more **integrated** or **systematic approach** to change.[11] OD consultants historically favored behavioral oriented interventions. Increasingly, OD consultants are oriented toward dealing with the total organization through an *integration* of behavioral, structural, and technical strategies. Figure 8.3 shows the integration of the three approaches to change.

Recent research suggests that technology alone is not the answer for a company to attain quality improvement.[12] To reach the true potential of technological changes, management must also carry out structural and behavioral changes. Similarly, a company that has set up finely tuned structural and behavioral innovations but uses outdated technology cannot operate at full potential.

FIGURE 8.3 An Integrated Approach to Change

Organizational Effectiveness and Excellence

The Corning Inc. plant at Blackburg, Virginia, has changed to a system that integrates people and technology. It decided against using robotics in certain places because they wanted humans to provide critical feedback. Plant Manager Robert Hoover says, "Even in boring and repetitive jobs, we moved away from automation because humans adapt and robots don't."[13] The plant removed time clocks, created one job classification, established one manager for 60 employees, and trained each employee to handle up to 15 different jobs. In the first year of changes, the plant was profitable and increased its productivity about 25 percent. So many Japanese, European, and U.S. companies wanted to look over the plant that Corning conducts tours once a month—and even charges a fee.

It is increasingly evident that organizations involve complexity and contingencies. Therefore, simple cause-and-effect diagnosis and intervention strategies may overlook some critical interrelationships which influence the change effort. As a result, it is often difficult to isolate changes to the relationship between any two single variables. The interrelationships between organizational variables are often complex and unclear, and the OD strategies must be comprehensive enough to provide interventions that deal with such situations.

A significant aspect to be considered in the selection of a change strategy is **second-order consequences**. This refers to the indirect or deferred consequences that result from the immediate change actions. A change in one aspect of a system to solve one problem may result in newly created problems.

The organization's problems should emerge from the diagnosis. From these findings, the most effective strategy is then selected. This can be termed an integrative approach to organization change and involves combining structural, technical, and behavioral change approaches to achieve the desired goals. After the consultant and the client determine the major strategy, they then decide upon the specific OD techniques to implement in the change effort.

In summary, the change strategy selected must consider organization, technological, individual, and work-team problems. The use of an inappropriate or limited strategy of change will probably lead to ineffective results and the emergence of new problems.

Stream Analysis

Stream analysis is one method used in planning the implementation and analysis of behavioral, structural, and technical changes.[14] Stream analysis begins with the consultant and the client identifying behavioral, technical, and structural interventions that they can implement as part of the OD program. Through the planning process, they schedule interventions to begin and end at specific times, and determine interrelationships between the interventions. Because of the number and complexities of variables (interventions, times, and interrelationships), a chart is built to better visualize the OD strategy. The chart is the major document used in stream analysis change strategy. It shows the interventions plotted over time with arrows showing the relationship of interventions to one another.

Figure 8.4 shows an example of a portion of a stream analysis chart for a hypothetical OD program. The key features in such a program could include installing a robotic production system (technical), implementing self-managed work teams (structural), and holding team-building sessions (behavioral). As an example, before a robotic production line can be installed and changes made in work teams, the consultant and client decide to use team building to introduce the new technology. Team building will begin at Month 0 and continue through Month 5. Robotic systems will be installed beginning Month 3 and completed by Month 5. A revised chain of command will be introduced Month 3, and so on. Stream analysis presents a visual representation of the OD program. Stream analysis charts bear some resemblance to a combination of modified PERT and Gantt planning charts.

Stream analysis is useful from several perspectives. It helps the practitioner and client diagnose and plan the interventions, and keeps track of progress once the change program is underway. The client is better able to keep the organization operating as effectively as possible during the change. It may show "holes" or periods of time when there is no activ-

FIGURE 8.4 Stream Analysis Chart

ity (Month 8) or periods when there is a good deal of activity (Month 4). This information may be used to redesign the change program or to schedule time appropriately. Stream analysis shows a pattern of triggers with one activity triggering or causing another activity to follow. For complex OD projects, it is especially helpful to represent visually the change program and show "where we've been and where we have to go." If modifications are required in the OD program, the consequences of the changes on other interventions can more easily be ascertained by referring to the stream analysis chart.

The authors were involved in a large OD program consisting of more than two dozen practitioners working with several operating divisions of a very large client system. Using the stream analysis approach, it was possible to plan and monitor the change program and build the necessary coordination among the practitioners and the operating divisions of the client system. It was also useful to top management because they could keep track of change activities as these occurred in the field. An entire room was devoted to charts wrapping around the walls so that top managers could drop by and see that the change program was moving on schedule. An additional benefit of this approach was that it gave legitimacy to the OD program because top management could see that something was going on out in the field.

Top management must be prepared to lead their company through a period when people are being asked to change not only structure, technology, and behaviors, but more importantly, their cultural values. Changing values is often a gut-wrenching and agonizing experience.[15] Once there is an awareness of a need for change and the consultant and client develop a change strategy, the question emerges as to the specific action intervention that will be most appropriate. There are a range of activities, practices, and techniques for intervening that are aimed at enhancing the effectiveness of the organization.

Selecting an OD Intervention

There are many strategies, methods, and techniques for intervening during the action phase of an OD program. An **OD strategy** involves the planning and direction of change programs, whereas **intervention techniques** deal with the operational aspects of the change—

the specific means by which the OD goals are attained. An **OD intervention** refers to the range of actions designed to improve the health or functioning of the client system. An awareness of the range of diverse intervention techniques available to be applied to a given target system is important to the practitioner. The major OD intervention techniques will be described in the next few chapters. All the OD interventions are aimed at changing some specific aspect of an organization: its climate, members, structure, or procedures. An organization practice is inefficient if it fails to further organization objectives; however, inefficiency may emerge slowly and become ingrained in the climate of the organization and the behaviors of the members. (See OD in Practice.)

OD IN PRACTICE
MONDAY MORNING MASSACRE AT McDONNELL DOUGLAS[16]

In the past Douglas Aircraft, a subsidiary of McDonnell Douglas Corporation, sold nearly half of the world's commercial aircraft. Today its sales have shrunk to 12 percent. But Douglas is trying to change. CEO John McDonnell says, "Rumors of our demise have proved to be greatly exaggerated."

Douglas Aircraft was totally restructured in secret sessions mandated by McDonnell. Selected corporate executives (none from Douglas Aircraft) were driven by chauffeurs, who held their destinations secret, and led down stairs to the basement of the home of Robert Hood, Jr., a senior executive. There they were told to "ponder the imponderables." No one at Douglas learned of the changes until a Monday morning in February when all 5,200 managers were bussed to a hanger in Long Beach, California.

The Firing

CEO John McDonnell introduced the new Douglas Aircraft president, Robert Hood, and three other top managers who were new to Douglas. McDonnell then told the managers they had all lost their jobs! They could, if they wanted, reapply for their jobs. Many managers did reapply for management positions and eventually 4,000 were rehired as managers; 1,000 fewer than before the reorganization. Management levels were cut from nine to five. Besides cutting immediate costs, the restructuring had another objective of improving communications by tearing down barriers between companies, departments, and people.

Many insiders, even at Douglas, were convinced that something extreme had to be done to ensure Douglas's survival. Since Douglas was taken over by McDonnell over 23 years ago, Douglas had earned a reputation for extravagant offices and holding expensive ceremonies, while corporate headquarters remained austere.

Total Quality Management System

The second part of the change program involved starting the total quality management system (TQM) at Douglas and other McDonnell operations. The purpose of TQM is that through the teamwork of production-line employees with less direct supervision, quality will improve and production mistakes will not have to be corrected at a later and more costly point. TQM is a teamwork based system intended to help build the highest quality products at the lowest possible competitive price. According to CEO McDonnell, "We're trying to make fundamental changes in how we conduct our business and how we work at our jobs."

TQM seems to be getting a lot of top management support; however, production floor supervisors directly involved in the program say management needs to be more supportive of team leaders by providing more communication and leadership skills and coaching their supervisors. Other supervisors report that employees don't want to take responsibility for anything. Even more ardent supporters of TQM on the floor say there are a lot of drawbacks and a lot of nonparticipation in the program. Bob Barnhart, a Senior Engineer and Field Service Representative to the U.S. Air Force says, "I think this TQM is a viable start, but don't let it stop. It needs to keep growing. We've got a long way to go"

The Results

Douglas Aircraft has been moderately profitable for the past ten quarters, though this has been partially attained by cutting its employees from a high of 125,000 to 78,000—all within two and one-half years. Morale, particularly among managers, is still low. John McDonnell said in a VCR tape sent to employees, "For years at DAC [Douglas Aircraft] we've tried Band-Aids as a way of patching outmoded systems and processes that were breaking down under the weight of rapid and sustained expansion . . . This time we're fixing the root causes of DAC's problems . . . But don't expect immediate bottom line results at DAC."

The success of the changes remains questionable. Recent indications suggest that management is growing increasingly concerned that the remedies are not working as well as planned. An internal memo from Deputy President John Capellupo cites a problem with "people who appear to be idle" at the job. Capellupo says, ". . . I conclude that we have a clear lack of discipline throughout our organization including all levels of management as well as our work force."

He went on to say that the total quality management program had led to a permissive system.

In another memo sent to all workers, Capellupo said, "I will demand that my management test you and your team's discipline to the limit of their physical and emotional stamina—but not beyond reason." One worker complained, "Who does he think he is running, the Marine Corps?"

Doug Griffith, President of the local UAW representing Douglas workers, says "You've got a cadre of people who were part of the traditional good-ol'-boy network, and now they're suddenly out of it. We've got a lot of them out on the floor, and they're a threat to what we're doing, like poison in the well."

Questions

1. What types of change approaches were used at McDonnell Douglas?
2. Did McDonnell Douglas appear to use an integrated approach?
3. What are the drawbacks of the change program?
4. What could McDonnell Douglas do to improve the chances of success?

When organizational inefficiency emerges, there must be a shift in the values, beliefs, and behaviors of the individuals who make the system work. OD intervention techniques are based upon the idea that the relationships between organization groups and organization members are one of the principal reasons for problems of inefficiency, and that certain activities do not contribute to organization objectives.

C. Northcote Parkinson in **Parkinson's Laws** summarizes the inherent problems of inefficient practices.[17] Parkinson proposed two principal reasons for organization inefficiency: (1) the law of multiplication of subordinates—a manager wants to increase the number of subordinates he or she directs rather than create rival organization members; and (2) the law of multiplication of work—members of the organization make work for each other. There are many similar kinds of inefficient operations that OD techniques seek to change.

In selecting a specific OD technique the consultant and the client consider several factors including the nature of the problem, the objectives of the change effort, the cultural norms of the client system, and the expected degree of resistance. Selecting a technique involves comparing and testing possible intervention techniques against some criteria. Three broad aspects are of concern to the OD consultant in selecting the appropriate intervention:

- *The potential results of the technique*
 - Will it solve the basic problems?
 - Does it have any additional positive outcomes?
- *The potential implementation of the technique*
 - Can the proposed technique actually work in a practical application?
 - What are the actual dollar and human costs of this technique and the impact of costs upon the client system?
 - How do the estimated costs of the technique compare with the expected results (costs versus benefit)?
- *The potential acceptance of the technique*
 - Is the technique acceptable to the client system?
 - Is the technique adequately developed and tested?
 - Has the technique been adequately explained and communicated to members of the client system?

These important facets should be considered before making a final decision on the selection of a technique. The selection of any given technique is usually a trade-off between advantages and disadvantages because there is no precise way to answer all these questions in advance. After comparing the advantages and disadvantages, specific techniques are selected for the action phase of the OD program.

It is common for consultants to use more than one technique in an OD program. In many OD programs, consultants use a multi-faceted approach by using a combination of interventions. Several studies have found that OD programs using more than one OD technique were generally superior in their results than programs relying on only one technique.[18]

The Major OD Intervention Techniques: An Overview

This section presents an overview of the basic OD intervention techniques. Since OD is a dynamic discipline, the boundaries of "what is" and "what is not" OD are ambiguous and changing. The interventions included in this discussion provide examples of the diverse techniques that exist, but they are not intended to be all-inclusive.

These planned activities or interventions are specifically aimed at correcting inefficiencies, solving problems, developing strengths, and creating areas of opportunity. A basic assumption underlying the intervention activity is that the client organization already contains most of the basic resources for change. The primary role of the OD practitioner is to energize these forces by helping the client system in diagnosing and resolving its own problems.

One way to categorize intervention techniques is in terms of the **target system** (see Table 8.1). OD intervention techniques include activities focusing on several organizational levels ranging from (1) the individual or interpersonal level, (2) the team or group level, (3) the intergroup level, to (4) the total organizational system level. The interventions, as previously discussed, are used in behavioral, structural, and technical strategies. Certain interventions are aimed primarily at individual improvement, while others are aimed at groups, but a single intervention may fit into several or all categories.

As explained, the consultant and the client select a technique that best fits the target system. The aspect of the organization that is being changed and the problem conditions then determine the type of intervention that is selected.

OD programs do not necessarily include all the intervention techniques listed in Table 8.1, but this grouping represents the range of possible activities. Usually, the specific intervention is dependent upon the nature of the target system. Certain techniques, such as Grid OD, systematically move from the individual to the total organizational system.

Table 8.1 OD Interventions: An Overview

Category	TYPES OF INTERVENTIONS			
	Individual	Team	Intergroup	Total Organizational System
Behavioral	Laboratory learning	Team building	Intergroup development	Goal setting
	Career planning	Process consultation	Third-party intervention	Grid OD (Phases 4,5,6)
	Managerial grid (Phase 1)	Quality control	Organization mirror	Survey feedback
	Stress management	Role negotiation	Process consultation	Action research
	Biofeedback	Role analysis	Grid OD (Phase 3)	Likert's System 4
	Management by objectives	Grid OD (Phase 2)	Total quality management	Quality of work life
	Goal setting	Goal setting		Total quality management
	Quality of work life	Third-party intervention		
Structural	Job enrichment	Job enrichment	Job enrichment	Grid OD (phases 4,5,6)
	Stress management	Team building	Goal setting	Survey feedback
	Quality of work life	Quality circles	Total quality management	Action research
	Management by objectives	Role negotiation		Likert's System 4
		Role analysis		Quality of work life
		Grid OD (Phase 2)		Total quality management
		Self-managed work teams		Restructuring
Technical	Job design	Job design	Job design	Grid OD (Phases 4,5,6)
		Quality control	Grid OD (Phase 3)	Survey feedback
		Grid OD (Phase 3)	Total quality management	Action research
				Likert's System 4
				Total quality management
				Reengineering

These different types of change techniques suggest the wide range of possible interventions available to the OD practitioner. Although this discussion includes the major categories, all possible interventions are not included. There are also differences among practitioners over what is and what is not an OD technique. In the following chapters major OD interventions will be described, moving from techniques aimed at the individual to system-wide applications.

REVIEW QUESTIONS

1. Compare and contrast the basic OD strategies.

2. Identify and give examples of OD interventions for various target systems.

3. Explain how stream analysis can be used in an OD program.

4. Describe an integrated approach to change.

5. Explain three factors that should be considered in selecting a technique.

KEY WORDS AND CONCEPTS

Define and be able to use the following:

Behavioral Change Approach
Downsizing
Integrated Approach
Intervention Techniques
OD Intervention
OD Strategy
Organization Structure

Parkinson's Laws
Second-Order Consequences
Stream Analysis
Structural Change Approach
Target System
Technical Change Approach
TQM

OD SKILLS SIMULATION 8.1
THE FRANKLIN COMPANY

Total time suggested: 1 hour, 10 minutes.

A. PURPOSE

In this simulation, you will be able to plan and implement structural, technical, and behavioral strategies in an organization. You will also critique and receive feedback on the effectiveness of your strategies. The goals include:

1. To determine appropriate intervention strategy.
2. To experience diagnosing and contacting a client system.
3. To provide feedback on consulting approaches.

B. PROCEDURES

Step 1. Everyone reads The Franklin Company Background (p. 217). Prior to class, divide the class into groups of six or seven members. Five of these members will serve as the Franklin Management Team and one or two as the OD Consultants. (Roles to be selected and read prior to the class meeting.) Each player reads only their role and marks decision on Franklin Company Decision Form, column 1 (p. 221). Any additional class members can become an observer. The consultants become familiar with the OD Consulting Guidelines (p. 220) and the Franklin Company Decision Form located on page 221. The roles are:

1. President
2. Vice President of Human Resources
3. Vice President of Manufacturing
4. Vice President of Marketing
5. Vice President of Finance
6. OD Consultants (one or two)

Step 2. The Franklin Management Team will meet with the consultant(s) to decide:

1. What are the major problems?
2. Should they use an OD consultant?
3. What strategies should be used to change?

The OD consultants will assist the committee in arriving at a decision using Franklin Company Decision Form, column 2.

Time suggested for Step 2: 30 minutes.

Step 3. The OD consulting team prepares an OD strategy and then presents it to the Franklin team, who may ask questions. A Decision Form is provided on page 221 to help the consulting team make a presentation.

Time suggested for Step 3: 15 minutes.

Step 4. Team members critique the Franklin team meeting and the role of the consultants. Discuss the following questions and complete the Team Rating Form on page 217.

TEAM RATING FORM

Based on the following scale, rate your team on how it performed on the following scale. Record your choice in the blank.

Low												High
1	:	2	:	3	:	4	:	5	:	6	:	7

Factor	Individual Rating	Team Rating
1. Cooperative teamwork	_____	_____
2. Member satisfaction	_____	_____
3. Team motivation	_____	_____
4. Information sharing	_____	_____
5. Consensual decision making	_____	_____
6. Conflict directly faced and resolved	_____	_____
7. Participative leadership	_____	_____
8. Clearly defined goals	_____	_____
9. Trust	_____	_____
10. Encouraged openness	_____	_____

1. How was a decision reached? (By consensus, vote, and so forth.)
2. What type of process skills did the consultants use? (Try to give examples.)
3. What did the consultants do or say that was helpful?
4. What did the consultant do or say that was dysfunctional?
5. Any suggestions of improvement for the Franklin team and the consultants?

Time suggested for Step 4: 15 minutes.

Step 5. As a class, discuss and evaluate the strategies presented by each of the consulting teams.

Time suggested for Step 5: 10 minutes.

THE FRANKLIN COMPANY BACKGROUND

The Franklin Company, a medium-size company with about 1,800 employees, manufactures radar units for use in small aircraft and in police cars. The company is actually more than 90 years old and initially manufactured wind vanes and lightning rods, but since World War II, it has manufactured only radar units. During the last four years, growth in sales has been stable and profits have decreased slightly, as contrasted to the previous 20 years of steady growth in sales and profits. Industry sales continue to show a steady growth, but new competitors have entered the field with new products and features, cutting into the firm's market share. Franklin has 12 distinct products with an average of three different models per product. New products have been brought on line but usually several years after the younger competitors. To make matters worse, several Franklin key managers, researchers, and sales people have joined the competition.

The current abbreviated organization chart is shown in Figure 8.5 (p. 218). All of the company's operations are conducted from the one site. Sales people are also physically based at the plant, but they make calls throughout the United States.

The President has called in an OD consulting team to diagnose and propose solutions to the current problems.

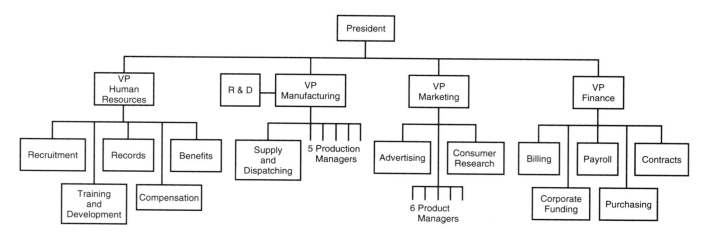

FIGURE 8.5 Franklin Organizational Chart

ROLE DESCRIPTIONS (READ **ONLY** *YOUR ROLE*)

Role 1—President. You have been the President of Franklin for the past 14 years and in large part its growth and success have been due to your own ability to select and motivate others. You are a college graduate, and have attended many executive seminars. You have tried to apply these concepts to Franklin. You still maintain close contact with day-to-day operations since you believe in "management by wandering around."

Over the past few years, growth has slowed, sales and earnings have declined, and turnover problems have emerged. You feel the rapid early growth may be the cause of current problems.

You are convinced that the lack of coordination between the four operating groups is the major problem and that a more decentralized operation will help resolve this. You also think a management information system (MIS) will improve coordination and communication. You have asked the Vice President of Finance to look into MIS.

You believe that the organization needs better morale and improved bottom-line results. Your Vice President of Human Resources has suggested that you try something new: an organization development program. The Vice President has invited a team of consultants to meet with your executive committee. You believe in modern techniques, so perhaps these consultants can get the various members to find an agreeable compromise to solve the problem.

Role 2—Vice President of Human Resources. You have an M.B.A. and you were brought in five years ago to serve in your current position. You see the key problem as poor structure, a lack of coordination among departments, and weak managerial competence and training of all levels.

All of the other Vice Presidents worked their way up to their present position, and you consider their professional managerial training somewhat remiss, with the exception of the Vice President of Marketing who has attended many of your management development training sessions. This is even more of a problem at the mid- and lower-level management ranks.

You feel that the answer to the problem is a decentralized operation with increased integration and coordination between departments and a participative, team style. You have read about OD and have talked to a colleague at another company who had high praise for their OD program. You even discussed implementing an OD program with the Vice President of Manufacturing, but there was little response. You feel a need to get conflicts out into the

open where they can be resolved rather than each unit seeking its own best interest. A unified team effort is needed.

You have attempted to initiate several training and change programs. These programs have been undercut by other managers. You got word that one Vice President was openly attacking the programs, even though the President has been strongly supportive. You suggested bringing in some OD consultants in hopes of initiating some badly needed changes. Even though they might add to costs in the short run, you are sure that long-term effectiveness will be improved.

Role 3—Vice President of Manufacturing. You have been with the company for 22 years and have worked your way up through the ranks. You have a degree in engineering and feel that you are competent, run a tight ship, and that your department is the main reason for past success. You believe that most problems are due to rapid growth that has resulted in loose structure, lack of coordination, and lack of control.

You feel that the company has too many meddling staff managers (particularly in marketing and human resources) who do not contribute to profits and only cause problems for the line managers. Several times the Vice President of Human Resources has tried to discuss with you management practices such as leadership and some new kind of OD program. You listened politely enough, but you got several good laughs out of it at your department meetings. The management training programs offered through the human resources division have been a waste of time, and you have told your people you prefer they stay on the job instead of going to more meetings. The Vice President of Marketing continually wants product modifications or comes up with some goofball idea for a new product. You have made it clear that you run manufacturing and that includes R&D. You can't run a smooth operation and keep costs down if you are constantly making special modifications. You believe you manufacture enough models to allow a customer to find a suitable product or the customer can easily make some minor modifications.

You feel the solution is to move into a more highly centralized structure and appoint an Executive Vice President to centralize cost control (like yourself, for example) and lay off some of the deadwood.

You hear that the President has invited some OD Consultants in, against your advice. You do not know much about OD, but it sounds like pouring money down a rathole to you. Besides, this OD business is a bunch of "touchie-feelie" nonsense anyway, which is the last thing you need.

Role 4—Vice President of Marketing. You have been with the company for 10 years. You are a college graduate with a major in psychology, but you have gained your knowledge of marketing from experience. You feel that marketing is the major factor in the company's growth, and if your product managers were given greater authority, they could turn the profit picture around.

You see the major problem as the lack of communication among departments and the failure to utilize talented managers. You have tried to get the manufacturing division to make some special modifications in radar units, but they have been willing to comply only on very large orders, and then it generally took them so long that you almost lost several of the orders from your customers. Several of your product managers have met with representatives of manufacturing to discuss new product ideas, but nothing comes of the meetings until your competitors come up with the identical product. Then it takes manufacturing a couple of years to design the unit.

Your people are bringing back word from the field that the excellent reputation once enjoyed by Franklin is beginning to fade. It has been discouraging for you and your people to fight an uphill battle with manufacturing for new products, and the real kicker is to learn that the competition comes out with your product idea.

Despite the problems with the manufacturing division, you find that if you treat your people well, they will perform for you. You have attended most of the management training sessions offered by the human resources department and have encouraged, though not

mandated, your managers to attend. Your department meetings even have follow-up discussions of the training sessions.

Even though marketing has been accused of being run like a "country club," you feel your department performs well. The answer, you believe, is to decentralize the firm into major independent groups and utilize more of the "whiz kids," the young M.B.A. types, in product management by giving them more authority over product operations. You would like to see yourself as Executive Vice President over the product managers.

You understand that some OD consultants are coming in and see this as a great opportunity to implement your ideas.

Role 5—Vice President of Finance. You have an M.B.A. from a major school. This and prior banking experience led to your successful 17 years at Franklin. You instituted all financial systems and made it a smooth operation.

You feel the problems are the result of too many changes in too short a time. The company has too many bright young kids and too many wasteful practices. You suggest going back to the basics by instituting a tighter centralized system of financial control and cutting about 10 percent of the deadwood. With yourself as an Executive Vice President (with other Vice Presidents reporting to you), this job could be done. You would set up some basic company rules, then force the department heads to enforce them.

You would like to see people be required to follow the chain of command. You have heard too many stories of people at lower levels cutting across the formal structure and meeting with employees in another division. This may sound good on the surface, but it usually screws up the operation later on. You would like to see all communications go up through their appropriate Vice President and then back down the chain of command. This type of centralized control is necessary to coordinate everything. You believe there are too many committees throughout the company, and you find it amazing that anything gets accomplished. Further, with all these committees making decisions, it's hard to figure out who to blame when something goes wrong. As far as you are concerned, a camel is a horse designed by a committee.

You realize that you are not as up-to-date on modern computerized systems as you might be. Though the president has asked you to look into a management information system (MIS), you consider it to be a waste of time and money. An MIS would call for a new computer and you have heard horror stories about computers and believe your current data processing system to be excellent.

You would like to avoid changes and keep things pretty much the way they are. You hear that some OD consultants are coming and your reaction is: Why do we need them? They represent just the kind of wasteful practice you oppose.

OD consulting guidelines. You hope to accomplish several things at this meeting:

1. To develop a consultant-client relationship with all of the committee members.
2. To make a preliminary diagnosis of possible problems.
3. To gain support for a possible OD project and convince them of the advantages.
4. To introduce them to some of the goals of OD, by doing some process consultation during the meeting.

FRANKLIN COMPANY DECISION FORM

Major Problems	Column 1 Individual	Column 2 Team
Managerial Style	_____	_____
Marketing	_____	_____
Manufacturing	_____	_____
Finance	_____	_____
Human Resources	_____	_____
Motivation	_____	_____
Communication	_____	_____
Team Work	_____	_____
Use Consultant	_____	_____
Change Strategy	_____	_____
Technical	_____	_____
Structural	_____	_____
Behavioral	_____	_____

CASE 8:
THE FARM BANK

The Farm Bank is one of the state's oldest and most solid banking institutions. Located in a regional marketing center, the bank has been active in all phases of banking, specializing in farm loans. The bank's president, Frank Swain, 62, has been with the bank for many years and is prominent in local circles.

The bank is organized into five departments as shown in Exhibit 1. Each department is headed by a Senior Vice President. They have been with the bank for years and in general reflect a stable and conservative outlook.

EXHIBIT 1 Partial Organization Chart

THE MANAGEMENT INFORMATION SYSTEM

Two years ago, President Swain felt that the bank needed to modernize its operation and with the approval of the Board of Directors, he decided to design and install a comprehensive management information system (MIS). The primary goal was to improve internal operations by supplying necessary information on a more expedited basis, thereby decreasing the time necessary to service customers. The system was also to be designed to provide economic operating data for top management planning and decision making. To head up this department, he selected Al Hassler, 58, a solid operations manager, who had some knowledge and experience in the computer department.

After the system was designed and installed, Al hired a young woman as his assistant. Valerie Wyatt was a young M.B.A. with a strong systems analysis background. In addition to being the only woman and considerably younger than any of the other managers at this level, Wyatt was also the only M.B.A.

In the time since the system was installed, the MIS has printed thousands of pages of operating information, including reports to all Vice Presidents, all Branch Managers, and the President. The reports include weekly, monthly, and quarterly summaries and include cost of operations, projected labor costs, overhead costs, and projected earnings figures for each segment of the bank's operations.

THE MIS SURVEY

Swain has been pleased with the system; however, he noticed little improvement in management operations. In fact, most of the older Vice Presidents tended to make decisions and function pretty much as they had before the MIS was installed. Swain then decided to have Wyatt conduct a survey of the users to try to evaluate the impact and benefits of the new system. Wyatt was glad to undertake the survey, since she had long felt the system was overelaborate for the bank's needs. She sent out a questionnaire to all department heads, branch managers, and so on, inquiring into the uses of the system.

As she began to assemble the survey data, a pattern began to emerge. In general, the majority of managers were strongly in favor of the system, but felt that there were a few minor modifications which could be made. As Valerie analyzed the responses several trends and important points came out: (1) 93 percent reported they did not regularly use the reports because the information was not in a useful form; (2) 76 percent reported the printouts were hard to interpret; (3) 72 percent stated they received more data than they wanted; (4) 57 percent reported finding some errors and inaccuracies; and (5) 87 percent stated they still kept manual records because they did not fully trust the MIS.

THE MEETING

Valerie Wyatt finished her report excitedly and rushed into Al Hassler's office and handed him the report. Hassler slowly scanned the report, then said, "You've done a good job here, Val. But now that we have the system operating, I don't think we should upset the apple cart, do you? Let's just keep this to ourselves for the time being and perhaps we can correct most of these problems. I'm sure Frank wouldn't want to hear this kind of stuff. This system is his baby, so maybe we shouldn't rock the boat with this report."

Valarie returned to her office feeling uncomfortable. She wondered what to do.

CASE ANALYSIS FORM

Name: _____

I. Problems

 A. Macro

 1. _____

 2. _____

 B. Micro

 1. _____

 2. _____

II. Causes

 1. _____

 2. _____

 3. _____

III. Systems affected

 1. Structural _____

 2. Psychosocial _____

 3. Technical _____

 4. Managerial _____

 5. Goals _____

IV. Alternatives

 1. _____

 2. _____

 3. _____

 4. _____

 5. _____

V. Recommendations

 1. _____

 2. _____

 3. _____

SUMMARY

This chapter examined some of the major organization development interventions. OD is a long-term effort to introduce planned change on a system-wide basis. Therefore, the selection of specific strategies and techniques is an important action step.

• **OD Strategy.** The OD strategy involves the planning and direction of the intervention activities. A comprehensive approach involves the way the organization is managed, the way jobs are designed, and the way people are motivated. The consultant and the client determine the appropriate strategy to best attain change objectives. There are also a number of OD techniques. Based upon the change strategy, specific action interventions that will best resolve problem conditions and increase organization effectiveness are then set in motion. A more detailed description of these techniques will be presented in the following chapters.

• **Change.** In this chapter, three basic approaches to change were identified: structural, technical, and behavioral. Structure provides the framework that relates elements of the organization. These units are engaged in some task or technical accomplishment and are also bound together in an interrelated network of social and behavioral relationships.

• **Interventions.** There are a variety of intervention techniques which may be used in organization development.

Although these techniques differ, they aim at the same basic goals: (1) to improve the functioning of the client system; (2) to increase the organization's adaptive capability toward a more anticipative system; and (3) to enhance the development and potential of the individual members of the organization.

• **OD Skills.** You have had an opportunity to diagnose a problem and to develop a specific set of strategies and techniques for executing an organization change program. You have probably found different departmental objectives which must be reconciled with organization goals. You may also have experienced different approaches to change among individuals. One person may view the problem as calling for a structural change, although another person may view it as requiring behavioral or technical change strategies. After a change strategy has been agreed upon, specific techniques for achieving change must then be designed and carried out.

• **Systems.** All the major variables are interrelated, and often a change in structure, for example, may have consequences on technical and behavioral elements. Therefore, a systems approach or integrative approach involves analyzing the way work is designed, the way the organization is managed, and the way people are motivated. The following chapters describe some specific OD interventions for changing organization conditions.

NOTES

1. Susan Sommersyn Brooks, "Managing a Horizontal Revolution," *HR Magazine* , vol. 40, no. 6, July 1995, p. 52.

2. Laura Rubach, "Downsizing: How Quality is Affected as Companies Shrink," *Quality Progress*: Vol. 28, No. 4, April 1995, p. 24.

3. F. Friedlander and L. D. Brown, "Organization Development," *Annual Review of Psychology*, 25 (1974), pp. 313–41; and Harold Leavitt, "Applied Organization Change in Industry: Structural, Technical and Humanistic Approaches," in *Handbook of Organizations*, ed. James March (Chicago: Rand McNally & Company, 1965).

4. Frederick Rose, "Job-Cutting Medicine Fails to Remedy Productivity Ills at Many Companies," *The Wall Street Journal*, June 7, 1994, p. A2.

5. Elizabeth Lesly and Larry Light, "When Layoffs Alone Don't Turn The Tide," *Business Week*, December 7, 1992, pp. 100–1.

6. Peter Nulty, "Kodak Grabs for Growth Again," *Fortune*, May 16, 1994, pp. 76–78; Brian Dumaine, "What's So Hot About Outsiders?," *Fortune*, November 29, 1993, pp. 63–5; and Joan E. Rigdon and Christian Hill, "Kodak Names Motorola Chief To Top Posts," *The Wall Street Journal*, October 28, 1993, pp. A3–A6.

7. Karen Pennar and Michael Mandel, "Economic Prospects for the Year 2000," *Business Week*, September 25, 1989, p. 162. Also see Nancy J. Perry, "The Workers of the Future," *Fortune*, Spring/Summer 1991, pp. 68–72.

8. Richard J. Selfridge and Stanley L. Sokolik, "A Comprehensive View of Organizational Development," *M.S.U. Business Topics*, Winter 1975, p. 46.
 Benten R. Schendler, "Japan is Changing for Good" *Fortune*, June 13, 1994, p. 125.

9. John F. Hulpke, California State University–Berkeley, 1994, sources: Jacob M. Schlesinger, Michael Williams, and Craig Forman, "Japan Inc., Wracked by Recession, Takes Stock of Its Methods," *The Wall Street Journal*, September 29, 1993, p. A1; Daniel Benjamin, "Germany Is Troubled By How Little Work Its Workers Are Doing," *The Wall Street Journal*, May 6, 1993, p. A1; Karen Lowry Miller, "Japan's New Credo: Average Can Be Good Enough," *Business Week*, May 3, 1993, p. 124; Krystal Miller and Jacqueline Mitchell, "After Years of Growth In U.S. Car Market, Japanese Surge Is Over," *The Wall Street Journal*, March 4, 1993, p. A1; Karen Lowry Miller, "Stress and Uncertainty: The Price of Restructuring," *Business Week*, March 29, 1993, p. 74; and Clay Chandler and Michael Williams, "A Slump in Car Sales Forces Nissan to Start Cutting Swollen Costs," *The Wall Street Journal*, March 3, 1993, p. A1.

10. Fred Luthans, "Conversation with Edgar H. Schein," *Organizational Dynamics*, Spring 1989, p. 66.

11. Jyotsna Sanzgiri and Jonathan Z. Gottlieb, "Philosophic and Pragmatic Influences on the Practice of Organization Development, 1950–2000," *Organizational Dynamics*, Autumn 1992, pp. 57–69.

12. Jayant V. Saraph and Richard J. Sebastian, "Developing a Quality Culture," *Quality Progress*, vol. 26, no. 9 (September 1993), pp. 73–8.

13. Amal Kumar Jaj, "Shifting Gears, Some Manufacturers Drop Efforts to Adopt Japanese Techniques," *The Wall Street Journal*, May 7, 1993, p. A1.

14. Jerry I. Porras, *Stream Analysis* (Reading, Mass.: Addison-Wesley Publishing Co., 1987); D. D. Warrick, ed., *Contemporary Organization Development, Current Thinking and Applications* (Glenview, Ill.: Scott, Foresman and Company, 1985); and Jerry I. Porras, Joan Harkness,

and Coeleen Kiebert, "Understanding Organization Development: A Stream Approach," *Training and Development Journal*, April 1983, pp. 52–63.

15. See Hugh Williamson, "What It Takes to be a Quality Consultant," *Quality Progress* , vol. 28, no. 4, April 1995, p. 33.

16. James E. Ellis, "McDonnell Bounces Through the Flak," *Business Week*, May 17, 1993, pp. 72–3; James E. Ellis, "Douglas Is Struggling for Altitude," *Business Week*, November 9, 1992, p. 71; Rick Wartzman, "McDonnell's Management Shake-Up Still Reverberates," *Wall Street Journal*, February 7, 1990, p. A8; Ralph Vartabedian, "The Remaking of Douglas by McDonnell," *Los Angeles Times*, October 15, 1989, p. D9;

and "90 Days, The Chairman's Quarterly Report," McDonnell Douglas Corporation, Video Cassette Tape, Number 1, September 1989.

17. C. Northcote Parkinson, *Parkinson's Laws* (Boston: Houghton Mifflin Company, 1957).

18. George A. Neuman, Jack E. Edwards, and Nambury S. Raju, "Organizational Development Interventions: A Meta-Analysis of Their Effects on Satisfaction and Other Attitudes," *Personnel Psychology*, vol. 42 (1989), p. 479; and R. A. Guzzo, R. D. Jette, and R. A. Katzell, "The Effects of Psychologically Based Intervention Programs on Worker Productivity: A Meta-Analysis," *Personnel Psychology,* vol. 38 (1985), pp. 275-91.

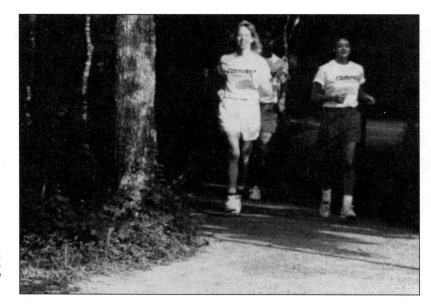

Recreational and fitness programs play a role at Compaq's Houston campus. *Photo reprinted with permission of Compaq Computer Corporation. All Rights Reserved.*

Employee Involvement and Empowerment: Interpersonal Interventions

9

OBJECTIVES

Upon completing this chapter, you will be able to:

1. Recognize the need for Employee Involvement (EI) interventions in an OD program.
2. Experience the dynamics involved in interpersonal communication.
3. Practice giving and receiving feedback on your personal communication style.
4. Describe career life planning and stress management as OD techniques.

PREMEETING PREPARATION

1. Read the Background Information.
2. Complete Step 1 of OD Skills Simulation 9.1. Form teams of five and assign roles the previous class meeting.
3. Complete Step 1 of OD Skills Simulation 9.2.
4. Complete Steps 1 and 3 of OD Skills Simulation 9.3.
5. Read and analyze Case 9: The Sundale Club.

BACKGROUND INFORMATION

In a growing number of today's organizations, power is shifting out of the office of managers and into the hands of lower level employees. Organizations such as AT&T, Delta Airlines, Federal Express, Hewlett-Packard, Motorola, and Wal-Mart are currently moving to empower their employees.[1] **Empowerment** is the process of giving employees the power to make decisions about their work.

One of the most critical elements in large-scale organization change is the individual. Excellence is going to be achieved by those organizations where risk taking and decision making are pushed down to the lowest possible level. This new culture is built upon the empowerment of the individual. The challenge is to empower the employee to take initiative and responsibility at all levels and functions of the organization. Organizations are designed to use the energy and ability of individuals to do work and realize goals. Members bring to the organization their values, assumptions, and behaviors. The success of future organizations, then, depends on how effectively the needs of individual members can be integrated with the vision and goals of the organization. People- or behavior-oriented changes are aimed at the **psychosocial system functioning** of the organization. The behavioral interventions may take various forms but all are intended to improve the basic skills that enhance employee empowerment, and thus underlie managerial effectiveness.

The results of a survey of major firms revealed that "firms that have transformed their culture claim to have increased productivity and number of clients, boosted employee camaraderie, made each employee feel a sense of ownership, and increased profits."[2] One essential factor in most OD programs is a greater openness of communication and improved conflict resolution, requiring the development of specialized skills among members.

There are a range of OD intervention activities aimed at enhancing the development and empowerment of the individual organization member. Essentially, the underlying assumption to these approaches is: if the individual becomes more effective, more involved, and more skilled, the total organization also will be improved. In a general sense, organization members attempt to improve their communication ability, interpersonal skill, and managerial performance. If managers can increase their interpersonal competence, the results should be improved organizational performance.[3]

In this chapter, we will discuss several interpersonal techniques that can be used to help organization members in becoming more empowered and involved. The techniques discussed include employee involvement, laboratory learning, the Johari Window Model, Transactional Analysis, career life planning, and stress management.

Empowerment/Employee Involvement

Employee involvement (EI), empowerment, and **buy-in management** are new techniques for unleashing human potential in organizations. The central idea is to delegate power and decision making to lower levels and, by using concepts like shared visions of the future, to engage all employees so that people develop in themselves a sense of pride, self-respect, and responsibility. Management is responsible for creating a supportive climate and removing barriers.[4]

Employee involvement attempts to move the organization from the traditional, "I just work here, I don't make the rules," type of culture, to one of shared vision and goals. The idea is to have the individual's purpose and vision congruent with that of organization. Employees develop a feeling of psychological ownership leading to concern, interest, commitment, and responsibility. A crucial element of employee involvement is that it must be genuine. To empower, managers have to talk giving power and then "walk the talk." It is not empowerment when the managers tell employees that they have authority and responsibility, while *not* allowing employees to make actual decisions and carry out actions. CEO Jack Welch of General Electric Company says, "The only way I know to create that kind of trust is by laying out your values and then walking the talk."[5]

One recent survey of 4,000 American managers reported:

- Only 46 percent give their best effort at work.
- Only 36 percent feel personally challenged by their jobs.
- 52 percent feel they have not attained their personal objectives.
- Over 43 percent feel trapped in their jobs.[6]

This suggests that many organizations lack a fully involved work force.

Officials at Ford believe that employee involvement has directly and significantly contributed to an improvement in quality. One year, Ford recalled more automobiles than the manufacturer built. But now, Ford claims to have the best quality of any U.S. automaker. Ford continues to use employee involvement and recently has begun to encourage its suppliers to set up similar programs.[7]

The potential power to be unleashed under EI and buy-in management is enormous. General Electric has implemented a version of employee involvement that they call "Work-Out." CEO Jack Welch says of Work-Out:

> The only way I see to get more productivity is by getting people involved and excited about their jobs. You can't afford to have anyone walk through a gate of a factory, or into an office, who's not giving 120 percent. I don't mean running and sweating, but working smarter. . . . It's a matter of seeing the importance of your role in the total process.
>
> The point of Work-Out is to give people better jobs. When people see that their ideas count, their dignity is raised. Instead of feeling numb, like robots, they feel important. They are important.[8]

Employee involvement has become in many organizations—including small and large, profit and not-for-profit, and domestic and international—a basic cornerstone of organization change and development programs. In Chapter 10, high-involvement work teams, employee involvement, and related change programs will be discussed in more detail.

Laboratory Learning

Laboratory learning programs (sometimes called encounter groups, training groups, or simply T-groups) evolved from the early group dynamics work of Kurt Lewin and the programs conducted by National Training Laboratories (NTL) in the United States and by Tavistock Institute in England.[9] In Japan, at the Group Dynamics Department of Kyushu University, research paralleled Lewin's and ideas were shared in what their researchers called **Performance Maintenance** (PM) theory.[10] Although reliable data on the extent of laboratory learning are not readily available, it grew rapidly through the mid-1970s. Recently, OD consultants are using laboratory learning less as a training technique, though they use some forms of it indirectly in other OD training techniques such as the Managerial Grid, team building, and Outward Bound.

The Objectives of Laboratory Learning

Managers have used *laboratory learning* to increase their interpersonal skills in leadership, group, and organization situations. The basic idea involves the use of a group as a laboratory for experimenting, learning, and discovering cause-and-effect relations in interpersonal communication. Laboratory learning programs usually include 10 to 12 participants who typically do not know one another and one or two experienced trainers or facilitators. The group sessions normally require a one- or two-week time span, although some last three days or less. Consultants usually conduct the programs at a location removed from the workplace.

The focus is on what goes on in the group and on the interpersonal dynamics between group members. The learning is unstructured in the sense that there is no appointed leader

and no assigned topic. The goal is for participants to develop self-insight and awareness, to increase sensitivity to one's effect on others, and to bring to the surface data on one's blind spots and hidden areas. The laboratory provides a safe climate away from the work organization where participants can try new behaviors and receive candid feedback from others on the effectiveness of those behaviors. Participants can then take back to their work new ways of behaving and working with others.

The Use of Laboratory Learning in OD Programs

Laboratory learning can be conducted independently of an OD program, but the problem of **fade out** is more likely to occur. Fade out occurs when participants, after having found some new ways of working with others, return to their work organizations where support is often lacking. Unless there is a supportive environment to reinforce the new behaviors in the workplace, there will be a high degree of degradation of laboratory learning on the job. Laboratory learning, when conducted as part of an OD program, provides a greater degree of support to the participant back in the work organization than when it is conducted as an isolated program.

Some 35 years ago, Robert Blake and Herb Shepard pioneered the use of laboratory learning in company-wide programs aimed at improving organization efficiency. To date, many major corporations (e.g., TRW, Texas Instruments, and Union Carbide) and the U.S. State Department have applied these techniques in organization development programs.

Results of Laboratory Learning

As already noted, some major corporations have applied laboratory learning methods as a part of management development and organization development programs. There is evidence to suggest that laboratory learning provides increased self-insight and awareness of impact upon others and that observable changes in behavior do occur on the job.[11]

Several studies have found laboratory learning to be one of the most effective OD interventions in providing employees with improvements in job satisfaction and self-development. It appears that laboratory learning improves organization productivity just as well as does technical and structural interventions.[12] In a report that reviewed empirical studies on the effect of OD, structured laboratory learning obtained the greatest impact. Laboratory learning interventions were responsible for a positive 80 percent overall change in hard-outcome measurements such as productivity, absenteeism, profits, and quality.[13]

One problem in evaluating most OD techniques is the lack of empirical data on the results of various interventions. This is changing with the increased use of OD and within the last decade the number of valid studies has increased.

Interpersonal Style—The Johari Window Model

An organization is made up of individuals, each with a unique set of values, behaviors, and motivations. Because of the interaction and communication between members, an organization's climate is formed. If the organization uses formal communications, lines of authority, and centralized decision making, most of the communications between members may be unauthentic. People will say what they think others want to hear or expect them to say. The communication, then is "mask to mask"; from one person's facade to another person's facade. Usually, such communication is distorted, inaccurate, and ineffective.

For example, it is reported that CEO Edwin Artzt of Procter & Gamble Company presents multiple images of himself. One retired executive says that while Artzt can turn on the charm, "he'll take you apart limb from limb" in an argument. Since Artzt became President, more than a dozen senior managers have left P&G in less than three years. An East Coast executive recruiter says he is receiving up to 50 calls a day from P&G managers. In another example of mask-to-mask communication, many managers who remain at P&G

"feel their behavior is being changed [public area], but their heart isn't being changed [closed area]," says one P&G manager.[14]

Communication is a critical dimension in determining the effectiveness of most organizations. The **Johari Window Model**, conceived by Joe Luft and Harry Ingram (the name Johari is formed by taking a portion of each of their first names), is one technique for identifying interpersonal communication style.[15] The model (see Figure 9.1) measures interpersonal style in terms of communication awareness by presenting a two-dimensional, four-celled figure based on the interaction of two sources of information—the self and others. In the model, each cell represents a particular area of knowledge about the self and illustrates the quality of the interpersonal communication process.

1. The public area. This area includes behavior, thoughts, and feelings that both the person and others know. This is the area of our public image and of interaction involving mutually shared perceptions (others see us as we see ourselves). One underlying assumption of the Johari Window Model is that interpersonal effectiveness is directly related to the amount of mutually shared information—or *congruence*. The larger this area becomes, the more effective will be the communication.

2. The blind area. This area represents aspects of the self (behavior, thoughts, and feelings) not known to oneself, but readily apparent to others. These include mannerisms and habits of which a person may be unaware, but others discover easily. The person who is red-faced and shouting "I'm not angry," or a person whose lip is twitching nervously, but words are saying "I'm in control," would be examples of this area. Some managers may try to be forceful and tough, rejecting any feelings of warmth as soft, yet such feelings might be highly visible to others.

3. The closed area. This area involves behavior, thoughts, and feelings known only to oneself, but not to others. This involves a protective facade intended to protect the ego or self-image. For others to become aware of this area, it must be disclosed by the person. This area includes feelings one may perceive as possibly harmful to one's self-image. For example, after hearing an off-color joke, a person makes a pretense at laughing though he or she may be repulsed by the humor.

The question arises: How effective are such facades and how effective are people in using them? When one is in a new situation or with strangers, the closed area usually rep-

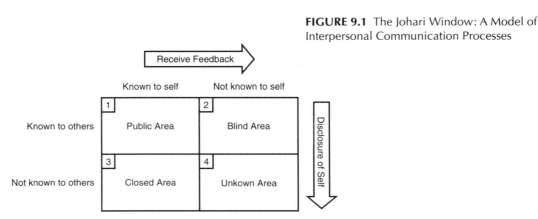

FIGURE 9.1 The Johari Window: A Model of Interpersonal Communication Processes

Source: Adapted from J. Luft, "The Johari Window," *Human Relations Training News,* Vol. 5 (1961), 6–7; *Of Human Interaction,* (Palo Alto, Calif.: National Press Books, 1961).

resents a large part of one's behavior because people do not know much about one another and trust is low. It is interesting that people go to great lengths to conceal this part of themselves, yet it is this element that makes each of us most human. It often takes years of knowing someone before we gain insights into this area.

4. The unknown area. Included here are behavior and feelings that are inaccessible both to oneself and to others. According to some psychologists, unconscious, deeply repressed feelings and impulses or other hidden aspects of the personality reside here. Over time, people may become aware of some of these aspects of themselves, but for our purposes this area is of less importance.

As indicated in Figure 9.1, movement along the vertical and horizontal dimensions enable the individual to change his or her interpersonal style by increasing the amount of communication in the public or shared area. To enlarge the public area, the person may move vertically by reducing the closed area. As a person behaves in less-defensive ways and becomes more open, trusting, and risk taking, others will tend to react toward him or her with increased openness and trust. This process, termed **disclosure**, involves the open disclosure of one's feelings, thoughts, and candid feedback to others. The openness of communication leads more to open and congruent relationships.

The behavioral process used to enlarge the public area horizontally, termed **feedback**, allows one to reduce the blind area. The only way to become aware of our blind spots is for others to give information or feedback to us about our behavior. The blind area can be reduced only with the help and cooperation of others, and this requires a willingness to invite and accept such feedback. Almost every organization finds that poor communication is the most important problem preventing organizational effectiveness.

The Johari Window Model is one technique for examining and improving the interpersonal communication process. The ideas of the Johari Window can be used with laboratory learning to help participants understand their effect on others (disclosure) and how their behavior comes across to others (feedback). (See Our Changing World.)

OUR CHANGING WORLD:
JOINT VENTURES AND THE JOHARI WINDOW[16]

The automobile companies of the United States compete with one another. Right? And the auto companies of the United States and those of Japan *really* compete? Much has been written about the fierce competition between Japanese and U.S. companies, especially in the auto industry.

Joint Ventures

While the evening TV news and the front pages of newspapers carried stories of those battles being played out in the marketplace, the business news was covering joint ventures. Toyota and General Motors, Mitsubishi and Chrysler, Isuzu and General Motors, and Mazda and Ford are a few of the joint ventures between the Japanese and the U.S. auto industries.

Mazda and Ford

Many ventures have not been successful. A lack of trust, misunderstanding, and little mutual benefit are some of the more significant problems confronting many joint ventures. Mazda and Ford have worked out a successful joint venture. But they have been working at their relationship for more than fifteen years.

The two companies cooperate on new vehicles and exchange valuable information. Both companies bring to the table different but complementary expertise. Mazda shares its engineering, manufacturing, and product development abilities. Ford offers international marketing, finance, and computer controlled measuring equipment.

Basic Business Principles

Ford and Mazda work hard at making it work. They chose what to work on jointly on a project-by-project basis. Through the years, Mazda and Ford have developed a set of Basic Business Principles:

1. Top management provides support; else middle management will resist ceding partial control of a project.
2. Meet often, informally, and at all levels. Socialization is important for building trust.
3. Use a third party to settle disputes.
4. Maintain independence and sharpen expertise.
5. Each project must be viable for each partner.
6. Appoint a monitor to take primary responsibility.

7. Anticipate cultural differences.

What is the secret to the Mazda-Ford relationship? The president of Mazda says, "The most important point is for people to meet face-to-face and talk freely."

The Johari Window

When you think of corporations as legal entities, then corporate behavior can be described in Johari Window terms. Corporations, as they interact with one another form a window with different size cells.

When Mazda and Ford work out a joint project, both companies present a "public area" to one another. According to the Basic Business Principles, the two companies work on enlarging the public area. They have also agreed up front to maintain certain areas as closed. For example, Ford has refused to manufacture a four-door Navajo for Mazda (though Ford does manufacture (for Mazda) a two-door model that is virtually the same as Ford's Explorer). Mazda has also kept its Miata model to itself.

Questions

1. Do you agree that corporations can have personalities?
2. If so, can they develop a Johari Window?
3. What do you think of the Basic Business Principles?

Transactional Analysis

Transactional Analysis (TA) is a practical and useful interpersonal relationship model that OD practitioners apply in organization change programs.[17] TA, originally developed by Eric Berne, is a way for people to understand themselves better. Although psychologists use TA, members of organizations have adapted the ideas to improve their communication and interpersonal relation skills. TA provides a model for analyzing and understanding human behavior using terminology familiar to many people.

Structural Analysis

In examining interpersonal communication, we can employ structural analysis or personality analysis to understand how we get to be who we are. According to **structural analysis**, every person has three separate sources of behavior called **ego states** (see Figure 9.2):

- *The Parent*. This ego state is a set of feelings, attitudes, and behaviors copied from those of a parental figure. Behavior may include prejudicial, critical, consoling, or nurturing actions.
- *The Adult*. This ego state is an independent set of feelings, attitudes, and behaviors involving the basis of objective facts. When the individual gathers facts, tests reality, and computes a rational, objective answer, he or she is in an adult state.
- *The Child*. This ego state is a collection of feelings, attitudes, and behaviors retained from the individual's childhood. The child ego state usually shows emotions of some kind, such as anger, excitement, sadness, and fear.

FIGURE 9.2 Ego States

Parent Ego State

Adult Ego State

Child Ego State

All three ego states exist within a person and are not related to a person's age. A certain amount of all ego states is necessary for a well-integrated personality. The best way to examine ego states is to look at the person, or at ourselves, for such behavioral clues as: What words are used? What gestures are used? What attitude is present? And what is the tone of voice?

By using structural analysis, a person can better understand the source of their values, behaviors, and thoughts. This increase in awareness of one's personal style can then help in improving his or her effectiveness in an organization.

Transactional Theory

The three ego states are present in every individual and directly affect the type of transactions the person will have with others. Every interaction between people involves a **transaction** between their ego states. When one person converses with a second person, the first person is in a distinct ego state and can direct the message to any of the three ego states in the second individual. A transaction is the basic unit of communication. Transactions may be classified as (1) complementary or open, (2) crossed or blocked, and (3) ulterior or hidden (see Figure 9.3).

FIGURE 9.3 Types of Transactions

COMPLEMENTARY TRANSACTION
1. Let me help you with the painting.
2. Gee, thanks. I'd like that.

CROSSED TRANSACTION
1. Are you ready to start work on the new assignment?
2. Get off my back!

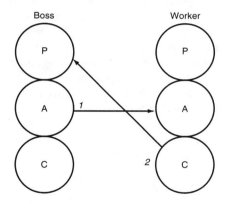

ULTERIOR TRANSACTION
1. Would you like to come up to my apartment and see my etchings?
2. I'd like to very much. I like art.

CROCK by Rechin, Parker and Wilder © Field Enterprises, Inc. by permission of American Syndicate, Inc.

A **complementary transaction** occurs when a message sent from one ego state receives an expected response from the other person's appropriate ego state. A **crossed transaction** occurs when a message from one ego state receives a response from an inappropriate or unexpected ego state. An **ulterior transaction** involves two ego states simultaneously: the literal words of the transaction, which may mean one thing, and the underlying intent, which may mean something entirely different.

Stroking is an important concept in transactional theory. A *stroke* is any form of recognition, including physical, verbal, or visual recognition, of one person by another. Strokes are given for "doing" and for "being." Strokes given for doing are *conditional*: they are tied to some type of performance of the receiver of the stroke. A manager ties a "thank you" to the desirable behavior by an employee. A stroke for being, or an *unconditional* stroke, is given to a person with no strings attached: it is given simply for being who they are. An example of an unconditional stroke was transmitted by CEO Herb Kelleher of Southwest Airlines, who has taken the airline into the industry's top 10, when he said of their employees ". . . its just the question of valuing individuals for themselves and always thinking of them as individuals instead of trying to classify them and lump them together. You know, each person at Southwest Airlines is of great importance to me as a person."[18] A manager who gives only conditional strokes may be regarded as artificial and "only says something when he wants something else in return." People in organizations generally need both performance and "being" strokes.

Strokes may be positive, negative, or crooked. **Positive strokes** (in TA language, warm fuzzies) are transactions that provide an expected response and reassure a person's worth, esteem, or competency: "You're OK!" **Negative strokes** (cold pricklies) are the reverse, resulting in an unexpected, unreassuring response with a "You're not OK" feeling. A **crooked stroke** has a double meaning like an ulterior transaction. It transmits a message different from the words that a person uses.

Organizations have stroking patterns that tend to be closely related to the organization's culture. Effective managers are usually those managers who know how to use conditional, unconditional, and positive strokes appropriately. (See CROCK comic strip.)

Psychological Positions and Scripts

Because of previous experiences, people make decisions about their worth and the worth of others. These feelings lead to **psychological positions** toward oneself and others, including:

- I'm OK, you're OK—this position suggests an acceptance of self and others; a healthy outlook.
- I'm OK, you're not OK—this position suggests a tendency to mistreat, blame, and to put down others.

- I'm not OK, you're OK—this position suggests low feelings of self-esteem or feelings of lack of power or inadequacy compared to others.
- I'm not OK, you're not OK—this position suggests feelings of hopelessness and loss of interest in living, with feelings of confusion and depression.

A person's life can be compared to the script in a play with the person being both the author and central actor of the play. This *script* is an ongoing life plan that an individual has decided to follow. Organizations and units of an organization also live out scripts. The accounting department personnel may be expected to be analytical, cold, and unfeeling in their relationships with other departments. The advertising department, on the other hand, may play the part of a "bunch of wild and crazy guys."

Authentic Communication and Relationships

In TA, the emphasis is upon open and authentic communications and relationships. Muriel James and Dorothy Jongeward have called a *winner* "one who responds authentically by being credible, trustworthy, responsive, and genuine both as an individual and as a member of society" and a *loser* "one who fails to respond authentically."[19] A loser is living in the past or future, intellectualizing and rationalizing. His or her potential remains dormant. When organization members are acting unauthentically, they begin to make mistakes, pass the buck, and complain about the inadequacies of other individuals of groups. TA provides one framework for carrying out change by examining how people relate, communicate, and work. Proponents of TA feel that Adult-to-Adult transactions make for a more effective organization and help develop employee involvement and empowerment.

Multinational corporations can also use TA in preparing managers to operate effectively within another culture. Cross-culture training programs can use the conceptual framework of TA by helping managers achieve an adult ego state.[20]

Perhaps a word of caution should be mentioned. Too often people having little exposure to TA play the "TA game": analyzing or using the jargon on others. TA is perhaps more wisely applied to oneself first before it is applied to others. If a person feels that TA can help solve a problem, it is probably better for that person to discuss it in terms of his or her feelings and reactions, such as "I'm responding like a Parent in this situation" or "I feel like a Child when you treat me that way." Too often people use TA in a one-upmanship game with such statements as "Aha! That's your Child showing now" or "Your Parent is talking now."

Despite such problems, the TA concepts are sometimes presented in training sessions by the OD consultant to the client. It has been found that for some people TA can be a useful framework for understanding and relating to others on and off the job.

Career Life Planning Interventions

OD is aimed at shifting the organization climate to increase the integration of organization and individual goals. The career development aspirations of the individual member are an important element. Managerial career development is an ongoing process of change in activities, positions, and values. People often feel caught in an **organizational trap** because their personal goals and sense of meaning become lost. Many of these individual career problems are symptoms of larger organization problems such as downsizing, closing plants, restructuring, a rigid bureaucratic structure, or intergroup conflict.

Career development in the 1990s has become an even more complicated issue. Companies are reducing the number of management levels and turning over more management responsibilities to rank-and-file employees. In addition, the 81 million baby boomers at a median age of 33 are crowding the management ranks. Echoing these ideas is a representative from recruiting firm Korn/Ferry International who says, "There is a grudging awareness and acknowledgement that there is a slowing down, that organizations are

flatter, and that there are fewer levels to go to. The younger managers I see are not happy about it."[21]

In Chapter 1, socialization was described as the entry of the individual into a new organization. Frequently, the initial entry or socialization process is an important phase leading to eventual career development and personal goals. In the socialization process, individual and organization expectations are exchanged. So, as an individual develops within the organization, his or her career path reaches crisis points where the individual faces a choice between jobs, between professions, or between organizations. At these points, there is a need for the individual to apply some form of career life planning to decide how best to achieve his or her career goals.

Career may be defined as "a continuing process through which a person engages in a sequence of developmental tasks necessary for personal growth in occupational life."[22] The purpose of career planning is to develop and promote high-potential employees in channels where their abilities will be used to the fullest.

Career life planning, one recent form of career development, involves the application of laboratory-learning techniques to career development. There are several different approaches to career life planning. However, all the approaches try to use the idea of goal setting and achievement motivation for the individual to gain greater control over his or her future career development.[23] Career life planning is the process of choosing occupation, organization, and career path.

Steps in a Typical Career Life Planning Program

Career life planning involves the following issues: (1) determining where you are now; (2) deciding where you want to be; and (3) developing a plan for getting where you want to be. The basic intervention involves a sequence of steps. Usually workshop participants work in consulting pairs, each helping the other in the following steps.

Step 1. Each person independently prepares a list of career life goals that usually includes career, professional, personal, and relational goals (List 1).

Step 2. Working in pairs, the consultant (partner) then goes through the list, reality testing (are the goals realistic?), helping set priorities, and looking for conflicting goals.

Step 3. Each person makes a list of important accomplishments or happenings, including peak experiences and satisfactions (List 2).

Step 4. The consultant then works through a comparison of the individual's goals (List 1) with the list of achievements (List 2), looking for conflicts or incongruencies between the two lists. For example, one's goal might be to become an accountant or a research scientist, jobs that involve indoor activities, whereas the list of past satisfactions may show an emphasis upon outdoor activities. The consultant points out the incongruencies to his or her partner. Each person prepares a new list of goals with relative importance of the goals (List 3) based on working with the consultant.

Step 5. Each person prepares a detailed plan of action specifying how to get from where he or she is to where the goals show that he or she would like to be.

Career planning can provide employees with information to enable them to make better career decisions. Although every individual needs to reassess continually his or her life goals and assess the progress toward them, individuals usually undertake career life planning at some crisis point such as when the individual faces possible alternative career patterns. These career goals need to be determined often because an individual's objectives and opportunities change during his or her lifetime.

The Results of Career Life Planning

There is little evidence to show the outcome of career life planning interventions, though there is some evidence to support the theory that career life planning may create a problem of high turnover. In one study, the findings suggest that a career management program was not related to increased satisfaction and commitment. If an organization cannot match its own opportunities to employee's goals, the situation may culminate in employees becoming alienated and leaving.[24] Another researcher concluded that today's workers are showing an increasing willingness to change jobs and careers if barriers block their goals.[25]

Despite the potential drawbacks of higher turnover, even if career life planning programs were abandoned, it is doubtful certain employees will cease to make career changes. It is likely that employee would have quit anyway, only later—after becoming increasingly frustrated and antagonistic.

Though many organizations have career life planning available, Coca-Cola USA set up a systems approach that helps avoid the previously mentioned problems of frustrated goal attainment and increased turnover.[26] Coca-Cola created a system based on performance plans, individual career planning, who succeeds whom upon promotions, and matching and selection criteria. The program helps the individual identify his or her career plans, provides skill and professional training to employees, and provides many ways to communicate to employees about careers and jobs available.

Stress Management and Burnout

Have you experienced job stress, being so completely overwhelmed by job demands, and pressured into doing more tasks than you can reasonably perform? If so, then, welcome to the club, you are like many American employees in the era of downsizing. One survey of 600 U.S. workers, reported that 46 percent said their jobs were highly stressful, and 34 percent reported that the stress was so bad they were thinking of quitting.[27]

Downsizing and other job demands cause incalculable levels of stress in workers who fear losing their jobs, have difficulty handling expanded job responsibilities, and are questioning their loyalty to the organization. **Stress** may be defined as the pattern of emotional and physiological reactions in response to demands from internal or external sources.

Stress is the interaction between an individual and the environment characterized by emotional strain affecting a person's physical and mental condition.[28] Stress is caused by **stressors** which are events that create a state of disequilibrium within an individual. The responses an individual has to the stress may be positive, as when it causes someone to be challenged in the performance of simple tasks or it may be negative, as when someone worries so much about doing a good job that a heart attack results.

The cost of too much stress to individuals, organizations, and society is extremely high. A Gallup Poll study "found that a full 25 percent of the workforce at companies may suffer from anxiety disorders or a stress-related illness, with about 13 percent suffering from depression. . . . In terms of days lost on the job, the study estimated that each affected employee loses about 16 work days a year because of stress, anxiety or depression."[29] In another survey, 36 percent of respondents cited their work situation as the largest cause of personal stress, more than any other cause.[30] As we have suggested, stress often has damaging effects on individuals.

Within the United States, 1.5 million people have heart attacks each year, more than 550,000 of them die, and high blood pressure afflicts 58 million people.[31] According to the National Heart, Lung, and Blood Institute, cardiovascular disease alone in one year accounted for $110 billion in health care and lost worker productivity.[32] Additional statistics exist for other stress-related illness such as ulcers and accidents.

Stress: Major Sources

What are the major sources of stress? Stress can be traced to on-the-job activities and to events occurring away from work. But because people cannot completely separate their

work and personal lives, the way people react and handle stress at work is a complex issue. Until recently, scientists had known with certainty that stressful events could raise blood pressure temporarily, but the long-term effects on heart disease was not definite.

A recent study published in the *Journal of the American Medical Association* concludes "that job strain may be a risk factor for both hypertension and structural changes of the heart in working men."[33] The study is the first time job characteristics have been related to both hypertension and structural changes in the heart. According to the report, jobs causing the most problems were *not* those with a great deal of pressure to work hard and fast such as high-powered executive jobs often associated with heart attacks. Instead, the types of jobs causing increases in blood pressure were lower-level jobs. These were jobs where there was high psychological demands coupled with little control over the workplace and little use of skills.

For "high stress" jobs, the researchers found workers were 3.09 times as likely to have chronic high blood pressure as the control group. But where a high-stress job included ways to control the situation, there was no increase in blood pressure. "What appears to matter is coming to a job every day where the demands are high and the control is down and having to biologically turn on to manage these threats," said Peter Schnall, an author of the report. "The implication of our work is that [in order to increase the health of workers] we should start thinking about job design, about moving toward enhancement of skills, about better job training and increasing worker participation in decision making."[34] Many of the OD interventions discussed in the remainder of this text try to solve these types of problems.

In another long-term study of stress, researchers found some significant areas of concern, particularly as they relate to the work environment.[35] The study explored emotional and mental ill health as it related to worklife. For the group of managers identified in this category, the typical manager tended to be of fairly high intelligence, tense, and suspicious. Further, there was a high degree of job insecurity (such as fear of being laid off), office politics, competition, and lack of teamwork and mutual support present in the job.

To summarize, factors in potentially stressful work activities include:

- Little control of the work environment.
- Lack of participation in decision making.
- Uncontrolled changes in policy.
- Sudden reorganizations and unexpected changes in work schedules (overtime).
- Conflicts with other people (subordinates, superiors, and peers) and other departments.
- Lack of feedback.
- Not enough time to do expected duties.
- Ambiguity in duties expected to be achieved.

Stressful events occurring away from work are extensive but often include problems related to marriage, children, a serious illness, death of a family member or friend, finances, change in social activities, impending retirement, life and career goals, and environmental pollution (noise, traffic, and air quality).

Job Burnout

Job burnout refers to "a syndrome of emotional exhaustion, depersonalization, and reduced accomplishment that can occur among individuals who do 'people work' of some kind. It is a response to the chronic emotional strain of dealing extensively with other human beings, particularly when they are troubled or having problems."[36] Job burnout commonly results in a state of physical, emotional, or mental exhaustion. For example, the burnout at Apple Computer, Inc., is reported to be significant. At a meeting considering a possible retirement plan for ordinary managers and employees, a human-resource staff member dismissed the

idea of a retirement plan with the comment that "we don't expect people to last that long," because the pace at Apple "burns out" many workers.[37]

Recently job burnout has become recognized as a major work stress problem. Burnout seems most common among professionals who must deal extensively with other people— clients, subordinates, and customers on the job. The professionals who seem most vulnerable to job burnout include managers, accountants, lawyers, nurses, police officers, and social workers. Recent studies, however, show burnout is a more widespread occurrence than has previously been thought.[38]

Those persons who experience job burnout seem to show few common personality characteristics, but they do show many significant and consistent job, work setting, and organization characteristics.[39] They tend to:

- Experience much stress because of job-related stressors.
- Be perfectionists or self-motivating achievers.
- Seek unrealistic or unattainable goals.

Under the stress of burnout, the individual can no longer cope with the demands of the job and the willingness to try drops dramatically. The costs of job burnout, both to the organization member suffering from this syndrome and the organization, can be high. Programs for coping with stress, which are examined in the last section of this chapter, are also useful in reducing causes and symptoms of job burnout.

Stress Management Interventions and Coping With Stress

A **stress management intervention** of an organization is any activity or program that attempts to reduce the cause of work related stresses or helps individuals to cope with the negative outcomes of exposure to the stress. The OD program itself is a stress management intervention as OD tries to create an organization that reduces the conditions that lead to harmful type of stressors being placed on its members. Research shows OD interventions are successful in reducing stress.[40] OD interventions such as team building, goal setting, self-managed work teams, and job design will be discussed in future chapters.

The disadvantage of having individuals learn to cope with stress is that it is not reducing the source of the stress. James Quick, a professor of organizational behavior at the University of Texas, says: "One of our concerns is that some of these programs can be used as substitutes for dealing with legitimate workplace issues that are creating stress. The burden of adjustment is often put on the worker. That's illegitimate. It should be shared."[41] Echoing this sentiment is Michael Jones of the California Worker's Compensation Institute who says, "If you can spot the factors that lead to stress and deal with them, you're better off than trying to manage it after it happens."[42]

With this caution in mind, there are things that can help individuals buffer the long-term effect of living with stress. Several methods used for stress management include **wellness programs, biofeedback, meditation, career life planning, stress management training,** and **job burnout seminars.**

Wellness programs. Wellness programs were initially associated with only physical fitness but recently wellness has come to include nutrition counseling and smoking cessation.[43] Johnson & Johnson Company's "Live for Life" program is probably the best-known wellness program and has become so popular with other companies that J&J has made their program commercially available (see OD in Practice). A company with a smoking-cessation program, U-Haul, deducts $5 every other week from the paychecks of employees who smoke, or are either overweight or underweight. "It's an incentive for employees to improve their state of wellness," said Executive Vice President Harry DeShong.[44] U-Haul's insurance plan pays for smoking-cessation and weight-loss programs.

OD IN PRACTICE
LIVE FOR LIFE[45]

Johnson & Johnson's "Live for Life" (LIF) program is a pioneer in health promotion. It is a "total immersion" approach including fitness, smoking cessation, moderation of drinking, nutrition, weight control, blood pressure control, and stress management. J&J also has altered the work environment by establishing a smoke-free corporate headquarters and regional offices, improving nutritional value in company cafeterias, and providing messages about the importance of a healthy lifestyle. The goals of the program are basic: stop smoking, eat more fruit and fewer fatty foods, exercise regularly, and buckle up your seat belt.

The LIF Program

The LIF program includes several levels of services. The first level is a confidential health screening program consisting of a 19-page questionnaire that becomes part of a health-risk profile. A nurse practitioner goes over the results with the employees, takes their blood pressure, and tests their pulse while they exercise. The second level of the programs, if an employee decides to continue with the program, consists of exercise, diet and weight control, and smoking cessation.

J&J headquarters has a gym on-site. At other company locations, facilities are provided on-site or at a local organization such as YMCA.

The Results

J&J has kept comprehensive records of the costs and benefits of the LIF program. Last year the program cost $200 per employee and saved $378 per employee by lowering absenteeism and by slowing the rise in health-care expenses.

In a study that lasted three years and involved 8,000 employees, J&J carefully tracked the program from its introduction. In the first year, the program cost more than it saved. In the second year, it broke even. In the third year, it saved enough to pay back losses incurred in the first year.

The LIF program has been so successful that J&J sells the program to other companies. To date, more than 60 companies with 850,000 employees participate in some form of the service.

The Credo

The LIF program at J&J is compatible with their corporate credo and culture. The Credo (a 44-year-old, 309-word statement created by Robert Johnson, son of the founder) stresses honesty, integrity, and putting people before profits.

As a consequence, *Fortune* named J&J as the most community and environmentally responsible company. J&J's current CEO Ralph Larsen says, "The Credo shouldn't be viewed as some kind of social welfare program. It's just plain good business."

Questions

1. What additions could be made to the J&J LIF program?
2. Must a company's culture be similar to J&J to implement a successful wellness program?
3. How can a company's culture help it to set up a wellness program?

A few companies have spent large sums of money to build gyms and elaborate training facilities to attract employees. Xerox, for example, has a $3.5 million fitness and recreation center in their Virginia training facility and General Foods has health and fitness efforts for 50,000 employees in 30 locations. Other organizations such as Kimberly-Clark, National Aeronautics and Space Administration (NASA), Control Data Corporation, Canada Life/North American Life, AT&T, and Blue Cross and Blue Shield of Indiana among others have some of the better-known wellness programs.[46] Smaller companies and non-profit organizations have also provided lower cost programs by using outside facilities such as those offered at a local college, YMCA, YWCA, or recreational center.

Relaxation techniques. Two commonly used relaxation techniques are biofeedback and meditation. A *biofeedback* course will usually take from several weeks to three or four months. The course takes place in a clinic with a trained technician and will normally begin with an analysis of the person's stress points: work, family, and so on. Instruments that can measure brain waves, heart activity, temperature, and muscle activity are connected to a person to measure physical reaction to stress. By receiving biological feedback from the monitoring machines, the person learns to consciously control his or her autonomic nervous system through decreasing pulse rate and blood pressure. With practice, the person no longer

needs the feedback from the monitoring devices and can practice "biofeedback" out of a clinic and in a work or personal activity that is stressful.

Meditation has reported outcomes similar to biofeedback except that instruments are not used to relax. People using meditation repeat in their mind a specific sound called a "mantra" during two 20-minute sessions a day—one in the morning and another in the late afternoon. Meditators often report higher energy and productivity levels, ability to get along better with others, lowered metabolic rates such as heart rate, and increased creativity.

Career life planning. Some cases of stress in people may need to be treated with career life planning. The sessions may be in a one-to-one or group session as previously explained in this chapter.

Stress management training. The training may include instruction in time management, goal setting, delegation, counseling of subordinates, self-awareness, relaxation techniques, conflict resolution, and identification of stress situations and symptoms. Participation in the programs is usually organization-wide on a voluntary basis and is often open to spouses as well.

Seminars on job burnout. Seminars to help employees understand the nature and symptoms of job problems, such as workshops on role clarity and analysis (see Chapter 10) have been used in many large companies, including Burlington Industries, Campbell Soup Company, IBM, Johnson & Johnson, and Xerox.

Results of Stress Management Interventions

The results of wellness programs are found on several levels: some more quantifiable than others. Medical research has shown the positive effect of exercise on health and the ability of a healthy individual to cope with increased levels of stress. Evidence to date shows a strong positive relationship between fit employees and increased productivity, higher morale, reduced absenteeism, less turnover, fewer worksite accidents, and reduced health care costs to the employer.[47] A five-year study by Blue Cross and Blue Shield of Indiana regarding the effect of wellness programs on earnings showed that it saved $1.45 in health care costs for each dollar spent.[48]

Stress management training, meditation, and biofeedback have been found to decrease pulse rate and blood pressure. One research study found that exercise, stress management, and a relaxation technique (such as meditation or biofeedback) showed significant decreases in pulse rate when used in combination with one another.[49]

In this chapter, the focus has been on interventions that can occur at an interpersonal level. The application of a specific intervention to a client will largely depend on the problems diagnosed. In the next chapter, interventions that are based on the development of the work team will be discussed.

REVIEW QUESTIONS

1. What are the objectives of laboratory training?

2. Identify and explain the four areas of the Johari Window Model.

3. How can you use the Johari Window Model as a tool to understand interpersonal communications?

4. What is the interrelationship between the Johari Window Model and laboratory learning?

5. Explain how Transactional Analysis can help you better understand your communication patterns.

6. Explain the steps in a career life planning program.

KEY WORDS AND CONCEPTS

Define and be able to use the following:

"Buy-in" Management
Biofeedback
Career Life Planning
Disclosure
Ego States
Employee Involvement
Empowerment
Fade Out
Feedback
Job Burnout
Johari Window Model

Laboratory Learning
Meditation
Performance Maintenance
Psychological Positions
Stress
Stress Management Interventions
Stressors
Stroking
Structural Analysis
Transactional Analysis
Transactions
Wellness Program

OD SKILLS SIMULATION 9.1
SACOG

Total time suggested: 1 hour.

A. PURPOSE

In this simulation, you will practice learning to recognize the dimensions of group effectiveness and to observe how these factors inhibit or facilitate group functioning. You will also learn to identify how OD interventions might be used to increase individual and group effectiveness. Factors such as relationships with peers, leadership, information sharing, communications, collaboration, competition, and problem solving will be studied.

B. PROCEDURES

Step 1. Form groups of five members the previous class period and assign roles. Extra class members can be observers or become an OD consulting team. Read the SACOG background information and your role description and make your decision in Column 1, SACOG Decision Form on page 247 before coming to class. The five roles are:

1. Mental Health Director
2. Marriage and Family Counseling Director
3. Job Training and Education Director
4. Drug Abuse Director
5. Alcohol Education and Rehabilitation Director
 OD Consultant (optional)
 Observer (optional)

Step 2. The administrator of SACOG has called a meeting of the five area directors. Because of an emergency Washington, D.C., meeting, the administrator will not be present and has delegated the task to the Directors. The OD consultant, if available, will be present to assist. The observer, if present, will not take part in the discussion. Through team discus-

sion, exploration, and examination, try to reach a *consensus decision* reflecting the integrated thinking and consensus of all members. Follow these instructions for reaching consensus:

1. Try to identify the best strategy.
2. Avoid changing your mind simply to reach agreement and to avoid conflict, but support solutions with which you are able to agree.
3. Avoid "conflict-reducing" techniques, such as majority vote, averaging, or trading in reaching your decision.
4. View differences of opinion as a help rather than a hindrance in decision making.

Enter team decision in Column 2, SACOG Decision Form on page 247.

Time suggested for Step 2: 30 minutes.

Step 3. Use the Team Effectiveness Profile and Transactional Analysis Form to critique the performance of your team. All team members are encouraged to critique the SACOG team meeting. (See pages 247, 248 for forms.)

Time suggested for Step 3: 10 minutes.

Step 4. Meeting with the entire class, compare the decisions made by each team. Then each team shares the results of their Team Effectiveness Profile and Transactional Analysis Form.

Time suggested for Step 4: 10 minutes.

SACOG BACKGROUND INFORMATION

SACOG, Southern Area Council of Governments, is a regional organization of several counties and their towns in a sparsely populated region. The area covers more than 20,000 square miles. SACOG is managed by a chief administrator who heads five social service areas which are in turn administered by directors. The areas are: (1) drug abuse, (2) alcohol education and rehabilitation, (3) marriage and family counseling, (4) mental health, and (5) job training and education. These five social agencies are organized such that they are separate from each other in terms of personnel and financing. They are administered from the central office located in the largest town in the region. Each of the directors of the five areas works out of this office, but they also have their own facilities located throughout the region.

Historically, the five agencies have worked closely together as they realize that in reality people's problems are interwoven. In other words, a person abusing alcohol or drugs is likely to have difficulty holding down a job and has family and mental problems.

SACOG receives financing from area, state, and federal governments and private grants. The total amount for this year is $15 million. The funds received have been increasing by an annual rate of seven percent for the past five years.

Several days ago SACOG received an invitation to apply for a special $1-million, five-year grant from a private foundation. The wording of the invitation indicated that only one application can be submitted and it will have to be very specific, which means that only one of the five agencies will be able to apply for the grant. Because of the large number of minority groups in the area and because SACOG is one of the most advanced, effective, and progressive social programs, there is a high probability of SACOG receiving the grant.

Aside from the substantial increase in funding, the director of the agency selected will have increased job responsibilities and be a much busier director. There will be a sizable pay increase, approximately 25 percent, which will place the salary close to that of the chief administrator.

One condition of the grant is that an advisory council be established to oversee the expenditures. The makeup of the council is to include part professionals (doctors, business people, educators, and so forth) and part community (including minority) representatives.

The group must arrive at a decision on these three items:

1. The agency to be named in the grant proposal.
2. A method of selecting the advisory council: either statewide or by county.
3. The length of term for council members: either two or four years.

The SACOG administrator decided to call a meeting of the five social service directors for the purpose of deciding which one of their areas will be selected to apply for the grant. The administrator did some homework and came up with six criteria believed to be relevant in the selection:

1. the past successes and failures,
2. the number of minorities served,
3. the number of people receiving services,
4. the availability of facilities in the region,
5. the anticipated results, and
6. the need of the community.

ROLE DESCRIPTIONS (READ ONLY YOUR ROLE)

Mental Health Director. As director of mental health, you are responsible for administering the outpatient facilities. The mental health area hires trained and experienced psychologists to staff the positions. The services are entirely on an outpatient basis. In fact, the area has no mental health facilities except the outpatient services provided by SACOG, so the community definitely needs the services. Records indicate that you have worked with 700 people in the past year.

The facilities are located in the three large towns in the area. If people needing services live in outlying areas, they must travel to one of the towns. Because of the large geographical area to be covered and the salaries of the staff, it has not been practical to provide mobile services.

The department has been as successful in its work as some of the better outpatient clinics in the country. Originally, there was some reluctance to use the facilities, but time and success seem to have changed this. Future programs will probably be just as successful. Various pilot programs have been tested in conjunction with a state university, and several have received wide attention. More extensive use of these new programs is planned.

There seem to be very few minority people seeking mental health services. This can partly be attributed to a long history of misunderstanding of the services offered. Furthermore, a study, although not conclusive, shows that there are few mental problems among the minority population. There seems to be a strong indication that many of the people using the services have been referred to you as a last resort.

You are strongly in favor of professionals running the council. Therefore, you support statewide selection so that the three large cities, rather than the rural areas, can dominate the selection process. As professionals are more likely to live in the cities, the statewide selection process will more likely produce professionals on the councils. You also prefer the shorter two-year term, since this will lessen the impact should nonprofessionals be selected.

Although your area is not perfect, you believe that it and the community could greatly benefit from the use of the grant.

Marriage and Family Counseling Director. As director of marriage and family counseling, you are responsible for administering counseling programs in such areas as child abuse, husband-wife relationships, and runaway children. The statistics show good past success for those cases in which your area has been involved. Follow-up studies are favorable. In cases of husband-wife counseling, the divorce rate is lower than the average. In most of

the child abuse cases, children are kept in the natural home instead of foster homes. Runaway children who have been located and brought back home usually do not run away again, and this has been attributed to counseling with the entire family.

There are centers in the three large towns, and several mobile trailers are used to serve the rural communities. The number receiving services has been increasing, up to 3,500 cases annually, although the facilities are geared to more. There seems to be a feeling among staff workers that people are hesitant to confide problems they may have with their marriage or children. Minorities use the services, although no more or no less than their numbers in the census figures would indicate.

Based on past data, there is a fairly high rate of success once a family comes in for help, but not all families who need help come in. The continued police reports of child abuse show a definite need for the services. The divorce rate is still high, although there are signs that it may be dropping. You would like to start working with families before their problems reach the stage of a runaway child or divorce, but you have not been successful in identifying these families and getting them to accept help. Despite this obstacle, it seems that with your past success rate and a definite need for continued services by the community, the future looks promising.

You can see no particular advantage to either statewide or county method of selection of the advisory council or length of term, so you seek to support anyone who will back your area for the grant.

Although your area is not perfect, you believe that it and the community could greatly benefit from the use of the grant.

Employee Training and Educational Director. As director of training and education, you are responsible for assisting the so-called unemployable and those seeking new skills in obtaining skills required for employment. Your department does not actually train people, but it arranges training and usually assists in the financing. Although the State Employment Commission and the Veterans Administration have similar services, there seem to be enough people unemployed and in need of the services that all help is welcomed. Yours and the other agencies often work together and coordinate programs.

As virtually all people for whom training has been arranged have been able to obtain employment, you feel your area has been successful even though there is still a fairly large unemployment rate, particularly among minorities. For those minorities needing the services that you have been able to reach, there has been a respectable, though not overwhelming, acceptance and use of the services. But as your facilities are in the three large towns, the large minority group living in the rural areas has received virtually no assistance. Furthermore, the statistics seem to indicate that if you could arrange training for that large minority group it might be difficult to find employment for them.

The other day you were looking at some statistics that showed that 1,400 people had used the services of your area within the past year. Even though this was only nine percent of the unemployed, it does seem to be a healthy indication that those needing the services are receiving them. Considering the increasing unemployment rate and your past success in training people, the future looks promising.

You feel that professionals should run the advisory council because nonprofessionals are generally less educated and more disorganized. You secretly favor statewide selection where the three large cities will control the selection. This more likely assures that professionals will be selected. Selection on a county basis will likely give more control to the rural areas, which will probably select nonprofessionals. You also want four-year terms so that you will have more time to develop a relationship with the council.

Although your area is not perfect, you believe that it and the community could greatly benefit from the use of the grant.

Drug Abuse Director. As director of drug abuse, you are responsible for administering various programs to reduce drug abuse. These programs include educational efforts in the schools, churches, and other parts of the community, as well as for persons who may

come in contact with a drug abuser—parents, teachers, police-officers, and so on. In educational efforts alone, you estimate that your area has talked to about 10,000 people in the past year. Other programs are specifically directed to the drug abuser, and these programs include one-to-one and group counseling and 24-hour hot-line service. Records indicate that you have worked with 900 people in these specific programs, and there is no information available on the hot-line service.

Research conducted by a private agency indicates that the harsher drugs are readily available, particularly in the larger towns. Also, the use of marijuana is increasing in school systems.

The facilities are concentrated in the three larger towns in the area. There is a toll-free number which is available 24 hours a day. Efforts are being made to serve the smaller towns and rural areas, but it is costly and there are low returns. As a result, you have decided to concentrate your efforts in the three large towns with well-equipped facilities. This strategy has caused some problems with serving minorities, as there is a large minority population living in the rural areas.

Despite some problems in gaining acceptance from the larger segments of the community, your area is making substantial progress. Although drug abuse is increasing, studies indicate that the situation could have been much worse if your area had not been active. Follow-up studies on people who have been counseled by your area indicate a favorable success rate. Considering the increasing availability of drugs and your area's past success, the future looks promising for continued help to the community.

You feel that minority involvement is desperately needed on the council. You support county-based selection which will give greater control to the rural areas where minorities are more likely to live. You also want a longer four-year term, to give the council more time to carry out their plans.

Although your area is not perfect, you believe that it and the community could greatly benefit from the use of the grant.

Alcohol Education and Rehabilitation Director. As director of alcohol rehabilitation, you are responsible for administering and coordinating the various programs. These programs include educational efforts directed at schoolchildren and other potential users as well as people who may interface with potential abusers, such as teachers, employers, and ministers. You estimate that your area has talked to about 10,000 people in the past year. Another phase of the programs includes working directly with alcoholics on an individual and on a group basis, and records show that about 1,100 people have used these services in the past year.

A recent independent study shows that alcoholism exists in all sections of the community and involves a variety of ages, occupations, economic levels, and ethnic backgrounds. As the community is being increasingly educated regarding the dangers of alcoholism, there is more of a willingness to recognize the problem and a motivation to solve it.

The past success has been outstanding. Various experimental rehabilitation techniques have been tried, and several have been successful and have received wide publicity. The more traditional programs have also been used extensively. Even though you have a well-trained staff, you rely to a great extent on volunteer workers.

The services are offered throughout the area. As much as possible you rely on facilities furnished by churches, individuals, and communities. The use of volunteer workers and available facilities has permitted service to the isolated rural communities where a large minority population lives. The number of minority members taking advantage of the facilities has been increasing, perhaps because minority members are now employed as part of the staff and as volunteers. Minorities are more likely to live in the rural areas, and your programs have made a strong attempt to set up programs outside the cities.

You favor a greater role for minorities, so you want the county basis for selection. Statewide selection gives more control to the three large cities where there are fewer minorities. You also favor the shorter two-year term to get more people involved rather than the longer four-year terms. You will compromise on the selection of the council so that you do not alienate possible grant support for your area.

Although your area is not perfect, you believe that it and the community could greatly benefit from the use of the grant.

OD Consultant. You hope to accomplish several things at this meeting:

1. To develop a consultant-client relationship with all the committee members. Try to use the concepts of the Johari Window and Transactional Analysis in working with the members.
2. To assist the committee by doing process consultation during the meeting.
3. To help them work more effectively as a team; however, avoid becoming involved in solving the problem for the team.

Observer Guidelines. You are not to take a part in the SACOG meeting. You are there as an observer so you can provide them information later in Steps 3 and 4. Use the Team Effectiveness Profile and Transactional Analysis Form to record your observations.

SACOG DECISION FORM

	Individual	Team
1. Agency to be named:		
Drug Abuse	_____	_____
Alcohol Education	_____	_____
Marriage/Family	_____	_____
Mental Health	_____	_____
Job Training	_____	_____
2. Method of Selecting		
Statewide	_____	_____
County	_____	_____
3. Length of Term		
Two years	_____	_____
Four year	_____	_____

TEAM EFFECTIVENESS PROFILE FORM

Based on the following scale, rate your team on how it performed on the following scale. Record your choice in the blank.

[Never 1 : 2 : 3 : 4 : 5 : 6 : 7 Always]

Factor	Individual Rating	Team Rating
1. Cooperative teamwork	_____	_____
2. Member satisfaction	_____	_____
3. Team motivation	_____	_____
4. Information sharing	_____	_____
5. Consensual decision making	_____	_____
6. Conflict directly faced and resolved	_____	_____
7. Participative leadership	_____	_____
8. Clearly defined goals	_____	_____
9. Trust	_____	_____
10. Encouraged openness	_____	_____

TRANSACTIONAL ANALYSIS FORM

What ego state was reflected by each Director and the consultant? Try to give specific examples.

	Parent	Adult	Child
Mental Health	_____	_____	_____
Marriage and Family	_____	_____	_____
Job Training	_____	_____	_____
Drug Abuse	_____	_____	_____
Alcohol Rehabilitation	_____	_____	_____
OD Consultant	_____	_____	_____

What kinds of transactions were used? Complementary? Crossed? Ulterior?

Kind of Transaction	Examples
_____	_____
_____	_____
_____	_____
_____	_____
_____	_____

Ego state diagrams can be used to explain an organization's behavior. As well, the organization can have different size circles to indicate the prevalence of Parent, Adult, and Child behavior. An example might be:

Example **SACOG**

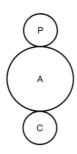

Think of the SACOG meeting in general terms instead of a couple of specific incidents. Do one or two ego states tend to be dominating? In the space above, draw an ego state diagram of different size circles for the team meeting.

OD SKILLS SIMULATION 9.2
JOHARI WINDOW

Total time suggested: 50 minutes

A. PURPOSE

This simulation is intended to provide you with information to compare your perceptions of your own Johari Window with perceptions of others. The survey can be a method to initiate further thought and self-exploration about your communications and interpersonal relations.

B. PROCEDURES

Step 1. After completing SACOG (another team activity such as a case or simulation can be substituted for SACOG), rate your team members by following the instructions in the Johari Window Survey. Additional surveys can be conducted with other team projects. Complete the Johari Window Survey and Table 1 before coming to class. In class, complete Table 2.

Time suggested for Step 1: 30 minutes.

Step 2. As a team and then with the class, discuss the following:

1. Are the results for feedback and disclosure similar for the way I see myself and the way others see me? If they are different, to what could this be attributed?

2. Do my scores seem reasonable?

3. Am I as public, blind, closed, and unknown in my interpersonal styles as I thought I was?

4. If I am not satisfied with my style, what can I do to change? Anything specific?

Time suggested for Step 2: 20 minutes.

JOHARI WINDOW SURVEY

Rating Scale and Instructions

Following is the six-point values scale that you are to use in rating all your team members on the ten Behavior Characteristics. First, become familiar with the criteria for the six-point values scale and then become familiar with the ten Behavior Characteristics.

Value Scale	Meaning
5	Does this consistently.
4	Does this most of the time.
3	Does this frequently.
2	Does this occasionally.
1	Does this on rare occasions only.
0	Never does this.

Then write the names of your team members along the top of the columns on the Rating Sheet (see p. 251). Be sure to notice that the last column is for yourself. Read over the Behavior Characteristics and determine how much each applies to the person you are rating.

Select a value from 0 to 5 that reflects the degree to which this behavior is characteristic of the person. If an item is not applicable, leave it blank. Keep in mind that a score of "0—Never does this" is not the same thing as "not applicable." (Try to avoid leaving an item blank.) Enter the value in the column for the person and the row for the Behavior Characteristic.

You may rate one person at a time on each of the ten Behavior Characteristics, or rate every person on each Behavior Characteristic as you go. Also feel free to use any value from the value scale as often or for as many members as is appropriate.

Be sure to evaluate each person on all ten Behavior Characteristics.

When you have completed your evaluations, cut the rating sheet into vertical strips and give your team members their rating strips. You will, as well, receive a rating strip from each member of your team.

BEHAVIOR CHARACTERISTICS

1. Openly tries to influence others and control the team activities. Is not manipulative in team action.

2. Interacts with the team in an open and candid manner. Is not closed and cautious in relations with others.

3. Listens to others and respects and accepts their comments. Does not dismiss or turn a deaf ear on the comments of others.

4. Says what he or she is thinking no matter how ridiculous it may be. Does not control remarks so they are in line with current ideas of others and thus be more acceptable to them.

5. If he or she feels that others are not leveling and being honest, he or she will press for additional information. Does not let the matter drop or change or allow the subject to be changed.

6. Makes sure that everyone on the team agrees and is committed to the team decisions by specifically testing or questioning them. Does not assume that members are in agreement just because they do not openly voice disagreement.

7. Takes risks in the team by exposing, when it is pertinent, highly personal information that may be both intellectual and emotional. Does not play it safe as though he or she does not trust others.

8. When others try to help him or her, no matter how critical to the point their comments may be, he or she welcomes and appreciates their efforts to help. Does not act hurt, angered, defensive, or rejective of their efforts.

9. Does things that allow others to participate, works to draw everyone into the team discussion, and is supportive of others. Does not just look out for self and leave participation up to each individual.

10. If he or she is angered or upset by others, he or she will openly confront them. Does not pretend to be unaffected or overcontrolled.

RATING SHEET

Behavioral Characteristics	Team Members						Self
1							
2							
3							
4							
5							
6							
7							
8							
9							
10							

SURVEY INSTRUCTION SHEET

On each of your feedback strips you were rated on ten Behavior Characteristics with a score of 0 to 5.

1. You have *two* types of feedback strips: you evaluating yourself and other people evaluating you. Divide the strips into these categories (notice that the word "self" identifies your self-evaluation).

2. Record in Table 1 the data from the feedback strip labeled "self." Move the value score to the rectangle in Column 2 (Feedback) or Column 3 (Disclosure) depending on the rectangle that is not shaded. If you have a microcomputer with Lotus 1-2-3 software available, your instructor may provide you with a spreadsheet template (name of template is SIM9-2.WK1) to calculate your scores.

3. Total Columns 2 and 3. Record the Column 2 Feedback part of the score on the chart by drawing a vertical line at the score. This is the degree to which you actively solicit information about yourself. Record Column 3 Disclosure part of the score by drawing a horizontal line at the score. This is the degree to which you are open and candid of your feelings and the degree to which you share factual information that you know.

4. Add all your points from the "other" strips for each of the ten behavior characteristics. Record the totals in Table 2, Column 1. See the example below.

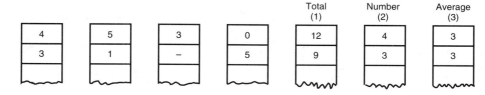

5. Determine the average for each Behavioral Characteristic and record this in Table 2, Column 3 (Average). If you were not evaluated on every Behavior Characteristic on every list, remember to consider this in your average. See the example for how to average a "0" and a blank.

6. Move the averages to the rectangle in Column 4 (Feedback) or Column 5 (Disclosure) depending on the rectangle that is not shaded.

7. Total Columns 4 and 5.

8. The total in Column 4 represents your feedback score. Record the score on the "feedback" part of the chart by drawing a vertical line at the score. Record the score on the "disclosure" part of the charts by drawing a horizontal line at the score.

9. Compare the scores of how you think about yourself from the graph in Table 1 to the scores of how others perceive you in the graph in Table 2.

	From Self Feedback List	Move Col. (1) to Col. (2) or (3) as indicated	
		Feedback	Disclosure
	(1)	(2)	(3)
Total →			

Behavior Characteristics	Total from "Other" Feedback Lists	Number of Times Evaluated on each Characteristic	Average for each Characteristic $\frac{Col. (1)}{Col. (2)}$ =	Move Averages in Col. (3) to Col. (4) or (5) as indicated	
				Feedback	Disclosure
	(1)	(2)	(3)	(4)	(5)
1					
2					
3					
4					
5					
6					
7					
8					
9					
10					
			Total →		

OD SKILLS SIMULATION 9.3
CAREER LIFE PLANNING

Total time suggested: 1 hour 25 minutes.

A. PURPOSE

This simulation will give you experience in preparing career and life plans and in acting as a helper for someone else formulating career life plans.

B. PROCEDURES

Complete Steps 1 and 3 before coming to class.

Step 1. Individually prepare a set of career life goals. The list can include school, career, professional, personal, and relationship goals (list 1).

Step 2. Divide into teams of two: participant and consultant. During the simulation you will be in each role position. The consultant goes through the list of career life goals testing for realistic goals, helping set priorities, and looking for conflicting goals. Revise the List 1 as necessary. When one person has completed, trade positions.
Time suggested for Step 2: 25 minutes.

Step 3. Individually list important accomplishments or happenings, including peak experiences, things that have made you feel happy or satisfied, or times when you felt most alive or real (List 2).

Step 4. Taking a turn at being a participant and consultant, work through a comparison of the individual goals (List 1) with the list of achievements (List 2). Look for conflicts or incongruencies between the two lists.
Time suggested for Step 4: 25 minutes.

Step 5. The outcome of Step 4 is a set of firm goals with relative priorities. Working individually, prepare a detailed plan of action specifying how to get from where you are to where the goals suggest you would like to be (List 3).
Time suggested for Step 5: 15 minutes.

Step 6. First in teams and then as a class, critique the usefulness of a career life planning session. Additional questions include:

• What things did the consultants say or do that were helpful?
• What things did the consultants think they did that were helpful?
• What things did the consultants do that were not helpful?
• What things would the consultants not do again?

Time suggested for Step 6: 20 minutes.

CASE 9
THE SUNDALE CLUB[50]

BACKGROUND

The Sundale Club is the largest athletic-social club in the city. It has been established for many years and has a prestigious reputation. Currently, the membership is slightly under 1,000. In the past, Sundale has had a waiting list for those wishing to join. However, in the past few months the list has been exhausted and the Director, Bob Watts, is considering a membership drive to fill unexpected membership vacancies.

STAFF DIRECTORY

Director - - - Bob Watts
Social Director - - - Carol Happ
Athletic Director - - - Ted Ellis
Asst. Athletic Director - - - Frank Havens
Women's Activities Manager - - - Pat Franklin
Mixed activities Manager - - - Jim Mercer
Men's Activities Manager - - - Chuck Johnson
Women's Fitness Coordinator - - - Alice Smith

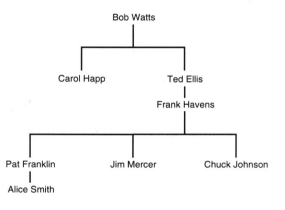

EXHIBIT 9.1

Alice Smith had been thinking about her modeling job on her way home that evening. Today had been a dandy. Ted Ellis, the athletic director, had fired Pat Franklin, who had worked for Sundale for nearly nine years (see Exhibit 1).

THE PROBLEM

The whole mess started five months ago when Ellis hired Chuck Johnson to become the men's activity manager. Shortly after Johnson arrived, rumors started that he was a homosexual. Although Johnson did not fit the stereotype of a homosexual, two of the members complained to Frank Havens, the assistant athletic director, that Johnson had made verbal passes at them.

Ted Ellis and Johnson were close friends, so Havens was reluctant to approach his boss with this problem. During the next few weeks more incidents concerning Johnson's behavior were reported by various staff members to Havens, in addition to complaints from club members.

Havens could sense that his staff was wondering why he had not done something about the situation, and he was aware that seven of the male members had withdrawn from the club. Finally, he requested a meeting with Ted Ellis.

The Meeting

The meeting with Ellis did not go well. Ted Ellis was extremely defensive about Johnson and shouted, "Chuck Johnson has more savvy about this business in his little finger than the whole bunch of you put together."

That night, Frank decided to go over Ellis's head and talk to Bob Watts. Watts was due to retire in the next year, so he did not want to rock the boat in the final days of his tenure with Sundale. Watts tried to convince Frank that it was just a silly rumor.

Frank's working relationship with Ellis was very strained and he continued to receive pressure from below. That week Frank quit the organization and went to work in the same capacity for the competition. The next day, Johnson, who had been working for Sundale five months now, was promoted as the new Assistant Athletic Director.

THE INCIDENT

Pat Franklin was bent! The entire athletic department, with the exception of Ellis, was shocked. Pat had been very dedicated to her job and the organization. Additionally, there was never a doubt that she would get Frank Haven's job when he moved up.

Pat Franklin burst into Ellis's office and demanded to know why she had not gotten the promotion. The next few minutes were rather ugly. Pat left Ellis's office, went to her own office, and began to cry. A knock at the door stopped the flow of tears, but after entering, Alice Smith could tell immediately something was wrong. Pat explained that she had just been fired, which started the tears again. Alice soon joined her.

On her way home, although very concerned about Pat, Alice was also concerned about her own future, and her part-time job as a model. Pat had allowed her to miss up to eight hours from the Sundale club each week to continue the modeling duties. Although she did not really need the modeling money, the job itself was very important to her from a personal satisfaction standpoint; she had to keep trim and well-groomed, which kept her thinking young. Also, the glamor aspect of the modeling profession satisfied her ego.

Carol Happ, the social director, was also starting to feel the effects of the turmoil created in the athletic department. Most of the Sundale Club's income was derived from the club's social activities. Further, Jim Mercer, the mixer activity manager, had noticed the impact of the turmoil within his own department.

Carol, acting on her own behalf, spoke privately to all the athletic department managers with the exception of Ted Ellis and Chuck Johnson. She had hoped to arrange a meeting with Bob Watts but found little support from that department because of their fear of Ted Ellis.

CASE ANALYSIS FORM

Name: _____

I. Problems

 A. Macro

 1. _____

 2. _____

 B. Micro

 1. _____

 2. _____

II. Causes

 1. _____

 2. _____

 3. _____

III. Systems affected

 1. Structural _____

 2. Psychosocial _____

 3. Technical _____

 4. Managerial_____

 5. Goals _____

IV. Alternatives

 1. _____

 2. _____

 3. _____

 4. _____

 5. _____

V. Recommendations

 1. _____

 2. _____

 3. _____

SUMMARY

- **Interventions.** This chapter has presented an overview of several OD interpersonal interventions. The consultant and the client must examine many factors in deciding upon an intervention. They must decide not only the depth of an intervention desired but also the relative advantages and disadvantages of various possible interventions. Employee Involvement (EI), empowerment, and buy-in management are powerful new techniques for unleashing human potential in organizations.

- **Lab Learning.** Although research on the effectiveness of laboratory learning programs shows mixed results, there is evidence to suggest that this technique can influence managerial behavior. OD practitioners have used it successfully in many change programs, such as the OD program at TRW.

- **Johari Window.** The Johari Window provides a way of thinking about ourselves in relation to other people. It also provides two major ways of getting to know and understand ourselves and others: self-disclosure and feedback. The purpose of these two strategies is to enlarge our open areas as much as possible by reducing the blind or closed areas. To the extent that we gain clearer and more accurate perceptions of ourselves and others, we can improve our ways of communicating and working together.

- **Transaction Analysis.** Transactional Analysis is a technique for changing the organization culture by getting people to think about their relationships with others and by providing a framework for improving their managerial style. One manager may assume that people are irresponsible and approach situations like a parent—critical, judgmental, and admonishing; another may act in ways that are dependent, powerless, or rebellious, like a child. Because the nature of people in any organization is changing, the manager or the OD consultant needs to develop new skills in relating to others. These relational skills involve transactions with others, and the way you come across to others may well influence your effectiveness.

- **Life Planning.** Career life planning also provides activities that helps the individual in reassessing his or her life and career goals and in redirecting his or her efforts toward new goals. You may now, or at some point in the future, be at a career decision point where you will want to use this technique to examine your career or life plan.

- **Stress.** Stress and burnout is increasingly having an impact upon organization members. Stress management programs set up by organizations for their members include biofeedback, meditation, career life planning, training in stress management, wellness programs, and seminars on job burnout. The purpose of most of these programs is to help the individual to increase coping skills. OD programs also have as one of their objectives improving organization situations causing harmful stress events.

- **Choice.** One important notion regarding behavior change is the idea of *choice*. Before becoming aware of the consequences of certain behaviors, we often are behaving in certain ways because it has been somewhat effective. Yet, this has been largely by habit and not by choice. As you begin receiving feedback on your "blind spots" and on the impact of your behavior on others, this opens up a choice. You can choose to continue behaving as you have and accept the consequences. Or you can choose to alter your patterns of behavior in hope of changing the consequences to more effective modes. Either way, once you have recognized the choices and take responsibility for your actions, more authentic and effective behavior is possible.

- **Organization efficiency.** Interpersonal interventions are based upon improving organization efficiency by increasing the individual's involvement, motivation, and competence. You have had a chance in the simulation to experience and practice these techniques. You may have gained some insights into your relational style and recognized how such techniques might be used in an OD program.

NOTES

1. Rahul Jacob, "The Struggle to Create an Organization in the 21st Century," *Fortune,* April 3, 1995 p. 90.
2. Barbara Block, "Creating a Culture All Employees Can Accept," *Management Review,* July 1989, p. 41.
3. See for example, Rosabeth Moss Kanter, *When Giants Learn to Dance: Mastering the Challenge of Strategy, Management, and Careers in the 1990s* (New York: Simon and Schuster, 1989); and W. Warner Burke, *Organization Development, A Normative View* (Reading Mass.: Addison-Wesley Publishing Company, 1987).
4. For additional information see: Robert Barner, "Enablement: The Key to Empowerment," *Training and Development Journal,* vol. 48, no. 6 (June 1994), pp. 33–36; Clay Carr, "Empowered Organizations,

Empowering Leaders," *Training and Development Journal,* vol. 48, no. 3 (March 1994), pp. 39–44; Erica G. Sorohan, "The Path to Empowerment," *Training and Development Journal,* vol. 47, no. 10 (October 1993), p. 12; Robert Frey, "Empowerment or Else," *Harvard Business Review,* vol. 71, no. 5 (September/October 1993), pp. 80–94; and Guy W. Wallace, "Empowerment is Work, Not Magic," *Journal for Quality and Participation,* vol. 16, no. 5 (September 1993, pp. 10–14; and Edward Betof and Frederic Harwood, "Raising Personal Empowerment," *Training and Development Journal,* vol. 46, no. 9 (September 1992), pp. 31–34.
5. "Jack Welch's Lessons for Success," *Fortune,* January 25, 1993, pp. 86–93.

6. Scott J. Simmerman, "The Square Wheels of Organization Development," Quality Progress, vol. 27, no. 10, October, 1994 p. 88.

7. Geoffrey Brewer, "Ford," *Incentive*, vol. 167, no. 2, (February 1993) pp. 22–3; and Keith D. Denton, "The Power of EI at Ford," *Journal of Managerial Psychology*, vol. 6, no. 3 (1991), pp. 23–31.

8. Welch, "Jack Welch's Lessons for Success."

9. See the following for a more detailed description: L. Bradford, J. Gibb, and K. Benne, *T-Group Theory and Laboratory Method* (New York: John Wiley & Sons, Inc., 1964); and K. Back, *Beyond Words: The Story of Sensitivity Training and the Encounter Movement* (New York: Russell Sage Foundation, 1972).

10. Mark F. Peterson, "PM Theory in Japan and China: What's in It for the United States?," *Organizational Dynamics*, Spring 1988, pp. 22–38.

11. See the following for a more detailed description: P. Buchanan, "Laboratory Training and Organization Development," *Administrative Science Quarterly*, vol. 14 (1969) pp. 466–80; and J. Campbell and M. Dunnette, "Effectiveness of T-Group Experience in Managerial Training and Development," in *Readings in Organizational Behavior and Human Performance*, eds. Larry L. Cummings and William E. Scott (Homewood, Ill.: Richard D. Irwin, Inc., 1969), p. 760.

12. George A. Neuman, Jack E. Edwards, and Nambury S. Raju, "Organizational Development Interventions: A Meta-Analysis of Their Effects on Satisfaction and Other Attitudes," *Personnel Psychology*, no. 42 (1989), pp. 461–89; and R. A. Guzzo, R. D. Jette, and R. A. Katzell, "The Effects of Psychologically Based Intervention Programs on Worker Productivity: A Meta-Analysis," *Personnel Psychology*, no. 38 (1985), pp. 275–91.

13. John M. Nicholas, "Organization Development Interventions on Hard Criteria Measures," *Academy of Management Review*, vol. 7, no. 4 (1982), pp. 531–42.

14. Zachary Schiller, "No More Mr. Nice Guy at P&G—Not by a Long Shot," *Business Week*, February 3, 1992, pp. 54–56; and Carol Hymowitz and Gabriella Stern, "At Procter & Gamble, Brands Face Pressure and So Do Executives," *The Wall Street Journal*, May 10, 1993, p. A1.

15. J. Luft, *Of Human Interaction* (Palo Alto, Calif.: National Press Books, 1961); and J. Hall, "Communication Revisited," *California Management Review*, vol. 15 (1973), pp. 56–67.

16. John F. Hulpke, CSUB, 1994, sources: Sam Jameson, "Well Connected," *Los Angeles Times*, March 1, 1994, p. 49; James B. Treece, Karen L. Miller, and Richard A. Melcher, "The Partners," *Business Week*, February 10, 1992, pp. 102–7; S. Mark Young, "A Framework for Successful Adoption and Performance of Japanese Manufacturing Practices in the United States," *Academy of Management Review*, vol. 17, no. 4 (October 1992), pp. 677–700; and Kevin Kelly, et. al., "Learning from Japan," *Business Week*, January 27, 1992, pp. 52–60.

17. The discussion is based upon descriptions in Julie Hewson, *Transactional Analysis in Management* (Bristol, England: Further Education Staff College, 1992); Eric Berne, *The Structure and Dynamics of Organizations and Groups* (New York: Grove Press, Inc., 1963); Maurice F. Villere, *Transactional Analysis at Work, A Guide for Business and Professional People* (Englewood Cliffs, N. J.: Prentice Hall Inc., 1981); Thomas Harris, *I'm OK, You're OK: A Practical Guide to Transactional Analysis* (New York: Harper & Row, Publishers, 1969); D. Jongeward and others, *Everybody Wins: Transactional Analysis Applied to Organizations* (Reading, Mass.: Addison-Wesley Publishing Co., 1973).

18. Interview on Cable News Network, Saturday, October 14, 1989.

19. M. James and D. Jongeward, *Born to Win* (Reading, Mass: Addison-Wesley Publishing Co., Inc., 1974), p. 1.

20. Hoon Park and J. Kline Harrison, "Enhancing Managerial Cross-Cultural Awareness and Sensitivity: Transaction Analysis Revisited," *Journal of Management Development*, Vol. 12, No. 3 (1993), pp. 20–29.

21. Joseph Weber "Farewell Fast Track," *Business Week*, December 10, 1990, p. 193. Also see Nancy J. Perry, "The Workers of the Future," *Fortune*, Spring/Summer 1991, pp. 68–72.

22. Allen Ivey and Weston Morrill, "Career Process: A New Concept for Vocational Behavior," *Personnel and Guidance Journal*, March 1968, p. 645.

23. Herbert A. Shepard, "Life Planning," in *The Laboratory Method of Changing and Learning: Theory and Application*, ed. Kenneth D. Benne, et al. (Palo Alto, Calif.: Science and Behavior Books, 1975), pp. 240–51. For additional information see: Gilbert Fuchsberg, "Parallel Lines," *The Wall Street Journal*, April 21, 1993, p. R4; Jacklyn Fierman, "Beating the Midlife Career Crisis," *Fortune*, September 6, 1993, pp. 53–62; and Victor S. Barocas, "Life Planning: Creating the Employer-Employee Partnership," *Employee Benefits Journal*, vol. 18, no. 2, (June 1993), pp. 2–5.

24. Cherlyn Skromme Granrose and James D. Portwood, "Matching Individual Career Plans and Organizational Career Management," *Academy of Management Journal*, vol. 30, no. 4 (1987), pp. 699–720.

25. M. J. Driver, "Career Concepts—A New Approach to Career Research," in *Career Issues in Human Resource Management*, ed. R. Katz (Englewood Cliffs, N.J.: Prentice Hall, 1982), pp. 23–32.

26. Lynn Slavenski, "Career Development: A Systems Approach," *Training and Development Journal*, February 1987, pp. 56–60.

27. Cited in A. Farnham, "Who beats stress best—and how" *Fortune*, October 7, 1991 p. 71.

28. For additional information see: John M. Ivancevich, Michael T. Matteson, Sara M. Freedman, and James S. Phillips, "Worksite Stress Management Interventions," *American Psychologist*, vol. 45, no. 2 (February 1990), p. 252; R. J. Burke and E. R. Greenglass, "Psychological Burnout Among Men and Women in Teaching: An Examination of the Cherniss Model," *Human Relations*, vol. 42, no. 3 (1989), pp. 261–73; J. H. Leigh, G. H. Lucas, and R. W. Woodman, "Effects of Perceived Organizational Factors on Role Stress-Job Attitude Relationships," *Journal of Management*, vol. 14, no. 1 (198), pp. 41–58; and S. M. Puffer and J. T. Brakefield, "The Role of Task Complexity as a Moderator of the Stress and Coping Process," *Human Relations*, vol. 43, no. 3 (1989), pp. 199–217.

29. Robin Goldwyn Blumenthal, "Survey Finds 25% of Work Force Has Anxiety Disorder, Stress-Linked Illness," *The Wall Street Journal*, October 20, 1989, p. A9B.

30. Jonathan Peterson, "Feeling Tense? You're Probably Doing Your Job," *Los Angeles Times*, April 29, 1990, p. A1.

31. President's Council on Physical Fitness and Sports, *Fitness in the Workplace, A Corporate Challenge* (Washington, D.C.:. United States Government).

32. National Heart, Lung, and Blood Institute, *The National Heart, Lung, and Blood Institute Fiscal Year 1986 Fact Book*, (Bethesda, Maryland: Department of Health and Human Services, National Institutes of Health, 1988).

33. Peter L. Schnall, et al., "The Relationship Between 'Job Strain,' Workplace Diastolic Blood Pressure, and Left Ventricular Mass Index," *Journal of the American Medical Association*, vol 263, no. 14 (April 11, 1990), pp. 1929–35.

34. Malcolm Gladwell, "Study Links Job Stress To High Blood Pressure" *The Washington Post*, April 11, 1990, p. 15.

35. Cary L. Cooper and Marilyn J. Davidson, "The High Cost of Stress on Women Managers," *Organization Dynamics*, Spring 1982, p. 45. For the original study see Cary L. Cooper and Andrew Melhuish, "Occupational Stress and Managers," *Journal of Occupational Medicine*, September 1980.

36. C. Maslach, *Burnout: The Cost of Caring* (Englewood Cliffs, New Jersey: Prentice Hall, 1982.)

37. G. Pascal Zachary, "Bruised Apple: Computer Firm's Chief Faces Slowing Growth, Discord in the Ranks," *The Wall Street Journal*, February 15, 1990, p. A1.

38. Cynthia L. Cordes and Thomas W. Dougherty, "A Review and an Integration of Research on Job Burnout," *Academy of Management Review*, vol. 18, no. 3 (October 1993), pp. 621–56.

39. R. T. Golembiewski, R. F. Munzenrider, and J. G. Stevenson, *Stress in Organizations: Toward a Phase Model of Burnout* (New York: Praeger, 1986).

40. R. T. Golembiewski, R. Hilles, and R. Daly, "Some Effects of Multiple OD Interventions on Burnout and Work Site Features," *The Journal of Applied Behavioral Science*, vol. 23, no. 3 (1987), pp. 295–313.

41. Amanda Bennett, "Is Your Job Making You Sick?," *The Wall Street Journal*, April, 22, 1988, Section 3, p. 11R.

42. Peterson, "Feeling Tense?," p. A1.

43. For more information see: Mary A. Papale and Grant D. Lawless, "The Impact of Lifestyle Health Risk on the Bottom Line: A Case Study," *Employee Benefits Journal*, vol. 18, no. 3 (September 1993), pp. 19–21 and Chris Roush, "Wellness Can Mean a Trim Bottom Line," *Business Week*, August 16, 1993, p. 112.

44. Rhonda L. Rundle, "U-Haul Puts High Price On Vices of Its Workers," *The Wall Street Journal*, February 14, 1990, p. B1.

45. Susan M. Seidler, "The Health Project: Using Model Program Data to Design Effective Health Promotion Programs," *Compensation and Benefits Review*, vol. 25, no. 4, (July/August 1993), pp. 30–37; and Neal Templin, "Johnson & Johnson 'Wellness' Program for Workers Shows Healthy Bottom Line," *The Wall Street Journal*, May 21, 1990, p. B1;

46. Sandra L. Fisher, "Vital Signs: Practical Plans to Promote 'Wellness'," *Sales and Marketing Management*, vol. 144, no. 11 (September 1992), pp. 121–22; and Julie C. Mason, "Healthy Equals Happy Plus Productive," *Management Review*, vol. 81, no. 7 (July 1992), pp. 33–37.

47. For a review of research studies, see Chris Roush, "Wellness Can Mean a Trim Bottom Line," *Business Week*, August 16, 1993, p. 112; Glenn E. Haughie, "Corporate Wellness Programs: Are They a Cost-Effective Benefit?" *Pension World*, vol. 29, no. 7, (July 1993), pp. 14–15; and Deborah L. Gebhardt and Carolyn E. Crump, "Employee Fitness and Wellness Programs in the Workplace," *American Psychologists*, vol. 45, no. 2 (February 1990), pp. 262–72.

48. Kathleen Doherty, "Is Worksite Wellness Good Business?" *Business and Health*, vol. 7, no. 2 (February 1989), pp. 32–36.

49. Nelia S. Bruning and David R. Frew, "Effects of Exercise, Relaxation, and Management Skills Training on Physiological Stress Indicators: A Field Experiment," *Journal of Applied Psychology*, vol. 72, no. 4 (1987), pp. 515–21.

50. This case was written by Captain Pete Farmer, USAF, Fairchild AFB, and is used by permission.

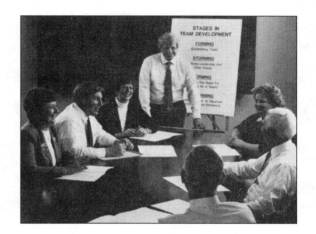

Employee Involvement at Ford. Steering committee members review team-development and participative management ideas. *Photo courtesy of Ford Motor Company*

Team Development Interventions

10

OBJECTIVES

Upon completing this chapter, you will be able to:

1. Identify how team-development techniques fit into an OD program.
2. Recognize team problems and why teams may not be operating at optimum capacity.
3. Understand and experience the process of team development.

PREMEETING PREPARATION

1. Read the Background Information.
2. Complete Steps 1 and 2 of OD Skills Simulation 10.1. Assign roles of five members the preceding class meeting.
3. Read and analyze Case 10: Steele Enterprises.

BACKGROUND INFORMATION

"All right. All right. Green right pitch twenty-nine wing T pull. On two."

My heart jumped and my mouth went dry at the call. I would have to crack back on Whitman, the outside linebacker on the right-hand side. Crawford would try to get outside of my block with the help of the strongside tackle.

Whitman moved toward the sideline in a low crouch, stringing the play out and watching Andy and the leading tackle. At the last second, he felt me coming back down the line at him. I dove headlong as he turned. He tried to jump the block and his knees caught me in the forehead and the side of the neck. We went down in a jumble of arms and legs, my shoulder went numb, and a hot burn shot up my neck and into the back of my head. The play gained eight yards.[1]

The excerpt above describes the team effort involved in running one football play for an eight-yard gain. Most of us have either participated in or watched games that involve teamwork. A **team** is a group of individuals with complementary skills who depend upon one another to accomplish a common purpose or set of performance goals for which they hold themselves mutually accountable.[2] **Teamwork** is work done by members, all subordinating personal prominence for the good of the team. In effective teams, members are open and honest with one another, there is support and trust, there is a high degree of cooperation and collaboration, decisions are reached by consensus, communication channels are open and well developed, and there is a strong commitment to the team goals.[3]

Many management theorists suggest that the team-based organization is the wave of the future. The self-managed team (discussed in Chapter 13) should be one of the basic building blocks of the organization and may well become the productivity breakthrough of the 1990s. Management consultant, W. Edwards Deming (management guru to the Japanese and responsible for much of Japanese post-war industrial success), once said in interview, "An example of a system well managed is an orchestra. The various players are not there as prima donnas—to play loud and attract the attention of the listener. They're there to support each other. In fact, sometimes you see a whole section doing nothing but counting and watching. Just sitting there doing nothing. They're there to support each other. That's how business should be."[4]

In this chapter, we examine some reasons for using team building and discuss several work-team interventions, including team development, outdoor experiential laboratory training, role negotiation, and role analysis techniques. Other team and intergroup interventions, such as goal setting and self-managed work teams, are discussed in succeeding chapters.

The Team Approach

Many organizations are attempting to increase productivity by implementing team based programs. It is reported that almost 80 percent of all U.S. companies have some type of team-based, employee involvement program in place.[5] As an example, several years ago the U.S. Army replaced the method they used of assigning soldiers on an individual basis to their units with a method that keeps soldiers together for their entire tour of duty. The Army believes that individuals perform better when they are part of a stable group; they are more reliable and they take responsibility for the success of the overall operation.

The coordination of individual effort into task accomplishment is most important when members of a team are interdependent. **Interdependence** refers to situations where one person's performance is contingent upon how someone else performs. Sports, such as baseball, football, and basketball, provide some useful parallels for understanding the workings of teams in other types of organizations. Among the three major professional sports, baseball, football, and basketball, according to Robert W. Keidel, basketball is more of a team sport than the other two.[6]

Baseball is a game of pooled interdependence where team-member contributions are somewhat independent of each other. Players are separated geographically on a large field, not all players on the field are actively involved in every play, and each player comes to bat one at a time.

Football, however, involves sequential interdependence where there is a flow of plays and first downs required to score. The players are closer geographically than baseball, and there is a greater degree of interdependence. Players are normally grouped together functionally (i.e., offense and defense) and the two groups do not contact one another. Unlike baseball, all players on the field are involved in every play.

Basketball exhibits the highest degree of interdependence. The players are closely grouped together and the team moves together on the court. Each player is likely to contact any other player and the member roles or functions are less defined than football. All players are involved in offense, defense, and trying to score.

Keidel suggests that organizations could use sport teams as a model for their organization. Some organizations require close teamwork similar to basketball, while other organizations require team involvement similar to baseball. A production manager at Procter & Gamble expressed his vision for his work team using sport terminology when he said, "I have a picture of an ideal basketball team in my head that I compare to the production team. When I see people not passing to each other or when I see somebody taking all the shots, I know we have to work on teamwork. When we're not using the backboard, we need to work on skills. When only part of the team can get rebounds, we have to do cross-training.[7]

One major OD technique, termed **team building** or **team development** (the two terms are generally used interchangeably), is used for increasing the communication, cooperation, and cohesiveness of units to make them more productive and effective.[8] Team building is a databased intervention where a work group examines such things as their goals, structure, procedures, culture, norms, and interpersonal relationships to improve their ability to work together effectively and efficiently. Ford Motor Company has recently begun to stress the team approach for all levels of employees from production line workers to top executives. (See OD in Practice.)

OD IN PRACTICE
PERESTROIKA COMES TO FORD[9]

Ford Motor Company has pulled off what many consider one of the most successful cultural revolutions in corporate America. At one point Ford recorded losses totalling $3.7 billion and nearly went bankrupt. Their products were out of touch with the market and poorly built.

But things have changed at Ford. In recent years, Ford has had a greater net annual income than General Motors—Despite lower sales than GM. Ford's labor cost per vehicle is $1,563, compared with $2,358 for GM and $1,872 for Chrysler. Ford has also been willing to share the wealth. One year, the average hourly worker received a $2,800 bonus.

Much of the success is attributed to a radical departure from a culture that encouraged competing personalities, factionalism, and autocratic management, to a culture that stresses teamwork through employee involvement and participative management. A retired Ford CEO said, "We don't want stars. Being part of a team is a much more productive environment."

Employee Involvement

Ford's success was not won without hard work through several years. The OD program at Ford was first introduced at the bottom with the formation of "Employee Involvement" (EI) teams consisting largely of line workers. The EI process involved teamwork training. One convert to the team process is Jim Bradley, a longtime pipe fitter at a Ford plant and a UAW member, who says "I used to come to work eight years ago and I would get out of my car, get back in and go home. Now I love to come to work. Things have turned around here 180 degrees."

At about the same time EI was introduced at the bottom levels, there was pressure to change placed on upper and middle management by the CEO and President. According to Ford's Chuck Tyson (an internal OD consultant), "They [EI teams] began to make suggestions about how to reorganize the work and how to lay out the plants. The ideas would bub-

ble up into middle management and into upper management. There was concern within Ford Motor Company that as this happened, those ideas would be blocked by a culture that rewarded very authoritarian kinds of behavior."

Participative Management

To ensure that the new ideas would take hold, the OD division at Ford introduced "Participative Management: Phase I." These were five-day management seminars for top teams of managers at Ford plants to experience participative management and to build support for the change programs. The seminars normally involved 100 participants from three or four management levels.

The seminars were designed to raise the dissatisfaction level of the status quo to the surface so that it was commonly expressed. At the seminars the participants created a common vision of where they wanted to go and to begin planning some first steps. About one year later "Leadership for Change: Phase II" seminars were introduced to teach specific participative management skills to carry out the goals made during Phase I.

Top Management Support

Ford made an up-front decision not to try to quantify the success of the program. This was a departure from Ford's tendency to put a dollar figure on everything. The programs were supported from the top and were constantly plugged at plant visits by the CEO and President. The symbolism was backed with cash and, though many programs were cut because of hard times, the budget for the employee-involvement and participative-management programs were never cut.

Questions

1. Why did Ford start an OD program?
2. What are some reasons for Ford's success with their OD program?
3. At what levels did team building occur?

Team building grew out of the application of laboratory learning (see Chapter 9) used principally during the 1950s and 1960s. The participants in laboratory learning groups were traditionally strangers. When laboratory learning was first used in organizations, the groups were also traditionally composed of strangers, often coming from different organizations. As laboratory learning developed and changed over the years, participants who worked with one another were brought together to deal with interpersonal issues and team functioning. This arrangement was often called *family groups*. The results were often mixed and disappointing due largely to the lack of structure in laboratory groups. But the lack of structure gradually evolved into a defined process of training people to work effectively as a team.

There are several reasons for using team development to improve organization effectiveness. First, the work group is the basic unit of the organization and thus provides a supportive change factor. And second, the operating problems of work groups are often sources of inefficiency.

Teams or work groups often have difficulty in operating effectively. Problems that inhibit effective operation include lack of clear objectives, interpersonal differences or conflicts, ineffective communication, difficulty in reaching group decisions, and inappropriate power and authority levels in the group. Consequently, team-development techniques are used in change programs to increase work team effectiveness. The work team reviews and evaluates its own functioning and develops improved work and relational patterns. The emphasis is on exploring the team's functioning and processes by its own members, usually with the help of a process consultant.

The Need For Team-Development Techniques

The team or work group is the primary unit in the organization and there is an increasing reliance on project teams, task force groups, and committees to accomplish organization goals. For example, Chrysler Corporation has overhauled its top-down autocratic management structure that retired CEO Lee A. Iacocca encouraged and relied upon. According to some Chrysler employees, Iacocca talked so much that he often answered his own questions. The current CEO, Robert J. Eaton, uses a team leadership style and acts as a coach

and listener who dismisses the trappings of power in favor of teamwork and consensus-building.[10] American Airlines Chairman, Robert Crandall, predicts, "The very finest products and services are going to be produced with a team effort, rather than through the more hierarchical management approaches that have tended to characterize this country."[11]

Work teams may be of two basic types. The first type, the *natural work team*, refers to people coming together because of the related jobs or the structure of the organization design. The second type, the *temporary task team*, refers to groups meeting for limited periods of time to work on a specific project or problem, and after the solution of the problem they disband. As task teams are designated to work on organizational and technological problems, there is an increasing need for collaboration and coordination of the variety of resources that are brought together. Collaboration does not automatically happen, but it is possible with the use of *team-development techniques*. For example, General Motors recognizes the effort necessary for team development to take place at their new Saturn assembly plant. When the Saturn plant first opened, employees were required to attend five days of "awareness training" designed to teach them how to learn cooperative work-methods. Less than three years later, GM had cut team development training by 50 percent or more in an effort to cut costs. Some of the original workers have complained that the newer workers (who often came to Saturn from closed GM plants) tended to be less enthusiastic about team cooperation. The local UAW (United Auto Workers) has pressed for more up-front training so the new arrivals can quickly learn about Saturn's work teams, cooperation, and worker self-management.[12] A great deal of the Saturn's success has been attributed to the high quality performance of these highly autonomous work teams.

In deciding if team building is appropriate, Marvin R. Weisbord has described the process as somewhat straightforward.

> First, the boss calls a meeting, introduces the idea, states his or her personal goals and asks for discussion. If, as is common, a consultant has been hired, the parties need a "get-acquainted" meeting to decide whether to go forward. Often the consultant interviews team members to discover their basic concerns. Questions might include each person's objectives, the problems each faces, and the extent and kinds of help people need from each other. The consultant, then, presents a summary of interview issues to the whole team, inviting a discussion of priorities and the pros and cons of continuing the process. If the decision is made to proceed, the group schedules one or more longer meetings specifically for team building.[13]

The Use of Team Development

Some practitioners feel that team building is becoming an overused technique because many teams agree they don't want to work together, can't work together, and have no reason to work together.[14] Given these limitations, an important thing to accomplish before beginning a team development intervention is to examine the degree of team member interaction. Situations which require interaction tend to fall into three categories: (1) simple situations; (2) complex situations; and (3) problem situations. The kind of task to be performed, then, determines the requirement of a team (see Figure 10.1).

A *simple situation* is one that can be solved by an individual. For example, an electronic engineer may need to consult occasionally with colleagues to obtain technical information to design a routine component, but the project is one that the engineer is expected to complete alone based on technical expertise. There is no need to involve others except to pass along or obtain information. The involvement of others may slow down the organization's functions. Managers operating in a simple situation focus on their responsibilities, do not involve others in their work, and, therefore, avoid wasting valuable time. Good social skills are important, but team development is not needed for work groups involved with simple situations.

According to Rosabeth Moss Kanter,[15] teamwork and employee participation are not needed when:

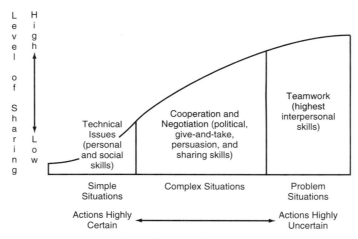

FIGURE 10.1 Situation Determines Teamwork

- There is one person who is obviously more of an expert on the subject than anyone else and those affected by the decision acknowledge and accept that expertise.
- There is an obvious correct answer.
- The task or problem is part of someone's regular job assignment, and it wasn't his or her idea to form the team.
- There is little or no interest in the issue.
- The involvement of others will not contribute to the issue nor would their knowledge or expertise be increased by the team experience.
- There is no time for discussion.
- Employees work more happily and productively alone.

Complex situations encompass the predominant portion of a group's work. There is a need to share information at a level that allows work to be accomplished, since the members cannot do the task on their own. However, input is not required from all group members and the level of the input is not deeply personal. These types of activities arise constantly in most organizations and members handle them by cooperating with one another. For example, members of a finance department of a large company will need to cooperate with each other in getting out the quarterly financial statements. Acting alone, no one person would have enough information or time to complete the statements, so information is shared and members help one another. Team development is not essential, but it is recommended because members need to cooperate and negotiate with each other and coordinate their activities. Good interpersonal skills are required including the ability to compromise, to see situations from another member's point of view, to negotiate, to persuade, to listen, and to share information.

Problem situations are atypical, consequential, unprecedented, and have an impact outside an individual's scope of influence. For example, a company that is planning to introduce a new product must work effectively not only within respective departments to formulate plans but also between departments to arrive at a general strategy. The uncertainty involved with these types of problems and the need to involve others in the solutions requires a team-building approach.

Different modes of working require different processes. Rosabeth Kanter contends that the team approach is appropriate:[16]

- To permit members to gain new expertise and experience and to develop and educate members.
- To allow those who know something about the subject to become involved.

- To build consensus and commitment on a controversial issue.
- To work on a problem that does not belong to any one person.
- To allow more creative discussions by pulling together people of unusual and different backgrounds and interests.
- To avoid the obvious decision and explore a variety of effects.

Operating Problems of Work Teams

When individuals are brought together to work on some problem or goal of the organization, there is likely to emerge a complex pattern of behaviors, interaction, and feelings between the members. A primary function will be to preserve the norms of the team and protect it from outside pressures perceived to be threats. Those people who receive rewards from the team and support the team's norms represent a core of "regular" members. At the other extreme are usually the "isolates," who have little to do with the others and seem to have little interest in and need for observing the norms.

The team also satisfies several important individual needs. If these needs are frustrated by organizational obstacles, then problems arise for both the individual and work organization. The satisfaction of social needs such as affiliation, acceptance, and status are important for most individuals and often these needs are partially met through the team. Work teams provide emotional support and identity for the individual. The lack of support is noticeable when work teams are dissolved such as in a reorganization or company takeover. Work teams also serve the valuable purpose of helping the individual in attaining goals and accomplishing the task.

A survey sponsored by the American Management Association found the principal causes of organization conflict included value differences, goal disagreements, poor cooperation, authority and responsibility disputes, poor personal performance, frustration, competition for organization resources, not following policies and work rules, misunderstandings, and personality clashes.[17] The sources of team operating problems shown in Figure 10.2, include the following elements.[18]

Goals. The individual often has difficulty in defining and clarifying his or her goals, and in work teams the problem is multiplied. Often objectives become misunderstood, confused, or changed without any definite clarification. Similarly, teams tend to lose their purpose and direction, and goals require testing from time to time to figure out whether they are going full steam, but in the wrong direction.

Member needs. As previously noted, teams also fill several needs of individuals, and frequently the satisfaction of completing the task is overemphasized at the expense of the social and personal needs of team members. There may be interpersonal differences, conflicts, or misunderstandings that hinder team effectiveness. Members may take sides and reject any compromise, or they may attack each other in subtle ways. Such interpersonal "garbage" or hang-ups need to be brought out and resolved.

FIGURE 10.2 Sources of Team Problems

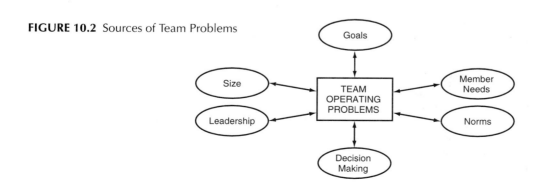

Norms. The team must develop norms about behavior patterns. Frequently, team members do not have the opportunity to communicate. Members need a chance to share problems, to discuss progress, and to touch base with one another.

Decision making. Another frequent source of difficulty in teams is the way decisions are made. Decisions may be made by authoritarian decree, by majority rules, or by unanimous rules. Each method has advantages and disadvantages. There is a good deal of evidence to show that members implement more effective decisions when they use consensus rules.[19]

Leadership. One key issue for teams is the degree of power and control that the members have over themselves and others. Consequently, groups sometimes suffer from a low level of participation, boredom, or apathy. Certain groups and individuals function better in a more structured, authoritarian situation, whereas others do not. For example, production units may operate better with more structure, while research groups probably do better with more independence.

Size. A work team can consist of as few as two members to as many as 25 or 30, but five to seven is generally considered the most effective size. Members of a small team behave differently than they would in a large team. A team of two or three generally is too small to be effective, whereas 12 members are probably the upper limit for the members to interact with every other member. With even larger teams there is a greater likelihood that subteams of five to seven will form to handle specific concerns.

Cohesiveness

The term **group (or team) cohesiveness** refers to the attractiveness a group has for its members. Some groups have more closeness and team spirit among members, and such groups are more cohesive than those where members are indifferent. Cohesiveness can act to improve group performance. But as Irving Janis has pointed out, group cohesiveness can make the need for uniformity greater than the need of high-quality decisions.

Groupthink is a theoretical framework postulated by Janis to describe the problems of group cohesiveness. Groupthink refers to "a mode of thinking that people engage in when they are deeply involved in a cohesive in-group, when the members striving for unanimity overrides their motivation to realistically appraise alternative courses of action."[20]

Eastman Kodak Company's insular management is an example of groupthink. The physical location of Kodak in Rochester, New York (where it has been located for over a century), means that managers have little chance to mix with counterparts from other companies. *Fortune* has called Kodak a champ, maybe *the* champ, of inbreeding and insularity. Many employees' social lives revolve around company events. At Kodak, consensus has become the norm, and confrontation is frowned upon.[21]

Groupthink often occurs when the members of groups avoid being too harsh in their judgments of their leaders' or their colleagues' ideas. In their behavior and thinking, they adopt a soft line of criticism. The members are friendly to one another and seek complete concurrence on every important issue. There is no disagreement or conflict to spoil the cozy, "we-feeling" atmosphere.

Janis identifies eight characteristics of groupthink and the problems tending to result from it:[22]

1. *Illusion of invulnerability.* Most or all the members share an illusion of invulnerability that masks obvious dangers and leads them to take extraordinary risks and causes them to fail to respond to clear warnings of danger.
2. *Rationalization.* Members construct rationalizations that allow them to discount warnings or other negative information.
3. *Illusion of morality.* Members unquestionably believe in the inherent morality of the group's position. Other groups with opposing views are thought of as evil. This type of thinking allows the group to disregard ethical or moral consequences of their actions.

4. *Shared stereotypes*. Views of opposing groups and especially their leaders are seen as evil or so stupid the opposing group could not possibly understand reasonable negotiations between differing groups.

5. *Direct pressure*. The group applies direct pressure to any other member who expresses doubts about the group's positions or who questions the validity of the arguments supporting a position.

6. *Self-censorship*. Avoidance of expressing views that differ from what appears to be a group consensus and minimize to themselves the importance of their doubts.

7. *Illusion of unanimity*. An illusion that all group members are in agreement. It is partly based on the false assumption that individuals who remain silent agree with the group.

8. *Mind guards*. Self-appointed members serve to protect the leader and other members from adverse information external to the group that might disrupt the cohesiveness of the group.

The consequences of group problems are usually not clearly understood, but most managers agree that these problems influence motivation, morale, and productivity. Empirical investigations of groupthink do not conclusively support Janis's theory. There are, however, studies that generally support the groupthink phenomenon, but suggest that many intervening factors are not included that influence decision outcomes.[23]

The Purpose of Team Development

A very broad objective of team development is integrating the goals of the individual and the group with the goals of the organization. To do this, work teams need to spend some time on the process of their team interaction, that is, *how* they work together and what they accomplish. When a baseball team executes a difficult cutoff play, a basketball team executes a precise fast break, or a football team scores on a long-pass play, it looks smooth and easy. Yet this ease and precision come from hours and hours of practice and attention to details of *how* to run the play.

The process of work teams in organizations is just as demanding and precise as in many sports activities (see B.C. comic strip), but how many work teams ever examine their performance?[24] Not very many do, and their reason is: "We're too busy." Yet, it is difficult to imagine any effective basketball or football team too busy to practice or review performance. This is what team development is all about. It is an intensive examination of team operation focusing upon *how* members function as a team, and how they can overcome operating problems and improve efficiency.

Each team has its own structure, norms, and values, and members of the team tend to do things in certain ways. Often, the loyalty of members is greater to fellow team members than to the organization. Because of these characteristics, team-development techniques are used to clarify goals and priorities, to examine how decision and communication are functioning, and to recognize how the relationships among team members influence output. The goals of team development include:

Source: By permission of Johnny Hart and Creators Syndicate, Inc.

- To identify objectives and set priorities.
- To examine the content or task performance of the team.
- To analyze group process; that is, how the group is functioning.
- To improve communications and relationships among group members.
- To improve the ability of the team in solving problems.
- To decrease unhealthy competition and increase cooperation among the team members.
- To work more effectively with other teams in the organization.
- To increase the team member's respect for each other's individual differences.

It should not be inferred that conflict within a team leads to organization ineffectiveness and, therefore, should be avoided. Conflict in some situations may be healthy and improve the performance of a work team.

Conflict is a natural social interaction and managers should be able to recognize the types of conflict and channel it in appropriate directions.[25] Conflict can be healthy when it is issue-oriented rather than personality-oriented, when it sharpens people's thought processes, when it is germane to the goals of the team, and when it does not produce winners and losers with the accompanying social stigma. The OD consultant's responsibility is to find effective methods to deal with the conflict and resolve any unhealthy conflict.

The Team-Development Process

Organizations are becoming increasingly complex. No one person can possess all the knowledge necessary to analyze satisfactorily and to solve such complex problems. In these instances, teams of work groups are used to bring together the expertise required for proper analysis and solution of the problem. Because of the nature of work groups, team-development interventions are probably the single most important and widely used OD activity. (See Our Changing World.)

OUR CHANGING WORLD
THE GOLD BADGE TEAM[26]

U.S. automobile companies have been working harder lately to instill a spirit of teamwork throughout their organizations. Team approaches can help develop the organizational culture needed to meet the global challenges of the twenty-first century. This is why *team building* or *team development* are major OD techniques. The team, for one thing, can be a supportive change factor in an organization.

Team Building in Japan

Sharp is one of many Japanese organizations to realize and take advantage of this potential. Sharp pushes and encourages teams throughout the organization, but with a special twist. To help insure an innovative corporate culture, something that is absolutely essential in the competitive and quick changing consumer electronics industries, Sharp has created a special way to reward top innovators. Sharp puts them on "Gold Badge Project Teams" which report directly to the company president. According to *Fortune* magazine, this special privilege instills pride in the elite Gold Badge Teams. Other workers set out scrambling for new ideas and new products hoping that they too might "make the team."

The Gold Badge Team

How does the Gold Badge Team idea work? *Fortune* is upbeat. "Something as simple as a reward can help make a culture more innovative," according to the magazine. The Gold Badge Teams at Sharp are doing more than just improving the corporate culture. Specific results are attained. "One result: the best-selling Wizard, an electronic organizer."

The Gold Badge Teams at Sharp offer one more perspective on the versatility and utility of the team approach. As the chapter points out, teams and teamwork can help management levels function better, can help communication and effectiveness between levels, and can work to mold a "Can Do" culture on the front lines. Through its use of elite Gold Badge Teams, Sharp shows another role of teamwork: encouraging an innovative culture. It's worth thinking about.

Questions

1. Do you agree with the Gold Badge Team Approach? Why or why not?

2. Do you think the Gold Badge Team approach could back-fire on Sharp? Support your position.

The team-development process, described by several practitioners, recognizes two separate types of activities.[27] *Family group diagnostic meetings*, one type of team development, are aimed at identifying group problems. *Family group team-building meetings*, another orientation of team development, are aimed at improving the team's functioning. The following description incorporates both activities.

Team development is an educational process of continually reviewing and evaluating team functioning and identifying and establishing new and more effective ways of operating. Team development is an ongoing experience; that is, it is occurring simultaneously with the work itself.

A team-development meeting has dual objectives: first, the task or work agenda of the group; and second, the processes by which members work on the task. Team-development meetings, normally guided by a consultant using process skills (see Chapter 7), focus on the process of the team, including the team's working relationship and its patterns for accomplishing tasks. In the team-development meetings, members learn how to look at their ways of behaving, diagnose any operating problems, and figure out new and more effective ways of functioning. It should be stressed that team development is not a one-time activity undertaken in the presence of a consultant. Once a team learns how to make process interventions, it can continue team development as an ongoing part of the group. The main purpose is to get team members involved in solving problems and in the decision-making process.

The procedure for team-development training meetings generally follows a similar format, although the specific contents and activities of the meetings can differ significantly. Such a procedure includes certain basic steps.

Step 1: Initiating the Team-Development Meeting

Within an organization the initiating of the team-development meeting may come from several different sources. Operating problems of a group may have been identified and diagnosed through the previous stages of the OD program. The team-development meeting may be initiated by a manager higher in the organization structure who is not a member of the team. The need for a meeting also may be apparent to the consultant, or the manager of the work group may initiate the team-development meeting. Although initiating the team-development meeting may come from any of these people, the decision to proceed is usually collaborative. The degree to which members support team development largely determines the success of the effort.

These topics include:

- Degree of team supporting.
- Deciding what tasks need to be done.
- Deciding if a team is necessary.

Step 2: Setting Objectives

After the decision to proceed, the next step is setting some broad objectives to be accomplished at the meeting. Such objectives might consist of evaluating the working processes of the team or improving their effectiveness. For an effective team-development meeting, there should be general agreement on the objectives before the meeting.

The consultant may want to ask some pertinent questions before proceeding any further, such as: What is the purpose of this meeting? What do the participants and I want to do? Why this group of people at this time? How does this meeting fit into the OD program? What is the priority given to this project? Is there real interest and commitment among team members?

These topics include:

- Evaluating team process.
- Determining team authority.
- Deciding on team's goals.
- Setting priorities.

Step 3: Collecting Data

Data may be collected from the team members in various ways, but as much information as possible is gathered before the meeting. One source is the information that was gathered in Stage 4 of the organization change process: the collection of information (see Chapters 2 and 5). The usefulness of this information depends on the extent to which it can be specifically identified with the team as opposed to the total organization. Additional questionnaires may be administered to the team members or members may be interviewed by the consultant. The consultant may have a minigroup meeting with the manager of the team and a few participants. The consultant also may have a two- to four-hour preteam-development meeting with all the members, designed especially to gather information.

These topics include:

- What resources are needed.
- Setting boundaries—who is and is not a team member.
- Clarifing the behaviors expected of each member.

Step 4: Planning the Meeting

The participants of the planning session may include any of the following: the consultant, the manager, and a few of the team members. Once the data have been analyzed, the actual planning may take place. An important point at this time is to restate the goals and objectives as specifically as possible considering information obtained during the previous step. The goals should be specific behavior objectives so that the remaining work of planning the sequence of events of the meeting may flow more easily and logically. Going through this process will better ensure a meeting that satisfies the needs of those involved.

These topics include:

- Providing time and place for meeting.
- Ensuring that all necessary personnel and resources are available.

Step 5: Conducting the Meeting

The meeting itself usually lasts two or three days. It is preferable that the physical setting be on "neutral territory," that is, away from the work area, such as at an isolated resort. A major reason for this is that it helps to place everyone—superior and subordinate—on a more equal level. It also lessens the opportunities for interruption. The nonwork setting also can help to create a climate for change and exploration of new ideas by the team members.

The meeting usually begins with a restatement of the objectives previously agreed upon. The data are presented to the entire team, with attention placed on problem areas or issues in which the team has expressed an interest, and then the team forms an agenda ranked in order of priority. At this point the team usually begins to work on the list of priority items. The team critiques its own performance to prevent dysfunctional actions and to improve functional activities. If the members feel that this is an opportunity for them to express open and honest feelings without fear of punishment, the superior or the leader of the team may come under attack. The pre-meeting interviews will have showed this possibility and the leader should be forewarned and prepared by the consultant for this eventuality. The way the manager reacts to the situation can mean success or failure to the team development meeting.

Once members have resolved interpersonal issues, the team members can deal with task issues that need to be discussed so that they may better solve their problems. The purpose is

for the team to develop specific action plans for improving the ways or processes it uses to reach its organization goals. Before the meeting ends, the team should list action items to be dealt with, who will be responsible for each item, and a time schedule. This will allow the team meeting to end officially, but it also allows the team-development effort to continue back in the work environment. The team further agrees on a future date to meet again to evaluate progress on the action items.

Topics include:

- Giving a concensus on all team goals and processes.
- Listing action items.

Step 6: Evaluating the Team-Development Process

In this meeting, the team examines the action items, exploring those that have been or are being carried out and those that are not working. Determination is made of how well the implemented action items have aided the team's operation and what further can be done. For those items that are not working, an evaluation is made about their necessity, and those action items that are not needed may be discarded. Items that appear to be helpful may then be given additional attention and support.

Topics include:

- Methods of resolving ongoing problems.
- Acquiring necessary resources.
- Continuous improvement.

Results of Team-Development Meetings

The research on the effectiveness of team building suggests that it is proving to be very positive, and it is currently a popular intervention being used in organizations. In an analysis of 126 studies that used OD interventions, they, in general, positively affected attitudes toward others, the job, and the organization. The analysis found team building to be the most effective OD intervention.[28] In a study of a team-building intervention in one major corporation, Donald F. Harvey and Neal Kneip found that team activities resulted in a greater clarification of problems and an awareness of a need for change in the organization.[29] For a different and high-tech approach to team development, see OD in Practice: Electronic Team Development.

OD IN PRACTICE
ELECTRONIC TEAM DEVELOPMENT[30]

Several companies are trying an unusual approach to meetings: one that encourages frank talk ("I've had enough—I'm looking for another job") and fast fingers. The approach calls for networking 20 to 50 personal computers around a horse shoe-shaped table. Participants sit at a personal computer and type in their messages for all to read. There is no talking as all communications are through the computers.

A computer program tracks and sorts topics typed in by participants. It then displays the messages on a central projection screen. The source of the message stays anonymous. To make up for lost nonverbal communications, the sender can add symbols to signify laughter, anger, boredom, and a smile. At the end of the meeting, everyone gets a printed synopsis.

Electronic Mail

DEC and a number of other companies have elaborate electronic mail systems which connect people around the world.

At DEC, about 75,000 people in 26 nations are linked together. DEC claims to be the best networked corporation in the world. It allows anyone on the system to "talk" to anyone else. This unrestricted approach differs from most organizations which restrict messages along organization lines. At DEC, a programmer sitting at a remote site on the Mojave desert near Death Valley can talk to another programmer in Australia or the company President.

Roar Like a Lion

The electronic meeting, however, is different from DEC's approach in that the participants are in the same room, looking at each other over their computer screens. No one knows who is typing in what. The approach can be brutally honest. One user says the anonymity of talking through a computer "turns even shy people powerful." Companies are finding they

can get valuable, unfiltered information. Managers get feedback that can be threatening or insightful, depending on what the manager chooses to do with the information. Some managers have taken improvement courses as a result of the feedback.

Even managers who shrink at the process give the meetings high marks for efficiency. When you have to type in everything that is communicated, the process tends to cut down on chitchat.

Users of the Electronic Meetings

A study by IBM and the University of Arizona found that the electronic meetings are as much as 55 percent faster than traditional meetings. Phelps Dodge Mining Co. held its annual planning meeting electronically. Usually the planning session takes days, but lasted only 12 hours when held electronically.

More companies like Greyhound Dial Corp., IBM, and Southwest Gas Corp. have tried the meetings. IBM is perhaps the biggest supporter of the idea. It has built 18 electronic meeting rooms and plans 22 more. Those taking part at IBM include the Chairman and 7,000 other IBMers. A project manager at IBM says the electronic meetings have "brought people together" who traditionally skirmished with one another.

The Drawbacks

Though anonymity has its advantages, there are also some drawbacks. Those people who are computer shy are reluctant to get heavily involved in the process. And the members find it helpful to be able to type. For those who come up with good ideas at the meetings, the system of anonymity makes it impossible to give credit to the person responsible.

One participant at a meeting typed in: "It's sad that we can't talk without sitting at terminals."

Questions

1. Do you think the electronic meeting could be used in an OD team-building session? If so, how?
2. What do you see as the advantages and disadvantages of the approach?
3. Do you think the electronic meeting could get people to talk verbally, face to face? Why or why not?

Outdoor Experiential Laboratory Training

Within the last few years, **outdoor experiential laboratory training** (sometimes called outdoor labs, wilderness labs, adventure learning, or the corporate boot-camp) has become a common technique used for team development and leadership training.[31] The idea is to take a group of people who normally work with one another and place them in an outdoor setting where they participate in experiential-learning exercises. The outdoor setting provides a different setting than the normal work environment and the learning exercises are typically foreign and varied enough to most participants' background that no one has a distinct advantage. Thus the outdoor lab puts most participants on an equal footing. This seems to hasten discussions surrounding leadership styles, teamwork, and interpersonal relationships.

The types of outdoor lab experiences run the spectrum from backpacking into wilderness areas to spas at luxury resorts. Some require extreme physical exertion in a setting of some physical danger. One type of outdoor lab has participants doing technical rock climbing where they are working in teams helping one another do climbs that none could do alone. Another outdoor lab has participants canoeing or rafting in white water. Rock climbing and canoeing involve physical conditioning and potentially dangerous situations in which not all employees would be willing or able to participate.

Other types of outdoor labs require very modest physical exertion with almost no element of danger. These labs rely upon props such as ropes stretched between trees that participants must cross. There is an element of perceived risk but the danger has been reduced by relying on safety ropes and nets. At these labs it is common to rely on the imagination of the participants to create the element of danger. For example, participants walking a twelve-foot long four-by-four inch board that is one foot off the ground can be an effective learning exercise. Participants are first told to imagine that the board is spanning a moat full of alligators. Then, having their fellow workers cheering them on to success can build the right kind of atmosphere for the learning exercise.

All the labs, despite the setting or the nature of the exercise, have participants involved in activities that require teamwork and allow opportunities to work on leadership and team development. After an exercise and in the evening, the team spends time with a consultant critiquing, debriefing, and discussing the exercise and the day's events with an emphasis upon what they learned. The learning normally provides participants with insights into their leadership and interpersonal styles. As a team, participants often learn how to improve their teamwork back on the job. Interpersonal barriers that inhibit effective teamwork are often broken down and members learn to trust and work with one another. Holding the lifeline for someone suspended off a cliff has a dramatic impact on both parties when they return to work where they need to trust and depend on one another in a less dramatic setting.

True physical risk taking is not the goal of most outdoor labs. Perceived physical risk makes the exercises exciting so that participants are challenged to do their best. One participant explained, "It felt great. Negotiating the elements takes ingenuity and teamwork. It's about having confidence and taking risks and supporting each other. People broke down a lot of barriers on the ropes course—some of the toughest ones in the office were scared to death up there. Now we're communicating in a whole new way."[32]

The Outdoor Lab Process

Outdoor labs are typically offered by training companies that specialize in them. Some organizations that use the labs extensively, such as Federal Express, operate their labs through the OD or human resource development divisions. To be something more than a company retreat that has only short-term gains, the outdoor lab needs to fit into a larger program that builds the ground work for the lab and follows through after the lab has ended. Many who have been active in outdoor labs say that the success of a lab is directly proportional to the amount of preplanning and follow-up.

Whether an outside provider or a company offers the labs internally, a preliminary assessment of the team and individual needs is made before the lab occurs. Goals and learning objectives of the outdoor lab are drawn up. When the outdoor lab is part of an OD team-development program, then this assessment has previously been made and the lab becomes an integral part of the OD program, similar to other OD interventions. An orientation meeting is held with participants at their work site before the lab is begun to explain what happens at the outdoor lab, the purpose of the lab, and calm fears. A videotape may be shown of other team sessions.

The internal or external OD consultant decides the type of outdoor lab experiences that would be appropriate to fit the desired goals and the physical abilities of the team. Assuming the lab will be offered by another company specializing in this type of training, a training program is arranged. Many providers of outdoor labs will design a training program to a team's specific objectives. Some providers will send their trainers to a company ahead of time to research the needs of the team. The team's OD consultant also may accompany them at the outdoor lab.

The type of training will dictate the location and facilities. A backpacking trip or rafting trip may take place in a wilderness or a National Park, a sail boat excursion may be in the Florida Keys, but most training programs take place at private, rural facilities where ropes, platforms, and other props are in place and sleeping and eating facilities are available. A good trainer will be well versed in corporate and bureaucratic jargon and use process consultation techniques.

After exercises and at the end of the day, trainers ask the work team to reflect on their process. Constructive feedback between participants is encouraged. They discuss how they operated as a team, what behaviors were helpful and dysfunctional, what it was like to take a risk and succeed or fail, how it felt to depend on other people, what it was like to give assistance, who acted in leadership roles, and how these observations might apply to the next exercise.

Before returning to the work place, participants spend time summarizing what they have learned and how it applies to work. Team members draw up goals for what they hope to do back at work and they make a plan for how they can accomplish the goals. Back at work, the team holds meetings to define the goals and develop more detailed plans. The trainer will often make a follow-up visit to the work site after several weeks to reinforce the learnings of the outdoor lab. The OD consultant also helps the team continue to work on their goals.

Cautions in Using Outdoor Labs

Outdoor labs are not without their risks to both the organization and to the individual. But by taking some modest precautions, most problems can be minimized.

It is beyond the scope of this discussion to present the legal consequences of outdoor labs but like any work activity, the employer is liable for the health and safety of its employees.[33] Safety should be a major concern and the safety record of the provider and safety training of the trainers should be investigated. In one lab, a participant of a youth-oriented outdoor lab died of dehydration and heat exposure when the trainers and their group got lost in a remote area north of the Grand Canyon. The group consisted of troubled youths and the trainers designed the program to help them gain self-esteem and self-control. Although there has not been a known death in a corporate outdoor lab, safety should be a major concern. For both liability and OD philosophical reasons, participants must be free to participate. There should be no coercive pressure to participate. Participants should also feel absolutely free to decline to participate in specific exercises.

There are fundamental questions about the value of outdoor labs as management training. AT&T spokesperson Burke Stinson says, "These programs can be a colossal waste of money if people don't return with new thinking and an expanded ability to take risks. Unless you follow up, the afterglow tends to wear off as soon as the scabs heal."[34]

Providers of outdoor labs are not regulated, and there is no professional organization that licenses them or serves as a reference. It is easy to get caught up in the flash of the exercises and not give attention to the experiential learning that should be taking place. There should be a balance of both exercises and opportunities to discuss the processes of the exercises. The trainers should be capable of more than guiding a group backpacking into a wilderness area. They should have much of the same training, skills, and experiences as an OD consultant, and should be selected with similar care.

The labs should not become too serious. Participants should have fun and do not need to be constantly drawing parallels between the lab and the work site. One trip leader on a backpacking trip in the Rockies recalled the story of a group consisting of a company's CEO and top executives. One manager halfway through the trip could no longer carry his pack. The lab leader pointed out that this was a team problem, just as it was in the work place. The CEO told the manager to pick up the pack or face being fired. The manager refused and the CEO subsequently fired him. Says the trainer, "That CEO thought everything out there related to the office. One thing it did mirror, for sure, is that the CEO is a _____ of a _____."[35]

Results of Outdoor Labs

Outdoor labs have become highly popular within the last few years as a team-development and leadership-training technique. Major corporations such as AT&T, Times Mirror, General Motors, IBM, Frito Lay, and Citicorp use outdoor labs and hundreds of smaller profit and not-for-profit organizations have sent their employees to the labs. Du Pont recently contracted with one provider for the training of 20,000 managers.

Although the popularity of the labs abounds, outdoor labs are new and studies documenting their effectiveness are limited. One study found that there was significant improvement that lasted over 15 months in the general functioning of the work teams.[36] There was, however, no significant change in individual behavior. Another study found that the suc-

cess of outdoor labs was unrelated to where the training was held.[37] This study found that the process, not the setting, facilitates behavior changes. The study also found that intact work teams, rather than teams of participants who did not work with one another, reported more benefit from outdoor labs.

A study at Martin Marietta conducted by a private consulting firm compared two work groups who had similar characteristics except one participated in outdoor labs and the other did not. The group that participated had an annual turnover rate of 1 percent and the other group had turnover of 11 percent, the company average. The study also found that those who participated had increased promotions and greater employee commitment.[38]

Though additional research needs to be conducted on outdoor labs, there is encouragement for use of the labs. Like many other OD interventions, when the techniques are taken out of the context of an OD program and become a fad, their effectiveness is diminished. When the labs are not introduced with planning and followed up correctly, they become expensive topics of conversation at cocktail parties.

Role Negotiation

Role negotiation, is directed at the work relationships among team members. The technique involves a series of controlled negotiations between participants. During the role negotiation, managers frankly discuss what they want from each other and explain why. The steps of role negotiation include the following:

1. *Contract setting*. Each member prepares a list for each other member with three headings: (a) things to do more, (b) things to do less, and (c) things to do the same.
2. *Issue diagnosis*. Each member writes out a master list combining the lists written about him or her, and posts this list on the wall. Members are then asked to clarify any items that need explanation.
3. *Role negotiation*. After the clarification, members decide which items they want most and form into pairs to negotiate, usually with a third party to help in the process.
4. *Written role negotiation agreement*. The outcome of the role negotiation is a set of written agreements spelling out the agreements and concessions which each party finds satisfactory.

Role Analysis

Another team-development intervention, called **role analysis technique** (RAT), is designed to clarify role expectations.[39] Because team norms influence member behavior, members form expectations about one another's behavior. The set of behaviors or attitudes associated with a particular position in a team is called a role. At times team members develop discrepancies between what is expected of each other. **Role analysis is** used to clarify such role discrepancies, leading to improved cohesiveness and functioning.

Role expectations are those behaviors of one member (role incumbent) expected or prescribed by other team members, while **role conception** refers to the focal person's own ideas about appropriate role behavior. **Role ambiguity** refers to the role incumbent's being unaware of or lacking sufficient knowledge of the expectations of others. In other words, he or she does not fully know what others expect.

When there is an incongruence or a discrepancy between the role expectations and the role conception, the **role conflict** occurs. Incongruence between formal job descriptions and actual role demands is another source of role conflict. Because the team members have a stake in each person's performance, they develop attitudes and expectations about what a member should or should not do in his or her role. Unfortunately, these expectations cannot always be in agreement, and role analysis provides a means for dealing with such problems. This intervention is based on the premise that consensual agreement about team member roles will lead to a more productive and satisfied team.

The steps of role analysis technique include the following:

1. *Role analysis.* The role incumbent sets forth the role as he or she perceives it, listing perceived duties, behaviors, and responsibilities: the role conception. Other team members add to or modify this list until all members are satisfied with the role description.

2. *The role incumbent's expectations of others.* The role incumbent lists his or her expectation of other group members. This list describes those expectations of others that affect the incumbent's role and impinge upon his or her performance. Again, the whole team adds to or modifies this list until they agree upon a complete listing.

3. *Role expectations by others.* The other members list their expectations of the role incumbent. This list includes what they expect him or her to do as it affects their role performance. The work team modifies this list until they all agree.

4. *Role profile.* Upon agreement of the role definition, the role incumbent is then responsible for making a written summary called a role profile. He or she distributes a copy of the completed role profile to each member.

5. The team follows the preceding procedure until each member has a written role profile.

6. Periodically, the team reviews role expectations and role profiles, since these may change over time and group mission or members also may change.

As with other OD techniques, there are reports of increased effectiveness from role-analysis techniques, but there is little empirical evidence upon which to base any conclusion. According to Dayal and Thomas, role analysis has been a useful technique for reducing role ambiguity and increasing group effectiveness.[40]

The focus of this chapter has been on developing team effectiveness. In the next chapter the discussion of OD will move to examining conditions for conflict and discuss several techniques for dealing with relations between teams.

REVIEW QUESTIONS

1. Identify the characteristics of effective teams. Is a golf team really a team, or just a group?

2. Identify and give examples of ways of increasing team effectiveness.

3. Identify the symptoms of groupthink. Explain how groupthink can be avoided through team development.

4. Identify the six steps in the team-development process.

KEY WORDS AND CONCEPTS

Define and be able to use the following:

Group Cohesiveness
Groupthink
Interdependence
Natural Work Team
Outdoor Experiential Laboratory
 Training
Role Ambiguity
Role Analysis Technique (RAT)

Role conception
Role conflict
Role negotiation
Team
Team development
Teamwork
Temporary task team

OD SKILLS SIMULATION 10.1
ORGANIZATION TASK AND PROCESS

Total time suggested: 1 hour, 10 minutes.

A. PURPOSE

The two parameters of group effectiveness include (1) the determination of the *one* best solution to the problem and (2) the completion in the shortest amount of time.

The purpose of this simulation is to experience and observe parameters of interpersonal and group issues that inhibit effective organization functioning. Specifically, it is to experience interdependence and to observe:

1. How task information is shared among team members.
2. How various problem-solving strategies influence results.
3. How collaboration and competition affect group problem solving.

B. PROCEDURES

Step 1. During the preceeding class, form groups of five members. Additional class members may serve as observers. Each individual is to select one general manager role from the following:

1. General manager, United States plant
2. General manager, Japan plant
3. General manager, Germany plant
4. General manager, Nigeria plant
5. General manager, Mexico plant
 Observers (optional)

Step 2. Following the Energy International Briefing Sheet you will find Role Descriptions and the Candidate Summary Sheet. Read the Briefing Sheet and your role description before coming to class. Make individual decision on E.I. Decision Form (Col. 1, p. 284).

Step 3. Your group is to select the correct candidate based upon the data you will receive. There is *one* correct solution, and decisions are to be reached independently of the other groups. Make Team Decision on E. I. Decision Form (Col. 2, p. 284).

The observers will not take an active part during this phase of the simulation. The observer will focus on answering the questions in Step 4 of this simulation. All groups will begin upon the signal from the instructor.

Time suggested for Step 3: 45 minutes.

Step 4. In your groups, consider the following questions with the observers (if available) guiding the discussion:

1. What behaviors seemed to help your group to successfully complete its task?
2. What factors inhibited problem solving?
3. How much time was spent on deciding *how* to solve the problem?
4. How was information shared among the group?
5. How did issues of authority or power affect the group?
6. How did collaboration/competition influence the outcome?
 Time suggested for Step 4: 10 minutes.

Step 5. Discuss the questions in Step 4 with the entire class.

Time suggested for Step 5: 15 minutes.

ENERGY INTERNATIONAL BRIEFING SHEET[41]

A. INSTRUCTIONS TO THE GROUP:

1. You are a committee made up of the general managers of Energy International (E.I.).
2. You have just flown into town.
3. This is the first meeting of the group.
4. You have just learned that E.I. will open a new Brazilian plant, and your first job is to select a general manager from among the seven applicants.
5. Basically, the data you bring with you are in your head.

B. ASSUMPTIONS THAT NEED TO BE MADE EXPLICIT:

1. Assume that there is one solution.
2. Assume that all data are correct.
3. You have 45 minutes to work the exercise.
4. Assume that today's date is April 1, 1995.
5. There must be substantial agreement when the problem has been solved.
6. You must work the problem as a group.

ROLE DESCRIPTIONS (READ ONLY *YOUR ROLE*)

General Manager, United States Plant. Your group is a committee made up of the general managers of Energy International, a young, medium-sized growing organization. The prime mission of E.I. is to locate and develop mineral claims (copper, uranium, cobalt, etc.).

The company's business has grown rapidly, especially in South America, where your organization has been made welcome by the various governments. In a recent meeting the Board of Directors decided to develop a new property near Fortaleza, in northeastern Brazil. This operation will include both mining and milling production.

The date is April 1, 1995. You have come from your respective plants in different locations. This is the initial session of your annual meeting. Your first order of business today is to select a new General Manager for the Brazilian plant from among the candidates on the Candidate Summary Sheet.

Fortaleza has a hot climate, one railroad, a scheduled airline, a favorable balance of trade, a feudal attitude toward women, considerable unemployment, a low educational level, a low literacy rate, and a strongly nationalistic regime.

The government has ruled that the company must employ Brazilians in all posts except that of General Manager. The government has also installed an official inspector who will make a monthly reports to the government. This report must be signed by the company's representative, who must be a Fellow of the Institute of Mineralogy.

There are a number of schools offering degrees in mineralogy; the most recently founded is the New Mexico Institute of Earth Sciences. This institute was established under a special grant and opened in 1965.

To earn a bachelor's degree in mineralogy, this school requires geology, seismology, and paleontology, in addition to the usual courses.

General Manager, Japan Plant. Your group is a committee made up of the general managers of Energy International, a young, medium-sized, growing organization. The prime mission of E.I. is to locate and develop mineral claims (copper, uranium, cobalt, etc.).

The company's business has grown rapidly, especially in South America, where your organization has been made welcome by the various governments. In a recent meeting the board of directors decided to develop a new property near Fortaleza, in northeastern Brazil. This operation will include both mining and milling production.

The date is April 1, 1995. You have come from your respective plants in different locations. This is the initial session of your annual meeting. Your first order of business today is to select a new General Manager for the Brazilian plant from among the candidates on the Candidate Summary Sheet.

Fortaleza has a hot climate, one railroad, a scheduled airline, a favorable balance of trade, a feudal attitude toward women, considerable unemployment, a low educational level, a low literacy rate, and a strongly nationalistic regime.

The government has ruled that the company must employ Brazilians in all posts except that of General Manager. It has also installed an official inspector who will make a monthly report, which must be countersigned by the General Manager. By law, the General Manager must have had at least three years' experience as a manager in charge of a mining operation.

There are a number of schools offering a degree in mineralogy, a degree essential to qualify for general membership in the Institute of Mineralogy. The smaller universities require three, the larger four, of the following special subjects as a part of their graduation requirements: geology, geophysics, oceanography, paleontology, seismology. The smallest is a women's university.

General Manager, Germany Plant. Your group is a committee made up of the general managers of Energy International, a young, medium-sized, growing organization. The prime mission of E.I. is to locate and develop mineral claims (copper, uranium, cobalt, etc.).

The company's business has grown rapidly, especially in South America, where your organization has been made welcome by the various governments. In a recent meeting the Board of Directors decided to develop a new property near Fortaleza, in northeastern Brazil. This operation will include both mining and milling production.

The date is April 1, 1995. You have come from your respective plants in different locations. This is the initial session of your annual meeting. Your first order of business today is to select a new General Manager for the Brazilian plant from among the candidates on the Candidate Summary Sheet.

Fortaleza has a hot climate, one railroad, a scheduled airline, a favorable balance of trade, a feudal attitude toward women, considerable unemployment, a low educational level, a low literacy rate, and a strongly nationalistic regime.

The government has ruled that the company must employ Brazilians in all posts except that of General Manager. It has also installed an official inspector who will make a monthly report, which must be countersigned by the company's representative. None of the government inspectors can read or write any language but Portuguese.

There are a number of schools offering degrees in mineralogy, and a passing grade in paleontology is essential to qualify for general membership in the Institute of Mineralogy. The largest university is the New York School of Mines, which requires the following special subjects for graduation: geology, paleontology, geophysics, and seismology.

General Manager, Nigeria Plant. Your group is a committee made up of the general managers of Energy International, a young, medium-sized, growing organization. The prime mission of E.I. is to locate and develop mineral claims (copper, uranium, cobalt, etc.).

The company's business has grown rapidly, especially in South America, where your organization has been made welcome by the various governments. In a recent meeting the Board of Directors decided to develop a new property near Fortaleza, in northeastern Brazil. This operation will include both mining and milling production.

The date is April 1, 1995. You have come from your respective plants in different locations. This is the initial session of your annual meeting. Your first order of business today is to select a new General Manager for the Brazilian plant from among the candidates on the Candidate Summary Sheet.

Fortaleza has a hot climate, one railroad, a scheduled airline, a favorable balance of trade, a feudal attitude toward women, considerable unemployment, a low educational level, a low literacy rate, and a strongly nationalistic regime.

The government has ruled that the company must employ Brazilians in all posts except that of General Manager. It has also installed an official inspector who will make a monthly report, which must be countersigned by the company's representative. None of the company's employees or staff can read or write any language but Portuguese.

There are a number of schools offering degrees in mineralogy, and a passing grade in seismology is essential to qualify for a general membership in the Institute of Mineralogy. The Massachusetts Institute of Sciences requires the following special subjects for graduation: geology, seismology, oceanography, and paleontology.

General Manager, Mexico Plant. Your group is a committee made up of the general managers of Energy International, a young, medium-sized, growing organization. The prime mission of E.I. is to locate and develop mineral claims (copper, uranium, cobalt, etc.).

The company's business has grown rapidly, especially in South America, where your organization has been made welcome by the various governments. In a recent meeting the Board of Directors decided to develop a new property near Fortaleza, in northeastern Brazil. This operation will include both mining and milling production.

The date is April 1, 1995. You have come from your respective plants in different locations. This is the initial session of your annual meeting. Your first order of business today is to select a new General Manager for the Brazilian plant from among the candidates on the Candidate Summary Sheet.

Fortaleza has a hot climate, one railroad, a scheduled airline, a favorable balance of trade, a feudal attitude toward women, considerable unemployment, a low educational level, a low literacy rate, and a strongly nationalistic regime.

The government has ruled that the company must employ Brazilians in all posts except that of General Manager. It has also installed an official inspector who will make a monthly report, which must be countersigned by the company's representative, who must be an American citizen.

Fellowship in the Institute of Mineralogy can be obtained by men over 35 years of age who have otherwise qualified for general membership in the institute. St. Francis University, which is not the smallest school, requires the following special courses for graduation: paleontology, geophysics, and oceanography.

ENERGY INTERNATIONAL DECISION FORM

	Criteria					(col. 1) Individual Decision	(col. 2) Team Decision
	1.	2.	3.	4.	5.		
R. Illin							
S. Hule							
T. Gadolin							
U. Samar							
V. Lute							
W. Noddy							
X. Lanta							

ENERGY INTERNATIONAL CANDIDATE SUMMARY SHEET

Name:	R. Illin
Date of Birth:	March 2, 1960
Passport:	L3452—U.S.A.
Education:	New York School of Mines, degree in mineralogy, 1980
Employment:	Research Assistant, New York School of Mines, 1981–1983
	Lecturer, Mineralogy, University of Bonn, 1989–1993
	Manager, Utah Copper Mining Co. Plant, 1993 to date
Language command:	English, French, German, Portuguese

Name:	S. Hule
Date of Birth:	May 4, 1952
Passport:	H4567—U.S.A.
Education:	New Mexico Institute of Earth Sciences, degree in mineralogy, 1978
Employment:	Uranium Unlimited, Management Trainee, 1978–1980
	Anaconda Copper Co. (Montana area), Geology Officer, 1981–1988
	Manager, Irish Mining Co. Ltd., 1985 to date
Language command:	English, French, Portuguese

Name:	T. Gadolin
Date of Birth:	June 5, 1953
Passport:	L7239—U.S.A.
Education:	New York School of Mines, degree in mineralogy, 1978
Employment:	United Kingdom Mining Board, Management Trainee, 1978–1980
	Assistant Manager, N.D.B. Cheshire Plant, 1981–1989
	Manager, Idaho Cobalt Minerals, 1989 to date
Language command:	English, Portuguese

Name:	U. Samar
Date of Birth:	April 6, 1961
Passport:	H6259—U.S.A.
Education:	Massachusetts Institute of Sciences, degree in mineralogy, 1982
Employment:	Jr. Engineer, West Virginia Mining Research Station, 1982–1991
	General Manager, Liberian State Mining Plant, 1991 to date
Language command:	English, German, Swahili, Portuguese

Name:	V. Lute
Date of Birth:	August 6, 1958
Passport:	K62371—U.S.A.
Education:	New York School of Mines, degree in mineralogy, 1979
Employment:	Jr. Development Mineralogist, Ontario Mining Constr. Ltd., 1979–1982
	Assistant Chief Mineralogy Officer, Canadian Dev. Board, 1983–1986
	Plant Manager, Welsh Mining Co. Ltd., 1987 to date
Language command:	English, French, Welsh, Pekingese

Name:	W. Noddy
Date of Birth:	August 7, 1951
Passport:	H63241—U.S.A.
Education:	St. Francis University, degree in mineralogy, 1976
Employment:	Assistant Manager, Société Debunquant d'Algerie, 1976–1980
	Manager, Kemchatka Mining Co., 1978 to date
Language command:	English, Portuguese, Russian, Arabic

Name:	X. Lanta
Date of Birth:	September 8, 1958
Passport:	Q123YB—Canada
Education:	University of Quebec, Diploma in English, 1978
	Massachusetts Institute of Sciences, degree in mineralogy, 1981
Employment:	Technical Officer, Sardinia Mining Corp., 1983–1991
	Manager, Moab Valley Mining Plant, 1991 to date
Language command:	Spanish, English, Portuguese

OD SKILLS SIMULATION 10.2A
TEAM DEVELOPMENT

Total time suggested: 1 hour, 20 minutes.

A. PURPOSE

To provide an opportunity for team members to diagnose and analyze their team functioning and to work on improving team processes.

B. PROCEDURES

Step 1. Form into the same teams, including the observers, as in Simulation 10.1. Working individually and using Simulation 10.1 as a source of information, complete the Team Development Profile and Decision Critique Form.

Step 2. Working with your team, collect data on team roles from Step 1 by summarizing and categorizing data using a blackboard or newsprint.

Time suggested for steps 1 and 2: 30 minutes.

Step 3. Team members analyze and discuss team functioning. Members may practice process consultant interventions (see Suggested Process Interventions).

The analysis may include the following questions:

1. How was our problem-solving capability?
2. How was our decision making done?
3. How well did we utilize team resources?
4. How did member behavior influence effectiveness?

Time suggested for Step 3: 20 minutes.

SUGGESTED PROCESS INTERVENTIONS

Try to focus your questions on the problem that seems to be emerging. Encourage the speakers to be specific. Be aware of who is and who is not talking; who talks to whom.

Questions about how people are feeling at the moment are appropriate. As an example, such a question to a member as "How did you feel when X said _____ to you?" might be appropriate. Explore feelings with the purpose of discovering how these are helping or hindering the problem solution. Additional questions include the following:

1. What behaviors seem to be aimed more at individual member needs than at task accomplishment?
2. What behaviors seemed to aid in task accomplishment?
3. How satisfied are members with current group functioning?

Step 4. Working in teams, develop a list of actions that will help improve group functioning for future team projects.
Time suggested for Step 4: 15 minutes.

Step 5. Each team shares its list and action plans from Step 4, and the class discusses team-development process.
Time suggested for Step 5: 15 minutes.

TEAM DEVELOPMENT PROFILE

Based upon the team problem-solving simulation, answer the following questions.

1. Name the two group members who had the most influence on the outcome.

2. Name the two group members who talked the least.

3. Name the two group members who talked the most.

4. Name the two group members who have tried to keep the group warm, happy, and comfortable.

5. Name the two group members who have competed or conflicted the most.

6. Name the two group members who have avoided or smoothed-over conflicts.

7. Name the two group members you would most like to work with on another project.

8. Name the two group members who have been most concerned with the accomplishment of the task.

9. If your team was a sports team, what sporting event would best describe your team behavior (for example: golf, football, roller derby, baseball, professional tag-team wrestling, track, or basketball)? Why did you choose this sport? What would be your and your opponent's score?

DECISION CRITIQUE FORM

Instructions: For each item, place a number in the blank to the right representing your reaction to how your group performed based on the following scale.

[Low 1 : 2 : 3 : 4 : 5 : 6 : 7 : 8 : 9 : 10 High]

1. Degree of cooperative teamwork: _____
2. Degree of team motivation: _____
3. Degree of member satisfaction: _____
4. Degree of information sharing (participation): _____
5. Degree of consensual decision making: _____
6. Degree of team conflict or competition (i.e., conflict directly faced and resolved): _____
7. Degree of quality of group decisions: _____
8. Degree of speed with which decision is made: _____
9. Degree of participating leadership: _____
10. Degree of clarity of goals: _____

OD SKILLS SIMULATION 10.2B
ROLE-ANALYSIS TEAM DEVELOPMENT

Total time suggested: 1 hour, 20 minutes.

A. PURPOSE

To give you practice in the role-analysis technique of team development.

B. PROCEDURES

Step 1. Form into the same teams as in Simulation 10.1. The observers in Simulation 10.1 will help the team using process interventions. (Observers: see Suggested Process Interventions in Step 3 of Simulation 10.2A) Select one manager at a time to serve as the role incumbent. Work through Steps 2 through 4 until a role profile has been made for each manager. Large newsprint pads will be helpful to record the information so all team members can see the recorded information.

Step 2. Role analysis. The role incumbent sets forth the role as he or she perceives it, listing on the newsprint perceived duties, behaviors, and responsibilities: the role conception. Other group members add to or modify this list until all team members are satisfied with the role description.

Step 3. The role incumbent's expectations of others. The role incumbent lists his or her expectation of other team members. This list describes those expectations of others that affect the incumbent's role and impinge upon his or her performance. Again, the whole team adds to or modifies this list until a complete listing is agreed upon.

Step 4. Role expectations by others. The other members list their expectations of the role incumbent. This list includes what they expect him or her to do as it affects their role performance. This list is also modified until it is agreed upon by the entire team.

Time suggested for Steps 2 through 4 for all managers: 50 minutes.

Step 5. Role profile. After all managers have participated in Steps 2 through 4, each manager working alone makes a written summary called a *role profile*. The managers share their profile with the rest of the group.

Time suggested for Step 5: 15 minutes.

Step 6. As a team and then with the entire class, critique the effectiveness of the role-analysis technique. Also consider the following questions:

1. What are its advantages and disadvantages?
2. How did the consultants help? Any suggestions for improvement?
3. What would be the next step in team development if your team was a management team at Energy International?
4. If your class participated in Simulation 10.2A: Team Development, compare that method with the role analysis technique.

Time suggested for Step 6: 15 minutes.

CASE 10: STEELE ENTERPRISES[42]

THE PR DINNER

Gene Robertson, Public Relations Director, Steele Enterprises, knew there was trouble as soon as he saw the room. Instead of bars set up with shiny glasses and fine liqueurs, and staffed by impeccably dressed bartenders, there was chaos. Tables of hors d'oeuvres were there, but with no semblance of order. Flowers had been delivered, but were not placed. Cocktail tables and other furniture were still stacked. Thank God I'm early, he thought.

Richard Leeman (Chemical, Public Relations Chief) and Donna Olson (Mechanical, Public Relations Chief) were arguing—really going at it—while Judy Fields and Joe Maxwell stood by uncertainly with looks of distress on their faces. Gene hurried over to intervene.

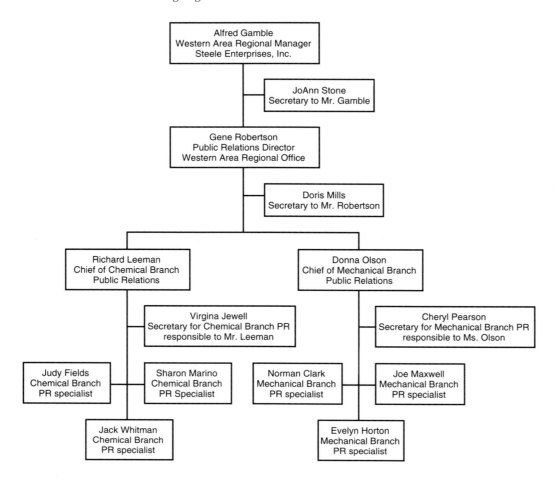

EXHIBIT 1 Steele Enterprises, Inc., Western Region, Public Relations Division

This was not the time for those two to get into it again. Not with more than 50 marketing representatives and buyers—ambassadors for 20 of the primary marketing outlets to which Steele Enterprises sold most of its goods—arriving in about an hour and a half. There is still time to put this thing together, he thought wearily (see Exhibit 1 for organization chart).

"OK, what's this all about?" Gene asked, as he carefully but easily slid between the two.

"God, am I glad to see you!" gasped Donna, as she tried to catch her breath. "Dick is just being unreasonable about this whole. . . ."

"Unreasonable!" yelled Dick. "If Judy and I hadn't happened by, the cost of the hors d'oeuvres alone would be more than we'd planned on for the whole works! As it is, we'll exceed the budget by nearly $4,000!"

"OK, calm down," Gene soothed, as he gently but firmly eased Dick a couple of more feet away from Donna. "Now, one at a time, you first, Donna. What is going on?"

Donna, still angry, was at least breathing more normally by this time. "You told us to get the best for this party," she said accusingly. "We told the catering manager to bring out his best stock and get us a classy spread of heavy hors d'oeuvres, but to stay within the $12,000 figure, with labor extra. Things were going great until Dick showed up. Then he started nosing around, asking questions, giving orders, and has things all fouled up! Just look!" She waved her arms around the room, indicating the mess.

"Not true!" gritted Dick through clenched teeth. "When Judy and I got here, neither one of these two were in sight, the catering manager was trying to find out what was going

on, and his cost sheet showed $16,500 instead of $12,000. I've canceled escargot, lobster tails, and the burgundy-soaked tenderloin strips, and told them to hold the liquor prices to a maximum of $25 a bottle, except for the liqueurs. Even with the cuts, food costs are going to be nearly $3,000 above our maximum estimate, because they've already got some oysters shelled, crab legs cracked, and shrimp peeled!"

"Hold it! Time out! Stop!" said Gene, appraising the situation. "We'll sort out who did what to whom later. Right now, we still have time to pull this thing back together and keep all our necks out of the nooses! Now, here's how we're going to handle this. . . ."

By the time the PR staff had been given their assignments (in clear, concise language, with no room for arguments), and by the time he had finished haggling with the catering manager (which cost him $100 under the table), getting the party cost down to within $2,000 of the estimated tab, *and* by the time the party was over (2:30 AM), Gene was really beat. It will be good to get home, he thought.

THE AFTERMATH

Gene came in about 11 AM the next day, and after finishing up the paper work from the morning's mail, went to lunch. Something has to give around here, he thought. His secretary, Doris Mills, could see the consternation on his face as they sat down at the table.

"Are those two going at it again?" she asked when he finally came back to earth.

"If you mean Dick and Donna, yes," he replied. "I've just got to do something with them. I've never had two more capable people running those branches, and I don't think they've ever had a more capable staff. But this constant fighting between them just has to stop or I'm going to have to get rid of somebody, and I really wouldn't like to do that. Especially with that kind of talent. Even Mr. Gamble has kind of joked around the fact that the competition must be fierce in the PR business!" Gene looked thoughtfully at Doris. "Have you heard anything from JoAnn Stone?"

"Not about the bickering between Dick and Donna," replied Doris. "And if anything was wrong at the party, it never got passed down through the grapevine."

"Well, that's something," sighed Gene. "The one hundred bucks I slipped to that jerk at the hotel to fix up the bill can at least be taken care of on the expense account. I'll call it incidental expenses or something." As Doris ordered, Gene thought: How lucky I am to have an efficient, competent secretary, who keeps her eyes and ears open and her mouth shut. I think she's about due for a raise.

THE PROBLEM

Later that afternoon, in the privacy of his office, Gene thought about the problems that he was having with his staff: Dick, Ginny, Judy, Jack, and Sharon in Chemical PR, and Donna, Cheryl, Norm, Ev, and Joe in Mechanical. We have the business and the budget to need that many people; the boss seems pleased with what we do; good, sharp people, every one of them, and yet a hell of a lot of fighting between the two branches. So far the staff under Dick and Donna haven't taken up the battle flags, but if I don't do something pretty soon, that could even happen, thought Gene. And the chemical-mechanical split suggested by Mr. Gamble, even though it's not working as it should, is out of my hands. Isn't it? worried Gene as he reviewed the backgrounds of the respective branch leaders. Something's wrong here, but what? he wondered. Maybe it's the technical breakdown, maybe we're not definite enough about which branch should work with which companies. And that fiasco last night— why did Dick come roaring in and try to take over when I thought I had made it pretty clear that Donna and her staff were to run that show? My orders *were* pretty clear, thought Gene, as he tried to assure his nagging conscience that he was doing a good job directing the PR efforts in the western region.

Good grief, I need a referee! thought Gene as he reviewed seven cases in the last six months in which he had had to intervene between Dick and Donna. Maybe I should try to trade one of them for Bob Lyons at the central region office at St. Louis, he mused, still feeling that he was, somehow, responsible for the conflicts.

CASE ANALYSIS FORM

Name: _____

I. Problems

 A. Macro

 1. _____

 2. _____

 B. Micro

 1. _____

 2. _____

II. Causes

 1. _____

 2. _____

 3. _____

III. Systems affected

 1. Structural _____

 2. Psychosocial _____

 3. Technical _____

 4. Managerial _____

 5. Goals _____

IV. Alternatives

 1. _____

 2. _____

 3. _____

 4. _____

 5. _____

V. Recommendations

 1. _____

 2. _____

 3. _____

SUMMARY

• **Team Development.** One major OD intervention is termed *team development* and it is a useful and successful vehicle for bringing about significant changes in a team. Team development includes outdoor experiential training, role negotiation, and role analysis techniques. These techniques are used to increase the communication, cooperation, and cohesiveness of work teams resulting in increased organization efficiency. It is important to remember that team development is only a part of an organization-wide change program that values participation, collaboration, and the maximization of the use of human resources.

• **Team Skills.** *Interdependence* refers to situations where one person's performance is contingent upon how someone else performs. In the simulation, you had a chance to experience interdependence, since it required the combined inputs of all team members to solve the problem. You also experienced and observed differences in how problem-solving information is communicated and shared within a team. Some teams may have taken a very open and systematic approach to the problem, whereas others showed the effects of closed or reactive behaviors. In the problem-solving process, much time may have been spent on irrelevant topics, on going off on tangents, or on nonconstructive arguments among members, whereas very little time was spent on deciding how best to solve the problem. Some members may have talked too much when they had nothing helpful to say; others may have unintentionally withheld important information by their silence. Authority or lack of authority, and cooperation or competition, also may have influenced your team effectiveness.

• **Feedback.** In the simulations, you also had an opportunity to participate in a team activity, and experience the team-building process. You have had a chance to see the influence of leader behavior and member behavior on a task outcome and to diagnose team problems and behavior. The feedback from the simulation should help you identify ways of being a more effective team member and should show how important team work and coordination are to organization efficiency.

NOTES

1. Peter Gent, *North Dallas Forty* (New York: William Morrow & Co., Inc., 1973), p. 264. Also a motion picture.
2. For additional information see Anthony R. Montebello and Victor R. Buzzotta, "Work Teams That Work," *Training and Development Journal*, vol. 47, no. 3, (March 1993), pp. 59–64; and Jon R. Katzenbach and Douglas K. Smith, "The Discipline of Teams," *Harvard Business Review*, March–April 1993, pp. 111–120.
3. Karen Benowski, "What Makes American Teams Tick?" *Quality Progress* vol. 28, no. 1, January, 1995, p. 39.
4. For additional information see Lee G. Bolman and Terrence E. Deal, "What Makes a Team Work?" *Organizational Development*, vol. 21, no. 2, (Autumn 1992), pp. 34–44; and Richard Hackman, *Groups that Work (and Those That Don't): Creating Conditions for Effective Teamwork* (San Francisco: Jossey-Bass, 1990).
5. "Is Industry Ready for Adult Relationships?" *Industry Week*, January 1991, p. 18.
6. Robert W. Keidel, "Baseball, Football, and Basketball: Models for Business," *Organizational Dynamics*, Winter 1984, pp. 5–18.
7. K. Kim Fisher, "Managing in the High-Commitment Workplace," *Organizational Dynamics*, Winter 1989, p. 38.
8. For additional information: see William G. Dyer, *Team Building, Issues and Alternatives* (Reading, Mass.: Addison-Wesley Publishing Company, 1987); and Richard E. Walton, *Managing Conflict, Interpersonal Dialogue and Third-Party Roles* (Reading, Mass.: Addison-Wesley Publishing Company, 1987).
9. Kathleen Kerwin and James B. Treece, "Crisis at GM," *Business Week*, November 9, 1992, pp. 84–86; Keith D. Denton, "The Power of EI at Ford," *Journal of Managerial Psychology*, vol. 6, no. 3 (1991), pp. 23–31; Melinda Guiles, "Ford's 1991 Escort Symbolizes Future," *The Wall Street Journal*, February 27, 1990, p. A8; Beverly Geber, "The Resurrection of Ford," *Training*, April 1989, pp. 23–32; and Gary Jusela, et. al, "Work Innovations at Ford Motor," in *Quality Productivity and Innovation*, Y. K. Shetty and Vernon M. Buehler, eds. (New York: Elsevier Science Publishing Co., Inc., 1987), pp. 123–45.
10. Douglas Lavin, "Robert Eaton Thinks 'Vision' Is Overrated and He's Not Alone," *The Wall Street Journal*, October 4, 1993, p. A1.
11. Ruth Simon and Graham Button, "What I Learned In the Eighties," *Forbes*, January 8, 1990, p. 100.
12. David Woodruff, "Saturn: Labor's Love Lost?" *Business Week*, February 8, 1993, pp. 122–24; and James B. Treece, "Here Comes GM's Saturn," *Business Week*, April 9, 1990, p. 60.
13. Marvin R. Weisbord, "Team Effectiveness Theory," *Training and Development Journal*, January 1985, p. 27.
14. See David Casey, "When Is a Team Not a Team?," *Personnel Management*, January 1985, p. 26 and Brian Dumaine, "The Bureaucracy Busters," *Fortune*, June 17, 1991, pp. 36–50.
15. Rosabeth Moss Kanter, *The Change Masters: Innovation for Productivity in the American Corporation* (New York: Simon & Schuster, 1983); and Rosabeth Moss Kanter, "Dilemmas of Managing Participation," *Organizational Dynamics*, Summer 1982, pp. 6–7.
16. *Ibid.*
17. K. W. Thomas and W. H. Schmidt, "A Survey of Managerial Interest with Respect to Conflict," *Academy of Management Journal*, vol. 19, no. 2 (1976), pp. 315–18.
18. For example, see E. A. Mannix, L. L. Thompson, M. H. Bazerman, "Negotiation in Small Groups," *Journal of Applied Psychology*, vol. 74, no. 3 (1989), pp. 508–17.
19. For example, see L. L. Thompson, E. A. Mannix, and M. H. Bazerman, "Group Negotiation: Effects of Decision Rule, Agenda, and Aspiration," *Journal of Personality and Social Psychology*, 54 (1988), pp. 86–95.
20. Irving Janis, *Groupthink* (Boston: Houghton Mifflin Company, 1982, 2nd ed.), p. 9.
21. Carol J. Loomis, "The Battle to Shape Up Kodak," *Fortune*, May 13, 1993, pp. 62–63; and Mark Maremont and Elizabeth Lesly, "The

Revolution That Wasn't at Eastman Kodak," *Business Week*, May 10, 1993, pp. 24–25.

22. Janis, *Groupthink*.

23. Glen Whyte, "Groupthink Reconsidered," *Academy of Management Review*," vol. 14, no. 1 (1989), pp. 40–56; and Gregory Moorhead and John R. Montanari, "An Empirical Investigation of the Groupthink Phenomenon," *Human Relations*, vol. 39, no. 5 (1986), pp. 399–410.

24. Richard Rapport, "To Build a Winning Team: An Interview with Head Coach Bill Walsh," *Harvard Business Review*, January–February 1993, pp. 111–20.

25. Gordon Lippitt, Ronald Lippitt, and Clayton Lafferty, "Cutting Edge Trends in Organization Development," *Training and Development Journal*, July 1984, pp. 59–62.

26. John F. Hulpke, California State University, Bakersfield, California. See also Brian Dumaine, "Creating a New Company Culture," *Fortune*, January 15, 1990, p. 130.

27. For a more detailed discussion, see Paul Brauchle and David Wright, "Training Work Teams," *Training and Development Journal*, vol. 47, no. 3 (March 1993), pp. 65–68; Paul Thornton, "Teamwork: Focus, Frame, Facilitate," *Management Review*, vol. 81, no. 11 (November 1992), pp. 46–47; R. Beckhard, *Organization Development: Strategies and Models* (Reading, Mass.: Addison-Wesley Publishing Co., Inc., 1969); and Jack Fordyce and Raymond Weil, *Managing with People* (Reading, Mass.: Addison-Wesley Publishing Co., Inc., 1971).

28. G. A. Neuman, J. E. Edwards, and N. S. Raju, "Organizational Development Interventions: A Meta-Analysis of Their Effects On Satisfaction and Other Attitudes," *Personnel Psychology*, 42 (1989), pp. 461–89; and R. A. Guzzo, R. D. Jette, and R. A. Katzell, "The Effects of Psychologically Based Intervention Programs On Worker Productivity: A Meta-Analysis," *Personnel Psychology*, vol. 38 (1985), pp. 275–91.

29. Donald F. Harvey and Neal Kneip, "The Results of an Integrated OD Program for Training and Team Building," a paper presented at Western Academy of Management, 1980.

30. Maryam Alavi, "An Assessment of Electronic Meeting Systems in a Corporate Setting," *Information and Management*, vol. 25, no. 4 (October 1993), pp. 175–82; Gerry Blackwell, "You, Too, Can Be an Einstein," *Canadian Business*, vol. 66, no. 5 (May 1993) pp. 66–99;

Bruce C. Merniter, *et. al.*, "Computers Improve Efficiency of the Negotiation Process," *Personnel Journal*, vol. 72, no. 4 (April 1993), pp. 93–99; and Jim Bartimo, "At These Shouting Matches, No One Says a Word," *Business Week*, June 11, 1990, p. 78.

31. For a more complete description of outdoor labs, see Jack Szwergold, "When Work Has You Climbing Trees," *Management Review*, vol. 82, no. 9 (September 1993), p. 6; Glenn Tarullo, "Making Outdoor Experiential Training Work," *Training*, vol. 29, no. 8 (August 1992), pp. 47–52; Robert Carey, "Go Take a Flying Leap (for the Company)," *Successful Meetings*, vol. 41, no. 7 (June 1992), pp. 59–62; Jennifer Laabs, "Team Training Goes Outdoors," *Personnel Journal*, vol. 70, no. 6 (June 1991), pp. 56–63; and Alex Prud'homme, "Management Training No Longer Means Seminars in Self-Discovery," *Business Month*, March 1990, pp. 61–66;

32. Prud'homme, "Management Training," p. 61.

33. For a more detailed discussion of legal risks, see: Susan Chesteen, Lee Caldwell, and Larry Prochazka, "Taking Legal Risks Out of Adventure Training," *Training and Development Journal*, July 1988, pp. 42–46.

34. Prud'homme, "Management Training," p. 66.

35. *Ibid.*

36. Betsy Wiesendanger, "Games Managers Play," *Sales and Marketing Management*, vol. 145, no. 2 (February 1993), pp. 36–41.

37. Richard J. Wanger and Christopher Roland, "How Effective Is Outdoor Training?" *Training and Development Journal*, vol. 46, no. 7 (July 1992), pp. 61–66.

38. Gall, "You Can Take the Manager," p. 58.

39. Wendell L. French and Cecil H. Bell, Jr., *Organization Development: Behavioral Science Interventions for Organization Improvement* 2nd ed. (Englewood Cliffs, N. J.: Prentice Hall, Inc., 1978).

40. I. Dayal and J. Thomas, "Operation KPE: Developing a New Organization," *Journal of European Industrial Training*, vol. 6, no. 7 (1982), pp. 25–27.

41. From J. William Pfeiffer and John E. Jones, eds., *The 1972 Annual Handbook for Group Facilitators* (La Jolla, Calif.: University Associates, Inc., 1972). Used by permission.

42. This case was written by Major K. Funk, USAF, Fairchild AFB, and is used by permission.

The team appoach has long been a part of Hewlett-Packard Company's corporate philosophy. *Photo courtesy of Hewlett-Packard Company.*

Intergroup Development Interventions 11

OBJECTIVES

Upon completing this chapter, you will be able to:

1. Identify problems of intergroup conflict and suboptimization.
2. Experience the negative effects of competition on organization effectiveness.
3. Observe and develop strategies for collaborative intergroup relations.
4. Diagnose the causes of cooperative versus competitive group relations.

PREMEETING PREPARATION

1. Read the Background Information.
2. Prepare for OD Skills Simulation 11.1. Read and familiarize yourself with the rules and procedures of the Disarmament Game. Compete Step 1.
3. Read and analyze Case 11: The Exley Chemical Company.

BACKGROUND INFORMATION

In a world of change, American companies are reexamining and reinventing the way their firms are organized and managed. In order to improve competitiveness, increase productivity, and reduce costs, managers are focusing efforts on shared responsibilities among work teams.[1] At GE Medical Systems, for example, interrelated teams are formed around core processes focusing on customer satisfaction. A team of engineers, production associates, and service staff reduced the time needed to install complex X-ray machines by one-third.[2]

One key area in the improvement of organization effectiveness involves the relation between operating groups or departments. Complex organizations tend to create situations of **interdependence,** where the performance of one group is contingent upon another group. Manufacturing depends upon engineering, production upon purchasing, marketing upon production, and so on. Consequently, managers must operate and function in an interdepartmental environment. General Electric Corporation focuses both on teamwork and cooperation between teams. CEO Jack Welch says, "If you can't operate as a team player, no matter how valuable you've been, you really don't belong at GE. . . . What we value most is boundary-lessness. It's the ability to work up and down the hierarchy, across functions and geographies, and with suppliers and customers."[3] Clearly, an important dimension in organization development is the interface between operating groups. As a customer or an employee, you might expect people to recognize that they are interdependent: What happens in one department or group affects the others. But, as obvious as this seems, people and groups in organizations often fail to cooperate with others, and in fact may be in open conflict. Have you ever gone to an organization with a problem and been shunted back and forth among departments? Each employee saying, "Its not my job," take this problem to another department. These situations can be very frustrating, and one may wonder, do these people ever talk to one another? As a result you may just take your business to a competitor elsewhere.

Also, you have probably worked on a team project in one of your college courses, where your success is dependent upon member cooperation. You would think everyone would be in agreement, but often there are conflicts—incompatibility of goals, differing expectations of one another, differing motivational levels, and differences over interpretations of facts. These are the operating problems that often lead to intergroup conflict.

Each organization is a system formed of subsystems: division, function, departments, and work teams. Each work team develops its own norms, goals, and behaviors, and these forces contribute to the cohesiveness and morale of that group. When two teams are highly interdependent misunderstandings, low coordination, or conflict may develop between the teams. Groups in conflict with one another spend a high degree of their effort, time, and energy directed toward the conflict instead of toward goal accomplishment.

Because of these problems, one set of OD interventions aims specifically at the improvement of these interdepartmental interface and intergroup operating problems. Such interventions attempt to bring to the surface underlying problems, to use joint problem solving, to correct misperceptions between groups, and to reopen channels of communication.

In this chapter, we examine conditions for conflict and discuss several techniques for dealing with intergroup relations. Although the organization may have different functional or operating groups, each with specialized tasks and goals, there must be coordinated effort if it is to achieve organizational excellence.

Collaboration and Conflict

An *organization* is a large system consisting of subsystems. The subsystems have internal boundaries across which members of the subsystems exchange information and materials. The points of intersection between departments are termed **interfaces**. The organization requires cooperation among its departments and divisions if it is to be effective. *Teamwork* implies that all members are contributing to an overall objective, even if it means subordinating personal prominence. In sports, a group of individuals play together as a team and

usually their degree of success depends on how well they cooperate and collaborate. The same is true of organization departments and groups. The climate of collaboration and the interface between work groups often determines organization effectiveness.

Richard Beckhard notes that "one of the major problems affecting organizational effectiveness is the amount of dysfunctional energy expended in inappropriate competition and fighting between groups that should be collaborating."[4] This competition and conflict originate with differences in objectives, values, efforts, and interests between groups. Some aspects of competition are consciously recognized and intentionally produced, whereas others are unconscious or unintentional. The interdependence of functions is one potential source of conflict.

Because of these potential group conflicts, and because work teams are often interdependent, the relationship between work teams is a crucial element in organization efficiency. Within the organization there is a need for competition between these elements, but there is also a need for cooperation and collaboration. Success often depends upon sharing resources effectively and many groups are interdependent; that is, they depend upon the exchange of resources with other elements to attain their objectives. **Interdependence** is the mutual dependence between groups. Often, however, these interdependencies introduce conflict into the organization system.

To reduce the conflict between operating divisions, departments, and teams, General Electric subscribes to interdependent teams by emphasizing the concept of being **boundaryless**. CEO Jack Welch says being boundaryless is "an open, trusting, sharing of ideas. A willingness to listen, debate, and then take the best ideas and get on with it. If this company is to achieve its goals, we've all got to become boundaryless. Boundaries are crazy."[5]

There is competition among divisions for all sorts of resources (capital, labor, management, and so forth), and often it becomes a win–lose situation. If the company decides to build a new manufacturing plant in Texas, it cannot build a new research laboratory in California. Such examples are many.

Conflict is increasingly perceived as inevitable and is all too common in today's organization. Managers report that they spend approximately 20 percent of their time dealing with conflict and its impact.[6] It has also been reported that corporate managers spend one quarter of their time dealing with conflict, while public administrators (in schools, hospitals, cities, and so on) spend almost one-half of their time dealing with conflict.[7] Therefore, a manager's ability to manage conflict is becoming much more important.[8] The horizontal organization structure is becoming increasingly common and this design intentionally builds in controlled conflict for integrating diverse activities.

Certain implications for the organization development consultant stem from this view of interdependent subsystems. First, the OD consultant must be able to recognize the interdependence of organization units. He or she also must be aware that these interactions result in conflicts between the units. Finally, elements often operate without **feedback**, or **open loop** as it is termed. When this is the case, there is no mechanism for corrective action to take place.

One important aspect of the organization is **intergroup competition**. Relations between groups often leads to conflict or dysfunctional behavior affecting operating efficiency. As a result, one objective of OD is to increase cooperation among organization subsystems. These **intergroup interventions** have been described as "the deliberate interaction of two or more complex social units which are attempting to define or redefine the terms of their interdependence."[9]

Intergroup Operating Problems

The potential for **conflict** depends on how incompatible the *goals* are, the extent to which required resources are scarce and shared, and the degree of interdependence of task activities (see Figure 11.1, on p. 298). The chance of **goal conflict** is somewhat low between groups that have their own resources and perform entirely different tasks directed toward

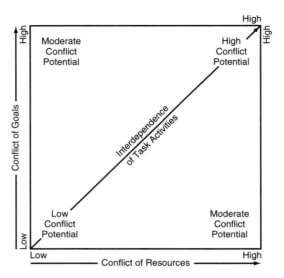

FIGURE 11.1 Factors Involved in the Potential for Conflict

completely separate goals. Electrical engineers and janitors seldom conflict because their tasks are largely separate. The potential for conflict is much higher between engineers and production managers or between sales people and credit managers. This is because such units tend to rely on common resources, their tasks are interdependent, and they frequently pursue incompatible goals (e.g., increasing sales versus reducing credit losses). The key, says Douglas Reid of Xerox, is identifying and building "the linkages between groups that don't normally work together."[10]

Intergroup relationships are complex, so OD consultants need to recognize the conditions that lead to the emergence of problems or conflicts. The conditions that are considered in this chapter are not exhaustive or mutually exclusive, but the important factors present in determining group relationships are discussed. The symptoms of these conflicts include complaints, gripes, verbal battles, inefficiency, and possibly sabotaging the other group in some way. (See CROCK comic strip.)

Suboptimization

When the goals of operating divisions are interdependent, optimization by one group may result in decreased goal attainment for other groups and the organization. As an example, engineering may design a product very quickly and inexpensively, but the product is difficult, time consuming, and costly for the manufacturing department to produce. The financial group, by limiting hiring or overtime, may cut costs and optimize its objective, but other departments and the organization may lose profits or customers to the extent that there is a net reduction in profits. This is called **suboptimization**. Suboptimization occurs when a group optimizes its own subgoals, but loses sight of the larger organization goals.

General Motors, before their recent reorganization, had significant problems of suboptimization. Their engineering and production divisions were so autonomous that they did not interface except through the President. A car body would be designed to meet appearance and safety requirements but could not be manufactured because of physical limitations of stamping or bending metal. The design would have to be sent back to engineering to be redone. Roger Smith, the CEO at the time, described the process: "Guys in Fisher Body would draw up a body and send the blueprint over and tell the guy, 'Okay, you build it if you can, you. . . .' And the guy at GMAD [production] would say, 'Well, J____, there's no damn way you can stamp metal like that, and there's no way we can weld this stuff together.' "[11] Obviously, to be effective, the old functionally oriented structures need to be altered to bring down barriers.

CROCK by Rechin, Parker and Wilder. © Field Enterprises, Inc. by permission of North America Syndicate, Inc.

The objectives of OD interventions are aimed at decreasing suboptimization by increasing collaboration or integration between interdependent groups. OD consultants Paul Lawrence and Jay Lorsch found that effectiveness measures were closely related to the degree of integration.[12] From these data it may be hypothesized that suboptimization, or lack of integration, is a contributing factor to decreased organization performance. Many organizations are becoming acutely aware of how important integration is. For years, some of America's largest corporations like IBM, General Motors, and Sears failed to see the problems caused by suboptimization.[13]

Intergroup Competition

A second condition causing intergroup problems involves groups with conflicting purposes or objectives. This condition emerges when a group desires or pursues one goal while directly opposing values that exist in another group. One example of this type of conflict is the conflict that occurs between the Air Force and the Army over tactical air support. The Army has acquired helicopters and several fixed-wing aircraft for this function, but the Air Force feels that this function is under its jurisdiction and the result is conflict. In other types of organizations, similar situations occur. Engineering may need special hand-tooled prototypes built and developed by a small manufacturing operation. Manufacturing, on the other hand, may see this as usurping its function and field of expertise. Each subsystem of the organization has its own special function or area, and these are usually jealously guarded against intrusion as almost a territorial right.

Perceived Power Imbalance Between Groups

Another condition that appears to influence intergroup conflict is the difference of power between two groups. The problem emerges where there is a perceived imbalance between units or when some previously established relationship is altered. This can particularly be a problem in today's environment of corporate mergers and takeovers. Where one group is overpowering and its views and objectives are consistently favored, a deterioration of relations with the other group is likely to result. This often forces the submissive or losing group to try manipulative tactics to revise the power balance. These may take the form of delay tactics or insistence of adherence to policies and procedures.

Role Conflict, Role Ambiguity

Role conflict (as explained earlier in Chapter 10) also exists when an individual belongs to or identifies with two or more groups whose goals or values are in conflict. This is more typical in a matrix or project form of organization where an individual may belong to several work groups and report to several bosses. Where directives are vague or incompatible, intergroup conflict may result.

Role ambiguity exists when an individual or the members of a group are not clear about their functions, purposes, and goals within the organization. Staff groups such as personnel or accounting often encounter vague or unclear situations where their functions tend to interfere or conflict with line operations. Personnel, for example, may want to control all hiring and promotion decisions, but other departments may want to have total control over such decisions. An individual or the members of a group may face a situation in which their job scope is being reduced for the good of the organization, but because of the intangible and multifaceted nature of what is good for the organization, this may result in noncompliance or conflict.

In the real work-day world, employees are faced with role conflict and ambiguity in some very traumatic ways. Many managers and line workers have been enrolled in work improvement programs that became so effective that they were laid off. *Business Week* reports on such an incident at Boeing Company. "Many employees recognize that Boeing needs to change. But some roll their eyes at the slogans and endless meetings and training sessions. Blue-collar workers and union members are especially leery. Boeing aims to 'empower' them to suggest ways to do their jobs more efficiently. Yet the more efficiently they make things run, the more likely they are to render their own jobs unnecessary."[14]

Personality Conflict

A final source of intergroup problems arises from interpersonal differences between members, usually the managers. Two individuals may be competing for promotion, rewards, or resources and may elevate this to a situation of intergroup conflict. Such conflicts may result from conflicting functions, objectives, career aspirations, or personalities.

Cooperation versus Competition

Competition is normally thought of in positive terms, especially in a market driven economic system. The rationale of some managers has been to introduce competition into their organizations to cause a "lean and mean" operation.

IBM has an industry reputation for internal strife and competition between divisions. For example, managers responsible for large, mainframe computers, afraid that their computers would become obsolete, weilded enough power to delay the introduction of more advanced personal computers into the marketplace. Of course, IBM's competitors had no such reluctance. Now IBM is battling Sun Microsystems and Hewlett-Packard to capture a share of the high-end personal computer market. The new CEO at IBM, Louis Gerstner, fumes, "We should have dominated. Where have we been?"[15] (For an approach that Hewlett-Packard is using, see OD in Practice.)

Research into the results of competition and cooperation among groups is mixed.[17] It is not as simple an issue as some contend. On the positive side of group competition, members have more self-esteem for their groups than noncompetitive groups. The competition produces more task orientation in groups and places additional pressure on groups to work. Though groups competing with one another are more highly oriented toward accomplishing the task than noncompetitive groups, there is a lack of evidence that intergroup competition results in greater productivity than cooperation. Further, groups in competition may experience a degradation in their internal cohesion.

Group behavior research suggests that cooperation in some situations promotes productivity. This seems true when the task is complicated and requires coordination and sharing of information.[18] In somewhat simple tasks, however, competition often is superior to cooperation as it heightens interest and provides incentive. Therefore, competition can be effective between groups who do not need to share information or resources.

Just as there are problems with competitive work groups, managers also must carefully structure cooperative groups. The task of the groups should be complicated enough to

OD IN PRACTICE
HEWLETT-PACKARD'S MANY BOARDS OF DIRECTORS[16]

The company that brought us MBWA (Management by Wandering Around) now has more "board of director" meetings than just about any other large company. In fact, HP has created many boards that are responsible for maintaining the timing and integration required for bringing out new and complex projects. "Board of directors" is a term HP has given to teams that are made up of representatives from every department involved on a project. HP implemented the practice at their Greeley, Colorado site which produces computer disk drives and the ScanJet scanner.

New Structure

In the past, HP relied on a highly decentralized structure. They organized divisions along product lines that were so autonomous that each division had its own marketing, manufacturing, R&D, personnel, and finance functions. Because of increasingly complicated products and technological overlap, there was emerging unhealthy conflict between divisions. HP created a group structure that put divisions with similar products together under one management. HP keeps the divisions small to speed up development and give participants a feeling of entrepreneurship. To help coordinate the operations involved in introducing dozens of new products a year at the Greeley site, HP established the board of directors idea.

A project's board of directors might include lab engineers, marketing people, writers responsible for user manuals, accountants, representatives from manufacturing, and others who can add to the project. The board oversees details such as product design, material expense, packaging, sales projections, and manufacturing schedules. Everyone is aware of break-even points, profit margins, and other accounting information to the extent that they often talk like a comptroller. Corporate planning is mainly bottom up.

Some members of the boards have criticized the meetings for being time consuming, stormy, and even boring at times. Says one HP manager, "Most of us get our own work done in the evenings and on weekends. Our time at the plant is mostly 'people-time.' "

Idea Works

But many at HP say the board idea works and is keeping HP competitive and profitable. The time it takes to bring a new printer to the marketplace is 22 months; down from 54 months. More than 70 percent of HP's new orders received last year were for products introduced less than two years ago. Mike Kelly, a public relations manager, says, "The front-line workers are the experts. They can tell us what process works, which approach is easier or smoother and how we can save money. Their input helps managers make good decisions."

Questions

1. What is HP's approach for integrating department functions?
2. What are advantages and disadvantages of their approach?
3. What else could HP be doing to build cooperation between their divisions?

justify the group effort. The formal reward system and the norms should encourage persons and groups to help others, to share information and resources, and to work on the task together.

In a summary of the effects of competition among groups, Edgar Schein, an OD consultant, predicts that competing groups see the best in itself and the worst in the other group.[19] Communication decreases between groups, and hostility increases toward the other group. Within a competing group, it becomes more cohesive, structured, and organized. Also within the group, concern for task accomplishment increases, while concern for psychological needs of members decreases. Leadership styles become more autocratic and less democratic.

After the groups complete the task and there is a winner and a loser, Schein predicts the wining group will become more cohesive but, with their self-image of being better than the other group, they will become complacent. The winning group will become more concerned for members' psychological needs and less concerned for task accomplishment. The losing group denies the loss if the situation is ambiguous enough or rationalizes the loss by blaming it on bad luck or unclear rules. Initially, the group splinters, tries to find someone to blame, and has less concern for members' psychological needs. Over time, however, the losing group usually learns more about itself because its preconceived ideas about being the best group are upset. The long-term result of the loss can have positive outcomes if the losing group realistically accepts its loss.

Managing Conflict

Organizational conflict must not necessarily be reduced or eliminated, but managed to enhance individual, group, and organizational effectiveness.[20] In a research project, it was the conclusion of the authors that a high degree of competitive conflict can be very damaging whereas a cooperative approach to conflict that encourages people to argue freely about the best way to attain goals is more likely to lead to constructive effects.[21]

IBM's CEO, Louis Gerstner, recognizes the importance of a cooperative approach. Gerstner became outraged when he learned that the IBM group selling personal computers (PCs) to schools had been told it would have to pay royalties to the IBM PC unit if it labeled its computers "IBM." In a message to employees, he said: "Henceforth, it will be our policy to share with our IBM colleagues, enthusiastically and without cost, *whatever* we develop." Gerstner has zeroed in on what he calls "a classic Pogo-type problem: We have met the enemy and it is us." At a meeting of IBM employees, Gerstner angrily complained of the rivalry among divisions: "We have people who will not respond to a customer because one unit is debating with another how they're having to share the revenue. That's ludicrous!"[22] IBM and an increasing number of other companies are aware that it is important for managers to promote cooperative, healthy conflict, while simultaneously discouraging competitive conflict.

One element of diagnosing conflict situations involves learning basic conflict styles used in dealing with interpersonal or intergroup conflict. Robert Blake, Herbert Shepard, and Jane Mouton first developed a conceptual scheme for classifying conflict styles, and the scheme was reinforced by K. W. Thomas.[23] The styles are identified based on two dimensions: (1) desire to satisfy self; and (2) desire to satisfy others (see Figure 11.2). There are five styles representing differing levels of cooperative versus assertive behaviors:

1. **Avoiding.** This style involves a low concern for both self and others; avoids conflict by withdrawing, buckpassing, or passive agreement.
2. **Obliging.** With a low concern for self and high concern for others, this style is concerned with people satisfaction, harmony, and smoothing over conflicts.
3. **Dominating.** With high concern for self and low concern for others, this style attempts to attain personal objectives and often ignores the needs of others, forcing win–lose situations.
4. **Compromising.** This style has moderate concern for self and moderate concern for others, tending to seek out compromise between conflicting parties or elements.
5. **Integrating.** With high concern for self and others, this style is concerned with problem solving; uses openness, sharing of information, and the examination of differences to reach a consensus solution.

Although some behavioral scientists suggest that there is one best style, most suggest an examination of styles, so that the most appropriate style for a given situation can be applied.[24]

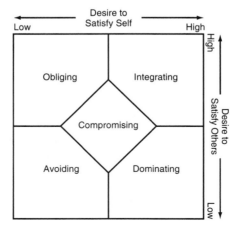

FIGURE 11.2 Conflict Styles

Intergroup Techniques

There seems to be an increasing awareness of conflict in organizations. The influx of women and minorities into the work force has resulted in new situations that cannot be managed by old structures. The increasing popularity of decentralized structures and matrix organization, in which many organization members wind up reporting to two or more bosses, has reduced the executives' reliance on authority and increased the reliance on interpersonal conflict management skills. Dick E. Milholland, an executive at Johnson Wax, says of his company's use of matrix organization: "In the matrix organization you serve two bosses, and work in two different directions. Therefore, the people who are part of the manufacturing organization are also part of the business organization. . . . We [can] share resources, focus, and do all kinds of things. . . . Now people are sitting down and talking to each other. Instead of each doing their own thing, the business team or other teams develop decisions together."[25] Milholland cautioned that the matrix organization was nine months in preparation and almost two years in execution.

Anthony Downs has suggested a law of interorganizational conflict: "Every group or organization is in partial conflict with every other group it deals with."[26] Although this may not be completely true, intergroup conflicts, including those of line and staff, interdepartment, and union-management, are very common. Motorola, Inc., recognizing this problem, is encouraging more team spirit by tearing down walls that isolate various departments. Now people from each discipline, such as design, manufacturing, and marketing, get involved in new projects early on. Products are designed from the outset to be cost-effective to build and to provide the features that customers want. Similar barriers between business units are also coming down. Collaborations involving two, three, or more divisions are common.[27] There are also barriers in multinational organizations, as suggested in Our Changing World on page 302.

Dealing with conflicts openly provides a way to manage tensions creatively, whereas unresolved conflict usually erodes away the effectiveness of an organization. To deal with intergroup conflict, the OD consultant seeks interventions that increase interaction, negotiation, and the frequency of communication between groups.

To deal with intergroup conflicts that inhibit cooperation, the consultant seeks strategies that aim at several goals. OD intergroup techniques seek to identify areas of commonality and **meta goals**—the superordinate organization goals. These techniques are aimed at avoiding the "win–lose" situations while emphasizing the "win–win" aspects of the situation. They attempt to apply strategies that encourage interaction and negotiation and to increase frequency of communication. It has been hypothesized that frequent contact between groups reduces the degree of conflict. Reasons for this are that intergroup contacts allow for biases of other groups to be reduced, encourage external loyalties by group members, reduce the importance of group membership, and reduce the pressures for conformity to group norms. Also frequent contact between groups permits points of potential conflict to be resolved as they occur instead of allowing the conflict to build.[29]

The world's largest independent software maker, Microsoft Corporation, encourages all employees to communicate and share ideas with one another. Microsoft is determined to avoid the typical big-company problem of conflict and lack of communications between divisions. According to senior executive Michael Maples, "We spend a lot of energy thinking about how to keep the place feeling small."[30]

To reduce conflict between groups, the consultant examines group-to-group working relationships, applying joint problem-solving efforts that confront intergroup issues. The OD techniques for dealing with intergroup problems include third-party consultation, organization mirror, and intergroup team building.

Third-Party Consultation

One method of increasing communication and initiating intergroup problem solving is the intervention of a third party, usually an outside consultant, although the person also may be

OUR CHANGING WORLD
FUJI-XEROX AND THE INTERGROUP CHALLENGE[28]

One key to organizational effectiveness involves relations between operating groups and departments, as noted in this chapter. Certainly, this challenge is at once greater and more complex in the growing area of cross cultural and of multinational operations. Although much is written of the successes of firms doing business away from home, it is no secret that sometimes it is tough to establish strong teamwork with "foreigners."

Team Management

Japan, for example, is noted for team management at home, but has not consistently followed the same principles when operating on alien turf. The Sogo and Daimaru department store chains both encourage employee suggestions and practices such as quality circles in Japan, but not with their successful retail stores in Hong Kong. In the United States, a study of 133 top executives working for Japanese firms found "no visible effort" to involve U.S. executives in the kind of "open communication and collaborative decision-making characteristic of the management culture in Japan." In fact, many American managers felt "locked out" of decision making.

Cross-Cultural Team Building

While cross-cultural team building and collaboration pose special challenges, there are also special payoffs to those who can pull it off. Some would say the joint venture between Fuji and Xerox provides a noteworthy example. Although Fugi-Xerox hasn't been a total winner, one would have to say they

have shown their share of successes. As of the early 1990s, half of all the copies made in Japan are made on Fuji-Xerox machines. President Yotaro Kobayashi feels his firm is one of the "most successful joint ventures in Japanese history."

How have they accomplished this? A clear sense of mission or vision is obviously good for starters, as well as a sense of modesty. Kobayashi also warned of complacency. Don't ever assume the market won't change.

Fuji-Xerox also adheres to some familiar yet noteworthy ideals:

- Broad agreement on basic issues at the top level.
- Dedication to quality.
- Uniqueness of technology and sales system.
- Full autonomy from parent organizations.
- Mutual trust and respect.

This last point may be obvious, but this makes it no less critical. The Fuji side has enjoyed an excellent relationship with the people at Xerox "with mutual respect and support running all the way through the various organizational levels." Conflict and differences may indeed be unavoidable when groups work together. The Fuji-Xerox example suggests that a dose of "mutual respect" may help turn those differences into positive energy for progress.

Question

1. How might multinational firms deal with such problems?

a superior, a peer, or a representative from another unit. **Third-party interventions** have the potential to solve such conflicts. One basic feature of this technique is confrontation.[31] **Confrontation** refers to the process in which the parties directly engage each other and focus on the conflict between them.

The goals of interventions include achieving increased understanding of the issues, accomplishing a common diagnosis, discovering alternatives for resolving the conflict and focusing on the common or meta goals. The third party attempts to make interventions aimed at opening communications, equalizing power, and confronting the problems.

Ensuring mutual motivation. Each group needs some incentive for resolving the conflict. This may entail arranging for some formal rewards by the organization for participating groups. Any organization rewards that inadvertently reward win–lose competitive behavior should be reconsidered by upper management.

Achieving a balance in situational power. If the situational power of the groups is not approximately equal, it is difficult to establish trust and maintain open lines of communication. In such a case, it may be possible to arrange for a third group, such as another work unit, to provide support to the groups with less power. For groups who have leaders who are less articulate or forceful in their presentations, the third party may need to regulate the discussion.

Coordinating confrontation efforts. One group's positive overtures must be coordinated with the other group's readiness to reciprocate. If one group is more highly motivated than the other, the discussion may be protracted by the third party or the higher-motivated group may be encouraged to moderate their enthusiasm. A failure to coordinate positive initiatives and readiness to respond can undermine future efforts to work out differences. A less-motivated group may even perceive a higher-motivated group as weak and willing to capitulate.

Developing openness in communication. The third party can help to establish norms of openness, provide reassurance and support, and decrease the risks associated with openness.

Maintaining an appropriate level of tension. If threat and tension are too low, the incentive for change or finding a solution is small. Yet, if threat and tension are too high, the parties may be unable to process information and see creative alternatives. They may become polarized and take rigid positions.

The third party provides an objective intervention for confronting or resolving issues between two disputing parties, since conflict situations are often tense and emotion-laden. Diagnostic insight is provided that is nonevaluative and a source of emotional support. The third party also aids in identifying conflict factors and then helps facilitate some changes in the relationships.

Organization Mirror

The **organization mirror** is a technique designed to give work units feedback on how other elements or customers of the organization view them.[32] This intervention is designed to improve relationships between teams and increase effectiveness.

A work team (which could be in personnel, engineering, production, accounting, and so on) that is experiencing interface problems with related work teams may initiate a feedback session. A consultant or other third party obtains specific information, usually by questionnaire or interview, from other organization groups that the work team contacts daily. The work team (also called the host group) meets to process the feedback. At this meeting, it is important that one or two spokespersons from each contacted group be present. The outside key people and the consultant discuss the data collected in an inner circle, while the host group "fishbowls" and observes on the outside (therefore the term organization mirror). Following this, the host group may ask questions of clarification (i.e., Why did you say this?) but may not argue or rebut. The host unit, with the assistance of the consultant, then discusses the data to identify problems.

Subgroups are formed of host-group members and key visitors to identify specific improvements that will increase operating efficiency. Following this, the total group hears a summary report from each subgroup, and they outline action plans and make specific task assignments. This completes the meeting, but a follow-up meeting to assess progress is usually set up for evaluation.

The organization mirror provides a means for a work team to improve its operating relations with other groups. It allows the team to obtain feedback on what it is doing, to identify key problems, and to search for specific improvements of operating efficiency.

Intergroup Team Building

One intervention technique, originally developed by Robert Blake, Herb Shepard, and Jane Mouton, is termed **intergroup team building** or **confrontation**.[33] Key members of conflicting groups meet to work on issues or interface. "An interface is any point at which contact between groups is essential to achieving a result."[34] The groups may be two interdependent organization elements such as architects and engineers, purchasing and production, or finance and other department heads.

Role playing is a frequently used method for gaining cross-group understanding. As in all confrontation, the consultant must intervene to open communications, balance power, and shift from hostile to problem-solving confrontation.

Intergroup team-building meetings usually take one or two days. Members are brought together to reduce misunderstanding, to open communication, and to develop mechanisms for collaboration. Most OD practitioners advise intragroup team development (see Chapter 10) before intergroup team building. The purpose of this is to clear out any team issues or "garbage" before getting to work on interface problems. The intergroup team building meeting usually involves the following steps:

Step 1. Two work groups who have identified intergroup operating problems first make three lists each before meeting together (see Table 11.1):

1. How do we see ourselves?
2. How we think the other department sees us?
3. How do we see the other department?

The groups prepare their lists written in large legible print on sheets of newsprint.

Step 2. The groups then meet together and tape their lists to the wall. A spokesperson for each group presents that group's lists. While one department is making its presentation, the other department may not defend itself, argue, or rebut; but it does have the opportunity to ask clarifying questions (What do you mean by inflexible? Could you be more specific on autocratic?).

Step 3. The groups then meet separately to discuss the discrepancies in perception and react to the feedback. The feedback allows for correcting perceptions and behaviors to a more effective mode.

Step 4. In the next phase, the groups divide into subgroups of five or six by mixing members of the two departments. These cross groups have the objectives of agreeing upon a diagnosis of interface problems and the development of conflict-reducing or problem-solving alternatives with action plans and follow-up activities. Together the groups develop an action plan for solving problems and assigning responsibilities for the action plan.

Step 5. Usually, they schedule a follow-up meeting to evaluate progress and to make sure that the actions have achieved their purpose.

Table 11.1 Sample Intergroup Meeting Listings

1. How do we see ourselves?	
a. Agreeable	e. Teamwork
b. Friendly	f. Participative
c. Trusting	g. Productive
d. Helpful	

2. How we think the other department sees us?	
a. Aggressive	e. Competitive
b. Communicative	f. Winners
c. Leaders	g. Independent
d. Rational	

3. How do we see the other department?	
a. Authoritarian	d. Opinionated
b. Sneaky	e. Inflexible
c. Loud	f. Unrealistic

Although little hard evidence is available, there have been subjective reports of positive results from intergroup meetings. Blake, Shepard, and Mouton reported improved relationships in their study, and French and Bell also reported working successfully with three tribal groups.[35] Bennis also reported improved relationships between two groups of officials within the U.S. Department of State.[36]

In the next two chapters, additional ideas of team and intergroup development will be discussed. First, goal setting as it relates to OD programs, and second, high-involvement work teams will be covered.

REVIEW QUESTIONS

1. Identify major sources of organizational conflict.

2. Many people approach conflict as a "win-lose" situation. Why is a "win-win" approach more likely to work?

3. What are the anticipated behaviors of competitive conflict that occurs among work teams?

4. Identify and compare the five major conflict styles.

5. Compare and contrast the methods used in the different approaches to resolving intergroup conflict.

KEY WORDS AND CONCEPTS

Define and be able to use the following:

Avoiding Style
Boundaryless
Conflict Styles
Compromising Style
Confrontation
Dominating Style
Feedback
Goal Conflict
Integrating Style
Interdependence

Interfaces
Intergroup Competition
Intergroup Interventions
Intergroup Team Building
Meta Goals
Obliging Style
Open Loop
Organization Mirror
Role Ambiguity
Suboptimization
Third-Party Intervention

OD SKILLS SIMULATION 11.1
THE DISARMAMENT GAME

Total time suggested: 1 hour, 45 minutes.

A. PURPOSE

The purpose of this exercise is to simulate a situation of intergroup conflict within an organization, to observe and experience the feelings generated by such competition, and to examine strategies for developing collaboration between organization units.

B. PROCEDURES

Step 1. Form teams of three to six players each. Before class, read the Disarmament Game Rules. Cut out the "play money" at the end of the simulation or, if the situation allows, use real money and play for lesser amounts (say 10 percent of the suggested amounts). Assign one person to serve as an observer. Make sure all participants understand the game rules.

Step 2. Begin playing Disarmament Game, keeping track of moves on the Record of Results. Play as many sets as you can within a one-hour-time limit. The observer can use the Observer Form found at the end of the simulation.
Time suggested for Steps 1 and 2: approximately 1 hour, 30 minutes.

Step 3. At the conclusion of the game and after all profits and losses have been calculated, get together with your competing team and discuss the following questions. The observers provide feedback to the teams on the Conflict Styles Form.
Time suggested for Step 3: 15 minutes.

1. To make an analogy, if one of the teams was the accounting department and the other team was the production department of a manufacturing enterprise, and the World Bank was the marketplace, what types of conclusions might you make about this company and the two departments?

2. What was the goal of your team? What kind of strategy to accomplish your goal did your team adopt? Did the strategy change at all during the simulation?

3. Was your team aware of the need for and advantages of collaborating with the other team? If so, how did you communicate the need for collaboration to the other team?

4. What part does trust play between the two teams in this simulation?

5. How is trust built? How does it start? Where does it come from?

6. Did your team trust and wait to collaborate with the other team so that you could try to break the World Bank? If so, what happened as a result of your trust?

7. If the simulation were to run again, would you do anything differently?

DISARMAMENT GAME RULES[37]

The Disarmament Game is played between two teams. A World Bank, which has funds, is also part of the game. Each team can win or lose money, and in this exercise your objective, as a team, is to win as much money as you can. Each team will consist of six to nine players. If there are uneven numbers of players, one person will assist the instructors, who are referees, thus making equal the number of players on each team.

The Funds

1. Each player will furnish $20 to be allocated as follows (see the end of this simulation for a description of "play money"):
 a. Initially, $15 (of your $20) will be given to your team treasury to be used in the exercise. You may need to contribute more money to the treasury, depending on the performance of your team. At the end of the game the funds remaining in your team's treasury will be divided equally among members of the team.
 b. The remaining $5 will be used to supplement the funds of the World Bank, managed by the referees.

 Example: Seven players on a side.

 Allocation of funds:

 Each team—$105

 World Bank—$35 from each team
2. The World Bank will deposit, from its own funds, an amount equal to the deposit of both teams. This money can be won by the teams.

Special jobs. You will have 15 minutes from the time the general instructions are completed until the first set begins. During this time you may read and discuss the instructions and plan team strategy. You must select persons to fill the following jobs. No person may hold more than one job at any one time. The jobs can be reassigned at any time by a majority vote of the team.

1. Two negotiators—functions stated below.
2. A team representative—to communicate group decisions to referees regarding initiation and acceptance of negotiations, moves, attacks, etc.
 a. You must elect a team representative.
 b. Referees will listen only to the team representative.
3. One recorder—to record moves of the team (on the Record of Results), specifically (a) the action taken by the team in each move; and (b) weapon status at the end of each move. He or she should also record who initiates decisions and how the team arrives at decisions.

The weapons. Each team will be given 20 cards, or "weapons." Each card will be marked on one side with an X to designate an "armed" condition. The blank side of the card signifies that the weapon is "unarmed." To begin the game, each of the two teams will place all 20 of its weapons in an "armed" condition. During the course of the entire game, the weapons will remain in your possession and out of sight of the other team.

The Procedure

1. The Set
 a. As many sets as possible will be played in the allocated time (from the time the first set begins). Payments will be made after each set.
 b. Each set consists of no more than 10 moves for each team. An attack following any move ends a set. If there is no attack, the set ends after the tenth move. Each team has two minutes to make a move. At the end of two minutes, you must have moved two, one, or none of the weapons from "armed" status. If you fail to move in the allotted time, the *status quo* counts as a move. In addition, you must decide whether or not to attack and whether or not you want to negotiate (see below). Your decision must be communicated to the referee within 15 seconds after the end of a move.
 c. Each team may announce an attack on the other team following any two-minute move period except the third, sixth, and ninth. You may not "attack" during negotiations.
 d. Once a set ends, begin a new set with all weapons armed. Continue with as many sets as the time allotted for the exercise will permit.
2. The Negotiations
 a. Between the moves, you will have the opportunity to communicate with the other team through negotiations.
 b. You may call for negotiations during the 15 seconds between move periods. The other team may accept or reject your request to negotiate. Negotiations can last *no longer* than two minutes.
 c. When the negotiators return to their teams, the next two-minute move period will start.
 d. Negotiators may say whatever is necessary to most benefit their team.
 e. The team is not necessarily bound by agreements made by its negotiators.
 f. Your negotiators *must* meet with those of the other team after the third, sixth, and ninth moves.

The Payoff

1. If there is an attack, the set ends. The team with the greater number of armed weapons will win 50 cents per member for each armed weapon it has *over and above* the number of armed weapons of the other team. This is paid directly from the treasury of the losing team to the treasury of the winning team. The World Bank is not involved in the transaction when there is an attack. If both teams have the same number of armed weapons when there is an attack, both teams pay the World Bank 50 cents per member.
2. If there is no attack, the set ends after 10 moves. If your team has more disarmed weapons than armed weapons, it will be awarded 20 cents per excess disarmed weapon, per member, by the World Bank. If your team has *fewer* disarmed weapons than armed weapons, your team will pay 20 cents per excess armed weapon, per member, to the World Bank.
3. The actual dollar payoff should occur at the end of each set.

Notes to Referee

1. Try to arrange separate rooms so that the teams cannot overhear each other.
2. In keeping the time, a timer that will ring accurately at two-minute intervals will be helpful.
3. Be sure to permit the teams only the specified times. You will probably need to be somewhat harsh toward the teams when directing them in order to keep them on the time schedule.
4. You will manage the funds of the World Bank and check the accuracy of the teams' record keeping.
5. You should not assist either team.

RECORD OF RESULTS

Move	Set 1 — Actual number of armed weapons	Set 1 — Action taken for this move (attack, not attack, negotiate)	Set 2 — Actual number of armed weapons	Set 2 — Action taken for this move (attack, not attack, negotiate)	Set 3 — Actual number of armed weapons	Set 3 — Action taken for this move (attack, not attack, negotiate)	Set 4 — Actual number of armed weapons	Set 4 — Action taken for this move (attack, not attack, negotiate)	Set 5 — Actual number of armed weapons	Set 5 — Action taken for this move (attack, not attack, negotiate)	Set 6 — Actual number of armed weapons	Set 6 — Action taken for this move (attack, not attack, negotiate)	Total of all sets
1.													
2.													
3.													
4.													
5.													
6.													
7.													
8.													
9.													
10.													
Ending number of armed weapons of other team													
Line 1 $ paid to other team													
Line 2 $ paid to World Bank													
Line 3 $ received from other team													
Line 4 $ received from World Bank													

Total Results
(Lines 3 + 4 − 1 − 2)

OBSERVER FORM

Based on the following scale, rate your team on how it performed on the following scale. Record your choice in the blank.

[Low 1 : 2 : 3 : 4 : 5 : 6 : 7 High]

Factor	Rating
1. Cooperative teamwork	_____
2. Member satisfaction	_____
3. Team motivation	_____
4. Information sharing	_____
5. Consensual decision making	_____
6. Conflict directly faced and resolved	_____
7. Participative leadership	_____
8. Clearly defined goals	_____
9. Trust	_____
10. Encouraged openness	_____

CONFLICT STYLES FORM

Rate members on their conflict style (Figure 11.2)

	Individual Rating	Team Rating
1. *Avoidance*—this style involves avoiding conflict by withdrawing.	_____	_____
2. *Obliging*—this style is concerned with harmony, smoothing over conflict.	_____	_____
3. *Dominating*—this style competes for one's own objectives in a win-lose mode.	_____	_____
4. *Compromising*—this style seeks to compromise.	_____	_____
5. *Integrating*—this style uses problem solving and openness to form a consensus.	_____	_____

OD SKILLS SIMULATION 11.2
INTERGROUP TEAM BUILDING

Total time suggested: 1 hour, 15 minutes.

A. PURPOSE

To provide an opportunity for group members to clarify and analyze their interrelationships and to work on improving intergroup processes.

B. PROCEDURES

Step 1. Form the same groups as in Simulation 11.1, and meet separately using a blackboard or newsprint to make these lists:

1. How do we see ourselves?
2. How we think the other group sees us?
3. How do we see the other group?

Do not share or let the other group see the lists until Step 2.

Step 2. The groups then meet together. A representative for each group presents his or her group's lists. While one Group is making its presentation, the other Group may not defend itself, argue, or rebut; but it does have the opportunity to ask clarifying questions (i.e., What do you mean by cutthroat? Could you give an example of two-faced?) The other group then makes its presentation.

Time suggested for Steps 1 and 2: 30 minutes.

Step 3. The groups then meet separately to discuss the discrepancies in perception.

Time suggested for Step 3: 10 minutes.

Step 4. Form subgroups of five or six by mixing members of the two groups. These cross groups have the objective of agreeing upon a diagnosis of interface problems and the development of conflict-reducing or problem-solving alternatives, with action plans and follow-up activities.

Time suggested for Step 4: 20 minutes.

Step 5. The subgroups report their findings including action plans and follow-up activities to the entire group.

Time suggested for Step 5: 15 minutes.

CASE 11:
EXLEY CHEMICAL COMPANY

The Exley Chemical Company is a major chemical manufacturer making primarily industrial chemicals, plastics, and consumer products. Company sales and profits have grown, and its ratio of net profits to sales is about average for the industry, but in the last year or so both sales and profits have been disappointing (see Table 1).

TABLE 1

Year	Sales
5 years ago	$ 81,000,000
3 years ago	93,000,000
2 years ago	108,000,000
Last year	111,000,000

Since new products are constantly being introduced into the line and methods of use are constantly changing, the relative importance of different product groups is constantly shifting. For example, changes in percentage of total sales were experienced by the major product groups over a five-year period (see Table 2).

TABLE 2

	PERCENT OF SALES	
	5 Years Ago	Last Year
Chemicals	61	55
Plastics	31	33
Consumer	8	12
	100	100

THE ORGANIZATION

The general structure is shown in Exhibit 1. Production is carried on in four plants across the United States, each of which has a plant manager. The marketing manager handles sales and marketing services, including the field sales force, with 20 district managers, and industrial sales representatives, who total 25.

All research is administered and done at the corporate research laboratory, including the development section, which is responsible for the development and improvement of production processes. The engineering department handles all planning and construction and the development of new processes and pilot-plant operations.

In addition, to manage the increasing amount of new products being developed, a product development division was established about three years ago. Prior to this, as new products were developed by the research division, they were passed on to the engineering division from the pilot-plant operation. Unfortunately, this method was inadequate for the complex coordination of these projects, so the new division was established. The product development division was to coordinate efforts in developing new products, including recommending manufacturing capacity, sales programs, and so on. The division was to conduct surveys to analyze market potential for new products and recommend the development

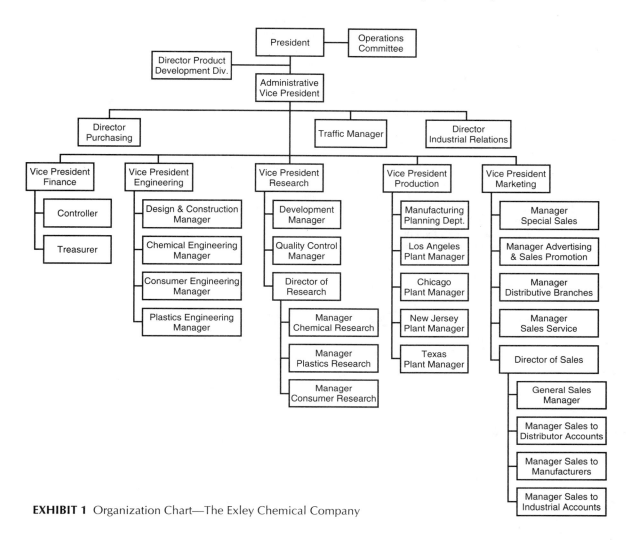

EXHIBIT 1 Organization Chart—The Exley Chemical Company

or production based on these surveys. During the period following the creation of the product development division, problems emerged.

THE SITUATION

Conflicts were created with several other departments. For example, the product development division started using a small force of specialty salespeople to conduct pilot marketing programs. This did not go over well with the marketing department. Also, the product division was given responsibility for market research, but the tasks of sales analysis and forecasting remained in the marketing division. Finally, a product manager was appointed for each separate group of products responsible for the coordination of all company activities for the product. This resulted in more problems.

1. The product manager often needs to visit customers in order to get more realistic input on market conditions, but this is resented by marketing executives. They feel that all customer relations should be handled through marketing, because these visits tend to confuse the customer. "Judging from what I've seen, Product Development couldn't care less about what we are doing in terms of integrating our markets," said the marketing vice president.

2. Sales executives tend to question the sales estimates issued by the product managers. These estimates are usually based on the total product market rather than on Exley's share, which often tends to inflate sales estimates. "The product development group is aggressive and they

want to grow, but you have to grow within guidelines. The product guys are going to have to learn to work with the other divisions," said a sales manager.

3. At a recent meeting of the Chemical Manufacturers Association, a product manager learned that a competitor was about to patent a new process for the production of polymers, which presumably will reduce costs by about one-third. Exley's research person in charge of polymers said that they had several interesting possibilities which might break in a few months. "I think corporate headquarters needs to integrate operations better. We can't be a bunch of entrepreneurs around here. We've got to have more teamwork on these projects." said the project manager.

4. The manager of sales proposed to the consumer projects group that Exley's antifreeze be promoted to retail outlets. He has forwarded a proposal to the project manager with a note: "Our customers feel this is a hot idea; can production supply the needed quantities at a competitive price?" The product manager has found that the two people in research and engineering who are most knowledgeable regarding this product are now deeply involved in a new project, so little has been done to date. "The big frustration is that you can't get help from other departments, if it doesn't have a large return for them. Each division head works on the project that makes the most for their division, but these are not necessarily the best from a corporate standpoint," said the product manager.

CASE ANALYSIS FORM

Name: _____

I. Problems

 A. Macro

 1. _____

 2. _____

 B. Micro

 1. _____

 2. _____

II. Causes

 1. _____

 2. _____

 3. _____

III. Systems affected

 1. Structural _____

 2. Psychosocial _____

 3. Technical _____

 4. Managerial _____

 5. Goals _____

IV. Alternatives

 1. _____

 2. _____

 3. _____

 4. _____

 5. _____

V. Recommendations

 1. _____

 2. _____

 3. _____

SUMMARY

• **Conflict.** Conflict is inevitable in organizations. Large organizations are divisionalized, departmentalized, and segmented to increase control and effectiveness. This creates boundaries between geographic areas or functional units, such as manufacturing, engineering, and marketing. Yet cooperation and collaboration among all units is essential to attaining objectives. This chapter discusses such problems of intergroup relations or interface and describes several OD interventions. The complexity and size of modern organizations often leads to competition or conflict between organization units. Large-scale organizations generate increased problems of dependence between groups, which often result in a condition of suboptimization and a decrease in general efficiency. Such problems as intergroup conflict, power imbalance, or personal conflicts inhibit coordination between groups.

• **Intergroup Interventions**. To deal with intergroup problems, the OD consultant seeks interventions that emphasize improving communication and relations between operating units. These interventions stress the involvement of the individual and the members of the group in the relation between what they do and what others are doing. The consultant uses strategies that identify areas of commonality, increase communication, and emphasize the "meta" goals. These interventions include third-party intervention, organization mirror, and intergroup team building and provide mechanisms for getting collaboration between competing groups. The major objectives of intergroup interventions include a better way of working together, and increased recognition of interdependence, a decrease in competition, and an increase in collaboration.

• **Win-Win**. You have had a chance in the Disarmament Game to experience a situation involving intergroup competition and conflict. Though the conditions and opportunity for a win–win collaboration are present, many inherent factors lead to defining it as a win–lose situation. You may have experienced what happens under condition of conflict and observed the consequences: communication between groups decreases, negative stereotypes are formed, hostility and distrust toward the other group increases while internally you may become more single-minded and cohesive. The net result is usually dysfunctional in terms of total effectiveness. The conflict between your groups may have escalated, with each group attempting to win its point by fair means or foul. Imagine what happens when such a misunderstanding arises between two departments within an organization.

• **Consequences**. You have also had a chance in the second simulation to observe how intergroup interventions might be used to reduce the dysfunctional consequences of win–lose conflict. These intergroup approaches attempt to identify the forces that restrict cooperation and open lines of communication. The outcome should be increased understanding and insight into problem issues and how win–win opportunities can be obscured when a fixed position is held and how facts can become distorted under such conditions. The intergroup intervention provides a framework for a win–win relationship. In this simulation, therefore, you have begun to explore ways of developing more collaborative relations between interdependent groups.

NOTES

1. Laura Rubach, "Downsizing: How Quality Is Affected as Companies Shrink," *Quality Progress*, vol. 28, no. 4, April, 1995, p. 24.

2. Rahul Jacob, "The Struggle to Create an Organization for the 21st Century," *Fortune*, April 3, 1995 p. 98.

3. John F. Welch, "A Master Class in Radical Change," *Fortune*, December 13, 1993, pp. 82–90. Also see, Noel Tichy and Stratford Sherman, "Talk at GE," *Training and Development Journal*, vol. 47, no. 6 (June 1993), pp. 26–35.

4. Richard Beckhard, *Organization Development: Strategies and Models* (Reading, Mass.: Addison-Wesley Publishing Company, Inc., 1969), p. 33.

5. "Jack Welch's Lessons for Success," *Fortune*, January 25, 1993, pp. 86–93.

6. K. W. Thomas and W. H. Schmidt, "A Survey of Managerial Interests with Respect to Conflict," *Academy of Management Journal,* vol. 10, 1976, p. 315.

7. Gordon Lippitt, Ronald Lippitt, and Clayton Lafferty, "Cutting Edge Trends in Organization Development," *Training and Development Journal*, July 1984, p. 60.

8. For additional information, see Paul H. Ephross and Thomas V. Vassil, *Groups That Work: Structure and Process* (New York: Columbia University Press, 1988), pp. 75–98.

9. Richard C. Walton and Robert B. McKersie, *A Behavioral Theory of Labor Negotiations—An Analysis of a Social Interaction System* (New York: McGraw-Hill Book Company, 1963).

10. Kenneth Labich, "Making Over Middle Managers," *Fortune*, May 8, 1990, p. 60.

11. Maryann Keller, *Rude Awakening: The Rise, Fall, and Struggle for Recovery of General Motors*, (New York: William Morrow and Company, Inc., 1989) p. 101.

12. Paul R. Lawrence and Jay W. Lorsch, *Organization and Environment: Managing Differentiation and Integration* (Boston: Graduate School of Business Administration, Harvard University, 1967), p. 40.

13. Carol J. Loomis, "Dinosaurs?" *Fortune*, May 3, 1993, pp. 36–42.

14. Dori J. Yang and Andrea Rothman, "Reinventing Boeing, Radical Changes Amid Crisis," *Business Week*, March 1, 1993, pp. 60–67. Also see Dori J. Yang, "When the Going Gets Tough, Boeing Gets Touchy-Feely," *Business Week*, January 17, 1994, pp. 65–67.

15. David Kirkpatrick, "Gerstner's New Vision of IBM," *Fortune*, November 15, 1993, pp. 119–26.

16. Alan Deutschman, "How H-P Continues To Grow and Grow," *Fortune*, May 2, 1994, pp. 90–100; Catherine Arnst, "Now, HP Stands for Hot Products," *Business Week*, June 14, 1993; Robert D. Hof, "Suddenly, Hewlett-Packard Is Doing Everything Right," *Business Week*, March

23, 1992, pp. 88–89; and Christine Ferguson, "Hewlett-Packard's Other Board," *The Wall Street Journal*, February 26, 1990, p. A10.

17. For a comprehensive review of the research literature on competition and cooperation, see Tjosvold, "Cooperation Theory and Organizations," *Human Relations*, vol. 37, no. 9 (1984), pp. 743–67; and A. Myers, "Team Competition and the Adjustment of Group Members," *Journal of Abnormal and Social Psychology*, vol. 65 (1962), pp. 325–32.

18. P. R. Laughlin, "Ability and Group Problem Solving," *Journal of Research and Development in Education*, vol. 12 (Fall 1978), pp. 114–20; and M. Okun and F. DiVesta, "Cooperation and Competition in Coacting Groups," *Journal of Personality and Social Psychology*, vol. 31 (April 1975), pp. 615–20.

19. Edgar H. Schein, *Process Consultation Volume I: Its Role in Organization Development* (Reading, Mass.: Addison-Wesley Publishing Company, 1988), pp. 109–12. Also see Barbara Meeker, "Cooperation, Competition, and Self-Esteem: Aspects of Winning and Losing," *Human Relations*, vol. 43, no. 3 (1990), pp. 205–19.

20. M. Afzalur Rahim, "A Strategy for Managing Conflict in Complex Organizations, *Human Relations*, vol. 18, no. 1 (1985), pp. 81–86.

21. Jeffrey Barker, Dean Tjosvold, and I. Robert Andrews, "Conflict Approaches of Effective and Ineffective Project Managers: A Field Study in a Matrix Organization," *Journal of Management Studies*, March 1988, pp. 167–78.

22. Kirkpatrick, "Gerstner's New Vision for IBM," p. 120.

23. Robert R. Blake, H. Shepard, and J. Mouton, *Managing Intergroup Conflict in Industry* (Houston, Tex.: Gulf Publishing Company, 1964); and K. W. Thomas, "Conflict and Conflict Management," in M. D. Dunnette, ed. *Handbook in Industrial Organizational Psychology* (Chicago: Rand McNally & Company, 1984). See also M. A. Rahim, "A Measure of Styles of Handling Interpersonal Conflict," *Academy of Management Journal*, vol. 26 (1983), pp. 368–76.

24. For a critique of conflict style literature and an alternative viewpoint, see Mark L. Knapp, Linda L. Putnam, and Lillian J. Davis, "Measuring Interpersonal Conflict In Organizations: Where Do We Go from Here?" *Management Communication Quarterly*, vol. 1, no. 3 (February 1988), pp. 414–29.

25. Dick E. Milholland, "Johnson Wax Regains a Competitive Edge Through Manufacturing," in Y. K. Shetty and Vernon M. Buehler, eds., *Quality Productivity and Innovation, Strategies for Gaining Competitive Advantage*, (New York: Elsevier Science Publishing Co., Inc., 1987) pp. 384–85.

26. A. Downs, *Inside Bureaucracy* (Boston: Little, Brown and Company, 1968).

27. Kenneth R. Thompson (interviewer), "A Conversation with Robert W. Galvin," *Organization Dynamics*, Winter 1993, pp. 56–69; and Lois Therrien, "The Rival Japan Respects, Motorola's Secret: Strong R&D,

Built-In Quality, and Zealous Service," *Business Week*, November 13, 1989, pp. 108–18.

28. John F. Hulpke, California State University, Bakersfield, California. Sources: Henny Sender, "Yotaro Kobayashi of Fuji Xerox: Managing a Cross-Border Joint Venture," *Institutional Investor*, vol. 25, no. 10 (September 1991), pp. 29–31; Michael Selwyn and Lori Valigra, "Making Marriages of Convenience; Fuji-Xerox: Example Worth Copying," *Asian Business*, vol. 27, no. 1 (January 1991), pp. 26–29; Wayland Hicks, "How Xerox Zapped the Japanese," *Business Month*, June 1989, pp. 80–82; and Gene Koretz, "Japanese Employers are 'Locking Out' Their U.S. Managers," *Business Week*, May 7, 1990, p. 24.

29. Reed E. Nelson, "The Strength of Strong Ties: Social Networks and Intergroup Conflict in Organizations," *Academy of Management Journal*, vol. 32, no. 2 (1989), pp. 377–401.

30. Kathy Rebello and Evan Schwartz, "Microsoft," *Business Week*, February 24, 1992, pp. 60–65. See also "Millionaires at Work," *Fortune* April 3, 1995, p. 21.

31. Loraleigh Keashly, *et. al.*, "The Comparative Utility of Third Party Consultation and Mediation Within a Complex Simulation of Intergroup Conflict," *Human Relations*, vol. 46, no. 3 (March 1993), pp. 371–93; Richard E. Walton, *Managing Conflict: Interpersonal Dialogue and Third-Party Roles* (Reading, Mass.: Addison-Wesley Publishing Company, 1987); B. H. Sheppard, "Third Party Conflict Intervention: A Procedural Framework," in L. L. Cummings and B. M. Staw, eds., *Research in Organizational Behavior*, vol. 6 (Greenwich, Conn.: JAI Press, 1984); and R. J. Fisher, "Third Party Consultation as a Method of Intergroup Conflict Resolution," *Journal of Conflict Resolution*, vol. 27 (1983), pp. 301–34.

32. To our knowledge this technique was probably developed by Sheldon Davis and his colleagues at TRW.

33. Blake, Shepard, and Mouton, *Managing Intergroup Conflict*; and Robert R. Blake and Jane S. Mouton, *Solving Costly Organizational Conflicts* (San Francisco: Jossey-Bass, Inc., Publishers, 1984).

34. Robert R. Blake and Jane S. Mouton, "Out of the Past . . . How to Use Your Organization's History to Shape a Better Future," *Training and Development Journal*, November 1983, p. 60.

35. Blake, Shepard, and Mouton, *Managing Intergroup Conflict* and Wendell L. French and Cecil H. Bell, Jr., *Organization Development: Behavioral Science Interventions for Organization Improvement* 3rd ed. (Englewood Cliffs, N. J.: Prentice Hall, Inc., 1984), p. 11.

36. Warren Bennis, *Organization Development: Its Nature, Origins and Prospects* (Reading, Mass.: Addison-Wesley Publishing Company, Inc., 1969).

37. We are indebted to Norman Berkowitz of Boston College and Harvey Hornstein of Columbia University for the design of this game. Used by permission of the authors.

Team meeting sessions help companies such as Compaq in goal setting. *Photo reprinted with permission of Compaq Computer Corporation. All Rights Reserved.*

Goal Setting

12

OBJECTIVES

Upon completing this chapter, you will be able to:

1. Recognize how goal setting can be used as part of an OD program.
2. Apply the major findings of research on goal setting to develop organizational and personal goals.
3. Understand how management by objectives (MBO) can be applied as a management system.
4. Experience and practice goal-setting approaches.

PREMEETING PREPARATION

1. Read the Background Information.
2. Complete Step 1 of OD Skills Simulation 12.1. Form teams of six and assign roles the preceding class period.
3. Complete Step 1 of OD Skills Simulation 12.2.
4. Read and analyze Case 12: Western Utilities Company.

BACKGROUND INFORMATION

At GE, CEO, Jack Welch has employees aiming at 'stretch goals'. Stretch goals at GE means having employee teams trying for huge gains in productivity and quality, without having any clear idea of how to get there, but knowing that employees will use their ingenuity to find ways to reach these goals. In Toshiba's plant, they set a stretch goal of producing a new VCR with half the parts, in half the time, at half the cost. They ended up exceeding these goals.[1]

Goals give direction to an individual's life and provide purpose; goals also give direction to an organization. It is difficult to imagine an organization without some form of goal setting. In a recent survey of Fortune 500 companies, those interviewed mentioned goal setting as a technique often used by successful managers.[2] Goal setting for a large and established company may be a formal program such as the development of an ideal model of the organization or the implementation of a management by objectives program. On the other hand, for an owner of a newly opened business, goal setting may take the form of a mental image of what the business will be like in a year and then five years from now.

OD programs rely heavily upon the goal-setting process. OD, by its definition, is planned change and in order for that change to take place goals need to be set. At an earlier stage in the implementation of the OD program, managers and other employees developed with a consultant ideas for what the organization would be like—that is, they developed goals. They then planned a series of steps to move the organization along to accomplish the goals.

As we have just seen, goal setting is used as a method to carry out the OD program. But goal setting also exists as a process that can be used on an individual, team, interteam, and organization wide basis. Team building and interteam building have set the foundation of trust and cooperation that are important for the establishment of goal setting.[3]

There have been several approaches to goal setting used within organizations. **Management by objectives (MBO)** has been a widely used method. While some OD consultants would be reluctant to include MBO as an OD intervention, it is an approach that can be and has been used to improve total organization effectiveness. When used properly, MBO produces a system of mutual target setting and performance review and enhances planning, communicating, and motivation. In this chapter, we will first discuss goal-setting concepts and then focus on management by objectives.

Goal-Setting Theory

Goal setting is a process intended to increase efficiency and effectiveness by specifying the desired outcomes toward which individuals, teams, and the organization should work. Goal setting may be used as an intervention strategy within an OD program. An analysis of the organization may determine that divisions are not unified in their efforts, that a division or divisions have little or no direction, or that individuals are dissatisfied with their performance and their careers. Besides team building, intergroup development, and other intra and interpersonal interventions, the OD consultant and the client may decide that goal setting may be beneficial. The goal-setting program may be carried out on the individual level to help employees improve their productivity or to help them advance their careers. Goal setting also may be carried out on a group basis, especially if individuals are required to work with one another. Goal setting set up on a departmental level serves to improve productivity and gives direction to the department's efforts.

The basic premise of goal-setting theory discussed here, which Edwin Locke and Gary Latham formulated, is that an individual's conscious intentions and values regulate his or her actions.[4] A *goal* is what an individual is trying to accomplish and it is the object or aim of action. Goals include deadlines, budgets, or other standards for behavior and performance. The following provides a summary of the major findings about goal-setting theory.

More difficult goals produce better performance. Also, it has been found the assignment of an easy goal results in no better performance than no goal at all. In general, goals must be difficult and challenging to have an effect.

Specific hard goals are better than "do your best" goals. Besides goals being difficult and challenging, they also should be specific. Specific goals serve to show exactly what constitutes acceptable performance. Motorola, Inc., which has made quality a top priority, set a goal of "Six Sigma" quality for all their products within five years. *Six Sigma* is a statistical term for 3.4 defects per million products—near-perfect manufacturing.[5] Goals, such as Motorola's, which are specific, are expressed in quantitative terms or as specific events; that is, they include time frames, standards, quotas, monetary amounts, and the like. Recent research suggests that, when the task is complex and there are many optimum strategies, goals should be expressed in general terms.[6] For example, a manager who is in charge of a department that is in a constant state of change may find that setting specific goals leads to rigid behavior and neglecting new opportunities. (See Our Changing World.)

People may abandon goals if the goals become too hard. Though goals should be difficult, people must be able to attain or at least approach their goals; otherwise, they tend to view the goal as impossible, become discouraged, and may abandon the goal. An individual is more likely to accept or choose a goal when there is high, instead of low, expectations of reaching it.[8] In several studies where goals were perceived to be impossible, performance decreased. The difficulty of the goals suggests the goals were not accepted in the first place.[9]

OUR CHANGING WORLD
GOAL MIXUP AT AIR INDIA[7]

Goal setting can be specific or general. Either way, it is pretty important that the *right* goals are stressed. Sometimes specific sales targets, for example, can backfire. The huge U.S. retail store chain W.T. Grant stressed increased sales throughout the organization and smart store managers quickly figured out that one way to increase sales was to give credit to literally *anybody*. A credit sale counted the same as a cash sale, and what's more, all credit collections were the responsibility of the head office. Sales zoomed, but accounts payable zoomed faster. The firm literally killed itself by stressing the wrong goal.

Non-Quantified Goals

Air India provides an example of how an organization can confuse a non-quantified goal, too. In an effort to increase patronage from world business travelers, the firm declared in ads and in company propaganda that "we'll treat you like a Maharajah!" Unfortunately, staffers on board the company's aircraft translated the goal slightly. In practice, the cabin attendants treated Western passengers as Maharajahs, while basically ignoring the Indian passengers that had long been taken for granted. Air India had great loyalty already from Indian customers, so why worry?

The Misidentified Goals

The misidentified goal illustrates potential problems of the wrong goal. On a flight from Bombay to Rome, 25-year-old TeJpreet Khungher, who looks like and is a proud Indian, asked for a soft drink. Hearing the request, a 10-year-old Western kid, asked for a Coke also. A few minutes later, the stewardess returned with a full 355 milliliter can of Coke. She proceeded to treat the 10-year-old white kid like a Maharajah, giving him the full 355 ml unopened can. Then she plopped a half-consumed smaller can on Khungher's tray, not bothering to apologize for its size nor the fact that it was already opened. In fact, she didn't even smile. Apparently the goal "Treat customers like Maharajahs" had been received on the working level as "treat Western passengers like Maharajahs, but don't worry about your fellow Indians." Needless to say, this goal displacement was probably not what was intended by top management. But, this no longer bothers Mr. Khungher. "It doesn't bother me a bit," he says. "I like flying now that I'm flying Air France."

Question

1. Can you identify other examples of problems in goal setting?

Participation in setting goals increases commitment and attainment of goals.
Commitment to difficult goals is higher under conditions when goals are self-set than under conditions when goals are assigned such as by a manager. Also, job satisfaction increases when a person participates in setting their goals.[10] As was discussed in Chapter 9, participation puts an employee more in control of their environment and helps to reduce stress.

Feedback and goals improve performance. Feedback on an individual's performance combined with goal setting has a positive effect on performance; yet, just giving feedback on a person's performance, without having previously set goals, does not lead to improved performance.[11] Information concerning the outcome of the performance, such as whether a goal was met, should be included, but it is also important to include information concerning how to adjust in order to accomplish the goal better. Also frequent, relevant, and specific feedback is important for goal setting to be a success. The feedback should occur as soon after the work activity as possible so the individual remembers the event and its details.[12]

Individual differences tend not to affect goal setting. Studies have shown goal-setting programs to be successful despite the education and job position of the subjects. Some goal-setting programs in organizations are limited to upper and middle management, but research findings suggest that goal setting is just as successful for positions requiring minimum education and skills. CEO David D. Glass of Wal-Mart Stores, Inc., echoes this theme when he said, "There are no superstars at Wal-Mart. We're a company of ordinary people overachieving."[13]

Goal setting has been used successfully by production workers, logging crews, managers, clerical workers, students, engineers, scientists, and maintenance workers. The success of a goal-setting program is also not contingent upon the number of years of service an employee has with an organization.[14]

There are some individual differences that should be considered in goal-setting programs. Individuals with a high need for achievement and with high self-esteem are more likely to commit themselves to difficult goals than are individuals with a low need for achievement and with low self-esteem. For individuals low in need for achievement, commitment will not be forthcoming just because they have participated in setting their goals. Probably only external rewards or punishment will be successful in building commitment for this type of individual.[15]

Goal setting in teams deserves special consideration. Setting difficult individual goals on an interdependent team task will likely result in poorer performance than when a team goal is set or even when there is no team goal at all. People engaged in individual goal setting tend to be more competitive and less cooperative—two conditions that were discussed in previous chapters as dysfunctional for team and interteam performance.[16] When people are engaged in interdependent work, it is important that individual goals are set such that they facilitate the attainment of the team goal.

Cooperation in goal setting can be accomplished by a manager explicitly specifying which goal is more important. Another way to get cooperation is through participative goal setting within the context of a team-building session. IBM, aware of a special need for goal setting in teams, implemented a technique they call PQM or *process quality management*. This approach relies heavily upon goals established by a team through consensus decision making. The team approach continues through a follow-up procedure to decide how well goals were met.[17]

Support of management is critical. Support by all levels of management in goal-setting programs is crucial to their success. Supervisors should be present to encourage the acceptance of goals by employees, to provide help in improving skills, and to give timely feedback on how the goals are being accomplished.

A Model For Goal Setting

Based upon the research findings previously cited, Latham and Locke[18] have developed a useful model for goal setting (see Figure 12.1). For goal-setting to be successful, goals need to be properly developed and the individuals trying to achieve the goals need to be committed to them. A goal-setting program in an organization requires careful planning.

As seen in Figure 12.1, the first three factors in the goal-setting process are determining the goal, achieving goal commitment, and overcoming resistance to **goal acceptance**. Goals can be determined in a variety of ways. Time and motion studies can provide the basis for goals involving repetitive and standardized tasks. Another approach sometimes used to establish goals is to base standards on past performance, but this may not result in a challenging goal, especially when past performance has been poor. Goals also may be set by joint participation between the employee and the supervisor. This method often leads to employee commitment, a crucial ingredient in effective goal-setting.

Goal commitment can be achieved in a variety of ways. Trust in upper management, as well as support by management and an effective reward and incentive system, is helpful in obtaining commitment.[19] The previous work that has been undertaken in the OD program should have built mutual trust between employees of all levels of the organization. Past successes of accomplishing goals build excitement and a positive feeling toward future goal accomplishment. Competition between employees may be useful in some cases, but managers should avoid designing competitive situations, especially in interdependent situations. There is also a danger employees may become so involved in competing with one another that they may lose sight of the goals.

Resistance to goal acceptance can be overcome by several methods and a combination of methods will likely result in a more successful goal-setting program. Providing special training for employees in new techniques and procedures and providing rewards and incentives can help encourage goal acceptance. Participation in setting goals can lead to goal acceptance for some employees.

For goals to work best, they should conform to certain attributes or characteristics. Goals should be difficult and challenging, but not impossible to accomplish. They should be specific and measurable, as well as compatible with goals formulated at higher levels of the organization. As an example of goal setting, Bell Canada's telephone operators are required to answer calls within 23 seconds, while Federal Express customer agents are

FIGURE 12.1 Goal Setting

expected to answer customer questions within 140 seconds. Both goals were considered very difficult when initially set, but employees eventually met and exceeded these goals.[20]

After specific performance goals have been set, a period of performance follows. During this time, managers must be prepared to provide support. To achieve specific goals, employees may require training or additional resources, such as new equipment or information. Managers may need to work with employees in developing action plans. Finally, managers should provide timely and objective feedback upon completion of the goal.

The results of the employees' performance can be beneficial or negative. The benefits may incur to the organization or the individual. When individuals succeed at meeting a goal, they feel competent and successful. Higher performance and pride in achievement of successes can be expected. Employees are more likely to have clearer roles as they more fully realize the performance expected of them. Negative consequences can be expected, when the goals are not achieved. This particularly seems to be a problem in situations where specific and measurable goals could not be set.

Results of Goal Setting

Research on the effects of goal setting has shown positive results on both the personal and organizational level.[21] One study found that in 90 percent of the cases, specific and challenging goals led to higher performance than easy goals, "do your best" goals, or no goals.

In a review of goal-setting studies, the median improvement in performance resulting from goal setting was 16 percent. The same study found goal setting, when combined with the use of monetary incentives, improved performance by more than 40 percent. Another study found goal setting to have significantly affected attitudes toward others, the job, and the organization. In a review of total company strength, results revealed that the performance of a company is strongly related to the extent of goal-setting and planning activities.

The remainder of this chapter will look at a specific type of goal-setting program: management by objectives.

Management By Objectives

Management by objectives (MBO) is a specific technique used by organizations for setting goals. It is a process aimed at the integration of individual and organization goals.[22] MBO may be defined as a system of management set up to help in planning, organizing, problem-solving, motivating, and other important management activities. It involves the participation of the subordinate and his or her manager in setting and clarifying the subordinate's goals. George Odiorne (a leading MBO consultant) defines MBO as "a process whereby the superior and subordinate managers of an organization jointly identify its common goals, define each individual's major areas of responsibility in terms of results expected, and use these measures as guides for operating the unit and assessing the contribution of each of its members."[23] The goals of this approach include an improved level of performance, increased communication and participation, higher morale and job satisfaction, and a better understanding of organization objectives at all levels.

MBO approaches goal setting on the assumption that people possess higher-level needs for competence and achievement, and that they want to satisfy these higher-level needs in their work. In addition, people will work harder and perform better if they participate in setting their goals. The assumptions conclude with the idea that management, then, must create a climate that encourages self-development by individuals.

The Purposes of MBO Programs

There are two underlying purposes for implementing MBO in an organization. One is to clarify organization goals and plans at all levels; the other is to gain increased motivation and participation among organization members. MBO provides a means of increasing the

clarity of organization planning and of enhancing the subordinate's knowledge and understanding of his or her job. MBO may be used to identify organization goals at all levels and to encourage participation in setting the standards that will be used to evaluate subordinate performance. Participation in the goal-setting process allows managers to control and monitor performance by measuring performance and results against the objectives subordinates helped to set.

The late Douglas McGregor also suggested a modified approach to MBO under the concept of "management by integration and self-control."[24] According to McGregor, the MBO concept could be used to provide a mutual opportunity for managers and subordinates to define and agree upon areas of responsibility, specific performance goals, and the terms of the expected outcomes. He suggested that managers establish their performance goals after reaching agreement with their superior regarding major job responsibilities. Then accomplishments would be appraised after a short period, usually six months. This self-appraisal would be in cooperation with the superior, after which another set of performance goals would be established. McGregor aimed at the commitment of organization members by the "creation of conditions such that the members of an organization can achieve their own goals best by directing their efforts toward the success of the enterprise."[25] He advocated this concept for appraising performance, since it shifted the emphasis from weakness and criticism to an analysis of strength and potential. In this application of MBO, the supervisor's role is one of counseling, coaching, or process consultation.

The MBO Process

Although opinions vary on the specific implementation of MBO, most consultants emphasize the need for top management's commitment to MBO. As with the overall OD program, MBO starts at the top of the organization and works down through successive layers of the organization. The MBO program of Bridgestone Corporation's tire plant in Tennessee begins with the President proposing a preliminary policy statement to the executive committee. This committee draws up a final presidential policy statement that is presented to department managers. Each department manager working with their superior draws up for their department an implementation plan, in detail, based on the President's policy statement.[26]

As is the case at Bridgestone, the MBO process begins with the top management team studying the operating system. From this study, the team sets up broad measures of organizational performance. Goal-setting sessions are then held from one organization level at a time from the top down. Within divisions and at each successive level the goals are more specifically defined.

Management by objectives may be described as a process consisting of a series of interrelated steps (see Figure 12.2):

- *Step 1.* The subordinate proposes to his or her manager a set of goals for the upcoming time period that are formulated to be congruent with goals set at the next higher level. This proposal sets forth specific goals and performance measures.
- *Step 2.* The subordinate and the manager jointly develop specific goals and targets. These goals must be specific, measurable objectives for each area of responsibility and they must be *mutually* agreed upon by subordinate and manager. The major responsibility, of course, should lie with the subordinate. These objectives should include both performance goals and personal career goals.
- *Step 3.* There is a period of performance in which the individual involved is attempting to accomplish the individual goals.
- *Step 4.* The manager feeds back results to the subordinate and gives appropriate rewards for performance. This individual performance review involves an appraisal and discussion of accomplishments and variances of overall performance compared with targets.
- *Step 5.* The outcome of the performance review provides the basis for setting new performance goals and recycling of the goal-setting process.

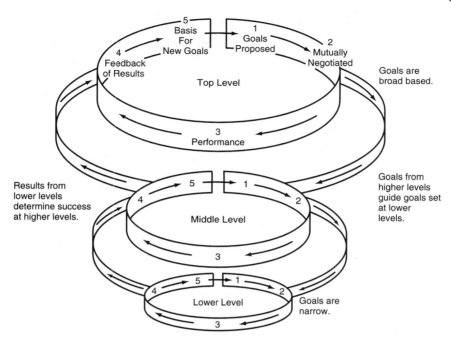

FIGURE 12.2 Steps in the MBO Process

MBO is a continuing self-renewal process. The time each complete cycle takes varies with MBO programs, though it is common for programs to have quarterly reviews of objectives with a major review and new objectives set annually. By having quarterly reviews, problems can be corrected quickly and changes in the situation can be considered. The central focus of any MBO program is the development of agreement between supervisor and subordinate about objectives and targets.

As happens with other OD interventions such as team building, MBO programs are set up in many organizations independently of an OD program. Yet, MBO and goal setting are processes many OD specialists introduce into organizations. For MBO to be used as an OD intervention, it should include (1) a team approach to setting and reviewing targets; (2) real participation by subordinates in setting goals, with an emphasis upon mutually agreed goals; (3) shared trust between the subordinate and manager; and (4) a real concern for personal career goals as well as for organization goals. With such a team orientation, MBO logically follows team and inter-team building in an OD program. When MBO is used in this sense, it can provide individual satisfaction and motivation, and increased organization attainment.

Many guidelines used for setting objectives are the same that are used in other types of goal-setting programs. Every effort should be made by the manager and the subordinate to make the goals as precise and specific as possible. There must be agreement and acceptance of these objectives by both the individual and his or her manager. These interactions between a manager and a subordinate also provide a counseling and coaching opportunity and in this manner provide for management development. Although these specific steps in the MBO process may vary among organizations and OD consultants, the goals are similar, including increased levels of performance and increased understanding at all levels of organization objectives. For an example of how one company, Boehringer Mannheim Corporation, installed MBO, see OD in Practice.

OD IN PRACTICE
BOEHRINGER MANNHEIM CORPORATION[27]

Boehringer Mannheim (BM) Corporation employs about 2,500 people and is involved in the fast-changing area of medical diagnostics equipment, orthopedic implant devices, and pharmaceuticals. BM set up a nontraditional MBO program that focused on having every key professional specify how much he or she will contribute to next year's profits.

The MBO Program

The program was phased in over two years. MBO began with a two-day training session conducted by an external consultant and attended by every member of management, including the CEO. The training program continues for future and new managers. To emphasize that MBO is not a one-shot program, the CEO still stresses MBO in employee publications and annual state-of-the-company presentations.

Employees formulate objectives for each year's budget and the direct supervisor reviews performance at quarterly intervals. A new feature of BM's program is to calculate the dollar value of written objectives. BM also introduced "stretch" objectives. These are objectives identified by an employee's manager that are most critical to the organiza-

tion's goals. A cash bonus system is tied to attaining stretch objectives.

Reasons for Success

The company claims success with their program on several levels. It is said that within BM there is a greater emphasis on results, improved teamwork, a growth in entrepreneurism, and a greater sense of contribution. BM traces their success with MBO to:

- Implementing MBO the right way.
- Tying MBO to company strategy.
- Establishing a financial perspective to MBO.

Questions

1. How does BM's approach compare to standard MBO programs?
2. Do you think tying MBO to financial objectives is a good idea?

Criticisms of MBO

The implementation of MBO usually requires large quantities of time, money, and effort for successful adaptation. Because of these limitations, managerial and professional employees have traditionally used MBO. For employees performing more routine work at the lower levels of an organization, obtaining benefits that exceed costs has been more difficult.

Some MBO programs also may have problems because management fails to recognize that proper implementation of MBO requires new improved managerial skills and competence (see B.C. comic strip). Critics question whether joint goal-setting among unequals is possible and whether subordinates at lower levels are free to select their objectives. In some applications, MBO may be too quantitative and setting objectives as explicitly as possible may not always be functional. In other MBO programs, communication may come from the top dictating to the bottom instead of open communication and mutual goal-setting. There is also a danger that MBO will focus on only certain aspects of the job (such as sales) and ignore other responsibilities (for example, customer satisfaction.)[28]

MBO has been used widely in organizations and in one study of Fortune 500 companies, 86 percent report using or having used MBO.[29] However, 11 percent report not using MBO at the time of responding to the survey, mirroring somewhat of an industry trend toward discontinuing MBO programs. MBO received a good deal of publicity in the 1970s and 1980s and expectations of some managers rose to unrealistic levels. Still, MBO remains an often used goal-setting process though it may go by a variety of names such as goal setting and target setting.

MBO is a technique that includes a multitude of different types of programs, and many OD consultants question whether MBO should be considered an OD intervention. Some critics feel that MBO is a manipulative approach and, therefore, should not be classified as an OD intervention, whereas others feel that OD and MBO are consistent approaches. Arthur

Source: B.C. by permission of Johnny Hart and Creators Syndicate, Inc.

Beck and Ellis Hillmar are among those who feel that OD and MBO do fit together. In fact, they do not believe it is possible to have one without the other.[30] It is their contention that one of the major assumptions underlying organization development is the need to have goal setting at all levels, and so they feel that MBO is a legitimate OD intervention.

Some consultants believe that properly designed MBO programs, based upon McGregor's ideas, can have positive organization results. Others believe that MBO can be improved by placing a greater emphasis upon individual goals and examining the underlying assumptions of motivation within these programs. There also should be an emphasis on mutual goal setting, and frequent feedback and interaction between superior and subordinate. Research evidence also suggests that less paperwork leads to improved effectiveness of MBO programs. In summary, MBO programs can, when implemented correctly, be effective in systematically engaging individuals in target setting and performance improvement.

The Results of MBO

Many different types of organizations have tried MBO. One difficulty in appraising these approaches is that MBO has become an all-purpose term implying many different things in many different organization settings. In a study of 87 organizations using MBO, the researchers concluded that there are at least 10 different approaches to MBO, ranging from motivational to coercive.[31]

Most research on MBO programs has reported mixed results. Some studies show that MBO has increased organization performance, while others show inefficiency and weakness in application. Although research on the effectiveness of MBO is not conclusive, the trend of findings is generally favorable. Several studies have found that goal-setting results in improved performance and increased motivation. The studies "have found that those managers working under MBO programs were more likely to have taken specific actions to improve performance than were those who continued with the traditional performance appraisal approach."[32] Other evidence suggests that MBO seems associated with positive attitudes toward the work situation and that participation by subordinates in decision making can improve performance level and job satisfaction.

In a two-part study at Purex Corporation, MBO reversed production rates from a 0.4 percent decline per month to an increase of 0.3 percent per month. In a second follow-up study, however, he found that participants felt that the program overemphasized production, was used as a whip, and did not involve all levels of management.[33]

This chapter has focused on what individuals, work teams, and organizations can do through OD goal-setting programs to improve performance. The next chapter deals with improving work processes for individuals and work teams through interventions including job design, self-managed work teams, and total quality management.

REVIEW QUESTIONS

1. Identify and discuss the major factors in effective goal setting.

2. Discuss the role of participation in goal setting.

3. Describe Locke and Latham's goal-setting model.

4. What are the typical steps in a MBO program?

5. Compare and contrast the reasons for successful and unsuccessful MBO programs.

KEY WORDS AND CONCEPTS

Define and be able to use the following:

Goal
Goal Acceptance
Goal Commitment
Process Quality Management

Goal Setting
Management by Objectives (MBO)
Resistance
Six Sigma

OD SKILLS SIMULATION 12.1
ORGANIZATION GOAL SETTING

Total time suggested: 1 hour.

A. PURPOSE

This simulation is intended to allow you the opportunity to set goals within an organization setting and observe how personal and organizational goals can be in conflict. You will experience how conflicting goals can sometimes be resolved.

B. PROCEDURE

Step 1. Prior to class form teams of six (extras act as observers), select roles, and read the Vernal Corporation Background Information and your role description. Read only your role and mark your individual decision in Col. 1 of Vernal Corporation Decision Form (p. 337). The roles are:

1. Project Manager
2. Accounting Systems Consultant
3. Information Systems Consultant
4. Technical Support Consultant
5. Government Contracts Consultant
6. OD Consultants
 Observer (optional)

Step 2. Meet with your team members and the project manager, who conducts the meeting. The OD Consultant will also be present to help with group process. Place Team Decision in Col. 2 of Decision Form (p. 337).

Time suggested for Step 2: 30 minutes.

Step 3. Critique your team meeting and the quality of the meeting. The consultant and observer will provide feedback. See the Observer Form (p. 337) at the end of this simulation. Also consider the following:

1. Were individual goals made public or were they concealed? Share at this point any information not previously disclosed in the team meeting.
2. Were both individual and organization goals adequately met?
3. To what extent did the personality of an individual influence the decision?
4. Do members currently support the decision?
5. Was the OD Consultant helpful? Dysfunctional? What suggestions for improvement can you give?

Time suggested for Step 3: 15 minutes.

Step 4. Meet with the other teams to compare decisions.
1. Each team presents their decision and the factors most important in arriving at the decision.
2. To what extent was there member support for the final decision? How could support have been increased?
3. How closely did differing teams achieve goal agreement? If there were differences, to what could the differences be attributed considering all teams had the same base of information?
4. Did the OD Consultants make content suggestions or provide process interventions?

Step 5. The class should discuss the process of goal setting and conflict resolution.

Time suggested for Steps 4 and 5: 15 minutes.

VERNAL CORPORATION BACKGROUND INFORMATION

Vernal is a medium-size company offering consulting services for accounting systems and information systems, and a special unit specializing in local and federal government contracts. Until now Vernal has had only one facility for all operations, and the majority of the business was conducted for clients in the metropolitan area. Because of substantial contracts recently obtained in another city 200 miles away in the same state, Vernal has decided to open a field office there. The office will be headed by a project manager and will consist of representatives from Accounting Systems, Information Systems, the Technical Support Unit, and the Government Contracts Unit.

The headquarters of Vernal is a new facility located in a planned suburban community, almost a rural setting, with the most up-to-date facilities. The company has a complete health facility which is part of its "wellness" program, day care, company-provided van pools, bicycle paths connected to the communities' extensive bicycle paths, covered and free parking lots, and a company-subsidized restaurant and cafeteria.

ROLE DESCRIPTION (READ ONLY YOUR ROLE)

Role 1—Project Manager. You have been selected as the Project Manager for the new facility across state. The four representatives will report directly to you, and your job will be to coordinate their activities with the home office. You applied for the position. The move will mean an advancement for all those selected. The assignment is expected to last about five years, and then you will be transferred back to company headquarters.

One of the first tasks facing you and your team before making the move is to select an office. Although you have reserved the right to make the final decision, you have called a meeting of those making the move to receive their input so that you can make a more informed decision. You are also interested in getting off to a good start with the other people as your success is largely determined by how well they do their job; therefore, you would like to have them agree upon a decision which best meets both the individual and company goals.

You have drawn up a summary of the available offices you obtained on a recent fact-finding trip (see the Office Alternative List). The four alternative offices on the summary sheet are the only choices available and the information on the sheet, though incomplete, is all that is available.

You have been informed that the maximum the company is willing to spend is $12,000 a month, though you would like to reserve $1,000 for last-minute lease changes. The offices have a monthly base lease rate and a group of options available. Most of the options have specific costs and you will have to select options that will not exceed $12,000 less the $1,000 reserve. Also, you would like to keep costs to a minimum.

You would personally like the office to be located close to the suburbs where you hope to buy a house. A private office area, such as a converted conference room, is important to you as it will lend respect to your position with the other team members. Otherwise you are not big on amenities such as a prestige office and furnishings. You are interested in bottom-line results that look good back at the home office, not a plush office.

All Representatives. You have been selected as the representative from your division to move to the new facility across the state. You will report directly to the project manager but you will retain close ties with your division. You applied for the position and the move will mean an advancement for all those selected. The assignment is expected to last about five years before you are transferred back to company headquarters.

The project manager has called a meeting of those making the move to help select an office. The project manager has reserved the right to make the final decision, but he/she would like to get your input. The manager has given you a summary of the offices with pertinent information he/she obtained on a recent fact-finding trip. (See the Office Alternative List.) The four alternative offices on the summary sheet are the only choices available and the information on the sheet, though incomplete, is all that is available.

The project manager has informed you that the maximum the company is willing to spend on the new office space is $12,000 a month. The offices have a monthly base lease rate and a group of options available. Most of the options have specific costs, and you will have to select those options that will not exceed $12,000.

Role 2—Accounting Systems Consultant. Your goal is to select an office reasonably close to your clients, many of whom are located in the downtown area. Clients will be coming to the office so it is important to have an impressive office, at least two conference rooms, adequate parking, and proximity to restaurants. You don't like to drive so some kind of transportation other than driving is important or else you would consider an apartment within walking distance. You will also need to build support for your choices with the other representatives and most certainly try to convince the project manager of your decision. You may say anything in order to build this support.

Role 3—Information Systems Consultant. You will often entertain your clients at the office. You believe that to entertain clients in meetings, you need a prestigious office with a good view, good furnishings, three conference rooms, and dining facilities. A downtown location close to your clients is desirable. You prefer to live in an apartment near your office. You will also need to build support for your choices with the other representatives and most certainly try to convince the project manager of your decision. You may say anything in order to build this support.

Role 4—Technical Support Consultant. You believe that health and recreation are the most important factor. Therefore, your goal is to select an office with full recreational and health facilities like those at the company headquarters. It would be ideal if there were amenities such as a hair stylist and restaurants. As your work requires you to call on clients at their offices to work out technical problems, you see no reason to have a lavish office. You would like to be able to purchase a house reasonably close to the office. You will also need to build support for your choices with the other representatives and most certainly try to convince the project manager of your decision. You may say anything in order to build this support.

Role 5—Government Contracts Consultant. You think it is important to have functionally adequate quarters, reasonably well furnished, and with a small kitchen, because you normally eat in the office. You are normally in and out of the office a lot to call on your clients, so parking close to the office is important. You also want health facilities similar to those at the home office. Because your time is important to you, you would like to get an apartment close to your work so you can ride your bike. You will also need to build support for your choices with the other representatives and most certainly try to convince the project manager of your decision. You may say anything in order to build this support.

Role 6—OD Consultant. You hope to accomplish several things at this meeting:
1. To develop a consultant-client relationship with all committee members.
2. To help the committee members in their task by making appropriate process interventions.
3. To remain uninvolved with the content of the problem.

Role 7—Observer. You will only observe during the role play session so that you can help the team critique their meeting in Steps 3 and 4. The Observer Form may assist you in providing feedback.

Office Alternative List, Decision Form, and Observer Form follow.

OFFICE ALTERNATIVE LIST

Type	Suburban Shopping Center Office	Regional Office Building	Downtown Office Building	Downtown High Rise
Base lease	$7,000	$9,000	$8,000	$10,000
Size	Large, 4 rooms.	Adequate, 1 moderate size room.	Adequate, 1 moderate size room.	Large, 1 room.
Custodial service	$200	$300	$300	$400
Furnishings	Used carpet and furniture, fair condition, $300. New carpet and furniture, $550.	Used carpet and furniture, good condition, $400. New carpet and furniture, $550.	Used carpet and furniture, good condition, $300. New carpet and furniture, $600.	Nearly new carpet and furniture, $500. New furniture, $700.
Conference rooms including furnishings	Not available but office space has 4 rooms.	Up to 5 available, $1,000 each.	Up to 2 available, $700 each.	Up to 4 available, $1,100 each.
Prestige of building	Little.	Moderately high.	Some.	High.
Windows and view	Small windows with limited view. No cost.	Large windows with view, $200. Lower 5 floors, windows with poor view, no cost.	Average windows with poor view. No cost.	Large windows, with excellent view, top 5 floors, $500. Lower floors with moderate view, no cost.
Size of building	2 story	25 story	10 story	40 story
Location	Suburban area. Nice housing nearby.	Large regional business center in suburban area. Various types of housing in area within 1/4 hour.	Downtown business district. Few and expensive apartments in area. Driving time to affordable housing, 3/4 hour.	Downtown business district. Apartments in building and area expensive. Driving time to affordable housing, 1/2 hour.
Parking	Street and small lot in rear. No cost.	One parking lot, $50 monthly per car. Street readily available.	One car allowed in building garage, no cost. Unlimited garage space 1 block away, $30 monthly per car. No street parking.	Unlimited in building. No cost for tenants and guests. No street parking.
Mass transportation system	None. Some bicycle paths.	None. Car pools. Some bicycle paths.	Bus. Building-sponsored van pools, $50 per office. Car pools.	Bus. Car pools.
Dining in building	Not available. Fast food next door.	Coffee shop in building. Okay restaurants in area.	Coffee shop and restaurant in building. Excellent restaurants in area.	Coffee shop and excellent restaurants in building. Catering available for offices.
Coffee machine, refrigerator, stove, kitchen	Small kitchen with all appliances, $100.	Small kitchen, appliances, lunch area, $200.	No kitchen. Coffee machine, $50.	Small kitchen, appliances and dining area, $300.
Miscellaneous services	Health club (gym and hot tub), 2 blocks away, $75 per member. Hair styling, 1 block away.	Hair styling. Complete health and recreation club next door, $200 per member.	Hair styling. No recreation facilities.	Hair styling. Hot tub, gym, pool, $200 per office. Guests allowed.

VERNAL CORPORATION
DECISION FORM

Decision Factors	Col. 1 Individual	Col. 2 Team
1. Lease	_____	_____
2. Size	_____	_____
3. Custodial	_____	_____
4. Furnishing	_____	_____
5. Conference	_____	_____
6. Prestige	_____	_____
7. View	_____	_____
8. Location	_____	_____
9. Parking	_____	_____
10. Mass Transit	_____	_____
11. Dining	_____	_____
12. Kitchen	_____	_____
13. Miscellaneous	_____	_____
Total		
Alternatives		
1. Suburban	_____	_____
2. Regional	_____	_____
3. Downtown	_____	_____
4. High Rise	_____	_____

OBSERVER FORM

Instructions: For each item, place a number in the blank to the right representing your reaction to how your group performed based on the following scale.

[Low 1 : 2 : 3 : 4 : 5 : 6 : 7 : 8 : 9 : 10 High]

	Individual Rating	Team Rating
1. Degree of cooperative teamwork	_____	_____
2. Degree of team motivation	_____	_____
3. Degree of member satisfaction	_____	_____
4. Degree of information sharing (participation)	_____	_____
5. Degree of consensual decision making	_____	_____
6. Degree of team conflict or competition (i.e., conflict directly faced and resolved)	_____	_____
7. Degree of quality of group decisions	_____	_____
8. Degree of speed with which decision is made	_____	_____
9. Degree of participating leadership	_____	_____
10. Degree of clarity of goals	_____	_____
Total ranking	_____	_____

OD SKILLS SIMULATION 12.2
MANAGING BY OBJECTIVES

Total time suggested: 1 hour.

A. PURPOSE

In this simulation, you will have an opportunity to practice goal setting and apply it to your own objectives. You will be able to practice MBO-type coaching and counseling relationships, and to receive feedback in your own consulting style.

B. PROCEDURES

Step 1. Before class, review your list of Personal Objectives for Course from Simulation 2.1, Chapter 2, and determine the progress toward the goals.

Step 2. Form groups of three. Each individual will have an opportunity (1) to review his or her objectives (client), (2) to act as consultant, and (3) to observe.

During class the consultant will act as a process consultant, helping the client determine specific, mutual objectives, providing feedback, and reviewing progress toward goals.

The observer is to carefully note the interaction of the consultant and client (see the Observer Form), looking for actions that would facilitate or inhibit the MBO process, and which might indicate the consultant's style.

Step 3. Rotate roles until each person has reviewed his or her objectives.

Time suggested for Steps 1–3: 45 minutes.

Step 4. The total group should then discuss the process of consulting or coaching another individual in the goal-setting situation.

Time suggested for Step 4: 15 minutes.

OBSERVER FORM

Instruction: Based on the following scale, select the number that indicates your observation of the following areas. Record your choice in the blank to the right.

Very Little 1 : 2 : 3 : 4 : 5 : 6 : 7 Very Much

Did the consultant

1. Establish a relationship? _____
2. Take over the problem? _____
3. Focus on feelings? _____
4. Encourage the client to be specific? _____
5. Allow the client to talk? _____
6. Lead and direct the conversation? _____
7. Show indications of judging the client? _____

CASE 12:
WESTERN UTILITIES COMPANY

Western Utilities Company, a privately owned utility company, has been faced with an expansion of its facilities resulting in financial inefficiencies. President Robert Delgado has requested a review of all operating standards. He requested that John Givens and Hilda Hirsh set out a broad outline of MBO performance standards that would identify key standards with which to control performance. Three years ago, Western Utilities, under the direction of a management consulting firm, implemented a system of management by objectives (MBO) for the purpose of evaluating department managers, sales engineers, and consumer service employees.

The advantage of such a system of controls is that top management can very rapidly scan a printout and detect any trouble spots in the department. Givens and Hirsh attempted to set the standards as if the personnel were working at a normal pace. After review, Givens and Hirsh raised the performance level on several items. Their justification was that if a standard can be achieved without a challenge, it is probably too low. Delgado had specifically asked for goals that were not easily attainable. There was a certain amount of negative reaction, but in the end the departments agreed.

THE SITUATION

During the past year, however, a significant degree of dissatisfaction has emerged. In the first year participation was encouraged and rewards were obtained. The employees set their goals high and productivity increased.

Now, however, problems are being reported in the evaluation of performance, and many managers are claiming that the standards set by Hirsh were too tight or unfair. The President said: "Yes, we have had a few operating problems, but no system is perfect." Hirsh noted that the consumer department had exceeded their monthly labor cost standards, so she called Bill Walton and "red-lined" his performance report. Walton hit the roof. He called Givens and said: "The system is grossly unfair and inaccurate as a measure of performance. The real objective is to control total costs. My department has done this, even though we were over in labor costs. There was a heavy snowstorm last month with lots of frozen lines, and we had to get people out there on overtime. The real need is to maximize customer service and to keep costs to a minimum, which we have done."

Two other department managers complained that the system was unfair, and several engineers are threatening to resign. In their complaints to Givens, they pointed out that it appeared that Hirsh was only looking for failures to report, under the cover of the MBO system. Robert Delgado thought: We may need to take another look at our system; maybe MBO doesn't work in a utility.

Case Analysis Form follows

CASE ANALYSIS FORM

Name: _____

I. Problems

 A. Macro

 1. _____

 2. _____

 B. Micro

 1. _____

 2. _____

II. Causes

 1. _____

 2. _____

 3. _____

III. Systems affected

 1. Structural _____

 2. Psychosocial _____

 3. Technical _____

 4. Managerial _____

 5. Goals _____

IV. Alternatives

 1. _____

 2. _____

 3. _____

 4. _____

 5. _____

V. Recommendations

 1. _____

 2. _____

 3. _____

SUMMARY

- **Goals**. Goal setting and management by objectives have been described in this chapter. Goal setting can have highly beneficial results for both individuals and organizations as reported in the research findings. However, goal setting requires careful planning if it is to be used in an OD program. There are certain characteristics of a goal that tend to result in a more effective goal-setting program. The goal should be difficult, specific, measurable, and achievable. When goal setting is set up in an organization, feedback should be provided by management to the employee. Commitment by the individual is crucial and participation in designing the goal is an effective way to assure acceptance.

- **MBO**. Management by objectives has been widely used in organizations but its success has been mixed. The failure of MBO programs can partially be traced to unrealistic expectations by management and to improper implementation. Despite some negative reports of MBO, it incorporates some very sound techniques of goal setting and should not be overlooked as an OD goal-setting technique.

- **Practice Skills**. In the simulations, you had an opportunity to experience and practice the concept of goal setting. You set your individual goals and acted much as a manager or OD consultant would do in negotiating team goals. In the simulation, you also experienced a situation where employees with different goals were confronted with a common problem.

NOTES

1. "Jack Welch Lets Fly on Budgets, Bonuses, and Buddy Boards," *Fortune*, May 29, 1995, p. 145.

2. Eric Stephan, Gordon E. Mills, R. Wayne Pace, and Lenny Ralphs, "HRD in the 500, A Survey," *Training and Development Journal*, January 1988, pp. 26–32.

3. For additional information see Michael P. O'Driscoll and James L. Eubanks, "Behavioral Competencies, Goal Setting, and OD Practitioner Effectiveness," *Group and Organization Management*, vol. 18, no. 3 (September 1993), pp. 308–27.

4. For summaries of goal setting see: Gary P. Latham and Edwin A. Locke, "Self-Regulation Through Goal Setting," *Organizational Behavior and Human Decision Processes*, vol. 50, no. 2 (December 1991), pp. 212–47; E. A. Locke, G. P. Latham, and M. Erez, "The Determinants of Goal Commitment," *Academy of Management Review*, vol. 13, no. 1 (1988), pp. 23–39; and E. A. Locke, L. M. Saari, K. N. Shaw, and G. P. Latham, "Goal Setting and Task Performance: 1969–80," *Psychological Bulletin*, vol. 90, no. 1 (1981), p. 125–52.

5. Kenneth R. Thompson, "A Conversation with Robert W. Galvin," *Organizational Development*, Winter 1994, pp. 56–69; and Mark Gill, "Stalking Six Sigma," *Business Month*, January 1990, pp. 42–46.

6. E. A. Locke, D. C. Chah, S. Harrison, and N. Lustgarten, "Separating the Effects of Goal Specificity from Goal Level," *Organizational Behavior and Human Decision Processes*, vol. 43 (1989), pp. 270–87; and P. C. Earley, T. Connolly, and G. Ekegren, "Goals, Strategy Development, and Task Performance: Some Limits on the Efficacy of Goal Setting," *Journal of Applied Psychology*, vol. 74, no. 1 (1989), pp. 24–33.

7. John F. Hulpke, California State University, Bakersfield, Bakersfield, California, 1994.

8. M. Erez and I. Zidon, "Effect of Goal Acceptance on the Relationship of Goal Difficulty to Performance," *Journal of Applied Psychology*, vol. 69 (1984), pp. 69–78.

9. G. P. Latham and G. A. Yukl, "A Review of Research on the Application of Goal Setting in Organizations," *Academy of Management Journal*, vol. 18, no. 4 (December 1975), p. 833.

10. M. Erez, P. C. Earley, and C. L. Hulin, "The Impact of Participation on Goal Acceptance and Performance: A Two-Step Model," *Academy of Management Journal*, vol. 28 (1985), pp. 50–66; and J. R. Hollenbeck, C. R. Williams, and J. Klein, "An Empirical Examination of the Antecedents of Commitment to Difficult Goals," *Journal of Applied Psychology*, vol. 74, no. 1 (1989), pp. 18–23.

11. P. C. Earley, G. B. Northcraft, C. Lee, and T. R. Lituchy, "Impact of Process and Outcome Feedback on the Relation of Goal Setting to Task Performance," *Academy of Management Journal*, vol. 33, no. 1 (1990), pp. 87–105; and R. Vance and A. Colella, "Effects of Two Types of Feedback on Goal Acceptance and Personal Goals," *Journal of Applied Psychology*, vol. 75, no. 1 (1990), pp. 68–76.

12. J. R. Larson, "The Dynamic Interplay Between Employees' Feedback-Seeking Strategies and Supervisors' Delivery of Performance Feedback," *The Academy of Management Review*, vol. 14, no. 3 (July 1989), p. 408.

13. Wendy Zellner, "O.K., So He's Not Sam Walton," *Business Week*, March 16, 1992, pp. 56–58.

14. Locke, Saari, Shaw, and Latham, "Goal Setting," p. 125.

15. Hollenbeck, Williams, and Klein, "An Empirical Examination"; and J. R. Hollenbeck and A. P. Brief, "The Effects of Individual Differences and Goal Origin on Goal Setting and Performance," *Organizational Behavior and Human Decision Processes*, vol. 40 (1987), pp. 392–414.

16. Jon R. Katzenbach and Douglas K. Smith, "The Discipline of Teams," *Harvard Business Review*, March–April 1993, pp. 111–20; T. R. Mitchell and W. S. Silver, "Individual and Group Goals When Workers Are Interdependent: Effects on Task Strategies and Performance," *Journal of Applied Psychology*, vol. 75, no. 2 (1990), pp. 185–93; and E. E. Gist, E. A. Locke, and M. S. Taylor, "Organizational Behavior: Group Structure, Process, and Effectiveness," *Journal of Management*, vol. 13, no. 2 (1987), pp. 237–57.

17. Maurice Hardaker and Bryan K. Ward, "Getting Things Done, How to Make a Team Work," *Harvard Business Review*, November–December 1987, pp. 112–20.

18. G. P. Latham and E. A. Locke, *Goal Setting: A Motivational Technique That Works* (Englewood Cliffs, N.J.: Prentice Hall, 1964); and G. P. Latham and E. A. Locke, "Goal Setting—A Motivational Technique That Works," *Organizational Dynamics*, Autumn 1979, pp. 68–80.

19. J. A. Riedel, D. M. Nebeker, and B. L. Cooper, "The Influence of Monetary Incentives on Goal Choice, Goal Commitment, and Task Performance," *Organizational Behavior and Human Decision Processes*, vol. 42 (1988), pp. 155–80.

20. A. Bernstein, "How to Motivate Workers: Don't Watch 'em," *Business Week*, April 29, 1991 p. 56.

21. Locke, Saari, Shaw, and Latham, "Goal Setting," p. 125; E. A. Locke, D. B. Feren, V. M. McCaleb, K. N. Shaw, and A. T. Denny, "The Relative Effectiveness of Four Methods of Motivating Employee Performance," *Changes in Working Life*, eds. K. Duncan, M. Gruneberg, and D. Wallis (New York: John Wiley & Sons, Inc., 1980).

22. For additional information see George S. Odiorne, "MBO Means Having a Goal and a Plan, Not Just a Goal," *Manage*, vol. 44, no. 1, September 1992, pp. 8–11; Paul Mali, *MBO Updated* (New York: John Wiley and Sons, 1986); S. Carroll and W. Tosi, Jr., *Management by Objectives, Applications and Research* (New York: Macmillan, Inc., 1973); George Odiorne, *MBO II* (Belmont, Calif.: Fearon-Pitman Publishing Inc., 1979); and Anthony Raia, *Managing by Objectives* (Glenview, Ill.: Scott, Foresman & Company, 1974).

23. Odiorne, *MBO II*, p. 53.

24. Douglas M. McGregor, *The Human Side of Enterprise* (New York: McGraw-Hill Book Company, 1960), p. 61. Also Douglas M. McGregor, "An Uneasy Look at Performance Appraisal," *Harvard Business Review*, May–June 1957, pp. 89–94.

25. McGregor, *Human Side*, p. 62.

26. Kazuo Ishikure, "Achieving Japanese Productivity and Quality Levels at a U.S. Plant," *Long Range Planning*, vol. 21, no. 5 (October 1988), pp. 10–17.

27. Albert W. Schrader, "MBO Makes Dollar Sense," *Personnel Journal*, July 1989, pp. 32–37.

28. For a critique of MBO see Philip E. Quigley, "Can Management By Objectives be Compatible with Quality?" *Industrial Engineering*, vol. 25, no. 7 (July 1993), p. 14; Jim M. Graber, *et. al.*, "Performance Appraisals and Deming: A Misunderstanding?" *Quality Progress*, vol. 25, no. 6 (June 1992), pp. 59–62.

29. Stephen R. Michael, "Organizational Change Techniques: Their Present, Their Future," *Organizational Dynamics*, Summer 1982, p. 77.

30. Arthur Beck and Ellis Hillmar, "OD to MBO or MBO to OD: Does It Make a Difference?" *Personnel Journal*, November 1972, pp. 827–34.

31. Carroll and Tosi, *Management by Objectives*.

32. Raia, *Managing by Objectives*; and H. Meyer, E. Kay, and J. French, "Split Roles and Performance Appraisal," *Harvard Business Review*, January–February 1965, p. 123.

33. M. T. Midas Jr. and T. L. Duvine "A Look at Continuing Improvement at Northwest Airlines," *National Productivity Review*, vol. 10, no. 3 Summer, 1991 p. 379.

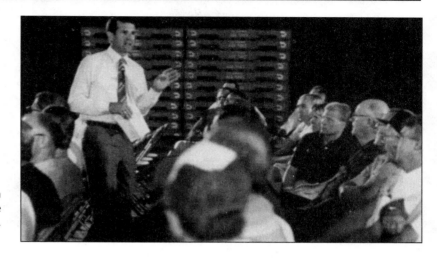

The president of Dana's North American Operations, John E. Doddridge, addresses the people at Spicer Universal Joint in Lima, Ohio. *Photo Courtesy of Dana Corporation.*

Total Quality Management: Quality and Productivity Interventions

13

OBJECTIVES

Upon completing this chapter, you will be able to:

1. Describe the major OD quality and productivity interventions.
2. Identify the similarities and differences in total quality management, self-managed work teams, and job design.
3. Diagnose job design problems as part of an OD program.
4. Experience how an OD consultant can help an organization in making productivity changes.

PREMEETING PREPARATION

1. Read the Background Information.
2. Complete Step 1 of OD Skills Simulation 13.1. Assign supervisor and observer roles the preceding class period.
3. Complete Step 1 of OD Skills Simulation 13.2. Form teams of five, assign roles the preceding class provided.
4. Read and analyze Case 13: Wengart Aircraft.

BACKGROUND INFORMATION

In the organization of the twenty-first century, there is an increasing emphasis being placed upon quality and productivity. To increase quality levels, enhance productivity, and reduce costs, executives are fundamentally reexamining the way companies are being managed.[1] Currently, many organizations are making changes in the way they operate: to their culture, technology, structure, and the way they relate to customers and employees. The message is clear: change or face elimination.[2] A key issue facing these organizations is the way in which they respond to a changing environment of "world class competition." OD interventions leading to improved productivity, efficiency, and quality have evolved to help organizations meet these challenges.

One widely used quality and productivity intervention is TQM. **Total Quality Management (TQM)** is having organization members who are committed to continuous improvement in meeting or exceeding customer expectations. During a time of downsizing and restructuring, many American companies are finding that they must learn to manage more effectively, and TQM involves all levels of the organization in developing practices that are customer oriented, flexible, and responsive to changing needs. At Motorola, the change involved a top to bottom overhauling of its corporate culture. The company is becoming a leader by driving relentlessly for market share, focusing on high quality, cutting manufacturing costs, investing in research and development, and pouring heavy resources into training and empowering its employees.

Business enterprises and nonprofit organizations are increasingly confronted with problems of stable or declining productivity, worker dissatisfaction and alienation, and increased domestic and foreign competition. Many federal regulations that once tended to protect inefficient operations are being removed and companies are now confronted with increased competition. Businesses no longer receive the degree of trade protection once afforded by their national government. As an example, for every $5 worth of goods or services a country produces, they sell about $1 abroad. The marketplace is truly a global market and with it comes increased competition. Witness the rapid changes in the services and products offered by the telecommunications industry, the rapid expansion and mergers of airline carriers, the expansion of services offered by the once conservative banking industry, and the change in the way health care is offered.

It is common to read newspaper reports daily about the decline in U.S. competitiveness, another U.S. market being lost to foreign industry, or the continued deterioration in the quality of U.S. products. The United States is no longer leading the world in technological innovations. But the problems are not only in the technology-based industries. Local, state, and federal governments are also trying to maintain or increase services despite budget reductions.

This chapter deals with improving work processes for individuals and work teams. The trend in many profit and not-for-profit organizations is toward decentralization, horizontal organizations, fewer levels of management, a decrease in staff positions, and broader spans of control. More of the decision-making authority is being pushed down to the lowest levels in the organizations where people are most aware of the problems. The work team and not the individual is becoming the mechanism in which work is organized. Through high-involvement management, line workers are planning, organizing, controlling, and directing. In a real sense, they are all managers.[3]

Much of the material in the discussion that follows applies the ideas and techniques presented in previous chapters, particularly team-building and intergroup development. The OD consultant uses structural changes like work design concepts to help organizations make productivity changes while simultaneously improving the work life of employees. In this chapter, we discuss three specific quality and high-involvement, **productivity interventions**: total quality management, self-managed work teams, and job design.

A Definition of Total Quality Management (TQM)

Total quality management has been defined as the management of activities involving improving the quality of the organization's product or service. TQM involves moving toward corporate excellence by integrating the desires of individuals for growth and development with organizational goals. TQM is a philosophy and a set of guiding principles for continuous improvement.

TQM applies human resources and analytical tools to focus on meeting or exceeding customer's current and future needs. It integrates these resources and tools into management efforts, by providing planned, systematic approaches to improving organizational performance. This involves everyone in programs aimed at improving the total organization, so that it is more customer oriented, quality conscious, flexible and responsive. The purpose of a TQM program is to increase the effectiveness of the organization, and to develop the potential of all individual members. Finally, there are a series of planned improvements which will ultimately influence the quality and productivity of the organization.

Total Quality Management has become a key concern of management. Much of this attention was initially focused on the auto industry which experienced declining sales and increasing product defects. Companies in many other industries also became concerned. The Malcolm Baldrige National Quality Award, created by the U.S. Congress in 1987, served to increase attention to quality.

Today's managers are being challenged to provide leadership in new and changing conditions. Customers, competitors, employees, and stockholders are all placing pressures on management for innovation and change at a rapid pace. One approach which has emerged to meet these changing forces is termed Total Quality Management (TQM). Total Quality management may be defined as an organizational strategy of commitment to improving customer satisfaction by developing techniques to carefully manage output quality. TQM is not so much a special OD technique, as it is an aspect of a reinvented corporate culture—a culture with a strong commitment to improving quality in all organizational processes.

THE CHARACTERISTICS OF TQM

Although there is some disagreement about what makes up TQM, there are several widely recognized key characteristics of TQM systems. TQM is regarded to be an organization-wide system that focuses on the customer, and increases efficiency and reliability of work.[4] TQM is planned and broad based. Organizations that are practicing TQM usually have several common principles or key components:[5]

TQM is organization wide. The production line is a natural and obvious place to improve quality. TQM also takes place in the accounting, marketing, human resources management, information systems, engineering, housekeeping departments, and other service and staff areas of an organization.

The CEO and other top managers visibly support it. Everyone, from top managers to hourly employees, operates under TQM. There is a reward system in place that ensures continual support.

TQM is ingrained as a value in the corporate culture. Continuous improvement penetrates the culture and values of the organization. Quality is seen as "how we do things around here."[6]

Partnership with customers and suppliers. Partnership with suppliers and customers is encouraged by the organization. The product or service must meet or exceed the customer's expectations. Results—not slogans—represent quality.

Source: CROCK by Rechin, Parker and Wilder. © Field Enterprises, Inc. by permission of North America Syndicate Inc.

Everyone in an organization has a customer. The customer may be internal or external. The next person in the production line, another department, or someone outside the organization who purchases the product or service is a customer.

Reduced cycle time. Cycle times for products and service, as well as support functions, focus on doing the job faster.

Techniques of TQM range in scope. Techniques used in TQM include statistical quality control, job design, empowerment, and self-managed work teams.

Do it right the first time. Quality is not obtained by rejecting a product when it gets to the end of a production line. Every stage of the production process builds in quality (see CROCK comic strip). Nothing leaves a department unless it is right, even though the poor quality might have originated in another department. Instead of relying on an inspection, the people making the product are responsible for product quality.

Corporate citizenship. The organization values and respects everyone, both in the organization and those it serves. This includes customers, suppliers, employees, owners, the community, and the environment. These parties are often called stakeholders.

No single formula works for everyone. Each organization is unique and off-the-shelf programs tend not to work. American managers often subscribe to the "follow-the-crowd" or "lemming" approach, but what was successful at one company may not work in another.

Quality

Harvard professor David Garvin has identified several dimensions of quality.[7] (See Table 13.1.) Garvin's eight dimensions help define the perspective of the quality concept. Customers, managers, engineers, line operators, and employees at every level of an organization must be involved in improving and managing quality.

Compatibility of TQM and OD

TQM and OD share similar values. Both are system wide, they depend on planned change, they believe in empowerment and involvement, they are self-renewing and continuous, they base decision making on data-based activities, and they view people as having the inherent desire to contribute in meaningful ways.

There are differences, however, between OD and TQM. Some OD consultants argue there are some core value differences, and they caution against OD consultants assuming the role of "quality management expert."[8] The OD consultant needs to be sure to enter the

TABLE 13.1 Dimensions of Quality

1. PERFORMANCE	A product's/service's primary operating characteristic (e.g., a car's acceleration performance, the comfort of a user using long-wear contact lenses).
2. FEATURES	Add-ons or supplements (e.g., the student study guide for a course, power locks on a car).
3. RELIABILITY	A probability of not malfunctioning or breaking down for a specified period of time (e.g., a 5-year, 60,000-mile warranty).
4. CONFORMANCE	The degree to which a product's design and operating characteristics meet established standards (e.g., a product test shows that the product is within 0.001 inches of the standard).
5. DURABILITY	A measure of a product's life (e.g., 10 years).
6. SERVICEABILITY	The speed and ease of repair (e.g., a panel that can be replaced by an untrained user).
7. AESTHETICS	A product's look, feel, taste, and smell (e.g., a rose has a delicate feel, a desired color, and a distinctive scent).
8. PERCEIVED QUALITY	Quality as viewed by a customer, client, or student (e.g., a parent uses a disposable diaper because it's sanitary, convenient, and reasonably priced).

relationship as a neutral party and resist advocating any particular method of change. TQM consultant's view organization problems as having TQM solutions. OD consultants view organization problems as having a variety of causes with no predefined solutions.

TQM can be applied as one change methodology along with an accompanying array of other interventions. According to some theorists, OD is becoming more of a "Checklist" or "technology driven approach."[9]; TQM approaches often lead even more in this direction. The OD consultant needs to be careful not to bring in prepackaged solutions to a client. Not all approaches of change are equally effective with all client systems at all points in time.

The OD consultant is often involved in setting up the TQM program. In this situation, the OD consultant is being asked to act in the role of an expert consultant and facilitator. Clients are usually more comfortable with expert-style consultants; however, the OD approach is to build the client's self-renewal capability.

TQM is in danger of becoming the latest management casualty of the 1990s.[10] To many employees, it represents the "flavor of the month" in a long line of management flops. The number of applicants for the Malcolm Baldrige National Quality Award peaked in 1991 and has since fallen sharply.[11] An Arthur D. Little, Inc., survey of 500 companies that use TQM turned up only 36 percent that felt it was significantly boosting their competitiveness. Another consultant company, Rath & Strong Inc., rated 95 companies' TQM efforts. Members of the firm gave more than half of the programs Ds and Fs, and only 26 percent rated an A or a B.[12]

Self-Managed Work Teams

One of the largest manufacturing operations using self-managed teams is General Motors' Saturn Plant in Tennessee which has been very successful and it is noted for its reliance on the self-managed team approach. These work teams are responsible for creating their own budgets, inventory and control systems, and the hiring of personnel. The Saturn teams are also responsible for organizing work quality and productivity. The Saturn plant has very low turnover, with high quality, and reduced costs.[13]

A **self-managed work team** is an autonomous group whose members decide how to handle their task.[14] The task of the team is an identifiable task, service, or product. The groups may be permanent work teams or temporary teams brought together to solve a problem or develop a new product. Often teams are composed of people from different parts of the organization with different skills and backgrounds. Authority has been vested in them by upper management to manage their group processes, including production and personnel matters, in order to accomplish their objectives. A diversified background of members

and the necessary authority gives the teams the ability to move around the bureaucratic organization and get the job done.

Increased responsibility is placed on team members. Work teams are assigned a wide range of tasks including budgeting, making job assignments, hiring and selecting team members, assessing job performance of fellow members, scheduling, purchasing equipment, and controlling quality.[15] (See Our Changing World.)

OUR CHANGING WORLD
THE TEAM APPROACH, SWEDISH STYLE[16]

Much is written about the emphasis on the work group in Japan. But there are numerous success stories involving worker participation from other parts of the globe, too.

Worker Involvement

Sweden provides a number of examples. The Kockems Shipyard in Malmo had what might have been the world's highest turnover rate in the 1970s, partly due to the blue-collar revolt that seemed to sweep the United States and Europe, and partly because of Sweden's liberal social security safety net: Nobody starved in Sweden, whether or not one worked. But these external factors were just part of the problem. Management pretty much had its head in the sand, too. Executives were far from the dust and noise, far from the areas where individuals had to cope with the day-to-day grind. Kockems turned itself totally around when management discovered the workers. Moving executives closer to the work force led to improvements in lighting, ventilation, and most important, attitudes. Workers began to think management cared. Why? Management *did* care!

Team Approach and Culture

In another example, Saab managed to take a tough industry, producing cars, and convince the Swedish workers that everyone counted. MIT professor Edgar Schein, one of the all-time greats when it comes to understanding organization change, credits Saab's autonomous work teams. "Before, Saab had very high worker turnover. Now it has virtually none. A happy, motivated work force not only saves a company retraining costs, but it makes it much more open to innovation," says Schein.

If the team approach can be used making automobiles in Sweden, one might think it could work anywhere. Schein says, "Such systems work better in national cultures that are more team oriented, such as the Scandinavian and some Asian countries. In the United States, it's much harder to convince people that it's better to pull their resources together and operate as a group. I don't think we value groups and teams for their own sake as much as other cultures do."

Can the team approach work anywhere or only where the idea fits the national culture? Apparently the team approach is easier to pull off in some countries. But, this is no excuse to give up. This chapter suggests that it *can* be done. Organizational development is like most other valuable commodities: you have to work at it. Nothing worth having seems to come easily.

Question

1. What do you think are the most important factors in increasing productivity?

Though self-managed work teams are still-controversial, Texas Instruments CEO Jerry Junkins says, "No matter what your business, these teams are the wave of the future."[17] However, Edward Lawler, who has consulted and written extensively on the subject, is more reserved and says, "You have to ask, 'How complex is the work?' The more complex, the more suited it is for teams."[18]

Self-managed work teams also go by other names including self-regulating work groups, cross-functional teams, socio-technical systems, autonomous work groups, high-performance work teams, and high-commitment work teams. Such companies as Digital Equipment Corporation, Aetna Life & Casualty, Procter & Gamble, Xerox, Boeing, Du Pont, Texas Instruments, General Motors, Cummins Engine Company, Dana Corporation, W. L. Gore, and TRW use them either throughout their companies or in specific facilities.

Du Pont's plant in Towanda, Pennsylvania, is a good example of self-managed work teams. The plant lets employees find their own solutions to problems, set their own production schedules, and have a say in hiring. Managers call themselves "facilitators." Their main job is to coach workers and help them understand the external market forces which

demand quality, teamwork, and speed. Says Du Pont Group Vice President Mark Suwyn: "These people manage their lives well outside the factory. They sit on school boards or coach Little League. We have to create a culture where we can bring that creative energy into the work force."[19]

Most companies, such as Du Pont, Procter & Gamble, and Boeing that use self managed teams, do not do so organization wide. They typically choose specific sites. Some companies, like General Motors in its Saturn division, build new plants to house the teams. Though the teams are more common in production facilities than the service sector, they have been successfully applied in service-oriented organizations such as life insurance companies and government agencies.

A recent survey of 476 "Fortune 1,000" companies shows that presently about one in five companies use self-managed work teams. The study also found that half the companies questioned say they will be relying significantly more on them in the years ahead.[20]

The Characteristics of Self-Managed Work Teams

When the self-managed work team approach is used at a company, there are several characteristics that are common to other self-managed work team sites.

The structure of the organization is based on team concepts. There are few management levels in the plant or work site structure and few job descriptions.

There is an egalitarian culture and a noticeable lack of status symbols. There are no management dining rooms, no assigned parking places, and no special furniture or decor for managers' offices. Managers may not have offices or, if they do, they often become team meeting rooms. There are no special dress codes so that if uniforms are required, such as at Honda's U.S. plant, everyone including the plant superintendent wears the uniform. In other sites, no one wears ties, special badges, or other signs of power.

A work team has a physical site. There are functional boundaries which members can identify.

The number of people in a team is kept as small as possible. Typical sizes range from five to 15 members.

Work teams order material and equipment. They set goals, profit targets, and decide their production schedule. They also help set rewards for their team members. They have a voice in whom is hired and fired in the work team and the hiring of managers. Says Robert Hershock, a Group Vice President at 3M, "You need to have a sense of who's not buying in and let the teams kick people off who aren't carrying their weight."[21]

Team members have a sense of vision of their team and their organization. A vision provides direction and energizes team behavior to accomplish goals. Most companies have a simple, understandable creed that is well communicated to all employees.

There is strong partnership between team members and management. If there is a labor union, the union is also a member of the partnership.

Team members are different enough in their backgrounds, cultural experiences, and training so that a variety of viewpoints will be represented and skills will be varied enough so that members can learn from one another.

Information of all types is openly shared. The information system needs to be well developed and available to all members. Members are knowledgeable in accounting and statistical concepts so they can use the financial and production information to make decisions.

Team members should be skilled and knowledgeable in their areas. Team members should have good interpersonal skills and a desire and ability to work with others.

Training, and especially cross training, is a major requirement of self-managed work teams. A Vice President of Tektronix says, "The growth and development of individual employees is the primary vehicle for advancing the company's long-term interests."[22] The success of a team depends on members being skilled and knowledgeable in a variety of areas including technical skills, finance and accounting, competition in the marketplace, and group process.

Team members are knowledgeable of customers, competitors, and suppliers. The primary emphasis is to focus on customers. To the team, a customer may be someone within their organization who uses their product or someone external to the organization. Some organizations enter joint-training ventures with their suppliers. They recognize that the finished product is no better than components supplied by other companies.

The Design of Jobs

The five core job dimensions of skill variety, task identity, task significance, autonomy, and feedback discussed in the job design section of this chapter can help in evaluating the degree to which a work team is genuinely a self-managed work team.

Skill variety will be present in a self-managed work team when the team and team members use many different skills and talents. Many organizations that have self-managed work teams have few job classifications reflecting the ability of people to do a variety of kinds of work.

Task identity occurs when the team is responsible for a complete and identifiable piece of work. Examples of task identity occur when work teams do market research, engineering and design of the product, production, budgeting, and handling customer questions and complaints. Engineers' desks are on the production floor and team members take calls from customers on the floor. At Tektronix's plant in Vancouver, customers' questions and complaints are taken over a phone located on the manufacturing floor.

Task significance occurs in a self-managed work team when the members see that their performance makes an impact on other team members, other people within the organization, and customers. Work teams are kept small so members can identify more closely with their contributions. Members have ready access to accounting and production figures so their individual contributions can be seen.

Self-managed work teams have **autonomy** when they have freedom to set goals, make work schedules, discipline and reward team members, and decide work methods. At the General Mills' plant in Lodi, California, the night shift does not have a manager present as the work teams are self-sufficient.

Feedback occurs in self-managed work teams when members see the effect of their work through accounting and production figures, information coming to the team from outside managers and customers, and by doing the work itself. Group work that includes the five job dimensions are more likely to have fully functional self-managed work teams.

New Organizational Structures

The structure that results from self-managed work teams is one that is flat with few levels of managers and little support staff. Considerable changes are also required in organizational policies and managerial practices to support the teams. It is not something that happens just to the employees on the lowest level but involves the entire hierarchy. Self-managed work teams are not superimposed upon the existing structure. For most organizations, they represent a substantial change in the way an organization is structured and managed.

One company, W. L. Gore & Associates, Inc. (manufacturer of the Gore-Tex fabric), has been experimenting with a free-form management structure for more than 32 years. Leaders, not bosses, head teams. The leaders must share decisions regarding hiring, discipline, and firing associates with peer committees. Gore refers to their chain of command as a "lattice system." In this system, an associate (all employees including the President are associates) may take an idea or complaint to any other. "We can learn a great deal from companies like Gore," says Du Pont Co. CEO Edgar S. Woolard, Jr., a major customer and supplier.[23]

One of the best ways to assure that decisions are made within the work team is to have few levels of managers so the remaining managers do not have time to make all the decisions. Functions that are normally performed by upper management are carried out by the work team. Few levels of management are needed because the work team is doing most of the work.

There is fewer support staff such as engineering, planning departments, and purchasing because these jobs are performed by the work team. Functional structures along such lines as accounting, personnel, engineering, production, and the like are counterproductive as they encourage a system where workers do not identify with the final product. These functional departments do not exist in some organizations that have implemented self-managed work teams. It does not mean that engineers and accountants are not needed, but it does mean these functions are integrated into the work team.

Management and Leadership Behavior

Within a work site that has implemented self-managed work teams, there are usually three distinct levels of management: upper management, coordinator, and work-team leader. The work team has an internal leader who is usually elected by the members, but sometimes higher management appoints the leader. The work team has an external leader that is sometimes called a **coordinator**. This is a position that is similar in position to that of a first-level supervisor in a traditional organization, though the behavior of the two is considerably different. The coordinator may have a few to several dozen teams to coordinate.

Upper management, sometimes called the **support team**, is similar to a site manager or plant manager in traditional organizations. This level is responsible for general planning, making broad goals, dealing with outside parties (such as the rest of the organization for multiple-site organizations and outside clients).

Sometimes organizations have created a council consisting of representatives from throughout the company to deal with substantive organization-wide concerns. The council may be elected by all members of the organization or appointed by management.

A common question that continually comes up for organizations using self-managed work teams is: if these are self-managed teams, what is the role of external leaders and managers? Organizing, planning, and directing, which are normal management functions are predominately carried out by the work team. The external coordinator's role and the internal leader's role is ambiguous, especially for the people in the positions.

The *coordinator's role* is an innovative one and there are no parallels to draw upon in a traditional organization. The coordinator behaves largely as an encourager, energizer, teacher, and facilitator for the team. He or she encourages teams in self-managing behaviors, learning, goal setting, creativity, self-evaluation, feedback to one another, new ways of problem solving, and group problem solving. The coordinator acts in many respects similar to a process consultant. The objective is to promote independence of the team. The coordinator helps the team obtain equipment and training, provides communication to and from management, and provides channels of communications between teams.

Some organizations refer to this person as a "chimney buster" or "barrier buster" to describe how this person runs interference for the team by breaking up the rigid and narrow (therefore, the term chimney) bureaucratic obstacles. The coordinator helps build trust and openness within the team, helps to fashion the organization's culture, helps the team develop a sense of direction, and gives an awareness of the total organization's vision to the work team.

The internal *team leader* acts to make sure equipment and supplies are available, helps the team organize itself, and serves as an additional team member who is doing work similar to other members. Like the external coordinator, the team leader also serves as an encourager and facilitator.

The Reward System

The reward system is usually different from traditional organizations for all employees. Usually, hourly workers no longer exist and all employees are salaried. Rewards are made in a manner so that individual members can identify their work and contributions with their pay. Self-managed work teams normally reward people based on skills, gain sharing, employee ownership, or some combination of these methods.

Pay based on skills or knowledge involves paying a member more for additional skills or tasks he or she can do.[24] Gain sharing is rewards paid to a team based on the team's contributions. The team is small enough so that an individual's performance is obviously reflected in their own pay check—as well as the pay check of everyone else in the team. Profit sharing is a reward based on the entire organization's performance so that people understand the importance of everyone working together. Normally, the relevancy to the individual and work team for this type of reward is lost because of the bigness of the organization. Consequently, organizations often combine some form of skill-based pay, gain sharing, and profit sharing.

Role of Labor Unions

If there is a union present, it will need to be highly involved from the very beginning including the planning stages. Facilities that have self-managed work teams do not have the typical adversarial relationship between management and worker. The success of creating a collegial relationship will depend on the support and acceptance of self-managed work teams by the union.

Often unions serve to keep management honest about participative management, make sure that all sides to an issue are heard, and give support to self-managed work teams that helps in the acceptance of the teams. Most union contracts covering plants that have self-managed work teams are very brief and open ended. GM's approach to setting up self-managed work teams at their new Saturn plant was to work with the UAW from the planning stages of the plant. The agreement calls for gain sharing, and skill-based pay. Policies are set by a joint union-management structure similar to the council discussed previously.[25]

Red Flags

There are several problems associated with self-managed work teams. However, usually the problems can be solved or circumvented. Some problems and cautions that should be considered follow.[26]

Self-managed work teams may not be appropriate to the task, people, and context. Where people and jobs are not interdependent, work teams may not be necessary. Many companies are finding that with increased complexity of technology and rapid development of products and services brought on by higher levels of competition, self-managed work teams are becoming more appropriate.

The organization does not perceive a need to change. This does not mean that installing self-managed work teams should be abandoned, but the driving forces within the organization for change will need to be set in motion.

Managers and leaders are vague and confused about their role. Training for managers, leaders, and team members can resolve the confusion.

Organizations that do not reward performance are likely to run into problems. A "thank you" and a wall plaque are not enough. Team work is time consuming and companies that add team responsibilities on to a person's existing responsibilities probably will face resistance. Organizations that share the wealth are more likely to have successful teams.

A lack of training can cause self-managed work teams to fail. Some consultants believe lack of training is a major reason for failure, especially for team members in group process and team building.

Since there are fewer layers in an organization, there are fewer opportunities for advancement into management positions. Companies that have not altered their career-planning programs to address shorter career ladders will face long-term resistance with their workers. Some companies can get the team to focus on building an effective team, the challenge of the product, and beating the competition.

Building self-managed work teams is not a one shot activity. Once the teams are installed, people can get back to work at their old job. The team *is* their job.

Results

There is a lack of empirical evidence on the effectiveness of self-managed work teams for several reasons. The idea is new and the techniques used in them are still being developed. Many organizations, because of competitive reasons are unwilling to allow academicians in to study their plants. As far as some companies are concerned, they know self-managed work teams are positively affecting earnings, and they are not inclined to give their techniques away.

According to most consultants who specialize in helping organizations implement self-managed work teams, the quality of the work is high and productivity is increasing. Stories from plant managers, employees, and unions abound about their effectiveness. A former Vice-President of Procter & Gamble said of their results, "At P&G there are well over two decades of comparisons of results—*side by side*—between enlightened work systems and those I call traditional. It is absolutely clear that the new work systems work much better—for example, with 30 percent to 50 percent lower manufacturing costs. Not only are the tangible, measurable, bottom-line indicators such as cost, quality, customer service, and reliability better—so are the harder-to-measure attributes such as quickness, decisiveness, toughness, and just plain resourcefulness. The people in these organizations are far more self-reliant and less dependent upon hierarchy and control systems than are people in the traditional organization."[27]

General Mills says that at sites that have self-managed work teams, productivity is as much as 40 percent higher than at its traditional factories. They also found that teams sometimes set higher productivity goals than management. At a Ford car assembly plant in Hermosillo, Mexico, where there is only one job classification, workers established a lower defect rate than most Japanese automobile makers.

Another company, Butler Manufacturing Company, put self-managed work teams in place in one of their plants. In this plant, absenteeism is less than one-fourth of normal for factory employment and turnover is one-third of normal. Profits have run 20-percent higher than expected for the first two years of the program and they estimate their profits are 10-percent higher than comparable operations.[28] See OD in Practice on page 352 for an example of how Dana Corporation has set up their version of high involvement work teams.

Job Design

Job design has been a concern of managers for many years, but it was Frederick Taylor, who first proposed the scientific design of a job. The scientific management ideas that came from the industrial engineers tended to break a job down into its smallest and simplest task to reduce the human error, the training, and the skill required to do the task. Through time-and-motion studies, productivity was expected to increase. There was little regard for the human element other than to make sure that it was adequately controlled and supervised. More recently, organizations are discovering there is often a high price to pay in absenteeism, turnover, apathy, poor work quality, or even sabotage when the human element is not considered.

The current trend is to redesign jobs to improve worker satisfaction and productivity. There are, still, no easy solutions to redesigning jobs because there are many variables: the worker, the nature of the work, the organization climate, and the manager's style. Some successes in job design do provide guidelines. The following is a discussion of two closely related theories of job design: job enrichment theory and job characteristics theory.[30]

Job Enrichment Theory

Frederick Herzberg found, through interviews, that employees at all levels in the organization were interested in two facets about their work—the quality of the work itself and the benefits or rewards of the job (money, status, and so forth).[31] Of the two, the quality of the

OD IN PRACTICE
DANA CORPORATION[29]

What is the name of the company cited in *In Search of Excellence*, listed in *The 100 Best Companies to Work for in America*, listed among the top 10 companies for women to work for, and has a plant named by *Fortune* magazine as a top 10 plant in the United States? The company is the Dana Corporation. But who is Dana? And what are they doing to get all the accolades?

Dana is a worldwide corporation employing 26,000 people, with headquarters in Toledo, Ohio. With $3.6 billion a year in sales, the diversified company primarily makes transmissions, clutches, drive lines, and axles for vehicles. It also builds condos and is into banking, insurance, and real estate.

The Structure

Dana has spent a good bit of effort building a flat, highly decentralized organization. It has only five levels of management. Dana's corporate office staff has decreased in number from 400 to 84. It pushed responsibilities down to lower levels of management. But just changing an organization chart is no guarantee that improvements will follow.

The Auburn plant, which manufactures clutches, is indicative of the programs at Dana. Though in 1981 they had a good reputation for quality, they also recognized they had many people problems. Maury Hagan, the plant manager, says "There was a huge wall between the front office and the people working on the floor." They decided improvements in their communication system could help solve many of their problems.

Communications System

The improvements in communications are directed at four areas: special events, mass communication, group communication, and individual communication. Special events are activities intended to communicate the importance of employees. These include an open house and a free physical examination for the employee and spouse every six months. Retirees are also included, as Dana believes that how you treat your retirees is an indication of what you really think of your active employees. The gain-sharing plan at the plant also communicates in a unique way how employees are performing.

Mass communication is formalized one-way communication coming from several managers to the employees. The supervisor has a minimum of one meeting each month to explain what is happening to the market, profits, deliveries, and quality. The area manager meets with all his or her people at least once a month. The plant manager meets at least four times a year with everyone in the plant in a mass meeting or groups of 20 to 30. The next manager up, the division manager, has a meeting twice a year with everyone. The President or Chairman of the Board meets everyone once a year. So the five levels of managers have had a meeting on a regular basis with everyone in the plant including line and staff employees.

Group communication consists of weekly staff meetings and quality circles for the 80 percent of employees who have chosen to participate in the circles. According to Mr. Hagan, "It is not the answer to everything, but is strictly a tool that opens avenues for your people."

Individual communication occurs with the open-door policy that the managers have. Unless there is another meeting going on, someone coming to see even the plant manager, Maury Hagan, will not have to wait more than five minutes. The philosophy is that for the person coming to see a manager, that is the most important thing on the person's mind at the moment. If it means the manager has to work overtime in the evening to get their other work done, then that is the way it goes.

Results at the Auburn Plant

Some significant changes in the plant are the changes in attitude. Before the communication program began, no hourly worker would sign up or apply for a management job. Hagan says, "They viewed management as an enemy, and they had no interest in joining management." Recently they had 47 hourly employees apply for a management position. Work habits have improved and productivity increased 16 percent in two years. They recognize they still have problems but they believe they are turning the corner. "Our competition is not within the plant anymore, it is on the outside and it is worldwide, and that is where we have to concentrate," says Hagan.

Questions

1. What type of productivity interventions does the communications program use? Is it quality circles, self-managed work teams, or something else?
2. Describe how the program at Dana's Auburn plant can be used at other organizations.

work leads to job satisfaction. *Job satisfaction* occurs when employees experience work situations that entail increases in achievement, recognition, challenging work, responsibility, and advancement. **Job enrichment theory** holds that jobs should be redesigned to improve the motivators related to a job by permitting employees to attain increased levels of responsibility and achievement. Employees also can be given appropriate recognition and advance-

ment in their careers for a job well done. And the work itself should be challenging, interesting, and meaningful. There are many techniques for improving these motivational factors and they must be tailored to fit specific situations. Several suggestions include:

- Give an employee or work group a natural and complete unit of work. This is in contrast to the practice of specialization of labor that has dominated the structure of most organizations in this century.
- Add more difficult assignments to an employee's job while providing appropriate training.
- Give an employee additional authority. For example, an employee could be allowed to make increasingly more important or difficult decisions.
- Allow a peer in a work group or team to become an expert in a specialized area. Very likely, a work team could have several specialists that other employees could go to for information and help.
- Make information, including company reports, directly available to an employee instead of editing or censoring the information. This is particularly important where the information is related to the employee's work.
- Remove controls over an employee while still holding the employee accountable.

Job enrichment theory holds that extrinsic rewards such as money are important to accompany changes to the jobs. It also emphasizes that a system that only provides rewards will not improve worker performance. Improvements in both quality of the work and rewards are required to make a change in job design successful.[32]

Job Characteristics Theory

Another approach to job design is the job characteristic model conceived of by J. R. Hackman, G. R. Oldham, R. Janson, and K. Purdy[33] and based on the work of A. N. Turner and P. R. Lawrence.[34] The model attempts to develop objective measures of job characteristics that can directly affect employee attitudes and work behaviors. According to the model, five core job dimensions that affect work motivation and satisfaction are skill variety, task identity, task significance, autonomy, and feedback.

Skill variety is the degree to which a job requires a variety of activities and involves the use of different skills and talents. Employees usually see tasks that require the use of several different skills, especially challenging skills, as being meaningful.

Task identity refers to the degree to which the job requires completion of a whole and identifiable piece of work. It is doing a job from beginning to end with a visible outcome. An employee probably will find a task more meaningful if it entails producing the entire product rather than a small component.

Task significance is the degree to which the job has a substantial impact on the lives of other people, whether in the same organization or in the external environment. Work will likely be more meaningful when an employee perceives the results to have a substantial effect on other people.

Autonomy is the degree to which the job provides substantial freedom, independence, and discretion to the individual in scheduling the work and in determining the procedures to be used in carrying it out. Autonomy allows employees to take a larger part in planning and controlling their work. Generally, employees will have greater commitment to and ownership in their jobs when they have autonomy over their work.

Job feedback refers to the degree to which carrying out the work activities required by the job results in the individual obtaining direct and clear information about the effectiveness of his or her performance. Customers or other people internal to the organization who use the product or service can provide feedback if communication channels are provided to the employee. The feedback is directly based on how well the task was done and not on the evaluations of a peer or supervisor.

The five core job dimensions can be mathematically combined to derive a score which reflects the motivational potential of a job. As skill variety, task identity, and task significance jointly determine a job's meaningfulness, these three dimensions are treated as one dimension in the formula:

Motivating Potential Score (MPS) = Job Meaningfulness × Autonomy × Job Feedback.

The first variable in the formula, job meaningfulness is a function of skill variety, task identity, and task significance so the formula can further be refined:

$$\textit{Motivating Potential Score (MPS)} = \left[\frac{\textit{Skill Variety} + \textit{Task Identity} + \textit{Task Significance}}{3} \right] \times \textit{Autonomy} \times \textit{Job Feedback.}$$

Based on the formula, a score of near zero on either the autonomy or job feedback dimensions will produce a **motivating potential score (MPS)** of near zero, whereas a number near zero on skill variety, task identity, or task significance will reduce the total MPS, but will not completely undermine the motivational potential of a job.

When the core job dimensions are present in a job, the job characteristics model predicts certain positive effects in an employee's psychological state. High scores in skill variety, task identity, and task significance result in an employee experiencing meaningfulness in the job, such as believing the work to be important, valuable, and worthwhile. A high score in the autonomy dimension leads to an employee feeling personally responsible and accountable for the results of the work he or she does. And a high score in the job feedback dimension is an indication that the employee has an understanding of how he or she is performing the job.

There are several suggestions made by the authors of the model and other authorities. They suggest using research from the behavioral sciences to enrich jobs and produce a positive impact on the five core job dimensions. One approach is to take existing, fractionalized tasks and put them back together to form a new and larger module of work. This will increase the skill variety and task identity job dimensions of the work. General Motors has used this method for several years in their successful NUMMI plant, a joint venture with Toyota in Fremont, California. Teams of workers are responsible for auto subassemblies such as door or transmissions.

A second approach is to form natural work units by giving an employee a task that is an identifiable and meaningful whole. An employee will have greater ownership in and will more closely identify with the work and will understand the significance of the work. A third approach is to permit the employee to have direct contact with the people who use their product or service. This would mean directing complaints or questions from customers directly to the involved employee or employees.

A fourth approach is to load jobs vertically by giving employees functions such as deciding work methods, when to take breaks, how to train new employees, formulating budgets, and managing crises. For an employee to undertake successfully these new responsibilities, which improve autonomy, it may be necessary to provide employee skill training in such areas as budgets, training techniques, and time management.

A fifth approach is to open or create feedback channels so employees can learn how well they are performing their work.

Results of Job Design Programs

The results of job design programs suggest that they can be successful if they are managed correctly and have employee involvement. In a review of the literature on work-restructuring methods, William Pasmore found that 90 percent of the reports of work-restructuring interventions cited improvements in productivity, costs, absenteeism, attitudes, or quality and that an increasing number of organizations are setting up such methods.[35]

The results of job design efforts using Herzberg's job enrichment theory are not conclusive, although there have been a number of studies. In a study conducted by R. N. Ford

at AT&T, it was shown that 18 of 19 job enrichment projects resulted in improvements in productivity, quality, and job satisfaction.[36]

Several studies generally have confirmed the validity of the job characteristics theory.[37] Additional research into this theory is warranted, but until it is available the basic ideas of the theory serve as a foundation for many changes in job design within organizations.

REVIEW QUESTIONS

1. Explain Total Quality Management and how it can be used to improve quality and productivity.

2. Would you like to work in a self-managed work team? Are classroom group project teams like a self-managed team? Why or why not?

3. What are the characteristics of self-managed work teams?

4. What are some problems that organizations might have in implementing Total Quality Management?

KEY WORDS AND CONCEPTS

Define and be able to use the following:

Autonomy
Coordinator
Job Design
Job Enrichment Theory
Motivating Potential Score (MPS)
Productivity Interventions

Self-Managed Work Teams
Skill Variety
Support Team
Task Identity
Task Significance
Team Leader
Total Quality Management (TQM)

OD SKILLS SIMULATION 13.1
PAPER HOUSE PRODUCTION

Total time suggested: 2 hours, 40 minutes.

A. PURPOSE

This simulation is designed to give you an opportunity to participate in a complex situation involving a great deal of interaction among competing teams, each striving to accomplish a specific objective. You will work in a traditional production environment and then in a self-managed work team. This will provide you with some experience to compare the two different methods of managing. In the process of interaction, you will have an opportunity to experience:

1. Leadership patterns.
2. Evaluation of jobs using the job characteristic model.
3. Implementation of a self-managed work team and the redesign of jobs.
4. Group process skills in a stress situation.
5. Interaction patterns among competing teams.

In addition, you will have the opportunity to analyze your team behavior as a member of a system engaged in a complex task.

B. PROCEDURE

Step 1. Before class form into teams of equal size, with six to eight members. The number of people producing the houses should be the same on each team. Extra class members can serve as observers. Select one person from each to be a supervisor/team leader and another to be an observer. The supervisor reads the Note to Supervisor and Note to Team Leader near the end of this simulation. The observer reads the Note to Observer at the end of the simulation and also refers to the Observer Form located at the end of this simulation. Everyone reads the Paper House Production Description and becomes familiar with the remaining steps in this simulation before coming to class.

Step 2. In a team meeting, plan for Production Period 1. The meeting should be formal and structured with the supervisor conducting the meeting. The production of the houses should show a high division and specialization of labor among the tasks involved in house production. The observer during the planning and production stages is not to make any suggestions or to help in any manner. The equipment and supply purchases will be made and recorded on Lines 2 through 7 of the Cash Position Statement—Production Period 1.

Time suggested for Step 2: 25 minutes.

Step 3. Teams will construct houses for 20 minutes. Closely adhere to the plans made during Step 2. At the end of the production period, the FHA will purchase houses meeting the specifications. Complete the Cash Position Statement—Production Period 1, and determine the winning team. Return all equipment, supplies, and houses.

Time suggested for Step 3: 30 minutes.

Step 4. Looking at the job as a whole (excluding the supervisor), evaluate the jobs using the job characteristics model and determine the Motivating Potential Score (MPS) by using a ranking from 1 (low) to 7 (high).

Skill variety: _____

Task identity: _____

Task significance: _____

Autonomy: _____

Job feedback: _____

$$\textit{Motivating Potential Score (MPS)} = \left[\frac{\textit{Skill Variety} + \textit{Task Identity} + \textit{Task Significance}}{3} \right] \times \textit{Autonomy} \times \textit{Job Feedback.}$$

Time suggested for Step 4: 10 minutes.

Step 5. Plan for Production Period 2. Using the same teams as Production Period 1, form a self-managed work team with the meeting closely following the suggestions for self-managed teams discussed in the text. The supervisor from Production Period 1 will be the team leader and operate as close as possible to the description in the text of a team leader. The team leader should read the Note to Team Leader at the end of this simulation. Redesign the jobs using suggestions from the theory of job enrichment and the job characteristics model. The observer will not assist in the meeting. The equipment and supply purchases will be made and recorded on lines 2 through 7 of the Cash Position Statement—Production Period 2. No cash, supplies, or equipment will be carried forward from Production Period 1.

Time suggested for Step 5: 25 minutes.

Step 6. Teams will again construct houses for 20 minutes. Closely adhere to the plans made during Step 5. At the end of the production period, the FHA will purchase houses meeting the specifications. Complete the Cash Position Statement—Production Period 2, and determine the winning team.

Time suggested for Step 6: 30 Minutes.

Step 7. As you did in Step 4, look at the jobs as a whole (excluding the team leader), evaluate the jobs using the job characteristics model, and determine the Motivating Potential Score (MPS).

Skill variety: _____

Task identity: _____

Task significance: _____

Autonomy: _____

Job feedback: _____

$$\textit{Motivating Potential Score (MPS)} = \left[\frac{\textit{Skill Variety} + \textit{Task Identity} + \textit{Task Significance}}{3} \right] \times \textit{Autonomy} \times \textit{Job Feedback}.$$

Time suggested for Step 7: 10 minutes.

Step 8. With the observer leading the discussion in your team and then with the other teams, focus on feedback from the Observer Form and the following questions:

1. Was there any difference in the MPS for the two production periods?
2. Was there any difference in the Cash Position Statements of the two production periods? How do you explain this?
3. If there was an improvement in the Cash Position Statement in Period 2 over Period 1, to what extent could the improvement be the result of the experience of having built the houses during the first production period? And to what extent could the improvement be the result of any changes made in the job design during the team meeting?
4. What kinds of problems did you encounter in improving the job design?
5. Were there compromises made between improving the quality of the jobs and improving productivity?
6. Try to project working in this company for several years. What would be the advantages and disadvantages of the two different production procedures?

Time suggested for Step 8: 20 minutes.

PAPER HOUSE PRODUCTION DESCRIPTION

The members of this team have just formed a corporation. You must decide on a name for your corporation. At this point you do not have any organization structure or production plans. Take the next 25 minutes to become better acquainted with this business. You should organize your corporation and plan your strategies for the 20-minute production period which will immediately follow this planning period.

Your corporation is, needless to say, in the paper house construction business. You produce quality paper houses, but in large quantities. Your goal is, very simply, to make the most money you can. Your corporation has $500,000 in cash available to purchase certain supplies and equipment. It may not spend more than this amount. The *only* source of supplies and equipment is your instructor (you may not use your own pen, ruler, etc.), and the supplies and equipment are available during this planning period and during the 20-minute production period (but at a higher price).

Following is a price list of supplies and equipment available.

	PRICE WHEN PURCHASED DURING	
Equipment	Planning Period	Production Period
Scissors	$ 7,000	$ 8,000
Cellophane tape	4,000	5,000
Ruler	5,000	6,000
Marking pen	2,000	3,000

| | PRICE WHEN PURCHASED DURING | | |
Supplies	No. of 5"×8" Cards per Package	Planning Period	Production Period
Micro pkg.	1	$ 2,000	$ 3,000
Mini pkg.	5	8,000	10,000
Poco pkg.	10	15,000	18,000
Medi pkg.	20	25,000	30,000
Maxi pkg.	40	45,000	53,000
Mogo pkg.	80	80,000	90,000

Any number or combination of packages may be purchased. Equipment and supplies unused at the end of this production period will be considered as unrecoverable salvage and will be collected. Completed houses built according to specifications will sell for $20,000 each, and you will be able to sell all you can build. Houses deviating from the specs as judged by the FHA (the FHA could be your instructor or an extra class member) are not marketable. The house plans provided are your specifications. Your house should appear as described except that your house should not have any dimensions written on it. Your company's name should be neatly printed on the roof.

House Specifications

1. The sides of the house each measure 4" high by 7" long. The front and back each measure 5" wide and 4" high (or 7 1/8" high at the top of the gable).
2. The total height of the house is 7 1/8" from the base to the highest point of the roof.
3. The roof is V-shaped and is 7" long. It measures 4" along the ends.
4. Your corporation's name appears in 1/2"-high letters on both sides of the roof. Neatly print name with the marking pen.
5. The two sides each have one window measuring 2" long and 1 1/2" high, centered. Draw the windows.
6. There is a door at the front (a gable end) measuring 3" high and 1 1/2" wide centered along the base of the wall. Draw the door.
7. There is no floor.

A Cash Position Statement for the first and second production periods is provided for you to keep a record of your financial status.

You have 20 minutes for the first production period. At the end of this time, qualifying houses will be bought and the cash position determined.

NOTE TO SUPERVISOR—FIRST PLANNING MEETING

(Other class members should not read.)

Conduct the meeting in Step 2 in a highly formal and structured manner. You should have the production procedures carefully planned before coming to the meeting. During the meeting you will simply tell others of your plans and make sure your subordinates know what is expected of them. You may choose to let others make suggestions, but the decision to implement them is yours. You may perform your job as a supervisor in a fairly autocratic manner. During the production stage you are not to do the work of producing the houses (production is the job of your workers). You are to make sure your subordinates are doing their jobs correctly.

NOTE TO TEAM LEADER—SECOND PLANNING MEETING

(Other class members should not read.)

Conduct the meeting in Step 5 using the discussion in the text on the role of the coordinator and internal team leader in a self-managed work team as your guide. You are to make sure equipment and supplies are available, help the team organize itself, and serve as an additional team member who is doing work similar to other members. You will also serve as an encourager and facilitator.

CASH POSITION STATEMENT—PRODUCTION PERIOD 1
_____ CORPORATION

1. Beginning cash $500,000

2. Cost of purchases during planning period:

3. Scissors _____

4. Cellophane tape _____

5. Ruler _____

6. Marking pen and pencil _____

7. Supplies (cards) _____

8. Total cost of purchases during

 planning period: (add Lines 3 through 7) _____

9. Cost of purchases during

 production period:

10. Scissors _____

11. Cellophane tape _____

12. Ruler _____

13. Marking pen and pencil _____

14. Supplies (cards) _____

15. Total cost of purchases during

 production period: (add Lines 10

 through 14) _____

16. Total cost of purchases:

 (add Lines 8 and 15) _____

17. Adjusted cash balance after purchases:

 (subtract Line 16 from 1) _____

18. Cash inflow from sale of houses:

19. Number of houses sold times selling price equals Sales receipts

 _____ × $20,000 = $ _____

19. Ending cash balance:

 (add Lines 17 and 18) _____

CASH POSITION STATEMENT—PRODUCTION PERIOD 2

_____ *CORPORATION*

1. Beginning cash $500,000

2. Cost of purchases during planning period:

3. Scissors _____

4. Cellophane tape _____

5. Ruler _____

6. Marking pen and pencil _____

7. Supplies (cards) _____

8. Total cost of purchases during

 planning period: (add Lines 3 through 7) _____

9. Cost of purchases during

 production period:

10. Scissors _____

11. Cellophane tape _____

12. Ruler _____

13. Marking pen and pencil _____

14. Supplies (cards) _____

15. Total cost of purchases during

 production period: (add Lines 10

 through 14) _____

16. Total cost of purchases:

 (add Lines 8 and 15) _____

17. Adjusted cash balance after purchases:

 (subtract Line 16 from 1) _____

18. Cash inflow from sale of houses:

 Number of houses sold times selling price equals Sales receipts

 _____ × $20,000 = $ _____

19. Ending cash balance:

 (add Lines 17 and 18) _____

NOTE TO OBSERVER

As an observer, you are *only to observe* during both production periods. Note the differences in the behaviors of members during the two production periods. Read the Notes to the Supervisor and Team Leader just proceeding this note to you so you will understand the roles of the supervisor and leader. Record your observations on the Observer Form located at the end of this simulation. Read the questions in Step 8, and be prepared to help the team discuss them.

OBSERVER FORM

Based on the following scale, rate your team on how it performed on the following scale. Record your choice in the blank.

[Low 1 : 2 : 3 : 4 : 5 : 6 : 7 High]

Factor	Production Period 1	Production Period 2
1. Cooperative teamwork	_____	_____
2. Member satisfaction	_____	_____
3. Team motivation	_____	_____
4. Information sharing	_____	_____
5. Consensual decision making	_____	_____
6. Conflict directly faced and resolved	_____	_____
7. Participative leadership	_____	_____
8. Clearly defined goals	_____	_____
9. Trust	_____	_____
10. Encouraged openness	_____	_____

OD SKILLS SIMULATION 13.2
TQM IN THE UNIVERSITY SETTING

Total Suggested Time: Time 1 hour

A. PURPOSE

If there is one constant in today's world, it is constant change. The purpose of this simulation is to apply the TQM process to your university, or organization. The goals are:

1. To compare decisions made by individuals with those made by the group.
2. To practice effective consensus-seeking techniques.
3. To gain insights into the concept of TQM values.

B. PROCEDURES

Step 1. Prior to class, form into teams of five members, each group constituting an executive committee. Assign each member of your group as one of the committee members. (Extras act as observers.) Use the TQM Decision Form. Observers may use Observer Form located at the end of this simulation to gather data on group process.

1. Dean
2. Professor
3. Student
4. Student
5. Student
 Observer (extras)

Participants are to enter their decisions in column (1) on the TQM Decision Form.

Step 2. Executive Committee Meeting. Through group discussion, exploration, and examination, try to reach a *consensus decision* reflecting the integrated thinking and consensus of all members. Remember, a consensus decision involves reaching mutual agreement by discussion until all agree on the final decision.

Follow these instructions for reaching consensus:

1. Try to reach the best possible decision, but at the same time defending the importance of your department.
2. Avoid changing your mind simply to reach agreement and to avoid conflict, but support solutions with which you are able to agree.
3. Avoid "conflict-reducing" techniques, such as majority vote, averaging, or trading in reaching your decision.
4. View differences of opinion as a help rather than a hindrance in decision making.

At this point, meet together as the Executive Committee and enter your results in column (2) on the TQM Decision Forms.

Time suggested for Step 2: 35 minutes.

Step 3. Each team lists its results on the blackboard, and the instructor leads a comparison of TQM approaches.

Time suggested for Step 3: 15 minutes.

Step 4. Team discusses Team process using Team Profile Observer Form.

Time suggested for Step 4: 10 minutes.

TEAM PROFILE/OBSERVER FORM

Team Profile: Rate the team on these dimensions.

	(Low)				(Moderate)					(High)
(A) Involvement	1	2	3	4	5	6	7	8	9	10
(B) Leadership	1	2	3	4	5	6	7	8	9	10
(C) Competence	1	2	3	4	5	6	7	8	9	10
(D) Communication	1	2	3	4	5	6	7	8	9	10
(E) Goals	1	2	3	4	5	6	7	8	9	10
(F) Decision-Making	1	2	3	4	5	6	7	8	9	10
(G) Collaboration	1	2	3	4	5	6	7	8	9	10
(H) Openess	1	2	3	4	5	6	7	8	9	10
(I) Listening	1	2	3	4	5	6	7	8	9	10
(J) Motivation	1	2	3	4	5	6	7	8	9	10

OBJECTIVES

1. Identify the ways in which time is currently being wasted.
2. Identify ways which one can plan time better.
3. Identify ways to organize work to achieve faster results.
4. Identify ways to control interruptions.
5. Identify ways to communicate quickly.
6. Identify ways to maximize the customer's satisfaction.
7. Identify ways to make informed decisions faster and effectively.

TQM DECISION FORM

Individual (Col. 1) Team (Col. 2)

1. *Process Improvement*

 How can we make an administrative processes faster, easier, and better?

 1. _____ _____
 2. _____ _____
 3. _____ _____

2. *Quality Improvement*

 How can we improve quality of education?

 1. _____ _____
 2. _____ _____
 3. _____ _____

3. *Customer Student Satisfaction*

 How can we measure and improve customer satisfaction levels and attract new customers

 1. _____ _____
 2. _____ _____
 3. _____ _____

4. *Other Ideas for Improvement*

 1. _____ _____
 2. _____ _____
 3. _____ _____

CASE 13:
WENGART AIRCRAFT

President Ralph Larsen of Wengart Aircraft has become increasingly concerned about profits. Though he is not fearful of a company takeover, he does feel an obligation to maximize shareholders' return on their investment. He and about a dozen top executives receive sizable stock bonuses, so it is to their advantage to obtain a high share price.

Wengart manufactures commercial and military aircraft. It is number two in its industry, which is composed of nine companies. Its profits however are ranked as seventh. It is disturbing to Larsen and his top management team that they are not able to maximize profits.

QUALITY PROBLEMS

Quality has been identified by the top management team as one of the major problems at Wengart. Aircraft have to be reworked even after they are sent to the customer. The federal government, one of Wengart's largest customers, shares the concern for quality to the extent that several letters have been sent to Larsen from the Secretary of Defense warning him that unless quality is improved by 20 percent within six months, the government will exercise its contract provision to withhold partial payment as a penalty. This will place even more pressure on profits. Nongovernment customers have also expressed serious concerns about quality. There have been major stories in *The Wall Street Journal* and *Business Week* about Wengart's quality problems and its deteriorating financial condition.

The Department of Defense, in its latest letter to Larsen, said it would look favorably upon Wengart implementing a "total quality management" (TQM) program similar to programs at other aircraft, automobile, and electronic firms. By Presidential Executive Order 12552 applying TQM to all federal executive agencies, the Department of Defense is encouraging all defense contractors to adopt TQM.

TOTAL QUALITY MANAGEMENT AND THE CONSULTANT

Larsen, in an effort to learn more about TQM, hired a management consultant to explain TQM. The consultant made several points at a two-hour meeting with Larsen:

- Customer, engineering, production, and product support functions are integrated into a team.
- The customer is the next person in line. The customer can, therefore, be the next person on the production line for someone within the company or it can be the purchaser of Wengart's planes. Everyone in the company is both a customer and a producer.
- Quality is giving customers what they have a right to expect.
- Substantial increases in education and training are required.
- Teamwork is a basic building block of TQM.
- As the CEO, Larsen and his top management team must be committed to TQM and communicate its importance by word and deed at every opportunity.
- TQM will have to become part of Wengart's culture. The CEO must believe in humanistic work principles that include improved leadership, working conditions, and job security.

Larsen thanked the consultant and said he would take it from here. To Larsen, TQM was a matter of common sense. It was what they were doing or should be doing.

Larsen decided that they had no other choice but to implement TQM. He called a meeting of his vice presidents and explained TQM. Kent Kelly, Vice President of Production, was placed in charge of the program by Mr. Larsen. However, Maria Lopez, Vice President of Human Resources, tried to convince him that TQM should be a joint project between Human Resources and Production with the President's office coordinating the program. Larsen explained to them that he didn't have time to get involved with TQM personally as he wanted to spend his time and energies improving profits.

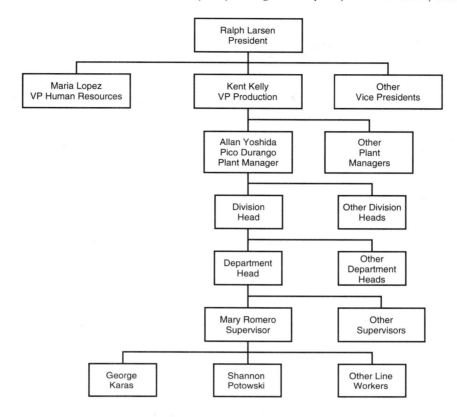

PICO DURANGO F-24 PLANT

Mary Romero, a supervisor of the wire harness assembly team for the F-24 aircraft, is responsible for 11 people on the swing shift. Her people put together the thousands of color-coded electrical wires that make up a "harness." Another production team places the harness in place in the aircraft by running the harness from the aircraft's central computer to the other sections of the aircraft. The F-24 is a new and highly advanced fighter aircraft for the U.S. Air Force using the latest in electronic and computer controls in combination with a stealth design. Romero's team, like every team on the F-24, is critical to the plane's ability to fly.

Two months ago, all managers and supervisors within the Pico Durango plant including Romero attended a meeting called by the Plant Supervisor, Allan Yoshida, where he explained TQM. Supervisors came away from the meeting with various interpretations of TQM so line workers tended to get different ideas about TQM. Within a day after the meeting, all workers in the plant received a brief memo from Yoshida in which he outlined TQM, said that supervisors had details, and that everyone was to support the program.

Romero was very enthusiastic about TQM. She was taking a management course through a local university, and her class had recently spent several class meetings learning about TQM. She was, however, confused at the brevity of the TQM information she and the other supervisors got from Yoshida.

Two of Romero's veteran workers, George Karas and Shannon Potowski, said it sounded just like the other management programs where the union workers did all the work and management, especially top management, got the credit—and the bucks. Both of the workers made some rough calculations and figured that, under the old system, at least 20 percent of their time was spent reworking a defective harness after it had been installed in a plane, waiting on products coming from the previous production team, or waiting on delayed inventory items. The waiting time, which was also common with other teams, was a good opportunity to go to the company store, take a little longer coffee break, or visit with

friends on other production teams. After comparing notes with other workers around the plant, plant workers generally concluded that Alan Yoshida was trying to speed up production so that the midnight shift could be cut.

This morning, Romero and several other supervisors went around their department and division heads to see Yoshida. They explained the rumors they had heard from workers about a worker plan to get the job done right the first time, but to make sure it took so long that no one would be laid off. Yoshida, unsure about what to do, referred to the seven-page memo Kent Kelly had sent him on how to implement TQM. Yoshida's knowledge about TQM was limited to the memo he had received from Kelly. The situation the supervisors were explaining was valid, said Yoshida. Unfortunately, Kelly's memo did not address the problem.

After looking at the way Kelly had set up the plant goals, Yoshida decided that quality was what mattered most. Yoshida quickly reasoned his next promotion was dependent on meeting his quality goals—not improving productivity. Getting the workers mad at you could be a sure-fire way to lose both quality and production. He told the supervisors at the meeting to pass the word that layoffs were not the purpose of TQM and just make sure quality was top-notch.

After the meeting, Yoshida wondered if he should call Kelly and see if there was any more to TQM he should know about. But then he decided after several minutes that if the program was very important, he surely would have heard something more. Best not to make waves.

QUESTIONS

1. Identify the driving and restraining forces toward acceptance of the TQM program at the top management level.
2. What are the driving and restraining forces of accepting the TQM program at the line worker level? Are the forces different from those at the top level?
3. Evaluate the way top management communicated the change program to the lower levels.
4. What was the vision of Wengart communicated by the President and other managers?
5. If you were an OD consultant to Wengart's top management, what would be your recommendations for implementing the TQM program?

(Case Analysis Form follows)

CASE ANALYSIS FORM

Name: _____

I. Problems

 A. Macro

 1. _____

 2. _____

 B. Micro

 1. _____

 2. _____

II. Causes

 1. _____

 2. _____

 3. _____

III. Systems affected

 1. Structural _____

 2. Psychosocial _____

 3. Technical _____

 4. Managerial _____

 5. Goals _____

IV. Alternatives

 1. _____

 2. _____

 3. _____

 4. _____

 5. _____

V. Recommendations

 1. _____

 2. _____

 3. _____

SUMMARY

• **TQM.** Quality issues have become a key concern of management. This concern has resulted in management programs called total quality management (TQM). TQM programs are comprehensive, integrated, and led by top management. TQM is regarded to be an organization-wide system that focuses on the customer, and increases efficiency and reliability of work.

• **Productivity.** In this chapter, we have examined several quality and productivity interventions that are often part of an OD program. Some interventions have been used over a period of several years with varying degrees of success, while other methods are somewhat new.

• **Self-managed.** Self-managed work teams represent a significantly new method of organizing and managing an organization. Most businesses that use this approach choose to apply it to specific plants or work sites instead of the entire organization. Self-managed work teams require a major commitment from the organization: both managers and workers. The long-term effectiveness of the teams has not been clearly established, but many organizations and their members are enthusiastic about the approach. Self-managed work teams are one of the most popular interventions and one that major corporations are hoping will make them competitive as we approach the twenty-first century.

• **Job design.** Two views of job design include job enrichment and job characteristics. The results of both theories are mixed, but both can be useful to the practicing manager and the OD consultant.

• **Team skills.** In the simulation, you had an opportunity to participate in a traditional organization and one based on using the ideas of job design and self-managed work teams. Though the experiment was limited in size and time, you perhaps drew some conclusions of your own about the application of job design and self-managed work teams.

In the last several years, productivity and quality interventions have received much more attention and seem to be having a positive impact in improving organizations. There are several methods that will help managers and consultants in improving productivity, but there is a definite need for additional research into work-design programs.

NOTES

1. See Laura Rubach, "Downsizing: How Quality Is Affected as a Company Shrinks," *Quality Progress*, vol. 28, no. 4 April 1995, p. 23.

2. Thomas Stewart, "Welcome to the Revolution," *Fortune*, October 13, 1995, p. 68.

3. For a more detailed view of the workplace of the future, see Walter Kiechel III, "How We Will Work in the Year 2000," *Fortune* May 17, 1993, pp. 38–52.

4. For detailed information see Philip B. Crosby, *Quality is Free: The Art of Making Quality Certain* (New York: McGraw-Hill, 1979); W. Edwards Deming, *Out of Crisis* (Cambridge: MIT Press, 1986); and Joseph M. Juran, *Juran on Leadership for Quality: An Executive Handbook* (New York: Free Press, 1989). For a current review of TQM see *The Academy of Management Review*, vol. 19, no. 3 (July 1994). This is a "Total Quality" Special Issue.

5. Additional information can be found in Richard M. Hodgetts, Fred Luthans, and Sang M. Lee, "New Paradigm Organizations: From Total Quality to Learning to World-Class," *Organizational Dynamics*, Winter 1994, pp. 5–18; George S. Easton, "The 1993 State of U.S. Total Quality Management: A Baldrige Examiner's Perspective," *California Management Review*, Spring 1993, pp. 32–54; Rahul Jacob, "TQM, More Than a Dying Fad?" *Fortune*, October 18, 1993, pp. 66–72; David E. Bowen and Edward E. Lawler III, "Total Quality-Oriented Human Resources Management," *Organizational Dynamics*, Spring, 1992, pp. 29–41; and Sang M. Lee, Fred Luthans, Richard M. Hodgetts, "Total Quality Management: Implications for Central and Eastern Europe," *Organizational Dynamics*, Spring 1992, pp. 42–55.

6. Robert M. Grant, Rami Shani, and R. Krishnan, "TQM's Challenge to Management Theory and Practice," *Sloan Management Review*, vol. 35, no. 2 (Winter 1994), pp. 25–35.

7. See J. Bank, *The Essence of Total Quality Management*, Englewood Cliffs, N.J.: Prentice Hall, 1992.

8. Ira M. Levin and Jonathan Z. Gottlieb, "Quality Management: Practice Risks and Value-Added Roles for Organization Development Practitioners," *The Journal of Applied Behavioral Science*, vol. 29, no. 3 (September 1993), pp. 296–310.

9. Edgar H. Schein, "Back to the Future: Recapturing the OD Vision," in *Advances in Organization Development, Vol. 1*, ed. F. Massarik (Norwood, N.J.: Ablex, 1990), pp. 13–26.

10. For additional information see Rhonda K. Reger, L. T. Gustafson, S. M. Demarie and J. V. Mullane, "Reframing the Organization: Why Implementing Total Quality Is Easier Said Than Done," *Academy of Management Review*, vol. 19, no. 3 (July 1994), pp. 565–84.

11. Rahul Jacob, "TQM: More Than a Dying Fad?" *Fortune*, April 3, 1995, p. 90.

12. Otis Port *et al.*, "Quality," *Business Week*, November 30, 1992, pp. 66–7.

13. See D. Woodruff, "Where Employees Are Management," *Business Week*, October 23, 1992.

14. For additional information on self-managed work teams, see: Brian Dumaine, "Who Needs a Boss?" *Fortune*, May 7, 1990, pp. 52–60; Edward E. Lawler III, *High-Involvement Management*, (San Francisco: Jossey-Bass Publishers, 1986) pp. 170–233; K. Kim Fisher, "Managing in the High-Commitment Workplace," *Organizational Dynamics*, Winter 1989, pp. 31–50; Charles C. Manz and Henry P. Sims, *Administrative Science Quarterly*, vol. 32 (1987), pp. 106–28; and Hackman and Oldham, *Work Redesign*, pp. 161–90.

15. For additional information see Lee G. Bolman and Terrence E. Deal, *Reframing Organizations: Artistry, Choice, and Leadership*, (San Francisco: Jossey-Bass Inc., Publishers, 1991).

16. John F. Hulpke, California State University–Bakersfield, 1995. Sources: Edgar H. Schein, "Corporate Culture is the Real Key to Creativity," *Business Month*, May, 1989, pp. 73–75.

17. Dumaine, "Who Needs a Boss?" p. 52.

18. Dumaine, "Who Needs a Boss?" p. 53.

19. Brian Dumain, "Creating a New Company Culture," *Fortune*, January 15, 1990, p. 130.

20. J.S. Lublin "Trying to Increase Worker Productivity," *The Wall Street Journal*, February 13, 1992, p. 131.

21. Dumaine, "Who Needs a Boss?" p. 55.

22. Joseph Weber, "No Bosses. And Even 'Leaders' Can't Give Orders," *Business Week*, December 10, 1990, pp. 196–97.

23. Frank Shipper and Charles C. Manz, "Employee Self-Management Without Formally Designated Teams: An Alternative Road to Empowerment," *Organizational Dynamics*, vol. 20, no. 3 (Winter 1992), pp. 48–61.

24. For more information on knowledge-based pay, see Bradley R. Hill, "A Two-Component Approach to Compensation," *Personnel Journal*, vol. 72, no. 5 (May 1993), pp. 154–161; and Henry Tosi and Lisa Tosi, "What Managers Need to Know About Knowledge-Based Pay," *Organization Dynamics*, Winter 1986, pp. 52–64.

25. Harry Berstein, "Saturn's 'Classless' Workplace," *Los Angeles Times*, May 22, 1990, p. D3.

26. For additional information see Brian Dumaine, "The Trouble With Teams," *Fortune*, September 5, 1994, pp. 86–92; Lawrence Holpp, "Five Ways to Sink Self-Managed Teams," *Training*, vol. 30, no. 9 (September 1993), pp. 38–42; Hans D. Allender, "Self-Directed Work Teams: How Far Is too Far?" *Industrial Management*, vol. 35, no. 5 (September/October 1993), pp. 13–15; and Frank J. Navran, "Four Roadblocks to Empowerment," *Executive Excellence*, vol. 10, no. 3 (March 1993), p. 15.

27. Fisher, "Managing in the High-Commitment Workplace," p. 33.

28. Hackman *Work Redesign*, p. 167–68.

29. Maury Hagan and Dave Warders, "Human Resources: Key to Excellence at Dana," in *Quality Productivity and Innovation*, eds. Y. K. Shetty and V. M. Buehler (New York: Elsevier Science Publishing Co., Inc., 1987), pp. 111–20; Edward Lawler III, *High Involvement Management* (San Francisco: Jossey-Bass Publishers, 1986), pp. 156–59; and John J. Sherwood, "Creating Work Cultures With Competitive Advantage," *Organizational Dynamics*, Winter 1988, pp. 5–27.

30. For an alternative to the theories discussed here, see Augustine O. Agho, Charles W. Mueller, and James L. Price, "Determinants of Employee Job Satisfaction: An Empirical Test of a Causal Model," *Human Relations*, vol. 46, no. 8 (August 1993), pp. 1007–27.

31. For additional information see: Frederick Herzberg, Bernard Mausner, and B. Snyderman, *The Motivation to Work* (New York: John Wiley & Sons, Inc., 1959); Frederick Herzberg, *Work and the Nature of Man* (Cleveland, Ohio: World, 1966); Frederick Herzberg, "One More Time: How Do You Motivate Employees?" *Harvard Business Review*, January–February 1968, pp. 53–62; M. Scott Meyers, "Conditions for Manager Motivation," *Harvard Business Review*, January–February 1966, pp. 58–71; and M. Campion, "Interdisciplinary Approaches to Job Design: A Constructive Replication With Extensions," *Journal of Applied Psychology*, vol. 73, no. 3 (1988), pp. 467–81.

32. Michael Campion and Carol L. McClelland, "Follow-up and Extension of the Interdisciplinary Costs and Benefits of Enlarged Jobs," *Journal of Applied Psychology*, vol. 78, no. 3 (June 1993), pp. 339–51.

33. J. R. Hackman, G. R. Oldham, R. Janson, and K. Purdy, "A New Strategy for Job Enrichment," *California Management Review*, Summer 1975, pp. 57–71. Also see Hackman and Suttle, Improving *Life at Work* (Santa Monica, Calif.: Goodyear Publishing Co., Inc., 1977), pp. 130–31.

34. A. N. Turner and P. R. Lawrence, *Industrial Jobs and the Worker* (Boston: Harvard Graduate School of Business Administration, 1965).

35. Also see William A. Pasmore, "Designing Work Systems for Knowledge Workers," *Journal for Quality and Participation*, vol. 16, no. 4 (July/August 1993), pp. 78–84; and William A. Pasmore, "Overcoming the Roadblocks in Work-Restructuring Efforts," *Organizational Dynamics*, Spring 1982, p. 55.

36. R. N. Ford, *Motivation Through the Work Itself* (New York: American Management Association, 1969).

37. Gary Johns, *et al.*, "Mediating and Moderating Effects in Job Design," *Journal of Management*, vol. 18, no. 4 (December 1992), pp. 657–76); Turner and Lawrence, *Industrial Jobs and the Worker*; M. R. Blood and C. L. Hulin, "Alienation, Environmental Characteristics, and Worker Responses," *Journal of Applied Psychology*, vol. 51 (1967), pp. 284–90; J. R. Hackman and E. E. Lawler III, "Employee Reactions to Job Characteristics," *Journal of Applied Psychology Monograph*, vol. 55 (1971), pp. 259–86; Y. Fried and G. Ferris, "The Validity of the Job Characteristics Model: A Review and Meta-Analysis," *Personnel Psychology*, vol. 40 (1987), pp. 287–322; P. Bottger and I. Chew, "The Job Characteristics Model and Growth Satisfaction: Main Effects of Assimilation of Work Experience and Context Satisfaction," *Human Relations*, vol. 39, no. 6 (1986), pp. 575–94; and E. Hogan and D. Martell, "A Confirmatory Structural Equations Analysis of the Job Characteristics Model," *Organizational Behavior and Human Decision Processes*, vol. 39 (1987), pp. 242–63.

Teamwork is an integal part of Hewlett-Packard Company's philosophy and style of doing business. While recognition is based on individual contribution, the company emphasizes working together and sharing rewards. *Photo courtesy of Hewlett-Packard Company.*

High Performing Systems: Systemwide Interventions

14

OBJECTIVES

Upon completing this chapter, you will be able to:

1. Recognize how system approaches are used in organization development change programs.
2. Identify several basic OD intervention techniques.
3. Experience and practice these system approaches.

PREMEETING PREPARATION

1. Read the Background Information. Prior to class form groups of seven and select roles.
2. Complete Step 1 of OD Skills Simulation 14.1.
3. Read and analyze Case 14: Tucker Knox Corporation.

BACKGROUND INFORMATION

In today's "nanosecond nineties," successful organizations are doing what was once considered impossible. They are increasing customer satisfaction, shortening process cycles and response times, reducing costs *and* developing innovative new products and services—all at the same time.[1] Boeing Co. for example, has been facing global competition and economic recession in the Airline Industry. In recent years, Boeing has reengineered, and downsized, including the elimination of 40,000 jobs. As a result, Boeing is radically reinventing itself. The entire process of downsizing and manufacturing an airplane is being reengineered, to do things better, faster, and more efficiently.[2]

In the past, managers aimed for success in a relatively stable and predictable world. Today, however, approaching the hyperturbulent environment of the twenty-first century, managers confront accelerating change. They are facing constant innovation in computer and information technology and a chaotic world of changing markets and consumer lifestyles. Today's organization must be able to transform and *renew* to meet these changing forces.[3]

In many organizations, empowerment has become a buzzword. Although the term is used often, it's not always understood. Empowerment is usually vaguely characterized as "something managers do to their employees." Despite the lack of a specific definition, many organizations have recognized that empowerment is critical to the achievement of total quality, customer satisfaction, and continuous improvement.[4]

All OD interventions are aimed at improving organization effectiveness, but certain interventions are aimed at the successful implementation of change within the total system. As noted, OD is essentially a system approach to the complex set of group, functional, and interpersonal relationships that are found in organizations. The system-level intervention may be described as a structural design framework for viewing the organization which examines (1) the way the organization is designed; (2) the work process of the organization; and (3) the interaction of individuals and groups within the flows and structures of the system. The major system-level interventions are aimed at developing high performing systems, and include TQM, reengineering, Likert's system 4 approach, survey feedback, and Grid® organization development.

Organizations inevitably change because they are open systems in constant interaction with their environment. Although the impetus for change may arise from internal or external forces, the underlying factor is the degree of openness of the organization to the changing demands, technologies, and values that influence the system.

In this chapter, an overview of the most widely used total organization change techniques is presented. It should be noted that the system may be an organization or a reasonably well isolated unit such as a large segment or subsystem within the total organization.

Total Quality Management

One systemwide approach to change (presented in Chapter 13) is termed Total Quality management (TQM). TQM is dedicated to having organization members who are committed to continuous improvement and meeting or exceeding customer expectations. During a time of downsizing and restructuring, many American companies are finding that they must learn to manage more effectively, and TQM involves all levels of the organization in developing practices that are customer oriented, flexible and responsive to changing needs. Total Quality management has been the most widely adopted system change strategy to improve productivity and competitiveness during the past five years.[5] This concept began with Deming's work with Japanese management, and its initial focus was on improving quality. But as it is now being applied, TQM represents a systemwide change approach which is being used by leading companies around the world.

Total quality management (TQM) involves all organization members in ensuring that every activity related to the production of goods or services relates to product quality. In essence, all organization members focus performance on maintaining the quality of products offered by the company. In TQM, all organization members work both individually and in teams to improve the quality of products. Although the TQM movement actually began in the United States, the establishment, growth, and development of the movement throughout the world began with the Japanese.

Top managers and workers all work together to ensure that all company operations improve product quality, as described earlier. The key themes of the quality movement are continuous improvement and constant innovation. Last year's best performance may not be good enough today, and today's best may not be good enough next month or next week.

Reengineering: A Radical Redesign

Although it is too early to predict the long term results of reengineering change programs, many companies including Boeing, Ford, Hallmark, Kodak, and PepsiCo. have applied reengineering to work processes.[6]

Reengineering, like TQM, is a system wide change approach focusing on changing the basic processes of an organization. Reengineering (as set forth by Michael Hammer and James Champy) may be defined as "the fundamental rethinking and radical redesign of business processes to achieve drastic improvements in performance.[7]

Reengineering, as the name implies, focuses on the design of work activities or processes: how the task is accomplished. It is like designing a circuit, examining the flows or sequences of activities from input to output in an attempt to eliminate inefficiences, and improve productivity. Reengineering seeks to make all processes more efficient by combining, eliminating or restructuring tasks without regard to traditional methods: the way things have always been done around here. The idea is to gain a large or quantum leap in performance, improvements of 100 percent or more.[8]

Like TQM, the main focus is the customer. Companies such as AT&T and Pacific Bell have reengineered the process used to implement telephone service to new customers. The result has been faster, better, and easier for both employees and customers, cutting down customer service time by one half. Reengineering does not refer to minor modifications of current practices. Instead it means starting with a clean sheet of paper, identifying the way things can be done best, right now. This includes radical changes in work processes and work relationships. The main emphasis on reengineering is making the customer happy.

The first step is to identify the key business processes of a department or work team. The next step is to identify performance measures in terms of customer satisfaction and to examine current processes to meet these measures. The customer doesn't care about internal rewards, or "turf wars"; the customer just wants the product or service done right, and on time. The third step is to reengineer the process, organizing work around the process, not functions or departments. Work is simplified by combining related tasks and eliminating any elements that do not directly add customer value. Finally, the redesigned process is implemented and all activities undergo a continuing reevaluation. As technlogy, competitors, and customers change, work processes are continually reexamined.

Reengineering examines each process and evaluates the process in terms of how it impacts the customer. In this sense it is similar to job design. It is different in that job design usually focuses on incremental changes, while reengineering is seeking a radical reexamination aimed at large scale increases in productivity. While reengineering has been criticized by some OD practitioners as a top down, or numbers approach, this approach lends itself to use in OD by involving all employees in the reengineering process. In its use of employee involvement, empowerment, and teams, reengineering is similar to the sociotechnical approach to change.

High-Performance Systems (HPS)

One of the more recent developments in large-scale change is the concept of **high performing systems, (HPS)** a term originated by Peter Vaill.[9] The idea is that today's organizations need continuing excellence and renewal as a way of bringing innovation into our systems.

In order to be effective, HPS leaders must see that the excessive layers of structure within the organization are removed and create a climate which emphasizes participation and communication across functional barriers. The most important key to creating a successful HPS is the leaders' ability to display energy and zest for the task being worked on, the product being built and one's fellow team members. Leading by example is a popular way for managers to create excitement and electricity within the workplace. Displaying enthusiasm tends to greatly impact the morale and productivity of the workforce.[10] A *high-performing system* has been defined as an excellent human system—one which performs at an unusually high level of excellence. But, as Peter Vaill points out, how we define excellence and performance depends upon our values.

HPS Criteria

Vaill has identified a set of eight criteria which may be used to examine systems:

1. They are performing excellently against a known external standard.
2. They are performing excellently against what is assumed to be their potential level of performance.
3. They are performing excellently in relation to where they were at some earlier point in time.
4. They are judged by informed observers to be doing substantially better qualitatively than other comparable systems.
5. They are doing whatever they do with significantly less resources than it is assumed is needed to do what they do.
6. They are perceived as exemplars of the way to do whatever they do, and thus they become a source of ideas and inspiration for others.
7. They are perceived to fulfill at a high level the ideals for the culture within which they exist.
8. They are the only organizations that have been able to do what they do at all.[11]

The OD consultant, then, can examine client systems and identify how well the system measures up to these criteria.

HPS Characteristics

Based on his experience, Vaill has also set for the right characteristics of HPSs. It should be noted that these may be organizations or subsystems (departments, divisions) within a larger organization.

1. HPSs are clear on their broad purposes and on nearer-term objectives for fulfilling these purposes. They know why they exist.
2. Commitment to these purposes is never perfunctory. Motivation, as usually conceived, is always high.
3. Teamwork in HPSs is focused on the task.
4. Leadership in HPS is strong and clear.
5. HPSs are fertile sources of inventions and new methods within the scope of the task they have defined.
6. HPSs have clear boundaries which separate them from their environments. There is a strong consciousness that "we are different."
7. HPSs are often seen as "a problem" by other subsystems in their environment; even those elements that may have power over them. HPSs avoid external control and produce to their own standards.
8. Above all, HPSs are systems that have "jelled," are cohesive units, such as Steve Job's "pirates" at Apple Computer, and the "skunk works" at Lockheed.

As Vaill suggests, the phenomenon of the HPS poses a complex conceptual challenge—how to analyze human interdependency in more descriptively accurate terms. Vaill also notes what he terms his "Time-Feelings-Focus" theory of high-performing systems. He has derived this because HPS leaders tend to put in extraordinary amounts of time, have very strong feelings and dedication to attain in the system's goals, and focus on key issues and variables. (See Our Changing World.)

OUR CHANGING WORLD
NO MORE PHILIPS WELFARE STATE[12]

"When I joined this company some 17 years ago, it was not the style of Philips to ask ourselves what we were doing badly but rather to congratulate ourselves on what we were doing well. We used to say 'we organize things better than anybody else. Let's not discuss it,'" said one long-time Philips manager.

A Cultural Revolution

No more. According to *Long Range Planning*, "In the last 15 years, Philips has undergone a more profound cultural revolution than any other European company." Why? According to the same article, "It is perfectly clear what has provoked this remarkable change: the Japanese Invasion."

The changes are obvious, but not yet complete by any means. Sometimes the surface changes, even those which look most spectacular, are the easiest. Twenty years ago, for example, the children of Philips' employees were delivered by Philips' midwives, attending Philips' nursery schools, and cared for by Philips' physicians. It was as paternalistic, and self-satisfied, as a company should be.

All that is gone now. Philips' employees find their own doctors and choose their own schools. But the mentality inside has not yet completely changed. As one executive put it, "If you take an organization of 344,000 people, you can't expect to change their attitudes and ways of working overnight, because the average human being resists change. It can't be done overnight, but it has to happen."

System Changes at Philips

What has changed so far? Philips has gotten leaner, going for economies of scale, partly by eliminating some 40 factories in Europe alone. More effort is going into product innovation. Employees have learned not to count on job security nor on automatic cost-of-living pay increases. The workforce is changing as more and more intellectuals—knowledge workers—play major roles in Philips.

Although the transformation at Philips may indeed be the most profound" in Europe, there is still room for change. In words that anyone contemplating OD system-wide interventions should memorize, one manager comments this reorganization "is more like a marathon than a quick sprint. It will go on for years and years, and we shall move forward steadily."

Question

1. Why do companies like Philips find a need to change?

The Grid® OD Program

One of the most widely used approaches to system-wide planned change is *Grid organization development*, a change model designed by Robert R. Blake and Jane S. Mouton and marketed by Scientific Methods, Inc.[13] This program is a systematic approach aimed at achieving corporate excellence. Blake and Mouton feel that in order to increase the effectiveness of managers and the organization, change must take place in the basic culture of the system.

Grid organization development starts with a focus on individual behavior, specifically on the managerial styles of executives using what Blake and Mouton call The Managerial Grid. The program then moves through a series of sequential phases involving the work team, the relationships between groups or subunits, and finally to the culture of the organization itself. The **Managerial Grid** and **Grid OD** represents one of the most extensively applied approaches to organization improvement and, administered by Scientific Methods, Inc., have been used by such major U.S. corporations as Procter & Gamble, Conoco, Merck, and Whirlpool, as well as by a number of foreign organizations. Westinghouse, for exam-

ple, has run more than 7,000 managers through the Grid starting in 1975 through 1990. Blake estimates that perhaps 750,000 managers have been involved with the Grid in one way or another and that perhaps 5,000 companies have engaged in Grid development activities. These are necessarily estimates, as there is no realistic basis for a head count. It is known that the *Managerial Grid* book has sold approximately 500,000 copies in English and more than 100,000 copies in Japanese. The book has also been translated into a number of other languages and has enjoyed wide popularity.[14]

Blake and Mouton assembled data on corporate excellence from some 200 organizations. They found that two common problems were planning and communication. Blake and Mouton found that the Managerial Grid seminars could be used as a starting point for a planned change program called Grid OD. Grid OD has as its objectives the maximizing of its managers' concerns for both their subordinates and the organization. In order to increase the effectiveness of an individual manager dealing with his or her subordinates, change must take place in the organization culture itself. The Grid OD program consists of the following six **grid phases**.

Phase 1: Grid Seminars

Organizations get involved in a Grid OD program in various ways, but involvement usually begins with someone in a responsible management position reading an article or book on the Managerial Grid. He or she may decide to become more familiar with the Grid by attending a public seminar to gain firsthand knowledge. These seminars last a week, are held both day and evening, and are conducted at various locations around the country and the world. There are about 30 to 40 hours of prework in addition to the work at the seminar. The learning objectives of the week include:

- Learning the Grid as a way to analyze thinking.
- Increasing personal objectivity in appraising oneself.
- Achieving clear and candid communication.
- Learning and working effectively in a team.
- Learning to manage intergroup conflict.
- Analyzing one's corporate work culture by applying the Grid framework.
- Gaining understanding of the phases of Grid OD.

The seminar is highly structured, with most of the activities devoted to short lectures and team projects. It is highly intensive and emotionally demanding, since it encourages competition between teams and confrontation between team members. Participants who leave the seminar committed to the precepts of the Grid will probably encourage other key members of their organization to attend a similar seminar.

The sessions include investigation by each person of his or her own managerial approach and alternative ways of managing which can be learned about, experimented with, and applied. Participants study methods of team action. They measure and evaluate team effectiveness in solving problems with others. A high point of seminar learning is reached when each participant receives a critique of his or her style of managerial performance from other members of the team. Another is when managers critique the dominant style of their organization's culture, its traditions, precedents, and past practices. A third is when participants consider steps for increasing the effectiveness of the whole organization.

Phase 2: Teamwork Development

An organization is composed of many subgroups or teams whose members range from top management to assembly-line workers. Phase 2 is concerned with improving teamwork and includes a boss and his or her immediate subordinates meeting together for a 1-week session. *Teamwork development* begins with the top manager in the organization and the

employees who report directly to him or her. These people later attend another team meeting with their own subordinates. This continues down through the entire organization.

Teamwork development is a planned activity that begins with each team member completing various Grid instruments. The teams deal with subjects directly relevant to their daily operations and behaviors. The team members are also getting feedback from participants on their Grid styles in real situations. Before the conclusion of the week, the team sets group and individual goals.

Phase 3: Intergroup Development

The Phase 2 teamwork development meetings have cut vertically through the organization encompassing natural work teams, but people also relate with others along a horizontal dimension: people interact with others in different teams, departments, divisions, and sections. Unintended competition between departments may develop into a win-lose contest resulting in a loss of organization effectiveness. Coordination, cooperation, and collaboration between elements are necessary for an effective organization, and to accomplish this *intergroup development* meetings are held and attended by the key members of two segments or divisions where barriers exist. Intergroup development involves group-to-group relationships where members of interfacing teams meet for three or four days to identify those things that would be present in an ideal relationship between their two segments. The objective is for the two segments to agree on the elements for an ideal relationship and then develop specific actions to attain the ideal. As in Phase 2, participants leave the meetings with actual goals and objectives plus an increased understanding of communication with one another.

Phase 4: Development of an Ideal Strategic Model

The development of an **ideal strategic model** provides an organization with the knowledge and skills to move from a reactionary approach to one of systematic development. This phase is concerned with the overall norms, policies, and structure of the organization. The responsibility for these matters is with the top manager and those reporting to him or her. During a week of study, the key people in the organization define what the organization would be like if it were truly excellent. It is not unusual for a moderate-sized organization to spend six months to a year perfecting the ideal strategic model. During this time other people at various levels have the opportunity to contribute to the model. This helps build commitment to the model needed for implementation.

Phase 5: Implementing the Ideal Strategic Model

The manner in which the ideal strategic model is implemented determines the success of Grid OD in the organization. An edict coming from above will probably fall on deaf ears and be doomed to failure from the beginning. The Grid OD program has an implementation model that can be adapted to any organization. An organization can be divided into identifiable segments such as products, profit centers, or geographical areas. Once the segments are identified, the top management team assigns one planning team to each segment, one team to the corporate headquarters, and a coordinator of Phase 5. The coordinator recommends tactics of implementation to the top-line executive. The task of each planning team is to analyze all aspects of its section's operations and determine how that section would act ideally. The design is based on the ideal strategic model determined in Phase 4 but is interpreted and implemented for each section by the planning team. The task is aided by the skills attained during Phase 1, 2, and 3. The studies to convert the ideal model into reality for each section may take three months to a year, and the actual conversion may take six months to five years or even longer.

Phase 6: Systematic Critique

The final phase in Grid OD is a systematic examination of progress toward change goals. The *systematic critique* determines the degree of organization excellence after Phase 5 compared with measurements taken *before* Phase 1. The basic instrument is a 100-question survey investigating managerial behavior, teamwork, intergroup relations, and corporate strategy. Through the use of instruments administered at each phase, it is possible to observe the degree of change and gain insight into the total process of change. It is gratifying for people to see the movement they have made toward their goals, as success may not be readily apparent considering that the entire Grid OD program may have been implemented over a period of five to ten years. Because change never ceases, this discovery sets the stage for a new beginning.

The Results of Grid OD Programs

As with many OD intervention techniques, there is a great deal of anecdotal evidence regarding Grid OD programs but little empirical evidence. The results of one Grid OD program have been reported in an article by Blake, Mouton, Barnes, and Greiner.[15] Their findings can be summarized as follows:

1. The analysis of data showed within a three-year period an increase in productivity of 30 percent and a decrease in costs of 14 percent.
2. Subordinates reported a 12 percent improvement in ratings of their managers' style and ability to manage.
3. The study suggests that managerial and team effectiveness can be improved and that Grid OD can make significant contributions to organization effectiveness.

Two other studies present some results from two different organizational settings on the application of this intervention. H. John Bernardin and Kenneth M. Alvares question the Grid's effectiveness, while Howard Hart presents findings which suggest that the Grid can be an effective development tool.[16] Another study of the Grid at Union Mutual Life Insurance Company also reported positive results.[17] In summary, there is at least some evidence which supports the contention that organizations which have applied Grid OD have become more efficient. But there are other studies, however, which report mixed or unfavorable results.[18]

Survey Research and Feedback

Employee attitude surveys are gaining popularity worldwide. IBM, Abbey National, Digital Equipment, and the BBC are just a few of the organizations sending questionnaires to their employees. The key to a successful survey is for management to clearly define the purpose of the survey and explain what will be done with the results. Once the data are collected, the results must then be translated into action plans.[19]

Federal Express is one company that is using a company wide survey system. Its Survey-Feedback-Action (SFA) uses a computerized survey to assess the attitudes, reactions, and suggestions of some 68,000 employees. Fed Ex found that the system was an important element for employee morale as well as producing many substantial cost-saving ideas.[20]

Employee Attitude Surveys serve two important functions:

1. **An Improvement Tool.** Surveys identify opportunities for improvement and evaluate the effectiveness of change programs.
2. **A Communication Tool.** Surveys also provide a communications channel and facilitate dialogue between managers and employees.

Employee surveys may be used to

- Assess the state of the organization, department or work team.
- Evaluate policies, procedures and work processes.
- Assess job satisfaction and morale.
- Identify problems that hinder employees in doing their jobs and satisfying customers.[21]

The questions on the survey should cover areas such as: do employees know in what direction the organization is going, what the organization's objectives are, and how their department fits into these goals. It is the manager's responsibility to provide their employees with feedback once the survey is conducted. After the results are collected, the organization should not fall into the common trap of comparing scores with other companies. Instead, the data should be analyzed to see how the results relate to the overall needs of the organization.

Survey research and feedback is a process in which the OD practitioner and members of the organization collaboratively collect data and use the data as a basis for changing organization relationships.[22] The survey feedback method, as developed by the Survey Research Center at the Institute for Social Research, University of Michigan, consists of collecting data by questionnaire on a number of organization dimensions and then feeding these data back to work groups at successively lower levels. The work group then uses these data to diagnose problems and to generate action plans altering organization structure and work relationships. The questionnaire probes into such dimensions as leadership, communication, decision making, superior-subordinate relations, and job satisfaction. The data generated by the questionnaire are then used as a basis for further change efforts.

Therefore, this method provides techniques for changing work relationships and also a means for measuring the effects of such changes within organizations. The client system is usually involved in the data collection activities, and members of management and other organization members are usually asked to submit questions for the survey and to plan the data collection itself. The data are usually fed back to the organization through work teams, that is, the superior and those immediately reporting to him or her in a work-related group. These feedback conferences then provide the client system with data about problems, leading to specific action plans and programs to improve work team effectiveness.

The Steps in Survey Feedback

The survey feedback approach as developed by the Survey Research Center usually includes the following steps:

Step 1. The involvement of top management in preliminary planning of the survey questionnaire. Other organization members may be involved if appropriate.

Step 2. The survey questionnaire is administered by the outside staff to all organization members.

Step 3. The data are summarized by the outside staff and then fed back to work teams throughout the hierarchy of the organization, usually beginning with the top management team and flowing down to successive levels of the organization, a so-called waterfall effect. Some guidelines for providing survey results include:

- Each manager should receive the results from his/her own work team.
- Results should be shared with the whole work team.
- Everyone should see the results for the organization as a whole.

Step 4. Each manager then has a meeting of his or her own work team to diagnose problems from the data presentation and to develop action plans and programs for improvement. An outside consultant involved in the survey usually attends each work team meeting act-

ing as a process consultant or resource person. This process may be described as a series of interlocking conferences or meetings structured in terms of organizational family units—the superior and immediate subordinates—considering the survey data together. The data presented to each group were those pertaining to their own group or for those subunits for which members of the organizational unit were responsible. The purposes of survey feedback include the following: (1) to develop an understanding of the problems, (2) to improve working relationships, and (3) to identify factors and opportunities for change or to determine areas where more research is required.

In one such company-wide study of employee and management attitudes and opinions over a period of two years, three different sets of data were fed back: (1) information on the attitudes and perceptions of 8,000 nonsupervisory employees toward their work, promotions opportunities, supervision, fellow employees, and so on; (2) first- and second-line supervisors' feelings about various aspects of their job and supervisory beliefs; and (3)information from intermediate and top levels of management about their supervisory philosophies, roles, policy information, problems of organizational integration, and so on.[23]

The Results of Survey Research and Feedback

Most of the evidence regarding the results of survey research and feedback methods has been obtained by the Survey Research Center and indicates positive changes in employee attitudes and perceptions.[24] The observations of the Survey Research Center indicate that these methods are a powerful process for creating and reporting changes within an organization. It also found that the greater the involvement of all members of the organization, the greater the change. Other conclusions are more ambiguous but suggest that a process of change did begin as a result of survey feedback, although quantitative measures did not show more than chance fluctuations.[25] When survey feedback interventions are the only type of intervention used, the success is usually short-range; but when feedback is combined with other interventions, the effects are usually more substantial and long-range. Survey feedback techniques have been widely used in organization change. John C. Aplin and Duane E. Thompson describe this process and they suggest that the returns from increased efficiency offset the costs of the survey activities.[26]

The survey research and feedback process is therefore based upon two elements: (1) the collection of data from all organization members, (2) the feedback of data to work teams in group meetings so that the group learns to better understand its own behavior during the survey feedback sessions. Although relatively little empirical evidence has been generated, the results seem to indicate that survey research and feedback can be an effective intervention approach to organization change.

Likert's System 4 Management

Another system-wide intervention developed by Rensis Likert is called **system 4 management.**[27] Likert found through extensive research that organizations can be described on a continuum with traditional bureaucratic organizations (ineffective) at one end and participative (effective) organizations at the other. (See CROCK comic strip, p. 384.) Likert then identified four systems as follows:

- **System 1**—exploitive-authoritative (autocratic, top down approach).
- **System 2**—benevolent-authoritative (top down/less coercive-autocratic).
- **System 3**—consultative.
- **System 4**—participative (based upon participative methods of decision making and supervision, this system emphasizes high degrees of employee involvement and participation).

Likert devised a measurement device to determine the degree to which an organization approximates the system 4 parameters. This is a 51-item questionnaire on which employ-

Source: CROCK By Hechin, Parker and Wilder. ®Field Enterprises, Inc. by permission of North America Synicate, Inc.

ees indicate their perception of the organization. The results are then plotted on a profile, as shown in Figure 14.1 The profile illustrates the differences that can occur in organizational functioning. According to Likert's model, the profile indicated by Organization A tends toward system 1 design; Organization B tends toward system 4 functioning. Likert has found that system 1 organizations tend to be least effective, whereas system 4 organizations tend to be highly effective. Consequently, to improve organizations, the OD practitioner tries to move the pattern of functioning closer to the right, toward the system 4 operation.

In today's changing environment, organizations that encourage individual abilities and hold employees accountable for achieving goals are more likely to succeed. These empowered organizations attract high performance from the outside. This empowerment approach to system 4 management allows decisions to be made by subordinates, rather than by managers, and gives employees personal responsibilities, instead of strict rules to follow. These organizations also promote individual abilities and encourage members to grow personally and professionally.

In analyzing empowered organizations, there are several elements to look for:

- Action opposed to further analysis
- Decisions involving subordinates rather than by superiors
- Individual accountability in place of rigid policies
- Specific recognition of team and individual accomplishments, rather than blanket expressions of thanks

Managers in these empowered system 4 organizations are demonstrating the importance of these values to themselves as individuals and as managers. Empowerment is not the simplest or easiest option available to managers. In fact, it requires an extensive commitment if its benefits are to be fully realized.[28]

OD programs in utilizing system 4 approaches, then, measure the present state of the system and design training interventions emphasizing empowerment, participative goal setting and shared decision making. In this way, one attempts to shift the key organizational factors toward the system 4 framework. Likert presents evidence that system 4 is the most effective management system for all organizations, and explains how a system 4 organization in contrast to systems 1 and 2 leads to greater effectiveness in an organization. Likert also suggests that the causal variables that form system 4 management practices can be altered or changed by members of the organization to affect the end-result variables related to performance and quality. Several organizations have reported using system 4 theory as an approach to change, including one OD program using system 4 approaches at General Motors. GM reported finding that grievances were reduced, waste costs were cut, and operating efficiencies were improved.[29]

The Third Wave Organization

The **third wave organization** is a concept originated by Alvin Toffler, who foresaw the managerial third wave. The first wave companies were built in the agricultural age. Second

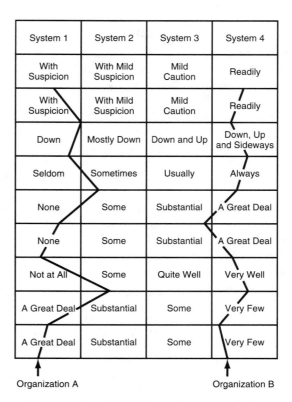

	System 1	System 2	System 3	System 4
Communication:				
1. How is downward communication accepted?	With Suspicion	With Mild Suspicion	Mild Caution	Readily
2. How is upward communication accepted?	With Suspicion	With Mild Suspicion	Mild Caution	Readily
3. What is direction of communication?	Down	Mostly Down	Down and Up	Down, Up and Sideways
Leadership:				
4. Are ideas of subordinates sought and used?	Seldom	Sometimes	Usually	Always
5. What is the degree of warmth and support between subordinates and their leaders?	None	Some	Substantial	A Great Deal
6. To what extent are the rewards and encouragements given to subordinates?	None	Some	Substantial	A Great Deal
Policies:				
7. Are the policies clearly understood?	Not at All	Some	Quite Well	Very Well
8. Are there a lot of rules, polices, and procedures a person has to know to get his job done?	A Great Deal	Substantial	Some	Very Few
9. Are there unnecessary procedures?	A Great Deal	Substantial	Some	Very Few

Organization A Organization B

Source: Adapted from Rensis Likert and Jane Gibson Likert, *New Ways of Managing Conflict* (New York: McGraw-Hill Book Company, 1976).

FIGURE 14.1 Profile of Organization Characteristics

wave companies evolved in the industrial age and emphasized mass production and growth. Third wave companies are evolving in the information age—to meet changing times, to be able to transform their products and organizations in response to changes in economic and social needs.[30]

The third wave organizations are developed for success in the information age including such characteristics as: flexibility, creativity, and innovations. (See Table 14.1.)

Table 14.1 Second Wave versus Third Wave Management

Characteristic	Second Wave	Third Wave
Organization	Hierarchy	Network
Output	Market Share	Market Creation
Focus	Institution	Individual
Style	Structured	Flexible
Source of Strength	Stability	Change
Structure	Self-Sufficiency	Interdependencies
Culture	Tradition	Genetic Code
Mission	Goals/Strategic Plans	Identity/Directions/Values
Leadership	Dogmatic	Inspirational
Quality	Affordable Best	No Compromise
Expectations	Security	Personal Growth
Status	Title and Rank	Making a Difference
Resource	Cash	Information
Advantage	Better Sameness	Meaningful Difference
Motivation	To Complete	To Build
International	Multinational	Multilocal
Outlook	Tactical	Strategic

Source: Adapted from J. Sculley, *Odyssey*, p. 95.

Flexibility. The third wave organization is flat, lean and flexible. The culture provides immense flexibility to reorganize. People expect buildings, offices, and people to change. Structure has no permanence.

Creativity. People are the life blood of the third wave organization. Third wave people are motivated by the commitment to a vision or cause, by the chance to be personally involved in projects that can change the world and the chance for personal growth. The third wave organization uses the idea of "buy-in" management—the idea that people actually influence the long-term vision and buy-in to the goals of the organization.

Innovation. The third wave organization supports risk taking and innovation. The goal is to make yourself and your product obsolete. The difference between the traditional second wave company and a third wave organization requires a revolution in attitudes, values, and behavior. For an example of organizations operating more from a system (or first wave) perspective see OD in Practice.

OD IN PRACTICE
FIRST WAVE? SECOND WAVE? THIRD WAVE?[31]

One way of looking at HPSs is to identify what is not a high-performing system. In this regard, we present two actual examples of organizations in action—Where would you classify them—second wave, third wave, or possibly first wave organizations? One example is taken from the U.S. Post Office, the other from the U.S. Navy.

The U.S. Postal Service

The U.S. Postal Service has asked for a record 19 percent increase in postal rates. After all the previous increases and service cuts and all the emphasis on high-tech automated equipment, why another increase?

Postal Operations

An answer may be indicated by examining the 900,000 square foot postal "factory" where 610 workers were getting out four million pieces of mail.

At one end of the factory stands six new optical character readers capable of sorting up to 35,000 letters an hour, but these machines sort only 42 percent of the letters. The rest are handled in the more traditional ways—mechanical sorting at 3,500 letters per hour and hand sorting at 500 letters per hour.

The postal service is operating with one foot in the future, automated mail processing and the other foot in the past, hand sorting operations. Labor costs still account for 83 percent of all costs and one of the reasons for working in the postal service is job security.

The Problems

The Post Office is also reducing service at the same time it is increasing rates and facing escalating competition. The Post Office standards generally call for overnight delivery within 150 miles, two days up to 500 miles, and three days for longer distances. But officials will stretch out many schedules so that average delivery time will increase.

Service has also slipped. The number of window hours has been reduced and Sunday mail pickups have ended.

These problems seem to emerge out of a clash between the new techniques and the traditional workforce that is relied upon to deliver an increasing avalanche of mail. Another challenge is to keep up with competitors such as United Parcel Service and Federal Express who dominate the express mail and parcel business.

McHale's Navy II—The Sequel

The experience of a Navy submarine commander would make a great movie—a new McHale's Navy except it is probably too unbelievable. The commander of a nuclear-powered submarine that accidentally sunk a tug boat off Long Beach has been relieved of his command after the latest in a series of incidents. The nuclear-powered submarine, Houston, has been plagued by a series of accidents that had one sailor saying that the sub was jinxed.

The Navigation Error

While operating off the coast of San Diego, the Houston's navigation officer misread chart information and failed to warn the officer-in-command of the submarine that an underwater object lay directly in their intended course.

The officer, to save the ship, stopped the engines to avoid a collision with a charted underwater mountain. But trailing behind the Houston was the sonar array used to detect other ships. When the sub stopped, the sonar cable did not. It went directly into the ship's propeller, slicing it off. The $2 million sonar array dropped to the ocean floor, along with the Captain's career.

The Hunt for Red October

A second incident occurred when the sub was sent to Long Beach to star in the movie production of "The Hunt for Red October." The night before the Houston's movie debut, how-

ever, the submarine's periscope struck a tow cable strung between the tugboat Barcona and two barges it was towing.

The commanding officer saw a dark bulky object—the Barcona (the tugboat)—when the periscope he was looking through broached the ocean surface. As he sighted the tug, he heard its cable strike the sub's antenna, so he followed standard procedure and yelled "emergency deep!" and the submarine with the Barcona and the two barges in tow, submerged, pulling the tug under with it. The tug's pilot was drowned. The commander was pretty upset said a crew member. "We were all pretty upset." A day later as they were returning from the filming, the Houston shredded a fishing net.

The Open Valve

In the third incident, the ship was submerged just below the ocean surface at periscope depth. The sub's powerful ventilating fans were pulling in fresh air through an induction mast located next to the periscope. Outside the seas were rough, which caused a valve on top of the induction mast to noisily open and shut. The valve shuts to prevent flooding when it senses water in the induction pipe, but the valve stuck in the open position. Gallons of sea water began pouring into the five-inch opening, filling the fan rooms, stopping the giant fans, and shorting out electrical connections. The water gushed into the operations compartment and flowed down into the submarine's lowest level.

The sub went down at a dangerous steep angle—about 30 degrees—causing most of the water to shift forward to the torpedo room. The sub remained in a nose dive until an emergency blow slowed the descent.

Almost as rapidly as it had sunk, the Houston started rising back to the surface and screamed out of the water with at least a 20 degree up-angle. But the water shifted to the rear of the sub, causing it to sink again. They did another emergency blow and stopped sinking at 350 feet. Crew members were screaming. It was pandemonium. The sub bobbed like a cork in heavy seas for two hours.

The commander, a dedicated submariner who exuded only confidence and competence, was removed from his command. One Navy source said, "Good managers make good choices on which challenges to take on, on which problems they need to solve. The commander focused on engineering."

These were obviously not high-performing systems, but they perform critical functions and probably need to consider change programs to increase overall functioning.

Questions

1. Would you say these meet the criteria of high-performing systems, and should they be? Why?
2. What types of changes might be needed?
3. How might system-wide OD approaches be used in transforming these systems?

As Minnesota Power CEO Arend "Sandy" Sandbulte has commented: Remember, developing a new corporate culture for your organization will take years. And the process never ends, because it is a process of continuous improvement. But the benefits are enormous: a vital, growing organization that people are proud to be part of; a work environment that promotes trust, creativity, and job satisfaction; and employees who view supervisors not as tyrants, but as coaches and barrier-busters who provide them with resources so they can get their work done in a better way."[32]

Most important, a participative work culture means that your organization has a better shot at beating the competition. Your workers can help make all of these things happen. And your organization's managers and supervisors can help employees realize their untapped potential by becoming true leaders, not just managers.

In this chapter, we have presented several of the major system-wide approaches to OD. Several of these models present contradictory approaches to change, and perhaps emphasize that there is no one best way for all organizations to manage change. Among the more popular approaches are TQM, reengineering, Grid OD and survey feedback; however, the research evidence supporting any one approach or model makes it difficult to make meaningful comparisons. It is clear that our knowledge of system-wide approaches to change and high-performing systems is incomplete. Our purpose here is to make you aware of these new approaches and models. Given a certain situation or set of conditions, you may decide that one approach may be more effective than others for that particular application.

REVIEW QUESTIONS

1. Identify and give examples from your experience of the major system-wide OD intervention techniques.

2. Compare and contrast the reasons for successful and unsuccessful change programs.

3. How can managers develop an organizational culture that encourages a high performing system or third wave organization?

KEY WORDS AND CONCEPTS

Define and be able to use the following:

Grid OD
Grid Phases
High-Performing Systems (HPS)
Ideal Strategic Model
Managerial Grid

Reengineering
Survey Research and Feedback
System 4 Management
Third Wave Organizations
Total Quality Management (TQM)

OD SKILLS SIMULATION 14.1
THE BRENTWOOD DIVISION

Total time suggested: 1 hour, 15 minutes.

A. PURPOSE

The purpose of this simulation is to provide a situation where you will need to influence others and to observe how information affects team decision making. During and after the simulation, you are encouraged to become aware of the processes you use in your attempts to influence and relate with others. You will also be provided the opportunity to design an OD program. You will experience:

- How task information is shared.
- How problem solving strategies influence results.
- How collaboration and competition affect team problem-solving.

B. PROCEDURES

Step 1. All participants read Brentwood Division Background Information. Form groups of seven to act out the executive committee role play. (Roles should be selected prior to the class meeting.) Additional class members will serve as observers. Each player should read only their role and the background information. Make individual decisions in col. 1 of Brentwood Division Decision Form on page 394.

1. Brentwood General Manager.
2. Director, Marketing.
3. Director, Production.
4. Director, Human Resources.
5. Director, Engineering.
6. OD Consultant Team (two). (Consultants also act as observers.)

Step 2. Executive committee meeting. Your team is to use the information to arrive at a decision. Each consultant and the executive committee meet in an executive meeting. The meeting is scheduled to last 30 minutes. The consultants use the Team Profile/Observer Form (on p. 394) to analyze the organization.

The decisions facing the committee are:

1. What should be the basic goal—efficiency or effectiveness; short-term profit or long-term market share?
2. What should the decision be on pricing policy—to stay with the policy or to become more flexible?
3. How should people be retained—by increasing salaries, bonuses, or other ways?

Time suggested for Step 2: 30 minutes.

Step 3. After the executive meeting, each consulting team completes the diagnosis and formulates an OD program to present to the executive committee for their consideration. While the consultants are designing the OD program, the executive committee of Brentwood should discuss questions to ask the consultants and the criterion for rating the proposal and filling out the Team Profile for the consultant.

Time suggested for Step 3: 10 minutes.

Step 4. The consultants present the diagnosis and OD program to their respective companies. Then each company with their consultant jointly develop an OD program.

Time suggested for Step 4: 15 minutes.

Step 5. At the conclusion of the role play, the consultants will feed back observations. Complete the Team Profile/Observer Form (p. 394) and discuss results and observations of team process and consulting style.

Time suggested for Step 5: 10 minutes.

Step 6. As a class, each consultant should present their company's OD program for class discussion and critique, and discuss the seven questions in the Team Profile/Observer Form.

Time suggested for Step 6: 10 minutes.

BRENTWOOD DIVISION BACKGROUND INFORMATION

The Continental Manufacturing Company is a leading manufacturer of industrial and military equipment. The company is divided into several major functional groups, each headed by a vice president. One of these groups is the Products Group which is divided into a number of product divisions, each headed by a division general manager (see Figure 14.2 on p. 390).

The Brentwood Division's General Manager oversees the directors for Engineering, Marketing, Production, and Human Resource Development. Brentwood's performance has been excellent, especially over the past ten years, but with the exception of the most recent

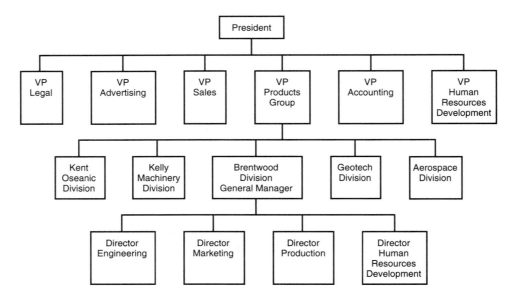

FIGURE 14.2 Continental Manufacturing Company

two years. In fact, Brentwood has a record of being one of the most profitable divisions of Continental in terms of amount of profit and return on investment. However, two years ago profits dropped by four percent and last year they dropped by 11 percent reflecting a decline in sales of 6 percent and 13 percent respectively. Continental uses cost centers with each division relatively autonomous in its operations; however, each division is expected to be self-supporting.

Brentwood employs about 1,200 people and operates from one plant location. The increase in employees has been rapid within the past ten years but the increase leveled off this year because of the sales decline. So far there have not been any layoffs but if the current sales trend continues, layoffs may have to be considered as a possibility to reduce costs. The employees are unionized as is common in this industry, but both Brentwood and Continental have exceptionally positive relationships with the unions. This is due largely to the diligent work at corporate headquarter's Human Resource Development Department where the contracts are formulated. At the local level, leadership training has been helpful, but the quality circles had some problems after a half year and were discontinued.

The major problem with sales has been attributed to the new major competitors who have entered the field. To date, the product line has faced little competition, probably because of the expensive and technologically advanced processes used in the fabrication. Because of the technological orientation of the products, it is important that Brentwood be able to respond quickly to the changing demands of their customers. Also, for Brentwood to be really competitive it is increasingly necessary for it to outguess the needs of its customers and bring in technologically superior products before its competitors. Most recently, Brentwood's ability to effectively respond to its competitors has been diminished because several dynamic middle managers and other key employees were lost to its competitors.

Recently, a key engineer left Brentwood and formed a competing company—Infiniti. He has been recruiting many key people from Brentwood—mainly engineers, marketing, and production specialists. Infiniti offers a bonus, but mainly recruits based on their free-form corporate culture and upon personal growth for the individual. But they often work much longer hours than employees at Brentwood.

Brentwood has recently submitted a proposal to one of its major customers (a large aerospace corporation) for a very large order involving 1,000 to 10,000 machines and could

involve much more over the long term. This company has always used the Brentwood product because of its fine support systems—its training and customer service. But the purchasing agent of the aerospace firm has recently informed Brentwood that it has bids from two competing firms—one of which is Infiniti—which are lower than Brentwood's standard $12,900 price—by as much as 20 to 25 percent. Basically, the bottom line is, if Brentwood cannot meet the competition, then the bid will probably go to a competitor.

Brentwood products are used as work stations in a variety of industrial and military products. The military contracts have been declining but at no greater rate than the civilian sales. The products themselves are very high tech and require strong engineering and software support. Many of the materials used in the manufacturing process are exotic metals and plastics that are very difficult to fabricate. In many cases the products must be extremely lightweight and have high strength. In some cases the composition of the products and the processes used in manufacturing are the result of inventions developed at Brentwood to which it owns the patent rights.

Corporate headquarters has recently formed a new OD division. It has been suggested by the vice president of the Products Group that Brentwood Division consider using the services of the OD group. As Continental believes it is important to allow its division to be fairly autonomous, Brentwood has the authority to choose to participate and help design an OD program that best fits its own culture and needs.

ROLE DESCRIPTIONS (READ ONLY YOUR ROLE)

Role 1—Brentwood General Manager. You have been with the company for eight years, five in your current job. Although you started fast, things have slowed down for the past two years. Your goal is to be promoted to group vice president, and to do this you need to turn things around right now and show a good profit profile. To accomplish this, you want to cut labor costs by 10 percent, cut expenses to the bone, and get rid of any fat or deadwood that exists. You operate best in a directive, structured, and centralized situation and feel that the current problems stem from a lack of control and coordination among departments. Your goal now is to increase short-run profits at any cost.

You basically would like to retain the pricing policy because the real question is value which your company has always provided. But, in this instance, you'd rather cut price than lose the order because Infiniti is involved. You feel the way to keep people from leaving is to appeal to their loyalty to Brentwood.

During the meeting you want to convince the directors to voluntarily cut costs by 10 percent, which will directly affect the bottom line. You also hope to sell them on a more centralized and controlled operation: a "taut ship." You feel that the basic causes of the current problems are the operating relations between departments and the lack of proper controls on spending.

You see the OD consultant as a possible ally in achieving your goal of promotion. A good word back at corporate headquarters would undoubtedly increase your chances. Consequently, you want to appear to be highly competent, dynamic, a "mover and a shaker," and an integrative manager.

Role 2—Director of Marketing. You are an M.B.A., and have been with the company for four years. You feel that a decentralized organization is most effective and believe that dividing Brentwood into major product groups instead of the current functional form would be best suited for the company. You are very concerned with good relationships as well as goal accomplishment and are known as a "super salesperson." You feel strongly that what the organization needs to solve its problems is an increased marketing and promotional effort. You recognize that the established market is important, but also that a firm must be innovative and adapt to changing markets with new products and promotions. A decentralized, product-oriented organization will best allow Brentwood to respond quickly to changing markets.

You feel that competitors are forcing you to change your pricing policies, therefore, you must change or lose the business. This does not mean that Brentwood will compete on price alone, but rather that you must change to meet new competition. You feel that growth and being the best is the way to hold people—you can't keep good people with money alone, they need a challenge.

In the meeting, you wish to push strongly for an aggressive marketing campaign aimed at increasing market share as a way to solve current problems. This requires increasing the sales force by 10 percent, and a 15 to 20 percent increase in advertising. The only way to halt a sales decline is to increase the marketing effort. You feel strongly that a decentralized, product-oriented organization is the way to go, with a product manager responsible for each major product line. The past problems were largely due to high manufacturing costs, poor product quality, and an inability to respond to the customers' demands. You hope to convince the OD consultant to support the major products group structure.

Role 3—Director of Production. You have been with the company for over 20 years. You worked your way up through the ranks and have found that a structured, decisive leadership style works best. You see increased efficiency as the major goal, since excessive spending in marketing and engineering is needlessly raising costs. You are convinced that costs can be reduced drastically by limiting engineering changes, limiting the number of products, and by slowing down the introduction of new products (which marketing always wants). This will allow a more stable and efficient production-line operation, rather than the hectic, constantly changing situation you have now.

You feel that Infiniti and others will go out of business from price cutting, therefore, Brentwood should stick with its pricing policy. This policy has been critical to its success over the years. You feel employees should be loyal to Brentwood, we should keep our key people by providing bonuses or stock options, and anyone who threatens to leave should be fired for disloyalty.

In the meeting, you are going to push for some "no nonsense" cost controls on overhead, particularly in marketing and engineering. You strongly oppose any layoffs in production, because skilled workers are hard to get and you are forced to pay overtime now. You also need a more automated assembly line, which in the long run will cut production costs and reduce the need for overtime. You would like to cut out the employee development programs initiated by the human resource director. Although the leadership programs were helpful, the self-managed team idea nearly caused a small rebellion when you did not approve of some production changes. You suggest a more centralized operation with tighter financial controls. For example, you feel that sales people pad their expense reports beyond reason. You hope to get support from the consultant for a more efficient and centralized form of operation.

Role 4—Director of Human Resource Development. You have a master's degree in human resource management, and have been with the company for five years. You favor a more decentralized organization and a type of leadership that is concerned with human needs and have been working toward this goal. You feel strongly that the most important resource in the organization is people. Morale and the satisfaction of individuals are the primary goals as you see it. You have already initiated several OD-type programs (communication, team building, and leadership training) and would like to see more innovative OD programs to improve the organization's long-term effectiveness. All of the programs you consider successful except for the quality circles. Some production line employees got upset when their suggestions were not implemented by the Director of Production. They came to see you about initiating the manufacturing changes they had proposed, but you had to explain it was the production director's decision to make.

You see a real problem in the changing competitive market place and feel that pricing policies may need to be changed. You wish to retain key people and feel Infiniti is a real threat because they have informal networks to find out who the key people are and then go

after them. You feel that Brentwood has to offer a better culture and more personal growth for its employees as well as financial incentives, if it is to retain and attract good people.

In the meeting, you strongly oppose any form of layoffs. The negative effects on morale would be almost irreversible. What is needed, you feel, is a raise in pay and improved coordination between departments instead of the constant bickering and fighting which prevails. You want to urge implementation of *self-managed work teams* (SMWT), which will solve these problems. This would improve the communication and coordination between groups. Naturally, you would be designing the SMWT program. If it is successful, this could lead to the application of the teams in the whole company. You see the OD consultant as an ally in gaining support for the SMWT program, and you hope to make a favorable impression as a dynamic manager who could head up a company-wide SMWT program.

Role 5—Director of Engineering. You have an M.S.E.E.and have been with the company for three years. You feel that a highly decentralized structure with a participative leadership is most effective. You see long-term effectiveness as the most important goal. Both profit and market share depend on the ability to remain innovative in R & D. You feel that the company must become more innovative and improve product marketability to survive.

You feel that the key to sustained performance is the relationship between Brentwood and its customers—the ability to meet customer needs with innovative new products and to produce them at competitive values. You feel that we must get this order in an attempt to stop Infiniti before they can get their foot in the door. You see the key to increasing markets and retaining key people is the challenge of being on the leading edge—of designing and producing the best, where new approaches and risk taking is encouraged.

In the meeting you wish to propose increased expenditures in R & D for the next two years. You also need two new engineers (in stress analysis and thermal dynamics) for these advanced projects. You feel that a reduction in manufacturing costs, less overtime, and reducing advertising budgets will allow for this. You feel that the current problems are due to stagnant, low-risk management, low-risk strategies, front-office interference, and a lack of R & D in emerging fields. The production department is old and obsolete, both in methods and equipment. You have suggested new methods, but your advice has been rejected. You hope to gain the consultant's support in creating a more innovative, R & D-oriented organizational climate. Recently you have lost several of your key researchers to other companies. You think Brentwood's lack of an incentive system tends to stifle any innovation. You would like to see the company use some of the techniques you used when you were at TRW, such as team building and reengineering.

Role 6—OD Consultant-Observer Guidelines. You are the consultant team from the company's newly formed OD consulting group. You hope to accomplish several things at this meeting:

1. To develop a consultant-client relationship with all the committee members.
2. To make a preliminary diagnosis of possible problems.
3. To assist the committee by doing process consultation during the meeting.

Use the Team Profile/Observer Form to analyze group processes and conflict styles.

TEAM PROFILE/OBSERVER FORM

Team Profile: Rate the team on these dimensions.

		(Low)				(Moderate)					(High)
(A)	Involvement	1	2	3	4	5	6	7	8	9	10
(B)	Leadership	1	2	3	4	5	6	7	8	9	10
(C)	Competence	1	2	3	4	5	6	7	8	9	10
(D)	Communication	1	2	3	4	5	6	7	8	9	10
(E)	Goals	1	2	3	4	5	6	7	8	9	10
(F)	Decision-Making	1	2	3	4	5	6	7	8	9	10
(G)	Collaboration	1	2	3	4	5	6	7	8	9	10
(H)	Openess	1	2	3	4	5	6	7	8	9	10
(I)	Listening	1	2	3	4	5	6	7	8	9	10
(J)	Motivation	1	2	3	4	5	6	7	8	9	10

Did the Consultant

1. Establish a relationship?
2. Take over the problem?
3. Focus on feelings?
4. Encourage the client to be specific?
5. Allow the client to talk?
6. Lead and direct the conversation?
7. Show indications of judging the client?

BRENTWOOD DIVISION DECISION FORM

	Individual Decision	Team Decision
1. Goal		
Profit	_____	_____
Market Share	_____	_____
Other	_____	_____
2. Pricing Policy		
Increase Price	_____	_____
Keep Price Stable	_____	_____
Decrease Price by ____%	_____	_____
3. Employee Retention		
Money	_____	_____
Responsibility	_____	_____
Involvement	_____	_____
Other	_____	_____
4. Other Factors		
Costs	_____	_____
Re-organization	_____	_____
Quality	_____	_____
Morale	_____	_____
Risk Taking	_____	_____

CONFLICT MANAGEMENT FORM

How did team members deal with conflict? Rate them on the form below:

	Individual	Team
1. Avoidance style (withdrawing, passive agreement)	_____	_____
2. Dominating, competing style (win/lose, fighting for one's position)	_____	_____
3. Compromising style (finding a mid point)	_____	_____
4. Obliging, accomodating style (smoothing over, giving in)	_____	_____
5. Integrating style (openness, sharing, consensus)	_____	_____

CASE 14: TUCKER KNOX CORPORATION[33]

INTRODUCTION

Ed Leonard sat slumped behind his desk at Tucker Knox Corporation. It was 6:00 PM and everyone else had left for the day. Ed recalled the progress he had made over the last four years. He had joined TKC to help the company develop a new Automation Design Department. In the first two years, he had designed and developed the new department and had helped to automate the production process to the point where new products were very competitive and profitable. The final year had been filled with political turmoil due to changes in top management.

A new challenge and a new set of goals were what Ed needed. He sat there at his desk staring at a phone call message from another company. Ed had been pursuing his personal goals with Tucker Knox, but felt that the phone message was the moment he had been waiting for. Ed had been planning a move away from Tucker Knox and this was his chance. Where did it all go wrong, he wondered.

COMPANY BACKGROUND

Tucker Knox Corporation is a world leader in keyboard design and manufacturing, supplying keyboards to computer "system" producers. Since 1981, TKC held the number one position in the market share (sales volume) of the capacitive switch keyboard design for private manufacturers. However, Tucker Knox is not just in competition with private key-

board manufacturers, it is also in competition with the captive keyboard manufacturing divisions of such "system" giants as IBM, Sperry,and Honeywell. The number 1 position was not easy to come by for a company that was founded by a retired corporate executive in a rented garage in 1969.

Larry Henderson, a strong-willed entrepreneur, pledged his personal assets, mortgaged his home, and called on five of his closest friends and business associates to build and grow the company into a world market leader with sales over $110,000,000 (see Organization Chart on p. 399). Larry, president and CEO, had always clearly been the father figure for TKC and for all of those whom he had personally selected to join him at the senior management level. Like sons answering to their faither, each of the senior vice presidents would always look to Larry for his "nod of the head" of approval or disapproval.

TUCKER KNOX GOALS

During an executive board meeting, the major topic of discussion was once again focused on a continual challenge to retain its market share in an aggressive price-competitive market. "Our current challenge is: (1) to compete in the world market with private and captive manufacturers; (2) have efficient manufacturing facilities in locations in the United States and overseas as required to meet price/cost demands; and (3) retain our corporate headquarters in the U.S. while the other manufacturers are moving their entire operations overseas." Larry started the meeting as he always had, by setting the issues directly on the table.

"These challenges mean that besides the usual corporate functions of marketing, sales, finance, and engineering,we will also have to provide those functions required to support our unique product design." In the keyboard business, the major areas of product uniqueness is the design of the "piece parts" comprising the physical and mechanical portion of the keyboard. The unique features in each manufacturer's part design leads to very high labor costs for assembly. These unique designs lead to no readily available automated assembly machines on the market that will aid in reducing the high cost of assembly labor. "I've waited patiently for you boys to provide a solution to this world competition issue, and I trust that the solution will be presented today," continued Larry.

Much to Larry's pleasure, the skilled fatherly coaching would pay off once again as the decision was announced by Howard Watson that, "beginning next year, I will develop a corporate Automation Engineering Department. The new department will be responsible for the concept, design, manufacture, installation, and maintenance of all custom automation for TKC's five manufacturing facilities: three in the United States, one in Ireland, and one in Taiwan." Larry was pleased, not only with the decision, but because Howard had been the one to announce it. With this new advanced technology department, Larry Henderson envisioned keeping his company ranked number one in world keyboard sales.

DEVELOPMENT OF THE DEPARTMENT

Howard Watson, Director of Manufacturing Engineering, worked closely with Larry in developing the Automation Engineering Department. Howard not only knew of Larry's fondness for equipment but Howard was also eager to move up in TKC. Howard was a very aggressive manager with a positive attitude toward his job, traits which Larry liked in his management staff. While his responsibilities were many, and growing, Howard had not yet selected a manager to develop and run the new department.

In fact, Howard had not filled either of the two vacant manager positions in his division. Howard was not a distrusting manager, but a great deal of convincing was always required before he would delegate control. Howard knew that for the Automation Engineering Department to be successful he would need a manager with a strong technical background as well as a good understanding of the business.

The manager he hired would be very visible to the corporate staff, including Larry. The manager would eventually have to develop and "sell" his own cost savings automation

programs to the Vice Presidents. There were several people within the Manufacturing Engineering Department that had the qualifications to manage the new department, but none with the technical background and none with the desire to have such a visible position.

Through a friend of his at Tucker Knox, Ed Leonard learned of the decision to develop an Automation Engineering Department. In June, Ed began discussing with Howard the need to build the new department and the potential of joining the TKC team. Ed was a Mechanical Engineer with an M.B.A. and both management and manufacturing experience who was seeking a new career challenge. Ed's engineering degree and experience easily satisfied the technical requirements of the position. However, his management skills were mainly in the project management area with some personnel management. Ed's managerial style was not as aggressive as Howard's, but his highly motivated, hard-work ethic, and commitment to the project appeared to be the balance that Howard was looking for. In November, Ed joined the Tucker Knox team, not as the Automation Engineering Department Manager, but as a Machine Design Engineer.

Howard wanted Ed to first prove his technical abilities in the seven person Machine Design Department that Howard had created as a beginning for the Automation Department. Ed would then progress through the step of department supervisor before moving to manager and further developing the department. This progression was important to Howard for two reasons. "The performance and success of this department is very important to the future of TKC. The employees in the department must function as a close knit team. It is essential that each team member accept and be accepted by every other member. Therefore," Howard continued, "each person functions in their new position for a period of time to demonstrate their ability and to become accepted by the team."

The second reason for this slow progression (which Howard did not discuss) was his nature of being very slow to delegate and relinquish authority. This play, being agreed upon by both Ed and Howard, was the beginning of a very strong management team that was about to develop within Tucker Knox. Within a year, Ed had proven his abilities and was promoted to Supervisor of Machine Design.

Soon after Ed Leonard's arrival at Tucker Knox, the machine design team was divided in two by Howard's boss, Jack Donaldson. Jack was a relatively new member of the Tucker Knox team that Larry Henderson had brought in as the Vice President of Technology. Larry Henderson was planning on retiring in a few years and had tried to groom several candidates for taking over his position. Jack Donaldson was the latest of these candidates. In attempting to establish his "signature" on the Tucker Knox organization, Jack decided to reduce some of the power that Howard possessed within TKC by splitting the machine design team.

The multiple copy manufacturing group was split off from the R & D group and assigned to Matt Jackson, Plastics Engineering Director. Matt was not only one of Howard's peers, but also his strongest rival.

Howard was not the type to take such change lightly. Howard disagreed with the decision not just because some of his organization was given to his strongest rival, but because the decision was not founded, in his opinion, on sound financial information. Howard and Ed worked closely developing cost savings justifications which Ed used to convince Larry Henderson and Jack Donaldson to recombine the multiple copy manufacturing group with the R & D group. By allowing Ed Leonard to present the data and plan to Jack, Howard once again demonstrated his ability to achieve his own goals through his skillful managing of people at all levels within the organization. He also put Ed Leonard in the middle of an internal political conflict.

GROWTH OF THE DEPARTMENT

Ed continued to build the Machine Design Department into a twenty-three-person Automation Engineering Department through corporate organization streamlining. The Test

Equipment Department, responsible for designing and building custom test equipment was merged with the automation group in January of year three. The Plastics Engineering Department, part of Matt's division, was merged into the Automation Department six months later. The Plastics Automation Department, also part of Matt's division, was merged into the Automation Department in December of the following year. This rapid growth of the Automation Engineering Department was due to the efforts of both Ed and Howard. Ed provided the technical expertise for the department growth. He also resented the justifications for cost reduction, increased output, and increased response to the ever-changing customer demands in the market place for new keyboard designs.

New keyboard designs resulted in demands from the Vice Presidents that the production facilities have the automation in place at the same time the new keyboard design arrived in production. The automation was viewed to be essential to provide the low production costs necessary to stay ahead of the competition. Howard's contribution to the team was not only his position as Director, but more so his natural ability to understand people almost better than they understand themselves and his ability to use internal politics to achieve his goals.

Howard had the ability to know how to deal with each of his peers and superiors in a way that bordered on manipulation. His intent was to influence decisions by communicating with each person in a unique way, so that each person was comfortable with the decisions. Howard used his position and communication skills to present the development steps to Larry Henderson and Jack Donaldson for their approvals. He often presented the idea to Larry Henderson first, and then to Jack Donaldson, as a *fait accompli*!

CHANGE IN SENIOR MANAGEMENT

In June of year two, a change took place in the Vice President assignments. Jack Donaldson was promoted to a newly created position of Senior Vice President. But as the corporate staff members were expecting Howard and Ed to also be promoted, trouble arose in the Ireland plant.

The managing director of the Ireland plant was unexpectedly forced to retire for health reasons with no time to groom a replacement. The Ireland plant played a major role in the European market. Howard possessed the most in-depth knowledge of the manufacturing part of the plan because he was responsible for having set it up. Jack Donaldson, being a relatively new member of the Tucker Knox top management team (and possibly being displeased with Howard for his political maneuvers in the Machine Design Department) decided to assign Howard to the Ireland plant.

Howard moved to Ireland in August of the second year. Jack Donaldson filled his own vacated position of Vice President of Technology with Sam Martin. Jack hand picked Sam from outside TKC so that he could begin building his own loyal management team. Sam came from a high-tech firm in California with the experience of high volume manufacturing of custom products comprised of "standard piece parts." Sam also brought several years of experience in worldwide competition including the creation of two foreign production facilities.

During his first couple of months at TKC, Sam Martin made no changes, no promotions, and no attempts of any kind to fill the personnel vacancies. After acquainting himself with his new departments, Sam Martin recommended promoting Ed Leonard to the position left vacant by Howard, but was overruled by Jack Donaldson. There was much discussion between Jack and Sam over Ed Leonard's record of continued cost reductions and excellent performance of timely installations of new equipment in the critical manufacturing facilities. However, without giving any explanation for his decision, Jack Donaldson overruled Sam. Sam Martin was ordered to fill the vacancy from outside the company. (See Organization Chart on p. 400.)

CONCLUSION

Within the next few weeks it became apparent that Jack was trying to fill the vacant positions in the senior management staff with people who would be loyal to him. Another newcomer, Art Hodges, would be brought in to fill Howard Watson's position. While Jack was hand selecting his own team he made sure that Sam Martin actually did the hiring so that it would appear that the "team" was selecting its own members. Art had been the manager of a packaging design department for a scientific instruments company in Portland, Oregon, where he had worked since graduating from college 10 years previously. He did not have the years of management experience that Sam had and would therefore be easily manipulated by Jack.

Three weeks after arriving at TKC, Art Hodges (at the direction of Jack Donaldson) reassigned Ed Leonard to the company's largest manufacturing facility to set up a maintenance department. Ed was told by Jack and Art that after successfully completing the assignment he would be able to return to his department. With virtually no experience at TKC, Art followed Jack's direction without question and four weeks later assigned Ed's Automation Engineering Department to Matt Jackson. Within three months, Jack Donaldson had managed to rearrange the Manufacturing Engineering Department and surround himself with managers that he had hand selected and who he felt would be loyal to him. Six months after being given the assignment to set up the maintenance department, Ed was brought back to the corporate facility and given six weeks to find another job within the company or be laid off.

Ed Leonard sat slumped behind his desk at the keyboard manufacturing company. It was late in the day and everyone had gone home. Ed recalled the progress he had made over the last few years as well as the lessons in management that he had so painfully been taught. Routine was not what Ed wanted and routine is certainly not what he got.

Tucker Knox Corporation Organization Chart (Early)

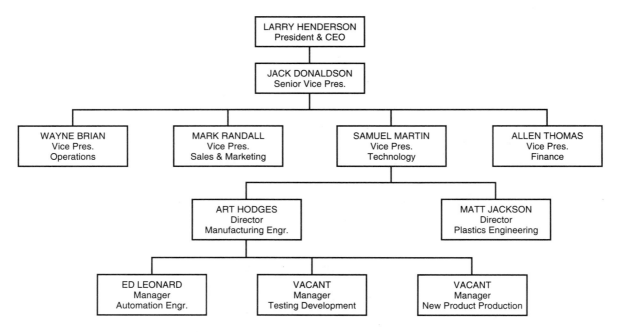

Tucker Knox Corporation Organization Chart (Later)

TUCKER KNOX CORPORATION FINANCIALS

Consolidated Statement of Income

	Year End June 30, (in thousands, except shares)
Net Sales	$111,655
Operation Costs and Expenses:	
Cost of sales	78,658
Research, development and engineering	8,431
Selling	8,598
General and administrative	13,008
Plant consolidation	2,053
Total operating costs and expenses	110,748
Operating Income	907
Interest Income (Expense)—net	(66)
Income Before Income Taxes	841
Provision for Income Taxes	280
Net Income	$561
Net Income per Commn Share	$.06
Weighted Average Shares Outstanding	8,843,121

Liabilities and Shareholders Equity

	(in thousands, except shares)
Current Liabilities	
Current portion of long-term obligations	$2,820
Accounts payable	5,246
Employee compensation and accrued vacation	1,844
Taxes other than income taxes	1,513
Commissions payable	1,469
Other	2,588
Total current liabilities	15,480
Long-term Obligations, less current portion above	3,629
Deferred Income Taxes	2,949
Commitments and Contingencies	
Shareholdes' Equity	
Common stock, no par value	38,789
Retained earnings	26,596
Foreign currency translation adjustment	235
Total shareholder' equity	65,620
	$87,678

CASE ANALYSIS FORM

Name: _____

I. Problems

 A. Macro

 1. _____

 2. _____

 B. Micro

 1. _____

 2. _____

II. Causes

 1. _____

 2. _____

 3. _____

III. Systems affected

 1. Structural _____

 2. Psychosocial _____

 3. Technical _____

 4. Managerial _____

 5. Goals _____

IV. Alternatives

 1. _____

 2. _____

 3. _____

 4. _____

 5. _____

V. Recommendations

 1. _____

 2. _____

 3. _____

SUMMARY

• **Systemwide.** In this chapter, we have examined several system-wide approaches to organization development: (1) TQM; (2) Reengineering; (3) high-performing systems; (4) Grid OD; (5) survey research and feedback; (6) Likert's system 4 model; and (7) the third wave organization.

• **Grid OD** is an approach to change focusing on efforts to improve managerial skills and to develop a new strategic model. These approaches use some of the methodologies similar to those of the action research model. They often involve the collection of data, the feeding back of these data to appropriate individuals, and the generation of action plans by system members. Although the research evidence on the results of these systemwide approaches is incomplete, it does indicate positive results in certain organization settings. More research evidence is needed to determine under what conditions one approach is more effective than another and why certain approaches are more appropriate within certain organization settings or on certain organization problems.

• **Survey Feedback** uses attitude surveys of employees as a means of identifying and communicating organizational problems. The survey data are then provided to work teams as away of improving performance.

• **OD Consulting Skills.** In the simulation, you have had an opportunity to experience and practice the concepts of systemwide change approaches. You also had a chance to experience an organizational meeting, which provides a method for rapidly generating information, identifying problems, and designing action solutions. You had an opportunity to apply concepts from this chapter as a means of diagnosing system problems, and as a framework for recommending action plans. You also had a chance to experience the consultant role and practice your consulting skills.

Developing a new corporate culture is a process of continuous improvement. But, a more participative, empowered, high performing system can lead to a successful organization.

• **TQM** is one of the most widely used organizational strategies for improving quality and productivity. TQM focuses on commitment to quality as key part of the corporate culture.

• **Reengineering** is another systemwide approach to change that is a fundamental and radical redesign of all business processes to achieve a higher level of performance.

NOTES

1. Ruban Jacob,"The Struggle to Create An Organization for the 21st Century," *Fortune*, April 3, 1995, p. 90.
2. D. J. Young, "Reinventing Beoing," *Business Week*, March 1, 1993, p. 60
3. Ruban Jacob, "The Struggle to Create An Organization for the 21st Century," *Fortune*, April 3, 1995, p. 90.
4. John H. Dobbs, "The Empowerment Environment," *Training and Development Journal,* February 1993, p. 55.
5. Howard E. Butz, Jr., "Strategic Planning: the Missing Link in TQM," *Quality Progress*, vol 28, no. 6, June, 1995, p. 105.
6. See Michael Hammer and James Champy, *Re-engineering the Corporation*, New York, HarperBusiness 1993.
7. "The Promise of Reengineering," *Fortune*, May 3, 1993, p. 97.
8. M. Hammer, "Reengineering Your Company," *Nations Business*, February, 1994, p. 16.
9. See Peter Vaill, "The Purposing of High-performing Systems," *Organizational Dynamics,* (Autumn 1982), p. 23.
10. "To electrify your firm, pull the plug yourself," *The Chicago Tribune*, July 6, 1994, p. 8.
11. Vaill, p. 25.
12. John P. Hulpke, CSUB, 1995 see also Graham Turner, "Inside Europe's Giant Companies: Cultural Revolution at Philips," *Long Range Planning*, August 1986, pp. 12–17.
13. Robert R. Blake and Jane Srygley Mouton, *The Managerial Grid III* (Houston, TX: Gulf Publishing Company, 1985), p. 182.
14. Robert S. Blake, Jane S. Mouton, L. Barnes, and L. Greiner, "Breakthrough in Organization Development," *Harvard Business Review*, November–December 1964, pp. 133–55.
15. Robert S. Blake, Jane S. Mouton, L. Barnes, and L. Greiner, "Breakthrough in Organization Development," *Harvard Business Review*, November–December 1964, pp. 133–55.
16. H. John Bernardin and Kenneth M. Alvares, "The Managerial Grid as a Prediction of Conflict Resolutions and Managerial Effectiveness," *Administrative Science Quarterly*, March 1976; and Howard Hart, "Grid Appraisals - Phases 1 and 2," *Personnel*, (September 1976).
17. "Using the Managerial Grid to Ensure MBO," *Organizational Dynamics*, Vol. 2, No. 4 (Spring 1974), p. 54–65.
18. See for example, M. Beer and S. Kleisath, "The Effects of Managerial Grid on Organizational and Leadership Dimensions," in *Research on the Input of Using Different Laboratory Methods for Interpersonal and Organizational Change*, ed. S. S. Zalkand, symposium presented at American Psychological Association, Washington, D.C., September 1976.
19. Diane Summers, "The right attitude—Staff surveys are increasingly popular," *The Financial Times Ltd.*, June 14, 1993, p. 11.
20. B. Smith, "Fed Ex's Key to Success," *Management Review*, July, 1993, p. 24.
21. Ronald D. Snee, "Listening to the voice of the employee," *Quality Progress*, vol 28, no 1, January, 1995, p. 91.
22. See Tony Condeni, "The Survey Solution," *Management World*, Vol. 12, No. 4a, (May 1983), pp. 30–31, which describes the use of an "OES" Survey.
23. *Ibid.*
24. *Ibid.*
25. M. Mils and others, "The Consequences of Survey Feedback: Theory and Evaluation," in *The Planning of Change*, 2nd ed., ed. W. Bennis, K. Benne, and R. Chin (New York: Holt, Rinehart & Winston, 1969), p. 466.

26. J. Apliin and D. Thompson, "Feedback: Key to Survey-Based Change," *Personnel Management*, (November 1974). See also Edward J. Conlon and Lawrence O. Short, "Survey Feedback as a Large Scale Change Device: An Empirical Examination," *Group and Organizational Studies,* Vol. 9, no. 3, (September 1984, pp. 399-416.

27. Rensis Likert and Jane Gibson Likert, *New Ways of Managing Conflict,* (New York: McGraw-Hill Book Company, 1976).

28. George Boyadjis and Earl Merkel, "Empowerment Managers Promote Employee Growth," *Healthcare Financial Management*, March 1990, p. 58.

29. William Dowling, "System 4 Builds Performance and Profits," *Organizational Dynamics*, Vol. 3, No. 3, (Winter 1975), pp. 23–38.

30. See John Sculley, *Odyssey*, (New York: Harper & Row, 1987), pp. 92-98.

31. Albert R. Karr "Letter Bomb," *The Wall Street Journal*, March 7, 1990, p. 1. Tom Burgess "Submarine Commander Loses Post," *The San Diego Union*, December 10, 1989, p. 1.

32. Arend Sandbulte, "Lead, Don't Manage," *Industry Week*, November 1, 1993, p. 18.

33. This case was written by Don Harvey and Mel Hartwig, Eastern Washington University, 1991.

The use of computers plays a part in forming corporate strategy at IBM. *Photo courtesy of International Business Machines Corporation.*

Organization Transformation: Strategy Interventions

15

OBJECTIVES

Upon completing this chapter, you will be able to:

1. Identify and define organization transformation (OT) in relation to the change process.
2. Understand the basic strategy-culture matrix and other approaches to changing the culture to fit the strategy.
3. Recognize the importance of corporate culture and its relation to strategy.
4. Experience these concepts in a management simulation.

PREMEETING PREPARATION

1. Read the Background Information.
2. Complete Step 1 of OD Skills Simulation 15.1. Form teams of five, select roles.
3. Read and analyze Case 15: The Space Electronics Corporation.

BACKGROUND INFORMATION

In a world of unpredictability and rapid change, what makes one organization a winner, while another fails to adjust to the same opportunities? How do some smaller companies move forward and seize new product and market opportunities, while other larger companies fail to take advantage of their size and situation? How did Bill Gates and others lead Microsoft from virtual obscurity to the Fortune Top 500, while at the same time Gulf Oil (once the ninth largest U.S. corporation) was taken over by another company? The answer lies in the firm's ability to change its strategy to meet changing conditions.[1]

According to John R. Graham, "When the year 2000 rolls around, the nation's corporate landscape will have changed more in the previous seven years than it did in the [century's] first 93 years." His argument is that the overwhelming success of many great companies starts to work against them when the "pride of position" starts to erode its base. Customers become fuzzy entities, then nonentities as corporations stop earning their loyalty. Then, Graham asserts, corporate visions become blurred as well; the idea banks for new products and services become overdrawn; and bloated corporate bureaucracies hinder employees from doing "productive work."[2]

Organizational transformation refers to these drastic changes to how an organization functions and relates to its environment.[3] Good management does not mean trying harder by using old, out-of-date methods. It involves developing strategies for coming up with new products, making sure they are what the customer wants, and getting the new products to market in time to gain a competitive advantage. Accelerating changes in technology, shorter product life cycles, and new unexpected competition contribute to make succeeding in business harder than ever. The evidence indicates that managers play a major role in whether or not an organization performs. Managers make strategy and strategy determines business success or failure.

Author/consultant Tom Peters offers a bold and daring approach in transforming a firm's corporate culture to create a strategically effective organization. With the world changing at ever-faster speeds, getting off the corporate endangered list requires nothing short of "disorganizing" the "organization," a word Peters sandwiches between quotes to emphasize that there's no liberation when much more than a semblance of the superstructure remains. He feels large corporations must not only revamp their entire organizational structure to adapt the corporate culture to the environment, but in fact says, "destroy your company before a competitor does."[4]

The new excellent companies must be able to transform the way they operate and recognize the importance of corporate culture in devising and executing new strategies. In fact, the biggest stumbling block in the path of strategic change is usually an old and inflexible corporate culture. A culture that prevents a company from meeting competitive threats, or from adapting to changing economic or social environments, can lead to the company's stagnation and ultimate failure unless it makes a conscious effort to change. These cultural change efforts include activities which are designed to improve the skills, abilities, structure, or motivational levels of organization members. The goals are improved technical skills (planning, and so forth) more effective work processes, improved interpersonal competence, and faster communications. Such implementation efforts may also be directed toward improved leadership, decision making, or problem solving among organization members. The assumption underlying such efforts is that by developing an improved culture, a more effective organization will result.

The **strategy-culture matrix** provides one model that can be used to assess the readiness of a corporate culture for strategic changes. A growing body of research has indicated that the culture does indeed affect strategy formulation and implementation, as well as the organization's ability to achieve a high level of corporate excellence. **Strategic change management**, another type of intervention, involves integrating the organization's strategy with its structure technology and people and aligning these factors to the competitive environment.

In this chapter, several of the major OD strategic interventions will be described including:

- Organizational Transformation
- Corporate Culture Change
- The Strategy-Culture Matrix
- Strategic Change Management

Organizational Transformation

In a general sense, OD strategies represent more gradual approaches to strategic change, focusing on developmental and participative change processes. **Organizational transformation (OT)**, on the other hand, may be defined as drastic, abrupt change to total structures, management processes, and corporate cultures.[5] It is important to note that since transformations aim for organizational survival in a competitive environment, the changes may or may not be developmental in nature and, in many instances, are not accomplished by using participative processes. Organizational transformations include such changes as takeovers, mergers, and plant closures which often involve large-scale downsizing, layoff of employees, and massive restructuring.

One example of such change was when new CEO Linda J. Wachner took over Warnaco. She had "to change things radically." The company very badly needed new direction, and it needed new thinking and enthusiasm. What Wachner did was impose a philosophy she calls "Do it now." "If we didn't make our people understand that the consumers are our bosses and make them look where the consumers are going and what they will want to buy, in five years and ten years, we would not have been able to set the new directions. So we changed. And that started at the top.[6]

Directive Approaches to Change. Another feature of OT approaches is that they tend to use directive rather than participative approaches. Typically, a senior manager initiates the transformational change: he or she decides when to initiate change, what the changes shall be, how change is to be implemented, and who is responsible for the change program. This is usually a top down, top management driven process.

Albert J. Dunlop, CEO of Scott Paper Co., provides an example of such a transformation. The day he became CEO, he brought in three of his former trusted associates as members of his top management team. On Day 2 he disbanded the previous Executive Committee. On Day 3 he fired 9 of 11 members of the old management team and on Day 4 he threw out his predecessers strategic plans. Within one year he had engineered one of the fastest turn arounds in corporate history. Many CEO's spend years struggling to change an inefficient company, but some, like Dunlop, are able to get an immediate transformation. This requires a clear; shared vision, a willingness to clean house, to reengineer and restructure, and the ability to tackle many problems at once.[7]

Research evidence suggests that the political dynamics of transformational change tend to be shaped more directively or coercively (by use of power) rather than by using more collaborative, participative approaches. It appears that under immediate threat, this may be the best way (or the only way) to rapidly bring the organization back into fit with its environment. There is also evidence to indicate that outsiders (or externally recruited executives) are more likely to initiate transformational change than the existing management team. Larry Bossidy's performance at Allied-Signal provides an object lesson in corporate transformation. In his first 15 months the New Jersey company's operating profits increased 28.5 percent. Return on shareholders' equity leaped from 8.9 percent to 17 percent. And the stock, at $29 when Bossidy's appointment was announced, recently soared to $55.[8]

Strategies of Change

There are several possible approaches to large-scale change programs depending upon the existing conditions. One approach, which may be termed the **incremental approach**, refers to long-term planned change which relies upon collaboration and participation from organization members. The second approach, **transformative change**, usually refers to immediate, drastic change accomplished by directive methods.

Dunphy and Stace have identified a model of large scale change strategies based upon three key dimensions: the time frame of the change, long or short; the level of support of the organization culture; and the degree of discontinuity with the environment.[9] From these three dimensions, four process change strategies or topologies have been identified, as shown in Figure 15.1.

1. **Participative Evolution.** This incremental strategy is used to keep an organization in fit with its environment in anticipation of changes, when minor adjustments are needed, and when sufficient time is available. Such change is achieved by collaborative means with the support and participation of organization members.
2. **Charismatic Transformation.** This transformative strategy is used to accomplish radical change in a short time frame, with support from the organization culture. Fred Smith of Federal Express and Steve Jobs, founder of Apple Computer, are two examples of leaders who used such strategies to accomplish change.
3. **Forced Evolution.** This strategy is used to make minor adjustments over longer time frames but without the support of the organization culture. The programs of David Roderick, former chairman at USX, Donald Peterson at Ford Motor Co., and Charles Parry, former chairman at Alcoa, would typify such changes. The organization culture did not support the changes and, in fact, Charles Parry was replaced by a CEO who returned Alcoa to its basic businesses.
4. **Dictatorial Transformation**. This transformative change strategy is used in times of crisis, when a major restructuring is needed which may run counter to the entrenched interests of the internal culture. In these conditions, authoritative direction may be the only option to ensure organizational survival. When Jack Welch, Jr. became CEO of General Electric, he wanted to make GE into a world class competitor. To accomplish this Welch set goals for each of GE's products to become number one or two in its markets or became a candidate for divestiture.

FIGURE 15.1 Strategies for Planned Organizational Change

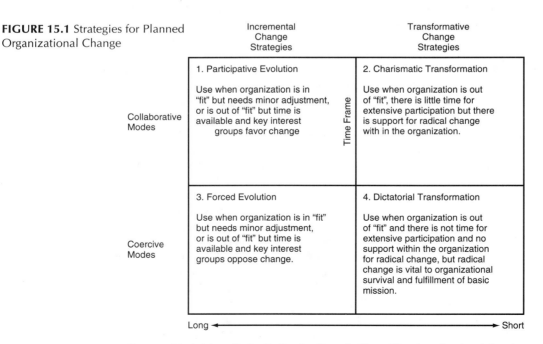

Source: Adapted from Dexter C. Dunphy, Doug A. Stace, "Transformational and Coercive Strategies for Planned Organizational Change Beyond the OD Model." *Organizational Studies.* vol. 9. no. 3. (1988). pp. 317 – 34.

The key point for OD consultants is that the selection of appropriate change strategies depends on a strategic analysis of the change situation. OD consultants, then should select the most effective change process and strategy, rather than relying solely on a strategy that is compatible with their own personal values. However, just as important is the fact that large-scale change in times of crisis can be more effectively implemented if it is combined with the behavioral skills of the OD approaches. (See Our Changing World.)

OUR CHANGING WORLD
A NEW CULTURE AT SAS[10]

When Jan Carlzon, newly named Scandinavian Airlines (SAS) Chief Executive Officer, had to change planes in Copenhagen (an SAS hub), he noted with curiosity and a bit of anger that the plane he got off of had docked at Gate A–1 (or the equivalent), but the connecting SAS flight was at Gate Z–99. As Carlzon noted a large group of his fellow passengers trudging to connect to the same plane, his fury grew. Gates, it turned out, were chosen to make life easy on the ground crew with little or no concern for the passengers. Something Carlzon decided, had to change.

A Culture Change

In a successful organizational development campaign, Carlzon managed to shift the entire airline towards a "customer first" attitude and take SAS from an annual deficit of $20 million to a profit of $54 million in one year. And, he got the gates changed.

Prior to the Carlzon inspired shakeup, "SAS was very rigid and its employees could do little more than follow rules and regulations." In a comprehensive effort to turn around the business, SAS carried out both group and individual counseling. Employees at the customer service level were given more responsibility, and more authority. Even the canned script to be read before takeoff was no longer sacrosanct: whoever read the welcome and safety message could improvise as long as the essentials were covered.

The Results

The end result was not only good for the employees, who felt and looked more responsive in their jobs, but was good for the traveling public as well. Ask anyone who flew SAS then, and has flown SAS since the change. The customer service strategy, matched by a change to a customer service culture, has made a world of difference at SAS.

Question

1. Do you agree with the changes? Suggest some ways that Carlzon might use to change the culture.

The Corporate Culture

The concept of **corporate culture** has become increasingly important as a factor in large-scale interventions. Each organization forms its own culture. As noted in Chapter 3, an organization's culture includes the shared values, beliefs, and behaviors formed by the members of an organization over time. The leadership style of top management and the norms, values, and beliefs of the organization's members combine to form the corporate culture. Organization effectiveness can be increased by creating a culture that achieves organizational goals and at the same time satisfies member needs.

The CEO's words alone do not produce culture; rather the actions of managers do: a corporation's culture can be its major strength when it is consistent with its strategies. Some of the most successful companies have clearly demonstrated that fact, including Goodyear where the word employee was replaced with the word associate. This leveling approach to management quickly became a part of the firm's corporate culture after an encounter with a black associate. Three or four black associates came up to the CEO, Stanley Gault, and one of them, quite embarrassed, said hesitantly, "Does the word associate apply to me?" He was told very quickly that the word associate applied to everybody, his job and the CEO's alike.[11]

Kotter and Heskett find that highly profitable companies like PepsiCo, Wal-Mart, and Shell have adaptive cultures that serve the interests of all three of their main constituencies—employees, customers, and stockholders. Over an 11-year period, companies that successfully satisfied these groups boosted employee productivity, satisfied customers and increased sales by an average of four times more than those who satisfied only one or two.[12]

The corporate culture reflects the organization's past and is often deeply rooted in the firm's history and mythology. Many cultures were started by the firm's founder, such as Fred Smith of Federal Express, and have been reinforced by successful operations and strategies. The corporate culture influences how managers approach problems, react to competition, and implement new strategies.

The Strategy-Culture Fit

Corporate culture is important because of its relationship to organizational effectiveness. There is increasing evidence that firms with effective corporate cultures claim to have increased productivity, boosted employee camaraderie, increased employee's sense of ownership, and increased profits.[13]

Strategy refers to a course of action used to achieve major objectives. This includes all the activities leading to the identification of the objectives and plans of the organization and is concerned with relating the resources of the organization to opportunities in the larger environment. Organizations are finding it increasingly necessary to change business strategy to meet emerging discontinuities in the environment.

Culture provides a set of values for setting priorities on what is important, and "the way things are done around here." Because of this, culture is a critical factor in the implementation of a new strategy. An organization's culture can be a major strength when there is a fit with the strategy and can be a driving force in implementing a successful change. Former CEO Louis Gerstner of RJR Nabisco, Inc. (recognizing the importance of culture in his strategy to revitalize the food and tobacco giant) said, "One of the key issues is culture. We have to free up the culture from the enormous, bureaucratic, overstuffed organization it became over the last few years, one that never talked about its problems."[14]

The challenge of the new millenium is the need to replace bureaucratic obstacles with speed, simplicity, constant change, and improvement. Carol Pasmore, manager of organizational effectiveness at General Electric Co.'s GE Lighting operations in Cleveland said,

> We are in a cultural revolution where the change of pace is going to be faster and competition will not stop. As a result, businesses will need an organization that is very different from the hierarchical one that exists today. They will need an adaptive organization that senses change in both the internal and external environments, as well as one that entrusts power and decision-making to workers. Without that no other strategy will succeed in the long run.[15]

Each organization evolves a unique culture. But this culture must also change to meet changing conditions. A number of studies have indicated that corporate strategy alone cannot produce winning results. Management consultants have suggested that only one company in ten can successfully carry out a complex change in strategy. But the need for devising and executing strategic changes is rapidly increasing. A study by Daniel R. Denison reported that firms whose cultures support employee participation in decisions performed significantly higher than those who did not.[16] It has been suggested that the best way to execute strategic change is through empowering employees. An action by a single employee is critical to the achievement of total quality, customer satisfaction, and continuous improvement.[17]

Culture: A Definition

There is widespread agreement that organizational culture refers to a system of shared values held by members that distinguishes one organization from another. An organization's culture may be described by a set of core characteristics that include:

- *Individual autonomy*—the degree of responsibility, independence, and the opportunities for exercising initiative for members of the organization.
- *Sensitivity to the needs of customers and employees*—the degree of responsiveness to changing needs.
- *Support*—the degree of assistance and warmth provided by managers.
- *Interest in having employees initiate new ideas*—the degree to which employees are encouraged and empowered to come up with better quality and productivity suggestions.
- *Openness of available communication channels*—the degree of freedom of communication between members and teams and levels.
- *Risk behavior*—the degree to which members are encouraged to be aggressive, innovative, and risk seeking.[18]

By combining each of these characteristics, then, a composite picture of the organization's culture is formed. The culture becomes the basis for the shared understanding that members have about the organization, how things are done and the way members are supposed to behave.

A company's success rests on its ability to change strategy in order to meet rapidly changing market conditions. Under these conditions the culture must be adjusted so the firm can confront and deal with factors that may contribute to its failure, stagnation, or success. The culture influences each member's adjustment to these changes. Productive corporate changes increase the company's capacity to meet new challenges. To be effective, managers must be able to motivate their employees and help them adapt to changing conditions. Success depends on management's skills and strategy, and on the acceptance of change by the organization members.

Organizations operating in different environments with differing competitive situations may need to develop different cultures, each one focused upon the goals of its strategy and competitive arena. Similarly, organizations existing in several markets may need to have differing subcultures to meet the unique strategies of each specific business environment. A corporate culture reinforcing innovation, entrepreneurship, and participation, for example, may be necessary for a high-tech firm competing in a highly dynamic and complex industry. On the other hand, a more traditional firm in a mature, smokestack industry may develop a culture focusing on stability, quality, and productivity.

Sharing the Vision

One important element in organizational and *culture change* is the development of a vision. Many management theorists feel that vision is the very essence of leadership. Any attempt at cultural change should begin with a clear vision of the new strategy and what it will take to make it work. Organizations are driven by a vision, not by directives from the chain of command.

A widely used definition of **vision** is "a mental image of a possible and desirable future state of the organization. . . (which) articulates a view of a realistic, credible, attractive future for the organization, a condition that is better in some important ways than what now exists."[19] The vision provides a sense of identity, purpose, and direction for organization members. An effective vision should be challenging, inspiring, and aimed at empowering people at all levels.[20]

In one study it was found that sharing the vision, that is making certain that all levels of the organization are involved and communicated with, is critical.[21] The fact of the matter is that the McDonald's employee flipping burgers and waiting on the customer is the one who will ultimately carry out the vision, not owner Joan Kroc and her management team at McDonald's Corporate Headquarters. One example of how a shared vision can impact an organization would be the vision of Steve Jobs, founder of Apple Computer, who galvanized his whole organization into revolutionizing the way people processed information by sharing the dream that personal computing and what they were doing could change the world.

Developing a shared vision involves several stages, as shown in Figure 15.2.[22]

FIGURE 15.2 Sharing the Vision

- *Share the Vision.* People will buy into a clear challenging vision that has meaning for them and will improve society.
- *Empower the Individual.* People need to feel they have a stake in the outcome and that they have participated in defining the vision. The idea is to have individual purpose congruent with the organization's vision.
- *Develop Trust.* An effective vision must set goals for challenging performance, but must allow people to "buy in" to the vision and provide feedback on performance.
- *Reward Performance.* An effective vision also rewards the achievement of outstanding performance. At Apple Computer, for example, along with financial awards, MacIntosh team members were included and recognized at product launch meetings and other award ceremonies. This element also includes support for taking risks, providing the freedom to fail, and pushing decision-making information downward to the lower levels.

A shared vision provides a starting point for cultural and organizational transition. As we have seen from our examples of leaders of corporate change (such as Bill Gates of Microsoft and Jack Welch of GE) a shared vision provides the starting point for cultural and organizational transformation. The vision should be simple, easily understood, clear and energizing.

Strong versus Weak Cultures

Every organization has a culture, but some cultures are stronger than others. IBM, for instance, has a more tightly held culture than does a conglomerate of newly acquired companies, or a very young firm. Harvard University has a more cohesive culture than many newer universities. In strong culture, the behavior of members is constrained by mutual accord rather than by command or rule.

It has become increasingly popular to differentiate between strong and weak cultures. The evidence suggests that strong cultures have a greater impact on employee behavior and are more directly related to reduced turnover. Research evidence also suggests that a strong culture helps workers march to the same drummer, create high levels of employee loyalty and motivation; and provide the company with structure and controls without the need for an innovation-stifling bureaucracy.[23]

A **strong culture** is characterized by the organization's basic values being both intensely held and widely shared, as shown in Figure 15.3. Each dimension can be envisioned as existing along a continuum from low to high. The more members sharing these basic values and the greater their commitment to those values, the stronger the culture.

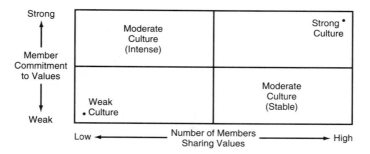

FIGURE 15.3 Relative Strength of Corporate Cultures

By this definition, IBM and AT&T would be assigned as having strong cultures, whereas relatively young companies or ones which have had a high turnover of executives and employees would be considered to have a **weak culture.** It should also be noted that once an organization develops a "strong" culture, there is a high resistance to changes which affect the culture. The organization can survive high turnover at lower ranks because new members can be strongly socialized into the organization.

It is important to recognize that **cultural strength** does not necessarily guarantee corporate effectiveness. Though many current writers argue that strength is desirable, the fact remains that the relationship between culture and effectiveness is not simple. The definition of the culture and the degree to which its solutions fit the problems posed by the environment seem to be the critical variables here, not strength alone.

Managers often have a difficult time in recognizing the relationship between culture and the critical performance factors on which excellence depends. There are several key components of the organization—structure, systems, people, style—that influence the way key managerial tasks are performed. Culture is the product of these components. Strategic change is largely concerned with adjustments in these components to accommodate the perceived needs of a new strategy. So, managing the strategy-culture relationship requires sensitivity to the interaction between the changes necessary to implement strategy and the compatibility or "fit" between those changes and the organization's culture. General Electric, an organization undergoing cultural change is described in OD in Practice.

OD IN PRACTICE
GE'S CROTONVILLE: A STAGING GROUND FOR CORPORATE REVOLUTION[24]

Today, General Electric is far and away the biggest U.S. investor in India, with $100 million sunk into factories making medical-imaging equipment, plastics, kitchen appliances, and lamps. Sales in India have gone from almost nothing to $400 million. The goal: $1 billion before the decade's end.

The way C.E.O. Jack Welch sees it, GE's aggressive pushes into India, China, and Mexico are no longer a matter of choice: they could well determine the future of the $57 billion titan, America's third-most-profitable company. Total revenues have climbed a mere 3 percent in each of the past two years, and the prospects for strong U.S. growth are marginal. Welch set out once and for all a strategy that would shift the company's "center of gravity" from the industrialized world to Asia and Latin America. By 2000, those markets could provide more than $20 billion in revenues, double the current level—and more than 25 percent of GE's total sales.

Changing the Culture

The first act of transformation is creating a sense of urgency for change and dealing with the inevitable resistance to a new order. Welch worked to delayer, downsize, and change GE's portfolio. A new breed of leader was required to transform the organization, develop global product and service strategies, strategic alliances, global coordination and integration, and global staffing and development. Toward that end, managers were required to attend Crotonville, GE's Management Development Institute. Welch felt that the chain of command, with its vested interests, is where much of the resistance to change resides. The GE "blue books" were symbolically burned, recognizing that there are no more textbook answers; leaders must write their own textbooks.

Culture Shock

The CEO and top managers came to Crotonville to conduct workshops on key GE strategic challenges. Along the way, participants found the development experiences increasingly unsettling and emotionally charged. They felt uncomfortable with feedback from their back-home organization, and wrestled with very difficult, unresolved, real-life problems, not case studies. Jack Welch, a very tough person, spent a great deal of time and energy in coaching and developing team players and team building. Those who had to depart though, he insisted, be treated compassionately; that is, "a soft landing." The cornerstone of Welch's strategy for building an organization and a winning team was this blending of hard issues (budget, manufacturing, marketing, distribution, head count, finance, and so forth) and the soft issues (values, culture, vision, leadership, style, innovative behavior, and so on).

Taking Chances—GE's Brave New World

Certainly GE is no stranger to international business, the big GE push into China, India, and Mexico—with Southeast Asia close behind—was summed up this way by Welch: "If it's right, it's the future of the next century for this company." Welch continued, "We're a company with great infrastructure strengths and, therefore, a company that ought to go where

the growth is. It's clear to anyone that the growth will be in the Pacific Rim, India, and Mexico.

Unmistakably, GE is telegraphing the message that for the company to remain competitive and profitable, it has to establish deep manufacturing, technological, and financial roots elsewhere, even if that's at the expense of some factory jobs in the United States, tied to slower markets. The modern company has to spread its brains, its centers of excellence.

To make this management mix work, GE is exporting the training programs, concepts, and managers developed at Crotonville. Ready or not, GE's focus on lean management, quick response, speeded-up product cycles, and productivity is now moving offshore along with its capital and technology. GE will be what Welch calls a multipolar and multicultural company.

Questions

1. Corporate executives have been quoted as saying that the greatest challenge GE faces is to change its culture. Do you agree?

2. Summarize the characteristics of the old and new cultures.

3. Suggest some ways to change the culture.

The Strategy-Culture Matrix

Strategic changes can more effectively be implemented when the culture of the organization is considered. In an effort to minimize the risks inherent in a proposed change, the extent of the need for change and the degree to which the change is compatible with the culture should be viewed together as each impacts upon the other. Four basic alternatives in determining strategy changes are:

1. Manage the change (manageable risk).
2. Reinforce the culture (negligible risk).
3. Manage around the culture (manageable risk).
4. Change the strategy to fit the culture (unacceptable risk).[25]

The need for strategic change and the compatibility of the change, viewed together as a strategy-culture matrix, will largely influence the method used to manage the strategic change (see Figure 15.4).

Manage the change (manageable risk). An organization in quadrant 1 (Figure 15.4) is implementing a strategy change that is important to the firm, where the changes are compatible with existing corporate culture.

Therefore, the company can pursue a strategy requiring major changes and should manage the change by using the power of cultural acceptance and reinforcement. The change strategies should emphasize these basic elements:

• Share the vision. The changes must be related to the overall goals and mission of the organization. This builds on existing strengths and makes any changes legitimate to members.

FIGURE 15.4 The Strategy-Culture Matrix

- Reshuffle power to raise key people to positions important in implementing the new strategy. Key people make visible the shared values and norms that lead to cultural compatibility.
- Reinforce the new value system. If the new strategic direction requires changes in marketing, production, and so forth, the changes should be reinforced by the organization's reward structure.

Reinforce the culture (negligible risk). An organization in quadrant 2 needs relatively little strategic change, and the changes are highly compatible with the existing culture. Here the consultant should emphasize several factors:

- Forge a vision of the new strategy that emphasizes the shared values, to make it work.
- Reinforce and solidify the existing culture.

At Apple Computer, former CEO John Sculley made changes to the firm's competitive position, but he was also determined to reinforce the existing culture in carrying out the new strategy.

Manage around the culture (manageable risk). Organizations in quadrant 3 need to make some strategic changes, but these changes are potentially incompatible with the corporate culture. Here the critical point is whether these changes can be implemented with a reasonable probability of success. The key element is to manage around the culture, without confronting direct cultural resistance (see B.C. comic strip). The approaches include:

- Reinforce the value system.
- Reshuffle power to raise key people.
- Use any available levers of change such as the budgeting process and reorganization.

B.C. by permission of Johnny Hart and Creators Syndicate, Inc.

H. Ross Perot, a former vice-president and member of the board of directors at General Motors, commenting on GM's inability to alter its culture said, "I come from an environment where, if you see a snake, you kill it. At GM, if you see a snake, the first thing you do is organize a committee on snakes. Then you go hire a consultant who knows a lot about snakes. Then you talk about it for a year."[26]

Change the strategy (unacceptable risk). An organization in quadrant 4 faces a different challenge because the strategic change is important to the company, but the changes are incompatible with the entrenched corporate culture.

First Chicago Bank, for example, illustrates the dilemma faced by an organization under these conditions. The company faced the challenge of attempting to change its culture from an "aversion for risk" to an "aggressive risk-taking style." The challenge of changing the culture is an expensive long-term undertaking that is practically impossible to achieve.

When an organization is in this situation, facing large-scale change with a high probability of cultural resistance, the OD consultant and management must determine whether strategic change is really a viable alternative. The key question is: Can the strategic change be made with any possibility of success? If the answer is no, the organization should modify its strategy to fit more closely with the existing culture.

Strategic Change Management

Noel Tichy proposed the **strategic change management** model which provides an important integration of the strategic interventions discussed earlier.[27] Tichy's model seeks an alignment among an organization's strategy, structure, and human resource systems, and a fit between them and the organization's environment. Strategic change is a function of how well an organization manages these alignments.

Tichy proposes that organizations are composed of **technical, political, and cultural** systems. Three basic management tools, including organizational strategy and structure, and human resource management, may be used to align the three systems with each other and with the larger environment (see Figure 15.5).

Organizations are perpetually experiencing increasing amounts of environmental change and uncertainty. This turbulence often causes existing structures and strategies to become obsolete, requiring major strategic changes. For example, the banking industry, long regarded as a stable and unchanging industry has faced monumental changes because of deregulation and electronic banking.

Tichy describes the three organizational systems as follows:

- *The technical system* is designed to solve the organization's production problems. It includes the mission, strategy, and organizational structure necessary to become effective.
- *The political system* resolves the allocation problem: how to distribute resources and power, including reward systems, career succession, budgets and power structure.
- *The cultural system* is designed to solve the value/belief problem—what values members share, what objectives should be pursued, and so forth.

The technical, political, and cultural systems are interrelated and form an organizational system, as discussed in Chapter 2. Strategic change management, then, involves the alignment of these systems to meet environmental pressures.

Tichy's approach to change suggests the following steps:

Step 1. Develop an image of desired organization with the technical, political, and cultural systems aligned. Change must start with a strategic vision of a desired organizational state. This vision should include a futuristic view of each of the three systems, as well as what the organization will look like when the systems are aligned.

FIGURE 15.5 Environmental Forces and Organizational Systems

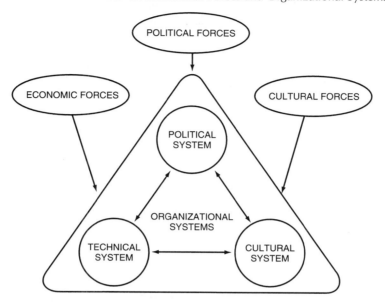

Source: Reproduced by permission From N. Tichy. "Strategic Change Management" (Working paper. GSBA. The University of Michigan. April 1982). p. 17.

Step 2. Separate the three systems and intervene separately in each one. Because each of the systems tends to be mutually reinforcing, it is necessary to unlock the systems from each other before strategic change can occur.

Step 3. Plan for reconnecting the three systems. After strategy interventions have been made in the three systems separately, it is necessary to determine how they will be reconnected. This reconnecting plan determines how the three systems will achieve the desired state or strategic vision in step 1.

Changing the Culture

There is a general agreement that an effective corporate culture can result in superior performance. There is also considerable agreement that organizations facing discontinuity—out of fit with the environment—may need large-scale cultural change. However, **changing the corporate culture** is often very difficult because the culture is based upon past successes.[28] Therefore, organization members may hold deeply entrenched beliefs and strong personal investments in the existing culture. There is research by Jay B. Barney which suggests that a firm's culture can be a source of sustainable competitive advantage if it is difficult to imitate, thus making it difficult for less successful organizations to imitate a more successful culture.[29]

The organization culture may inhibit the implementation of a strategy and prevent a firm from meeting competitive threats or from adapting to changing economic conditions. This can lead to the firm's decline, stagnation, or even ultimate demise unless the culture is changed. One company that has systematically changed its cultural emphasis is PepsiCo, Inc.

At one time, the company was content in its number two position, offering Pepsi as a cheaper alternative to Coca-Cola. But today, a new employee at PepsiCo quickly learns that beating the competition, whether outside or inside the company, is the surest path to success. In its soft-drink operation, for example, Pepsi's marketers now take on Coke directly, asking consumers to comprehend the taste of the two colas. That direct confrontation is reflected inside the company as well. Managers are pitted against each other to grab more

market share, to work harder, and to wring more profits out of their businesses. Because winning is the key value at Pepsi, losing has its penalties. Consistent runners-up find their jobs gone. Employees know they must win merely to stay in place—and must devastate the competition to get ahead.[30]

Another company that has changed its cultural emphasis is General Electric Corporation under CEO Jack Welch. When he looked at the books, Mr. Welch was appalled. Two-thirds of sales were made by aging businesses. Sales were dropping for the first time in 22 years. GE was increasing productivity by a mere 1.5 percent a year compared with the 8 percent of its Japanese competitors. Pay and bonuses depended on seniority, not merit. He gave managers of every GE business an ultimatum: make your business number one or number two in its industry or get out.[31]

Terrence Deal and Allan Kennedy suggest that there are only five reasons to justify large-scale cultural changes.

1. When the company has strong values that do not fit a changing environment.
2. When the industry is very competitive and changes with lightning speed.
3. When the company is mediocre or worse.
4. When the firm is about to join the ranks of the very largest.
5. When the firm is small but growing rapidly.[32]

Organizations facing these situations may need to change their culture in order to adapt to a changing environment or to perform at higher levels of effectiveness. But implementing cultural change can be extremely difficult and time consuming. Given the problems associated with culture change, most OD consultants suggest that major changes to the culture should be attempted only after less difficult and costly solutions have been ruled out.

There are also problems of meshing different cultures or subcultures within the same organization. Pillsbury Co. (as noted earlier) had problems of internal conflict between subcultures. At Pillsbury's high-rise corporate headquarters in Minneapolis, managers tend to be very formal and traditional—dark three-piece suits are the uniform. But at the Burger King subsidiary's tropical headquarters on Biscayne Bay in Miami, pink is the exterior color, they favor flashier cars, more colorful clothes, and no ties, forming a low-key, laid-back, informal culture. These cultural differences have led to the factional nicknames "Minneapolis Ice" and "Miami Vice."[33]

This cultural clash becomes even more evident in the case of mergers or takeovers when two differing cultures must be integrated. In one case in the author's experience, one high-tech firm, Company B, with a very innovative, participative culture, was acquired by Company A, a larger competing firm with a very formal, traditional, top-down culture.

At the time the acquisition was announced, Company A stated that no major changes were planned, and that Company B would continue operating as a separate company. But within six months, 80 percent of the Company B management team was replaced, large-scale layoffs were instituted, and the Company A corporate culture was imposed on Company B. The results included: loss of key people; loss of sales (including one $60 million customer); a decrease in morale and productivity; an increase in turnover; and a lack of trust among remaining employees.[34] The integration of differing corporate cultures during merger situations appears to provide a very cost-effective area for the use of OD cultural change interventions in the future.[35]

For many businesses, changing the culture is not in the best long-term interest of the firm. For example, Apple Computer management recognizes that its most important challenge will be to retain its small-company culture even though it has grown into a top Fortune 500 firm.

In summary, leadership in today's fast changing world involves developing an innovative corporate culture: a culture which recognizes employees' needs, the firm's history, the marketplace, and the company's products and services. Top managers invariably try to develop a framework for transmitting the corporate culture and for adapting to change.

Unfortunately, often a strong culture may prove to be a liability if it fails to respond to changing market forces. When the corporate culture is resistant to change, then OD strategies may be used to move the culture in a more innovative direction.[36]

REVIEW QUESTIONS

1. Compare and contrast organization development and organization transformation. How are they similar or dissimilar?

2. Suppose you are receiving a new job offer, what cultural factors would you consider in making a decision?

3. How does the culture affect an organization's ability to change?

4. Can you identify the characteristics that describe your organization's culture?

5. Find an article from *Business Week, Fortune, The Wall Street Journal,* or another publication that discusses an organization's culture and identify the strength of the corporate culture using Figure 15.3 as a frame of reference.

KEY WORDS AND CONCEPTS

Define and be able to use the following:

Changing Cultures
Corporate Culture
Cultural Strength
Culture Characteristics
Empowerment
Incremental Approach
OD Strategy Interventions
Organization Culture

Organizational Transformation (OT)
Strategic Change Management
Strategy
Strategy-Culture Matrix
Technical, Political, and Cultural Systems
Transformative Change
Vision

OD SKILLS SIMULATION 15.1
THE GENTECH COMPANY

Total time suggested: 1 hour 10 minutes

A. PURPOSE

The purpose of this simulation is to experience and observe how information affects strategic discussion making. In this simulation, you will be able to develop strategy and culture in an organization. You will receive feedback on your risk-taking level. The goals include:

- Comparing strategic decisions made by individuals with those of the team.
- Learning how task information is shared among group members.
- Identifying how individual risk-taking levels influence results.
- Learning how collaboration and competition affect team problem solving.

B. PROCEDURES

Step 1. Prior to class, form GenTech teams of five. Additional members may serve as observer/consultants. Each member selects one role and reads company and strategy information. The roles include:

1. Executive Vice President, Corporate Strategy.
2. Vice President, Human Resources.
3. Vice President, Manufacturing.
4. Vice President, Marketing.
5. Vice President, Engineering.
 Extras: OD Consultant/Observer

Individually, read the GenTech Company background, terminology,and strategy descriptions that follow. There are four basic strategies and within each strategy there are two implementation alternatives. For the four strategies, allocate a percentage of investment to each strategy that reflects the degree of emphasis you want to place on that strategy. Record your choices on Form 1: My Individual Strategic Decisions, Column 1 (Individual Strategy). The four strategies should add vertically to 100 percent.

Then for each of the four basic strategies, allocate a percentage of resources between Implementation Alternatives A & B. Record your percentages in Column 2 (Alternatives A & B). The sum of the percentages for Alternatives A & B within each of the four strategies will total 100 percent. (As an example, you may give "Market Penetration" 30 percentage points and within this strategy you may give Alternative A 80 percentage points and Alternative B 20 percentage points. You would then go through the other three strategies and allocate percentage points in a similar manner.) See Form 1 on page 423.

Step 2. The Executive Committee Meeting. The committee meets to select a strategy. Through team discussion, exploration, and examination, try to reach a consensus decision reflecting the integrated thinking and consensus of all members. The two parameters of team effectiveness include: (1) the determination of an optimal strategy; and (2) the completion of the task in the least amount of time.

Follow these instructions for reaching consensus:

1. Try to identify the best long-term strategy.
2. Avoid changing your mind simply to reach an agreement and to avoid conflict, but support solutions with which you are able to agree.
3. Avoid "conflict-reducing" techniques such as majority vote, averaging, or trading in reaching your decision.
4. View differences of opinion as a help rather than a hindrance in decision making.

There are at least three possible strategies that your team can follow:

- High risk, high growth.
- Low risk, low growth, cost control.
- Some trade-off between the first two strategies.

At this point, meet together as the Executive Committee and enter your committee's decision on Form 2: Executive Committee Strategic Decisions (page 424).

Time suggested for Step 2: 30 minutes.

Step 3. Each team lists its results on the blackboard and compares and discusses the team decision rankings.

Time suggested for Step 3: 10 minutes.

Step 4. Based upon your own decision style, individually rate your risk-taking level on Form 3: Individual Risk Assessment (on p. 424). If you feel you are a low risk taker (risk averse), select a rating at the low end of the scale; if you feel you are a high risk taker (risk taking), then you will rate yourself on the high end of the scale. On Form 4: Risk Taking—Individual and Team write in team member names, and on an individual basis rate the other team members' risk level relative to yourself and record it in Column 1: My Assessment of Others (page 425).

Time suggested for Step 4: 10 minutes.

Step 5. Meeting with your team, reach a team consensus on each member's risk level and record it in Form 4, Column 2 (Team Consensus). Share feedback and collect ratings from each member on your style. Record this risk level assessment made by others on Form 5: My Risk Taking Summary (page 425).

Time suggested for Step 5: 10 minutes.

Step 6. You now have three risk level ratings: (1) your own; (2) the team consensus rating; and (3) ratings from other individuals. Calculate an average of the ratings and compare the assessments of your risk taking levels on Form 5.

Individual and team risk can be compared based on these scores. However, individuals have varying degrees of risk taking and the final score may not reflect how decisions were made during the team discussion.

Time suggested for Step 6: 10 minutes.

Step 7. With the class, consider the following questions with the consultant leading the discussion.

1. What behaviors seemed to help your group to successfully complete its task?
2. How was information shared among the group? Draw a rough sociogram for the team.
3. How did issues of risk taking affect the decision?
4. How did collaboration/competition influence the outcome?

THE GENTECH COMPANY BACKGROUND

The GenTech Company is a medium-sized high-tech firm selling computers, computer components, software, and information systems. GenTech has had a strong and steady growth record and its products have traditionally been highly rated by customers. GenTech has a sound financial position but during the last five years it has been losing its market share because of new competitors entering the field with more advanced products and at lower prices.

In the past, GenTech has been particularly noted for its fast growth. People always know where they stand around GenTech. However, recently several of the newer and more promising managers and engineers have quit to join competitors. As a relative newcomer to the computer industry (GenTech was founded 11 years ago), GenTech is still a medium-sized company in its industry, but it has been modestly successful in competing with big firms like DEC and IBM. GenTech is a fast-moving company and employee behavior is somewhat unorthodox in that it is highly flexible. GenTech has always operated on the concept of "Let's get it done now and we'll worry about rules and regulations tomorrow."

The executive vice president has called a meeting of key managers to form a new corporate strategy based upon the goals of the company. One key factor is how to allocate the investment funds into a total company strategy.

TERMINOLOGY

1. A market penetration strategy involves an attempt to increase market share in an existing market niche, one in which the firm already offers a product or service.

2. Market development introduces an existing product or service into new market areas, often by expansion into new market segments or geographic areas.

3. Diversification involves the development of new products and services and entry into new markets. The degree of change often makes this a high-risk strategy.

4. Product development is a technology-based strategy that involves developing new or advanced products for existing markets.

EXHIBIT 15.1 Strategy Matrix

The Board of Directors has suggested four basic strategies with two implementation alternatives within each basic strategy as follows:

Strategy 1. Market Penetration.

A. Increase advertising expenditures, number of sales reps, and promotional activities, and possibly cut prices. This strategy will focus on the products with greatest profit margin (printers, keyboards). There is an 80 percent estimated probability that this strategy will increase demand for currently profitable products.

B. Increase advertising and introduce new high-end "Cadillac" products into existing lines. This new, improved company image may lead to customer acceptance of these higher margin products in existing and increased market share and profits with an estimated 75 percent probability of success.

Strategy 2. Market Development.

A. Identify and develop new markets for existing products by promoting products in markets not currently served, new demographic or geographic markets. Market research estimates a 75 percent probability that increasing demand in new markets would add to sales growth, profits about the same (possibly slightly lower), but with increased volume of sales.

B. Identify and develop new markets by differentiating our existing products to tailor them to new geographic markets, or new market niches. The profit margins are likely to be high on this strategy, even with relatively low volume of sales with an estimated 70 percent probability of success, since uncertainty in the industry could result in low sales.

Strategy 3. Product Development.

A. The production group has proposed new product development aimed at designing a new low-cost, low-price keyboard and disk drive to meet competition. In the past, the firm has been a high-quality product, with an investment in manufacturing efficiency. A low-cost product could be developed resulting in increased sales to the low-end market, estimated at a 70 percent probability of success.

B. A second new product would involve the development of a new high-performance keyboard and laser printer. This would provide an increase in market share at the high end market against foreign competition. This requires up-front design investment, but has a 65 percent probability of considerably higher profit margins and increased market.

Strategy 4. Diversification.

A. There is an opportunity to acquire a competing firm making color monitors which would fit with our line of products. This would allow a complete line of peripherals and would increase volume, but involves an industry in which we have little expertise; the estimate of success is rated at about 65 percent, but could increase total sales volume and profitability.

B. The company has a chance to develop a new laptop or notebook size computer by acquiring a small company in this field. This would move the company into entirely new markets and increase its potential return and profitability. This builds on existing expertise, although much of the technology comes from the acquired company, thus its estimated probability of success is only 60 percent, but it has become a very attractive, high-growth industry, (representing the fastest growing segment of the market), thus offers high rewards if successful. Our risk is that of alienating some current customers.

FORM 1: MY INDIVIDUAL STRATEGIC DECISION

Strategy	Individual Strategy (Column 1)	Implementation Alternatives A & B (Column 2)	
1. Market Penetration	_____ %	A _____ %	
		B _____ %	
		100%	
2. Market Development	_____ %	A _____ %	
		B _____ %	
		100%	
3. Product Development	_____ %	A _____ %	
		B _____ %	
		100%	
4. Diversification	_____ %	A _____ %	
		B _____ %	
		100%	
Total	100%		

FORM 2: EXECUTIVE COMMITTEE STRATEGIC DECISIONS

Strategy	Team Strategy (Column 1)	Alternatives A & B (Column 2)

1. Market Penetration _____ % A _____ %

 B _____ %
 100%

2. Market Development _____ % A _____ %

 B _____ %
 100%

3. Product Development _____ % A _____ %

 B _____ %
 100%

4. Diversification _____ % A _____ %

 B _____ %
 100%

Total 100%

FORM 3: INDIVIDUAL RISK ASSESSMENT

In the space below, indicate whether you are a risk seeker or risk averter. If you avoid risk in most or all situations, pick a number closer to 0. If you are a high risk taker, choose a number close to 100. Circle the number that best describes your approach to risky situations.

	Risk Level	
Risk Averse Cautious	0 10 20 30 40 50 60 70 80 90 100%	Risk Taker

This is your "individual risk estimate."

FORM 4: RISK TAKING—INDIVIDUAL AND TEAM

Risk Taking. (Ability to take risks to accomplish what one feels is necessary, to dare to be different, to follow one's conscience, to be creatively different.)

Risk Averse Cautious	0	10	20	30	40	50	60	70	80	90	100%	Risk Taker

Team Members' Names	Column 1 Individual Risk Level (My Assessment of Others)	Column 2 Risk Level of Members (Team Consensus)
1. _____	_____	_____
2. _____	_____	_____
3. _____	_____	_____
4. _____	_____	_____
5. _____	_____	_____
6. _____	_____	_____
7. _____	_____	_____
8. _____	_____	_____

FORM 5: MY RISK TAKING SUMMARY

Record the Risk Level Assessment made by other individuals and the team from Form 4.
Record your self assessment from Form 3.

From Team Member	Risk Level Rating
1. _____	_____
2. _____	_____
3. _____	_____
4. _____	_____
5. _____	_____
6. _____	_____
7. _____	_____
Individual Average	_____
Team Assessment (Form 4. Column 2)	_____
My Assessment (Form 3)	_____

CASE 15:
THE SPACE ELECTRONICS
CORPORATION

The Space Electronics Corporation is a subsidiary of a major firm with sales in excess of $200 million. The company held substantial positions in commercial and military electronic system markets; however, profitability and market position have been declining. About a year ago it became apparent that two R&D projects were coming up: the stealth bomber and the Star Wars proposals. These appeared to be the only two major projects coming up in the next few years. The executive committee was to decide whether or not they should pursue these two projects. This would involve taking a radically new course of action, going after the prime contract, whereas in the past they had operated as a subcontractor to other primes.

THE EXECUTIVE COMMITTEE MEETING

In mid-September, Reade Exton, the president, opened the meeting. "As you all know, our profitability and market position have been declining. We have landed only one new proposal during this period, and there is great pressure from headquarters to go after these major projects. We have all had an opportunity to review a copy of the proposals, and I'll let Glenn start the discussion."

Glenn Overton, Vice President, Engineering. "About a year ago it became obvious that our engineering activity was going to decline. The decision was made that a joint effort with marketing would be undertaken and after a series of meetings, it was decided that our best course of action was to aggressively pursue these two large contracts."

Oliver Whittier, Vice President, Finance. "Frankly, Glenn, I have reservations about such a major departure from our past policies and by the magnitude of these projects. I'm worried about the increased overhead and the drain on our current profits. And I have a gut feeling that our probabilities of getting those contracts is less than you seem to think."

Ted Byron, Vice President, Marketing. "Although you may estimate that the probability of gaining these projects is low, the payoff is enough to turn our whole picture around. These contracts will put us on the map. My best 'guesstimate' is that our chances are closer to 75 percent than 60 percent. Don't forget, I have a lot of personal contacts back in Washington, and while that is no guarantee, it sure doesn't hurt."

Paul Brown, Vice President, Industrial Relations. "I agree with Oliver: I have my doubts as to our chances of getting such a large-scale project, and I am worried about our people. If we should fail to get these contracts, people could get hurt. We may have to have layoffs and that is a bad business. I think we have a certain responsibility to the people here."

Mort Jensen, Vice President, Manufacturing. "Let's face it, if we pull these two proposals out of the hat, they will love us at headquarters. We'll be superstars! But on the other hand, we could take a real beating if these projects fizzle out. I think we have to consider the risk factor and what might happen to the company if we fail. And, like Paul says, a number of our line employees could take a beating if things don't work out."

Glenn Overton. "Listen, fellows, there are no lead-pipe cinches in this business. But don't you think Ted and I have a better feel for our probabilities than people in personnel? If a downturn were to occur, our company will be hard pressed anyway. Frankly, I'm not quite as optimistic as Ted here, but I still think our chances are in the 60 percent range. Even at that it seems like a good risk because even if we only get one of the projects, our company will benefit greatly. Plus our R&D will stand to gain a heck of a lot by being involved in the state of the art. We'll be able to attract new talent."

Mort Jensen. "One of our past problems was the isolation of R&D from the rest of the organization. I feel that we should seek to achieve more interdepartmental cooperation. So I think it is important to get all the differing viewpoints out on the table."

Reade Exton. "I think we have had a good discussion, but now what is our decision? As you know, there is a lot of pressure from headquarters to go after these projects, but it has to be a group decision. Frankly, we are between a rock and a hard place. There will have to be a significant expenditure just to pursue these major contracts, and our R&D activity will be almost exclusively devoted to the proposals for about 3 months, and that will include 10-hour days and 7-day work weeks. There definitely is a degree of risk involved, although the exact odds are hard to predict. One thing is sure: if we don't go after the projects, we won't get them."

Case Analysis Form follows on page 428

CASE ANALYSIS FORM

Name: _____

I. Problems

A. Macro

1. _____

2. _____

B. Micro

1. _____

2. _____

II. Causes

1. _____

2. _____

3. _____

III. Systems affected

1. Structural _____

2. Psychosocial _____

3. Technical _____

4. Managerial _____

5. Goals _____

IV. Alternatives

1. _____

2. _____

3. _____

4. _____

5. _____

V. Recommendations

1. _____

2. _____

3. _____

SUMMARY

• **Organization Transformation.** This chapter has presented several interventions for helping organizations transform to meet new strategic directions. Such large-scale change programs typically occur in response to, or in anticipation of, fundamental environmental or technological changes. Environmental discontinuities often require a dramatic shift in organizational strategy, which in turn necessitate changes to organization structure, corporate culture, and managerial processes. These strategy interventions are aimed at relating the organization to its broader environment and achieving a higher level of corporate excellence.

• **Corporate Culture.** Corporate culture includes the shared values and beliefs of organization members and determines how members perform. Corporate culture is a key determinant of how an organization implements strategic change and what strategies and techniques the OD consultant may bring to such interventions. Changing the corporate culture starts with developing a shared vision, the empowerment of members, and the development of a trust relationship at all levels.

• **Strategy.** The strategy-culture matrix provides one tool that the OD practitioner can use in implementing strategic changes. Changing the corporate culture can be an extremely challenging task. Such change requires clear strategic vision, reinforcement of new values, and reshuffling the power-reward systems to fit the new strategy. Strategic change management presents another systems view of the organization as technical, political, and cultural systems, and involves aligning these systems with the environment.

• **OD Skills.** In the simulation you had the chance to experience the meshing of different goals and risk taking in forming a strategy. One important point is the difficulty and complexity of strategic change programs, and the need for OD practitioner skills in implementing change programs in organizations.

• **Organizational Excellence.** Organizational excellence in a rapidly changing world requires an innovative and adaptive corporate culture. Strategic change has become increasingly important in recent years, and often influences the very survival of an organization in a volatile environment. The corporate culture can be a force in reinforcing or resisting strategic changes. Therefore, when the culture is resistant to innovations, OD techniques and strategies may be used to enhance successful strategic changes.

NOTES

1. See Rahul Jacob, "The Struggle to Create an Organization for the 21st Century," *Fortune*, April 3, 1995, p. 90.
2. Thomas J. Higginson and Robert P. Waxler, "Corporate Cultures for the 1990's: What is Needed?", *Industrial Management*, January/February 1993, p. 13.
3. Richard Leifer, "Understanding Organizational Transformation Using a Dissipative Mode," *Human Relations*, vol. 42, no. 10, (1989), pp. 899–916.
4. Tom Peters, *Liberation Management: Necessary Disorganization for the Nanosecond Nineties*, (New York: Random House, 1992), pp. 6–14.
5. Leifer, p. 900.
6. "Leaders of Corporate Change," *Fortune*, December 14, 1992, p. 105.
7. Joann S. Lublin and Alex Mickels, "How Three Companies Achieved Fast Turnarounds," *The Wall Street Journal*, July 21, 1995, p. 81.
8. Thomas A. Stewart, "Allied-Signal's Turnaround Blitz," *Fortune*, November 30, 1992, pp. 72–76.
9. Dunphy and Stace, "Transformational and Coercive Strategies," *Organization Studies*, vol. 9, no. 3, 1988, pp. 317-334.
10. John F. Hulpke, Cal. State Univ., Bakersfield, 1995;see also Jan Carlzon, "Moments of Truth," *Industry Week*, July 27, 1987, pp. 40–44.
11. Jacqueline M. Graves, "Leaders of Corporate Change," *Fortune*, December 14, 1992, pp. 104–114.
12. John P. Kotter and James L. Heskett, *Corporate Culture and Performance*, (New York: The Free Press, 1992), p. 150.
13. See Barbara Block, "Creating a Culture All Employees Can Accept," *Management Review*, (July 1989), p. 41.
14. Judith Dobrzynski, "Running the Biggest LBO," *Business Week*, October 2, 1989, p. 79.
15. Michael A. Verespej, "When Change Becomes the Norm," *Industry Week*, March 16, 1992, pp. 35–38.
16. Daniel R. Denison, "The Climate, Culture, and Effectiveness of Work Organizations," (Ph.D. Dissertation, University of Michigan: Ann Arbor, 1982).
17. John H. Dobbs, "The Empowerment Environment," *Training & Development*, February, 1993, p. 55–57.
18. See J. Martin, *Culture in Organizations*. New York, Oxford Press, 1992.
19. John R. Latham, "Visioning: The Concept, Trilogy and Process," *Quality Process*, vol 28, no, 4, April, 1995, p. 65.
20. Joseph V. Quigley, "From Vision to Reality: Strategic Management Getting Value from Strategic Planning," *The Executive Speaker*, vol. 13, no. 2, January 1991, p. 10.
21. Howard E. Butler, "Strategic Planning: the Missing Link in TQM," *Quality Process*, vol . 28, no. 5, May 1995, p. 105.
22. John W. Alexander, "Sharing the Vision," *Business Horizons*, (May–June 1989), pp. 56–59.
23. John Kotter and James Heskett, "Corporate Culture and Performance," *The Economist*, June 1992, p. 75. See Noel Tichy, "GE's Crotonville: A Staging Ground for Corporate Revolution," *The Academy of Management Executive*, 1989, vol. 111, no. 2, pp. 99–106; Tim Smart, Pete Engardio, and Geri Smith, "GE's Brave New World," *Business Week*, November 1993.
24. See Noel Tichy, "GE's Crotonville: A Staging Ground for Corporate Revolution," *The Academy of Management Executive*, 1989, vol. 111, no. 2, pp. 99–106; Tim Smart, Pete Engardio and Geri smith, "GE's Brave New World," *Business Week*, November 1993.
25. Howard Schwartz and Stanley M. Davis, "Matching Corporate Culture and Business Strategy," *Organizational Dynamics*, Summer 1981, p. 43.
26. Maryann Keller, *Rude Awakening: The Rise, Fall, and Struggle for Recovery of General Motors*, (New York: William Morrow and Company, Inc ., 1989), p. 181.

27. Noèl Tichy, "Revolutionize your Company or Someone Else Will," *Fortune*, December 13, 1993, p. 114.

28. See Donald F. Harvey and R. Wald, "Changing the Organizational Culture."

29. Jay B. Barney, "Organizational Culture: Can It Be a Source of Competitive Advantage?" *Academy of Management Review*, vol. 11, no. 3 (1986), pp. 656–65.

30. See M. McCarthy, "PepsiCo to Consolidate Its Operations," *The Wall Street Journal*, October 30, 1990, p. 4.

31. Noel Tichy and Stratford Sherman, "Control Your Destiny or Someone Else Will," *The Economist*, February 1993, p.94.

32. Terence E. Real and Alan A. Kennedy, *Corporate Cultures*, Reading, MA: Addison-Wesley, 1982.

33. "Cultural Clash at Pillsbury," *The Wall Street Journal*, October 23, 1986, p. 1. (Note: Since then Pillsbury has been acquired by a British conglomerate.)

34. Donald F. Harvey, and Gayle Ogden, "The Impact of Corporate Culture in an Acquisition Situation," Working Paper, 1995.

35. Anna Bell, "The Honeymoon That Never Was," *Restaurant Business*, March 20, 1992.

36. Myerson, Paul and Robert D. Hamilton, III, "Matching Corporate Culture and Technology," *Advanced Management Journal*, vol. 51, Winter 1986, p. 8.

Teamwork takes on a high-tech flavor at XEROX Design teams are trained in the company's Leadership Through Quality precepts and given advanced engineering tools such as this integraph design terminal, which can display three-dimensional images. *Photo courtesy of XEROX Corporation.*

Organization Development: The Challenge and the Future

16

OBJECTIVES

Upon completing this chapter, you will be able to:

1. Understand the basic issues in using organization development as an approach to planned change.
2. Recognize ways of maintaining, internalizing, and stabilizing a change program.
3. Identify some of the future trends and problems facing the OD consultant.
4. Understand the process of terminating the consultant-client relationship.

PREMEETING PREPARATION

1. Read the Background Information.
2. Complete Part A Steps 1 and 4, and Part B Step 1 of OD Skills Simulation 16.1. (Reform consulting trios from OD Skills Simulation 2.1.)
3. Complete Steps 1 and 2 of OD Skills Simulation 16.2.

BACKGROUND INFORMATION

Tomorrow's organization will be different from today's. In a world of global competitiveness and technological innovation, organizations are reengineering, restructuring, and flattening the hierarchy to meet market pressures. Leading companies now envision an endlessly changing organization. The new term is **reconfigureable**: an organization that is flexible and able to change on an annual, monthly, weekly, daily, even hourly time frame. Unchanging systems will become dinosaurs.[1] Tom Peters suggests that in today's world, "Excellence isn't—there are no excellent companies. The old saw, 'If it ain't broke don't fix it' needs revision. I propose: If it ain't broke, you just haven't looked hard enough.' Fix it anyway."[2]

There is a continuing need for long-range strategies to improve organizational decision making and work relationships to meet these changing conditions. From these needs, organization development, the newest discipline in planned change techniques, has emerged. Clearly, OD is being viewed by organizations of all types—industrial, governmental, and health care—as a field of expertise that can provide results. Still, there are issues and challenges facing this discipline if it is to continue to provide a viable option for planned change.

Change is a continuing process. Every organization exists in a continuous state of adapting to change. Downsizing changes are usually caused by external competitive forces, whereas other changes to work processes emerge as a result of shifting forces within the organization.[3] Many management theorists feel that authoritarian or bureaucratic systems are too rigid to adapt to this increasing rate of change and therefore become reactive organizations—reacting drastically after problems emerge. Motorola for example, continues to focus on quality, cycle time reduction, and teamwork in a change process that most companies can only try to emulate. Thirteen years after initiating a quality change program, TQM is still being used to invigorate the company. As Rosabeth Kantor, of Harvard, says, "A lot of companies have used TQM as a device to discipline its workforce. Motorola has taken it as a way to examine what everyone does, including managers."[4]

More and more organizations are finding that employees are no longer satisfied with simply filling a slot in the organization chart. In a survey of American workers conducted for the U.S. Labor Department, the University of Michigan's Survey Research Center found that 41.5 percent responded "very true" when asked if they had interesting work with the freedom to decide how to do the job. This is 9.8 percent lower than the results in an earlier survey. Also, when asked about having enough information and authority to accomplish their job, workers responded 52.4 percent "very true." This was down 10.9 percent from the earlier survey.[5] It is not likely that jobs are getting worse. Rather, employees are probably getting better; that is, people are achieving higher educational levels, with a resulting increase in the level of motivational needs.

Because organizations are in a continuous state of change, OD is a continuing process. As one set of change objectives is achieved, new standards of excellence and new challenges arise. As a result, the OD practitioner has two primary criteria of effectiveness. One criterion is the stability of the OD effort after the practitioner stops working with the client system; the other is the ability of the client system to maintain innovation within the system or the development of a self-renewal capability.

Since an OD program is an approach to improving effectiveness, there is a need for an evaluation of the results. The organization members involved in the change process need feedback on the results of their efforts in order to determine whether to modify, continue, or discontinue these activities. At this point there is also usually a disengagement between the OD practitioner or consultant and the client—a termination of the change program relationship.

Organization development is an ongoing process because an organization cannot remain static and be effective. In today's changing environment, organizations must develop adaptive mechanisms and anticipative management systems. To cope with these changing conditions, an OD practitioner needs to be able to monitor and assess progress toward change

goals and to recognize when these efforts may be phased out. The participants and teams involved in an OD program need feedback to measure their progress toward goals and to stabilize change efforts. This continuing assessment also acts to prevent deterioration or degradation to prior behavior, attitudes, or values. An organization might implement a total quality management program and initially feel that the program is successful. A year later, however, most managers may have discarded TQM and returned to prior management methods unless there is some stabilization of the TQM program.

Because OD is a continuous improvement process, the completion of one change cycle leads into another cycle in the process of development. In this chapter, we examine the evaluation and termination process, discuss several emerging issues, and examine the future of the OD field.

Monitor and Stabilize Action Programs

After the OD program has been implemented, then emphasis must be placed upon internalizing and stabilizing the changes so that the new behavior becomes part of the cultural norms. In Chapter 2, a five-stage model of the organization development process was presented. Stage five of OD involves three factors: (1) feedback—generating and communicating data to participating members so they can measure their progress; (2) stabilizing or "freezing" the change or desired behavior so that it will be continued; and (3) evaluating the OD program results.

The Feedback of Information

The organization members involved in an OD program need feedback on the results of the change in order to determine whether to modify, continue, or discontinue their activities. If the client system obtains no feedback on the consequence of a change program, it may be perceived as a failure and be discontinued. Therefore, part of the OD consultant's job is to see that necessary information is made available to participating members and groups. In research conducted on TQM programs, it was found that more successful programs had early payoffs that the participants could see and be encouraged by.[6]

The feedback of information is important because it also can create commitment among organization members. Commitment to change emerges from open communications and management's ability to reinforce new behaviors so that members can see how their contribution affects outcomes.

One criterion for determining the effectiveness of a change program is whether or not system problems have been corrected. In certain instances, data will be readily available, particularly around operational indices of performance or productivity. In other instances, the consultant may gather after-the-fact interview or questionnaire data to verify the degree of change in less tangible factors such as morale, leadership style, or job satisfaction. At McKinsey Consulting (former employer of *In Search of Excellence* co-authors Tom Peters and Robert Waterman), for example, client firms are first evaluated by developing hypothesis problem statements about the client firms current operations. These hypotheses are then researched and proven or disproven with factual information, not opinions. This research process includes all of the possible alternative actions that could logically be incorporated into the firms culture. From this review and elimination process, recommendations are then forwarded and suggested for adoption by their client.[7] At Chaparral Steel, team meetings are held to share information on productivity, back log, and man hours per ton. Each month financial statements, including a chart tracking operating profits (the key measure for profit sharing) are posted for all members.[8]

Work teams may also use such techniques as the "organization mirror" to gain information on how other organization groups view their changed status. Some systematic and periodic appraisal of results should be designed into the change effort to determine when desired levels have been achieved. This requires the setting of some type of "benchmark"

to measure the extent or degree of change over time. The OD practitioner and the managers also need to provide reinforcement and support for change by giving recognition, encouragement, and approval for positive change. Receiving information or performance data is important, but a major factor in the deterioration of performance is lack of recognition or reinforcement. (See Our Changing World.)

OUR CHANGING WORLD
MEXICO'S SLEEPY BORDER TOWNS?[9]

Remember the sleepy little border towns of Tijuana, Ciudad Juarez, Nogalez, Mexicali? Well, they're gone. Not the towns, but the "sleepy" aspect. The transformation along the U.S.-Mexico border points out once again that change is everywhere.

The Maquiladoras

Nearly 2,200 U.S. firms have set up assembly operations near Mexico's northern border, employing some 450,000 people in a $6 trillion business. Maquiladoras, as the plants are called, provide Mexico with its second largest source of foreign exchange, just behind oil, benefitting the workers and residents. The U.S.-Mexico agreement that set up the program has benefitted non-U.S. firms also including Nissan, Hitachi, Sony, Philips, and Siemens. These firms are taking advantage of the special duty forgiveness provisions offered by that agreement. Additional benefits to be afforded under the North American Free Trade Agreement (NAFTA) are sure to attract even heavier participation from outside firms.

Under such agreement everyone wins, right? Maybe. It depends on who you talk to. And, once again, we see that organizational health is a day-to-day thing. What looked good yesterday may not fit at all today. New influences on the organization, such as NAFTA provisions, permit cohesive cooperation without hindrance of global retaliation by "rival" firms. Therefore, organizational health will depend on joint efforts that benefit both the provider and user of North American output.

Potential Problems

The potential problem seems to stem from personnel practices. Workers are often not paid well, even by Mexican standards. Then there is the occasional obvious screw up, like the firm Acapulco Fashions. Workers were so fed up with pay and conditions that they went out on strike. Acapulco Fashions simply pulled out, not even paying already-earned back pay. Too many Maquiladoras seem to favor young unmarried female workers, who are willing to accept low wages. Turnover stays high, approaching levels that Scandinavia worried about in the 1970s. But, too few employers seem to care. It is as if the human resources management policy of these organizations is to exploit people until they are burned out and then discard them, according to some critics.

Most observers feel that the program has the potential to help everyone concerned, if it is run more effectively. Once again, we see why Organizational Development must be an ongoing process. No organization can remain static and remain effective. Maquiladoras, take note.

Questions

1. What are the causes of the problems and what would you suggest to correct these problems?

The Stabilization of Change

When a performance problem has been corrected and the change objectives have been achieved, some means must be devised to ensure that the new performance level is stabilized. If this is not done, the tendency is for the individual or the system to deteriorate and revert to previous ineffective behaviors. As an example, an individual may desire to discontinue some habit, such as smoking, and actually change for a short period of time. However, the change objective is not accomplished if the person begins smoking again six months later. One criticism of laboratory learning is called "fade-out." This occurs when a manager develops new behaviors while at a seminar, but the change erodes away back on the job because the work environment has not changed and is not supportive. Fade-out, or deterioration of change, may occur in an OD program when the change is not stabilized into

the system and behavior gradually slips back into previous ineffective modes. Obviously, one measure of success is whether or not the change is permanently assimilated into and accepted by the client system. Northrop Corporation had such a difficult time maintaining change, they developed Integrated Product Teams (IPT) to constantly reinforce the changes. These teams changed the "status quo," but unlike other OD programs, they never disassembled—so there was always a reinforcement.

The change program itself may have a **stabilizing** effect because of its advantages and support. At TRW, team development has become so widely accepted that many project managers request a team building session every time a new project is assembled. There is also a sort of "Hawthorne effect" surrounding many change methods, such as self-managed work teams or TQM techniques, so participating employees feel they are an elite group and sell the benefits of the OD program to other members, thus stabilizing the acceptance of change. Sometimes an OD program is initiated in one division or subsystem of an organization, and the performance results may be used to demonstrate the effectiveness of the new techniques to another division. Where results are obtainable, such as those relating to decreased turnover or costs, this recognition may act as a stabilizing force.

Once a change effort is fully accepted, the change may become institutionalized or internalized by group members. The acceptance and adoption of a change effort depend upon practice and familiarity, so that the innovation becomes a routine part of organization activity. At Motorola, TQM is a continuing innovation. Managers continue to level with one another over on-the-job performance, and they are constantly critiquing one another over quality goals. In other words, the change has been integrated into the organization structure, norms, and culture.

Finally, some form of continuing assessment of the change effort during later periods should be included to guard against degradation over time. The greater the investment in the OD program, the more detailed the reappraisal mechanisms should be.

The Evaluation of OD Programs

One major problem in OD lies in the need for the development of better research designs and methods. As Frank Friedlander and L. Dave Brown have pointed out, if the practice and theory of OD is to merge into a broader field of planning change, research will play a crucial role.[10]

Many OD practitioners feel that the evaluation method should be designed into the change process itself. Researchers have surveyed OD practitioners to see what evaluation practices were being used. From this data, a set of guidelines was developed. They suggested that OD evaluations will be important in the future for three groups:

1. the key organizational decision makers: to show them that OD expenditures are providing the desired results;
2. the OD participants: to provide feedback about their change efforts; and
3. the OD specialists: to develop their expertise and reputations based upon their experiences.

The authors point out that the evaluative practice will be determined by three factors: "(1) the training of the OD specialist, (2) the cooperation of the organizational members involved in the effort, and (3) the willingness of organizational decision makers to pay for a rigorous evaluation."[11] Remember, "what gets rewarded, gets done."

Evaluating OD program outcomes involves making an assessment about whether the OD intervention has been satisfactorily implemented, and, if so, whether it is bringing about the desired outcomes. When client systems invest resources in major OD efforts, there is an increasing need for data on the results. OD consultants are frequently being asked to justify the OD program in terms of basic productivity, cost savings, or other bottom line measures. Consequently, organizations are constantly seeking a more rigorous evaluation of OD interventions.[12]

Termination of the Consultant-Client Relationship

The final stage of the OD process occurs in an OD program when the basic change objectives have been accomplished and either the consultant or the client or both feel that members of the system can continue the change effort without outside assistance. Perhaps that place has been reached when there is a diminishing rate of return for efforts expended. The practitioner may feel that little more can be accomplished; the evaluation indicates that desired change levels have been achieved, and the client system feels able to continue renewal processes on their own. The change program should have as part of its strategy some provision for a gradual disengagement of the consultant's help and a transition to internal resources as the primary focus of change (see B.C. comic strip). The focus here is to ensure that the changes are not short term or temporary but are followed by a regression to former operating patterns. Then prepare for continuous improvement with periodic follow-ups and a gradual phasing in of new change objectives.

Developing a Self-Renewal Capacity

One of the basic objectives of the OD consultant is to develop the ability to innovate within the client system. The client system needs a self-sustaining capability to devise and implement change programs without outside support. Watson and Glaser have noted that

> . . . following any important change comes a period during which the new equilibrium is being stabilized. Yet that condition, too, is only temporary. The organization that has accepted an innovation may need a breathing spell in which to consolidate what it has learned. But if the organization is geared to continued growth, its members will value forward-moving change as a recurrent and desirable phenomenon. From the plateau on which equilibrium is regained, the cycle of change can be launched again.[13]

Self-renewal means building innovation and commitment to change into the organization's values. Change is the only constant in today's world, and transformational leaders need to find continuing ways to renew and revitalize their teams, departments, and organizations. As an example, the Air Force has taken on W. Edward Demming's total quality movement. With training from OD consultants specializing in TQM theory, the Air Force has developed Process Action Teams (PATs), rewritten regulations into guidelines, and streamlined structures and processes. The rewards for the changes and results include recognition at the National Quality Review in Washington, DC as well as Air Force and DOD Quality Awards. PATs have turned into **Integrated Product Team (IPTs)**, to continue the change process and make long range improvements. The aerospace community has followed the Air Force in this effort, including Northrop, where they have developed IPTs that have the power of change and the power of executive boards—a tremendous amount of power.

B. C. by permission of Johnny Hart and Creators Syndicate, Inc.

Usually, the mechanism for this self-renewal capacity is some internal OD practitioner or group. Such internal consultants can continue with new data collection, diagnosis, and evaluation to determine the need for further change strategies and programs. The OD consultant needs to continue to provide members' awareness of emerging competitive problems and using this as a means of developing a willingness to move rapidly to introduce needed changes. The self-renewing organization is constantly able to initiate new strategies leading to continued innovation and adaptation. As Tom Peters has commented, "Now, with the life expectancy of a new product going from half a dozen years to six or eight months, you'd better have an organization with virtually zero impedance in a structural sense. My philosophy these days can be boiled down to a single sentence: it's a crazy world, so you'd better have a crazy organization."[14] In a changing, chaotic world, there is a need for constant innovation and continuous change.

Termination and Disengagement from the Client System

As the client system develops a self-renewal capability, the need for an external consultant should decrease. If the client system has successfully developed a self-renewal capacity, then a gradual termination of the consultant-client relationship should be a smooth transition; however, if the client system has become overdependent upon the OD practitioner, termination of the relationship may be difficult.

The OD consultant considers **disengagement** when the benchmarks used to evaluate change have been achieved and the client system appears capable of continuing innovation; that is, the client system has the resources and competence necessary to continue change efforts. In order to form a self-renewal capability, the OD consultant needs to develop highly motivated people. The organizational culture, and empowered employees emerge from five steps to successful change.

1. **Determine the world standard.** When Digital Equipment benchmarked its manufacturing operations, it discovered its costs were 30% to 40% too high.
2. **Use process mapping.** Break down the organization's activities to their jobs component. Identify the inefficiencies, then redesign each process from scratch.
3. **Communicate with employees.** Get employees focused on customers and competitors. Define a clear vision that creates a sense of urgency.
4. **Distinguish what needs to be changed from how hard it is to do it.** Don't let difficulty stop the climb. If something really needs to be done—the difficulty of doing it is irrelevant.
5. **Set stretch targets.** There's nothing wrong with asking people to perform as well as the best in the world. Don't tell them how to do it though; their ideas may be better than managements. GE's CEO Jack Welch adds one rule: Don't punish people for failing to reach stretch targets.[15]

It should be emphasized that continued involvement is usually advisable. The consultant is available for emergency help or special consultation. Continued formal or informal contacts are always possible, and the consultant may become involved again in some new change effort.

Some Conditions for Success of OD Efforts

Several OD practitioners have attempted to identify conditions leading to possible success of OD efforts, as follows:

- **Pressure to change.** The organization is generally under considerable external or internal pressure to improve. Top management has been aroused to action and is searching for solutions.
- **Change initiation.** Change begins at the top of the organization in the form of a consultant to the top team. This generally induces reorientation and reassessment of past practices and current problems.
- **Top management involvement.** Top management is involved and takes a responsible role in the process. Several levels of management generally participate in the collection of data and the analysis of specific problems.

- **Commitment to change.** Ideas and methods for developing solutions are generated at a number of levels in the organization. This results in some level of commitment to change by organization members.
- **Beta testing.** Some experimentation with innovation takes place. The proposed solutions are generally developed, tested, and found acceptable before the scope of the change is expanded to include larger problems or the entire system.
- **Results.** The organization development program is generally reinforced by positive results. The change effort spreads with each successful experience and, as management support grows, is gradually accepted as a way of life.[16]

Organization development, then, involves long-term, system-wide application of behavioral science techniques to increase organization effectiveness. OD works on the idea that improving the way people work together and the way work groups cooperate increase performance. The management style needed to work in an innovative manner differs from traditional concepts, and OD programs are designed to focus upon the manager's attitudes and upon a managerial style that encourages action in the presence of risk. OD strategies try to increase the manager's tolerance for ambiguity and uncertainty and the ability to communicate with and motivate others.

The field of OD has grown rapidly. Many innovative techniques have been developed, and many more are still being developed. Because of this rate of growth, there are also many problems and disagreements among practitioners over what is and what is not an OD technique and what interventions or strategies are most used. Although initially OD strategies emphasized the behavioral aspects of change, OD practitioners are increasingly using an integrated, eclectic, or systems approach which includes structural and technical strategies.

One thing, is clear—the field of OD is itself developing and changing. You must decide for yourself what rings true in terms of your own experience and what does not. Organization development has been described as a process designed to increase organization effectiveness by integrating the needs of the individual members for growth and development with organization goals. In a changing environment, OD provides strategies to alter beliefs, attitudes, values, and structures of organizations, making them more anticipative and adaptive to deal with problems of "future shock."

What OD is, though, is "beyond"—beyond anything and everything ever presented in traditional methods. Tom Peters suggests these seven "beyonds:"

- **Beyond decentralization.** Most big companies decentralized years ago—on paper. Yet the market's demand for speed, innovation, and responsiveness mocks yesterday's timid "divisionalization."
- **Beyond empowerment.** Although empowerment is still a dream at most outfits, giving workers a strong voice is insufficient. We need to turn every employee into a "business person," as one executive puts it, or a "90 percent entrepreneur" in the words of another.
- **Beyond disintegration.** Blowing up the headquarters (maybe literally) and cutting middle management are musts. But so is hooking up to create a new form of organization that routinely changes shape.
- **Beyond reengineering.** Reengineering means linking formerly separate functions, then stripping most steps from old cumbersome business processes.
- **Beyond learning.** "Learning organizations" are a hot topic these days. But even organizations that keep getting smarter fall short. Enter the "curious corporation." The average firm is dull as doornails, which simply will not do in a decidedly non-dull marketplace.
- **Beyond total quality management.** TQM is about reducing TGWs (things gone wrong—an important quality measure in the motor industry). That's essential. But in a crowded market, increasing TGRs, or things gone right, is the real trick. Cutting TGWs is mechanical, but increasing TGRs requires artistry.
- **Beyond change.** The previous six "beyonds" add up to revolution. Today's message is quantum leap...from 5 or 6 percent to 40 or 50 percent (improvement). The time for plodding forward is past. The moment for revolution and revolutionaries is at hand.[17]

Organization development represents a major change from traditional methods of management development and training. OD is a means for changing organization systems and revitalizing them in line with the needs of the individuals within the system and environmental constraints. Because of the changing environment, it is important that individual managers be aware of and understand the advantages and disadvantages of the techniques and strategies available for managing in this changing context. OD is not a panacea; however, it does provide a dynamic and powerful methodology for helping people and organizations collaboratively work together and become a winning team.

Emerging Issues and Values

OD is a growing, developing, and changing field of study. Consequently, there are a number of evolving theories and concepts which have contributed to the field, and a number of approaches which have emerged from OD. At this stage, the field is still in transition, which makes it difficult to define exact boundaries of what is or is not an OD intervention. As a result, there are two key issues which will be examined in the following sections: (1) OD: fad or discipline? and (2) the role of values.

OD: Fad or Discipline?

A number of writers have presented arguments concerning whether OD will emerge as a long-term *contribution* to management and organization theory, or will soon fade away into the dusty archives together with scientific management and other short-lived trends. This is a little like asking the question: "Is air travel a fad?" After all, it has only been around for 60 years or so. Similarly, OD now has some 40 years of background history and if anything, at this point, has not yet reached its apex either in quantity or quality of effort.

OD has already developed and experimented with a variety of new approaches to organization innovation and renewal and the state of the art is still evolving. OD is an exciting new field. As with any discipline, there are unsolved issues, problems, and controversy.

> Rather than being a fad, OD appears to be one of the primary methods for helping organizations adjust to accelerated change. As a result, OD is not a fad, but an emerging discipline. Bennis points out that OD rests on three basic propositions. The first is the hypothesis that each age adopts an organizational form which is most appropriate to that particular age and that changes taking place in that age make it necessary to "revitalize and rebuild our organizations." The second basic proposition is that the only real way to change organizations lies in changing the "climate" of the organization—the "way of life," a system of beliefs and values, an accepted form of interaction and relating. It is more important to change the climate of the organization than the individual if organizations are to develop. The third basic proposition is that "a new *social* awareness is required by people in organizations," since social awareness is essential in our current world. In short, the basic thrust behind OD is that the world is rapidly changing and that our organizations must follow suit.[18]

A lot of executives these days would like to latch on to almost any new concept that promises a quick fix for their problems:

- Having trouble developing new products? Try "Entrepreneurship" the process for getting entrepreneurial juices flowing in a big company.
- Having a tough time competing against foreign competition? Try "Quality Circles," a way to involve workers in finding ways to increase productivity and ensure quality.[19]
- Having trouble building team-work, increasing communication skills or boosting self-esteem? Try "outdoor experiential training," a way to build trust and instill teamwork through off-the-job exercises.[20]
- Having trouble linking a firm's daily operations to its vision? Try "performance pyramids," a new paradigm that comprises the firms key results in terms of both financial and market measures.[21]

There is nothing inherently wrong with any of these theories, but too often managers use them as gimmicks or quick fixes, rather than facing the basic problems. Unless such solutions are systematically thought out and supported by the commitment of top management, they may become mere fads. A similar situation has occurred with the management concepts advocated in the best selling book *In Search of Excellence* (see OD in Practice.)

George Strauss, however, some twenty years ago took a more pessimistic view of OD's future:

> There is a real chance that the term itself will become as anachronistic as "scientific management" and "human relations" are today. Yet, like these earlier movements, which were also controversial in their time, OD will have left its mark on managerial practice.[22]

OD IN PRACTICE
WHAT WENT WRONG IN THE SEARCH FOR EXCELLENCE?[23]

For the foreseeable future, it is difficult to find a firm that has a solid or sustainable lead over its competitors. The rate of change is too rapid for organizations to become complacent. In fact, the cycles between winner and loser are becoming increasingly immediate and drastic.

At least 15 of the 43 excellent companies highlighted by Thomas Peters and Robert Waterman in their book, *In Search of Excellence*, lost their luster soon after the book's publication. And one, People Express, which had been considered an example of what to do right in an organization, just escaped bankruptcy by being purchased by its rival, Texas Air.

Companies such as Eastman Kodak and Texas Instruments, if judged on their performance during the last decade, would not pass the financial tests for excellence laid down in the book. Others, including Atari, Avon, and Levi Strauss, have suffered significant earnings declines stemming from serious business or management problems.

Failure of U.S. businesses is at its all-time high since the Great Depression. Though the entrepreneurial drive is strong—a year ago there were 250,456 new businesses started—57,067 businesses went bankrupt that year and more than half of them were less than five years old.

Excellent Companies in Trouble

In Search of Excellence suggested that U.S. firms needed to regain their competitive edge by placing more emphasis on the people side of business—customers and employees—and by sticking to what they do best. Then why have so many excellent companies had problems? One criticism has been that companies have ignored such fundamental factors as technology, fundamental changes in markets, and broad economic and business trends.

Companies such as Lockheed learned their lessons the hard way. In the initial stages of the L-1011 Tristar, production with high costs coupled with losses in defense contracts, Lockheed was saved from bankruptcy by federal loan guarantees. Yet when the crisis was passed and it was clear to analysts that there was not a large enough market to support the

Tristar, Boeing's 747, and McDonnel Douglas' DC-10, Lockheed continued with production. To Lockheed the Tristar was a symbol of getting back in the commercial aircraft business and they hung on despite the lack of enough firm orders to see the project to the breakeven point. Eventually, Lockheed gave up and took a $400 million write-off.

Excellence in a Changing World

The excellent companies of today do not have a guarantee on remaining excellent. Companies that have followed one set of rules such as those espoused in *In Search of Excellence* have tended to get into trouble just as companies did when they followed the strict rules of the financial number crunchers.

Leading management consultants, including Tom Peters, have suggested two ways to respond to this changing era of unsustainable excellence. One is reactive: to buy and sell businesses in hope of staying in front of the industry growth curve.

The second strategy is proactive and involves meeting uncertainty by becoming a "world-class competitor": with high-quality, enhanced responsiveness, and continuous, short-cycle innovation aimed at creating new markets for both new and mature products and services.

If the word "excellence" is to be meaningful in the future, it may require major redefinition: as Tom Peters has noted, "Excellent firms don't believe in excellence—only in constant improvement and constant change. That is, excellent firms of tomorrow will cherish impermanence—and thrive on chaos."

Questions

1. Were the companies illustrated in the book excellent in the first place?
2. Are there universal rules of excellence or are they specific to an organization?
3. For organizations having problems, what can be done to pull them out of their problems?

It is our contention that organization development is not a passing fad. OD is contributing a technology that will be required even more as the rate of change increases. It is our view that OD emerged as a response to the needs of organization and individuals for innovative ways to adapt to change. OD presents the technology for creating and seeking **organizational excellence**, which is the underlying goal of the modern manager and organization. The successful managerial organizations are seeking the need to practice "anticipative" management styles rather than using "reactive" styles, that is, waiting until after the fact to react to change.

As the rate of change has increased, so has the range of interventions used in OD. Organization Development has moved far beyond its historical antecedents and is continually adding new approaches and techniques as new problem areas emerge. As noted earlier, new system-wide approaches are needed to tie together the basic OD approaches. Each OD intervention is aimed at solving technical or human problems, but what is needed are comprehensive, long-term approaches which integrate the systems into long-term solutions.

The Role of Values

There is also a diversity among OD practitioners over how OD techniques should be applied to improve organizational functioning. In the application of OD, practitioners face several complex dilemmas, including the following.

The professionalism of OD. Many theorists question OD on the grounds that it is ill-defined and that it presents "a moving target." They point to the lack of a common body of knowledge, research, and techniques. It is generally recognized that because of its rapid emergence, there is not enough empirical evidence to provide scientific validation of all, or perhaps any, of the major OD intervention techniques, OD's basic thrust arises from its face validity: it seems to work in making the organization more competitive.

The certification of OD practitioners. There are currently a number of organizations with an OD orientation or an OD division but no single organization that accredits or certifies OD practitioners. Some theorists feel that the rapid growth of the OD field leads to the possibility that unqualified persons (or charlatans) may represent themselves as professionals and that a certifying agency might prevent this. Others feel that many certifying bodies are less than effective and suggest: "let the free enterprise system operate."

An overemphasis upon human and social intervention. A second issue is that OD approaches seem to overemphasize changing the behavioral patterns of members, with a consequent lack of recognition of other significant factors, such as structural and technological elements. Many practitioners suggest a broadening trend in OD practices to a more systematic, comprehensive, or integrated approach to change, as in TQM.

The reality of organization dynamics is a subject Jerry Harvey, an OD consultant, explores. Basically, Harvey is concerned that the area of OD has been reduced to a series of "mythical theoretical propositions." He confronts some basic OD propositions, stating that (1) *there is no such thing as resistance to change*; (2) *time is irrelevant*—if the consultant handles situations competently as they arise, significant changes can occur almost simultaneously; and (3) *OD should not exist as a noun*—it should be a verb or adjective describing an approach to change.[24] This last statement ascribes the same factors (emphasis of social responsibility, self-control, and democratic ideals) to the OD approach to change as it does to the goals sought by OD programs.

Whether or not Harvey's purported myths of OD are indeed myths or just "hair splitting" arguments aimed at phrases and definitions composed for convenience is not to be decided here. What is important is that we proceed with our study of OD with a questioning, inquiring, and irreverent attitude. Many practitioners join with Jerry Harvey in sug-

gesting that new vitality, potency, and creativity are needed if OD is to continue its own growth and evolution.

Dealing with power. Another criticism of OD is its reliance upon the use of collaboration models, which frequently increase cohesion within units but fail to deal with organization power issues or with relations to external systems. OD efforts seem to be successful under conditions of trust and collaboration but less able to deal with conditions of distrust, power, and conflict.

The limitations of time and terminality. Jerry Harvey has emphasized this point by suggesting that time is an irrelevant variable, or as George Allen, former coach of the Washington Redskins, states: "The future is now!" OD interventions are generally regarded as a long-term, two- to five-year process. What about a system that requires immediate change? OD, at this point, offers few short-term improvement techniques that allow rapid change to occur.

OD is usually undertaken in relatively healthy organizations that desire to become more effective. What does OD offer for the self-destructing system? What does it offer organizations in crisis that may be fighting for survival? Is there a need for short-term, crisis OD interventions which can help introduce change under conditions where urgency and survival may be the immediate concern?

Future Trends in Organization Development

The application of OD technology is growing rapidly. New models, techniques, and approaches are being constantly developed and old techniques discarded. OD itself is facing future shock.

An awareness of the complex environment in which organizations exist is evidenced by the popularity of new trend books in management, such as *Liberation Management, Megatrends 2000, Reengineering the Corporation,* and *The Greatest Management Principle in the World.* As shapers of change, OD practitioners will play a critical role in helping organizations adjust to the changing forces and trends that affect them.

These future trends include:

- **Organization transformation (OT).** This recent advance in change strategies is used in situations of drastic, abrupt change when the organization's survival is at stake. These include such changes as mergers, takeovers, product changes, and plant closures, which often involve large-scale layoffs and restructuring.
- **Shared vision.** This approach to organizational change involves getting all levels of management to identify the strategic vision of the future and what it takes to make it work.
- **Innovation.** Organizations are focusing more effort on innovating—creating new products, goods, and services—and also new ways of organizing and relating among organization members. 3M, for example, is known to have a corporate culture that encourages and supports innovation.
- **Trust.** The critical factor in changing organizations is the development of **trust** within and between individuals, teams, and organizational units and levels. Without trust, there can be no sustainable excellence with an organization.
- **Empowerment.** In order to develop high-performing systems, organization members must be empowered—given the autonomy to do things their own way, to achieve recognition, involvement, and a sense of worth in their jobs. This allows for member ownership of ideas and strategies, and for "buy in" management. The payoff to employee empowerment and involvement is that it allows individuals to discover and use their own potential.
- **Learning Organization.** A conceptual framework for the organization of the future, it's the notion that learning is central to success. Management needs to see the big picture, to escape linear thinking, and to understand subtle interrelationship.
- **Reengineering.** The term for a fundamental rethinking and radical redesign of a business system. Urges an overhaul of job designs, organization structures, and management systems. Work should be organized around outcomes, not tasks or functions.

- **Core Competencies.** The idea is for companies to identify and organize around what they do best. Corporate strategy should be based not on products or markets, but on competencies that give a company access to several markets and are difficult for competitors to imitate.
- **Organizational Architecture.** A metaphor that forces managers to think more broadly about organization in terms of how work, people, and formal and informal structures fit together. This often leads to autonomous work teams and strategic alliances.[25]

Because of the rapid changes, predicting the future trends in OD is difficult, if not impossible. However, there are a number of "cutting edge" trends which appear to be affecting the future directions of OD.[26]

Macrosystem Trends

These trends focus on the organizational system, including:

- *The impact of culture change.* It will become increasingly important to understand the impact of culture on morale, productivity, competence, organizational health, and especially the relationship of culture to strategy.
- *Total resource utilization.* Another trend which has emerged is the need for a system approach to ensure efficient use of the organization's resources. OD practitioners will increasingly be required to work with complex client systems.
- *Centralization vs. decentralization.* In organizations of the future, it will be necessary to both centralize and decentralize functions, structure, and governance.
- *Conflict resolution.* Conflict management has become an important element in today's complex organizations, and value and goal differences are continuing problems. Future OD activities should include helping managers to diagnose conflict and to resolve disputes.
- *Interorganization collaboration.* As limited resources and increased complexity confront the manager of the future, increased sharing, collaboration, and cooperation among organizations will be necessary. Networking offers alternative routes for organizational action.

Human Resource System Trends

These trends focus on group dynamics including:

- *Merging line and staff functions.* There is a trend toward reducing layers of management, increasing participation, and developing temporary systems for problem solving. OD specialists may be facilitating teamwork, assisting in "downsizing," and managing the transition to "do more with less" systems.
- *Resource linking.* As problems become more complex, it becomes important to develop ad hoc problem solving groups.
- *Integrating TQM and productivity.* An increasing emphasis on productivity and quality suggest future trends for OD practitioners to develop links between the goals of management and improving productivity systems.
- *Diversity.* There are increasing trends toward greater diversity of the work force, including multinational corporations and a need for and integration of values and skills.
- *Networking.* In order for organizations to benefit from knowledge and innovation, efficient systems for identifying and accessing information will be needed.
- *Rewarding.* "You get what you reward" is the truism reminding managers to reward smart work, simplification, loyalty, teamwork, and risk taking. Rewards may include stocks, trips, bonuses, and fun.[27]

The Individual Trends

These trends focus on the individual:

- *Intrinsic worth.* Evidence suggests that intrinsic, not extrinsic, motivation is a factor in stress and its symptoms. The OD practitioner can assist in shared understanding and training to deal with these problems.

- *Change in individuals*. With an increased emphasis on corporate training and development efforts, the OD practitioner will need to make this process easier and more effective.
- *The effects of thinking*. The concept of the thinking individual raises the question of corporate values and cultures as belief systems, and offers the OD specialist a vehicle for creating a positive, research-based value system in the organization.
- *Health and fitness*. Currently, "fitness" models focus on organizational and individual health, and such models will provide an increase in self-selected excellence and fitness approaches for the OD practitioner in the future.
- *Interdependence*. Finally, the increasing complexity emphasizes the interdependent relationship between the individual and the organization. The OD practitioner attempts to develop synergy among organizational elements.

The Future of OD

In a world of innovation, Tom Peters suggests that "We must create the organizations that attempt, at least, to survive by getting close to the matter, putting zanies in charge, and staying small enough to shift focus fast."[28] The course of change anticipated for OD will predominantly surround the issues of a changing workforce, international competence, and transformation within the organization. The changing workforce will encompass a positive change toward productivity and involvement with enhanced training and technological awareness. International competence will mean shared values and similar organizational structures to compete in a highly competitive arena. Transformational management leaders will lend credence to the evolution of growth patterns associated with the emerging "self managing" work groups. In addition, advancing media communication technologies will influence all of these organization transformations.[29]

Organization development is an expanding and vital technology. A great deal has been accomplished during its past growth and certainly much more needs to be done in the future. OD is being applied in a multinational framework and in a variety of organizational settings, including industrial, governmental, and health-care institutions. It is agreed by most theorists that there is a need for more empirical studies on the relationship of various intervention processes to other organizational variables. It is widely acknowledged that techniques to deal effectively with external systems and power-coercive problems are yet to emerge. Yet, the very controversy and questioning of the myths and rituals of OD are themselves an indication of a healthy discipline. When OD practitioners become complacent, when controversy over various approaches and techniques subsides, and when the discipline becomes stagnant, then perhaps there will be an even deeper need to worry about the future of OD.

Managers need to understand that OD interventions have the potential to make the biggest difference in human development and bottom line performance. These interventions are based on the same truths that led us to consider democracy to be a superior form of governance in our society.[30]

REVIEW QUESTIONS

1. Identify some of the conditions for success of an OD program.

2. Is OD an emerging discipline or only a passing fad?

3. Do you agree or disagree with the criticisms of OD?

KEY WORDS AND CONCEPTS

Define and be able to use the following:

Core Competencies
Decentralization
Disengagement
Empowerment
Entrepreneurship
Evaluation of OD Programs
In Search of Excellence
Integrated Product Teams (IPT)
Learning Organization
Monitoring
OD Success Factors

Organization Transformation (OT)
Organizational Architecture
Organizational Excellence
Professionalism of OD
Reconfigureable Organization
Reengineering
Self-renewal Capacity
Shared Vision
Stabilizing
Teams

OD SKILLS SIMULATION 16.1
OD CONSULTANT BEHAVIOR PROFILE II

Total time suggested: 1 hour.

A. PURPOSE

In most organizations, there is a lot of untapped human potential. In an excellent, renewing organization, this potential can be released, resulting in personal growth for the individual. Personal development and organization renewal involve changes in attitudes and behavior which are related to your self-concept, role, goals, and values.

The purpose of this profile is to help you gauge for yourself some aspects of your behavior. During this course, you have gained additional opportunities to obtain information about yourself on how you behave in organization situations. This feedback may provide the impetus for you to change, but the ultimate responsibility for that change is with you.

In this simulation, you will experience:

- developing skills in goal setting and changing behaviors.
- developing skill in listening and using feedback.
- exploring the consulting role in an ongoing situation.
- increasing your self-renewal capability.

B. PROCEDURES

Part A: Profile Survey

Step 1. Before class, complete the Profile Survey.

How you respond reflects how you view yourself, which in turn reveals something of your behavioral style. Based on the following scale, select the number to indicate the degree to which you feel each description is characteristic of you. Record your choice in the blank to the right.

PROFILE SURVEY

1	2	3	4	5	6	7
Not at All Characteristic			Somewhat Characteristic			Very Characteristic

1. Having the ability to communicate in a clear, concise, and persuasive manner _____
2. Being spontaneous—saying and doing things that seem natural on the spur of the moment _____
3. Doing things "by the book"—noticing appropriate rules and procedures and following them. _____
4. Being creative—having a lot of unusual, original ideas, thinking of new approaches to problems others do not often come up with _____
5. Being competitive—wanting to win and be the best _____
6. Being able to listen to and understand others _____
7. Being aware of other people's moods and feelings _____
8. Being careful in your work—taking pains to make sure everything is "just right" _____
9. Being resourceful in coming up with possible ways of dealing with problems _____
10. Being a leader—having other people look to you for direction; taking over when things are confused _____
11. Having the ability to accept feedback without reacting defensively, becoming hostile, or withdrawing _____
12. Having the ability to deal with conflict and anger _____
13. Having written work neat and organized: making plans before starting on a difficult task: organizing details of work _____
14. Thinking clearly and logically; attempting to deal with ambiguity, complexity, and confusion in a situation by thoughtful, logical analysis _____
15. Having self-confidence when faced with a challenging situation _____
16. Having the ability to level with others, to give feedback to others _____
17. Doing new and different things; meeting new people; experimenting and trying out new ideas or activities _____
18. Having a high level of aspiration, setting difficult goals _____
19. Analyzing a situation carefully before acting; working out a course of action in detail before embarking on it _____
20. Being effective at initiating projects and innovative ideas _____
21. Seeking ideas from others; drawing others into discussion _____
22. Having a tendency to seek close personal relationships, participating in social activities with friends; giving affection and receiving it from others _____
23. Being dependable—staying on the job; doing what is expected _____
24. Having the ability to work as a catalyst, to stimulate and encourage others to develop their own resources for solving their own problems _____
25. Taking responsibility; relying on your own abilities and judgment rather than those of others _____
26. Selling your own ideas effectively _____
27. Being the dominant person; having a strong need for control or recognition _____
28. Getting deeply involved in your work; being extremely committed to ideas or work you are doing _____
29. Having the ability to evaluate possible solutions critically _____
30. Having the ability to work in unstructured situations, with little or no support and to continue to work effectively even if faced with lack of cooperation, resistance, or hostility _____

Step 2. Form into trios (same groups as in Simulation 2.1), with one person acting as the client, a second as the consultant, and the third as observer (see the Profile Form and Consultant Appraisal Form). Share the information from your Profile and obtain feedback and perceptions from your consulting partners. Compare the changes in your answers from Simulation 2.1 and, with your two partners, discuss whether or not the changes reflected on the profile seem accurate.

1. Were the desired client objectives actually achieved? If so, how?
2. Provide feedback of performance information by consultant to client—what changes in behavior were observed, and so on?
3. What outcomes have been used to assess and reinforce changes?
4. In what ways has the consultant been most helpful to the client?

The observer will observe the consulting relationship using the form and try to provide feedback on the consultant style.

Step 3. After the consulting sessions are completed, each observer shares information on the Consultant Appraisal Form.

Time suggested for Steps 2 and 3: 15-20 minutes rotating roles.

CONSULTANT APPRAISAL FORM

Your role during this part of the simulation is important because your goal is to give individuals feedback on their strategies of change. In giving feedback during the discussion, try to focus on the dimensions listed below.

Following are listed ten criteria of helping relationships. Rate the consultant by circling the appropriate number.

NOTES:
Words,
behaviors

1. Level of involvement:
 Cautious Low 1 : 2 : 3 : 4 : 5 : 6 : 7 : 8 : 9 : 10 High Interested _____

2. Level of communication:
 Doesn't listen Low 1 : 2 : 3 : 4 : 5 : 6 : 7 : 8 : 9 : 10 High Listens _____

3. Level of openness, trust:
 Shy, uncertain Low 1 : 2 : 3 : 4 : 5 : 6 : 7 : 8 : 9 : 10 High Warm, friendly _____

4. Level of collaboration:
 Authoritative Low 1 : 2 : 3 : 4 : 5 : 6 : 7 : 8 : 9 : 10 High Seeks agreement _____

5. Level of influence:
 Gives in Low 1 : 2 : 3 : 4 : 5 : 6 : 7 : 8 : 9 : 10 High Convincing _____

6. Level of supportiveness:
 Disagrees Low 1 : 2 : 3 : 4 : 5 : 6 : 7 : 8 : 9 : 10 High Supports _____

7. Level of direction:
 Easygoing,
 agreeable Low 1 : 2 : 3 : 4 : 5 : 6 : 7 : 8 : 9 : 10 High Gives directions _____

8. Level of competence:
 Unsure Low 1 : 2 : 3 : 4 : 5 : 6 : 7 : 8 : 9 : 10 High Competent _____

9. Other:
 Never Low 1 : 2 : 3 : 4 : 5 : 6 : 7 : 8 : 9 : 10 High _____

10. Overall style:
 Ineffective Low 1 : 2 : 3 : 4 : 5 : 6 : 7 : 8 : 9 : 10 High Effective _____

Step 4. Complete Table 2.3 Profile Form (see page 53 in Chapter 2), by coloring in the bar graph for Chapter 16 in the appropriate line (or bring in computer printout) relative to the behavior profile you have just completed. Note that the 30 descriptions have been reordered to fit into five categories. The profile may indicate items on which your score is less desirable than you would like. You may also find categories in which you have generally low ratings. These may suggest areas for improvement in the future and for assessing the kinds of changes you may wish to make in order to become a more effective consultant or manager.

Part B. Goal Setting—Personal Objectives for Career

Step 1. After completing Table 2.3, Profile Form, outside of class list on the Performance Objectives Form some of the *specific* objectives and expectations you have for your career. These objectives should describe what you will be able to do and the time required. Refer to the Profile Form you have just completed and select some behaviors you would like to emphasize for change.

PERFORMANCE OBJECTIVES FORM

Communicating Skills: *Time Requirement*

1. _____

2. _____

3. _____

Interpersonal Skills:

1. _____

2. _____

3. _____

Aspiration-Achievement Levels:

1. _____

2. _____

3. _____

Problem-Solving Skills:

1. _____

2. _____

3. _____

Leadership Skills:

1. _____

2. _____

3. _____

Other:

1. _____

2. _____

3. _____

OD SKILLS SIMULATION 16.2
THE OD CONSULTANT

Total time suggested: 1 hour.

A. PURPOSE

To provide an opportunity to apply the skills you have learned in this course.

B. PROCEDURE

Step 1. Before class, read the Bob Knowlton case and complete individually the questions following the case. Record your answers on the Bob Knowlton Record Form (Column 1 on page 457).

Step 2. Using the steps in an OD program, develop a preliminary diagnosis and an OD intervention strategy and how you would suggest solving the problem if you were an OD consultant. Use the Diagnostic/Strategy Form at the end of the case as a guide.

Step 3. Form groups of five or six members each and come up with a team consensus on questions and OD strategies and techniques. Place your answers on the Bob Knowlton Record Form (Column 5). Each team writes its solution on newsprint or blackboard and discusses differences.

Time suggested for Step 3: 20 minutes.

Step 4. Individually complete the Team Process Profile (Individual Form) and tabulate the individual results on the Team Process Profile (Group Form). Discuss the results.

Time suggested for Step 4: 10 minutes.

Step 5. Using the answers given by the instructor (to be recorded in Column 3 of the Bob Knowlton Record Form), score your individual and team answers. Where the actual and correct answers match, put +10 in columns (2) and (4) on the Record Form. If the actual and correct answers do not match, put 0 points in columns (2) and (4). By totaling the points, an individual and a team score can be calculated.

Individuals and teams can be compared based on these scores. However, the score may not reflect how effectively decisions were made by the team.

Step 6. Compare and discuss group answers. How many different problems were identified? What different interventions might have been used? Can you come to a class consensus on an OD intervention strategy? Compare team solutions.

Time suggested for Step 6: 20 minutes.

CASE 16:
THE BOB KNOWLTON CASE[31]

Bob Knowlton was sitting alone in the conference room of the laboratory. The rest of the group had gone. One of the secretaries who had stopped and talked for a while about her husband's coming induction into the Army, had finally left. Bob, alone in the laboratory, slid a little further down in his chair, looking with satisfaction at the results of the first test run of the new photon unit.

He liked to stay after the others had gone. His appointment as project head was still new enough to give him a deep sense of pleasure. His eyes were on the graphs before him but in his mind he could hear Dr. Jerrold, the project head, saying again, "There's one thing about this place that you can bank on. The sky is the limit for a man who can produce!" Knowlton felt again the tingle of happiness and embarrassment. Well, dammit, he said to himself, he had produced. He wasn't kidding anybody. He had come to the Simmons Laboratories two years ago. During a routine testing of some rejected Clanson components he had stumbled on the idea of the photon correlator, and the rest just happened. Jerrold had been enthusiastic; a separate project had been set up for further research and development of the device, and he had gotten the job of running it. The whole sequence of events still seemed a little miraculous to Knowlton.

He shrugged out of the reverie and bent determinedly over the sheets when he heard someone come into the room behind him. He looked up expectantly; Jerrold often stayed late himself, and now and then dropped in for a chat. This always made the day's end especially pleasant for Bob. It wasn't Jerrold. The man who had come in was a stranger. He was tall, thin, and rather dark. He wore steel-rimmed glasses and had on a very wide leather belt with a large brass buckle. Bob's wife Lucy remarked later that it was the kind of belt the Pilgrims must have worn.

The stranger smiled and introduced himself, "I'm Simon Fester. Are you Bob Knowlton?" Bob said yes, and they shook hands. "Doctor Jerrold said I might find you in. We were talking about your work, and I'm very much interested in what you are doing." Bob waved to a chair.

Fester didn't seem to belong in any of the standard categories of visitors: customer, visiting fireman, stockholder. Bob pointed to the sheets on the table. "There are the preliminary results of a test we're running. We've got a new gadget by the tail and we're trying to understand it. It's not finished, but I can show you the section that we're testing."

He stood up, but Fester was deep in the graphs. After a moment, he looked up with an odd grin. "These look like plots of a Jennings surface. I've been playing around with some autocorrelation functions of surfaces—you know that stuff." Bob, who had no idea what he was referring to, grinned back and nodded, and immediately felt uncomfortable. "Let me show you the monster," he said, and led the way to the work room.

After Fester left, Knowlton slowly put the graphs away, feeling vaguely annoyed. Then, as if he had made a decision, he quickly locked up and took the long way out so that he would pass Jerrold's office. But the office was locked. Knowlton wondered whether Jerrold and Fester had left together.

The next morning, Knowlton dropped into Jerrold's office, mentioned that he had talked with Fester, and asked who he was. "Sit down for a minute," Jerrold said. "I want to talk to you about him. What do you think of him?" Knowlton replied truthfully that he thought Fester was very bright and probably very competent. Jerrold looked pleased. "We're taking him on," he said. "He's had a very good background in a number of laboratories, and he seems to have ideas about the problems we're tackling here." Knowlton nodded in agreement, instantly wishing that Fester would not be placed with him. "I don't know yet where he will finally land," Jerrold continued, "but he seems interested in what you are doing. I thought he might spend a little time with you by way of getting started." Knowton nodded

thoughtfully. "If his interest in your work continues, you can add him to your group." "Well, he seemed to have some good ideas even without knowing exactly what we are doing," Knowlton answered. "I hope he stays; we'd be glad to have him."

Knowlton walked back to the lab with mixed feelings. He told himself that Fester would be good for the group. He was no dunce, he'd produce. Knowlton thought again of Jerrold's promise when he had promoted him—"the man who produces gets ahead in this outfit." The words seemed to carry the overtones of a threat now.

That day Fester didn't appear until mid-afternoon. He explained that he had had a long lunch with Jerrold, discussing his place in the lab. "Yes," said Knowlton, "I talked with Jerry this morning about it, and we both thought you might work with us for awhile." Fester smiled in the same knowing way that he had smiled when he mentioned the Jennings surfaces. "I'd like to," he said. Knowlton introduced Fester to the other members of the lab. Fester and Link, the mathematician of the group, hit it off well together, and spent the rest of the afternoon discussing a method of analysis of patterns that Link had been worrying over for the last month.

It was 6:30 when Knowlton finally left the lab that night. He had waited almost eagerly for the end of the day to come—when they would all be gone and he could sit in the quiet rooms, relax, and think it over. "Think what over?" he asked himself. He didn't know. Shortly after 5:00 PM they had all gone except Fester, and what followed was almost a duel. Knowlton was annoyed that he was being cheated out of his quiet period, and finally resentfully determined that Fester should leave first.

Fester was sitting at the conference table reading, and Knowlton was sitting at the desk in the little glass-enclosed cubby that he used during the day when he needed to be undisturbed. Fester had gotten the last year's progress reports out and was studying them carefully. The time dragged. Knowton doodled on a pad, the tension growing inside him. What the hell did Fester think he was going to find in the reports?

Knowlton finally gave up and they left the lab together. Fester took several of the reports with him to study in the evening. Knowlton asked him if he thought the reports gave a clear picture of the lab's activities. "They're excellent," Fester answered with obvious sincerity. "They're not only good reports; what they report is damn good, too!" Knowlton was surprised at the relief he felt, and grew almost jovial as he said goodnight.

Driving home, Knowlton felt more optimistic about Fester's presence in the lab. He had never fully understood the analysis that Link was attempting. If there was anything wrong with Link's approach, Fester would probably spot it, "And if I'm any judge," he murmured, "he won't be especially diplomatic about it."

He described Fester to his wife, who was amused by the broad leather belt and the brass buckle. "It's the kind of belt that Pilgrims must have worn," she laughed. "I'm not worried about how he holds his pants up," he laughed with her. "I'm afraid that he's the kind that just has to make like a genius twice each day. And that can be pretty rough on the group."

Knowlton had been asleep for several hours when he was jerked awake by the telephone. He realized it had rung several times. He swung off the bed muttering about damn fools and telephones. It was Fester. Without any excuses, apparently oblivious of the time, he plunged into an excited recital of how Link's patterning problem could be solved. Knowlton covered the mouthpiece to answer his wife's stage-whispered "Who is it?" "It's the genius," replied Knowlton.

Fester, completely ignoring the fact that it was 2:00 in the morning, proceeded in a very excited way to start in the middle of an explanation of a completely new approach to certain of the photon lab problems that he had stumbled on while analyzing past experiments. Knowlton managed to put some enthusiasm in his own voice and stood there, half-dazed and very uncomfortable, listening to Fester talk endlessly about what he had discovered. It was probably not only a new approach, but also an analysis which showed the inherent weakness of the previous experiment and how experimentation along that line would certainly have been inconclusive. The following day Knowlton spent the entire morning with

Fester and Link, the mathematician, the customary morning meeting of Bob's group having been called off so that Fester's work of the previous night could be gone over intensively. Fester was very anxious that this be done and Knowlton was not too unhappy to call the meeting off for reasons of his own.

For the next several days Fester sat in the back office that had been turned over to him and did nothing but read the progress reports of the work that had been done in the last six months. Knowlton caught himself feeling apprehensive about the reaction that Fester might have to some of his work. He was a little surprised at his own feelings. He had always been proud—although he had put on a convincingly modest face—of the way in which new ground in the study of photon measuring devices had been broken in his group. Now he wasn't sure, and it seemed to him that Fester might easily show that the line of research they had been following was unsound or even unimaginative.

The next morning, as was the custom, the members of the lab, including the secretaries, sat around a conference table. Bob always prided himself on the fact that the work of the lab was guided and evaluated by the group as a whole and he was fond of repeating that it was not a waste of time to include secretaries in such meetings. Often, what started out as a boring recital of fundamental assumptions, to a naive listener, uncovered new ways of regarding these assumptions that would not have occurred to the researcher who had long ago accepted them as a necessary basis for his work.

These group meetings also served Bob in another sense. He admitted to himself that he would have felt far less secure if he had had to direct the work out of his own mind, so to speak. With the group-meeting as the principle of leadership, it was always possible to justify the exploration of blind alleys because of the general educative effect on the team. Fester was there; Lucy and Martha were there; Link was sitting next to Fester, their conversation concerning Link's mathematical study apparently continuing from yesterday. The other members, Bob Davenport, George Thurlow, and Arthur Oliver, were waiting quietly.

Knowlton, for reasons that he didn't quite understand, proposed for discussion this morning a problem that all of them had spent a great deal of time on previously, with the conclusion that a solution was impossible, that there was no feasible way of treating it in an experimental fashion. When Knowlton proposed the problem, Davenport remarked that there was hardly any use of going over it again, that he was satisfied that there was no way of approaching the problem with the equipment and the physical capacities of the lab.

This statement had the effect of a shot of adrenalin on Fester. He said he would like to know what the problem was in detail and, walking to the blackboard, began setting down the "factors" as various members of the group began discussing the problem and simultaneously listing the reasons why it had been abandoned.

Very early in the description of the problem it was evident that Fester was going to disagree about the impossibility of attacking it. The group realized this and finally the descriptive materials and their recounting of the reasoning that had led to its abandonment dwindled away. Fester began his statement which, as it proceeded, might well have been prepared the previous night although Knowlton knew this was impossible. He couldn't help being impressed with the organized analogical way that Fester was presenting ideas that must have occurred to him only a few minutes before.

Fester had some things to say, however, which left Knowlton with a mixture of annoyance, irritation and, at the same time, a rather smug feeling of superiority over Fester in at least one area. Fester was of the opinion that the way that the problem had been analyzed was really typical of group-thinking and, with an air of sophistication which made it difficult for a listener to dissent, he proceeded to comment on the American emphasis on team ideas, satirically describing the ways in which they led to a "high level of mediocrity."

During this time, Knowlton observed that Link stared studiously at the floor, and he was very conscious of George Thurlow's and Bob Davenport's glances toward him at several points of Fester's little speech. Inwardly, Knowlton couldn't help feeling that this was one point at least in which Fester was off on the wrong foot. The whole lab, following Jerry's lead, talked if not practiced the theory of small research teams as the basic organization for

effective research. Fester insisted that the problem could be approached and that he would like to study it for a while himself.

Knowlton ended the morning session by remarking that the meetings would continue and that the very fact that a supposedly insoluble experimental problem was now going to get another chance was another indication of the value of such meetings. Fester immediately remarked that he was not at all averse to meetings for the purpose of informing the group of the progress of its members—that the point he wanted to make was that creative advances were seldom accomplished in such meetings, that they were made by the individual "living with" the problem closely and continuously, a sort of personal relationship to it.

Knowlton went on to say to Fester that he was very glad Fester had raised these points and that he was sure the group would profit by reexamining the basis on which they had been operating. Knowlton agreed that individual effort was probably the basis for making the major advances, but that he considered the group meetings useful primarily because of the effect they had on keeping the group together and on helping the weaker members of the group keep up with the ones who were able to advance more easily and quickly in the analysis of problems.

It was clear as days went by and meetings continued that Fester came to enjoy them because of the pattern which the meetings assumed. It became typical for Fester to hold forth and it was unquestionably clear that he was more brilliant, better prepared on the various subjects which were germane to the problems being studied, and that he was more capable of going ahead than anyone there. Knowlton grew increasingly disturbed as he realized that his leadership of the group had been, in fact taken over.

Whenever the subject of Fester was mentioned, in occasional meetings with Dr. Jerrold, Knowlton would comment only on the ability and obvious capacity for work that Fester had. Somehow he never felt that he could mention his own discomforts, not only because they revealed a weakness on his own part, but also because it was quite clear that Jerrold himself was considerably impressed with Fester's work and with the contacts he had with him outside the photon laboratory.

Knowlton now began to feel that perhaps the intellectual advantages that Fester had brought to the group did not quite compensate for what he felt were evidences of a breakdown in the cooperative spirit he had seen in the group before Fester's coming. More and more of the morning meetings were skipped. Fester's opinion concerning the abilities of others of the group, with the exception of Link, was obviously low. At times, during morning meetings or in smaller discussions, he had been on the point of rudeness, refusing to pursue an argument when he claimed it was based on the other person's ignorance of the facts involved. His impatience of others led him to also make similar remarks to Dr. Jerrold. Knowlton inferred this from a conversation with Jerrold in which Jerrold asked whether Davnport and Oliver were going to be continued on; and his failure to mention Link, the mathematician, led Knowlton to feel that this was the result of private conversations between Fester and Jerrold.

It was not difficult for Knowlton to make a quite convincing case on whether the brilliance of Fester was sufficient recompense for the beginning of this breaking up of the group. He took the opportunity to speak privately with Davenport and with Oliver and it was quite clear that both of them were uncomfortable because of Fester. Knowlton didn't press the discussion beyond the point of hearing them in one way or another say that they did feel awkward and that it was sometimes difficult for them to understand the arguments he advanced, but often embarrassing to ask him to fill in the background on which his arguments were based. Knowlton did not interview Link in this manner.

About six months after Fester's coming into the photon lab, a meeting was scheduled in which the sponsors of the research were coming in to get some idea of the work and its progress. It was customary at these meetings for project heads to present the research being conducted in their groups. The members of each group were invited to other meetings which

were held later in the day and open to all, but the special meetings were usually made up only of project heads, the head of the laboratory, and the sponsors.

As the time for the special meeting approached, it seemed to Knowlton that he must avoid the presentation at all cost. His reasons for this were that he could not trust himself to present the ideas and work that Fester had advanced, because of his apprehension as to whether he could present them in sufficient detail and answer such questions about them as might be asked. On the other hand, he did not feel he could ignore these newer lines of work and present only the material that he had done or that had been started before Fester's arrival. He felt also that it would not be beyond Fester at all, in his blunt and undiplomatic way— if he were present at the meeting, that is—to make comments on his [Knowlton's] presentation and reveal Knowlton's inadequacy. It also seemed quite clear that it would not be easy to keep Fester from attending the meeting, even though he was not on the administrative level of those invited.

Knowlton found an opportunity to speak to Jerrold and raised the questions. He remarked to Jerrold that, with the meetings coming up and with the interest in the work and with the contributions that Fester had been making, he would probably like to come to these meetings, but there was a question of the feelings of the others in the group if Fester alone were invited. Jerrold passed this over very lightly by saying that he didn't think the group would fail to understand Fester's rather different position and that he thought that Fester by all means should be invited. Knowlton then immediately said he had thought so, too; Fester should present the work because much of it was work he had done; and, as Knowlton put it, that this would be a nice way to recognize Fester's contributions and to reward him, as he was eager to be recognized as a productive member of the lab. Jerrold agreed, and so the matter was decided.

Fester's presentation was very successful and in some way dominated the meeting. He attracted the interest and attention of many of those who had come, and a long discussion followed his presentation. Later in the evening—with the entire laboratory staff present—in the cocktail period before the dinner, a little circle of people formed about Fester. One of them was Jerrold himself, and a lively discussion took place concerning the application of Fester's theory. All of this disturbed Knowlton, and his reaction and behavior were characteristic. He joined the circle, praised Fester to Jerrold and to others, and remarked on the brilliance of the work.

Knowlton, without consulting anyone, began at this time to take some interest in the possibility of a job elsewhere. After a few weeks he found that a new laboratory of considerable size was being organized in a nearby city, and that the kind of training he had would enable him to get a project head job equivalent to the one he had at the lab, with slightly more money.

He immediately accepted it and notified Jerrold by a letter, which he mailed on a Friday night to Jerrold's home. The letter was quite brief, and Jerrold was stunned. The letter merely said that he had found a better position; that there were personal reasons why he didn't want to appear at the lab any more; that he would be glad to come back at a later time from where he would be, some forty miles away, to assist if there was any mixup at all in the past work; that he felt sure that Fester could, however, supply any leadership that was required for the group; and that his decision to leave so suddenly was based on some personal problems—he hinted at problems of health in his family, his mother and father. All of this was fictitious, of course. Jerrold took it at face value but still felt that this was very strange behavior and quite unaccountable, for he had always felt his relationship with Knowlton had been warm and that Knowlton was satisfied and, as a matter of fact, quite happy and productive.

Jerrold was considerably disturbed, because he had already decided to place Fester in charge of another project that was going to be set up very soon. He had been wondering how to explain this to Knowlton, in view of the obvious help Knowlton was getting from Fester and the high regard in which he held him. Jerrold had, as a matter of fact, considered

the possibility that Knowlton could add to his staff another person with the kind of background and training that had been unique in Fester and had proved so valuable.

Jerrold did not make any attempt to meet Knowlton. In a way, he felt aggrieved about the whole thing. Fester, too, was surprised at the suddenness of Knowlton's departure and when Jerrold, in talking to him, asked him whether he had reasons to prefer to stay with the photon group instead of the project for the Air Force which was being organized, he chose the Air Force project and went on to that job the following week. The photon lab was hard hit. The leadership of the lab was given to Link with the understanding that this would be temporary until someone could come in to take over.

QUESTIONS

1. The self-managed work team violates which of the following principles:
 a. Importance of decentralization.
 b. Unity of command.
 c. Keeping the chain of command limited.
 d. Mixing types of departmentation.
2. Fester's role in the organization was determined by:
 a. A set of expectations.
 b. The formal organization structure.
 c. Based on the authority of the position.
 d. Largely his personality.
3. Jerrold's approach to leadership included:
 a. Providing direction and performing management functions.
 b. Influencing others and setting goals.
 c. Providing direction and influence.
 d. Influencing and pressuring to produce.
4. Jerrold's decision to promote Fester was based upon:
 a. Leadership traits.
 b. Leadership behavior.
 c. Situational factors.
 d. Contingency factors.
5. In Bob's group, which is most correct:
 a. Conflict was successfully managed.
 b. Conflict indicates that problems exist in the organization.
 c. Conflict is something to be avoided.
 d. Conflict is only damaging when it is unresolved.
6. In this organization one problem was:
 a. Getting too many people with conflicting opinions involved in the decisions.
 b. Collecting "yes" men who did not encourage diversity of opinion.
 c. Considering how others would react to decisions.
 d. Delegating too many decisions for others.
7. Jerrold's managerial style (see Chapter 4) is predominately:
 a. Craftsman
 b. Jungle fighter
 c. Company man
 d. Gamesman
8. Bob's managerial style is predominately:
 a. Craftsman
 b. Jungle fighter
 c. Company man
 d. Gamesman
9. Fester's style is predominately:

 a. Craftsman
 b. Jungle fighter
 c. Company man
 d. Gamesman
 10. The main cause of the problem is:
 a. Jerrold
 b. Knowlton
 c. Fester
 d. The organization

DIAGNOSTIC/STRATEGY FORM

		A. Problem	B. Target System	C. Intervention
Individual	1.	_____	_____	_____
	2.	_____	_____	_____
	3.	_____	_____	_____
	4.	_____	_____	_____
	5.	_____	_____	_____
Team Consensus	1.	_____	_____	_____
	2.	_____	_____	_____
	3.	_____	_____	_____
	4.	_____	_____	_____
	5.	_____	_____	_____

BOB KNOWLTON RECORD FORM

Question	(1) Individual Answer	(2) Individual Score	(3) Correct Answer	(4) Team Score	(5) Team Answer
1					
2					
3					
4					
5					
6					
7					
8					
9					
10					
	Individual Score		Team Score		

TEAM PROCESS PROFILE
(INDIVIDUAL FORM)

Low : : : : : : High
 1 2 3 4 5 6 7

Instructions: For each item, place a number in the blank to the right representing your reaction to how your group performed based on the scale above.

Factor	Rating
1. Degree of cooperative teamwork	_____
2. Degree of member satisfaction	_____
3. Degree of team motivation	_____
4. Degree of information sharing	_____
5. Degree of consensual decision making	_____
6. Degree of conflict directly faced and resolved	_____
7. Degree of participative leadership	_____
8. Degree of clearly defined goals	_____
9. Degree of trust	_____
10. Degree of encouraged openness	_____
Total Ranking	_____

TEAM PROCESS PROFILE
(GROUP FORM)
INDIVIDUAL RATINGS

Item	Names of Individuals									Total	Average
1											
2											
3											
4											
5											
6											
7											
8											
9											
10											
Totals											

OD SKILLS SIMULATION 16.3
UNFINISHED BUSINESS

A. PURPOSE

You will soon be leaving this organization, and this simulation is intended to provide an opportunity to bring the class to a close. More specifically, it will allow you to clear up any questions you may have about the content of the subject matter.

B. PROCEDURE

You are encouraged to share any thoughts, feelings, opinions, and so forth, that you may have relative to the class and its members. There is no format to this simulation. It is suggested that it be conducted as an informal discussion.

SUMMARY

- **Organization Development.** In this book, we have examined the practice and application of organization development as an approach to planned change. It seems fair to say that despite criticism and controversy, OD is a growing, developing, and workable discipline. OD has come a long way in the past four decades, since its inception by Douglas McGregor, Richard Beckhard, Robert Blake, and Herbert Shepard in their early work with organizational systems. Since that time, an array of new intervention techniques, methodologies, and applications have evolved. Still, many practitioners feel OD has become too ritualized, that the field lacks rigorous empirical foundations, and that it fails to deal with critical issues. As you have probably noted, there is a wide divergence of opinion over what are or should be called OD interventions and also whether or not certain interventions lead to successful outcomes.

- **Research.** One problem is that much of the research supporting various OD activities has either been biased or failed to be replicated with similar results. Consequently, one study may suggest that a certain intervention has been very effective within an organization, whereas a second similar study finds just the opposite: a complete lack of positive impact. Given much conflicting data, how is one to evaluate the various methodologies, strategies, and interventions that may be utilized in an OD program?

- **Generalization.** A second problem is that of over-generalization on limited or short-term data. In a number of instances, very positive initial reports have initiated a "halo

effect," so that everyone tries to duplicate an apparent success only to discover later that the final outcome is not as positive as initial reports appeared. One example of this at a food plant involved an OD program based upon the team concept, in which self-managed work teams were assigned areas of responsibility. The program had some very positive results, but other pressures emerged and analysts reported later that the program seemed to be deteriorating. The OD program resulted in lower unit costs, decreased turnover, and lower accident rates, but external pressures from the power system seemed to be posing new problems, which may have affected long-term results.

- **Future.** In conclusion, OD is not merely a passing fad. We are optimistic about the future of OD and believe that it will continue to grow and be more widely used. This growth will not result from more practitioners moving into the OD field or because more techniques become available, but because the problems of adapting to a more rapidly changing world create the need for expanded use of OD. The increasing need for organization transformation, high-performing systems, innovation, and empowerment suggests that speed in making transitions is the critical issue facing organizations. OD consultants must be able to develop new and innovative ways of adapting organizations to high-speed change. As more organizations seek to achieve organizational excellence, there will be a parallel growth in the need for new OD models, new OD strategies, new OD interventions, and new OD practitioner roles in the future.

NOTES

1. See Rahul Jacob, "The Struggle to Create an Organization for the 21st Century," *Fortune*, April 3, 1995, p. 90.

2. Tom Peters, "Facing up to the Need for a Management Revolution," *California Management Review*, (Winter, 1988), pp. 7–37.

3. See Laura Rubach, "Downsizing: How Quality is Affected as Companies Shrink," *Quality Progress*, vol 28, no. 4, April, 1995, p. 25.

4. Ronald Henkoff, "Keeping Motorola On a Roll," *Fortune*, April 18, 1994, p. 72.

5. See Laura Rubach, "Downsizing: How Quality is Affected as Companies Shrink," *Quality Progress,* vol 28, no. 4, April, 1995, p. 25.

6. See Howard E. Butz, Jr., "Strategic Planning: The Missing Link in TQM," *Quality Progress*, vol. 28, no. 5, May, 1995, p. 166.

7. John Huey, "How McKinsey Does It," *Fortune*, November 1, 1993, vol. 128, no. 11, pp. 56–81.

8. Brian DuMaine, "Who Needs a Boss?" *Fortune*, May 7, 1990, p. 52.

9. John F. Hulpke, California State University, Bakersfield, Bakersfield, CA, 1995.

10. F. Friedlander and L. Brown, "Organization Development," *Annual Review of Psychology,* vol. 25, 1974, p. 336.

11. A. Armenakis, H. Field, and D. Mosley, "Evaluation Guidelines for the OD Practitioner," *Personnel Journal*, February 1975.

12. George A. Neuman, Jack E. Edwards, and Nambury S. Raju, "Organizational Development Interventions: A Meta Analysis of Their Effects," *Personnel Psychology*, vol. 42, 1989, p. 461. See also B. Macy and P. Mirvis, "Organizational Change Efforts: Methodologies for Assessing Organizational Effectiveness and Program Costs versus Benefits," *Evaluation Review*, vol. 6, June 1982, pp. 301–372.

13. G. Watson and E. Glaser, "What Have We Learned About Planning for Change?" *Management Review*, November 1967, p. 45.

14. Tom Peters interview, *Psychology Today*, March 1993, p. 56.

15. Stratford Sherman, "Are you as Good as the Best in the World?" *Fortune*, December 13, 1993, pp. 95–96.

16. Larry Greiner, "Patterns of Organizational Change," *Harvard Business Review,* May–June 1967, pp. 110–130.

17. Tom Peters, "Road to the Great Beyond," *The Independent*, November 7, 1993, pp. 22.

18. T. Cummings and E. Huse, *Organization Development*, (New York: West Publishing Co., 1989), 4th ed., p. 8.

19. "Business Fads—What's In and Out," *Business Week*, January 20, 1986, pp. 52–61.

20. Glenn Martin Tarullo, "Making Outdoor Experiential Training Work," Training, vol. 29, no. 8 (August 1992), pp. 47–52.

21. Kelvin F. Cross, "For Good Measures," *CMA Magazine*, vol. 66, no. 3 (April 1992), pp. 20–23.

22. G. Strauss, "Organization Development: Credits and Debits," in *The Management Process*, 2nd ed., S. Carrol, F. Pline, and J. Mower, eds. (New York: Macmillan Inc., 1977), p. 404.

23. Sources: Tom Peters, "Facing Up to the Need for a Management Revolution," *California Management Review*, Winter 1988, pp. 7–37; "Failure: Spotlight on a Neglected Side of Business," *The Wall Street Journal*, December 15, 1986, p. 29; and "Who's Excellent Now?" *Business Week*, November 5, 1984, pp. 76–86.

24. J. Harvey, "Eight Myths OD Consultants Believe In—and Die By," *OD Practitioner*, February 1975.

25. John A. Byrne, "Management's New Gurus," *Business Week*, August 31, 1992.

26. See Gordon Lippit, Ronald Lippitt, and Clayton Lafferty, "Cutting Edge Trends in Organization Development," *Training and Development Journal,* vol. 38, no. 7, July 1984, pp. 59–62.

27. Michael Leboeuf, Ph.D., *The Greatest Management Principle in The World*, (New York: Berkely Books, 1985), pp. 4–5.

28. Tom Peters, *Liberation Management*, 1992, p. 14.

29. Jonathan Z. Gottlieb and Jyotsna Sanzgiri, "Philosophic and Pragmatic Influences on the Practice of Organization Development, 1950–2000," *Organizational Dynamics*, vol. 21, no. 2 (Autumn 1992), pp. 57–69.

30. William A. Pasmore, "Participation, Individual Development and Organization Change: A Review and Synthesis," *Journal of Management*, vol. 18, no. 2 June 1992, pp. 375–397.

31. We are indebted to Professor Alex Bavelas, of Stanford University, for the use of this case and it is used with his permission.

INDEX